William Carew Hazlitt, Richard Price, Thomas Warton

History of English Poetry

From the 12th to the Close of the 16th Century

William Carew Hazlitt, Richard Price, Thomas Warton

History of English Poetry
From the 12th to the Close of the 16th Century

ISBN/EAN: 9783744674713

Printed in Europe, USA, Canada, Australia, Japan

Cover: Foto ©ninafisch / pixelio.de

More available books at **www.hansebooks.com**

HISTORY OF ENGLISH POETRY

FROM THE TWELFTH TO THE CLOSE

OF THE SIXTEENTH

CENTURY.

BY THOMAS WARTON, B.D.

FELLOW OF TRIN. COLL., OXFORD; F.S.A.; PROFESSOR OF
POETRY IN THE UNIVERSITY OF OXFORD.

WITH A PREFACE BY RICHARD PRICE, AND NOTES VARIORUM.

EDITED BY W. CAREW HAZLITT.

WITH NEW NOTES AND OTHER ADDITIONS BY SIR FREDERIC MADDEN, K.H., F.R.S.;
THOMAS WRIGHT, M.A., F.S.A.; W. ALDIS WRIGHT, M.A.; REV.
WALTER W. SKEAT, M.A.; RICHARD MORRIS, LL.D;
F. J. FURNIVAL, M.A.; AND THE EDITOR.

WITH INDEXES OF NAMES AND SUBJECTS.

IN FOUR VOLUMES.

VOL. III.

LONDON:
REEVES AND TURNER, 196, STRAND.
1871.

The History of English Poetry.

SECTION XVIII.

T is not my intention to dedicate a volume to Chaucer, how much soever he may deserve it; nor can it be expected that, in a work of this general nature, I should enter into a critical examination of all Chaucer's pieces. Enough has been said to prove that in elevation and elegance, in harmony and perspicuity, of versification he surpasses his predecessors in an infinite proportion: that his genius was universal, and adapted to themes of unbounded variety: that his merit was not less in painting familiar manners with humour and propriety, than in moving the passions, and in representing the beautiful or the grand objects of nature with grace and sublimity. In a word, that he appeared with all the lustre and dignity of a true poet, in an age which compelled him to struggle with a barbarous language and a national want of taste; and when to write verses at all was regarded as a singular qualification. It is true, indeed, that he lived at a time when the French and Italians had made considerable advances and improvements in poetry: and although proofs have already been occasionally given of his imitations from these sources, I shall close my account of him with a distinct and comprehensive view of the nature of the poetry which subsisted in France and Italy when he wrote: pointing out, in the mean time, how far and in what manner the popular models of those nations contributed to form his taste and influence his genius.

I have already mentioned the troubadours of Provence, and have observed that they were fond of moral and allegorical fables. A taste for this sort of composition they partly acquired by reading Boethius and the *Psychomachia* of Prudentius, two favourite classics of the dark ages: and partly from the Saracens their neighbours in Spain, who were great inventors of apologues. The French have a very early metrical romance *De Fortune et de Félicité*, a translation from Boethius, *De Consolatione* by Regnier de Saint-

Trudon, a Dominican friar.¹ From this source came the *Tournament of Antichrist* above mentioned, which contains a combat of the Virtues and Vices: the Romaunt of Richard de Lisle, in which Modesty fighting with Lust² is thrown into the river Seine at Paris: and above all, the *Romaunt of the Rose*, translated by Chaucer, and already mentioned at large in its proper place. Visions were a branch of this species of poetry, which admitted the most licentious excursions of fancy in forming personifications, and in feigning imaginary beings and ideal habitations. Under these we may rank Chaucer's *House of Fame*, which I have before hinted to have been probably the production of Provence.

But the principal subject of their poems, dictated in great measure by the spirit of chivalry, was love: especially among the troubadours of rank and distinction, whose castles, being crowded with ladies, presented perpetual scenes of the most splendid gallantry. This passion they spiritualised into various metaphysical refinements, and filled it with abstracted notions of visionary perfection and felicity. Here too they were perhaps influenced by their neighbours the Saracens, whose philosophy chiefly consisted of fantastic abstractions. It is manifest, however, that nothing can exceed the profound pedantry with which they treated this favourite argument. They defined the essence and characteristics of true love with all the parade of a Scotist in his professorial chair: and bewildered their imaginations in speculative questions concerning the most desperate or the most happy situations of a sincere and sentimental heart.³ But it would be endless, and indeed ridiculous, to describe at length the systematical solemnity with which they clothed this passion.⁴ The *Romaunt of the*

---

¹ See [Brunet, last edit. i. 1034-5. This was printed at Bruges in 1477.] I have before mentioned John of Meun's translation of Boethius. It is in verse. Jean de Langres is said to have made a translation in prose, about 1336. It is highly probable that Chaucer translated Boethius from some of the French translations. In the Bodleian library [and elsewhere] there is a gloss on Boethius by our countryman Nicholas Trivett [a Dominican,] who died before 1329. [This is not a rare MS.]

² Puterie. Properly bawdry, obscenity. Modesty is drowned in the river, which gives occasion to this conclusion, "Dont vien que plus n'y a Honte dans Paris." The author lived about the year 1300.

³ In the mean time the greatest liberties and indecencies were practised and encouraged. These doctrines did not influence the manners of the times. In an old French tale, a countess in the absence of her lord having received a knight into her castle, and conducted him in great state to his repose, will not suffer him to sleep alone; with infinite politeness she orders one of her damsels, "la plus courtoise et la plus belle," into his bed-chamber, "avec ce chevalier gesir." *Mem. Cheval.* ut supr. tom. ii. p. 70, not. 17.

⁴ This infatuation continued among the French down to modern times. "Les gens de qualité," says the ingenious M. de Sainte Palaye, "conservoient encore ce goût que leurs pères avoient pris dans nos anciennes cours: ce fut sans doute pour complaire a ce fondateur, que l'Academie Françoise traita, dans ses premiers séances, plusieurs sujets qui concernoient l'Amour; et l'on vit encore dans l'hotel du Longueville les personnes les plus qualifées et les plus spirituelles du siecle de Louis XIV. se disputer a qui commenteroit et raffineroit le mieux sur la delicatesse du cœur et des sentimens, a qui feroit, sur ce chapitre, les distinctions les plus subtiles." *Mem. Cheval.* ut supr. tom. ii. p. v. pag. 17.

Rose, which I have just alleged as a proof of their allegorising turn, is not less an instance of their affectation in writing on this subject: in which the poet, under the agency of allegorical personages, displays the gradual approaches and impediments to fruition, and introduces a regular disputation conducted with much formality between Reason and a lover. [The later prose work called the] *Testament of Love*[1] [which has been mistakenly attributed to Chaucer], is also formed on this philosophy of gallantry. It is a lover's parody of the work of Boethius *De Consolatione* mentioned above. [The] poem called *La Belle Dame sans Mercy*[2] and [the] *Assemble of Ladies*, [both thoughtlessly assigned to Chaucer by some writers,] are from the same school.[3] Chaucer's *Prioress* and *Monk*, whose lives were devoted to religious reflection and the most serious engagements, and while they are actually travelling on a pilgrimage to visit the shrine of a sainted martyr, openly avow the universal influence of love. They exhibit, on their apparel, badges entirely inconsistent with their profession, but easily accountable for from these principles. The Prioress wears a bracelet on which is inscribed, with a crowned A, *Amor vincit omnia*.[4] The Monk ties his hood with a true lover's knot.[5] The early poets of Provence, as I before hinted, formed a society called the *Court of Love*, which gave rise to others in Gascony, Languedoc, Poictou, and Dauphiny: and Picardy, the constant rival of Provence, had a similar institution called *Plaids et Gieux sous l'Ormel*. These establishments consisted of ladies and gentlemen of the highest rank, exercised and approved in courtesy, who tried with the most consummate ceremony, and decided with supreme authority, cases in love brought before their tribunal. Mareçhal d'Auvergne, an old French poet, for the diversion and at the request of the Countess of Beaujeu, [published a collection of these supposed Decrees in prose under the title of] *Arresta amorum*, or the Decrees of Love, which is a humorous description of the *Plaids* of Picardy. Fontenelle has recited one of their processes, which conveys an idea of all the rest.[6] A queen of France was appealed to from an unjust sentence pronounced in

---

[1] ["We do not propose here to dwell upon this question, but rather to throw out a hint, and to make a quotation from the end of the *Testament of Love*, in which the writer (if Chaucer) is made to bestow upon himself and upon one of his works most extravagant laudation. It seems to us impossible to suppose that a man of Chaucer's genius and modesty (always coupled) would thus have written of himself."—Collier, *Introd. to Seven Poetical Miscellanies*, 1867.]

[2] Translated or imitated from a French poem of Alain Chartier, v. 11:

"Which Maistir Alayne made of remembrance
Chief secretary to the king of France."

He was secretary to Charles the Sixth and Seventh. But he is chiefly famous for his prose. [Alain Chartier was certainly living near fifty years after Chaucer's death, which makes it quite incredible that the latter should have translated anything of his. In MS. Harl. 372, La belle Dame sans Mercie is attributed to Sir Richard Ros.—*Tyrwhitt*. Mr. Tyrwhitt also rejects the Assemble of Ladies from the list of Chaucer's works.—*Price*.]

[3] So is Gower's *Confessio Amantis*, as we shall see hereafter.

[4] v. 162.   v. 197.

[6] *Hist. Theat. Franc.* p. 15, tom. iii. *Oeuvr.* Paris, 1742.

the love-pleas, where the **Countefs** of Champagne prefided. The queen did not choofe to interpofe in a matter of fo much confequence, nor to reverfe the decrees of a court whofe decifion was abfolute and final. She anfwered, "God forbid, that I fhould prefume to contradict the fentence of the Countefs of Champagne!" This was about the year 1206. Chaucer has a poem called the *Court of Love*, which is nothing more than the love-court of Provence:[1] it contains the twenty ftatutes which that court prefcribed to be univerfally obferved under the fevereft penalties.[2] Not long afterwards, on the fame principle, a fociety was eftablifhed in Languedoc, called the *Fraternity of the Penitents of Love*. Enthufiafm was here carried to as high a pitch of extravagance as ever it was in religion. It was a contention of ladies and gentlemen, who fhould beft fuftain the honour of their amorous fanaticifm. Their object was to prove the excefs of their love, by fhewing with an invincible fortitude and confiftency of conduct, and with no lefs obftinacy of opinion, that they could bear extremes of heat and cold. Accordingly the refolute knights and efquires, the dames and damfels, who had the hardinefs to embrace this fevere inftitution, dreffed themfelves during the heat of fummer in the thickeft mantles lined with the warmeft fur. In this they demonftrated, according to the ancient poets, that love works the moft wonderful and extraordinary changes. In winter, their love again perverted the nature of the feafons: they then clothed themfelves in the lighteft and thinneft ftuffs which could be procured. It was a crime to wear fur on a day of the moft piercing cold; or to appear with a hood, cloak, gloves, or muff. The flame of love kept them fufficiently warm. Fires, all the winter, were utterly banifhed from their houfes; and they dreffed their apartments with evergreens. In the moft intenfe froft their beds were covered only with a piece of canvafs. It muft be remembered, that in the mean time they paffed the greater part of the day abroad, in wandering about from caftle to

---

[1] See alfo Chaucer's *Ten Commandments of Love*.

[2] *Vie de Petrarque*, tom. ii. not. xix. p. 60. Probably *the Cour d'Amour* was the origin of that called *La Cour Amoreufe*, eftablifhed under the gallant reign of Charles VI. in 1410. The latter had the moft confiderable families of France for its members, and a parade of grand officers, like thofe in the royal houfehold and courts of law. See *Hift. Acad. Infcript.* tom. vii. p. 287, *feq.* 4to. See alfo *Hift. Laugued.* tom. iii. p. 25, *feq.*

The moft uniform and unembarraffed view of the eftablifhment and ufages of this *Court*, which I can at prefent recollect, is thrown together from fcattered and fcarce materials by the ingenious author of *Vie de Petrarque*, tom. ii. p. 45, *feq.* not. xix. But for a complete account of thefe inftitutions, and other curious particulars relating to the ancient manners and ancient poetry of the French, the [reader may be referred to] the hiftory of the Provençal poets written by Sainte Palaye, who has copied moft of their MSS. with great care and expenfe. [The only authentic fource of information on this fubject is a work written about the year 1170 and publifhed (among other places) at Dorpmund in 1610. *Erotica feu Amatoria* Andreæ capellarii regis, &c. See [Raynouard's] *Poefies des Troubadours*, von Aretins *Aufpruche der Minnegerichte München*, 1813, and No. v. of the *Retrofpective Review*.—Price. See alfo Cochrane's *Foreign Quarterly Review* for 1835.—*Rye.*]

castle; insomuch that many of these devotees, during so desperate a pilgrimage, perished by the inclemency of the weather, and died martyrs to their profession.[1]

The early universality of the French language greatly contributed to facilitate the circulation of the poetry of the troubadours in other countries. The Frankish language was familiar even at Constantinople and its dependent provinces in the eleventh century, and long afterwards. Raymond Montaniero, an historian of Catalonia, who wrote about the year 1300, says that the French tongue was as well known in the Morea and at Athens as at Paris. "E parlavan axi belle Francis com dins en Paris."[2] The oldest Italian poetry seems to be founded on that of Provence. The word *sonnet* was adopted from the French into the Italian versification. It occurs in the *Roman de la Rose*, "Lais d'amour et *sonnets* courtois."[3] Boccaccio copied many of his best tales from the troubadours.[4] Several of

[1] See D. Vaisette, *Hist. du Languedoc*, tom. iv. p. 184, *seq.*
[2] *Hist. Arragon.* c. 261. [3] v. 720.
[4] Particularly from Rutebeuf and Herbers. Rutebeuf was living in the year 1310. He wrote tales and stories of entertainment in verse, [a collected edition of which was published by Jubinal, 1839, two vols., 8vo.] It is certain that Boccaccio took from this old French minstrel Nov. x. Giorn. ix. And perhaps two or three others. Herbers lived about the year [1260. See Raynouard, *ut supr.*] He wrote a French romance in verse, called *Dolopathos*. He translated it from the Latin of [Jean, moine de Hautesville:

"blans moinnes de bone vie,
De Haute-selve l'abaie,
A ceste estoire novellée;
Par biau latin l'a ordenée.
Herberz la velt en romanz trère,
Et del romanz . 1 . livre fere."
Dolopathos, edit. 1856, p. 4.]

It has great variety, and contains several agreeable stories, pleasant adventures, emblems, and proverbs. Boccaccio has taken from it four tales, viz., Nov. ii. Giorn. iii. Nov. iv. Giorn. vii. Nov. viii. Giorn. viii.; and the Tale of the Boy who had never seen a woman, since finely touched by Fontaine. An Italian book called *Erastus* is compiled from this *Romance of the Seven Sages*. It is said to have been first composed by Sandaber the Indian, a writer of proverbs: that it afterwards appeared successively in Hebrew, Arabic, Syriac, and Greek; was at length translated into Latin by the monk above mentioned, and from thence into French by Herbers. It is very probable that the monk translated it from some Greek manuscript of the dark ages, which Huet says was to be found in some libraries. Three hundred years after its composition, the *Roman* of Herbers was translated into Dutch, and again from the Dutch into Latin. There is an English abridgment of it, which is a story-book for children. See *Mem. Lit.* tom. ii. p. 731. Fauchet, p. 106, 160. Huet, *Orig. Fab. Rom.* 136. Fabric. *Bibl. Gr.* x. 339. Massieu, *Poes. Fr.* p. 137. Crescimben. *Volg. Poes.* vol. i. l, v. p. 332.

The ground-work of *Dolopathos* is a Greek story-book called *Syntipas*, often cited by Du Cange, whose copy appears to have been translated from the Syriac. See *Gloss. Med. et Infim. Græcitat.—Ind. Auctor*, p. 33. In Harl. MSS. 5560, is another, which is said to be translated from the Persic. Fabricius says, that *Syntipas* was printed at Venice, *lingua vulgari*. Bibl. Gr. x. 515. On the whole, the plan of *Syntipas* appears to be exactly the same with that of *Les Sept Sages*, the Italian *Erasto*, and our own little story-book the *Seven Wise Masters;* except that, instead of Dioclesian of Rome, the king is called *Cyrus of Persia;* and, instead of one Tale, each of the philosophers tells two. The circumstance of Persia is an argument, that *Syntipas* was originally an oriental composition. See what is collected on this

Dante's fictions are derived from the same fountain. Dante has honoured some of them with a seat in his Paradise:[1] and in his tract *De Vulgari Eloquentia*, has mentioned Thibault, King of Navarre, as a pattern for writing poetry.[2] With regard to Dante's capital work, the *Inferno*, Raoul de Houdane, a French bard, about the year 1180, wrote a poem, entitled *Le Voye ou le Songe d'Enfer*.[3] Both Boccaccio and Dante studied at Paris, where they much improved their taste by reading the songs of Thibault, King of Navarre, Gaces Brules, Chatelain de Coucy, and other ancient French fabulists.[4] Petrarch's refined ideas of love are chiefly drawn from those amorous reveries of the Provençals which I have above described; heightened, perhaps, by the Platonic system, and exaggerated by the subtilising spirit of Italian fancy. Varchi and Pignatelli have written professed treatises on the nature of Petrarch's love. But neither they, nor the rest of the Italians who to this day continue to debate a point of so much consequence, consider how powerfully Petrarch must have been influenced, to talk of love in so peculiar a strain, by studying the poets of Provence. His *Triomfo d'Amore* has much imagery copied from Auçelm Faydit, one of the most celebrated of these bards. He has likewise many imitations from the works of Arnaud Daniel, who is called the most eloquent of the troubadours.[5] Petrarch, in one of his sonnets, represents his mistress Laura sailing on the River Rhone, in company with twelve Provençal ladies, who at that time presided over the *Court of Love*.[6]

Pasquier observes, that the Italian poetry arose as the Provençal declined.[7] It is a proof of the decay of invention among the French in the beginning of the fourteenth century, that about that period

---

curious subject, which is intimately concerned with the history of the invention of the middle ages by [Tyrwhitt, Wright, and others]. There is a translation of this romance in octosyllable verse, MSS. *Cotton. Galb.* E ix. It is entitled *The Proces of the Seven Sages*, and agrees entirely with *Les Sept Sages de Rome* in French prose. MSS. *Harl.* 3860. See also MSS. C. C. Coll. Oxon. 252. The Latin book, called *Historia Septem Sapientum Romæ*, is not a very scarce MS.; it was printed before [1480], see Mr. Wright's *Dissert. on the Seven Sages*, prefixed to the present work, where the whole subject is much more systematically and satisfactorily handled than in the incidental and desultory note introduced by Warton here rather out of place.] Many of the old French minstrels deal much in tales and novels of humour and amusement, like those of Boccaccio's *Decameron*. They call them *Fabliaux*. [It is from these Fabliaux that Boccaccio has borrowed many of his tales, and not from the Troubadours, who were, more properly speaking, the poets of Provence.—*Douce*.]

[1] Compare Crescimben. *Volg. Poes.* l. i. c. xiv. p. 162.
[2] *Commed. Infern.* cant. 22.   [3] Fauch. *Rec.* p. 96.
[4] See Fauchet, *Rec.* pp. 47, 116; and Huet, *Rom.* pp. 121, 108.
[5] He lived about 1189. Beauchamps, *Recherch.* p. 5. Nostradamus asserts, that Petrarch stole many things from a troubadour, called Richard seigneur de Barbezeiuz, who is placed under 1383. Petrarch, however, was dead at that time.
[6] Sonnet clxxxviii. *Dodici Donne*, &c. The Academici della Crusca, in their Dictionary, quote a MS. entitled *Libro d'Amore* of the year 1408. It is also referred to by Crescimbeni in his *Lives of the Provençal Poets*. It contains verdicts or determinations in the *Court of Love*.
[7] Pasq. *Recherch. de la France*, vii. 5, pp. 609, 611, edit. 1633.

they began to translate into prose their old metrical romances: such as the fables of King Arthur, of Charlemagne, of Ogier le Danois, of Renaud de Montauban, and other illustrious champions, whom their early writers had celebrated in rhyme.[1] At length, about 1380, in the place of the Provençal a new species of poetry succeeded in France, consisting of Chants Royaux,[2] Balades, Rondeaux, and Pastorales.[3] This was distinguished by the appellation of the New Poetry: and Froissart, who has been mentioned above chiefly in the character of an historian, cultivated it with so much success, that he has been called its author. The titles of Froissart's poetical pieces will alone serve to illustrate the nature of this poetry; but they prove, at the same time, that the Provençal cast of composition still continued to prevail. They are, *The Paradise of Love, A Panegyric on the Month of May, The Temple of Honour, The Flower of the Daisy, Amorous Lays, Pastorals, The Amorous Prison, Royal Ballads in honour of our Lady, The Ditty of the Amorous [Espinette, or little Thorn,] Virelais, Rondeaus, and The Plea of the Rose and Violet.*[4] Whoever examines Chaucer's smaller pieces will perceive that they

---

[1] These translations, in which the originals were much enlarged, produced an infinite number of other romances in prose; and the old metrical romances soon became unfashionable and neglected. The romance of *Perceforrest*, one of the largest of the French romances of chivalry, was written in verse about 1220. It was not till many years afterwards translated into prose. M. Falconet, an ingenious inquirer into the early literature of France, is of opinion, that the most ancient romances, such as that of the *Round Table*, were first written in Latin prose: it being well known that Turpin's *Charlemagne*, as it is now extant, was originally composed in that language. He thinks they were translated into French rhymes, and at last into French prose, *tels que nous les avons aujourduy.* See *Hist. Acad. Inscript.* vii. 293. But part of this doctrine may be justly doubted.

[2] With regard to the *Chaunt Royal*, Pasquier describes it to be a song in honour of God, the holy Virgin, or any other argument of dignity, especially if joined with distress. It was written in heroic stanzas, and closed with a *l'Envoy*, or stanza containing a recapitulation, dedication, or the like. Chaucer calls the *Chant royal* above mentioned a *Kyngis Note. Mill. T.* v. 111, p. 25. His *Complaint of Venus* [as well as the] *Cuckow and Nightingale* and *La belle Dame sans Mercy,* [both wrongly attributed to him] have all a *l'Envoy*, and belong to this species of French verse. Chaucer's *l'Envoy* to the *Complaint of Venus*, or *Mars and Venus*, ends with these lines:

"And eke to me hit is a grete penaunce,
Syth ryme in Englissh hath such skarceté,
To folowe worde by worde the curiosité
Of Graunson floure of hem that make, in Fraunce."

[Morris's *Chaucer*, vi. 247, v. 377.] *Make* signifies to *write poetry*; and here we see that this poem was translated from the French. See also [the poem called] *Chaucer's Dream*, v. 2204. Petrarch has the *Envoi*.

[3] About this time, a Prior of S. Genevieve at Paris wrote a small treatise entitled, *L'Art de Dictier Ballades et Rondelles.* See Beauchamp's *Rech. Theatr.* p. 88. Massieu says this is the first *Art of Poetry* printed in France. *Hist. Poes. Fr.* p. 222. See [Pelletier,] *L'Art Poétique*, 1555, liv. 11, ch. i. *De l'Ode.* [Compare *infra*, iv. 252-3.]

[4] Pasquier, *ubi supr.* p. 612. Who calls such pieces *Mignardises*. [In vol. vii. of the *Memoires de l'Academie des Inscriptions*, p. 287, there is an account of a manuscript describing a society called "La Cour amoureuse des Rois des Espinettes."—*Douce.*]

are altogether formed on this plan, and often compounded of these ideas. Chaucer himself declares that he wrote

<blockquote>
many an ympne for your holy dayes
¹That highten Balades, Roundels, Virelayes.²
</blockquote>

But above all, [the] *Flower and the Leaf*, [attributed to Chaucer, but most probably written many years after he died], in which an air of rural description predominates, and where the allegory is principally conducted by mysterious allusions to the virtues or beauties of the vegetable world, to flowers and plants, exclusive of its general romantic and allegoric vein, bears a strong resemblance to some of these subjects. The poet is happily placed in a delicious arbour, interwoven with eglantine. Imaginary troops of knights and ladies advance: some of the ladies are crowned with flowers, and others with chaplets of agnus castus, and these are respectively subject to *a Lady of the Flower and a Lady of the Leaf.*³ Some are clothed in green, and others in white. Many of the knights are distinguished in much the same manner. But others are crowned with leaves of oak or of other trees: others carry branches of oak, laurel, hawthorn, and woodbine.⁴ Besides this profusion of vernal ornaments, the whole procession glitters with gold, pearls, rubies, and other costly decorations. They are preceded by minstrels clothed in green and crowned with flowers. One of the ladies sings a bargaret, or pastoral, in praise of the daisy:

<blockquote>
A bargaret⁵ in praising the daisie⁶
For, as me thought, among her notes swete,
She said, *Si douse est la Margarete*.⁷
</blockquote>

---

¹ Here is an ellipsis. He means, *And Poems.*

² [*Prol. Leg. Good Women.* Morris's *Chaucer*, v. 289, ver. 422.] He mentions this sort of poetry in the *Frankelein's Tale*, ver. [218, edit. Morris.]

<blockquote>
"Of suche matiere [love] maden he many layes,
Songes compleigntes, roundeletes, virrelayes."
</blockquote>

Compare *Chaucer's Dreme*, ver. 973. In the *Floure and Leafe* we have the words of a French Roundeau, ver. 177.

³ In a decision of the Court of Love cited by Fontenelle, the judge is called *Le Marquis des fleures et violettes.* Font. *ubi supr.* p. 15.   ⁴ ver. 270.

⁵ Rather *Bergerette*. A song *du Berger*, of a *shepherd*. [Hence also perhaps the Barginet (or pastoral) of Antimachus in England's Helicon, 1600. Bargenet is mentioned as a dance by Sir T. Elyot and Geo. Gascoigne, whence Mr. Steevens conjectured that the phrase might be equivalent to our *Nancy Dawson's jig*, and might signify a short metrical performance as well as a dance. See note on the term in *Cens. Lit.* i. 422.—*Park.*]

⁶ [Morris's *Chaucer*, iv. 99, ver. 348.]

⁷ A panegyric on this flower is again introduced in the Prologue to the *Leg. of G. Wom.* ver. 180:

<blockquote>
"The longe day I shoope me for tabide
For nothing ellis, and I shal nat lye,
But for to loke upon the daysie;
That men by reson wel it callè may
The daisie, or elles the ye of day,
The emperice, and floure of floures alle," &c.
</blockquote>

Speght supposes that he means to pay a compliment to Lady Margaret, countess of Pembroke, King Edward's daughter, one of his patronesses. See the *Balade* beginning In Fevrere, &c., ver. 688. Froissart's song in praise of the daisy might

This might have been Froissart's song: at least this is one of his
subjects. In the mean time a nightingale, seated in a laurel-tree,
whose shade would cover an hundred persons, sings the whole service,
"longing to May." Some of the knights and ladies do obeysance
to the leaf, and some to the flower of the daisy. Others are represented as worshipping a bed of flowers. Flora is introduced " of
these flouris goddesse." The lady of the leaf invites the lady of
the flower to a banquet. Under these symbols is much morality
couched. The leaf signifies perseverance and virtue: the flower
denotes indolence and pleasure. Among those who are crowned
with the leaf, are the knights of King Arthur's round table, and
Charlemagne's Twelve Peers; together with the knights of the
order of the Garter [lately] established by Edward III.[1]

But these fancies seem more immediately to have taken their rise
from the Floral Games instituted in France in the year 1324,[2]
which filled the French poetry with images of this sort.[3] They
were founded by Clementina Isaure, countess of Toulouse, and annually celebrated in the month of May. She published an edict,
which assembled all the poets of France in artificial arbours dressed
with flowers: and he that produced the best poem was rewarded
with a violet of gold. There were likewise inferior prizes of flowers
made in silver. In the mean time the conquerors were crowned
with natural chaplets of their own respective flowers. During the
ceremony, degrees were also conferred. He who had won a prize
three times was created a doctor *en gaye Science*, the name of the
poetry of the Provençal troubadours. The instrument of creation
was in verse.[4] This institution, however fantastic, soon became
common through the whole kingdom of France: and these romantic
rewards, distributed with the most impartial attention to merit, at
least infused an useful emulation, and in some measure revived the
languishing genius of the French poetry.

---

have the same tendency: for he was patronized both by Edward and Philippa.
Marguarite is French for Daisy. Perhaps the same compliment is intended by the
" Margarite perle," *Test. Love*, p. 483, col. i. &c. Urr. See also *Prol. Leg. G. Wom.*
v. 218, 224. That Prologue has many images like those in the *Flower and the Leaf*.
See *Le dit de la fleur de lis et de la Marguerite*, by Gillaume Machaut, *Acad.
Inscript.* xx. p. 381, x. 669. On the whole, it may be doubted whether either
Froissart or Chaucer means Margaret, countess of Pembroke. For compare
Append. Pref. Canterb. Tales, vol. i. p. xxxiv. [edit. Tyrwhitt.] I add, that in
the year 1547, the poetical pieces of Margaret de Valois, queen of Navarre, were
collected and published under the title of *Marguerite de la Marguerite des princesses,
tres illustre royne de Navarre*, by [Symon] de la Haye, her valet de chambre. It
was common in France to give the title of Marguerites to studied panegyrics and
flowery compositions of every kind, both in prose and verse.

[1] ver. 516, 517, 519. [2] *Mem. Lit.* tom. vii. p. 422, 4to.
[3] Hence Froissart in the *Epinette Amoureuse*, describing his romantic amusements,
says he was delighted with
" Violettes en leur saisons
Et roses blanches et vermeilles," &c.
See *Mem. Lit.* x. 665, 287.
[4] *Recherches sur les poetes couronnez.* (*Mem. Lit.* x. 567.)

The French and Italian poets, whom Chaucer imitates, abound in allegorical perfonages: and it is remarkable that the early poets of Greece and Rome were fond of thefe creations. Homer has given us *Strife, Contention, Fear, Terror, Tumult, Defire, Perfuafion,* and *Benevolence.* We have in Hefiod *Darknefs,* and many others, if the Shield of Hercules be of his hand. *Comus* occurs in the *Agamemnon* of Æfchylus; and in the *Prometheus* of the fame poet *Strength* and *Force* are two perfons of the drama, and perform the capital parts. The fragments of Ennius indicate that his poetry confifted much of perfonifications. He fays, that in one of the Carthaginian wars the gigantic image of *Sorrow* appeared in every place: "Omnibus endo locis ingens apparet imago *Triftitias.*" Lucretius has drawn the great and terrible figure of *Superftition,* "Quæ caput e cœli regionibus oftendebat." He alfo mentions, in a beautiful proceffion of the Seafons, *Calor aridus, Hyems,* and *Algus.* He introduces *Medicine muttering with filent fear,* in the midft of the deadly peftilence at Athens. It feems to have efcaped the many critics who have written on Milton's noble but romantic allegory of *Sin* and *Death,* that he took the perfon of Death from the *Alceftis* of his favourite tragedian Euripides, where Θανατος is a principal agent in the drama. As knowledge and learning increafe, poetry begins to deal lefs in imagination: and thefe fantaftic beings give way to real manners and living characters.

[Of Laurence Minot, the contemporary of Chaucer, who in the beginning of the year 1352 wrote, or at leaft completed,[1] a feries of poems on the wars of Edward III., fome fhort account may be here not unfitly introduced. Minot appears to have been a native of one of the northern counties. "The lateft event they (his poems) commemorate, is the capture of Guifnes-Caftle, which happened, according to Avefbury, on St. Vincent's day, the 22nd of January, 1351-2."]

The ftanza of one of Minot's poems on the wars of Edward III. is the fame as Chaucer's *Sir Topas*:[2]

> Edward oure cumly king
> In Braband has his woning,
>   With mani cumly knight,
> And in that land, trewly to tell,
> Ordains he ftill for to dwell,
>   To time he think to fight.
>
> Now God that es of mightes mafte,
> Grant him grace of the Haly Gafte,
>   His heritage to win;
> And Mari moder of mercy fre,
> Save oure king, and his menʒe,
>   Fro forow, fchame, and fyn.
>
> Thus in Braband has he bene,
> Whare he bifore was feldom fene,
>   For to prove thaire japes;

---

[1] [Minot's *Poems,* ed. 1795, *Introd.*]   [2] MSS. Cott. *Galb.* E. ix.

Now no langer wil he spare,
Bot unto Fraunce fast will he fare,
  To consort him with grapes.

Furth he ferd into France,
God save him fro mischance,
  And all his cumpany;
The nobill duc of Braband
With him went into that land,
  Redy to lif or dy.

Than the riche floure de lice
Wan thare ful litill prise,
  Fast he fled for ferde;
The right aire [1] of that cuntre
Es cumen with all his knightes fre
  To schac [2] him by the berd.

Sir Philip the Valayse,
Wit his men in tho dayes,
  To batale had he thoght;
He bad his men tham purvay
Withowten lenger delay,
  Bot he ne held it noght.

He broght folk ful grete wone,
Ay sevyn ogains one,
  That ful wele wapind [3] were;
Bot sone when he herd asery,
That king Edward was nere tharby,
  Than durst he noght cum nere.

In that morning fell a myst;
And when oure Inglis men it wist,
  It changed all thaire chere:
Oure king unto God made his bone,
And God sent him gude consort sone,
  The weder wex ful clere.

Oure king and his men held the felde,
Stalworthly with spere and schelde,
  And thoght to win his right;
With lordes and with knightes kene,
And other doghty men bydene,
  That war ful frek to fight.

When sir Philip of France herd tell,
That king Edward in feld walld dwell,
  Than gayned him no gle;
He traisted of no better bote,
Bot both on hors and on fote,
  He hasted him to fle.

It semid he was ferd for strokes,
When he did fell his grete okes
  Obout his pavilyoune.
Abated was than all his pride,
For langer thare durst he noght bide,
  His bost was broght all doune.

---

[1] heir.   [2] shake.   [3] weaponed, armed.

The king of Beme had cares colde,
That was ful hardy, and bolde,
  A ſtede to umſtride :
[He and] The king als of **Naverne**
War faire ferd in the ferne
  Thaire heviddes for to hide.

And leves wele, it is no lye,
The felde hat Flemangrye
  That king Edward was in ;
With princes that war ſtif ande bolde,
And dukes that war doghty tolde,
  In batayle to begin.

The princes that war riche on raw,
Gert nakers ſtrikes and trumpes blaw,
  And made mirth at thaire might ;
Both alblaſt and many a bow,
War redy railed opon a row,
  And ful frek for to fight.

Gladly thai gaf mete and drink,
So that thai ſuld the better ſwink,
  The wight men that thar ware :
Sir Philip of Fraunce fled for dout,
And hied him hame with all his rout,
  Coward, God giff him care.

For thare than had the lely flowre
Lorn all halely his honowre,
  That ſo gat fled for ferd ;
Bot oure king Edward come ful ſtill,
When that he trowed no harm him till,
  And keped him in the berde.[1]

[A few other ſpecimens of Minot may here be added] :

  Men may rede in Romance[2] right,
  Of a grete clerk that Merlin hight ;
  Ful many bokes er of him wreten,
  Als thir clerkes wele may witten ;
  And ȝit in many prevé nokes
  May men find of Merlin bokes.
  Merlin ſaid thus with his mowth,
  Out of the north into the ſowth,
  Suld cum a bare over the ſe,
  That ſuld mak many man to fle ;
  And in the ſe, he ſaid ful right,
  Suld he ſchew ful mekill might ;
  And in France he ſuld bigin
  To mak tham wrath that er tharein :
  Untill the ſe his taile reche ſale,
  All folk of France to mekill bale.

---

[1] [This and the following ſpecimens from Minot have been corrected by Mr. Ritſon's edition of his poems.]

[2] In another place Minot calls the book on which his narrative is founded, the *Romance :*

    " How Edward, als the Romance ſaies,
    Held his ſege before Calais."

Thus have I mater for to make
For a nobill prince fake.
Help me god, my wit is thin,
Now Laurence Minot will bigin.

 A Bore es broght on bankes hare,
With ful batail bifor his breft,
For John of France will he noght fpare.
In Normondy to tak his reft.—
At Creffy when thai brak the brig,
That faw Edward with both his ine ;
Than liked him no langer to lig,
Ilk Inglis-man on others rig ;
Over that water er thai went,
To batail er thai baldly big,
With brade ax, and with bowes bent,
With bent bowes thai war ful bolde,
For to fell of the Frankifch-men.
Thai gert tham lig with cares colde.
Ful fari was fir Philip then
He faw the toun o ferrum bren,
And folk for ferd war faft fleand
The teres he lete ful rathly ren
Out of his eghen, I underftand.
Than cum Philip, ful redy dight,
Toward the toun with all his rowt
With him come mani a kumly knight,
And all umfet the bare obout :
The bare made tham ful law to lout,
And delt them knokkes to thaire mede
He gert tham ftumbill that war ftout.
Thare helpid nowther ftaf ne ftede
Stedes ftrong bilevid ftill
Bifide Creffy opon the grene
Sir Philip wanted all his will
That was wele on his fembland fene,
With fpere and fchelde, and helmis fchene
The bare than durft thai noght habide.
The king of Beme[1] was cant and kene,
Bot thare he left both play and pride.
Pride in prefe ne prais I noght.
Omong thir princes prowd in pall,
Princes fuld be wele bithoght
When kinges fuld tham tyll counfail call.

 The fame boar, that is, Edward [Baliol], is introduced by Minot as refifting the Scotifh invafion in 1347, at Nevil's Crofs, near Durham.[2]

---

[1] John, king of Bohemia. By Froiffart he is called inaccurately the king of Behaigne, or Charles of Luxemburgh. See Froiffart, *ut fupr.* fol. lxiv. b. The Lord Charles of Bohemia, his fon, was alfo in the battle and killed, being lately elected emperor. Holinfh. iii. 372.

[2] The reader will recollect that this verfification is in the ftructure of that of the *Lives of the Saints*, where two lines are thrown into one, viz. *Vndecim millia virginum*, MSS. Col. Trin. Oxon. 57.

  " Ellevene thoufand virgines, that fair companye was,
  Imartird wer for godis fone, ich wille telle that cas.
  A kyng ther was in Bretaygne, Maur was his name,
  A douȝter he hadde that het Vrfe, a mayde of good fame.

> Sir David the Bruse[1]
> Was at diftance,
> When Edward the Baliolfe,[2]
> Rade with his lance:
> The north end of Ingland,
> Teched him to daunce,
> When he was met on the more,
> With mekill mifchance.
> Sir Philip the Valayfe,
> May him noght avance.
> The flowres that faire war,
> Er fallen in Fraunce;
> The flowres er now fallen,
> That fers war and fell,
> A bare with his bataille,
> Has done tham to dwell.
> Sir David the Brufe,
> Said he fulde fonde
> To ride thurgh all Ingland,
> Wuld he noght wonde:
> At the Weftminfter Hall,
> Suld his ftedes ftonde,
> Whils oure king Edward
> War out of the londe.

Edward's victory over the Spaniards in a fea-fight, in 1350, was a part of Minot's general fubject:

> I wald noght fpare for to fpeke,
> Wift I to fpede,

> So fair woman me nyfte non, ne fo guod in none poynte,
> Criftene was al hire ken, fwithe noble and queynte:
> Of hire fairhede and guodneffe me told in eche fonde fide,
> That the word com into Engelonde, and felle wher wide.
> A kyng ther was in Engelonde, man of gret power,
> Of this maide he herde telle gret nobleife far and ner."

The minftrel, who ufed the perpetual return of a kind of plain chant, made his paufe or clofe at every hemiftick. In the fame manner the verfes of the following poem were divided by the minftrel. MSS. Cott. Jul. V. fol. 175. [The tranfcript is not later than the year 1300:]

> "Als y yod on ay Monday, by twene Wiltindon and Walle,
> Me ane after brade way, ay litel man y mette withalle,
> The lefte that ever y fathe, to fay oither in boure oither in halle,
> His robe was noither grene na gray, bot alle yt was of riche palle.
> On me he cald and bad me bide, wel ftille y ftode ay litel fpace;
> Fro Lanchefter the Parke fyde, yeen he come wel faire his pace: &c.
> I biheld that litel man, bi the ftrete als we gon gae,
> His berde was fyde ay large fpan, and glided als the fether of pae.
> His heved was wyte as any fwan, his higehen were gret and grai, &c.
> His robe was al golde biganne, well crittlik maked i underftande,
> Botones afurd everilke ane, from his elbouthe on til his hande."

They enter a caftle:

> "The bankers on the binkes lay, and faire lordes fette y fonde,
> In ilk ay hirn y herd ay lay, and levedys fouthe me loud fange."

[1] David Bruce, king of Scotland. See Langtoft, p. 116.
[2] [Edward de Baliol. Edward III. was not in England when the affair at Nevill's Crofs happened.—*Ritfon*.]

>   Of wight men with wapin,
>   And worthly in wede.
>   That now er driven to dale,
>   And ded all thaire dede,
>   Thai fail in the fee-gronde,
>   Fiffches to fede!
>   Fele Fiffches thai fede,
>   For all thaire grete fare,
>   It was in the waniand
>   That thai come thare.
>   Thai failed furth in the Swin
>   In a fomers tyde,
>   With trompes and taburns,
>   And mikell other pryde.

SECTION XIX.

F Chaucer had not exifted, the compofitions of John Gower, the next poet in fucceffion, would alone have been fufficient to refcue the reigns of Edward III. and Richard II. from the imputation of barbarifm. His education was liberal and uncircumfcribed, his courfe of reading extenfive, and he tempered his feverer ftudies with a knowledge of life. By a critical cultivation of his native language, he laboured to reform its irregularities, and to eftablifh an Englifh ftyle. In thefe refpects he refembled his friend and contemporary Chaucer:[1] but he participated in no confiderable portion of Chaucer's fpirit, imagination, and elegance. His language is tolerably perfpicuous, and his verfification often harmonious; but his poetry is of a grave and fententious turn. He has much good fenfe, folid reflection, and ufeful obfervation. But he is ferious and didactic on all occafions: he preferves the tone of the fcholar and the moralift on the moft lively topics. For this reafon he feems to have been characterized by Chaucer with the appellation of the *moral* Gower.[2] But his talent is not confined to Englifh verfe only. He wrote alfo in Latin, and copied Ovid's *Elegies* with fome degree of purity, and with fewer falfe quantities and corrupt phrafes than any of our countrymen had yet exhibited fince the twelfth century.

Gower's capital work [or, as he calls it, *Cronica Tripartita*,] confifts of three parts, only the laft of which properly furnifhes matter

---

[1] It is certain that they both lived and wrote together. But I have confidered Chaucer firft, among other reafons hereafter given, as Gower furvived him [feveral years.] Chaucer died October 25, 1400, aged 72 years. Gower died [between the 15th of Auguft and the 24th of October, 1408. See *Confeffio Amantis*, ed. 1857, i. xvii.-xviii.]

[2] *Troil. and Crefs.* ad calc.

for our present inquiry. It is entitled *Speculum Meditantis, Vox Clamantis, Confessio Amantis*. [The last] was finished in 139[2-3].[1] The *Speculum Meditantis* [is not known to exist.][2] The *Vox Clamantis*, or the *Voice of one crying in the Wilderness*, which [has been printed for the Roxburghe Club,] contains seven books of Latin elegiacs. This work is chiefly historical, and is little more than a metrical chronicle of the insurrection of the Commons in [1381.] The best and most beautiful manuscript of it is in the library of All Souls College at Oxford, with a dedication in Latin verse, addressed by the author, when he was old and blind, to Archbishop Arundel.[3] The *Confessio Amantis*, or the *Lover's Confession*, is an English poem, in eight books, first printed by Caxton in 1483. It was written at the command of Richard II. who, meeting our poet Gower rowing on the Thames near London, invited him into the royal barge, and after much conversation requested him to *book some new thing*.[4]

This tripartite work is represented by three volumes on Gower's curious tomb in the conventual church of Saint Mary Overy in Southwark, [lately restored to something like] its ancient state; and this circumstance furnishes me with an obvious opportunity of adding an anecdote relating to our poet's munificence and piety, which ought not to be omitted. Although a poet, he largely contributed to rebuild that church in its present elegant form, and to render it a beautiful pattern of the lighter Gothic architecture; at the same time he founded, at his tomb, a perpetual chantry.

It is on the last of these pieces, the *Confessio Amantis*, that Gower's character and reputation as a poet are almost entirely founded. This poem, which bears no immediate reference to the other two divisions, is a dialogue between a lover and his confessor, who is a priest of Venus, and, like the mystagogue in the *Table* of Cebes, is called Genius. Here, as if it had been impossible for a lover not to be a good Catholic, the ritual of religion is applied to the tender passion,

---

[1] *Confess. Amant.* Prol. fol. 1, a, col. 1. [Bulleyn, in his *Dialogue both plesaunt and pitefull*, first printed before 1564, introduces a visionary description of old "moral Goore," with pen in hand, commending honest love without lust, and pleasure without pride, &c. And the dedication to Henry VIII., before Berthelet's edition of the *Confessio Amantis*, superadds to his established *moral* epithet the terms "worthy olde writer, and noble autour."—*Park*.]

[2] [Gower's *Speculum Meditantis* has never, I believe, been seen by any of our poetical antiquaries, nor does it exist in the Bodleian Library. Campbell, the author of Gower's article in the *Biographia Brit.*, and Warton, who profess to give an account of its contents, were deceived by the ambiguity of a reference in Tanner; and, instead of the work in question, describe a much shorter poem or *balade* by the same author.—*Ellis*. See also Gower's *Confessio Amantis*, ed. 1857, Introd. xxv.-vi. "At the end of the Bodl. MSS. N. E F, 819, and Fairfax, 8, is subjoined," says Mr. Park, "a notice in Latin of Gower's three principal works, and so much as relates to the Speculum is given by Mr. Ellis."]

[3] MSS. Num. 26. It occurs more than once in the Bodleian Library, and, I believe, often in private hands. There is a fine MS. of it in the British Museum. It was written in the year 1397, as appears by the following line, MSS. Bodl. 294:

"Hos ego bis deno Ricardi regis in anno."

[4] *To the Reder*, in Berthelet's edition. From the *Prologue*.

and Ovid's *Art of Love* is blended with the breviary. In the course
of the confession, every evil affection of the human heart, which may
tend to impede the progress or counteract the success of love, is
scientifically subdivided, and its fatal effects exemplified by a variety
of apposite stories, extracted from classics and chronicles. The poet
often introduces or recapitulates his matter in a few couplets of Latin
long and short verses. This was in imitation of Boethius.

This poem is strongly tinctured with those pedantic affectations concerning the passion of love, which the French and Italian poets of the fourteenth century borrowed from the troubadours of Provence, and which I have above examined at large. But the writer's particular model appears more immediately to have been John of Meun's celebrated *Roman de la Rose*. He has, however, seldom attempted to imitate the picturesque imageries and expressive personifications of that exquisite allegory. His most striking portraits, which yet are conceived with no powers of creation, nor delineated with any fertility of fancy, are *Idleness*, *Avarice*, *Micherie* or Thieving, and *Negligence*, the secretary of *Sloth*.[1] Instead of boldly clothing these qualities with corporeal attributes, aptly and poetically imagined, he coldly yet sensibly describes their operations, and enumerates their properties. What Gower wanted in invention, he supplied from his common-place book, which appears to have been stored with an inexhaustible fund of instructive maxims, pleasant narrations, and philosophical definitions. It seems to have been his object to crowd all his erudition into this elaborate performance. Yet there is often some degree of contrivance and art in his manner of introducing and adapting subjects of a very distant nature, which are totally foreign to his general design.

In the fourth book our confessor turns chemist; and discoursing at large on the Hermetic science, developes its principles and exposes its abuses with great penetration.[2] He delivers the doctrines concerning the vegetable, mineral, and animal stones, to which Falstaff alludes in Shakespeare,[3] with amazing accuracy and perspicuity;[4]

---

[1] Lib. iv. f. 62, a, col. 1; lib. v. f. 94, a, col. 1; lib. iv. f. 68, a, col. 1; lib. v. f. 119, a, col. 2.

[2] Lib. iv. f. 76, b, col. 2.

[3] Falstaff mentions a philosopher's or chemist's two stones. See 2nd P. Henr. IV. act iii. sc. 2. Our author abundantly confirms Doctor Warburton's explication of this passage, which the rest of the commentators do not seem to have understood. See Ashm. *Theatr. Chemic.* p. 484, 1652.

The nations bordering upon the Jews, attributed the miraculous events of that people to those external means and material instruments, such as symbols, ceremonies, and other visible signs or circumstances, which by God's special appointment, under their mysterious dispensation, they were directed to use. Among the observations which the oriental Gentiles made on the history of the Jews, they found that the Divine will was to be known by certain appearances in precious stones. The Magi of the East, believing that the preternatural discoveries obtained by means of the Urim and Thummim, a contexture of gems in the breast-plate of the Mosaic priests, were owing to some virtue inherent in those stones, adopted the

---

[4] Lib. iv. f. 77, a, col. 1.

although this doctrine was adopted from systems then in vogue, as we shall see below. In another place he applies the Argonautic expedition in search of the golden fleece, which he relates at length, to the same visionary philosophy.[1] Gower very probably conducted his associate Chaucer into these profound mysteries, which had been just opened to our countrymen by the books of Roger Bacon.[g]

In the seventh book, the whole circle of the Aristotelic philosophy is explained; which our lover is desirous to learn, supposing that the importance and variety of its speculations might conduce to sooth his anxieties by diverting and engaging his attention. Such a discussion was not very likely to afford him much consolation: especially, as hardly a single ornamental digression is admitted, to decorate a field naturally so destitute of flowers. Almost the only one is the following description of the chariot and crown of the sun; in which the Arabian ideas concerning precious stones are interwoven with Ovid's fictions and the classical mythology:

> Of golde gliftrend spoke and whele
> The sonne his carte[3] hath faire and wele,
> In whiche he sitte, and is coroned
> With brighte stones environed,
> Of which if that I speke shall
> There be to-fore in speciall
> Set in the front of his corone
> Thre stones, whiche no persone
> Hath upon erthe, and the first is
> By name cleped licuchis.
> That other two be cleped thus
> Astrices and ceramius
> In his corone, also behinde,
> By olde bokes as I finde,
> There ben of worthy stones thre
> Set ech of hem in his degre,
> Wherof a cristall is that one,
> Which that corone is set upon.

---

knowledge of the occult properties of gems as a branch of their magical system. Hence it became the peculiar profession of one class of their sages, to investigate and interpret the various shades and coruscations, and to explain, to a moral purpose, the different colours, the dews, clouds, and imageries, which gems, differently exposed to the sun, moon, stars, fire, or air, at particular seasons, and inspected by persons particularly qualified, were seen to exhibit. This notion being once established, a thousand extravagancies arose, of healing diseases, of procuring victory, and of seeing future events, by means of precious stones and other lucid substances. See Plin. *Nat. Hist.* xxxvii. 9, 10. These superstitions were soon ingrafted into the Arabian philosophy, from which they were propagated all over Europe, and continued to operate even so late as the visionary experiments of Dee and Kelly. It is not in the mean time at all improbable, that the Druidical doctrines concerning the virtues of stones were derived from these lessons of the Magi: and they are still to be traced among the traditions of the vulgar, in those parts of Britain and Ireland, where Druidism retained its latest establishments. See Martin's *West. Isles*, p. 167, 225. And Aubrey's *Miscell.* p. 128. When Richard I. in 1191 took Cyprus, he is said to have found the castles filled with rich furniture of gold and silver, "necnon lapidibus pretiosis, et plurimam virtutem habentibus." G. Vines. *Iter Hierosol.* cap. xli. p. 328, *Hist. Anglic. Script.* vol. ii. Oxon. 1687.

[1] Lib. v. f. 101, a, *seq.*   [2] See *supra.*   [3] chariot.

>The feconde is an adamant.
>The thridde is noble and avenaunt,
>Which cleped is ydriades,
>And over this yet netheles
>Upon the fides of the werke,
>After the writing of the clerke,
>There fitten five ftones mo,
>The finaragdine is one of tho,
>Jafpis and elitropius
>And vendides and jacinctus.
>Lo, thus the corone is befet,
>Wherof it fhineth well the bet,
>And in fuch wife his light to fprede
>Sit with his diademe on hede
>The fonne fhinend in his carte.
>And for to lede him fwithe and finarte
>After the brighte daies lawe
>There ben ordeined for to drawe
>Four hors his chare and him withall,
>Wherof the names telle I fhall.
>Eritheus the firft is hote,
>The which is red and fhineth hote,[1]
>The fecond Acteos the bright,
>Lampes the thridde courfer hight,
>And Philogeus is the ferth,[2]
>That bringen light unto this erth
>And gone fo fwifte upon the heven, &c.[3]

Our author clofes this courfe of the Ariftotelic philofophy with a fyftem of politics: not taken from Ariftotle's genuine treatife on that fubject, but from the firft chapter of a fpurious compilation, entitled, *Secretum Secretorum Ariftotelis*,[4] addreffed under the name of Ariftotle to his pupil Alexander the Great, and printed at Bologna in 1516. This work was treated as genuine, and explained with a learned glofs by Roger Bacon:[5] and was of fuch high reputation in Gower's age, that it was tranfcribed, and illuftrated with a commentary, for the ufe of Edward III. by his chaplain Walter de Millemete, prebendary of the collegiate church of Glafeney in Cornwall.[6] Under this head, our author takes an opportunity of giving advice to a weak yet amiable prince, his patron Richard II., on a fubject of the moft difficult and delicate nature, with much freedom and dignity. It might alfo be proved, that Gower, through this detail of the fciences, copied in many other articles the *Secretum Secretorum*, which is a fort of an abridgment of the Ariftotelic philofophy, filled with many Arabian innovations and abfurdities, and enriched with an appendix concerning the choice of wines, phlebotomy, juftice, public notaries, tournaments, and phyfiognomy, rather than from the Latin tranflations of Ariftotle. It is evident, that he copied from this work the doctrine of the three chemical ftones,

---

[1] named. [2] fourth. [3] [C. F. ed. 1857, iii. 112-13.]
[4] [A profe tranflation (about 1450) is in Lambeth MS. 501.—F.]
[5] See Wood, *Hift. Antiquit. Univ. Oxon.* lib. i. p. 15, col. 1.
[6] Tanner, Bibl. p. 527. It is cited by Bradwardine, a famous Englifh theologift, in his grand work, *De Caufa Dei*. He died 1349.

mentioned above.¹ That part of our author's astronomy, in which he speaks of the magician Nectabanus instructing Alexander the Great, when a youth, in the knowledge of the fifteen stars, and their respective plants and precious stones, appropriated to the operations of natural magic, seems to be borrowed from Callisthenes, the fabulous writer of the life of Alexander.² Yet many wonderful inventions, which occur in this romance of Alexander, are also to be found in the *Secretum Secretorum:* particularly the fiction of Alexander's Stentorian horn, mentioned above, which was heard at the distance of sixty miles, and of which Kircher has given a curious representation in his *Phonurgia,* copied from an ancient picture of this gigantic instrument, belonging to a MS. of the *Secretum Secretorum,* preserved in the Vatican.³

It is pretended by the mystic writers, that Aristotle in his old age reviewed his books, and digested his philosophy into one system or body, which he sent, in the form of an epistle, to Alexander. This is the supposititious tract⁴ of which I have been speaking; and it is thus described by Lydgate, who has translated a part of it.

> Title of this boke Lapis Philosophorum,
> Namyd also De Regimine Principum,
> Of philosophres Secretum Secretorum.—
> The which booke direct to the kyng
> Alysaundre, both in the werre and pees,
> Lyke his requeft and royall commanding,
> Fulle accomplifhid by Ariftotiles.
> Feeble of age.

Then follows a rubric " How Aristotile declareth to kynge Alyfandre of the ftonys."⁵ It was early translated into French profe,⁶ and printed in English.⁷ This work will occur again under Lydgate. There is also another forgery consecrated with the name

---

¹ There is an Epiftle under the name of Alexander the Great, *De Lapide Philofophorum,* among the *Scriptores Chemici artis auriferæ,* Bafil. 1593, tom. i. See next note.
² Or from fictitious books attributed to Alexander the Great, *De feptem Herbis feptem Planetarum,* &c. See Fabric. *Bibl. Gr.* tom. ii. 206. See *fupra.* Callifthenes is mentioned twice in this poem, Lib. vii. f. 139, b. col. 2; and vi. f. 139, b. col. 2. See a chapter of Callifthenes and Alexander, in Lydgate's *Fall of Princes,* b. iv. ch. 1, *feq.* fol. 99, edit. *ut infra.*
³ Pag. 104. See *Secretum Secretorum,* Bibl. Bodl. MSS. D. i. 5, Cap. *penult,* lib. 5.
⁴ [Harl. MSS. 2251 and 7333; Sloane MS. 2027.—F.]
⁵ MSS. Bibl. Bodl. Laud, B. 24, K. 53. Part of this manufcript is printed by Afhmole, *Theatr. Chemic.* ut fupr. p. 397. See Julius Bartolocc. tom. i. *Bibl. Rabbinic.* p. 475; and Joann. a Lent, *Theol. Judaic.* p. 6.
⁶ *Mem. de Litt.* tom. xvii. p. 737, 4to.
⁷ [*The fecret of fecrets of Ariftotyle with the gouernale of princes,* &c., tranflated and printed by R. Copland, 1528, 8vo.] A work called [*Ariftotles Politiques, or Difcourfes on Gouernment*], from the French of Louis le Roy, printed in [1597], and dedicated to Sir Robert Sidney, is Ariftotle's genuine work. In Grefham college library there is " Alexandri M. Epiftolæ ad preceptorem Ariftotelem, Anglice factæ." MSS. 52. But [this can furely have nothing to do with] Lydgate's [imperfect] poem on the fubject, [printed by Afhmole].

of Aristotle, and often quoted by the astrologers, which Gower might have used: it is *de Regiminibus coelestibus*, which had been early translated from Arabic into Latin.[1]

Considered in a general view, the *Confessio Amantis* may be pronounced to be no unpleasing miscellany of those shorter tales which delighted the readers of the middle age. Most of these are now forgotten, together with the voluminous chronicles in which they were recorded. The book which appears to have accommodated our author with the largest quantity of materials in this article, was probably a chronicle entitled *Pantheon*, or *Memoriæ Seculorum*, compiled in Latin, partly in prose and partly in verse, by Geoffrey of Viterbo, a chaplain and notary to three German emperors, who died in the year 1190.[2] It commences, according to the established practice of the historians of this age, with the creation of the world, and is brought down to the year 1186. It was first printed at Basle in 1569.[3] The learned Muratori has not scrupled to insert the five last sections of this universal history.[4] The subject of this work, to use the laborious compiler's own expressions, is the Old and New Testament; and all the emperors and kings, which have existed from the beginning of the world to his own times: of whom the origin, end, names, and achievements are commemorated.[5] The authors whom our chronicler professes to have consulted for the gentile story, are only Josephus, Dion Cassius, Strabo, Orosius, Hegesippus, Suetonius, Solinus, and Julius Africanus, among whom not one of the purer Roman historians occurs. Gower also seems to have used another chronicle written by the same Godfrey, never printed, called *Speculum Regum* or the *Mirror of Kings*, which is almost as multifarious as the last; containing a genealogy of all the potentates, Trojan and German, from Noah's flood to the reign of the emperor Henry VI., according to the chronicles of the venerable Bede, Eusebius, and Ambrosius.[6] There are, besides, two ancient collectors of marvellous and delectable occurrences to whom our author is indebted, Cassiodorus and Isidorus. Cassiodorus[7] wrote, at the command of the Gothic King Theodoric, a work named *Chronicon*

---

[1] Hotting. *Bibl. Orient.* p. 255. See Pic. Mirandulan, *contra Astrolog.* lib. i. p. 284.
[2] Jacob. Quetif. i. p. 740.
[3] Again, among *Scriptor. de Reb. Germanicis*, by Pistorius, 1584. Lastly in a new edit. of Pistorius, by Struvius, Ratisbon, 1726, fol. There is a chronicle, I believe sometimes confounded with Godfrey's *Pantheon*, called the *Pantaleone*, from the creation to 1162, about which time it was compiled by the Benedictine monk of Saint Pantaleon at Cologne, printed by Eccard, with a German translation, in the first volume of *Scriptores Medii Ævi*, pp. 683, 945. It was continued to 1237, by Godfridus, a Pantaleonist monk. This continuation, which has considerable merit as a history, is extant in Freherus, *Rer. Germanicar.* tom. i. edit. Struvius, p. 335.
[4] [*Rerum Ital. Script.* vii. p. 346.
[5] *in proem.* [6] See Lambecc. ii. p. 274.
[7] See *Confes. Amant.* lib. vii. f. 156, b, col. 1. And our author to King Henry, v. 330. In the prologue to the *Fructus Temporum*, printed at St. Alban's in 1483, one of the authors is "Cassiodorus of the actys of emperours and bisshoppys."

Breve, commencing with our first parents, and deduced to the year 519, chiefly from Eusebius, the chronicles of Prosper and Jerom, and Aurelius Victor's Origin of the Roman nation.[1] An Italian translation by Lodovico Dolce was printed in 1561.[2] Isidorus Hispalensis, cited by [the author of the *Life of Alexander*] and by Chaucer, in the seventh century framed from the same author a Latin Chronicle, from Adam to the time of the Emperor Heraclius, first printed in [an Italian translation at Ascoli in 1477, and republished at Friuli in 1480. The original Latin was printed in 1593].[3]

These comprehensive systems of all sacred and profane events, which in the middle ages multiplied to an excessive degree, superseded the use of the classics and other established authors, whose materials they gave in a commodious abridgment, and in whose place, by selecting those stories only which suited the taste of the times, they substituted a more agreeable kind of reading: nor was it by these means only, that they greatly contributed to retard the acquisition of those ornaments of style and other arts of composition, which an attention to the genuine models would have afforded, but by being written without any ideas of elegance, and in the most barbarous phraseology. Yet productive as they were of these and other inconvenient consequences, they were not without their use in the rude periods of literature. By gradually weaning the minds of readers from monkish legends, they introduced a relish for real and rational history; and kindling an ardour for inquiring into the transactions of past ages, at length awakened a curiosity to obtain a more accurate and authentic knowledge of important events by searching the original authors. Nor are they to be entirely neglected in modern and more polished ages. For, besides that they contain curious pictures of the credulity and ignorance of our ancestors, they frequently preserve facts transcribed from books which have not descended to posterity. It is extremely probable that the plan on which they are all constructed, that of deducing a perpetual history from the creation of the writer's age, was partly taken from Ovid's *Metamorphoses*, and partly from the Bible.

In the meantime there are three histories of a less general nature, which Gower seems more immediately to have followed in some of his tales. These are Colonna's [*Gest Historial* of the *Destruction of*] *Troy*, the *Romance of Sir Lancelot*, and the *Gesta Romanorum*.

From Colonna's history, which he calls *The Tale of Troy*, *The Book of Troy*,[4] and sometimes *The Cronicle*,[5] he has taken all that relates to

---

[1] [*Chronica ab Adamo*, &c. *Opera*, 1729, i.]
[2] *Compendio di Sesto Ruffo, con la Cronica di Cassiodoro, de Fatti de Romani*, &c. 4to.
[3] [See Brunet, iii. 464.]
[4] Of Palamedes and Nauplius, "The boke of Troie whoso rede." Lib. ii. f. 52, b. col. 2. The story of Jason and Medea, "whereof the tale in speciall is in the *boke of Troie* writte." Lib. v. f. 101, a, col. 2. Of the Syrens seen by Ulysses, "which in the *tale of Troie* I finde." Lib. i. f. 10, b, col. 1. Of the eloquence of Ulysses, "As in the *boke of Troie* is funde." Lib. vii. f. 150, a, col. 1, &c. &c. See *supra*.
[5] In the story of the Theban chief Capaneus, "This knight as the *Cronike* seine."

the Trojan and Grecian ſtory, or, in Milton's language, *The Tale of Troy Divine*. This piece was firſt printed at Cologne [before] 1477.[1] An Italian tranſlation appeared at Venice in 1481. It was tranſlated into Italian ſo early as 1324 by Filippo Ceffi, a Florentine,[2] [according to ſome, or, as others ſay, not till 1333, and by Matteo Bellebuoni]. By ſome writers it is called the Britiſh as well as the Trojan ſtory;[3] and there are MSS. in which it is entitled the hiſtory of Medea and Jaſon. In the Italian tranſlation it is called *La Storia Trojana*. This hiſtory is repeatedly called the *Troie Boke* by Lydgate, who tranſlated it into Engliſh verſe.[4]

As to the romance of *Sir Lancelot*, our author, among others on the ſubject, refers to a volume of which he was the hero: perhaps that of Robert [de] Borron, altered ſoon afterwards by Godefroy de Leigny, under the title of *Le Roman de la Charette*, and printed with additions in 1494:

> For if thou wilt the *bokes* rede
> Of Launcelot and other mo,
> Then might thou ſeen how it was tho
> Of armes, for this wolde atteine
> To love, which, withouten peine
> Maie not be gette of idleneſs;
> And that I take to witneſſe
> An old cronique in ſpeciall
> The whiche into memoriall
> Is write for his loves ſake,
> How that a Knight ſhal undertake.[5]

He alludes to a ſtory about Sir Triſtram, which he ſuppoſes to be univerſally known, related in this romance:

> In every mannes mouth it is
> How Triſtram was of love drunke
> With Bele Iſolde, whan they dronke

Lib. i. f. 18, b. col. 2. Of Achilles and Teucer, "In a *Cronique* I fynde thus." Lib. iii. fol. 62, a, col. 1. Of Peleus and Phocus, "As the *Cronique* ſeithe." Lib. iii. f. 61, b, col. 1. Of Ulyſſes and Penelope, "In a *Cronique* I finde writte." Lib. iv. f. 63, b. col. 2. He mentions alſo the *Cronique* for tales of other nations. "In the *Cronique* as I finde, Cham was he which firſt the letters fonde, and wrote in Hebrew with his honde, of naturall philoſophie." Lib. iv. f. 76, a, col. 1. For Darius's four queſtions, Lib. vii. f. 151, b, col. 1. For Perillus's brazen bull, f. &c. See below.

[1] [See Brunet, laſt edit. ii. 169.]

[2] See Haym's Bibl. Italian. p. 35, edit. Venez. 1741, 4to.

[3] Sandius and Hallerwood, in their Supplement to Voſſius's Latin Hiſtorians, ſuppoſe Colonna's Trojan and Britiſh chronicle the ſame. In Theodoric Engelhuſen's *Chronica Chronicarum*, compiled about the year 1420, where the author ſpeaks of Troy, he cites Colonna *de Bello Trojano*. In the Preface he mentions Colonna's *Chronica Britannorum*. See Engelhuſen's firſt edit. Helmſt. 1671; or rather, *Scriptor. Brunſvic. Leibnit.* p. 977. See alſo Fabyan and other hiſtorians.

[4] Bochas, B. i. ch. xvi. *How the tranſlatoure wrote a booke of the ſiege of Troy, called Troye Boke*. And *ib*. St. 7, 17, 20, edit. Wayland, fol. xxx. b. xxxi. a. And in Lydg. *Deſtr. of Troy*.

[5] [Edit. 1857, ii. 70.]

> The drink, which Brangweine hem betok,
> Er that king Mark, &c.¹

And again, in the assembly of lovers:

> Ther was Tristram which was beleved
> With Bele Isolde, and Lancelot
> Stood with Gunnor,² and Galahot
> With his lady.³

The *Gesta Romanorum*, [of which a sufficiently ample account has been furnished in one of the preliminary Dissertations,] somewhat resembles the plan of Gower's poem. In the rubric of the story of Julius and the poor knight, our author alludes to this book in the expression, *Hic secundum* Gesta, &c.⁴ When he speaks of the emperors of Rome paying reverence to a virgin, he says he found this custom mentioned, "Of Rome among the *Gestes* olde."⁵ Yet he adds, that the Gests took it from Valerius Maximus. The story of Tarquin and his son Arrous is ushered in with this line, "So as these olde Gestes seyne."⁶ The tale of Antiochus, as I have hinted, is in the *Gesta Romanorum*; although for some parts of it Gower was perhaps indebted to Geoffrey's *Pantheon* above mentioned. The foundation of Shakespeare's story of the three caskets in the *Merchant of Venice* is to be found in this favourite collection: this is likewise in our author (yet in a different form) who cites a *Cronike*⁷ for his authority. I make no apology for giving the passage somewhat at large, as the source of this elegant little apologue, which seems to be of Eastern invention, has lately so much employed the searches of the commentators on Shakespeare, and that the circumstances of the story, as it is told by Gower, may be compared with those with which it appears in other books.

The poet is speaking of a king whose officers and courtiers complained that, after a long attendance, they had not received adequate rewards, and preferments due to their services. The king, who was

---

¹ [*Ibid.* iii. 17.] ² Geneura, Arthur's queen. ³ [*Ibid.* iii. 359.]
⁴ Lib. viii. f. 153, a, col. 1. And in other rubrics. In the rubric there is also *Gesta Alexandri*, lib. iii. f. 61, a, col. 1. And in the story of Sardanapalus, "These olde Gestes tellen us," lib. iii. 167, a, col. 1. [But, as Ritson pointed out, the term *Gesta*, here repeatedly used, may be applicable merely to the *histories* or *chronicles* consulted by Gower.]
⁵ Lib. v. f. 118, a, col. 2. ⁶ Lib. vii. f. 169, a, col. 1.
⁷ He refers to a *Cronike* for other stories, as the story of Lucius king of Rome, and the king's fool. "In a Cronike it telleth us." Lib. vii. f. 165, a, col. 2. Of the translation of the Roman empire to the Lombards. "This made an emperour anon, whose name, the Chronicle telleth, was Othes." Prol. fol. 5, b, col. 2. Of Constantine's leprosy. "For in Cronike thus I rede." Lib. iii. f. 46, b, col. 2. For which he also cites "the *bokes* of *Latine*," ib. f. 45, a, col. 1. In the story of Caius Fabricius, "In a Cronique I fynde thus." Lib. vii. f. 157, a, col. 2. Of the soothsayer and the emperor of Rome. "As in Cronike it is witholde."—"Which the Chronike hath autorized." Lib. vii. f. 154, b, col. 1, f. 155, b, col. 2. Of the emperour's son who serves the Soldan of Persia. "There was as the Cronique seith, an emperour," &c. Lib. ii. f. 41, b, col. 1. For the story of Carmidotoirus consul of Rome, he refers to these *olde bokes*. Lib. vii. f. 157, b, col. 2, &c.

no stranger to their complaints, artfully contrives a scheme to prove whether this defect proceeded from his own want of generosity, or their want of discernment.

> Anone he let two cofres make
> Of one semblaunce and of o make
> So lich, that no life thilke throwe
> That one may fro that other knowe.
> They were into his chambre brought,
> But no man wot why they be wrought.
> And netheles the king hath bede,
> That they be set in prive stede,
> As he that was of wisdom sligh.
> Whan he therto his time sigh
> All privelich, that none it wist,
> His owne hondes that o kist
> Of fine golde and of fine perrie,
> The which out of his treforie
> Was take, anone he filde full,
> That other cofre of strawe and mull
> With stones meind he filde also.
> Thus be they fulle bothe two.

The king assembles his courtiers, and shewing them the two chests, acquaints them, that one of these is filled with gold and jewels; that they should choose which of the two they liked best, and that the contents should instantly be distributed among them all. A knight by common consent is appointed to choose for them, who fixes upon the chest filled with straw and stones:

> This king than in the same stede
> Anone that other cofre undede,
> Where as they sighen great richesse
> Wel more than they couthen gesse.
> Lo, saith the king, now may ye se,
> That there is no defaulte in me,
> Forthy[1] my self I woll acquit
> And bereth ye your owne wit
> Of that fortune hath you refused.[2]

It must be confessed, that there is a much greater and a more beautiful variety of incidents in this story, as it is related in the *Gesta Romanorum* which Shakespeare has followed, than in Gower: and were it not demonstrable, that this compilation preceded our author's age by some centuries, one would be tempted to conclude, that Gower's story was the original fable in its simple unimproved state. Whatever was the case, it is almost certain that one story produced the other.

In speaking of our author's sources, I must not omit a book translated by the unfortunate Antony Widville, Earl Rivers, chiefly with a view of proving its early popularity. It is the *Dictes* [or *Sayengis*] of [the] *Philosophres*, which Lord Rivers translated from the French

---

[1] therefore.
[2] [Ed. 1857, ii. 206-7.] The story which follows is somewhat similar, in which the Emperor Frederick places before two beggars two pasties, one filled with capons, the other with florins. *Ibid.*

of William de Thignonville, provoſt of the city of Paris, [who died in 1414,] entitled *Les dictes moraux des philoſophes, les dictes des ſages et les ſecrets d' Ariſtote*.[1] The Engliſh tranſlation was printed [thrice] by Caxton, [with the date] 1477 [and again by W. de Worde in 1528]. Gower refers to this [book,] which firſt exiſted in Latin, more than once; and it is moſt probable, that he conſulted the Latin original.[2]

It is pleaſant to obſerve the ſtrange miſtakes which Gower, a man of great learning and the moſt general ſcholar of his age, has committed in this poem concerning books which he never ſaw, his violent anachroniſms, and miſrepreſentations of the moſt common facts and characters. He mentions the Greek poet Menander, as one of the firſt hiſtorians or "firſt enditours of the olde cronike," together with Eſdras, Solinus, Joſephus, Claudius Sulpicius, Termegis, Pandulfe, Frigidilles, Ephiloquorus, and Pandas. It is extraordinary that Moſes ſhould not be here mentioned, in preference to Eſdras. Solinus is ranked ſo high, becauſe he recorded nothing but wonders;[3] and Joſephus, on account of his ſubject, had long been placed almoſt on a level with the Bible. He is ſeated on the firſt pillar in Chaucer's *Houſe of Fame*. His *Jewiſh Hiſtory*, tranſlated into Latin by Rufinus in the fourth century, had given riſe to many old poems and romances:[4] and his *Maccabaics*, or Hiſtory of the ſeven Maccabees martyred with their father Eleazar under the perſecution of Antiochus Epiphanes, a ſeparate work tranſlated alſo by Rufinus, produced the *Judas Maccabee* of Belleperche in the year 1240, and at length enrolled the Maccabees among the moſt illuſtrious heroes of romance.[5] On this account too, perhaps, Eſdras is here ſo reſpectably remembered. I ſuppoſe Sulpicius is Sulpicius Severus, a petty annaliſt of the fifth century. Termegis is probably Triſmegiſtus, the myſtic philoſopher, certainly not an hiſtorian, at leaſt not an ancient one. Pandulf ſeems to be Pandulphus of Piſa, who wrote lives of the popes, and died in the year 1198.[6] Frigidilles is perhaps Fregedaire, a Burgundian, who flouriſhed about the

---

[1] See *Mem. de Litt.* xvii. 745, 4to.

[2] Among theſe other "*tales wiſe of philoſophers* in this wiſe I rede," &c. lib. vii. f. 143, a, col. 1, f. 142, b, col. 2, &c. See Walpole's *Cat. Royal and Noble Authors*. There is another tranſlation done in 1450, dedicated to Sir John Faſtolfe, knight, by his ſon-in-law *Stevyn Scrope Squyer*. MSS. Harl. 2265. William de Thignonville is here ſaid to have tranſlated this book into French for the uſe of King Charles VI. [See Blades' *Caxton*, ii. 37.]

[3] Our author has a ſtory from Solinus concerning a monſtrous bird, lib. iii. f. 62, b, col. 2.

[4] There is *Joſephus de la Battaille Judaique* [tranſlated from Latin into French, and printed at Paris, 1492, folio.] All Joſephus's works were printed in the old Latin tranſlation, at Verona, 1480, folio. They were tranſlated into French, German, Spaniſh, and Italian, and printed, between the years 1492 and 1554. See [Brunet, laſt edit. in v.] A French tranſlation was made in 1460, or 1463. MSS. Bibl. Reg. Paris. 7015.

[5] In the Britiſh Muſeum there is "Maccabeorum et Joſephi Hiſtoriarum Epitome, metrice." 10 A viii. 5. MSS. Reg. See MSS. Harl. 5713.

[6] See the ſtory, in our author, of Pope Boniface ſupplanting Celeſtine. "In a Cronyke of tyme ago." Lib. ii. f. 42, a, col. 2.

year 641, and wrote a Chronicle from Adam to his own times; this has been often printed, and contains the best account of the Franks after Gregory of Tours.[1] Our author, who has partly suffered from ignorant transcribers and printers, by Ephiloquorus undoubtedly intended Eutropius. In the next paragraph, indeed, he mentions Herodotus: yet not as an early historian, but as the first writer of a system of the metrical art, "of metre, of ryme, and of cadence."[2] We smile, when Hector in Shakespeare quotes Aristotle: but Gower gravely informs his reader, that Ulysses was a *clerke*, accomplished in a knowledge of all the sciences, a great rhetorician and magician: that he learned rhetoric of Tully, magic of Zoroaster, astronomy of Ptolemy, philosophy of Plato, divination of the prophet Daniel, proverbial instruction of Solomon, botany of Macer, and medicine of Hippocrates.[3] In the seventh book Aristotle, or the *philosopher*, is introduced reciting to his scholar Alexander the Great a disputation between a Jew and a Pagan, who meet between Cairo and Babylon, concerning their respective religions: the end of the story is to shew the cunning, cruelty, and ingratitude of the Jew, which are at last deservedly punished.[4] But I believe Gower's apology must be, that he took this narrative from some christian legend, which was feigned (for a religious purpose) at the expense of all probability and propriety.

The only classic Roman writers which our author cites are Virgil, Ovid, Horace, and Tully. Among the Italian poets, one is surprised he should not quote Petrarch: he mentions Dante only, who in the rubric is called "a certain poet of Italy named Dante," *quidam poeta Italiæ qui Dante vocabatur*.[5] He appears to have been well acquainted with the Homilies of Gregory the Great,[6] which were translated into Italian, and printed at Milan so early as 1479. I can hardly decipher, and must therefore be excused from transcribing, the names of all the renowned authors whom our author has quoted in alchemy, astrology, magic, palmistry, geomancy, and other branches of the occult philosophy. Among the astrological writers, he mentions Noah, Abraham, and Moses. But he is not sure that Abraham was an author, having never seen any of that patriarch's works: and he prefers Trismegistus to Moses.[7] Cabalistical tracts were however extant, not only under the names of Abraham, Noah, and Moses,

---

[1] See Ruinart. *Dissertat. de Fredegario ejusque Operibus*, tom. ii. *Hist. Franc.* p. 443. There is also Fridegodus, a monk of Dover, who wrote [a metrical version (from *Eddius Stephanus*) of the life of Wilfrid in 656. Other works are improperly attributed to him. See Wright's *Biog. Brit. Lit.* 1843-6, A-S. Per. 433-4.] Also a Frigeridus, known only by a reference which Gregory of Tours makes to the *twelfth book of his History*, concerning the times preceding Valentinian III., and the humiliation of Rome by Attila. Gregor. Turonens. *Hist. Francor.* lib. ii. cap. 8, 9. If this last be the writer in the text, a MS. of Frigeridus, now lost, might have existed in Gower's age.

[2] Lib. vi. f. 76, b, col. 1.   [3] Lib. vi. f. 135, a, col. 1.
[4] Lib. vii. f. 156, b, col. ii.   [5] Lib. vii. f. 154, b, col. 1.
[6] Prolog. f. 2, b, col. 1. Lib. v. f. 93, a, col. 1, 2, f. 94, a, col. 1.
[7] Lib. vii. f. 134, b, col. 1, vii. f. 149, b, col. 1.

but of Adam, Abel, and Enoch.¹ He mentions with particular regard Ptolemy's *Almagest*, the grand source of all the superstitious notions propagated by the Arabian philosophers concerning the science of divination by the stars.² These infatuations seem to have completed their triumph over human credulity in the age of Gower, who probably was an ingenious adept in the false and frivolous speculations of this admired species of study.

Gower, amidst his graver literature, appears to have been a great reader of romances. The lover, in speaking of the gratification which his passion receives from the sense of hearing, says, that to hear his lady speak is more delicious, than to feast on all the dainties that could be compounded by a cook of Lombardy. They are not so restorative

> As be the wordes of her mouth.³
> For as the windes of the south
> Ben most of alle debonaire,
> So whan her list⁴ to speke faire,
> The vertue of her goodly speche
> Is verrily min hertes leche.

These are elegant verses. To hear her sing is paradise. Then he adds:

> Ful ofte time it falleth so,
> Min ere with a good pitaunce
> Is fed of reding of romaunce
> Of Ydoine and of Amadas,
> That whilom were in my cas,
> And eke of other many a score,
> That loveden longe, er I was bore,
> For whan I of her loves rede,
> Min ere with the tale I fede
> And with the lust of her histoire.
> Somtime I drewe into memoire,
> How sorwe may nought ever last,
> And so cometh hope in ate last.

The romance of *Idoyne and Amadas* is recited as a favourite history among others, in the prologue to a [copy of the] *Cursor mundi*. I have already observed our poet's references to *Sir Lancelot*.

Our author's account of the progress of the Latin language is extremely curious. He supposes that it was invented by the old Tuscan prophetess Carmens; that it was reduced to method, to composition, pronunciation, and prosody, by the grammarians Aristarchus, Donatus, and Didymus: adorned with the flowers of eloquence and rhetoric, by Tully: then enriched by translations from the Chaldee, Arabic, and Greek languages, more especially by the version of the Hebrew bible into Latin by Saint Jerom in the fourth century: and that at length, after the labours of many celebrated writers, it received its

---

¹ See *supra*. And Morhof. Polyhist. tom. ii. p. 455, *seq.* edit. 1747.
² Mabillon mentions, in a MS. of the *Almagest* written before the year 1240, a drawing of Ptolemy, holding a mirror, not an optical tube, in his hand, and contemplating the stars. Itin. Germanic. p. 49.
³ [Ed. 1857, iii. 30, 31.]   ⁴ she chooses.

final consummation in Ovid, the poet of lovers. At the mention of Ovid's name, the poet, with the dexterity and addreſs of a true maſter of tranſition, ſeizes the critical moment of bringing back the dialogue to its proper argument.[1]

The *Confeſſio Amantis* was moſt probably written after Chaucer's *Troilus and Creſſida*. At the cloſe of the poem, we are preſented with an aſſemblage of the moſt illuſtrious lovers.[2] Together with the renowned heroes and heroines of love, mentioned either in romantic or claſſical hiſtory, we have David and Bathſheba, Samſon and Dalilah, and Solomon with all his concubines. Virgil, alſo, Socrates, Plato, and Ovid, are enumerated as lovers. Nor muſt we be ſurpriſed to find Ariſtotle honoured with a place in this gallant group: for whom, ſays the poet, the queen of Greece made ſuch a ſyllogiſm as deſtroyed all his logic. But, among the reſt, Troilus and Creſſida are introduced; ſeemingly with an intention of paying a compliment to Chaucer's poem on their ſtory, which had been ſubmitted to Gower's correction: although this famous pair had been alſo recently celebrated in Boccaccio's *Filoſtrato*. And in another place, ſpeaking of his abſolute devotion to his lady's will, he declares himſelf ready to acquieſce in her choice, whatſoever ſhe ſhall command: whether, if when tired of dancing and caroling, ſhe ſhould chooſe to play at [dice] or read *Troilus and Creſſida*. This is [probably] Chaucer's poem:

> That whan her liſt on nightes wake[3]
> In chambre as to carole and daunce,
> Me thenketh I may me more avaunce,
> If I may gone upon her honde,
> Than if I wonne a kinges londe.
> For whan I may her hond beclippe,
> With ſuch gladneſſe I daunce and ſkippe,
> Me thenketh I touche nought the floor.
> The roo, which renneth on the moor,
> Is thanne nought ſo light as I.
> * * * *
> And whan it falleth other gate,
> So that her like nought to daunce,
> But on the dees to caſte chaunce
> Or axe of love ſome demaunde
> Or elles that her liſt commaunde
> To rede and here of Troilus.

That this poem was written after [the] *Flower and Leaf*, [might be perhaps collected from the following paſſage, which appears to be an imitation of [that piece], and is no bad ſpecimen of Gower's moſt poetical manner, [if we were to forget that the *Flower and the Leaf* was in all probability not in exiſtence during Gower's life-time] Roſiphele, a beautiful princeſs, but ſetting love at defiance, the daughter of Herupus, king of Armenia, is taught obedience to the laws of Cupid by ſeeing a viſion of ladies:

---

[1] Lib. iv. f. 77, b, col. 2.   [2] Lib. viii. f. 158, a, col. 2.
[3] Lib. iv. [edit. 1857, ii. 95.]

Whan come was the month of may,[1]
She wolde walke upon a day,
And that was er the fonne arift,
Of women but a fewe it wift.
And forth fhe wente prively
Unto the park was fafte by,
All fofte walkend on the gras,
Till fhe came there the launde was,
Through which ther ran a great rivere.
It thought her faire and faide: Here
I woll abide under the fhawe,
And bad her women to withdrawe
And there fhe ftood alone ftille
To thenke what was in her wille.
She figh the fwote floures fpringe,
She herde gladde foules finge,
She figh the beftes in her kinde,
The buck, the doo, the hert, the hinde,
The male go with the femele.
And fo began there a quarele
Betwene love and her owne herte,
Fro which fhe couthe nought afterte.
And as fhe caft her eye aboute,
She figh clad in one fute a route
Of ladies, where they comen ride
A longe under the wodes fide.
On faire amblende hors they fet,
That were all white, faire and great,
And everychone ride on fide.
The fadels were of fuche a pride
With perle and gold fo well begone,
So riche figh fhe never none,
In kirtles and in copes riche
They weren clothed alle aliche
Departed even of white and blewe
With alle luftes, that fhe knewe,
They were embrouded over all,
Her bodies weren longe and fmall.
The beaute fair upon her face
It may none erthly thing deface,
Corounes on her hede they bere
As eche of hem a quene were,
That all the golde of Crefus halle
The lefte coronall of alle
Ne might have bought after the worth.
Thus comen they ridende forth.
The kinges doughter, which this figh,
For pure abafshe drewe her adrigh
And helde her clofe under a bough.

At length fhe fees riding in the rear of this fplendid troop, on a horfe lean, galled, and lame, a beautiful lady in a tattered garment, her faddle mean and much worn, but her bridle richly ftudded with gold and jewels: and round her waift were more than a hundred halters. The princefs afks the meaning of this ftrange proceffion, and is anfwered by the lady on the lean horfe, that thefe are fpectres

---

[1] [Ed. 1857, ii. 44-5.]

of ladies who, when living, were obedient and faithful votaries of love. " As to myself," she adds, " I am now receiving my annual penance for being a rebel to love :"

> For I whilom no love hadde,[1]
> My hors is now feble and badde
> And all to-tore is min array,
> And every yere this frefshe may
> Thefe lufty ladies ride aboute,
> And I muft nedes fue[2] her route
> In this maner, as ye now fe
> And truffe her halters forth with me
> And am but as her horfe knave.[3]

The princefs then afks her, why fhe wore the rich bridle, fo inconfiftent with the reft of her furniture, her drefs, and horfe? The lady anfwers, that it was a badge and reward for having loved a knight faithfully for the laft fortnight of her life:

> Nowe have ye herd all min anfwere,[4]
> To god, madame, I you betake,
> And warneth alle for my fake,
> Of love that they be nought idel
> And bid hem thenke upon my bridel.
> And with that worde all fodeinly
> She paffeth as it were a fkie[5]
> All clene out of this ladies fight.

My readers will eafily conjecture the change which this fpectacle muft naturally produce in the obdurate heart of the Princefs of Armenia. There is [an indication] that the [writer of the] *Floure and Leafe* [ftudied] the *Confeffio Amantis*. In the eighth book, our author's lovers are crowned with the Flower and Leaf:

> Min eye and as I cafte aboutes[6]
> To know among hem who was who,
> I figh where lufty youthe tho,
> As he, which was a capitein
> To-fore all other upon the plein,
> Stood with his route well begon,
> Her hedes kempt and therupon
> Garlondes, nought o colour,
> Some of the lefe, fome of the floure,
> And fome of grete perles were.
> The newe guife of Beawme[7] there.

I believe on the whole, that Chaucer had publifhed moft of his poems before this piece of Gower appeared. Gower, in a fort of Epilogue to the *Confeffio Amantis* [found only in certain MSS. of the work, and perhaps of doubtful authority,] is addreffed by Venus, who commands him to greet Chaucer as her favourite poet and difciple, as one who had employed his youth in compofing fongs and ditties to her honour. She adds at the clofe:

> Forthy now in his daies olde[8]
> Thou fhalt him telle this meffage,

---

[1] [Ed. 1857, ii. 48-9.]   [2] follow.   [3] their groom.
[4] [Ed. 1857, ii. 49.]   [5] a fhadow; Ixia, umbra.   [6] [Ed. 1857, iii. 358.]
[7] Boeme, Bohemia.   [8] [Ed. 1857, iii. 374.]

> That he upon his later age
> To fette an end of all his werke,
> As he, which is min owne clerke,
> Do make his teſtament of love,
> As thou haſt do thy ſhrifte above,
> So that my court it may recorde.

[But it is hardly to be ſuppoſed that here Gower intends the proſe work ſo called, erroneouſly aſcribed to Chaucer. He, it ſeems more likely, refers to ſome poetical labour, which he propoſed to Chaucer, and which was never produced.] Chaucer at this time was [about fifty-two] years of age. The Court of Love, one of the pedantries of French gallantry, occurs often [in Gower]. In an addreſs to Venus, "Madame, I am a man of thine, that in thy Court have long ſerved."[1] The [confeſſor] obſerves, that for want of patience, a man ought, "among the women alle in Loves Court, by jugement the name bere of pacient."[2] He declares, that many perſons are condemned for diſcloſing ſecrets, "In Loves Courte, as it is ſaide, that let her tunges gone unteide."[3] By Thy Shrift, the author means his own poem now before us, the Lover's Confeſſion.

There are alſo many manifeſt evidences which lead us to conclude, that this poem preceded Chaucer's *Canterbury Tales*, undoubtedly ſome of that poet's lateſt compoſitions, and probably not begun till after the year 1382. The *Man of Laws Tale* is circumſtantially borrowed from Gower's *Conſtantia*:[4] and Chaucer, in that Tale, apparently cenſures Gower for his manner of relating the ſtories of Canace and Apollonius in the third and eighth books of the *Confeſſio Amantis*.[5] The *Wife of Bath's Tale* is founded on Gower's *Florent*, a knight of Rome, who delivers the king of Sicily's daughter from the incantations of her ſtep-mother.[6] Chaucer, however, among other great improvements, has judiciouſly departed from the fable, in converting Sicily into the more popular court of King Arthur.

Perhaps, in eſtimating Gower's merit, I have puſhed the notion too far that, becauſe he ſhews ſo much learning, he had no great ſhare of natural abilities. But it ſhould be conſidered, that when books began to grow faſhionable, and the reputation of learning conferred the higheſt honour, poets became ambitious of being thought ſcholars, and ſacrificed their native powers of invention to the oſtentation of diſplaying an extenſive courſe of reading, and to the pride of profound erudition. On this account, the minſtrels of theſe times, who were totally uneducated, and poured forth ſpontaneous rhymes in obedience

---

[1] Lib. i. [ed. 1857, i. 47.]   [2] Lib. iii. [ibid. 303.]
[3] [Ibid. 307.] In the ſame ſtrain we have Cupid's parlement. Lib. viii. f. 187, b, col. 2.
[4] *Conf. Amant.* Lib. ii. f. 30, b, col. 2. See particularly, *ibid.* f. 35, b, col. 2, a, col. 1. And compare Ch. *Man of L. T.* v. 5505. "Some men wold ſayn, &c." That is, Gower.
[5] See Chaucer, *ibid.* v. 4500; and *Conf. Amant.* Lib. iii. f. 48, a, col. 1, *ſeq.* Lib. viii. f. 175, a, col. 2, *ſeq.*
[6] Lib. i. f. 15, b, col. 2.

to the workings of nature, often exhibit more genuine strokes of passion and imagination, than the professed poets. Chaucer is an exception to this observation: his original feelings were too strong to be suppressed by books, and his learning was overbalanced by genius.

This affectation of appearing learned, which yet was natural at the revival of literature, in our old poets, even in those who were altogether destitute of talents, has lost to posterity many a curious picture of manners and many a romantic image. Some of our ancient bards, however, aimed at no other merit than that of being able to versify; and attempted nothing more than to clothe in rhyme those sentiments, which would have appeared with equal propriety in prose.

In [the library at Trentham,] there is a thin oblong MS. on vellum, containing some of Gower's poems in Latin, French, and English. By an entry in the first leaf, in the hand-writing and under the signature of Thomas lord Fairfax, Cromwell's general, an antiquarian, and a lover and collector of curious manuscripts,[1] it appears that this book was presented by the poet Gower, about the year 1400, to Henry IV.; and that it was given by Lord Fairfax to his friend and kinsman Sir Thomas Gower knight and baronet, in the year 1656. By another entry, Lord Fairfax acknowledges to have received it, in the same year, as a present from that learned gentleman Charles Gedde Esquire, of St. Andrews in Scotland: and at the end are five or six Latin anagrams on Gedde, written and signed by Lord Fairfax, with this title: "In nomen venerandi et annosi Amici sui Caroli Geddei." By King Henry IV. it seems to have been placed in the royal library: it appears at least to have been in the hands of Henry VII. while Earl of Richmond, from the name Rychemond, inserted in another of the blank leaves at the beginning, and explained by this note, "Liber Henrici Septimi tunc Comitis Richmond, propria manu scripsit." This MS. is neatly written, with miniated and illuminated initials: and contains the following pieces. I. A Panegyric in stanzas, with a Latin prologue or rubric in seven hexameters, on Henry IV.[2]—II. A short Latin poem in elegiacs on the same

---

[1] He gave twenty-nine ancient MSS. to the Bodleian library, one of which [MSS. Fairf. No. 3] is a beautiful copy of Gower's *Confessio Amantis*. When the Record-tower in St. Mary's Abbey at York was accidentally blown up in the grand rebellion, he offered rewards to the soldiers who could bring him fragments of the scattered parchments. Luckily, however, the numerous original evidences lodged in this repository had been just before transcribed by Roger Dodsworth; and the transcripts, which formed the ground-work of Dugdale's *Monasticon*, consisting of forty-nine large folio volumes, were bequeathed by Fairfax to the same library Fairfax also, when Oxford was garrisoned by the parliamentary forces, exerted his utmost diligence in preserving the Bodleian library from pillage; so that it suffered much less than when that city was in the possession of the royalists.

[2] This poem is printed in Urry's edit. of Chaucer, 1721, p. 540. [The title is, Carmen de pacis commendatione quod ad laudem et memoriam serenissimi principis domini regis Henrici quarti suus humilis orator Johannes Gower composuit. Et nunc sequitur Epistola in quâ idem Johannes pro statu et salute dicti domini sui altissimi devocius exorat.—*Todd.*]

subject, beginning, "Rex cœli deus et dominus qui tempora solus."[1] This is followed by ten other very short pieces, both in French and [Latin] of the same tendency.—III. Cinkante Balades, or Fifty Sonnets in French. Part of the first is illegible. They are closed with the following epilogue and colophon:

> O gentile Engletere a toi iescrits,
> Pour remembrer ta ioie qest nouelle,
> Qe te survient du noble Roi Henris,
> Par qui dieus ad redresce ta querele,
> A dieu purceo prient et cil et celle,
> Qil de sa grace au fort Roi corone,
> Doignt peas, honour, ioie et prosperite.

"Expliciunt carmina Johis Gower que Gallice composita Balades dicuntur." IV. Two short Latin poems in elegiacs. The first beginning, "Ecce patet tensus ceci Cupidinis arcus." The second, "O Natura viri potuit quam tollere nemo." V. A French poem, imperfect at the beginning, *On the Dignity or Excellence of Marriage*, in one book. The subject is illustrated by examples. I transcribe one of the stories.

"Qualiter Jason uxorem suam Medeam relinquens, Creusam Creontis regis filiam sibi carnaliter copulavit. Unde ipse cum duobus filiis suis postea infortunatus decessit."

> Li prus Jason qeu lisle de Colchos
> Le toison dor pour laide de Medee
> Conquist dont il donour portoit grant loos
> Par tout le monde encourt la renomee
> La joesne dame ove soi ad amenee
> De son paijs en grece et lespousa
> Freinte espousaile dieus le vengera.
>   Quant Medea meulx quide estre en repos,
> Ove son mari et qelle avoit porte
> Deux fils de luy lors changea le purpos
> El quelle Jason primer fuist oblige
> Il ad del tout Medeam refuse
> Si prist la file au roi Creon Creusa
> Freinte espousaile dieus le vengera.
> Medea qot le coer de dolour cloos
> En son corous et ceo fuist grant pite
> Sas joesnes fils queux ot jadis en clos
> Deinz ses costees ensi com forseuee
> Devant ses oels Jason ele ad tue
> Ceo qeu fuist fait pecche le fortuna
> Freinte espousaile dieus le vengera.

Towards the end of the piece the poet introduces an apology for any inaccuracies which, as an Englishman, he may have committed in the French idiom:

> Al Universite de tout le monde
> JOHAN GOWER ceste balade envoie;
> Et si jeo nai de francois la faconde,
> Pardonetz moi qe jeo de ceo forsvoie.
> Jeo suis Englois : si quier par tiele voie

---

[1] [Another copy in MS. Cotton. Otho, D. i. 4.]

> Estre excuse mais quoiq, nulls endie
> Lamour parfit en dieu le justifie.

It is finished with a few Latin hexameters, viz. "Quis scit vel qualis sacer ordo connubialis." This poem occurs at the end of two valuable folio MSS., illuminated and on vellum, of the *Confessio Amantis*, in the Bodleian Library.[1]

But the *Cinquante Balades* or fifty French Sonnets, above mentioned, are the curious and valuable part of [the Gower MS.] They do not appear in any other MS. of Gower which I have examined. But if they should be discovered in any other, I will venture to pronounce that a more authentic, unembarrassed, and practicable copy than this before us, will not be produced, although it is for the most part unpointed, and obscured with abbreviations and with those misspellings which flowed from a scribe unacquainted with the French language.

To say no more, however, of the value which these little pieces may derive from being so scarce and so little known, they have much real and intrinsic merit. They are tender, pathetic, and poetical, and place our old poet Gower in a more advantageous point of view than that in which he has hitherto been usually seen. I know not if any even among the French poets themselves, of this period, have left a set of more finished sonnets; for they were probably written when Gower was a young man, about the year 1350. Nor had yet any English poet treated the passion of love with equal delicacy of sentiment and elegance of composition. I will transcribe four of these balades as correctly and intelligibly as I am able, although I must confess there are some lines which I do not exactly comprehend:[2]

BALADE XXXVI.

> Pour comparer ce Jolif tems de Maij,
> Jeole dirrai semblable a paradis;
> Car lors chantont et Merle et Papegai,
> Les champs sont vert, les herbes sont floris;
> Lors est nature dame du païjs:
> Dont venus poignt l'amant aut tiel assai,
> *Rencontre amour nest qui poet dire nai.*
> Quant tout ceo voi, et que jeo penserai,
> Coment nature ad tout le monde suspris,
> Dont pour le temps Se fait minote et gai,
> Et jeo des autres sui soulein horspris,
> Com til qui sanz amie est vrais amis,

---

[1] MSS. Fairfax iii.; and NE. F. 8. 9.; also in the MS. at All Souls' College, Oxford, xxvi., described and cited above; and in MSS. Harl. 3869. In all these and, I believe, in many others, it is properly connected with the *Confessio Amantis* by the following rubric: "Puisqu'il a dit cidevant en Englois, par voie dessample, la sotie de cellui qui par amours aimie par especial, dirra ore apres en Francois a tout le mond en general un Traitee selonc les aucteurs, pour ensamplier les amants marietz," &c. It begins,
"Le creature du tout creature."

[2] [*Balades and other Poems*, by John Gower. Printed from the original MS. in the library of the Marquis of Stafford at Trentham; printed for the Roxburghe Club, 1818, 4to.]

Neſt pas mervaile lors ſi jeo meſmai,
Qencontre *amour neſt qui poet dire nai.*
   En lieu de Roſe, urtie cuillerai,
Dont mes chapeals ferrai par tiel devis,
Qe tout joie et confort jeo lerrai,
Si celle ſoule eu qui jai mon coer mis,
Selonc le point qe jai ſovent requis,
Ne deigne alegger les griefs mals qe jai,
Qencontre amour *neſt qui poet dire nai.*
Pour pite querre et pourchacer mercis,
Vàt'en, balade, u jeo tenvoierai,
Qore en certein jeo lai treſbien apris
Qencontre amour *neſt qui poet dire nai.*

BALADE XXXIV.

Saint Valentin, lamour et la nature,
Des toutȝ oiſeals ad en governement,
Dont chaſcun deaux, ſemblable a ſa meſure,
Une compaigne honeſte a ſon talent
Eſliſt tout dun acord et dun aſſent,
Pour celle ſoule laiſt a covenir;
Toutes les autres car nature aprent
V li coers eſt le corps falt obeir.
Ma doulce dame, enſi jeo vous aſſure,
Qe jeo vous ai eſlieu ſemblablement,
Sur toutes autres eſtes deſſure
De mon amour ſi treſentierement,
Qe riens y falt pourquoi joiouſement,
De coer et corps jeo vous voldrai ſervir,
Car de reſon ceſt une experiment,
V li coers eſt le corps falt obeir.
Pour remembrer jadis celle aventure
De Alceone et Ceix enſement,
Com dieus muoit en oiſel lour figure,
Ma volente ſerroit tout tielement
Qe ſanȝ envie et danger de la gent,
Nous porroions enſemble por loiſir
Voler tout francs en noſtre eſbatement
V li coers eſt le corps falt obeir.
Ma belle oiſel, vers qui mon penſement
Seu vole ades ſanȝ null contretenir
Preu ceſt eſcript car jeo ſai voirement
V li coers eſt le corps falt obeir.

BALADE XLIII.

Plus tricherous qe Jaſon a Medee,
A Dejanire ou q' Ercules eſtoit,
Plus q' Eneas q' avoit Dido leſſee,
Plus qe Theſeus q' Adriagne[1] amoit,
Ou Demephon quant Phillis oublioit,
Je trieus, helas, qamer iadis ſoloie,
Dont chanterai deſore en mon endroit
Ceſt ma dolour qe fuiſt ancois ma joie.
Unqes Ector qama Pantaſilee,[2]
En tiele haſte a Troie ne ſarmoit,
Qe tu tout mid nes deinȝ le lit couche
Amis as toutes quelq: venir doit,
Ne poet chaloir mais qune femme y ſoit,
Si es comun plus qe la halte voie,
Helas, qe la fortune me deçoit,

---

[1] Ariadne.   [2] Pentheſilea.

Cest ma dolour qe fuist ançois ma joie.
De Lancelot[1] si fuissetz remembre,
Et de Tristrans, com il se contenoit,
Generides,[2] Florent,[3] Partonope,[4]
Chascun de ceaux sa loialte guardoit;
Mais tu helas qest jeo qe te forsvoit
De moi qa toi jamais mill jour falsoie,
Tu es a large et jeo sui en destroit,
Cest ma dolour qe fuist ançois ma joie.
Des toutz les mals tu qes le plus maloit,
Ceste coimpleignte a ton oraille envoie
Sante me laist, et langour me recoit,
Cest ma dolour qe fuist ançois ma joie.

BALADE [XXX].

Si com la Nief, quant le fort vent tempeste,
Pur halte mier se torne çi et la,
Ma dame, ensi mon coer manit en tempeste,
Quant le danger de vo parole orra,
Le Nief qe vostre bouche soufflera,
Me fait sigler sur le peril de vie,
Quest en danger falt quil merci supplie.
Rois Uluxes, sicom nous dist la geste,
Vers son païs de Troie qui sigla,
Not tiel paour du peril et moleste,
Quant les Sereines en la mier passa,
Et le danger de circes eschapa,
Qe le paour nest plus de ma partie,
Quest en danger falt quil merci supplie.
Danger qui tolt damour toute la feste,
Unques un mot de confort ne sona,
Ainz plus cruel qe nest la fiere beste
Au point quant danger me respondera.
La chiere porte et quant le nai dirra,
Plusqz la mort mestone celle oie
Quest en danger falt quil merci supplie.
Vers vous, ma bone dame, horspris cella,
Qe danger manit en vostre compainie,
Ceste balade en mon message irra
Quest en danger falt quil merci supplie.[5]

---

[1] Sir Lancelot's intrigue with Geneura, King Arthur's queen, and Sir Tristram with Bel Isoulde, incidents in Arthur's romance, are made the subject of one of the stories of the French poem just cited, *viz.*:
"Commes sont la cronique et listoire
De Lancelot et Tristrans ensemble," &c.

[2] [The hero of a romance and a ballad-poem under the same name, of which there is an account in *Handbook of Early English Literature*, in voce.]

[3] Chaucer's *Wife of Bathes Tale* is founded on the story of Florent, [as just stated]. His story is also in our author's *Confessio Amantis*, lib. iii. fol. 48, a, col. 1, *seq.* lib. viii. fol. 175, a, col. 2, *seq.* and in the *Gesta Romanorum*. [There is a well-known] romance called *Le bone Florence de Rome*, which begins:
"As ferre as men ride or gon."
[And which has been printed by Ritson in his *Romances*, 1802.] I know not if this be Shakespeare's Florentius, *Tam. Shr.* i. [2, Dyce's edit. 1868, iii. 122]:
"Be she as foul as was Florentius' love."

[4] [*Parthenope de Blois*, of which the old English version has been printed from an unique but imperfect MS. by Mr. Buckley, 1862, 4to.]

[5] For the use, and indeed the knowledge, of this MS. I am obliged to the unsolicited kindness of Lord Trentham; a favour which his lordship was pleased to confer with the most polite condescension. [The text has now been collated with that of 1818, and many errors of transcription thus removed.]

SECTION XX.

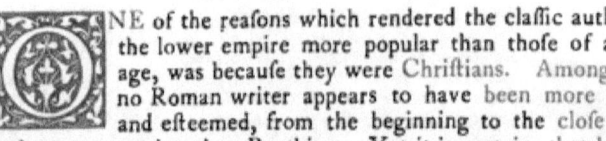NE of the reasons which rendered the classic authors of the lower empire more popular than those of a purer age, was because they were Christians. Among these, no Roman writer appears to have been more studied and esteemed, from the beginning to the close of the barbarous centuries, than Boethius. Yet it is certain, that his allegorical personifications and his visionary philosophy, founded on the abstractions of the Platonic school, greatly concurred to make him a favourite.[1] His *Consolation of Philosophy* was translated into the Saxon tongue by King Alfred, the father of learning and civility in the midst of a rude and intractable people, and illustrated with a commentary by Asser, bishop of Saint David's, a prelate patronized by Alfred for his singular accomplishments in literature, about the year 890. Bishop Grosseteste is said to have left annotations on this admired system of morality. There is a very ancient MS. of it in the Laurentian library.[2] There are few of those distinguished ecclesiastics, whose erudition illuminated the thickest gloom of ignorance and superstition with uncommon lustre, but who either have cited this performance, or honoured it with a panegyric.[3] It has had many imitators. Eccard, a learned French Benedictine, wrote in imitation of this Consolation of Philosophy a work in verse and prose containing five books, entitled the Consolation of the Monks, about the year 1120.[4] John Gerson also, a doctor and chancellor of the University of Paris, wrote the Consolation of Theology in four books, about the year 1420.[5] It was the model of [the]

---

[1] It is observable that this Spirit of Personification tinctures the writings of some of the Christian fathers about, or rather before, this period. Most of the agents in the *Shepherd of Hermas* are ideal beings. An ancient lady converses with Hermas, and tells him that she is the Church of God. Afterwards several virgins appear and discourse with him; and when he desires to be informed who they are, he is told by the Shepherd-angel, that they are Faith, Abstinence, Patience, Chastity, Concord, &c. Saint Cyprian relates, that the church appeared in a vision, *in visione per noctem*, to Colerinus; and commanded him to assume the office of Reader, which he in humility had declined. Cyprian. *Epist.* xxxix. edit. Oxon. The church appearing as a woman they perhaps had from the Scripture, *Rev.* xli. 1, *Esdras*, &c.

[2] Mabillon, *Itin. Ital.* p. 221.

[3] He is much commended as a catholic and philosopher by Hincmarus archbishop of Rheims, about the year 880. *De Prædestinat. contr. Godeschalch.* tom. i. 211, ii. 62, edit. Sirmond. And by John of Salisbury, for his eloquence and argument. *Policrat.* vii. 15. And by many other writers of the same class.

[4] See Trithem. cap. 387, de S. E. And *Illustr. Benedictin.* ii. 107.

[5] *Opp.* tom. i. p. 130, edit. Dupin. I think there is a French *Consolatio Theologiæ* by one Cerisier. [John de Tambaco wrote also a *Consolation of Theology* in fifteen books, 1366. It was very early printed, without name, date, signatures, paging, or catch-word.—Herbert, MS. note.—*Park*.]

Testament of Love. It was translated into French[1] and English before the [close of the fourteenth century].[2] Dante was an attentive reader of Boethius. In the *Purgatorio,* Dante gives Theology the name of Beatrix his mistress, the daughter of Fulco Portinari, who very gravely moralizes in that character. Being ambitious of following Virgil's steps in the descent of Eneas into hell, he introduces her, as a daughter of the empyreal heavens, bringing Virgil to guide him through that dark and dangerous region.[3] Leland, who lived when true literature began to be restored, says that the writings of Boethius still continued to retain that high estimation which they had acquired in the most early periods. I had almost forgotten to observe, that the Consolatio was translated into Greek by Maximus Planudes, the most learned and ingenious of the Constantinopolitan monks.[4]

I can assign only one poet to the reign of Henry IV., and this a translator of Boethius.[5] He is called Johannes Capellanus, or John the Chaplain, and he translated into English verse the treatise *De Consolatione Philosophiæ* in the year 1410.[6] His name is John Walton.[7] He was canon of Oseney, and died subdean of York. It appears probable, that he was patronized by Thomas Chaundler, among other preferments dean of the king's chapel and of Hereford cathedral, chancellor of Wells, and successively warden of Wykeham's two colleges at Winchester and Oxford. Chandler is cha-

---

[1] See Haym, p. 199.

[2] Besides John of Meun's French version of Boethius, printed [about 1485, and afterwards reprinted] with a translation of Virgil, there is one by De Cis, or Thri, an old French poet. Matt. *Annal. Typogr.* i. p. 171. Francisc. a Cruce, *Bibl. Gallic.* pp. 216, 247. [Brunet seems to indicate no fewer than three French metrical versions]. It was printed in Dutch at Ghent, 1485, fol. In Spanish at [Sevile, 1499], fol. Polycarpus Leyserus, in that very scarce book *De Poesi Medii Ævi,* [printed Halæ, 1721, 8vo.] enumerates many curious old editions of Boethius, pp. 95, 105. [Addit. MSS. Brit. Mus. 10, 340, and 16, 165, and Harl. MS. 2421, are copies of the prose translation of Boethius, said to be Chaucer's.—F. Printed by the Early English Text Society, ed. Morris, 1868, as above stated. As to Warton's bibliography of Boethius, the reader may compare the last edition of Brunet, i. 1035-8.]

[3] See *Purgat.* Cant. xxx.

[4] Montfauc. *Bibl. Coislin.* p. 140. Of a Hebrew version, see Wolf. *Bibl. Hebr.* i. pp. 229, 1092, 243, 354, 369.

[5] I am aware that Occleve's poem, called the *Letter of Cupid,* was written in this king's reign (1402). "In the yere of grace joyfull and joconde, a thousand fower hundred and seconde." Urry's Chaucer, p. 537, v. 475. But there are reasons for making Occleve, as I have done, something later. Nor is Gower's *Balade to Henry IV.* a sufficient reason for placing him in that reign. Ibid. p. 540. The same may be said of Chaucer.

[6] [Royal MS. 18. A. 13; Harl. MSS. 43-4; Rawlinson MSS. 151 (imperfect at beginning); Sloane MSS. 554. See also Bracegirdle's translation in hexameters and other metres, temp. Eliz. in Addit. MS. Brit. Mus. 11,401.—F.]

[7] [A manuscript of this work noticed by Mr. Todd (and now in the possession of Sir Thomas Philipps, Bart.) has the following colophon: "Explicit liber Boecii de consolacione philosophie de latino in Anglicum translatus anno dñi millesimo ccccx°. per Capellanum Johannem Tebaud alias Watyrbeche." *Illustrations of Gower and Chaucer* (1810), Introd. p. xxxi.]

racterized by Wood as an able critic in polite literature, and by Leland as a rare example of a doctor in theology who graced scholastic difputation with the flowers of a pure latinity.[1] In the Britifh Mufeum there is a correct MS. on parchment of Walton's tranflation of Boethius: and the margin is filled throughout with the Latin text, written by Chaundler above mentioned.[2] There is another lefs elegant MS. in the fame collection. But at the end is this note: "Explicit liber Boecij de Confolatione Philofophie de Latino in Anglicum tranflatus A.D. 1410, per Capellanum Joannem.[3] This is the beginning of the prologue: "In fuffifaunce of cunnyng and witte." And of the tranflation, "Alas I wretch that whilom was in welth." I have feen a third copy in the library of Lincoln cathedral,[4] and a fourth in Baliol college.[5] This is the tranflation of Boethius printed in the monaftery of Tavifto[ck] in 1525, and in octave ftanzas.[6] This tranflation was made at the requeft of Elizabeth Berkeley. I forbear to load thefe pages with fpecimens not original, and which appear to have contributed no degree of improvement to our poetry or our phrafeology. Henry IV. died in 1399.

The coronation of Henry V. was celebrated in Weftminfter Hall with a folemnity proportioned to the luftre of thofe great achievements which afterwards diftinguifhed the annals of that victorious monarch. By way of preferving order, and to add to the fplendour of the fpectacle, many of the nobility were ranged along the fides of the tables on large war-horfes at this ftately feftival which, fays my chronicle, was a fecond feaft of Ahafuerus.[7] But I mention this ceremony, to introduce a circumftance very pertinent to our purpofe; which is, that the number of harpers in the hall was innumerable,[8] and thefe undoubtedly accompanied their inftruments with heroic rhymes. The king, however, was no great encourager of the popular minftrelfy, which feems at this time to have flourifhed in the higheft degree of perfection. When he entered the city of London in triumph after the battle of Agincourt, the gates and ftreets were hung with tapeftry, reprefenting the hiftories of ancient heroes; and children were placed in artificial turrets, finging verfes.[9] But Henry, difgufted at thefe fecular vanities, commanded by a formal edict, that for the future no fongs fhould be recited by the harpers, or others, in praife of the recent victory.[10] This prohibition

---

[1] Wood, *Hift. Antiq. Univ. Oxon.* ii. p. 134. Leland, *Script. Brit.* art. *Chaundlerus.*
[2] MSS. Harl. 43, 1. And MSS. Coll. Trin. Oxon. 75.
[3] MSS. Harl. 44. [4] MSS. i. 53.
[5] MSS. B. 5. He bequeathed his *Biblia* and other books to this library.
[6] There is an Englifh tranflation of Boethius by one George Colvil or Coldewell, bred at Oxford, with the Latin, "according to the boke of the tranflatour, which was a very old printe." Dedicated to Queen Mary, and printed in 1556.
[7] Elmham, *Vit. et Geft. Henr. V.* edit. Hearne, cap. xii. p. 23. Compare Lel. *Coll.* Append. iii. 226, edit. 1770.
[8] Elmham, *ubi fupr.* p. 23. [9] *Ibid.* cap. xxxi. p. 72.
[10] "Cantus de fuo triumpho fieri, feu per Cithariftas vel alios quofcunque,

had no other effect than that of displaying Henry's humility, perhaps its principal and real design. Among many others, a minstrel-piece [attributed to John Lydgate],¹ soon appeared, evidently adapted to the harp, on the *Siege of Harflete and the Battle of Agincourt*. It was written about the year 1417. These are some of the most spirited lines:

> Sent Jorge be fore our kyng they dyd se,²
> They trompyd up full meryly,
> The grete battell to gederes ȝed;³
> Our archorys⁴ theiy schot ful hartely,
> They made the Frenche men faste to blede,
> Her arrowys they went with full good spede.
> Oure enemyes with them they gan down throwe
> Thorow breste plats, habourgenys, and basnets.⁵
> Eleven thousand was slayne on a rew.⁶
> Denters of dethe men myȝt well deme,
> So fercelly in ffelde theye gan fythe.⁷
> The heve upon here helmyts schene⁸
> With axes and with swerdys bryȝt.
> When oure arowys were at a flyȝt,⁹
> Amon the Frenche men was a wel sory schere.¹⁰
> Ther was to bring of gold bokylyd¹¹ so bryȝt
> That a man myȝt holde a strong armoure.
> Owre gracyus kyng men myȝt knowe
> That day foȝt with hys owene hond,
> The erlys was dyscomwityd up on a rowe,¹²
> That he had slayne understond.
> He there schevyd¹³ oure other lordys of thys lond,
> Forsothe that was a ful fayre daye.
> Therefore all England maye this syng
> Laws¹⁴ Deo we may well saye.
> The Duke of Glocetor, that nys so nay,
> That day full wordely he wroȝt,
> On every side he made goode waye,
> The Frenche men faste to grond they browȝt.
> The erle of Hontynton sparyd noȝt,
> The erle of Oxynforthe layd on all soo,
> The young erle of Devynschyre he ne rouȝt,
> The Frenche men fast to grunde gan goo.
> Our Englismen thei were ffoul sekes do
> And ferce to fyȝt as any lyone.
> Basnets bryȝt they crasyd a to,
> And bet the French banerys adoune;
> As thonder-strokys ther was a scownde,
> Of axys and sperys ther they gan glyd.
> The lordys of Franyse lost her renowne

Cantari, penitus prohibebat." *Ibid.* p. 72. And *Hearnii Præfat.* p. xxix. *seq.* § viii. See also Holinsh. *Chron.* iii. p. 556, col. 1, 40.
¹ [See the Percy Folio MS. ii. 159-60.—F.]
² "The French saw the standard of Saint George before our king."
³ This is Milton's "Together rush'd both battles main."
⁴ archers.   ⁵ breast-plates, habergeons and helmets.
⁶ row.   ⁷ fight.   ⁸ "They struck upon their bright helmets."
⁹ flying.   ¹⁰ much distress.   ¹¹ buckled.
¹² I believe it is "The earls he had slain were all thrown together on a heap or in a row;" [discomfited?]
¹³ shewed.   ¹⁴ laus.

> With grefoly wondys they gan abyde.
> The Frenfche men, for all here pryde,
> They fell downe all at a flyʒt:
> Ie me rende they cryde, on every fyde,
> Our Englys men they underftod noʒt ariʒt.
> Their pollaxis owt of her hondys they twiʒt,
> And layde ham along ftryte upon the graffe.
> They fparyd nother deuke, erlle, ne knyght.[1]

These verses are much less intelligible than some of Gower's and Chaucer's pieces, which were written fifty years before. In the mean time we must not mistake provincial for national barbarisms. Every piece now written is by no means a proof of the actual state of style. The improved dialect, which yet is the estimate of a language, was confined only to a few writers, who lived more in the world and in polite life, and it was long before a general change in the public phraseology was effected. Nor must we expect among the minstrels, who were equally careless and illiterate, those refinements of diction which mark the compositions of men who professedly studied to embellish the English idiom.

Thomas Occleve is the first poet that occurs in the reign of Henry V. I place him about the year 1420. Occleve is a feeble writer, confidered as a poet, and his chief merit seems to be that his writings contributed to propagate and establish those improvements in our language which were now beginning to take place. He was educated in the municipal law,[2] as were both Chaucer and Gower; and it reflects no small degree of honour on that very liberal profession that its students were some of the first who attempted to polish and adorn the English tongue.

The titles of Occleve's pieces, [several] of which have been [now] printed, indicate a coldness of genius, and on the whole promise no gratification to those who seek for invention and fancy. Such as, *The tale of Jonathas and of a wicked woman*.[3] *Fable of a certain em-*

---

[1] Printed [from MSS. Cotton. *Vitell*. D. xii. 11, fol. 214,] by Hearne, Elmham, ut fupr. Append. p. 359, Num. vi. See p. 371, *feq*. [Of another performance of the fame kind, copies are at Holkham, in Harl. MSS. 753 and 2256 (the laft partly printed in *Archæologia*, xxii. 350-78), MS. Bodley, 124 (imperf. and printed *ibid*. xxi. 43-78), and in one of the Egerton MSS. The latter, which is of later date, was purchafed for the Britifh Mufeum at Lord Charlemont's fale in 1865. But almoſt all the MSS. differ from each other; fee Sir F. Madden's remarks, *Arch*. xxii. 350 *et feq*. See *Rem. of the Early Pop. Poetry of England*, ii. 82. Another and lefs interefting narrative of the fame event is inferted in the collection juft quoted from an old printed copy in the Bodleian among Selden's books. The latter feems to be a fort of popular abridgment or *rifacciento*.] See *Obfervat. on Spens*. ii. 41. Dr. Percy has printed an ancient ballad on this fubject. *Reliques*, vol. ii. p. 24, edit. 1767. See Hearne's *Præfat*. ut fupr. p. xxx.

[2] He ftudied in Cheftres-inn, where Somerfet-houfe now ftands. See Buck, *De tertia Angliæ Accademia*, cap. xxv.

[3] *Ubi infr*. Bibl. Bodl. MSS. From the *Gefta Romanorum*. [A modernized verfion is in the *Shepheards Pipe*, 1614. by W. Browne, who tells us that he had *all* the writer's pieces by him. See Browne's *Works*, edit. Hazlitt, i. Introd. and Ritfon's *Bibl. Poetica*, v. Hoccleve, for a more ample lift of his works, and compare James's *Iter Lancaftrenfe*, ed. Corfer, lix. Sixteen of Hoccleve's poems were printed in 1796 by Mr. George Mafon from a MS. which he had bought at Dr.

perefs.[1] *A prologue of the nine leffons that is read over Allhalow-day.*[2] *The moſt profitable and holfomeſt craft that is to cunne,*[3] *to lerne to dye.*[4] *Confolation offered by an old man.*[5] *Pentaſticcon to the king. Mercy as defined by Saint Auſtin. Dialogue to a friend.*[6] *Dialogue between Occleef and a beggar.*[7] *The letter of Cupid.*[8] *Verſes to an empty purſe.*[9] But Occleve's moſt confiderable poem is a piece called a tranſlation of Egidius *De Regimine Principum,*[10] [addreſſed to Prince Henry, ſon of Henry IV., and confequently written before 1413.]

This is a ſort of paraphraſe of the firſt part of Ariſtotle's epiſtle to Alexander above mentioned, entitled *Secretum Secretorum,* by the ſaid Egidius, and of Jacobus de Caſſolis, whom he calls Jacob de Caſſolis. Egidius, a native of Rome, a pupil of Thomas Aquinas, eminent among the ſchoolmen by the name of Doctor Fundatiſſimus, and an archbiſhop, flouriſhed about the year 1280. He wrote this Latin tract in three books (*De Regimine Principum,* or the *Art of*

Aſkew's ſale, and which was afterwards in the Heber collection. At Heber's ſale it was bought for Sir Thomas Philipps.]

[1] Bibl. Bodl. MSS. Seld. *ſupr.* 53, Digb. 185, Laud. K. 78, MSS. Reg. Brit. Muſ. 17 D. vi. 2. This ſtory ſeems to be alſo taken from the *Geſta Romanorum.* Pr. "In the Roman actys writyn."

[2] *Ubi ſupr.* Bibl. Bodl. MSS. [3] know.

[4] MSS. Bodl. *ut ſupr.* and MSS. Reg. Brit. Muſ. 17 D. vi. 3, 4, the beſt manu-ſcript of Occleve.

[5] MSS. Digb. 185. More [Cant.] 427, [and ſee Horne's Catal. MSS. Queen's Coll. Camb. ii. 1000, *ut infra.*]

[6] MSS. Seld. *ut ſupr.* [7] MSS. Harl. 4826, 6.

[8] MSS. Digb. 181, MSS. Arch. Bodl., Seld. B. 24. It is printed in Chaucer's Works, Urr. p. 534. Bale [MS. Glynne] mentions one or two more pieces, par-ticularly *De Theſeo Athenienſi,* lib. i. Pr. "Tum effet, ut veteres hiſtoriæ tradunt." This is the beginning of Chaucer's *Knight's Tale,* and there are other pieces in the libraries.

[9] This, and the *Pentaſtichon ad Regem,* are in MSS. Fairf. xvi. Bibl. Bodl. and in the editions of Chaucer. But the former appears to be Chaucer's, from the twenty additional ſtanzas not printed in Urry's *Chaucer,* page 549. MSS. Harl. 2251. 133, fol. 298.

[10] [Pinkerton (*Anc. Scotiſh Poems,* ii. 472-3) notices a quite different verſion in Maitland's folio MS. in the Pepys Library, beginning at p. 96, "Richt as all ſtringis ar cupillit in ane harpe," and being in 2 Parts. Part 2 beginning, p. 101, "Juſtice will have ane general preſedent," and ending p. 105.—F. From the *Boke of Curteſye* or *Lytyll John,* printed by Caxton, and attributed to Chaucer by Urry:

"Beholde Ocklyf in his tranſlacion,
In goodly langage and ſentence paſſyng wyſe
How he gyueth his prynce ſuche exortacion
As to the hyeſt he coude beſt deuyſe:
Of trouthe, pees, mercy and Iuſtiſe,
And vertues leeting for no ſlouthe,
To do his deuoir and quite him of his trouthe."—*Park.*

De Regimine Principum has been edited for the Roxburghe Club by Mr. T. Wright, 1860. In the library of Queen's College, Cambridge, is an Engliſh poem by Occleve, entitled *Conſolatio ſibi Oblata,* MS. on vellum in folio, fourteenth century (Horne's Cat. ii. 1000). The *Boke of Curteſye,* above quoted by Park, has been printed by Mr. Furnivall from Caxton's edition (1477-8), with two other texts (Oriel MS. 79, and Baliol MS. 354), in the Early Engliſh Text Society's Extra Series, 1868.]

Government) for the use of Philip le Hardi, son of Louis, king of France, a work highly esteemed in the middle ages, and translated early into Hebrew, French,[1] and Italian. In those days ecclesiastics and schoolmen presumed to dictate to kings, and to give rules for administering states, drawn from the narrow circle of speculation, and conceived amid the pedantries of a cloister. It was probably recommended to Occleve's notice by having been translated into English by John Trevisa, a celebrated translator about the year 1390.[2] The original was printed at Rome in 1482, and at Venice 1498, and, I think, again at the same place in 1598.[3] The [Spanish] translation was printed at Seville, in folio, 1494, "Transladó de Latin en Romance Don Bernardo Obispo de Osma; impresso por Meynardo Ungut Alemano et Stanislao Polono companeros." The printed copies of the Latin are very rare, but the manuscripts innumerable. A third part of the third book, which treats *De Re Militari Veterum*, was printed by Hahnius in 1722.[4] One of Egidius's books, a commentary on Aristotle *de Anima*, is dedicated to our Edward I.[5]

Jacobus de [Cassolis,] or of Casali in Italy, another of the writers copied in this performance by our poet Occleve, was a French Dominican friar about the year 1290, and wrote in four parts a Latin treatise on chess, or, as it is entitled in some manuscripts, *De moribus hominum et de officiis nobilium super Ludo Scaccorum*. In a parchment manuscript of the Harleian Library, neatly illuminated, it is thus entitled, *Liber Moralis de Ludo Scaccorum, ad honorem et solacium Nobilium et maxime ludencium, per fratrem Jacobum de Cassulis ordinis Fratrum Prædicatorum*. At the conclusion, this work appears to be a translation.[6] It was printed at Milan in 1479. I believe it was as great a favourite as Egidius on Government, for it was translated into French by Jean Ferron [in 1347, and dedicated to Bertrand de Auberi, and also by] John Vignay, a monk Hospitaller of Saint [Jacques] du Haut-[pas],[7] under the patronage of [John, duke of Normandy (after-

---

[1] Wolf. Biblioth. Hebr. tom. iii. p. 1206. It was translated into French by Henry de Gand, at the command of Philip, king of France. *Mem. de Lit.* tom. xvii. p. 733, 4to.

[2] Bibl. Bodl. MSS. Digb. 233. *Princip.* "To his special, [&c.] politik sentence that is." In this manuscript there is an elegant picture of a monk or ecclesiastic, presenting a book to a king.

[3] All in folio. Those of 1482 and 1598 are in the Bodleian Library In All-Souls College Library at Oxford there is a manuscript, *Tabula in Ægidium de Regimine Principum*, by one Thomas Abyndon. MSS. G. i. 5.

[4] In the first tome of *Collectio Monumentorum veter. et recent. ineditorum.* E. Cod. MS. in Biblioth. Obrecktina. The curious reader may see a full account of Ægidius *de Regimine Principum* in Morlier, *Essais de Litterature*, tom. i. p. 198, *seq.*; and of the Venetian edition in 1498, in Theophilus Sincerus, *De Libris Rariorib.* tom. i. p. 82, *seq.*

[5] Cave, p. 755, edit. 1688.

[6] MSS. Harl. 1275, 1; [MSS. Magd. Coll. Oxf. (dated 1456, and transcribed by Symon Aylvard), MSS. No. 12.]

[7] Who also translated the *Golden Legend* of Jacobus de Voragine, and the *Specu-*

wards King of France), before the year 1350,] with the title of *Le Jeu des Echecs moralisé*, or *Le traité des Nobles et de Gens du Peuple selon le Jeu des Echecs*. This was afterwards translated by Caxton, who did not know that the French was a translation from the Latin, and who called his version the *Game of the Chess*. It was also translated into German verse by Conrad van Ammenhasca¹ [in 1337, and at a later period into German prose, the latter of which was printed in 1477.]

Occleve's poem was never printed [till lately.] This is a part of the [Address to the King:]²

>Ariftotle, moft famous philofofre,³
>His epiftles to Alifaundre fent;
>Whos fentence is wel bette than golde in cofre,
>And more holfumer grounded in trewe entent.
>For all that ever tho Epiftles ment,
>To fette was this worthy conquerour,
>In reule how to fuftene his honour,

>The tendir love and the fervent chiertie,
>That this worthy clerk ay to this kyng bere,
>Truftyng his welthe durable to be,
>Unto his hert ftak and fatte fo nere,
>That by writyng his counfeille yave he clere
>Unto his lorde to kepe hym fro myfchaunce,
>As witneffethe his booke of governaunce.⁴
>Of whiche and of Gyes of Regement⁵
>Of Prynces plotmele, thynke I to tranflete, &c.
>My dere maifter, God his foule quyte,
>And fader Chaucer fayne would me han taught,
>But I was dulle, and lernede right naught.

>Allas my worthy maifter honorable,
>This londes verray trefour and richeffe,
>Dethe by thy dethe hathe harme irreperable
>Unto us none: hir vengeable dureffe
>Difpoilede hathe this londe of the fwetneffe
>Of rettoryk, for unto Tullius
>Was never man fo like amonge us.

>Alfo who was heir in phylofofye
>To Ariftotle in our tunge but thow?

---

lum Hiftoriale of Vincent of Beauvais. *Vie de Petr.* tom. iii. p. 548, and *Mem. Lit.* xvii. 742, 746, 747, edit. 4to.

¹ See Jacob. Quetif. tom. i. p. 471, ii. p. 818. Lambecc. tom. ii. *Bibl. Vindob.* p. 848.

² [The prefent text has received fome emendations from Harl. MSS. 116 and 4866, and Royal MS. 17. D. vi.—*Price.* An imperfect MS. was fold among the books of the Rev. Thomas Corfer, of Stand, in 1869. The text ufed by Mr. Wright was the Royal MS.]

³ Gerard Langbaine, fpeaking of the *De Regimine Principum*, by Occleve, fays that it is "collected out of Ariftotle, Alexander, and Ægidius on the fame, and Jacobus de Caffolis (a fryar preacher) his book of chefs, viz. that part where he fpeaks of the king's draught," &c. Bibl. Bodl. MSS. Langb. Cod. xv. page 102. [In the fame Langbaine MS. fome lines occur, which form part of the Dialogue prefixed to Occleve's poem, as edited by Mr. Wright in 1860.]

⁴ Ariftotle's *Secretum Secretorum*.

⁵ Ægidius *de Regimine Principum*.

> The fteppes of Virgile in poyfye
> Thou folwedeft eke : men wote well ynow
> That combre-worlde[1] that the my maifter flowe :[2]
> Wolde I flayne were! dethe was to haftyfe
> To renne on the, and reve the thy lyfe :
>
> * * *
>
> She myght han taryede hir vengeaunce a while
> Til that fome man hade egal to theb be :
> Nay, lete be that! fhe knewe wel that this yle
> May never man bryng forthe like to the,
> And hir offis nedes do mote fhe ;
> God bade hir do fo, I trufte for the befte,
> O maifter, maifter, God thy foulè refte!

In [the Proem, which is partly in the form of a dialogue], we have thefe pathetic lines, which feem to flow warm from the heart, to the memory of the immortal Chaucer, who I believe was rather Occleve's model than his mafter, or perhaps the patron and encourager of his ftudies :

> But weleaway, fo is myne hert wo
> That the honour of Englifhe tonge is dede,
> Of whiche I was wonte have counfeeille and rede !
> O maifter dere and fader reverent,
> My maifter Chaucer, floure of eloquence,
> Mirrour of fructuous entendement,
> O univerfal fader in fcience,
> Allas, that thou thyne excellent prudence
> In thy bedde mortelle myghteft not bequethe,
> What eyled dethe ? allas why wold he fle the !
> O dethe, that didft noe harme fingulere
> In flaughtre of hym, but alle this londe it fmerteth :
> But natheles yit haft thow no powere
> His name to flee, his hye vertu aftertethe
> Unflayne fro the, whiche ay us lyfly hertethe
> Withe bookes of his ornat endityng,
> That is to alle this londe enlumynyng.[3]

Occleve feems to have written fome of thefe verfes immediately on Chaucer's death, and to have introduced them long afterwards into this Prologue.

It is in the royal manufcript of this Poem in the Britifh Mufeum

---

[1] [*i.e.* death.] The expreffion feems to be taken from Chaucer, where Troilus fays of himfelf, " I *combre-world*, that maie of nothing ferve." *Tr. and Crefs.* v. 279.

[2] flew.

[3] [Edit. 1860, p. 71.] MSS. Rawlins. 647. fol. This poem has at the end " Explicit Ægidius de Regimine Principum " in MSS. Laud. K. 78. Bibl. Bodl. See alfo *ibid.* MSS. Selden. fupr. 53. Digb. 185. MSS. Afhmol. 40. MSS. Reg. 17 D. vi. 1. 17 D. xviii. MSS. Harl. 4826. 7. and 4866. In fome of thefe [occurs a dialogue of fome length between an old man and the author, in which many curious biographical particulars refpecting the latter may be found, and which precedes the dedication in Mr. Wright's edition.] Occleve, in the [Addrefs or Dedication] cited in the text, mentions Jacobus de Caffolis as one of his authors, which in the Mufeum MSS. precedes the tranflation of Ægidius. [The work of Caffolis, to which Occleve reforted here, was the *Game of the Chefs* moralized, which from a French tranflation was rendered into Englifh, and printed by Caxton twice.]

that Occleve has left a drawing of Chaucer:[1] according to which Chaucer's portraiture was made on his monument, in the chapel of Saint Blaſe in Weſtminſter Abbey, by the benefaction of Nicholas Brigham in the year 1556.[2] From this drawing, in 1598, John Speed procured the print of Chaucer prefixed to Speght's edition of his Works; which [was ſubſequently] copied in a moſt finiſhed engraving by Vertue.[3] Yet it muſt be remembered, that the ſame drawing occurs in an Harleian MS. written about Occleve's age,[4] and in another of the Cottonian department.[5] Occleve himſelf mentions this drawing in his *Conſolatio Servilis*. It exactly reſembles the curious picture on board of our venerable bard, preſerved in the Bodleian gallery at Oxford. I have a very old picture of Chaucer on board, much like Occleve's, formerly kept in Chaucer's houſe, a quadrangular ſtone-manſion at Woodſtock in Oxfordſhire, which commanded a proſpect of the ancient magnificent royal palace, and of many beautiful ſcenes in the adjacent park: and whoſe laſt remains, chiefly conſiſting of what was called Chaucer's bed-chamber, with an old carved oaken roof evidently original, were demoliſhed [in the laſt century only.] Among the ruins they found an ancient gold coin of the city of Florence.[6] Before the grand rebellion, there was in the windows of the church of Woodſtock an eſcutcheon in painted glaſs of the arms of Sir Payne Rouet, a knight of Henault, whoſe daughter Chaucer married.

Occleve, in this poem and in others, often celebrates Humphrey, duke of Gloucester[7] who, at the dawn of ſcience was a ſingular promoter of literature, and (however unqualified for political intrigues) the common patron of the ſcholars of the times. A ſketch of his character in that view is therefore too cloſely connected with our ſubject to be cenſured as an unneceſſary digreſſion. About the year 1440, he gave to the univerſity of Oxford a library containing ſix hundred volumes, only one hundred and twenty of which were valued at more than one thouſand pounds. Theſe books are called *Novi Tractatus*, or New Treatiſes, in the univerſity-regiſter,[8] and ſaid to be *admirandi apparatus*.[9] They were the moſt ſplendid and coſtly copies that could be procured, finely written on vellum, and elegantly embelliſhed with miniatures and illuminations. Among the reſt was a tranſlation into French of Ovid's *Metamorphoſes*.[10]

---

[1] MSS. Reg. 17 D. vi. 1.
[2] He was of Caverſham in Oxfordſhire. Educated at Hart-Hall in Oxford, and ſtudied the law. He died at Weſtminſter, 1559.
[3] In Urry's edit. 1721, fol.
[4] MSS. Harl. 4866. The drawing is at fol. 91.
[5] MSS. Cotton. *Oth.* A. 18. [The Chaucer part is burnt.—F.]
[6] I think a Florein, anciently common in England. Chaucer, *Pardon. Tale*, v. 2290. "For that the Florains ben ſo faire and bright." Edward III., in 1344, altered it from a lower value to 6s. 8d. The particular piece I have mentioned ſeems about that value.
[7] As he does John of Gaunt.
[8] Reg. F. fol. 52, 53, b. *Epiſt*. 142.
[9] *Ibid*. fol. 57, b, 60, a, *Epiſt*. 148.
[10] Leland, *Coll*. iii. p. 58, edit. 1770

Only [four specimens] of these valuable volumes [have been] suffered to remain [and of them two are in the British Museum.] [One] is a beautiful MS. in folio of Valerius Maximus, enriched with the most elegant decorations, and written in Duke Humphrey's age, evidently with a design of being placed in this sumptuous collection. All the rest of the books which, like [these,] being highly ornamented, looked like missals, and conveyed ideas of popish superstition, were destroyed or removed by the pious visitors of the university in the reign of Edward VI., whose zeal was equalled only by their ignorance, or perhaps by their avarice. A great number of classics, in this grand work of reformation, were condemned as antichristian.[1] In the library of Oriel college at Oxford, we find a MS. *Commentary on Genesis*, written by John Capgrave,[2] a monk of Saint Austin's monastery at Canterbury, a

---

[1] Some however had been before stolen or mutilated. Leland, *Coll.* iii. p. 58, edit. 1770.

[2] [By favour of Mr. Bliss of the Bodleian Library I am enabled to add, that Capgrave appears from one of the Rawlinson MSS. No. 118, to have been a considerable maker of verse, and the translator of a life of St. Catherine, written by Athanasius in Greek, rendered from that language into Latin by a priest named Arreck, and finally into English verse by Capgrave. Prefixed is an account of the work written by Sir Henry Spelman, in whose possession probably the volume once was, and of whom it deserves therefore to be remembered that he had stored up the production of a poet of the fourteenth century, at a time when the scattered remains of our poetical writers were more than commonly neglected. His description of the nature of the poem and of its authors it may be desirable to give : " A preiste, which this author, Jo. Capgrave, nameth Arreck, having hearde much of St. Katherin, bestowed eighteen years to searche out her life : and, for that purpose, spent twelve of them in Greece. At last, by direction of a vision in the days of Peter K. of Cyprus and Pope Urban V., he digged up in Cyprus an old booke of that very matter, written by Athanasius byshop of Alexandria (but whether he that made the Creede or not the author doubteth) and hidden there 100 yeares before by Amylon Fitz Amarack. Then did this Arreck compile her story into Latyn, saithe this author :

  ' For out of Greek he hath it first runge
  This holy lyfe into the Latyn tounge.'

And then also did he make it into English verse ; but leaving it unperfected, and in obscure rude English, Capgrave not only enlarged it, but refyned it to the phrase of his tyme, as himselfe testifyethe, speaking of the preist to St. Katherin

  ' He made thy life in English tounge full wel,
  But yet he died or he had fully doo,
  And that he made, it is ful harde therto
  Right for strangnesse of his dark language.
  He is now dead ; thou hast give him his way,
  Now wil I, lady, more openly make thy life,
  Out of his worke yf thou wilt helpe therto.'

This preiste, as Capgrave also sheweth, died at Lynn, many yeares before his tyme, where Capgrave was a regular : for he saithe in his Prologue :

  ' Yf ye wil wite what that I am,
  My country is Norfolk, of the towne of Lynn.
  Out of the world, to my profit I cam,
  Unto the brotherhood which I am in.
  God send me grace never to blynn

learned theologist of the fourteenth century [and the reputed author of John of Tynemouth's *Nova Legenda Angliæ*, published in 1516.] It is the author's autograph, and the work is dedicated to Humphrey, duke of Gloucester. In the superb initial letter of the dedicatory epistle is a curious illumination of the author Capgrave, humbly presenting his book to his patron the duke, who is seated and covered with a sort of hat. At the end is this entry, [probably not] in the handwriting of Duke Humphrey. "*Cest livre est a moy Humfrey duc de Gloucestre du don de frere Jehan Capgrave, quy le me fist presenter a mon manoyr de Pensherst le jour . . . de l'an*. MCCCXXXVIII."[1] This is one of the books which Humphrey gave to his new library at Oxford, destroyed or dispersed by the active reformers of the young Edward.[2] John Whethamstede, a learned abbot of Saint Alban's, and a lover of scholars, but accused by his monks of neglecting their affairs, while he was too deeply engaged in studious employments and in procuring transcripts of useful books,[3] notwithstanding his unwearied assiduity in beautifying and enriching their monastery,[4] was in high favour with this munificent prince.[5] The duke was fond of visiting this monastery, and employed Abbot Whethamstede to collect valuable books for him.[6] Some of Whethamstede's tracts, MSS. copies of

---

To follow the steps of my faders before,
Which to the rule of Austen were swore.'"

These may afford sufficient specimens of the poet's style: of the subject chosen no notice can be required.—*Park*.]

[1] Cod. MSS. 32.

[2] He gave also Capgrave *super Exodum et Regum libros*. Registr. Univ. Oxon. F. fol. 67, b.

[3] *Supra*, vol. i. See *Dissertat*. i. We are told in this abbot's *Gesta*, that soon after his instalment he built a library for his abbey, a design which had long employed his contemplation. He covered it with lead, and expended on the bare walls, besides desks, glasing, and embatteling, or to use the expressions of my chronologer, *deducta vitriacione, crestacione, positione descorum*, upwards of one hundred and [forty] pounds. *Apud* Hearne's *Otterbourne*, vol. i. Præfat. Append. p. cxxiii. ed. 1732. He founded also a library for all the students of his monastery at Oxford. *Ibid*. p. cxiii. And to each of these students he allowed an annual pension, at his own expence, of thirteen shillings and four-pence. *Ibid*. p. cxviii. See also p. cxxix. A grand transcript of the *Postilla* of Nicholas de Lyra on the Bible was begun during his abbacy, and at his command, with the most splendid ornaments and hand-writing. The monk who records this important anecdote, lived soon after him, and speaks of this great undertaking, then unfinished, as if it was some magnificent public edifice. "God grant," says he, "that this work in our days may receive a happy consummation!" *Ibid*. p. cxvi.

[4] Among other things, he expended forty pounds in adorning the roof and walls of the Virgin Mary's chapel with pictures. *Gest*. ut supr. p. cx. He gave to the choir of the church an organ, than which, says my chronicler, there was not one to be found in any monastery in England, more beautiful in appearance, more pleasing for its harmony, or more curious in its construction. It cost upwards of fifty pounds. *Ibid*. p. cxxviii. His new buildings were innumerable: and the Master of the Works was of his institution, with an ample salary. *Ibid*. p. cxiii.

[5] Leland, *Script. Brit*. p. 437.

[6] Leland, *ibid*. 442, 432. See also Holinsh. *Chron*. f. 488, b. And f. 1234, 1235, 1080, 868, 662. Weever, *Fun. Mon*. pp. 562, 574. Whethamstede erected in his life-time the beautiful tabernacle or shrine of stone, now remaining, over

which often occur in our libraries, are dedicated to the duke:[1] who presented many of them, particularly a fine copy of Whethamstede's *Granarium*,[2] an immense work which Leland calls *ingens volumen*, to the new library.[3] The copy of Valerius Maximus, which I mentioned before, has a curious table or index made by Whethamstede.[4] Many other abbots paid their court to the duke by sending him presents of books, whose margins were adorned with the most exquisite paintings.[5] Gilbert Kymer, physician to Henry VI. among other ecclesiastic promotions dean of Salisbury and chancellor of the university of Oxford,[6] inscribed to Duke Humphrey his famous medical system *Diaetarium de sanitatis custodia* in the year 1424.[7] I do not mean to anticipate when I remark, that Lydgate, a poet mentioned hereafter, translated Boccaccio's book *De Casibus virorum illustrium* at the recommendation and command, and under the protection and superintendence, of Duke Humphrey, whose condescension in conversing with learned ecclesiastics and diligence in study the translator displays at large, and in the strongest expressions of panegyric. He compares the duke to Julius Cæsar who, amidst the weightiest cares of state, was not ashamed to enter the rhetorical school of Cicero at Rome.[8] Nor was his patronage confined only to English scholars. His favour was solicited by the most celebrated

---

the tomb of Duke Humphrey in Saint Alban's abbey church. Hearne's *Otterb*. ut supr. p. cxxi. *seq*. See also *ibid*. pp. cxix, cxvi.

[1] See Whethamstede, *De viris illustribus*, Brit. Mus. MSS. Cotton. *Tiber*. D. vi. i. *Oth*. B. iv. And Hearne, *Pref. Pet. Langtoft*. p. xix. *seq*.

[2] *Registr. Univ. Oxon*. F. f. 68.   [3] Leland, *ubi infr*.

[4] MSS. Bodl. NE. vii. ii.

[5] "Multos codices, *pulcherrime pictos*, ab abbatibus dono accepit." The Duke wrote in the frontispieces of his books, Moun bien mondain. Leland, *Coll*. iii. p. 58, *ut supr*.

[6] By the recommendatory letters of Duke Humphrey. *Registr. Univ. Oxon*. F. fol. 75. *Epist*. 180.

[7] See Hearne's *Append. ad Libr. Nigr. Scaccar*. p. 550. And *Præfat*. p. 34.

[8] *Prol*. Sign. A. ii. A. iii. edit. Wayland, *ut supr*. He adds:

> "And hath joye with clarkes to commune,
> And no man is more expert in langage,
> Stable in study.—
> His courage never dothe appall
> To study in bokes of antiquitie.—
> He studieth ever to have intelligence,
> Readyng of bokes.—
> And with support of his magnificence,
> Under the wings of his protection.—
> I shall proceed in this translation.—
> Lowly submittyng, every houre and space,
> My rude langage to my lordes grace."

See also fol. xxxviii. b, col. 2. Lydgate has an epitaph on the duke, MSS. Ashmol. 59, 2; MSS. Harl. 2251, 6, fol. 7. There is a curious letter of Lydgate, in which he sends for a supply of money to the duke, while he was translating Boccaccio. "Littera dom. Joh. Lydgate missa ad ducem Glocestrie in *tempore translationis Bochasii*, pro *oportunitate pecunie*." MSS. *ibid*. 5, fol. 6. See also *ibid*. 131, fol. 279, b, of the duke's marriage.

writers of France and Italy, many of whom he bountifully rewarded.[1] Leonard Aretine, one of the first restorers of the Greek tongue in Italy which he learned of Emanuel Chrysoloras, and of polite literature in general, dictates to this universal patron his elegant Latin translation of Aristotle's *Politics*. The copy presented to the duke by the translator, most elegantly illuminated, is now in the Bodleian Library at Oxford.[2] To the same noble encourager of learning Petrus Candidus, the friend of Laurentius Valla, and secretary to the duke of Milan, inscribed by the advice of the archbishop of Milan a Latin version of Plato's *Republic*.[3] An illuminated MS. of this translation is in the British Museum, with two epistles prefixed from the duke to Petrus Candidus.[4] Petrus de Monte, a learned Venetian, in the dedication of his treatise *De Virtutum et Vitiorum Differentia* to the duke of Gloucester, mentions the latter's ardent attachment to books of all kinds, and the singular avidity with which he pursued every species of literature.[5] A tract, entitled *Comparatio Studiorum et Rei Militaris*, written by Lapus de Castellione, a Florentine civilian, and a great translator into Latin of the Greek classics, is also inscribed to the duke at the desire of Zeno archbishop of Bayeux. I must not forget, that our illustrious duke invited into England the learned Italian, Tito Livio of Friuli, whom he naturalised, and constituted his poet and orator.[6] Humphrey also retained learned foreigners in his service, for the purpose of transcribing and translating from Greek into Latin. One of these was Antonio de Beccaria, a Veronese, a translator into Latin prose of the Greek poem of Dionysius Afer *De Situ Orbis:*[7] and him the duke employed to translate into Latin six tracts of Athanasius. This translation, inscribed to the duke, is now among the royal MSS. in the British Museum, and at the end, in his own hand-writing, is the following insertion: "Cest livre est a moi Homphrey Duc le Glouceftre: le quel je fis translater de Grec en Latin par un de mes secretaires Antoyne de Beccara, nè de Verone."[8]

An astronomical tract, entitled by Leland *Tabulæ Directionum*,

---

[1] Leland, *Script*. p. 442.
[2] See MSS. Bodl. D. i. 8, 10. And Leland, *Script*. p. 443.
[3] Leland, *Script*. p. 422. And Mus. Ashmol. 789, f. 54, 56, where also is a copy of the Duke's two Epistles to Petrus Candidus, [mentioned below.]
[4] P. Candidi Decembrii, Duci Mediolani a secretis, Translatio Politiæ Platonis, ad Humfredum Gloucestriæ Ducem, &c. Cui præfiguntur duæ Epistolæ Ducis Gloceftriæ ad P. Candidum. Most elegantly written, *ad fin*. "Cest livre est a moy Humfrey Duc de Gloceftre du don P. Candidus secretaire du duc de Mylan." Catal. MSS. Angl. tom. ii. p. 212, Num. 6858. [See MSS. Harl. 1705, and Muratori, *Rer. Ital. Script.* xx.]
[5] MSS. Nowic. More, 257, Bibl. Publ. Cantabrig.
[6] Author of the *Vita Henrici quinti* (printed by Hearne, Oxon. 1716) and of other pieces. See Holinsh. iii. 585.
[7] Printed at Venice 1477. *Ibid*. 1498. Paris, 1501. Basil. 1534, 4to.
[8] MSS. Reg. 5 F. [iii. 4to.] In the same library is a fine folio MS. of "Chronique des Roys de France jusques a la mort de S. Loys, l'an 1270." At the end is written with the Duke of Gloucester's hand, "Cest livre est a moy Homfrey duc de Gloceftre du don des executeurs le Sr de Faunhore." 16 G. vi.

is falsely supposed to have been written by Duke Humphrey.[1] But it was compiled at the duke's instance, and according to tables which he himself had constructed, called by the anonymous author in his preface, *Tabulas illustrissimi principis et nobilissimi domini mei Humfredi*, &c.[2] In the library of Gresham college, however, there is a scheme of calculations in astronomy, which bears his name.[3] Astronomy was then a favourite science: nor is it to be doubted, that he was intimately acquainted with the politer branches of knowledge, which now began to acquire estimation, and which his liberal and judicious attention greatly contributed to restore.

I close this section with an apology for Chaucer, Gower and Occleve: who are supposed by the severer etymologists to have corrupted the purity of the English language, by affecting to introduce so many foreign words and phrases. But if we attend only to the politics of the times, we shall find these poets, as also some of their successors, much less blameable in this respect than the critics imagine. Our wars with France, which began in the reign of Edward III. were of long continuance. The principal nobility of England, at this period, resided in France, with their families, for many years. John, king of France, kept his court in England, to which exclusively of these French lords who were his fellow prisoners or necessary attendants, the chief nobles of his kingdom must have occasionally resorted. Edward the Black Prince made an expedition into Spain. John of Gaunt, duke of Lancaster, and his brother the Duke of York, were matched with the daughters of Don Pedro, king of Castile. All these circumstances must have concurred to produce a perceptible change in the language of the court. It is rational therefore, and it is equitable, to suppose that, instead of coining new words, they only complied with the common and fashionable modes of speech. Would Chaucer's poems have been the delight of those courts in which he lived, had they been filled with unintelligible pedantries? The cotemporaries of these poets never complained of their obscurity. But whether defensible on these principles or not, they much improved the vernacular style by the use of this exotic phraseology. It was thus that our primitive diction was enlarged and enriched. The English language owes its copiousness, elegance and harmony to these innovations.

---

[1] See Holinsh. *Chron.* sub ann. 1461, f. 662, col. 2.
[2] MSS. More, 820.   [3] MSS. Gresh. 66. See MSS. Ashmol. 856.

SECTION XXI.

I CONSIDER Chaucer as a genial day in an English spring. A brilliant sun enlivens the face of nature with an unusual lustre: the sudden appearance of cloudless skies and the unexpected warmth of a tepid atmosphere, after the gloom and the inclemencies of a tedious winter, fill our hearts with the visionary prospect of a speedy summer: and we fondly anticipate a long continuance of gentle gales and vernal serenity. But winter returns with redoubled horrors: the clouds condense more formidably than before; and those tender buds and early blossoms, which were called forth by the transient gleam of a temporary sunshine, are nipped by frosts, and torn by tempests.

Most of the poets, who immediately succeeded Chaucer, seem rather relapsing into barbarism than availing themselves of those striking ornaments which his judgment and imagination had disclosed. They appear to have been insensible to his vigour of versification and his flights of fancy. It was not indeed likely that a poet should soon arise, equal to Chaucer: and it must be remembered that the national distractions, which ensued, had no small share in obstructing the exercise of those studies which delight in peace and repose. His successors, however, approach him in no degree of proportion. Among these, John Lydgate is the poet who follows him at the shortest interval.

I have placed Lydgate in the reign of Henry VI., and he seems to have arrived at his highest point of eminence about the year 1430.[1] Many of his poems, however, appeared before. He was a monk of the Benedictine Abbey of Bury in Suffolk, and an uncommon ornament of his profession. Yet his genius was so lively, and his accomplishments so numerous, that I suspect the holy father Saint Benedict would hardly have acknowledged him for a genuine disciple. After a short education at Oxford, he travelled into France and Italy,[2] and returned a complete master of the language and the literature of both countries. He chiefly studied the Italian and French poets, particu-

---

[1] In a copy of Lydgate's *Chronicle of English Kings*, there is a stanza of Edward IV. [added after Lydgate's death]. MSS. Harl. 2251, 3. In his poem *Ab inimicis nostris*, &c. Edward IV. his *Quene* and *Modir* are remembered. MSS. Harl. ibid. 9, fol. 10. But Lydgate was ordained a subdeacon, 1389; deacon, 1393; and priest, 1397. *Regiſtr. Gul. Cratfield, abbatis de Bury,* MSS. Cott. *Tiber.* B. ix. fol. 1, 35, 52. Edward came to the crown, 1461. Pits says, that our author died, 1482, [but the event must be placed much earlier, though after 1461]. Lydgate, in his *Philomela*, mentions the death of Henry Lord Warwick, who died in 1446. MSS. Harl. ibid. 120, fol. 255.

[2] See one of his *Ditties,* MSS. Harl. 2255, 41, fol. 148:
"I have been offte in dyvers londys," &c.

larly Dante, Boccaccio, and Alain Chartier, and became so distinguished a proficient in polite learning, that he opened a school in his monastery for teaching the sons of the nobility the arts of versification and the elegancies of composition. Yet although philology was his object, he was not unfamiliar with the fashionable philosophy: he was not only a poet and a rhetorician, but a geometrician, an astronomer, a theologist, and a disputant. On the whole I am of opinion, that Lydgate made considerable additions to those amplifications of our language, in which Chaucer, Gower, and Occleve led the way: and that he is the first of our writers whose style is clothed with that perspicuity, in which the English phraseology appears at this day to an English reader.

To enumerate Lydgate's pieces, would be to write the catalogue of a little library. No poet seems to have possessed a greater versatility of talents. He moves with equal ease in every mode of composition. His hymns and his ballads have the same degree of merit; and whether his subject be the life of a hermit or a hero, of Saint Austin or Guy earl of Warwick, ludicrous or legendary, religious or romantic, a history or an allegory, he writes with facility. His transitions were rapid from works of the most serious and laborious kind to sallies of levity and pieces of popular entertainment. His muse was of universal access; and he was not only the poet of his monastery, but of the world in general. If a disguising was intended by the company of goldsmiths, a mask before his majesty at Eltham, a may-game for the Sheriffs and Aldermen of London, a mumming before the Lord Mayor, a procession of pageants from the creation for the festival of Corpus Christi, or a carol for the coronation, Lydgate was consulted, and gave the poetry.[1]

About the year 1430, Whethamstede, the learned and liberal Abbot of Saint Alban's, being desirous of familiarising the history of his patron saint to the monks of his convent, employed Lydgate, as it should seem, then a monk of Bury, to translate the Latin legend of his life in English rhymes. The chronicler, who records a part of this anecdote, seems to consider Lydgate's translation as a matter

---

[1] See a variety of his pieces of this kind, MSS. Ashmol. 59. ii. Stow says, that at the reception of Margaret, queen of Henry VI. several pageants, the verses by Lydgate, were shown at Paul's gate, in 1445. *Hist.* p. 385. See also MSS. Harl. 2251. 118. fol. 250. b. See the prologue to Feyld's *Controversye betwene a Lover and a Jaye:*—

"Chaucer, floure of rethoryke eloquence,
Compyled bookes pleasaunt and mervayllous,
After hym noble *Gower*, experte in scyence,
Wrote moralytees harde and delycyous.
But *Lydgates* workes are fruytefull and sentencyous;
Who of his bookes hathe redde the fyne
He wyll hym cal a famous rethorycyne."—*Park.*

Mr. Ritson, in his *Bibliographia Poetica*, has furnished a list of 251 pieces written by Lydgate. Many of them, however, are attributed to him upon authority of no very early date, and he is doubtlessly made responsible for a large portion of the anonymous rhymes of his age.—*Price.*]

of mere manual mechanism; for he adds that Whethamstede paid for the translation, the writing, and illuminations, one hundred shillings. It was placed before the altar of the saint, which Whethamstede afterwards adorned with much magnificence, in the abbey church.[1]

Our author's stanzas, called the *Dance of Death*, which he translated from the French, at the request of [a French *clerk* or scholar,] to be inscribed under the representation of death leading all ranks of men about the cloister of (St. Paul's) church [London], in a curious series of paintings, are well known. But their history has not, I believe, yet appeared. These verses, founded on a sort of spiritual masquerade, anciently celebrated in churches,[2] were originally written by one Macaber in German rhymes, and were translated into Latin about the year 14[9]0 by Pierre Desrey. This Latin translation was [re-]published by Goldastus.[3] But a French translation was made much earlier than the Latin, and written about the walls of Saint Innocents' cloister at Paris; [and from this version] Lydgate formed his English one.[4]

---

[1] *Gest. Joh. Whethamst.* ut supra, pp. cxvi. cxxvii. cxxiv. It is added, that Whethamstede expended on the binding and other exterior ornaments of the MS. upwards of three pounds. Bale and Pits say, that Whethamstede himself made the translation, pp. 584. 630. It is in Trinity College at Oxford (MSS. 10) and in Lincoln Cathedral (MSS. I. 57). Among Lydgate's works is recited, *Vita S. Albani Martyris ad Joh. Frumentarium* [Whethamstede] *abbatem*. [A complete list of his printed works, including one or two unseen by Warton, will be found in *Handb. of E. E. Lit.* art. *Lydgate*. A selection from his Minor Poems has been printed for the Percy Society.]

[2] See *supra*, Note. A *Dance of Death* seems to be alluded to so early as in *Pierce Plowman*, written about [1362]:—

"Death came driving after and al to dust pashed
Kyngs, and kaisars, knights, and popes."

[3] At the end of the *Speculum omnium Statuum totius orbis terrarum* compiled by Rodericus [Sancius], and printed at Haynau in 1613.

[4] See the *Daunce of Macabre*, MSS. Harl. 116. 9. fol. 129. And *Observations on the Fairy Queen*, vol. ii. p. 116, *seq*. The *Dance of Death*, falsely supposed to have been invented by Holbein, is different from this, though founded on the same idea. It was painted by Holbein in the Augustine monastery at Basil, 1543. But it appeared much earlier. In the chronicle of Hartmannus Schedelius [usually called *The Nuremberg Chronicle*,] 1493; in the Quotidian Offices of the church, Paris, 1515, 8vo.; in public buildings at Minden, in Westphalia, so early as 1383; at Lubeck, in the portico of Saint Mary's church, 1463; at Dresden, in the castle or palace, 1534; at Annaberg, 1525; at Leipsic, &c. Paul Christian Hilscher has written a very learned and entertaining German book on this subject, printed at Dresden, 1705, 8vo. Engravings of Holbein's pictures at Basle were published [by Merian] at Francfort 1649 and 1725. The German verses there ascribed appeared in Latin elegiacs, in Caspar Laudismann's *Decennalia humanæ Peregrinationis*, A.D. 1584. [See Douce's work on the *Dance of Death*, 1833, 8vo, and a good paper in the *Athenæum*, Sept. 22, 1849.—Rye. The edition of the *Alphabet de la Mort*, by M. Anatole de Montaiglon, 1856, may also be consulted. The first edition of Holbein's *Dance of Death* appeared in 1538. But see a note in the last edition of Brunet, iii. 255.]

The most antient complete French copy of *La Danse Macabre* was [probably that published at Paris between 1486 and 1490, twelve leaves folio, in two columns,

In the British Museum is a most splendid and elegant MS. on vellum, undoubtedly a present to Henry VI.[1] It contains a set of Lydgate's poems in honour of Saint Edmund, the patron of his monastery at Bury. Besides the decoration of illuminated initials, and one hundred and twenty pictures of various sizes, representing the incidents related in the poetry, executed with the most delicate pencil, and exhibiting the habits, weapons, architecture, utensils, and many other curious particulars belonging to the age of the ingenious illuminator, there are two exquisite portraits of the king, one of William Curteis, Abbot of Bury, and one of the poet Lydgate kneeling at Saint Edmund's shrine.[2] In one of the king's pictures, he is represented on his throne, crowned, and receiving this volume from the abbot kneeling; in another he appears as a child prostrate on a carpet at Saint Edmund's shrine, which is richly delineated, yet without any idea of perspective or proportion. The figures of a great number of monks and attendants are introduced. Among the rest, two noblemen, perhaps the king's uncles, with bonnets or caps of an uncommon shape. It appears that our pious monarch kept his Christmas at this magnificent monastery, and that he remained here, in a state of seclusion from the world and of an exemption from public cares, till the following Easter [1433], and that at his

---

with woodcuts. There are many later impressions.] To this work Erasmus alludes in the third book of his *Ratio Concionandi*, where he says, "Quin et vulgares rhetoristæ censuerunt hoc decus, qui interdum versibus certo numero comprehensis, pro clausula, accinunt brevem et argutam sententiam, velut in Rhythmis quos Gallus quispiam edidit in *Choream Mortis*." Opp. tom. v. p. 1007. Naude calls this allegory, "Chorea ab eximio Macabro edita." *Mascur.* p. 224. The Latin edition of Pierre Desrey was printed at [Paris] in 1490. The French have an old poem, partly on the same idea, *La Danse des Aveugles*, under the conduct of Love, Fortune, and Death, written by Pierre Michault, [secretary to Charles, Duke of Burgundy]. See *Mem. Acad. Inscript. et Bel. Let.* ii. 742. And Goujet, *Bibl. Fr.* ix. 358. [The earliest edition of the *Danse Maccabre* mentioned in the last edition of Brunet is that of Paris, 1485, folio, but it is less complete than that described above.] In this edition the French rhymes are [erroneously] said to be by Michel Marot, *Bell. Lettr.* tom. i. p. 512, num. 3109. He has catalogued all the antient editions of this piece in French, which are many. Pierre Desrey, above mentioned wrote a French romance called *La Genealogie on Godfrey of Bouloign*. Paris, 1511. [Lydgate's poem is neither a literal nor complete translation of the French version, and this he avows:—

"Out of the French I drough it, of entant
Not word by word, but folowyng in substaunce."

Again, the number of the characters in Lydgate is much less than that in the French, and he has not only omitted several, but supplied their places with others; so that if these lines were inscribed under the painting at St. Paul's, it must have differed materially from that at St. Innocents', at Paris. All the ancient *Dances of Death*, though evidently deduced from one original, differed much in the number and designs of the characters; but they generally appear to have been accompanied with Macaber's verses, or with imitations of them.—*Park*.]

[1] MSS. Harl. 2278.

[2] There is an ancient drawing, probably coeval, of Lydgate presenting his poem called the *Pilgrim* to the Earl of Salisbury, MSS. Harl. 4826. 1. It was written 1426. Another of these drawings will be mentioned below.

departure he was created a brother of the chapter.¹ It is highly probable, that this sumptuous book, the poetry of which was undertaken by Lydgate at the command of Abbot Curteis,² was previously prepared, and presented to his majesty during the royal visit, or very soon afterwards. The substance of the whole work is the life or history of Saint Edmund,³ whom the poet calls the "precious charboncle of martirs alle."⁴ In some of the prefatory pictures, there is a description and a delineation of two banners, pretended to belong

---

¹ Fol. 6.

² Curteis was abbot of Bury between the years 1429 and 1445. It appears that Lydgate was also commanded, "Late charchyd in myn oold days," to make an English metrical translation of *De Profundis*, &c. To be hung against the walls of the abbey church. MSS. Harl. 2255. 11. fol. 40. See the last stanza.

³ *The Life and Acts of St. Edmond, King and Martyr*, by John Lydgate, a splendid MS. on vellum, illuminated throughout, and embellished by fifty-two historical miniatures, was in the library of Topham Beauclerk, Esq. It began thus:—

"The noble story to putte in remembraunce
Off Seynt Edmond, mayd martre and kyng,
With his suppoort my style I wyl avaunce
First to compyle afftre my konnyng:
His gloryous lyff, his birthe, and his 'gynnyng,
And by discent, how he that was soo good,
Was in Saxonye born, of the royal blood."

In the library of Mr. Dennis Daly, which was disposed of at Dublin in 1792, a MS. of Lydgate contained the life of St. Edmund, and with it the other legend by him of St. Fremund, presented to Edward IV. The latter began with these lines:—

"Off Burchardus folwe I shall the style,
That of Seynt Fremund was whileom secretarye,
Which of entent did his lyff compyle,
Was his regiftreer, and also his notarye,
And in desert was with him solytarye,
And with him ay present, remembryng every thing
Wroot lyff and myracles of this hooly kyng."

The metrical orisons of the poet are thus offered up for his sovereign:—

"Encreafe our kyng in knyghtly hygh prowesse,
With alle his lordys of the spiritualtie;
Pray God graunte conqueftes and worthynesse,
Be rightfull rule, to all the temporalte;
And to Edward the Fourte, joye and felicyte!
Off his two reemys, fayth love and obeyffance,
Longe to persever in his victoryesse
As just enherytor of Yngelond and France."—*Park.*]

⁴ The poet's *Prayer to Saint Edmund for his Assistance in compiling his Life*, fol. 9. The history begins thus, fol. 10, b:—

"In Saxonie whilom ther was a kyng
Callid Alkmond of excellent noblesse."

It seems to be taken from John of Tynemouth's *Sanctilogium*, who flourished about the year 1360. At the end, connected with St. Edmund's legend, and a part of the work, is the life of Saint Fremund, fol. 69, b. But Lydgate has made many additions. It begins thus:—

"Who han remembre the myracles merueilous
Which Crift Jhesu lift for his seyntes shewe."

Compare MSS. Harl. 372. 1. 2. fol. 1. 25. 43. b, [and preceding note.]

to Saint Edmund.¹ One of thefe is moft brilliantly difplayed, and charged with Adam and Eve, the ferpent with a human fhape to the middle, the tree of life, the holy lamb, and a variety of fymbolical ornaments. This banner our bard feigns to have been borne by his faint, who was a king of the Eaft Angles, againft the Danes: and he prophefies that King Henry, with this enfign, would always return victorious.² The other banner, given alfo to Saint Edmund, appears to be painted with the arms of our poet's monaftery, and its blazoning is thus defcribed:

> The' other ftandard, Feld fable, off colour ynde,³
> In which of gold been notable crownys thre,
> The firft toknè: in cronycle men may fynde,
> Grauntyd to hym for royal dignyte:
> And the fecond for his virgynyte:
> For martyrdam the thridde, in his fuffring.
>
> To thefe annexyd feyth, hope, and charyte,
> In toknè he was martyr, mayd, and kyng.
> Thefe three crownys⁴ kynge Edmund bar certeyn,
> Whan he was fent by grace of goddis hand,
> At Geynefburuhe for to fleyn kyng Sweyn.

A fort of office, or fervice to Saint Edmund, confifting of an antiphone, verficle, refponfe, and collect is introduced with thefe verfes:

> To all men prefent, or in abfence,
> Whiche to feynt Edmund have devocion
> With hool herte and dewe reverence,
> Seyn⁵ this antephnè and this orifon;
> Two hundred days is grauntid of pardoun,
> Writ and regiftred afforn his holy fhryne,
> Which for our feyth fuffrede paffioun,
> Blyffyd Edmund, kyng, martyr, and virgyne.

This is our poet's envoy:

> Go littel book, be ferfull, quaak for drede,
> For to appere in fo hyʒe prefence.⁶

Lydgate's poem, called the *Life of our Lady*, printed by Caxton [without date, and again in 1531],⁷ is opened with thefe harmonious and elegant lines, which do not feem to be deftitute of that eloquence which the author wifhes to fhare with Tully, Petrarch, and Chaucer.⁸ He compares the holy Virgin to a ftar:

> O thoughtfull hertè, plonged in diftreffe
> With flombre of flouth, this long wynters night!
> Out of the flepe of mortal hevineffe
> Awake anon, and loke upon the light
> Of thilke fterre, that with her bemys bright,
> And with the fhynynge of her ftremes meryè,
> Is wont to glad all our hemifperie!⁹
>
> This fterre in beautie paffith Pleiades,
> Bothe of fhynynge, and eke of ftremes clere,

---

¹ Fol. 2. 4. ² Fol. 2. ³ blue.
⁴ See fol. 103, b, f. 104. ⁵ [fay.]
⁶ Fol. 118, b. ⁷ See MSS. Harl. 629. fol. membran.
⁸ Cap. xxxiii. xxxiv. ⁹ hemifphere.

> Bootes, and Arctur, and alfo Iades,
> And Efperus, whan that it doth appere :
> For this is Spica, with her brightè fpere,[1]
> That towarde evyn, at midnyght, and at morowe,
> Downe from hevyn adawith[2] al our forowe.—
>
> And dryeth up the bytter terys wete
> Of Aurora, after the morowe graye,
> That fhe in wepying dothe on floures flete,[3]
> In lufty Aprill, and in frefshè Maye :
> And caufeth Phebus, the bryght fomers daye,
> Wyth his wayne gold-yborned,[4] bryght and fayre,
> To'[5] enchafe the myftès of our cloudy ayre.
>
> Now fayrè fterre, O fterre of fterrys all !
> Whofe lyght to fe the angels do delyte,
> So let the gold-dewe of thy grace yfall
> Into my brefte, lyke fcalys fayre and whyte,
> Me to enfpire ![5]

Lydgate's manner is naturally verbofe and diffufe. This circumftance contributed in no fmall degree to give a clearnefs and a fluency to his phrafeology. For the fame reafon he is often tedious and languid. His chief excellence is in defcription, efpecially where the fubject admits a flowery diction. He is feldom pathetic or animated.

In another part of this poem, where he collects arguments to convince unbelievers that Chrift might be born of a pure virgin, he thus fpeaks of God's omnipotence :

> And he that made the high and cryftal heven,
> The firmament, and alfo every fphere,
> The golden ax-tre,[6] and the ftarres feven,
> Citherea fo lufty for to' appere,
> And redde Marfe,[7] with his fterne here ;
> Myght he not eke onely for our fake
> Wythyn a mayde of man his kynde[8] take ?
>
> For he that doth the tender braunches fprynge,
> And the frefshe flouris in the gretè mede,
> That were in wynter dede and eke droupynge,
> Of bawmè all yvoyd and leftyhede ;
> Myght he not make his grayne to growe and fede,
> Within her breft, that was both mayd and wyfe,
> Whereof is made the fothfaft[9] breade of lyfe ?[10]

We are furprifed to find verfes of fo modern a caft as the following at fuch an early period ; and we fhould judge them to be a forgery, were not their genuinenefs authenticated, and their antiquity confirmed, by the venerable types of Caxton and a multitude of unqueftionable MSS.

> Like as the dewe difcendeth on the rofe
> With fylver drops.[11]

---

[1] fphere.   [2] [awakens.]   [3] *float;* drop.
[4] Burnifhed with gold. So in Lydgate's *Legend on Dan Joos,* a monk, taken from Vincent of Beauvais's *Speculum Hiftoriale,* the name Maria is *ful fayre graven* on a red rofe, in lettris of bournid gold. MSS. Harl. 2251. 39. fol. 71. b.
[5] prologue.   [6] of the fun.   [7] Mars.   [8] nature.
[9] true.   [10] Cap. xx.   [11] Cap. xix.

Our Saviour's crucifixion is expreſſed by this remarkable metaphor:

> Whan he of purple did his baner ſprede
> On Calvarye abroad upon the rode,
> To ſave mankynde.[1]

Our author, in the courſe of his panegyric on the Virgin Mary, affirms that ſhe exceeded Heſter in meekneſs, and Judith in wiſdom; and in beauty, Helen, Polyxena, Lucretia, Dido, Bathſheba, and Rachel.[2] It is amazing, that in an age of the moſt ſuperſtitious devotion ſo little diſcrimination ſhould have been made between ſacred and profane characters and incidents. But the common ſenſe of mankind had not yet attained a juſt eſtimate of things. Lydgate, in another piece, has verſified the rubrics of the miſſal, which he applies to the god Cupid, and declares with how much delight he frequently meditated on the holy legend of thoſe conſtant martyrs, who were not afraid to ſuffer death for the faith of that omnipotent divinity.[3] There are inſtances, in which religion was even made the inſtrument of love. Arnaud Daniel, a celebrated troubadour of the thirteenth century, in a fit of amorous deſpair, promiſes to found a multitude of annual maſſes, and to dedicate perpetual tapers to the ſhrines of ſaints, for the important purpoſe of obtaining the affections of an obdurate miſtreſs.

[Lydgate's *Court of Sapience* was printed by Caxton about 1481. It is a poem of conſiderable length, and comprehends not only an allegorical fiction concerning the two courts of the caſtle of Sapience in which there is no imagination, but a ſyſtem of natural philoſophy, grammar, logic, rhetoric, geometry, aſtronomy, theology, and other topics of the faſhionable literature. The writer's deſign is to deſcribe the effects of wiſdom from the beginning of the world: and the work is a hiſtory of knowledge or learning. In a viſion, he meets the goddeſs Sapience in a delightful meadow; who conducts him to her caſtle or manſion, and there diſplays all her miraculous operations. [Lydgate] in the poem invokes the *gylted goddeſs* and *mooſt facundyous lady* Clio, apologiſes to thoſe *makers* who delight in *termes gay* for the inelegances of language which as a foreigner[4] he

---

[1] Cap. ix.

[2] Cap. iv. In a *Life of the Virgin* in the Britiſh Muſeum, I find theſe eaſy lyrics introduced, MSS. Harl. 2382. 2. 3. fol. 75. fol. 86. b. Though I am not certain that they properly belong to this work:

> "A mery tale I telle yow may
> Of ſeynt Marie that ſwete may:
> Alle the tale of this leſſone
> Is of her Aſſumptione.—
> Mary moder, welle thee be!
> Mary mayden, thenk on me!
> Mayden and moder was never none,
> Togader, lady, ſave thee allone."

But theſe lines will be conſidered again.

[3] MSS. Fairfax, xvi. Bibl. Bodl.

[4] Caxton [who wrote the prologue] could only be deemed a *foreigner*, from having paſſed ſome time in foreign countries.—*Aſhby*. It ought to be obſerved,

could not avoid, and modestly declares that he neither means to rival nor envy Gower and Chaucer.

Lydgate also produced a poem called the *Temple of Glass*, which was likewise printed by Caxton about 1479.] On a comparison,[1] it will be found to be a copy of the *House of Fame* of Chaucer, in which that poet sees in a vision a temple of glass, on the walls of which were engraved stories from Virgil's Æneid and Ovid's Epistles. It also strongly resembles that part of Chaucer's *Assembly of Fowls*, in which there is the fiction of a temple of brass, built on pillars of jasper, whose walls are painted with the stories of unfortunate lovers. In [the] *Assembly of Ladies*, in a chamber made of beryl and crystal, belonging to the sumptuous castle of Pleasant Regard, the walls are decorated with historical sculptures of the same kind. The situation of [Lydgate's] Temple on a craggy rock of ice, is evidently taken from that of Chaucer's *House of Fame*. In [the poem called] *Chaucer's Dream*, the poet is transported into an island, where "wall and yate was all of glasse." These structures of glass have their origin in the chemistry of the dark ages. This is [Lydgate's] exordium:

> Me dyd oppresse a sodayne, dedely slepe:
> Within the whiche methought that I was
> Ravyshed in spyrite into a Temple of Glas,
> I ne wyst howe ful ferre in wyldernesse,
> That founded was, all by lyckelynesse,
> Nat upon stele, but on a craggy roche

---

that Mr. Blades (*Life and Typogr. of Caxton*, ii. 115) considers the authorship of Lydgate by no means established, and certainly there is a good deal to be said in favour of Mr. Blades's view. We must recollect, however, that the highly respectable authority of Stow is on the other side, and supports the monk of Bury's claim. Of direct evidence there is not a tittle.

[1] In the [Bodleian] library are two MSS. of this poem. MSS. Fairfax. xvi. without a name. And MSS. Bodl. 638. In the first leaf of the Fairfax MS. is this entry: "I bought this at Gloucester, 8 Sept. 1650, intending to exchange it for a better boke. Fairfax." And at the end, in the same hand. "Here lacketh seven leaves that are in Joseph Holland's boke." This MS., however, contains as much as Berthelet's edition. In the Bodleian MS. (Bodl. 638), this poem, with manifest impropriety, is entitled the *Temple of Bras*. It there appears in the midst of many of Chaucer's poems. But at the end are two poems, *The Chaunse of the Dyse*, by Lydgate, and *Ragmanys Roll*. [The latter is printed in *Remains of the E. P. Poetry of England*, i. 68, et seq.] And, I believe, one or two more of Lydgate's poems are intermixed. It is a miscellany of old English poetry, chiefly by Chaucer: but none of the pieces is respectively distinguished with the author's name. This MS. is partly on paper and partly on vellum, and seems to have been written not long after the year 1500. [In an imperfect copy from the press of Caxton of Chaucer's *Assembly of Fowls* the piece is called *The Temple of Brass*. See Blades, ii. 61-3.]

[The following argument, says Mr. George Mason, since occurring, may strengthen the strong claim of Lydgate to be regarded as the author. In one of the Paston letters, published by Sir John Fenn, vol. ii. p. 90, and dated 1471, the *Temple of Glass* is mentioned as if it had then been written some years. This circumstance must ill accord with its being attributed to Hawes; besides that the language is older in many particulars than that which Hawes used.—MS. note in W. de Worde's edit. of the book which does not give the poem to Hawes, as Mr. Warton had been led to believe, from the misrepresentation of Ames.—*Park*.]

>Lyke yſe yfroze : and as I dyd approche,
>Againe the ſonne that ſhone, methought, ſo clere
>As any cryſtall ; and ever, nere and nere,
>As I gan nyghe this griſely dredefull place,
>I wext aſtonyed, the lyght ſo in my face
>Began to ſmyte, ſo perſyng ever in one,
>On every parte where that I dyde gon,
>That I ne mighte nothing as I wolde
>Aboute me conſydre, and beholde,
>The wondre eſters,[1] for brightneſſe of the ſonne :
>Tyll at the laſte, certayne ſkyes donne,[2]
>With wynde[3] ychaſed, han their courſe ywent,
>Before the ſtremes of Titan and iblent,[4]
>So that I myght within and without,
>Where ſo I wolde, behelden me about,
>For to report the facyon and manere
>Of all this placè, that was circuler,
>In cumpace-wyſe rounde by yntale ywrought :
>And whan I had longe goon, and well ſought,
>I founde a wicket, and entred yn as faſte
>Into the temple, and myne eyen caſte
>On every ſide, &c.[5]

The walls of this wonderful temple were richly pictured with the following hiſtorical portraitures from Virgil, Ovid, King Arthur's romance, and Chaucer :

>I ſawe depeynted upon a wall[6]
>From eſt to weſt ful many a fayre ymage,
>Of ſondry lovers, lyke as they were of age
>I ſet in ordre after they were true ;
>With lyfely colours, wonders freſhe of hewe,
>And as methought I ſaw ſom ſyt and ſom ſtande,
>And ſome knelyng, with bylles[7] in theyr hande,
>And ſome with complaynt woful and pitious,
>With dolefull chere, to put to Venus,
>So as ſhe ſate fletynge in the ſee,
>Upon theyr wo for to have pite.
> And fyrſt of all I ſawe there of Cartage
>Dido the quene, ſo goodly of viſage,
>That gan complayne her auenture and caas,
>Howe ſhe diſceyued was of Aeneas,
>For all his heſtes and his othes ſworne,
>And ſayd helas that ſhe was borne,
>Whan ſhe ſawe that dede ſhe muſt be.
> And next her I ſawe the complaynt of Medee,
>Howe that ſhe was falſed of Jaſon.
>And nygh by Venus ſawe I ſyt Addon,
>And all the maner howe the bore hym ſloughe,
>For whom ſhe wepte and had pite inoughe.
> There ſawe I alſo howe Penelope,
>For ſhe ſo long ne myght her lorde ſe,
>Was of colour both pale and grene.

---

[1] The wonderful chambers of this temple.   [2] dun, dark.
[3] i. e. collected.   [4] blinded, darkened the ſun.
[5] This text is given from Berthelet's edition, collated with MSS. Fairfax, xvi.
[6] From Pr. Cop. and MSS. Fairf. xvi. as before.
[7] bills of complaint

> And alder next was the freshe quene;
> I mean Alceste, the noble true wife,
> And for Admete howe she lost her lyfe;
> And for her trouthe, if I shall nat lye,
> Howe she was turned into a daysye.
>   There was also Grisildis innocence,
> And all hir mekenesse and hir pacience.
>   There was eke Ysaude, and many other mo,
> And all the tourment and all the cruell wo
> That she had for Tristram all her lyue;
> And howe that Tysbe her hert dyd ryue
> With thylke swerde of syr Pyramus.
>   And all maner, howe that Theseus
> The minotaure slewe, amyd the hous
> That was forwrynked by craft of Dedalus,
> Whan that he was in prison shyt in Crete, &c.
>   And uppermore men depeinten might see,
> Howe with her ring goodlie Canace
> Of every foule the leden¹ and the song
> Could understand, as she hem walkt among:
> And how her brother so often holpen was
> In his mischefe by the stede of brass.²

We must acknowledge that all the picturesque invention, which appears in this composition, entirely belongs to Chaucer. Yet there was some merit in daring to depart from the dull taste of the times, and in choosing Chaucer for a model, after his sublime fancies had been so long forgotten, and had given place for almost a century, to legends, homilies, and chronicles in verse. In the mean time, there is reason to believe, that Chaucer himself copied these imageries from the romance of *Guigemar*, one of the Lays of Marie de France:³ in which the walls of a chamber are painted with Venus and the *Art of Love* from Ovid.⁴ Perhaps Chaucer might not look further than the temples of Boccaccio's *Theseid* for these ornaments. At the same time it is to be remembered, that the imagination of these old poets must have been assisted in this respect, from the mode which anciently prevailed of entirely covering the walls of the more magnificent apartments in castles and palaces with stories from Scripture-history, the classics, and romance. I have already given instances of this practice, and I will here add more.⁵ In 1277,

---

¹ language.   ² See Chaucer's *Squire's Tale*.
³ Fol. 141, MSS. Harl. 978. See supr. *Dissertat.* i. [It is evident, says Mr. Waldron, in a MS. note, from the conclusion of the passage above cited, that more of the *Squire's Tale* had been written than has been preserved.—*Park*.]
⁴ A passage in Ovid's *Remedium Amoris* concerning Achilles' spear is supposed to be alluded to by a troubadour, Bernard Ventadour, who lived about the year 1150. *Hist. Troubad.* p. 27. This Mons. Millot calls "Un trait d'erudition singulier dans un troubadour." It is not, however, impossible, that he might get this fiction from some of the early romances about Troy.
⁵ See *supr.* To the passages adduced from Chaucer these may be added from the poem of *Chaucer's Dream*, ver. 1320:

> "In a chamber *paint*
> Full of *stories old* and *divers*."

Again, *ibid*. ver. 2167:

Otho, duke of Milan, having restored the peace of that city by a signal victory, built a noble castle, in which he ordered every particular circumstance of that victory to be painted. Paulus Jovius relates that these paintings remained, in the great vaulted chamber of the castle, fresh and unimpaired so late as the year 1547.[1] That the castles and palaces of England were thus ornamented at a very early period, and in the most splendid style, appears from the following notices. [Walter de] Langton, bishop of Lichfield, commanded the coronation, marriages, wars, and funeral, of his patron Edward I. to be painted in the great hall of his episcopal palace, which he had newly built.[2] This must have been about the year 1312. The following anecdote relates to the old royal palace at Westminster. In the year 1322, one Symeon, a friar minor and a doctor in theology, wrote an Itinerary in which is this curious passage. He is speaking of Westminster Abbey. "Near this monastery stands the most famous royal palace of England; in which is that celebrated chamber, on whose walls all the warlike histories of the whole Bible are painted with inexpressible skill, and explained by a regular and complete series of texts, beautifully written in French over each battle, to the no small admiration of the beholder, and the increase of royal magnificence."[3] This

---

"For there was no lady ne creture,
Save on the walls *old portraiture*
Of horsemen, hawkis, and houndes," &c.

Compare Dante's *Purgatorio*, c. x. p. 105, *seq.* edit. Ald.

[1] "Extantque adhuc in *maximo testudinatoque conclavi*, incorruptæ præliorum cum *veris ducum vultibus* imaginibus, *Latinis elegis* singula rerum elogia indicantibus." *Vit. Vicecomit. Mediolan.* p. 56, edit. 1549.

[2] Erdswicke's *Staffordshire*, p. 101, [and Le Neve's *Fasti Eccl. Anglic.* edit. Hardy, i. 549. Bishop Langton succeeded in 1295-6, and died in 1321.]

[3] "Eidem monasterio quasi immediate conjungitur illud famosissimum palatium regium Anglorum, in quo illa vulgata camera, in cujus *parietibus* sunt omnes Historiæ bellicæ totius Bibliæ ineffabiliter *depictæ*, atque in Gallico completissime et perfectissime constanter conscriptæ, in non modica intuentium admiratione, et maxima regali magnificentia." " *Itinerarium Symeonis et fratris Hugonis Illuminatoris ex Hibernia in terram sanctam*, A.D. MCCCXXII." MSS. C. C. C. Cantabr. G. 6, Princip. "Culmine honoris spreto." It comprehends a journey through England, and describes many curiosities now lost. See *supr.*

The old palace at Westminster was consumed by fire in 1299, but immediately rebuilt, I suppose by Edward I. Stow's *London*, p. 379, 387, edit. 1599. So that these paintings must have been done between the years 1299 and 1322. It was again destroyed by fire in 1512, and never afterwards re-edified. Stow, *ibid.* p. 389. About the year 1500, the walls of the Virgin Mary's chapel, built by Prior Silkestede, in the cathedral of Winchester, were elegantly painted with the miracles and other stories of the New Testament in small figures, many delicate traces of which now remain.

Falcandus, the old historian of Sicily, who wrote about the year 1200, says that the chapel in the royal palace at Palermo, had its walls decorated " de lapillulis quadris, partim aureis, partim diverficoloribus veteris ac novi Testamenti depictam historiam continentibus." *Sicil. Histor.* p. 10, edit. 1550. But this was mosaic work which, chiefly by means of the Crusades, was communicated to all parts of Europe from the Byzantine Greeks; and with which all the churches and other public edifices at Constantinople were adorned. *Epist. de Comparat. Vet. et Nov.*

ornament of a royal palace, while it conveys a curious history of the arts, admirably exemplifies the chivalry and the devotion of the times united. That part of the Old Testament indeed, which records the Jewish wars, was almost regarded as a book of chivalry: and their chief heroes, Joshua and David, the latter of whom killed a giant, are often recited among the champions of romance. In France, the battles of the kings of Israel with the Philistines and Assyrians were wrought into a grand volume, under the title of "*Plusieurs Batailles des roys d'Israel en contre les Philistines et Assyriens.*"[1]

With regard to the form of [Lydgate's] poem, I am of opinion that Visions, which are so common in the poetry of the middle ages, partly took their rise from Tully's *Somnium Scipionis*. Had this composition descended to posterity among Tully's six books *De Republica*, to the last of which it originally belonged, perhaps it would have been overlooked and neglected.[2] But being preserved, and illustrated with a prolix commentary by Macrobius, it quickly attracted the attention of readers who were fond of the marvellous, and with whom Macrobius was a more admired classic than Tully. It was printed [at Venice] subjoined to Tully's *Offices*, in [1470.][3] It was translated into Greek by Maximus Planudes,[4] and is frequently quoted by Chaucer.[5] Particularly in the *Assembly of*

Romæ, p. 122. Man Chrysolor. See *supr.* Leo Ostiensis says, that one of the abbots of Cassino in Italy, in the eleventh century, sent messengers to Constantinople, to bring over artificers in mosaic, to ornament the church of the monastery, after Rome or Italy had lost that art for five hundred years. He calls Rome *magistra Latinitas. Chron. Cassin.* lib. iii. c. 27. Compare Muratori, *Antich. Italian.* 1752, i. Diss. xxiv. p. 279.

[1] MSS. Reg. [Brit Mus.] 19 D. 7. There is an Arabic book, containing the Psalms of David, with an additional psalm, on the slaughter of the giant Goliah. MSS. Harl. 5476. See above.

[2] But they were extant about the year 1000, for they are cited by Gerbert. *Epist.* 83. And by Peter of Poitou, who died in 1197. See Barth. *Advers.* xxxii. 5, 58. Leland says, that Tully *de Republica* was consumed by fire, among other books, in the library of William Selling, a learned abbot of Saint Austin's at Canterbury, who died in 1494. *Script.* v. *Cellingus.*

[3] [Brunet, *Man. du Libr.* last edit. ii. 19.]

[4] Lambeccius mentions a Greek MS. of Julian, a cardinal of S. Angelo, Ὁ σκιρος τοῦ Σκιπίωνος, 5, p. 153. The *Disputatio* of Favonius Elogius, a Carthaginian rhetorician, and a disciple of Saint Austin, on the *Somnium Scipionis*, was printed by G. Schottus, Antw. 1613, 4to.

[5] *Rom. Rose*, lib. i. ver. 7, [&c. edit. Morris.]
"An authour that highte Macrobes,
That halte nat dremes false ne lees,
But undoth us the avysyoun,
That whylom mette Kyng Cipioun."
Nonnes Pr. Tale, 303, edit. Morris.
"Macrobius, that writ the avisioun
In Auffrik of the worthy Cipioun."
Chaucer's Dreme, ver. 284. [Chaucer] mentions this as the most wonderful of dreams. *House F.* v. 407. He describes a prospect more extensive and various than that which Scipio saw in his dream:

Fowls, he suppofes himfelf to fall afleep after reading the *Somnium Scipionis*, and that Scipio fhewed him the beautiful vifion which is the fubject of that poem.[1] Nor is it improbable that not only the form, but the firft idea, of Dante's *Inferno* was fuggefted by this apologue which, in Chaucer's words, treats

> "of Hevene, and Helle,[2]
> And erthe, and of foules that therynne duelle."

Not to infift on Dante's fubject, he ufes the fhade of Virgil for a myftagogue, as Tully fuppofes Scipio to have been fhown the other world by his anceftor Africanus.

[Stephen Hawes, Lydgate's pupil, always fpeaks with affectionate refpect of him. In his *Joyfull Medytacyon* of the *Coronacyon of Kynge Henry the eyght* [1509] he alludes to him not inelegantly:

> The ryght eloquent poete and monke of bery
> Made many fayre bookes/ as it is probable
> From ydle derkenes/ to lyght and emyfpery
> Whofe vertuous paftyme/ was moche comendable
> Prefentynge his bookes/ gretely prouffytable
> To your worthy predeceffour the V. Kynge Henry
> Whiche regyftred is in the courte of memory.

And again, in the *Converfyon of Swerers*, 1509, there is this ftanza:

> Amonge all other my good mayfter Lydgate
> The eloquent poete and monke of bury
> Dyde bothe conteyne and alfo tranflate
> Many vertues bokes to be in memory
> Touchynge the trouthe well and fentencyoufly
> But fyth that his deth was intollerable
> I praye God rewarde hym in lyfe perdurable.

Nor muft we omit to take notice of Lydgate's *Stans Puer ad Menfam*, are of the earlieft codes of inftruction for behaviour at table. There are feveral MSS. of it. Caxton printed it once and Wynkyn de Worde feveral times. Two other writers, John Ruffell and Hugh Rhodes, founded fimilar treatifes upon it. The latter calls himfelf Lydgate's fcholar.

Lydgate's tranflation of *The Life of St. Alban* and *The Life and Paffion of St. Imphabel* was perhaps founded on the Latin elegiac poem compofed in the twelfth century by Robert of Dunftable, and firft printed at St. Albans in 1534, with many woodcuts. It is in feven-line ftanzas; it purports to have been publifhed at the inftigation of Robert Cotton, abbot of St. Albans. The poem feems to

---

> "That fawe in dreme, at point devife,
> Heven and erth, hell, and paradife."

And in other places.
[1] He makes Scipio fay to him, ver 109:

> "Thou haft the fo wel borne
> In lokenge of myn olde booke al to torne,
> Of which Macrobe roght noght a lyte," &c.

[2] [Morris's *Chaucer*, iv. 52, ver. 32.]

have been written in 1439, and there is a MS. of it in the library of Trinity College, Oxford.]

Lydgate's chief *prose* work was a translation in 1413 (with additions), of the *Pelerinage de la vie humaine* of Guillaume De Deguileville, prior of Chalis.[1]

The French book, [from which he translated], is a vision, and has some degree of imagination. In the colophon to Caxton's English copy of De Deguileville's *Second Pilgrimage* are these words: "Here endeth the dreme of *Pylgremage of the soule* translatid oute of Frenshe in to Englishe, with somwhat of addicions, the yere of our lord M.CCCC. & thyrten, and endeth in the Vigyle of seynt Bartholomew." The translator of this book, at least the author of the *Additions*, which altogether consist of poetry in seven-lined stanzas, I believe to be Lydgate. Not to insist on the correspondence of time and style, I observe, that the thirty-fourth chapter of Lydgate's metrical *Life of the Virgin Mary* is literally repeated in the thirty-fourth chapter of this Translation.[2] This chapter is a digression of five or six stanzas in praise of Chaucer; in which the writer feelingly laments the recent death of his "maister Chaucer, poete of Britaine," who used to "amende and correcte the wronge traces of my rude penne." No writer besides, in Lydgate's own life-time, can be supposed, with any sort of grace or propriety, to have mentioned those personal assistances of Chaucer in Lydgate's own words. And if we suppose that the Translation, or its "Addicions," were written by Lydgate, before he wrote his *Life of the Virgin*, the proof will be the same.[3]

[But besides Lydgate's metrical copy of De Deguileville in 1413, we have to notice one in prose, executed about the same time by an anonymous writer, who speaks of the original author merely as *Johan the Preeste*. This prose version was taken in fact from the French of Jean Gallopes, priest of Angers, who subsequently became Dean of the Collegiate Church of Saint Louis de Saulsoye, in Evreux, and chaplain to John, Duke of Bedford, Regent of France. Gallopes professes to have undertaken his labour at the request of Jeanne Maillart, dame de Savegines, who seems to be identical with

---

[1] [*The Booke of the Pylgremage of the Sowle*, &c. Edited by K. I. Cust, 1859. The English was printed by W. Caxton in 1483, and is partly republished in Miss Cust's volumes.]

[2] [De Deguileville produced three Pilgrimages, 1. *Of Man:* 2. *Of the Soul;* 3. *Of Christ.*—F. These appear to have been all written before 1358. Of the two former specimens have been afforded by Miss Cust, in the two volumes printed in 1859, with some interesting facsimiles. The prose English translation mentioned in the text (whether prior to Lydgate's metrical version or not, seems to be uncertain), is in the University Library, Cambridge, and has been edited by Mr. W. Aldis Wright for the Roxburghe Club, 1869. A beautiful, though not perhaps very early, MS. of the *Roman des Trois Pelerinages*, with very spirited and well-executed drawings, is in the possession of Mr. H. Huth. For further particulars as to the MSS. of De Deguileville's tripartite work, and of the early printed editions of it, see Mr. Aldis Wright's *Preface*.]

[3] Ad calc. Opp. Chauc. fol. 376, col. 1. Stow mentions Lydgate's *Pilgrimage of the World* "by the commaundement of the earle of Salisburie, 1426." [MS. Cotton. Vitell. C. xiii. part-printed.—F.]

Jeanne de Laval, the name given to the lady in another MS. of the work. Gallopes, who furvived till 1435, alfo accomplifhed, at the requeft of his patron the Regent Bedford, a profe tranflation of De Deguileville's *Second Pilgrimage* (*Pelerinage de l'ame*), which he dedicated to the duke.[1] In Bennet College Library there is an elegant illuminated MS. of Bonaventura's *Life of Chrift*, tranflated by the fame Gallopes, containing a curious picture of the tranflator prefenting his book to Henry V. ; this is the fame *Speculum Vitæ Chrifti*, which Caxton printed in Englifh (the tranflator unknown) about 1488.[2] The Englifh is not a rare MS.][3]

SECTION XXII.

LYDGATE'S [beft-known] poems are the *Fall of Princes*, the *Siege of Thebes*, and the *Deftruction of Troy*. Of all thefe I fhall fpeak diftinctly.

About the year 1360, Boccaccio wrote a Latin hiftory in ten books, entitled *De Cafibus Virorum et Feminarum illuftrium*. Like other chronicles of the times, it commences with Adam, and is brought down to the author's age. Its laft grand event is John, king of France taken prifoner by the Englifh at the battle of Poictiers, in the year 1359.[4] This book of Boccaccio was twice tranflated into French [in the firft inftance by an anonymous hand, whofe verfion appeared from the prefs of Colard Manfion at Bruges in 1476, and fecondly] by [Laurence de Premierfait: in this cafe] fo paraphraftically and with fo many confiderable additions, as almoft to be rendered a new work.[5] Laurence's French tranflation was

---

[1] [The Warton Club (fince diffolved) promifed an edition of an early Englifh tranflation of this fecond portion of De Deguileville from a MS. in the public library at Cambridge, with the title of the *Pylgrym*.]
[2] [See Blades, ii. 1946.]   [3] [*Ibid*. 196.]
[4] [Often printed in Latin and French. See a copious bibliography in the laft edit. of Brunet, i. 986, *et feqq*. A Spanifh tranflation appeared at Seville in 1495, and an Italian one at Venice in 1545.]
[5] In Lydgate's *Prologue*, B. i. fol. i. a, col. 1, edit. Wayland:

"He that fumtime did his diligence
The boke of Bochas in French to tranflate
Out of Latin he was called Laurence."

He fays that Laurence (in his Prologue) declares, that he avails himfelf of the privilege of fkilful artificers, "who may chaunge and turne, by good difcretion, fhapes and forms, and newly them devife, make and unmake, &c." And that old authors may be rendered more agreeable, by being clothed in new ornaments of language, and improved with new inventions. *Ibid*. a, col. 1. He adds, that it was Laurence's defign, in his tranflation into French, "to amende, correct, and declare, and not to fpare things touched fhortly." *Ibid*. col. 2. Afterwards he calls him this noble tranflatour. *Ibid*. b. col. 1. In another place, where a panegyric on France is introduced, he fays that this paffage is not Boccaccio's, but added, [firſt] printed at Lyons in 1483;[1] it is the original of Lydgate's poem. This Laurence or Laurent, ſometimes called Laurent de Premierfait, a village in the dioceſe of Troies, was an eccleſiaſtic and a famous tranſlator. He alſo tranſlated into French Boccaccio's *Decameron*, at the requeſt of Jeanne, queen of Navarre: Cicero *de Amicitia* and *de Senectute*; and Ariſtotle's *Oeconomics*, dedicated to Louis de Bourbon, the king's uncle. Theſe verſions appeared in the year[s] 1414 and 1416.[2] Caxton's [Engliſh verſions of Cicero *De Amicitiâ* and *De Senectute*] printed [together] in 1481, were tranſlated from Laurence's French verſion. Caxton, in the [colophon], calls him *Laurence de primo facto*.

Lydgate's poem conſiſts of nine books, and is entitled in the earlieſt edition: [*The Boke calledde Iohn Bochas Diſcriuinge the Falle of Princys*.][3] The beſt and moſt authentic MS. of this piece is in the Britiſh Muſeum; probably written under the inſpection of the author, and perhaps intended as a preſent to Humphrey, duke of Glouceſter, at whoſe gracious command the poem, as I have before hinted, was undertaken. It contains, among numerous miniatures illuſtrating the ſeveral hiſtories, portraits of Lydgate and of another monk habited in black, perhaps an abbot of Bury, kneeling before a prince, who ſeems to be Saint Edmund, ſeated on a throne under a canopy, and graſping an arrow.[4]

The work is not improperly ſtyled a ſet of tragedies. It is not merely a narrative of men eminent for their rank and misfortunes. The plan is perfectly dramatic, and partly ſuggeſted by the pageants of the times. Every perſonage is ſuppoſed to appear before the poet, and to relate his reſpective ſufferings: and the figures of theſe ſpectres

---

> " By one Laurence which was tranſlatour
> Of this proceſſe to commende France;
> To prayſe that lande was all his pleaſaunce."

B. ix. ch. 28, fol. 31, a, col. 1, edit. *ut infr*. Our author in the Prologue above cited, ſeems to ſpeak as if there had been a previous tranſlation of Boccaccio's book into French. *Ut ſupr*. a, col. 1:

> " Thus Laurence from him envy excluded
> Though toforne him tranſlated was this book."

[Alluding of courſe to the anonymous verſion of 1476.]

[1] MSS. Harl. See alſo *ibid*. MSS. Reg. 18 D. vii., and 16 G. v. And MSS. Bodl. F. 10, 2. [2465.] He is ſaid to have tranſlated this work in 1409. MSS. Reg. *ut ſupr*. 20 C. iv.] In folio. [In 1578, was publiſhed a third French verſion, " reduict en neuf livres, par Cl. Witart." See Brunet, *ut ſupr*. 988-9.]

[2] He died in 1418. See Martene, *Ampl. Collect.* tom. ii. 1405. And *Mem. de Litt*. xvii. 759, 4to. Compare du Verdier, *Biblioth*. Fr. p. 72. And *Bibl. Rom*. ii. 291. It is extraordinary that the piece before us ſhould not be mentioned by the French antiquaries as one of Laurence's tranſlations. Lydgate, in the Prologue above cited, obſerves that Laurence, who in " cunyng did excel," undertook this tranſlation at the requeſt of ſome eminent perſonages in France, who had the intereſt of " rhetorike" at heart. *Ut ſupr*. a, col. 2.

[3] [Lond. by R. Pynſon, 1494, folio.] There is a ſmall piece not connected with this, entitled: " The Tragedy of princes that were lecherous." MSS. Aſhmol. 59, ii.

[4] MSS. Harl. 1766, fol. 5.

are sometimes finely drawn. Hence a source is opened for moving compassion, and for a display of imagination. In some of the lives the author replies to the speaker, and a sort of dialogue is introduced for conducting the story. Brunchild, a queen of France, who murdered all her children, and was afterwards hewn in pieces, appears thus:

> She came, arayed nothyng lyke a quene,
> Her heer vntressed, Bochas toke good hede;
> In all his boke he had afore nat sene
> A more wofull creature in dede,
> With weping eyen, to-torne was all her wede:
> Rebuking Bochas cause he had left behynde
> Her wretchydnesse for to put in mynde.[1]

Yet in some of these interesting interviews our poet excites pity of another kind. When Adam appears, he familiarly accosts the author with the salutation of Cosyn Bochas.[2]

Nor does our dramatist deal only in real characters and historical personages. Boccaccio, standing pensive in his library, is alarmed at the sudden entrance of the gigantic and monstrous image of Fortune, whose agency has so powerful and universal an influence in human affairs, and especially in effecting those vicissitudes which are the subject of this work. There is a Gothic greatness in her figure, with some touches of the grotesque. An attribute of the early poetry of all nations, before ideas of selection have taken place. I must add, that it was the admired allegory of Boethius on the *Consolation of Philosophy*, which introduced personification into the poetry of the middle ages.

> Whyle Bochas pensyfe stode in his lybrary,
> With chere oppressed, pale in his vysage,
> Somdeale abasshed, alone and solytary;
> To him appeared a monstruous ymage,
> Parted on twayne of colour and corage,
> Her right syde full of sommer floures,
> The tother oppressed with winter stormy shoures.
>
> Bochas astonyed, fearfull for to abrayde,
> Whan he behelde the wonderfull fygure
> Of Fortune, thus to him selfe he sayd.
> " What may this meane? Is this a creature,
> Or a monstre transfourmed agayne nature,
> Whose brenning eyen spercle of their light,
> As do sterres the frosty wynter nyght?"
>
> And of her chere full good hede he toke;
> Her face semyng cruell and terrible,
> And by disdayne manacinge of loke;
> Her heare vntrussed, harde, sharpe, and horryble,
> Frowarde of shap, lothsome, and odyble:
> An hundred handes she had, of eche parte,[3]
> In sondry wyse her gyftes to departe.[4]

---

[1] [Book ix. chap. 3.]
[2] B. i. [ed. 1527.] In the same style he calls Ixion Juno's secretary. B. i. ch. xii. fol. xxi. b, col. 2.
[3] on either side.   [4] distribute.

> Some of her handès lyft vp men alofte,
> To hye eftate of worldly dignyte;
> Another hande griped full vnfofte,
> Whiche cafte another in great aduerfyte,
> Gaue one rycheffe, an other pouerte,
> Gaue fome alfo by reporte a good name,
> Noyfed an other of flaundre and diffame.
>
> Her habyte was of manyfolde colours,
> Watchet blewe of fayned ftedfaftneffe,
> Her golde allayed like fon in watry fhours,
> Meynt[1] with grene, for chaunge and doubleneffe.[2]

Her hundred hands, her burning eyes, and difhevelled treffes, are fublimely conceived. After a long filence, with a ftern countenance fhe addreffes Bochas, who is greatly terrified at her horrible appearance; and having made a long harangue on the revolutions and changes which it is her bufinefs to produce among men of the moft profperous condition and the moft elevated ftation, fhe calls up Caius Marius, and prefents him to the poet:

> Blacke his wede, and his habyte alfo,
> His heed vnkempt, his lockes hore and gray,
> His loke down-caft in token of forow and wo;
> On his chekes the falte teares lay,
> Whiche bare recorde of his deedly affray.
>
> His robe ftayned was with Romayne blode,
> His fworde aye redy whet to do vengeaunce;
> Lyke a tyraunt moft furyous and wode,[3]
> In flaughter and murdre fet all his plefaunce.[4]

She then teaches Bochas how to defcribe his life, and difappears:

> Thefe wordes fayd, Fortune made an ende,
> She bete her wynges, and toke her to flight,
> I can nat fe what way fhe dyd wende;
> Saue Bochas telleth, like an aungell bright,
> At her departyng fhe fhewed a great light.[5]

In another place Dante " of Florence, the laureate poete, demure of loke fullfilled with patience," appears to Boccaccio, and commands him to write the tale of Gualter, duke of Florence, whofe days, " for his tiranny, lechery, and covetyfe, ended in mifchefe." Dante then vanifhes, and only Duke Gualter is left alone with the poet.[6] Petrarch is alfo introduced for the fame purpofe.[7]

The following golden couplet, concerning the prodigies which preceded the civil wars between Cæfar and Pompey, indicates dawnings of that poetical colouring of expreffion and of that facility of verfification, which mark the poetry of [later] times:

> Serpentes and adders, fcaled fyluer-bright,
> Were ouer Rome fene flyeng all the nyght.[8]

---

[1] mingled.   [2] Book vi.
[3] mad.   [4] B. vi. ch. 1.   [5] Ibid.
[6] B. ix. In another place Dante's three books on heaven, purgatory, and hell, are particularly commended. B. iv. Prol.
[7] B. viii. Prol. He mentions all Petrarch's works, Prol. B. iv.
[8] B. vi. ch. 11.

These verses, in which the poet describes the reign of Saturn, have much harmony, strength, and dignity:

> Fortytude ſtode tho in his might,
> Defended wydowes, and cheryſhed chaſtyte;
> Knighthod in proweſſe gaue ſo clere a light,
> Gyrte with his ſworde of trouth and equite.[1]

Apollo, Diana and Minerva, joining the Roman army, when Rome was beſieged by Brennus, are poetically touched:

> Appollo firſt ſhewed his preſence,
> Freſhe, yonge, and luſty, as any ſonne ſhene,
> Armed all with golde; and with great violence
> Entred the felde, as it was well ſene:
> And Diana came with her arowes kene:
> And Mynerua in a bright haberioun;
> Which in their commyng made a terrible ſoun.[2]

The following lines are remarkable:

> God hath a thouſande handes to chaſtyſe,
> A thouſande dartes of punicion,
> A thouſande bowes made in dyuers wyſe,
> A thouſande arowblaſtes bent in his dongeon.[3]

Lydgate, in this poem, quotes Seneca's tragedies[4] (for the ſtory of Oedipus), Tully, Virgil and his commentator Servius, Ovid, Livy, Lucan, Lactantius, Juſtin[5] or "prudent Juſtinus an old croniclere," Joſephus, Valerius Maximus, Saint Jerom's chronicle, Boethius,[6] Plato on the immortality of the ſoul,[7] and Fulgentius the mythologiſt.[8] He mentions "noble Perſius," Proſper's epigrams, Vegetius on Tactics, which was highly eſteemed (as its ſubject coincided with the chivalry of the times), and which had been juſt tranſlated into French by [Chriſtine de Piſe], and into Engliſh by John Treviſa,[9] "the grene chaplet of Eſop and Juvenal," [10] Euripides "in his tyme a great tragician, becauſe he wrote many tragedies," and another called *Clarke* Demoſthenes.[11] For a catalogue of Tully's works, he refers to the *Speculum Hiſtoriale* [12] or *Myrrour Hyſtoriall*, of Vincent of Beauvais, and ſays that he wrote twelve books of Orations, and ſeveral "morall ditties." [13] Ariſtotle is introduced as teaching Alexander and Calliſthenes philoſophy.[14] With regard to Homer, he

---

[1] B. vii. ch. 10. [2] B. iv. ch. 23.
[3] tower; caſtle. B. i. ch. 3. [4] Ibid. ch. 9.
[5] B. i. ch. 11; B. ii. ch. 6; B. iii. ch. 14; ibid. ch. 25; B. iv. ch. 11. See Prol. B. i.
[6] B. ii. ch. 15; ibid. ch. 16; ibid. ch. 2; ibid. ch. 30; B. viii. ch. 24.
[7] B. iii. ch. 5.
[8] B. ix. ch. 1, from whom Boccaccio largely tranſcribes in his *Genealogiæ Deorum*, hereafter mentioned.
[9] MSS. Digb. Bibl. Bodl. 233. *Princip.* "In olde tyme it was the manere." Finiſhed at the command of his patron Thomas lord Berkeley. [Chriſtine de Piſe's verſion of Vegetius (with much additional matter interſperſed by the tranſlator) was tranſlated by Caxton 4 Hen. VII. See Blades, ii. 205-8.]
[10] Prol. B. iv. [11] B. ii. ch. 22.
[12] See *ſupra*. [13] B. vi. ch. 15.
[14] B. iv. ch. 9. This is from Ariſtotle's *Secretum Secretorum*, which Lydgate,

observes that "Grete Omerus, in Isidore ye may see, founde amonge Grekes the crafte of eloquence."[1] By Isidore he means the *Origines* or *Etymologies* of Isidorus [junior] Hispalensis, in twenty books; a system of universal information, the encyclopedia of the dark ages, and printed [at Augsburgh] before 1472.[2] In another place he censures the singular partiality of the book called *Omere*, which places Achilles above Hector.[3] Again, speaking of the Greek writers, he tells us that Boccaccio mentions a "scriveyn" or scribe, who in a small scroll of paper wrote the destruction of Troy, following Homer: he adds that this history was much esteemed among the Greeks on account of its brevity.[4] This was Dictys Cretensis or Dares Phrygius. But for perpetuating the achievements of the knights of the round table, he supposes that a clerk was appointed, and that he compiled a register from the pourfuivants and heralds who attended their tournaments, and that thence the histories of those invincible champions were framed, which, whether read or sung, have afforded so much delight.[5] For the stories of Constantine and Arthur he brings as his vouchers the romantic chronicle called *Brut* and Geoffrey of Monmouth.[6] He concludes the legend of Constantine by telling us that an equestrian statue in brass is still to be seen at Constantinople of that emperor, in which he appears armed with a prodigious sword, menacing the Turks.[7] In describing the Pantheon at Rome, he gives us some circumstances highly romantic. He relates that this magnificent fane was full of gigantic idols, placed on lofty stages: these images were the gods of all the nations conquered by the Romans, and each turned his countenance to that province over which he presided. Every image held in his hand a bell framed by magic; and when any kingdom belonging to the Roman jurisdiction was

---

as I have mentioned above, translated. But he did not finish the translation, for about the middle of it we have this note, "Here dyed this translator and notable poet John Lydgate, monk of Bury; and Fowler bygan his prolog in this wyse, 'Where floure of knighthood the bataile doth refuse.'" Fol. 336, MSS. Laud. K. 53. The Prologue consists of ten stanzas, in which he compares himself to a dwarf entering the lists, when the knight is foiled. But it is the *yong* Fowler in MSS. Laud. B. xxiv. In the Harleian copy of this piece I find the following note, at fol. 236: "Here deyde the translatour a noble poete Dan Johne Lydgate, and his *folowere* began his prologe in this wise. Per Benedictum Burghe. 'Where floure of,'" &c. MSS. Harl. 2251, 117. It must be observed that there was a Benedict Burghe coeval with Lydgate, and preferred to many dignities in the church, who translated into English verse, for the use of Lord Bourchier, son of the Earl of Essex, [*Magnus et Parvus Cato*, the latter being the later additions of Daniel Churche at the end of the twelfth century. Of this Caxton printed two editions in 4to., and a third in folio.] More will be said of [Cato] in its proper place.

[1] B. ii. ch. 15.
[2] See Gesner. *Bibl.* p. 468 and Matt. *Annal. Typ.* i. p. 100.
[3] B. iv. Prol. fol. 93, a, col. 1.   [4] B. ii. cap. 15, fol. 51, b, col. 1.
[5] B. viii. ch. 25. See *supra*.
[6] B. viii. ch. 13. See *supra*.
[7] B. viii. Boccaccio wrote the original Latin of this work, long before the Turks took and sacked Constantinople in 1453.

meditating rebellion againſt the imperial city, the idol of that country gave, by ſome ſecret principle, a ſolemn warning of the diſtant treaſon by ſtriking his bell, which never ſounded on any other occaſion.¹ Our author, following Boccaccio who wrote the *Theſeid*, ſuppoſes that Theſeus founded the order of knighthood at Athens.² He introduces, much in the manner of Boethius, a diſputation between Fortune and Poverty, ſuppoſed to have been written by Andalus the *blake*, a doctor of aſtronomy at Naples, who was one of Bochas's preceptors.

> At Naples whylom, as he dothe ſpecifye,
> In his youth when he³ to ſchole went,
> There was a doctour of aſtronomye.—
> And he was called *Andalus the blake*.⁴

Lydgate appears to have been far advanced in years when he finiſhed this poem: for at the beginning of the eighth book he complains of his trembling joints, and declares that age, having benumbed his faculties, has deprived him "of all the ſubtylte of curious makyng in Englyſshe to endyte."⁵ Our author, in the ſtructure and modulation of his ſtyle, ſeems to have been ambitious of rivalling Chaucer,⁶ whoſe capital compoſitions he enumerates, and on whoſe poetry he beſtows repeated encomiums.⁷

Lydgate's *Story of Thebes* was firſt printed [by Wynkyn de Worde, about 1500, with the *Temple of Glas* and the *Interpretacion of Godes and Goddeſſes*,⁸ in 4to, and was republiſhed] by William Thinne, at the end of his edition of Chaucer's Works in 1561.

The author introduces it as an additional Canterbury Tale. After a ſevere ſickneſs, having a deſign to viſit the ſhrine of Thomas à Becket at Canterbury, he arrives in that city, while Chaucer's pilgrims were aſſembled there for the ſame purpoſe; and by mere accident, not ſuſpecting to find ſo numerous and reſpectable a company, goes to their inn. There is ſome humour in our monk's travelling figure:⁹

---

¹ B. viii. ch. 1. ² B. i. c. 12. ³ Boccaccio.
⁴ B. iii. ch. 1. "He rede in ſcholes the moving of the heavens," &c. Boccaccio mentions with much regard *Andalus de Nigro* as one of his maſters in his *Geneal. Deor.* lib. xv. cap. vi. And ſays, that Andalus has extant many *Opuſcula aſtrorum cælique motus oſtendentia*. I think Leander, in his *Italia*, calls this Andalus, *Andalotius niger, curioſus aſtrologus*. See Papyrius *Maſſ. Elog.* tom. ii. p. 195.
⁵ B. vii. Prol. He calls himſelf older than ſixty years. ⁶ Prol. B. i.
[⁷ Among theſe, the following invites citation:

> "My maſter Chaucer with his freſh commedies,
> Is deade, alas, chiefe poete of Brytayne:
> That ſumtime made ful piteous tragedies.
> The fall of prynces he did alſo complayne,
> As he that was of makyng ſoueraynne,
> Whom al this lande of ryght ought prefarre;
> Sith of our language he was the lode-ſtarre."—*Park*.]

⁸ [*Handb. of E. E. Lit.* art. *Lydgate*.]
⁹ Edit. 1598, ad calc. *Chaucer's Works*, fol. 370, Prol.

> In a cope of blacke, and not of greene,
> On a palfray, flender, long, and lene,
> With ruftie bridell, made not for the fale,
> My man toforne with a void male.[1]

He fees, ftanding in the hall of the inn, the convivial hoft of the tabard, full of his own importance; who without the leaft introduction or hefitation thus addreffes our author, quite unprepared for fuch an abrupt falutation:

> Dan Pers,
> Dan Dominike, Dan Godfray, or Clement,
> Ye be welcome newly into Kent;
> Though your bridel haue nother boos, ne bell,
> Befeeching you that ye wil tell,
> Firft of your name, and what countre
> Without more, fhortly that ye be,
> That loke fo pale, all deuoid of blood,
> Vpon your head a wonder thredbare hood.[2]

Our hoft then invites him to fupper, and promifes that he fhall have made according to his own directions a large pudding, a round *hagis*, a French *moile*, or a *phrafe* of eggs: adding, that he looked extremely lean for a monk, and muft certainly have been fick, or elfe belong to a poor monaftery; that fome nut-brown ale after fupper will be of fervice, and that a quantity of the feed of annis, cummin, or coriander, taken before going to bed would remove flatulences. But above all, fays the hoft, cheerful company would be your beft phyfician. You fhall not only fup with me and my companions this evening, but return with us to-morrow to London; yet on condition, that you will fubmit to one of the indifpenfable rules of our fociety, which is to tell an entertaining ftory while we are travelling.

> What, looke vp, Monke! For by Cockes[3] blood,
> Thou fhalt be merrie, who fo that fay nay;
> For to-morow, anon as it is day,
> And that it ginne in the eaft [to] daw,[4]
> Thou fhalt be bound to a new law,
> At going out of Canterburie toun,
> And lien afide thy profeffioun;
> Thou fhalt not chefe,[5] nor thy felfe withdraw,
> If any mirth be found in thy maw,
> Like the cuftome of this company;
> For none fo proud that dare me denie,
> Knight, nor knaue, chanon, prieft, ne nonne,
> To tell a tale plainly as they konne,[6]
> When I affigne, and fee time oportune;
> And, for that we our purpofe woll contune,[7]
> We will homeward the fame cuftome vfe.[8]

Our monk, unable to withftand this profufion of kindnefs and feftivity, accepts the hoft's invitation, and fups with the pilgrims. The next morning, as they are all riding from Canterbury to Ofpringe, the hoft reminds his friend Dan John of what he had men-

---

[1] portmanteau. [2] Edit. 1598, ad calc. *Chaucer's Works*, fol. 370, Prol.
[3] God's. [4] dawn. [5] chufe.
[6] can, or know. [7] continue. [8] Fol. 370, back.

tioned in the evening, and without farther ceremony calls for a story. Lydgate obeys his commands, and recites the tragical deſtruction of the city of Thebes.[1] As the ſtory is very long, a pauſe is made in deſcending a very ſteep hill near the Thrope[2] of Broughton on the Blee; when our author, who was not furniſhed with that accommodation for knowing the time of the day, which modern improvements in ſcience have given to the traveller, diſcovers by an accurate examination of [the cylinder or pocket-dial (mentioned by Shakeſpeare, and in much more recent times uſed in ſome ruſtic diſtricts),] in which the ſun's horary progreſs along the equator was marked—that it was nine in the morning.[3]

It has been ſaid, but without any authority or probability, that Chaucer firſt wrote this ſtory in a Latin narrative, which Lydgate afterwards tranſlated into Engliſh verſe. Our author's originals are Guido di Colonna, Statius, and Seneca the tragedian.[4] Nicholas Trivetus, an Engliſh Dominican friar of London, who [died about 1529], has left a commentary on Seneca's tragedies.[5] [Seneca's works were] printed [at Naples] ſo early as [1475]. Lydgate in this poem often refers to " myne auctor" who, I ſuppoſe is Colonna.[6] He ſometimes cites Boccaccio's Latin tracts: particularly the *Genealogiæ Deorum*, a work which at the reſtoration of learning greatly contributed to familiariſe the claſſical ſtories: *De Caſibus virorum illuſtrium*, the ground-work of the *Fall of Princes* juſt mentioned; and *De Claris Mulieribus*, in which Pope Joan is one of the heroines.[7] From the firſt, he has taken the ſtory of Amphion building the walls of Thebes by the help of Mercury's harp, and the interpretation of that fable, together with the fictions[8] about Lycurgus, king of Thrace.[9] From the ſecond, as I recollect, the accoutrements of Polymites:[10] and from the third, part of the tale of Iſophile.[11] He alſo characteriſes Boccaccio for a talent, by which he is not now ſo generally known—

---

[1] Fol. 371.

[2] Or Thorpe. Properly a lodge in a foreſt. A hamlet. It occurs again, pag. 651, col. 1:

   " Bren townes, thropes, and villages."

And in the *Troye Boke*, he mentions, " provinces, borowes, vyllages, and thropes." B. ii. c. x.

[3] Pag. 630, col. 2. [Chilindre, or cylinder, a kind of pocket ſun-dial.—F.]

[4] See pag. 630, col. 1.

[5] MSS. Bodl. NE. F. 8, 6. Leland ſaw this Commentary in the library of the Ciſtercian abbey of Buckfaſt-Lees in Devonſhire. Col. iii. p. 257.

[6] Pag. 623, col. 2; 630, col. 1; 632, col. 2; 635, col. 2; 647, col. 2; 654, col. 1; 659, col. 1. See ſupra.

[7] Firſt printed, Ulm. 1473, fol. [For an account of an early Engliſh tranſlation by Henry Parker, Lord Moſley, temp. Hen. VIII., ſee *infra*, iv. 80.]

[8] Lydgate ſays, that this was the ſame Lycurgus who came as an ally with Palamon to Athens againſt his brother Arcite, drawn by four white bulls, and crowned with a wreath of gold. Pag. 650, col. 2. See *Kn. Tale*, v. 2131. Our author expreſsly refers to Chaucer's *Knight's Tale* about Theſeus, and with ſome addreſs, " As ye have before heard it related in paſſing through Deptford," &c.

[9] Pag. 623, col. 2; 624, col. 1; 651, col. 1.   [10] Pag. 634, col. 2.

[11] Pag. 648, col. 1, *ſeq*.

for his poetry; and styles him, "among poetes in Itaile stalled."¹ But Boccaccio's *Theseid* was yet in vogue. He says, that when Oedipus was married, none of the Muses was present, as they were at the wedding of *Sapience* with *Eloquence*, described by that poet "whilom so sage, Matrician inamed de Capella." This is Marcianus Mineus Felix de Capella, who lived about the year 470, and whose Latin prosaico-metrical work, *de Nuptiis Philologiæ et Mercurii*, in two books, an introduction to his seven books or system of the *Seven Sciences*, I have mentioned before: a writer highly extolled by Scotus Erigena,² Peter of Blois,³ John of Salisbury, and other early authors in corrupt Latinity;⁴ and of such estimation in the dark centuries, as to be taught in the seminaries of philological education as a classic.⁵ Among the royal MSS. in the British Museum, one occurs written about the eleventh century, which is a commentary on these nine books of Capella, compiled by Duncant an Irish bishop,⁶ and given to his scholars in the monastery of Saint Rhemigius.⁷ They were early translated into Latin leonine rhymes, and are often imitated by Saxo Grammaticus.⁸ Gregory of Tours has the vanity to hope, that no reader will think his Latinity barbarous: not even those, who have refined their taste, and enriched their understanding with a complete knowledge of every species of literature, by studying attentively this treatise of Capella.⁹ Alexander Neckam, a learned abbot of Cirencester, and a voluminous Latin writer about the year 1210, wrote annotations on Capella, which are yet preserved.¹⁰ His work was first printed in 1499, and [two or three other editions appeared during the sixteenth and seventeenth centuries.] This piece of Capella, dictated by the ideal philosophy of Plato, is supposed to have led the way to the celebrated Consolation of Philosophy¹¹ by Boethius.

The marriage of Sapience and Eloquence, or Mercury and Phi-

---

¹ Pag. 651, col. 1.   ² *De Divis. Natur.* lib. iii. pp. 147-8.   ³ Epist. 101.
⁴ See Alcuin. *De Sept. Artib.* p. 1256. Honorius Augustodunus, *De Philosophia Mundi*, lib. ii. cap. 5. And the book of Thomas Cantipratanus attributed to Boethius, *De Disciplina Scholarium.* Compare Barth. ad Claudian. p. 32.
⁵ Barth. ad Briton. p. 110. "Medii ævi scholas tenuit, adolescentibus prælectus," &c. See Wilibaldus, *Epist.* 147, tom. ii. *Vet. Monum.* Marten. p. 334.
⁶ Leland says he saw this work in the library of Worcester abbey. *Coll.* iii. p. 268.
⁷ MSS. Reg. 15, A. xxxiii. Liber olim S. Remig. Studio Gifardi scriptus. Labb. *Bibl. Nov. Manuscr.* p. 66. In imitation of the first part of this work, a Frenchman, Jo. Boræus, wrote *Nuptiæ Jurisconsulti et Philologiæ*, Paris, 1651, 4to.
⁸ Stephan. in Prolegomen. c. xix. And in the notes, *passim.* He is adduced by Fulgentius.
⁹ *Hist. Fr.* lib. x. *ad calc.* A MS. of Capella, more than 700 years old, is mentioned by Pez. *Thesaur. Anecdot.* [1721-9], tom. iii. p. 620. But by some writers of the early ages he is censured as obscure. Galfridus Canonicus, who flourished about 1170, declares, " Non petimus nos, aut lascivire cum Sidonio, aut vernare cum Hortensio, aut involvere cum Marciano." Apud Marten. *ubi supra*, tom. i. p. 506. He will occur again.
¹⁰ Bibl. Bodl. MSS. Digb. 221; and in other places. As did Scotus Erigena (Labb. *Bibl. Nov. Manuscr.* p. 45) and others of that period.
¹¹ See Mabillon. *Itin. Ital.* p. 221.

lology, as described by Capella, at which Clio and Calliope with all
their sisters assisted, and from which Discord and Sedition, the great
enemies of literature, were excluded, is artfully introduced, and
beautifully contrasted with that of Oedipus and Jocasta, which was
celebrated by an assemblage of the most hideous beings:

> Ne there was none of the Muses nine,
> But one accord to maken melody:
> For there song not, by heauenly armony,
> Neither Clio nor Caliope,
> None of the suftren in nomber thrife thre,
> As they did, when Philolaie,[1]
> Afcended vp high aboue the fkie,
> To be wedded: this Lady vertuous,
> Unto her Lord the God Mercurius.—
> But at his weddinge, plainly for to tell,
> Was Cerberus, chief porter of hell;
> And Herebus, fader to Hatred,
> Was there present with his wholl kinred,
> His wife alfo[2] with her browes blacke
> And her daughters, forow for to make,
> Hidoufly chered, and vgly for to fee,
> Megera and Thefiphonee,
> Alecto eke: with Labour and Envie,
> Drede, Fraude, and falfe Tretcherie,
> Trefon, Povert, Indigence, and Nede,
> And cruell Death in his rent wede:[3]
> Wretchedneffe, Complaint, and eke Rage,
> Fearfull Pale, Dronkenneſs, croked age:
> Cruell Mars, and many a Tigre wood,[4]
> Brenning[5] Ire, and vnkind blood,
> Fraternall hate, depe fet in the root,
> Sauf only death that there was no boot:[6]
> Affured othes at fine vntrew,[7]
> All thefe folke were at wedding new,
> To make the towne defolate and bare,
> As the ſtory after fhall declare.[8]

The bare conception of the attendance of this allegorical group on
thefe inceftuous efpoufals is highly poetical: and although fome of
the perfonifications are not prefented with the addition of any
picturefque attributes, yet others are marked with the powerful pencil
of Chaucer.

This poem is the *Thebais* of a troubadour. The old claffical tale
of Thebes is here clothed with feudal manners, enlarged with new
fictions of the Gothic fpecies, and furnifhed with the defcriptions, circumftances and machineries appropriated to a romance of
chivalry. The Sphinx is a terrible dragon, placed by a necromancer
to guard a mountain, and to murder all travellers paffing by.[9] Tydeus
being wounded fees a caftle on a rock, whofe high towers and crefted

---

[1] Philologia.   [2] Night.
[3] garment.   [4] the attendants on Mars.
[5] burning.   [6] "Death was the only refuge or remedy."
[7] "Oaths which proved falfe in the end."
[8] [*Story of Thebes* (Speght's *Chaucer*, 1598, fol. 374-5).]
[9] [*Ibid.* fol. 373.]

pinnacles of polished stone glitter by the light of the moon: he gains admittance, is laid in a sumptuous bed of cloth and of gold, and healed of his wounds by a king's daughter.[1] Tydeus and Polymite tilt at midnight for a lodging before the gate of the palace of King Adrastus, who is awakened with the din of the strokes of their weapons which shake all the palace, and descends into the court with a long train by torch-light: he orders the two combatants to be disarmed, and clothed in rich mantles studded with pearls; and they are conducted to repose by many a stair to a stately tower, after being served with a refection of hypocras from golden goblets. The next day they are both espoused to the king's two daughters, and entertained with tournaments, feasting, revels, and masques.[2] Afterwards Tydeus having a message to deliver to Eteocles, king of Thebes, enters the hall of the royal palace, completely armed and on horseback, in the midst of a magnificent festival.[3] This palace, like a Norman fortress or feudal castle, is guarded with barbicans, portcullisses, chains, and fosses.[4] Adrastus wishes to close his old age in the repose of rural diversions, of hawking and hunting.[5]

The situation of Polymite, benighted in a solitary wilderness, is thus forcibly described:

> Holding his way, of heart nothing light,
> Mate[6] and weary, till it draweth to night:
> And all the day beholding enuiroun
> He neither saw Castle, Towre, ne toun;
> The which thing greuéth him full sore,
> And sodainly the Sea began to rore,
> Wind and tempest hidoufly t'arise,
> The raine doun beat in full grisly wise;
> That many a beast thereof was adrad,
> And nigh for fere gan to wexe mad,
> As it sempte by the wofull sownes
> Of Tigres, Beares, Bores, and Liouns;
> Which to refute, and himselfe to saue,
> Euerich in hast draweth vnto his caue.
> But Polymite in this tempest huge
> Alas the while findeth no refuge.
> Ne him to shroud saw no where no succour,
> Till it was passed almost midnight houre.[7]

When Oedipus consults concerning his kindred the oracle of Apollo, whose image stood on a golden chariot with four wheels burned bright and sheen, animated with a fiend, the manner in which he receives his answer is touched with spirit and imagination:

> And when Edippus by great deuocion
> Finished hath fully his orison,

---

[1] [Ibid. fol. 382.]
[2] [Ibid. fol. 377, et seq.] Concerning the dresses, perhaps in the masques, we have this line [ibid. fol. 378, verso.]
  "And deuise of many a solein wede."
[3] [Ibid. fol. 379.]
[4] [Ibid. fol. 379, verso.]
[5] [Ibid. fol. 378.]
[6] afraid; fatigued.
[7] [Ibid. fol. 376.]

> The fiend anon, within inuifible,
> With a voice dreadful and horrible
> Bad him in haſt take his voiage
> Toward Thebes, &c.¹

In this poem, excluſively of that general one already mentioned, there are ſome curious mixtures of manners, and of claſſics and ſcripture. The nativity of Oedipus at his birth is calculated by the moſt learned aſtronomers and phyſicians.² Eteocles defends the walls of Thebes with great guns.³ The prieſt Amphiorax or Amphiaraus is ſtyled a biſhop, as in Chaucer;⁴ and his wife is alſo mentioned. At a council held at Thebes, concerning the right of ſucceſſion to the throne, Eſdras and Solomon are cited: and the hiſtory of Nehemiah rebuilding the walls of Jeruſalem is introduced.⁵ The moral intended by this calamitous tale conſiſts in ſhewing the pernicious effects of war: the diabolical nature of which our author ſtill further illuſtrates by obſerving, that diſcord received its origin in hell, and that the firſt battle ever fought was that of Lucifer and his legion of rebel angels.⁶ But that the argument may have the fulleſt confirmation, Saint Luke is then quoted to prove, that avarice, ambition and envy are the primary ſources of contention, and that Chriſt came into the world to deſtroy theſe malignant principles, and to propagate univerſal charity.

At the cloſe of the poem, the mediation of the holy virgin is invoked, to procure peace in this life and ſalvation in the next.⁷ Yet it ſhould be remembered, that this piece is written by a monk, and addreſſed to pilgrims.⁸

SECTION XXIII.

THE third of Lydgate's poems which I propoſed to conſider, is the *Troy Book* or the *Deſtruction of Troy*. It was firſt printed at the command of Henry VIII., in the year 1513, with this title: ["*The hyſtorye | Sege and dyſtruceyon of Troye.*" On D 4 verſo, occurs: "Here endette the Troye booke. Otherwiſe called the Sege of Troye / tranſlated by Iohn̄ Lydgate, monke of the Monaſtery of Bery."]⁹

---

¹ [*Ibid.* fol. 373.] ² [*Ibid.* fol. 372.]
³ [*Ibid.* fol. 383-4.] Great and ſmall, and ſome as large as *tonnes*.
⁴ [*Ibid.* fol. 384.] ⁵ [*Ibid.* fol. 378.] ⁶ [*Ibid.* fol. 395 *b*.]
⁷ [Pious invocations commonly conclude romances, as prayers for the king, &c. did plays and ſongs.—*Aſhby*.]
⁸ Lydgate was near fifty when this poem was written [fol. 370, edit. 1598].
⁹ Among other curious decorations in the title-page [of edit. 1555] there are ſoldiers firing great guns at the city of Troy. Caxton, in his *Recueill of the Hiſtoryes of Troye*, did not tranſlate the account of the final deſtruction of the city from his French author Raoul le Feure, "for as moche as that worſhifull and religyoˢ man dan Iohn lidgate monke of Burye dide *tranſlate hit but late*, after whos worke I fere to take vpon me," &c. At the end of B. ii.—[Blades, ii. 133.]

Another and a much more correct edition followed, under the care of [Robert] Braham, in the year 1555.[1] It was begun in 1414, the last year of the reign of Henry IV. It was written at that prince's command, and is dedicated to his successor. It was finished in 1420. In the Bodleian Library there is a MS. of this poem elegantly illuminated, with the picture of a monk presenting a book to a king.[2] From the splendour of the decorations, it appears to be the copy which Lydgate gave to Henry V.

This poem is professedly a translation or paraphrase of Guido di Colonna's romance, entitled *Historia Trojana*,[3] [and seems to have been taken from the French and Latin, one helping out the other, as was the usual practice with our old translators. The extreme probability is, that Lydgate was more familiar with the former language.][4] I have before observed, that Colonna formed his Trojan History from Dares Phrygius and Dictys Cretensis,[5] who perpetually occur as authorities in Lydgate's translation. Homer is, however, referred to in this work; particularly in the catalogue or enumeration of the ships which brought the several Grecian leaders with their forces to the Trojan coast. It begins thus, on the testimony of Colonna:[6]

---

[1] The full title may be seen in *Handb. of E. E. Lit.* art. *Colonna*. T. Heywood published a modernized version in 5-line stanzas, entitled *The Life and Death of Hector*, &c., 1614, folio.]

[2] MSS. Digb. 232. [Sir F. Madden seems to doubt whether Lydgate really was the translator. (Introd. to *Sir Gawayne*, xxxix.)]

[3] *Princip.* "Licet cotidie vetera recentioribus obruantur." [Of the original Latin, Panzer, in his *Annales Typographici*, enumerates about nine editions in the fifteenth century. See Dibdin's ed. of Herbert, i. 11.—*Park*.]

Of a Spanish version, by Petro Nuñez Degaldo, see [Brunet, last edition, ii. 171. This, however, was a romantic paraphrase, printed at Toledo in 1512. A translation of the work itself appeared at Seville in, if not before, 1502.]

[4] Yet he says, having finished his version, B. v. signat. EE i :

"I have no more of Latin to translate,
After Dytes, Dares, and Guydo."

Again, he despairs of translating Guido's *Latin* elegantly. B. ii. c. x. [Guido's *Latin* can hardly mean anything but the original Colonna's *Historia Trojana*.—*Ashby*.] See also B. iii. sign. R. iii.

[5] As Colonna's book is extremely scarce, and the subject interesting, I will translate a few lines from Colonna's Prologue and Postscript. From the Prologue. "These things, originally written by the Grecian Dictys and the Phrygian Dares, (who were present in the Trojan war, and faithful relators of what they saw,) are transferred into this book by Guido di Colonna, a judge. And although a certain Roman, Cornelius by name, the nephew of the great Sallustius, translated Dares and Dictys into Latin, yet, attempting to be concise, he has very improperly omitted those particulars of the history, which would have proved most agreeable to the reader. In my own book, therefore, every article belonging to the Trojan story will be comprehended."—And in his Postscript. "And I Guido de Colonna have followed the said Dictys in every particular; for this reason, because Dictys made his work perfect and complete in every thing. And I should have decorated this history with more metaphors and ornaments of style, and by incidental digressions, which are the pictures of composition. But deterred by the difficulty of the work," &c. Guido has indeed made Dictys nothing more than the groundwork of his story. All this is translated in Lydgate's Prologue.

[6] From Dict. Cretens. lib. i. c. xvii. p. 17, *seq.* edit. Dacer. Amstel. 1702. 4to.

> Mine auctour telleth howe Agamamnon,
> The worthi king, an hondred shippes brought.

And is closed with these lines:

> Full many shyppe was in this nauye,
> Mo than Guydo maketh rehersayle,
> Towarde Troye with grekes for to sayle:
> For as Homer in his discrypcion
> Of Grekes shippes maketh mencion,
> Shortly affyrmyng the man was neuer borne
> That such a nombre of shippes sawe toforne.[1]

In another place Homer, notwithstanding all his "rhetoryke and sugred eloquence," his "lusty songes" and "dytees swete," is blamed as a prejudiced writer, who favours the Greeks:[2] a censure which flowed from the favourite and prevailing notion held by the western nations of their descent from the Trojans. Homer is also said to paint with colours of gold and azure,[3]—a metaphor borrowed from the fashionable art of illumining. I do not however suppose that Colonna, who flourished in the middle of the thirteenth century, had ever seen

---

And Dar. Phryg. cap. xiv. p. 158, *ibid*. There [are two very ancient editions of Dares in quarto, without name or place. See Brunet, ii. 521.] Of Dictys [Cretensis there are also two very early editions, *absque notâ*, in 4to, and it was reprinted] at Milan, 1477, 4to. Dares is in German, with cuts, by Marcus Tatius, Auugst. Vindel. 1536, fol.; Dictys, by John Herold, at Basil, 1554. Both in Russian, at Moscow, 1712, 8vo. [A French version of Dares Phrygius was published in 1553, and was immediately translated into English by Thomas Paynel, Lond. 1553, 8vo. See also Brunet, ii. 522.]

[1] B. ii. c. xvi. [edit. 1555.]

[2] B. iv. cap. xxxi. In the *Prologue*, Virgil is censured for following the traces of Homer's style, in other respects a true writer. We have the same complaint in our author's *Fall of Princes*. See *supr*. In Chaucer's *House of Fame*, Colonna is introduced, among other authors of the Trojan story, making this objection to Homer's veracity. B. iii. ver. 387 [edit. Morris]:

> "Oon seyde that Omere made lyes,
> Feynynge in hys poetries,
> And was to Grekes favorable;
> Therfor held he hyt but fable."

[In the *Gest Hystoriale of the Destruction of Troy* (edit. 1869, ll. 103-24) there are two passages which bear on this point—that Homer was prejudiced, and favours the Greeks in all his statements, and that he did so simply because he was himself a Greek; our author thus writes:

> "Thow Omer, þat oft tymes openly writis
> Of þat buerne in þi boke [Achilles], as best of his hondes,
> Or wegh þat is worshipfull, & wight of his dedis;
> He comendith hym kyndly as a knight noble!
> How be reason, or right, or rewle, may þou prine
> To deme hym so doghty in dedis of armys?
> Lilly, thi lesynges þou lappis full faire,
> Thurgh affection & faithe þou fest with the grekes;
> As þou said by þi-selfe, þurgh sibradyn first
> Thou was aliet to þat lynage, as by lyne olde:
> Or ellis wodenes þe wrixlet, & þi wit failet,
> And no reason by rewle þat renke to comend."—*Donaldson*.]

[3] B. iv. c. xxxi. signat. X ii.

Homer's poems: he might have known these and many other particulars contained in the Iliad from those factitious historians whom he professes to follow. Yet it is not, in the mean time, impossible that Lydgate might have seen the Iliad, at least in a Latin translation. Leontius Pilatus, already mentioned, one of the learned Constantinopolitan exiles, had translated the Iliad into Latin prose, with part of the Odyssey, at the desire of Boccaccio,[1] about the year 1360. This appears from Petrarch's Epistles to his friend Boccaccio,[2] in which, among other curious circumstances, the former requests Boccaccio to send him to Venice that part of the new Latin version of the Odyssey by Leontius, in which the descent of Ulysses into hell and the vestibule of Erebus are described. He wishes also to see how Homer, blind and an Asiatic, had described the lake Avernus and the mountain of Circe. In another part of these letters he acknowledges the receipt of the Latin Homer, and mentions with how much satisfaction and joy the report of its arrival in the public library at Venice was received by all the Greek and Latin scholars of that city.[3] The Iliad was also translated into French verse by Jacques Milet, a licentiate of laws, about the year 1430.[4] Yet I cannot believe that Lydgate had ever consulted these translations, although he had travelled in France and Italy. One may venture to pronounce peremptorily that he did not understand, as he probably never had seen, the original. After the migration of the Roman emperors to Greece, Boccaccio was [one of the few Europeans] that could read Homer; nor [were] there perhaps [many copies] of either of Homer's poems existing in Europe till about the time the Greeks were driven by the Turks from Constantinople.[5] Long after Boccaccio's time the knowledge of the Greek tongue, and consequently of Homer, was confined only to a few scholars. Yet some ingenious French critics have insinuated that Homer was familiar in France very early; and that Christin[e de Pise,] in a poem written in the year 1398,

---

[1] It is a slight error in Vigneul [de] Marville [*i. e.* Bonaventure d'Argonne,] that this translation was procured by Petrarch [*Melanges d'Histoire*, &c., 1740,] tom. i. p. 21. The very ingenious and accurate author of *Memoires pour la Vie de Petrarque* is mistaken in saying that Hody supposes this version to have been made by Petrarch himself. Lib. vi. tom. iii. p. 633. On the contrary, Hody has adjusted this matter with great perspicuity, and from the best authorities. *De Græc. Illustr.* lib. i. c. 1, p. 2, *seq.*

[2] [*Epist.*] *Senil.* lib. iii. cap. 5.

[3] Hody, *ubi supra*, pp. 5, 6, 7, 9. The Latin Iliad in prose was published under the name of Laurentius Valla, with some slight alterations, in 1497.

[4] *Mem. de Litt.* xvii. p. 761, ed. 4to. [There is another translation into French verse, of the first ten books, by Hugues Salel, 1555: this was rendered into English in 1581 by Arthur Hall.]

[5] See Boccat. *Geneal. Deor.* xv. 6, 7. Theodorus, [a native of Tarsus, and] archbishop of Canterbury in the seventh century, brought from Rome into England a MS. of Homer which is now said to be in Bennet Library at Cambridge. See the Second Dissertation [and Wright's *Biogr. Brit. Liter.* A.-S. Per. 31 *et alibi.*] In it is written with a modern hand, "Hic liber quondam Theodori archiepiscopi Cant." But probably this Theodore is Theodore Gaza, whose book, or whose transcript, it might have been. Hody, *ubi supra*, lib. i. c. 3, pp. 59, 60.

and entitled *L'Epitre d'Othea a Hector*,[1] borrowed the word Othea or Wifdom from ω θεα in Homer, a formal appellation by which that poet often invocates Minerva.[2] [This epiftle occurs at the end of the early printed copies of the fame author's *Cent Hyftoires de Troye*.][3]

This poem is replete with defcriptions of rural beauty, formed by a felection of very poetical and picturefque circumftances, and clothed in the moft perfpicuous and mufical numbers. The colouring of our poet's mornings is often remarkably rich and fplendid:

> Whan that the rowes[4] & the rayes rede
> Eftward to vs full early gonnen fprede,
> Even at the twelyght in the dawnynge,
> When that the larke of cuftome gynneth fing,
> For to falue[5] in her heauenly laye
> The lufty goddeffe of the morowe graye,
> I meane Aurora, which afore the fonne
> Is wont tenchafe[6] the blacke fkyes donne,
> And the derkeneffe of the dymmy night:
> And frefhe Phebus, with cōforte of his light,
> And with the brightnes of his beames fhene,
> Had ouergylt the hye hylles grene.
> And floures eke agayn the morow-tyde,
> Vpō their ftalkes gā playn[7] theyr leues wide.[8]

Again, among more pictures of the fame fubject:

> Whan Aurora the fyluer droppes fhene,
> Her teares fhad vpon the frefhe grene;
> Complaynyng aye in weping & in forow,
> Her chyldrens death euery fomer morowe:
> That is to faye, when the dewe fo foote,
> Enbawmed hath the flouer and eke the roote
> With lufty lycoure in Aprill and in Maye:
> When that the larke, meffenger of daye,
> Of cuftome aye Aurora doth falue,
> With fundrye notys her forow to tranfmewi.[9]

The fpring is thus defcribed, renewing the buds or bloffoms of the groves, and the flowers of the meadows:

> And them whom winters blaftes have fhaken bare
> With fote blofomes frefhly to repare;
> And the meadows of many a fundry hewe,
> Tapitid ben with divers floures newe
> Of fundry motlefs,[10] lufty for to fene;
> And holfome balm is fhed among the grene.

---

[1] In the royal MSS. of the Britifh Mufeum this piece is entitled *La Chevalerie Spirituelle de ce monde*. 17 E. iv. 2.

[2] Sallier, *Mem. Litt.* xvii. p. 518.

[3] [Warton and his editors omit to mention that this work by an accomplifhed lady, a native of Venice, but born of Bolognefe parents, was tranflated about 1530 by R. W., who was probably the Robert Wyer who printed the book. See *Hand. of E. E. Lit.* art. *Chriftine de Pife*.]

[4] ftreaks of light. A very common word in Lydgate. Chaucer, *Kn. T.* ver. 597.
   "And while the twilight and the *rowis* red
      Of Phebus light."

[5] falute. [6] chafe. [7] open. [8] B. i. ch. vi. [edit. 1555.]
[9] change. B. iii. c. xxiiii. [10] colours.

Frequently in these florid landscapes we find the same idea differently expressed. Yet this circumstance, while it weakened the description, taught a copiousness of diction and a variety of poetical phraseology. There is great softness and facility in the following delineation of a delicious retreat:

> Tyll at the last amonge the bowes glade
> Of aduenture I caught a plesaunt shade;
> Ful smothe and playn and lusty for to sene,
> And soft as veluet was the yonge grene:
> Where fro my hors I did alight as fast,
> And on a bowe aloft his reyne cast.
> So faynte and mate of werynesse I was,
> That I me layde adowne vpon the gras,
> Upon a bryncke, shortly for to telle,
> Besyde the ryuer of a cristall welle;
> And the water, as I reherse can,
> Like quicke siluer in his streames ran,[1]
> Of whych the grauell and the bryght stone
> As any golde agayne the sonne shone.[2]

The circumstance of the pebbles and gravel of a transparent stream glittering against the sun, which is uncommon, has much of the brilliancy of the Italian poetry. It recalls to my memory a passage in Theocritus:

> Εὗρον ἀέναον κράναν ὑπὸ λισσάδι πέτρῃ,
> Ὕδατι πεπληθυῖαν ἀκηράτῳ· αἱ δ᾽ ὑπένερθεν
> Λάλλαι κρυστάλλῳ ἠδ᾽ ἀργύρῳ ἰνδάλλοντο
> Ἐκ βυθοῦ.

> They found a perpetual spring, under a high rock,
> Filled with pure water: but underneath
> The pebbles sparkled as with crystal and silver
> From the bottom.[3]

There is much elegance of sentiment and expression in the portrait of Creseide weeping, when she parts with Troilus:

> And fro her eyen the teares round drops tryll,
> That all fordewed haue her blacke wede;
> And eke vntrussed her heyre abrode gā sprede,
> Lyke golde wyre forrent and all to torne—
> And ouer this her freshe rosen hewe,
> Whylom ymeynt[4] with whyte lylyes newe,
> Wyth wofull wepynge pyteously disteyned;
> And like the herbes in April all bereyned,
> Or floures freshe with the dewes swete,
> Ryght so her chekes moyste were and wete.[5]

The following verses are worthy of attention in another style of

---

[1] [Perhaps the poet only means to express quick motion; but Swinburn tells us that in a room of the Moorish palace at Corduba, where water could not be had, there is a shallow cavity in the floor which was filled with quicksilver to give the appearance of water.—*Ashby*.]
[2] B. ii. cap. xii.
[3] Διοσκουρ. Idyll. xxii. v. 37. [4] mingled.
[5] B. iii. c. xxv. So again of Polyxena, B. iv. c. xxx.:
> "And aye she rente with her fingers smale
> Her golden heyre on her blacke wede."

writing, and have great ſtrength and ſpirit. A knight brings a ſteed to Hector in the midſt of the battle:

> And brought to Hector ſothly there he ſtode
> Amonge grekes all bathed in their bloud:
> The whiche in haſte ful knightly he beſtrode,
> And the amonge lyke Mars himſelfe he rode.[1]

The ſtrokes on the helmets are thus expreſſed, ſtriking fire amid the plumes:

> But ſtrokes felle, that men hardeen rynge,
> On baſſenettes the feeldes rounde about,
> So cruelly that the fyre ſprange oute
> Amonge the tuftes brode, bryght and ſhene,
> Of foyle of golde, & fethers whyte and grene.[2]

The touches of feudal manners, which our author affords, are innumerable: for the Trojan ſtory, and with no great difficulty, is here entirely accommodated to the ideas of romance. Hardly any adventure of the champions of the Round Table was more chimerical and unmeaning than this of our Grecian chiefs: and the cauſe of their expedition to Troy was quite in the ſpirit of chivalry, as it was occaſioned by a lady. When Jaſon arrives at Colchos, he is entertained by King Oetes in a Gothic caſtle. Amadis or Lancelot was never conducted to his fairy chamber with more ceremony and ſolemnity. He is led through many a hall and many a tower, by many a ſtair, to a ſumptuous apartment, whoſe walls, richly painted with the hiſtories of ancient heroes, glittered with gold and azure:

> Through many halle, and many riche toure,
> By many tourne, and many dyuers waye,
> By many gree[3] made of marbyll graye.—
> And in his chambre, engloſed[4] bright & cleare,
> That ſhone ful ſhene with gold & with aſure,
> Of many ymage that there was in picture,
> He hath commaunded to his offycers,
> Only in honour of the that were ſtraungers,
> Spyces and wyne.[5]

The ſiege of Troy, the grand object of the poem, is not conducted according to the claſſical art of war. All the military machines, invented and uſed in the Cruſades, are aſſembled to demoliſh the bulwarks of that city, with the addition of great guns. Among other implements of deſtruction borrowed from the holy war, the Greek fire (firſt diſcovered at Conſtantinople), with which the Saracens ſo greatly annoyed the Chriſtian armies, is thrown from the walls of the beſieged.[6]

---

[1] B. iii. c. xxii.   [2] B. ii. c. xviii.   [3] Greece, degree, ſtep, ſtair, gradus.
[4] Painted, or rather Englaſed. Skelton's [Garlande] of Laurell, [Works, edit. Dyce, i. 381]:

> "Where the poſtis wer embulyoned with ſaphiris indy blew
> Englaſid glittering," &c.

[5] B. i. c. v. See Colonna, ſignat. b.
[6] B. ii. c. xviii. In Caxton's Troy-Book Hercules is ſaid to make the fire "artificiall" as well as Cacus, &c. ii. 24.

§. 23. *Extravagant Incidents introduced into the Poem.* 87

Nor are we only presented in this piece with the habits of feudal life and the practices of chivalry. The poem is enriched with a multitude of oriental fictions and Arabian traditions. Medea gives to Jason, when he is going to combat the brazen bulls, and (to lull the dragon who guarded the golden fleece asleep) a marvellous ring, in which was a gem whose virtue could destroy the efficacy of poison, and render the wearer invisible. It was the same sort of precious stone, adds our author, which Virgil celebrates, and which Venus sent her son Eneas, that he might enter Carthage unseen. Another of Medea's presents to Jason, to assist him in this perilous achievement, is a silver image or talisman, which defeated all the powers of incantation, and was framed according to principles of astronomy.¹ The hall of King Priam is illuminated at night by a prodigious carbuncle, placed among sapphires, rubies and pearls on the crown of a golden statue of Jupiter, fifteen cubits high.² In the court of the palace, was a tree made by magic, whose trunk was twelve cubits high; the branches, which overshadowed distant plains, were alternately of solid gold and silver, blossomed with gems of various hues, which were renewed every day.³ Most of these extravagances, with a thousand more, are in Guido di Colonna, who lived when this mode of fabling was at its height. But in the fourth book, Dares Phrygius is particularly cited for a description of Priam's palace, which seemed to be founded by fayrie or enchantment, and was paved with crystal, built of diamonds, sapphires, and emeralds, and supported by ivory pillars, surmounted with golden images.⁴ This is not, however, in Dares. The warriors, who came to the assistance of the Trojans, afford an ample field for invention. One of them belongs to a region of forests, amid the gloom of which wander many monstrous beasts, not real, but appearances or illusive images, formed by the deceptions of necromancy to terrify the traveller.⁵ King Epistrophus brings from the land beyond the Amazons a thousand knights, among whom is a terrible archer, half man and half beast, who neighs like a horse, and whose eyes sparkle like a furnace, and strike dead like lightning.⁶ This is Shakespeare's "dreadful sagittary."⁷ The Trojan horse, in the genuine spirit of Arabian philosophy, is formed of brass;⁸ of such immense size, as to contain a thousand soldiers.

---

¹ B. ii. c. xviii. ² B. ii. c. xi. ³ *Ibid.*
⁴ Cap. xxvi. ⁵ B. ii. c. xviii.
⁶ So described by Colonna, sig. n 4, *seq.*
⁷ *Ibid.* And B. iii. c. xxiv. The Sagittary is not in Dictys or Dares. In whom also these warriors are but barely named, and are much fewer in number. See Dar. cap. xviii. p. 161. Dict. lib. ii. cap. xxxv. p. 51. The description of the persons of Helen, and of the Trojan and Grecian heroes [B. ii. c. xv.] is from Dares through Colonna. (Daret. *Hist.* c. xii. p. 156, *seq.*)
⁸ In Dicty's "tabulatis extruitur ligneis," lib. v. c. x. p. 113. In Gower he is also a "hors of braffe." *Conf. Amant.* lib. i. fol. xiiii. a, col. 1. From Colonna, signat. t 4. Here also are Shakespeare's fabulous names of the gates of Troy. Signat. d 4, *seq.*

Colonna, I believe, gave the Trojan ſtory its romantic additions. It had long before been falſified by Dictys and Dares; but thoſe writers, miſrepreſenting or enlarging Homer, only invented plain and credible facts. They were the baſis of Colonna, who firſt filled the faint outlines of their fabulous hiſtory with the colourings of Eaſtern fancy, and adorned their ſcanty forgeries with the gorgeous trappings of Gothic chivalry. Or, as our author expreſſes himſelf in his Prologue, ſpeaking of Colonna's improvements on his originals:

> For he enlumineth by crafte and cadence
> This noble ſtorye with many freſhe coloure
> Of rhetorik, and many ryche flouer
> Of eloquence, to make it ſounde the bett.[1]

Clothed with theſe new inventions, this favourite tale deſcended to later times. Yet, it appears, not only with theſe, but with an infinite variety of other embelliſhments not fabricated by the fertile genius of Colonna, but adopted from French enlargements of Colonna, and incorporated from romances on other ſubjects, in the French *Hiſtories of Troy*, written by a French eccleſiaſtic, Rauol le Fevre [in] 1464, and tranſlated by Caxton.[2]

The deſcription of the city of Troy, as newly built by King Priam, is extremely curious; not for the capricious incredibilities and abſurd inconſiſtencies which it exhibits,[3] but becauſe it conveys anecdotes of ancient architecture, and eſpecially of that florid and improved ſpecies which began to grow faſhionable in Lydgate's age. Although much of this is in Colonna. He avoids to deſcribe it geometrically, having never read Euclid. He ſays that Priam [ſent]

> For ſuch as coulde graue, groupe, or carue,
> Or ſuche as were able for to ſerue,
> With lime and ſtone for to reyſe a wall,
> With bataylyng and creſtes marciall,
> Or ſuch as had connynge in their head
> Alabaſter, other white or read,
> Or marbell grey, for to pullyſhe playne,
> To make it ſmothe of vaynes and of grayne;
> He ſente alſo for euery ymageour
> Both in entayle, and euery portreyour

---

[1] better.

[2] As for inſtance, Hercules having killed the eleven giants of Cremona, builds over them a vaſt tower, on which he placed eleven images of metal, of the ſize and figure of the giants. B. ii. c. 24. Something like this, I think, is in *Amadis de Gaul*. Robert Braham, in the *Epiſtle to the Reader*, prefixed to the edition of Lydgate's *Troy Book*, 1555, is of opinion that the fables in the French *Recuyell* ought to be ranked with the "trifeling tales" and "barrayne leurdries" of *Robyn Hode* and *Bevys of Hampton*, and are not to be compared with the "faythful" and "trewe" reports of this hiſtory given by Dares Phrygius and Dictys Cretenſis.

[3] It is three days' journey in length and breadth. The walls are two hundred cubits high, of marble and alabaſter, and machicolated. At every angle was a crown of gold, ſet with the richeſt gems. There were great guns in the towers. On each turret were figures of ſavage and monſtrous beaſts in braſs. The gates were of braſs, and each has a portcullis. The houſes were all uniform, and of marble, ſixty cubits high.

> For eche caruer and curious ioyner,
> To make knottes with many a queynt floure
> To sette on crestes within and eke without.—
> * * *
> And yf I should rehersen by and by,
> The corue knottes by craft of masonry;
> The freshe enbowing[1] with verges right as lynes,
> And the housyng ful of backewines,
> The ryche coyning, the lusty tablementes,
> Vinettes[2] ronning in casementes.
> * * *
> Nor howe they put, in stede of mortere,
> In the ioyntoures, coper gylte full clere;
> To make them ioyne by leuell and by lyne,
> Amonge the marbell freshely for to shyne
> Agaynst the sonne, whan his shene lyght
> Smote on the golde that was burned bright.

The sides of every street were covered with "freshe alures"[3] of marble, or cloisters, crowned with rich and lofty pinnacles, and fronted with tabernacular or open work,[4] vaulted like the dormitory of a monastery, and called *deambulatories*, for the accommodation of the citizens in all weathers:

> And euery house couered was with lead;
> And many gargoyle, and many hydous head,
> With spoutes thorough, &c.[5]—

And again, of Priam's palace:

> And the walles, within and eke without,
> Endlonge were with knottes grauen cleane,
> Depeynt with asure, golde, cinople, & grene.
> * * *
> And all the windowes and eche fenestrall
> Wrought were of beryl[6] & of cleare crystall.

With regard to the reality of the last circumstance, we are told that in Studley castle in Shropshire[7] the windows, so late as the reign of Elizabeth, were of beryl.

The account of the Trojan theatre must not be omitted, as it displays the imperfect ideas of the stage, at least of dramatic exhibition, which now prevailed; or rather the absolute inexistence of this sort of spectacle. Our author supposes that comedies and tragedies were first represented at Troy.[8] He defines a comedy to

---

[1] arching.
[2] [Sprigs or branches used in pictorial or architectural ornamentation.]
[3] ["The *alure* seems in its primary sense to have been the passage behind the battlements, *allorium, ambulacrum*, in French, *alleure* or *allée*."—Way, *Promptor. Parvulorum*.]
[4] Like the latticed stone-work, or *cancelli*, of a Gothic shrine.
[5] [See a note by Dallaway in Walpole's *Anecd. of Painting*, edit. 1862, i. 124.]
[6] [For a more striking description of Priam's palace see *The Gest Hystoriale of the Destruction of Troy*, edit. 1869, pp. 54-6.—*Donaldson*.]
[7] [Should we not read Sudeley Castle, near Winchcombe, in Gloucestershire? See Leland's *Itinerary*, iv. fol. 170, where it is said that "part of the windowes of it were glazed with berall." This, however, has been doubted by an intelligent friend in his account of Sudeley. See *Monthly Mag.*—*Park*.]
[8] Harrison's *Descript. Brit.* cap. xii. p. 188. The occupations of the citizens

begin with complaint and to end with "gladneſſe:" expreſſing the actions of thoſe only who live in the loweſt condition. But tragedy, he informs us, begins in proſperity, and ends in adverſity: ſhowing the wonderful viciſſitudes of fortune which have happened in the lives of kings and mighty conquerors. In the theatre of Troy, he adds, was a pulpit, in which ſtood a poet, who rehearſed the "noble dedes that were hyſtoryall of kynges, & prynces," and worthy emperors; and, above all, related thoſe fatal and ſudden cataſtrophes, which they ſometimes ſuffered by murder, poiſon, conſpiracy, or other ſecret and unforeſeen machinations:

> All this was tolde and red of the poete.
> And whyle that he in the pulpet ſtode
> With deadly face all deuoyde of blode,
> Synging his diteis with muſes all-to-rent;
> Amyd the theatre, ſhrowded in a tent,
> There came out men, gaſtfull of their cheres,
> Disfygured their faces with viſeres,
> Playing by ſygns in the peoples ſyght
> That the poet ſonge hath on heght:[1]
> So that there was no maner diſcordaunce,
> Atwene his ditees and their countenaunce.
> For lyke as he aloſte dyd expreſſe
> Wordes of ioye or of heauineſſe,
> So craftely they[2] coulde them[3] transfygure.[4]

It is added, that theſe plays, or "rytes of tragedyes old," were acted at Troy, and "in the theatre halowed and yholde," when the months of April and May returned.

In this detail of the dramatic exhibition which prevailed in the ideal theatre of Troy, a poet, placed on the ſtage in a pulpit, and characteriſtically habited, is ſaid to have recited a ſeries of tragical adventures; whoſe pathetic narrative was afterwards expreſſed by the dumb geſticulations of a ſet of maſqued actors. Some perhaps may be inclined to think, that this imperfect ſpecies of theatric repreſentation was the rude drama of Lydgate's age. But ſurely Lydgate would not have deſcribed at all, much leſs in a long and laboured digreſſion, a public ſhow which from its nature was familiar and

---

of Troy are mentioned. There were goldſmiths, jewellers, embroiderers, weavers of woollen and linen, of cloth, of gold, damaſk, ſattin, velvet, *ſendel*, or a thin ſilk like cypreſs, and double *ſamyte*, or ſatin. Smiths who forged poll-axes, ſpears, and *quarrel-heads*, or croſs-bow darts ſhaped ſquare. Armourers, bowyers, fletchers, makers of trappings, banners, ſtandards, penons, "and for the fielde freſhe and gaye getours." I do not preciſely underſtand the laſt word. Perhaps it is a ſort of ornamental armour for the legs. [We may refer, by way of compariſon, to the liſt of trades, as they ſtand in the *Geſt Hyſtoriale*. Some intereſt is attached to this particular; each verſion gives a different ſet, and many of them are not in Guido di Colonna at all; indeed the liſt as given by our author, and the deſcription of the tradeſmen, their ſhops and homes, are exactly thoſe of Edinburgh in the fifteenth century. See the Early Engliſh Text Society's edit. part i. pp. 53-4.—*Donaldſon.*]

[1] "That which the poet ſung, ſtanding in the pulpit."
[2] the actors.
[3] [Mr. Horne Tooke queried whether *them* did not refer to words in the lines preceding.—*Park.* Clearly.]
[4] Lib. ii. cap. x. See alſo, B. iii. c. xxviii.

notorious. On the contrary, he describes it as a thing obsolete, and existing only in remote times. Had a more perfect and legitimate stage now subsisted, he would not have deviated from his subject, to communicate unnecessary information, and to deliver such minute definitions of tragedy and comedy. On the whole, this formal history of a theatre conveys nothing more than an affected display of learning, and is collected, yet with apparent inaccuracy and confusion of circumstances from what the ancient grammarians have left concerning the origin of the Greek tragedy. [It was doubtless] borrowed by our author from some French paraphrastic version of Colonna's Latin romance.[1]

Among the ancient authors, beside those already mentioned as cited in this poem, are Lollius for the history of Troy, Ovid for the tales of Medea and Jason, and Ulysses and Polyphemus, the Myrmidons and other stories, Statius for Polynices and Eteocles, the venerable Bede, Fulgentius the mythologist, Justinian with whose institutes Colonna as a civilian must have been well acquainted, Pliny, and Jacobus de Vitriaco. The last is produced to prove that Philometer, a famous philosopher, invented the game of chess, to divert a tyrant from his cruel purposes in Chaldea: and that thence it was imported into Greece. But Colonna, or rather Lydgate, is of a different opinion; and contends in opposition to his authority that this game, "so sotyll and so marvaylous," was discovered by "prudent clerkes" during the siege of Troy, and first practised in that city. Jacobus de Vitriaco was a canon regular at Paris, and among other dignities in the church, bishop of Ptolemais in Palestine about the year 1230. This tradition of the invention of chess is mentioned by Vitriaco in his *History*.[2] The anecdote of Philometer is, I think, in Egidius Romanus above mentioned. [The author of the poem called *Chaucer's Dream*] calls Athalus, that is Attalus Philometer, who is often mentioned in Pliny, the inventor of chess.[3]

I must not pass over an instance of Lydgate's gallantry, as it is the gallantry of a monk. Colonna takes all opportunities of satirising the fair sex; and Lydgate with great politeness declares himself absolutely unwilling to translate those passages of this severe moralist, which contain such unjust and illiberal misrepresentations of the female character. Instead of which, to obviate these injurious reflections, our translator enters upon a formal vindication of the ladies; not by a panegyric on their beauty, nor encomiums on those amiable accomplishments, by which they refine our sensibilities, and give elegance to life; but by a display of that religious fortitude with which some women have suffered martyrdom; or of that inflexible chastity, by means of which others have been snatched up alive into heaven,

---

[1] Colonna calls him, "ille fabularius Sulmonensis,—fabulose commentans," &c. Signat. b, 2.

[2] ["Libri duo, quorum prior orientalis . . . alter occidentalis historiæ nomine inscribitur," Paris, 1597.]

[3] [Chaucer's Works, edit. 1721, p. 408. It is scarcely necessary to observe, that this view is erroneous.]

in a state of genuine virginity. Among other striking examples which the calendar affords, he mentions the transcendent grace of the eleven thousand virgins who were martyred at Cologne in Germany. In the mean time, female saints, as I suspect, in the barbarous ages were regarded with a greater degree of respect, on account of those exaggerated ideas of gallantry which chivalry inspired: and it is not improbable that the distinguished honours paid to the Virgin Mary might have partly proceeded from this principle.

Among the anachronistic improprieties which this poem contains, some of which have been pointed out, the most conspicuous is the fiction of Hector's sepulchre, or tomb: which also merits our attention for another reason, as it affords us an opportunity of adding some other notices of the modes of ancient architecture to those already mentioned. The poet (from Colonna) supposes that Hector was buried in the principal church of Troy near the high altar, within a magnificent oratory erected for that purpose, exactly resembling the Gothic shrines of our cathedrals, yet charged with many romantic decorations:

> With crafty archys raysyd wonder clene,
> Embowed over all the work to cure,
> So marveylous was the celature
> That al the rose, and closure envyrowne,
> Was of fyne golde plated up and downe,
> With knottes grave wonder curyous
> Fret ful of stonys rich and precious, &c.

The structure is supported by angels of gold. The steps are of crystal. Within is not only an image of Hector in solid gold, but his body embalmed, and exhibited to view with the resemblance of real life, by means of a precious liquor circulating through every part in golden tubes artificially disposed, and operating on the principles of vegetation.[1] This is from the chemistry of the times. Before the body were four inextinguishable lamps in golden sockets. To complete the work, Priam founds a regular chantry of priests, whom he accommodates with mansions near the church, and endows with revenues, to sing in this oratory for the soul of his son Hector.[2]

In the Bodleian library, there is a prodigious folio MS. on vellum,

---

[1] [I wonder nobody ever thought of proving that the circulation of the blood was known before Harvey, from this passage. However, it seems difficult to conceive how this liquor was seen to circulate through golden tubes let into a mummy. Had he made his *body* of crystal instead of the *steps*, with proper tubular passages, we might fancy the blood circulated, as it is seen to do in a great length of glass tube artificially twisted.—*Ashby*. If Dr. Ashby had lived to our time, he might have witnessed the expression of doubt as to Harvey's origination of the great discovery on grounds independent of the present passage.]

[2] B. iii. c. xxviii. Joseph of Exeter in his *Antiocheis* has borrowed from this tomb of Hector, in his brilliant description of the mausoleum of Teuthras, lib. iv. 451. I have quoted the passage in the [third] *Dissertation*. [For another description of Hector's tomb, and of his embalming, see the *Destruction of Troy*, edit. 1869, pp. 284-5.—*Donaldson*.]

a tranflation of Colonna's *Trojan Hiftory* into verfe,[1] which [of courfe will not be] confounded with Lydgate's *Troy-Book* now before us. It is an entirely different work, and is written in the fhort minftrel-metre. I have given a fpecimen of the Prologue above. It appears to me to be Lydgate's *Troy-Book* divefted of the octave-ftanza, and reduced into a meafure which might more commodioufly be fung to the harp.[2] It is not likely that Lydgate is its author: that he fhould

---

[1] MSS. Laud, K. 76, fol. [now Laud, 595. I am told that it is a fine MS. and worth printing.]

[2] It may, however, be thought, that this poem is rather a tranflation or imitation of fome French original, as the writer often refers to *The Romance*. If this be the cafe, it is not immediately formed from the *Troy-book* of Lydgate, as I have fuggefted in the text. I believe it to be about Lydgate's age; but there is no other authority for fuppofing it to be written by Lydgate than that, in the beginning of the Bodleian MS. now before us, a hand-writing, of about the reign of James I. affigns it to that poet [in this prefix: " Dares a Trojan haralte and Dictas a Grecian haralte, wrat this booke in Greeke, and lefte it in Athenes, and theare it was founde by Guido de Columpius, a notary at Rome, and digefted into Latyn, and in anno 1414 tranflated into Engglifhe by John Lidgate monke of Bury. Vide fo. 2."—*Park*.] I will give a few lines from the poem itfelf, which begins with Jafon's expedition to Colchos, the conftant prelude to the Trojan ftory in all the writers of this fchool:

> " In colkos Ile a Cite was,
> That men called thanne reconitas;
> Fair and mekel,[1] large and longe,
> With walles heye and wondir ftronge:
> Ful of toures and heye paleis,
> Off riche knystes and burgeis:
> A kyng that tyme that hete[2] Cetes
> Gouerned than that lond In pes,[3]
> With his baronage and his meyne,
> Dwelleden thanne in that Cyte:
> For al aboute that riche toun
> Stode wodes and parkis enviroun,
> That were replenyfched wondirful
> Off herte and hynde, bore and bul,
> And other many fauage beftis,
> Be-twix that wode and that foreftis,
> Ther was large contray & playn,
> Faire wodes & fair Champayn,
> Ful of femely-rennyng welles,
> As the romaunce the fothe[4] telles,
> With-oute the cete that ther fprong.
> Ther was of briddes michel fang
> Thorow alle the zer[5] and mykel cry,
> Off alle Ioyes gret melody.
> ¶ To that Cite & kyng Cetes
> Zode[6] Iafon and hercules,
> And alle the felawes that he hadde
> In clothes of gold, as kynges be cladde," &c.—fol. 8 *b*.

Afterwards, fol. 9 *b*. the forcerefs Medea, the king's daughter, is thus characterifed:

| [1] great. | [2] hight, named. | [3] peace. | [4] truth. |
| [5] year. | [6] came. | | |

either thus transform his own composition, or write a new piece on the subject. That it was a poem in some considerable estimation, appears from the size and splendour of the MS.: and this circumstance induces me to believe, that it was at a very early period ascribed to Lydgate. On the other hand, it is extraordinary that the name of the writer of so prolix and laborious a work, respectable

> "Sche coude the science of clergy,
> And mochel of Nigramauncy.—
> ¶ Sche coude with coniurisouns,
> With here scleyghte[1] and oresouns,
> The day, that was most fair & lyght,
> Make as derk es any nyght:
> Sche coude also In selcouth wyse
> Make the wynde bothe blowe & ryse,
> And make him so lowde blowe,
> As it scholde houses ouerthrowe.
> He couthe turne, verement,
> Alle wederes[2] and the firmament," &c.

The reader, in some of these lines, observes the appeal to *The romance* for authority. This is common throughout the poem, as I have hinted. But at the close, the poet wishes eternal salvation to the soul of the author of the *Romaunce*, fol. 275:

> "¶ And thus was Troye dryuen doun . . . .
> As In this romaunce men may rede . . . .
> ¶ And thus endis this stronge batayle . . . .
> As the romaunce ther-of doth say . . . .
> ¶ And he that this romaunce wroght & made
> Lord In heuene thow him glade."

[I think the word *Romance* does not occur any where else in the MS. except in the first page.]

If this piece is translated from a French romance, it is not from the ancient metrical one of Benoit [de Sainte More,] but perhaps from some later French romance, which copied or translated Colonna's book. This, among other circumstances, we may collect from these lines:

> "Dares the heraud of Troye says,
> And Dites that was of the Gregeis, &c.
> And after him cometh *maister* Gy,
> That was of Rome a notary."

This *maister Gy* or *Guy*, that is Guido di Colonna, he adds, wrote this history:

> "In the *manere* I schall telle."

That is " my author, or romance, follows Colonna." *Dares the heraud* is Dares Phrygius, and *Dites* Dictys Cretensis.

This poem, in the Bodleian MS. aforesaid, is finished, as I have partly observed, with an invocation to God, to save the author and the readers or hearers, and ends with this line:

> "Seythe alle Amen for charite."

But this rubric immediately follows, at the beginning of a page: "Hic bellum de Troye Ffinit et Greci transierunt versus patriam suam." Then follow several lineated pages of vellum, without writing. I have never seen any other manuscript of this piece.

[See the Alliterative *Troy-Book* from the MS. in the Hunterian Museum, Glasgow, printed for the Early English Text Society, 1869, and M. Joly's admirable edition of Benoit de Saint More's *Roman de Troie*, Paris, 1870, with an essay on the author's works (already quoted).— F.]

---

[1] sleight, art.   [2] weathers.

and conspicuous at least on account of its length, should have never transpired. The language accords with Lydgate's age, and is of the reign of Henry VI.: and to the same age I refer the hand-writing, which is executed with remarkable elegance and beauty.[1]

[To the same reign belongs William Lichfield, Parson of All-Hallows, Thames Street, who died in 1447. He is the author of a poem in seventy-two eight-line stanzas, entitled *The Complaint between God and man*. There was an edition of it, printed by Wynkyn de Worde, and it occurs in more than one MS.[2]]

SECTION XXIV.

TWO more poets remain to be mentioned under the reign of Henry VI., if mere translation merit that appellation. These are Hugh [de] Campeden and Thomas Chestre.

The first was a great traveller, and translated into English verse the French romance of *Sidrac*, [of which there is a copy in MS. Egerton, 751.] This translation, [which is not very uncommon in MS.] was printed with the following title at the expense of Robert Saltwood, a monk of Saint Austin's convent at Canterbury [about 1530]: "The History of Kyng Boccus and Sydracke how he confounded his lerned men and in the syght of them dronke strong venym in the Name of the Trinite and dyd him no hurt. Also his dyuynyte that he lerned of the Boke of Noe. Also his profycye that he had by Revelacyon of the aungell," &c.] There is no sort of elegance in the diction, nor harmony in the versification. It is in the minstrel-metre. [It begins:][3]

> Men may fynde in olde bookes,
> Who soo yat in them lookes,
> That men may mooche here,
> And yerefore yff yat yee wolle lere,

---

[1] [Mr. Heber had a poetical tract, printed by W. de Worde, entitled *The Proverbes of Lydgate*. In the colophon it is termed *The Proverbes of Lydgate upon the fall of prynces*. It begins

"To kysse the steppes of them that were fortheryng
Laureate poetes which had foveraynte."

It consists of several detached poems gathered from Lydgate's imitation of Boccaccio. The whole are composed in stanzas which have the peculiarity of closing with a similar line in each piece. The third of these bears relation to a song which is in abeyance between Chaucer and Lydgate.—*Park*. But the piece referred to by Mr. Park is the *Good Counsel of Chaucer*. See Bell's ed. viii. 143.]

[2] MSS. Caius Coll. Camb. E 147, b. This writer, who shone most in prose, is said to have written 3083 English sermons [in a note to a copy of his *Complaint* in a folio MS. of the early part of the fifteenth century in the possession of Mr. Henry Huth.] See T. Gascoigne MS. Dict. art. *Predicator*; Stow's *Survey of London*, 251, 386; and Newcourt's *Repertorium*, i. 819.

[3] Bibl. Bodl. MSS. Laud, G. 57, [which differs literally from the old printed copy.]

> I shall teche yoowe a lytill jeste
> That befell oonys in the este,
> There was a kynge that Boctus hyght
> And was a man of mooche myght.
> His londe lay be grete Inde:
> Bectorye hight hit as we fynde,
> After the tyme of Noee even
> VIIJ^{te} hundred yere fourty and seven
> The kynge Bochus hym be thought
> That he would have a citee wrought
> The rede Jewes fro hym spere
> And for to mayntene his were
> Ayenst a kyng that was hys foo,
> And hath moste of Inde longyng hym too:
> His name Garaab the kyng.
> Bocchus tho proved all this thing,
> And smartly a towre begenne he,
> There he wolde make his citee;
> And it was right at the incomyng
> Of Garabys londe the kyng.
> The masons with grete laboure
> Beganne to worke uppon the toure;
> And all that they wroghten on day
> On night was hit done away.
> On morn when Bochus hit herde,
> Hee was wroth that hit so ferde,
> And dyd hyt all new begynne.
> At even whan they shuld blynne
> Off worke when they went to reste
> In the night was all downe heste.
> Well vii monthes this thei wrought,
> And in the night avaylid yt nought.
> Boccus was wroth wonderly
> And callid his folke that was hym by.
> Councellith me lordinges, seyde hee,
> Howe I may beste make this citee.
> They sayde: sir, sendith a noon
> Aftir your philosophers everychon,
> And the astronomers of your londe;
> Of hem shall yee counseill fonde—

Afterwards King Tractabare is requested to send

> The booke of astronomye
> That whilom Noe had in baylye,

together with his astronomer Sidracke. At the end:

> And that Hugh of Campedene
> That this boke hath thorogh soght,
> And untoo Englyssh ryme hit brought.

Sidrack, who is a Christian, at length builds the tower *in Nomine S. Trinitatis*, and he teaches Bocchus, who is an idolater, many articles of true religion.[1]

Thomas Chestre appears also to have been a writer for the minstrels. No anecdote of his life is preserved. He has left a poem entitled *Sir Launfal*, one of Arthur's knights, who is celebrated with

---

[1] [For copious extracts from the printed edition, see Corser's *Collectanea Anglo-poetica*, ii. 289, *et seq.*]

other champions in the French lays, [which is a tranflation from a lay written on the fame ftory by Marie de France. But the tranflator has introduced occafional additions and variations]. It is opened with a feaft celebrated at Whitfuntide by King Arthur at Kardoyl, a French corruption from Carliol, by which is meant Cairleon in Wales, fometimes in romances confounded with Cardiff:[1]

> Jei commence le Lay de Launval.
> Laventure de un Lay,
> Cum ele avint vus cunteray,
> Fait fu dun gentil vaffal,
> En Bretaigne lapelent Launval:
> A Kardoyl fuiornont li reys
> Arthur, li prouz, e li curteys,
> Pur les Efcot, e pur les Pis,
> Ki deftrueient les pays;
> En la terre de Logres[2] le trououent,
> Mult fouent le damagouent
> A la Pentecufte en eftè,
> I aveit li reys fojournè,
> A les i dona riches duns,
> E al cuntes,[3] e al baruns,
> A ceus de la Table Runde, &c.

That is, Here begins the Lay of Launval.—[I will relate to you] the Adventure of a certain Lay, made of a gentle vaffal, whom in Bretaigne they called Launval. The brave and courteous King Arthur fojourned at Kardoyl, for making war againft the Scots and Picts, who deftroyed the country. He found them in the land of Logres, where they committed frequent outrages. The king was there at the feaft of Pentecoft, where he gave rich gifts to the counts and barons, and the knights of the round table, &c.[4]

[The Englifh] begins thus:

> LAUNFAL MILES.
> Be douȝty Artours dawes
> That held Engelond yn good lawes,
> There felle a wondyre cas,
> Of a ley[5] that was y-fette,
> That hyȝt Launval and hatte ȝette.
> Now herkeneth how hyt was.
> Douȝty Artoure fom whyle
> Sojournede yn Kardevyle,[6]

---

[1] [See *Geoffr. Monm.* ix. 12.]
[2] Logres, or Loegria, from Locrine, was the middle part of Britain.
[3] counts. So in *Robert of Gloucefter*, we have Contafs for countefs. On which word his editor Hearne obferves, that King James I. ufed to call a countefs a cuntys. He quotes one of James's letters, "Come and bring the three Cuntys [for counteffes] with you." *Glofs.* p. 635.
[4] The writing of this MS. of *Launval* feems about 1300. The compofition is undoubtedly much earlier. There is another (MSS. Harl. 978, § 112). This I have cited in the Firft Differtation. From the Englifh *Launfall*, I have given extracts in the Differtation on the *Gefta Romanorum*, fupr. pp. 261, 267, of vol. i. See alfo vol. iv. p. 108.]
[5] [lay.]
[6] [Mr. Halliwell fays: "The old romance of Merlin calls it, 'la ville de Cardueil en Galles [Wales],'" and the editor believes that Carlion-on-Ufk (the *Ifca*

Wyth joye and greet folas,
And knyʒtes that were profitable,
With Artour of the rounde table,
Never noon better ther was.
Sere Perſevalle, and ſyr Gawayn,
Syr Gyheryes, and ſyr Agrafrayn,
And Launcelet du Lake,
Syr Kay, and ſyr Ewayn,
That welle couthe fyʒte yn plain,
Bateles for to take.
Kyng Ban Booʒt, and kyng Bos,
Of ham ther was a greet los,
Men ſawe tho nowhere¹ her make,²
Syr Galafre, and ſyr Launfale,
Wherof a noble tale
Among us ſchalle a wake.

With Artoure ther was a bachelere
And hadde y-be welle many a ʒere,
Launfal for ſoth he hyʒt,
He gaf gyftys largelyche
Gold and ſylver, and clodes ryche,
To ſquyer and to knyʒt.
For hys largeſſe and hys bountè
The kynges ſtuward made was he
Ten yer, y you plyʒt,
Of alle the knyʒtes of the table rounde
So large ther nas noon y-founde,
Be dayes ne be nyʒt.

So hyt by-fylle yn the tenthe ʒere
Marlyn was Artours counſalere,
He radde hym fore to wende
To kyng Ryon of Irlond ryʒt,
And fette hym ther a lady bryʒt
Gwennere hys douʒtyr hende, &c.

In the concluſion occurs:

Thomas Cheſtre made thys tale
Of the noble knyʒt ſyr Launfale,
Good of chyvalrye:
Jheſus that ys hevene kyng
Yeve us alle hys bleſſyng
And hys modyr Marye. *Amen.*
EXPLICIT LAUNFALE.³

[There does not ſeem to be any real] evidence to prove, that Cheſtre was the [tranſlator] of the metrical romance called the *Earle of Tholouſe*.⁴ This is [alſo] one of the romances called *Lais*, as appears from theſe lines:

Silurum of the Romans) is the place intended. Carliſle, which Ritſon conjectured, is ſurely very improbable.]
¹ ther.   ² match.
³ [Printed twice by Ritſon in his *Romances*, 1802, and again by Halliwell. A later verſion, where the hero is called *Sir Lambwell*, is in the lately edited Percy MSS.; and, of courſe, the ſtory is among the *Fabliaux*.]
⁴ MSS. Aſhmol. Oxon. 45 [6926]. And MSS. More, Camb. 27. Princip.:

"Jeſu Criſt in trinite,
Only god in perſons thre, &c.

> In romance this gest
> A Ley[1] of Britayn callyd I wys, &c.

That it is a translation, appears from the reference to an original, "The Romans telleth so." I will, however, give the outlines of the story, which is not uninteresting, nor inartificially constructed.

Dioclesian, a powerful emperor in Germany, has a rupture with Barnard, earl of Touloufe, concerning boundaries of territory. Contrary to the repeated persuasions of the empress, who is extremely beautiful, and famous for her conjugal fidelity, he meets the earl with a numerous army in a pitched battle, to decide the quarrel. The earl is victorious, and carries home a great multitude of prisoners, the most respectable of which is Sir Tralabas of Turkey, whom he treats as his companion. In the midst of their festivities they talk of the beauties of the empress; the earl's curiosity is inflamed to see so matchless a lady, and he promises liberty to Sir Tralabas, if he can be conducted unknown to the emperor's court, and obtain a sight of her without discovery. They both set forward, the earl disguised like a hermit. When they arrive at the emperor's court, Sir Tralabas proves false: treacherously imparts the secret to the empress that he has brought with him the Earl of Touloufe in disguise, who is enamoured of her celebrated beauty, and proposes to take advantage of so fair an opportunity of killing the emperor's great and avowed enemy. She rejects the proposal with indignation, enjoins the knight not to communicate the secret any farther, and desires to see the earl next day in the chapel at mass. The next day the earl in his hermit's weeds is conveniently placed at mass. At leaving the chapel, he asks an alms of the empress; and she gives him forty florins and a ring. He receives the present of the ring with the highest satisfaction, and although obliged to return home, in point of prudence and to avoid detection, comforts himself with this reflection:

> Well is me, I have thy grace,
> Of the to have thys thyng!
> If ever I have grace of the,
> That any love betweene us be,
> This may be a Tokenyng.

He then returns home. The emperor is called into some distant country, and leaves his consort in the custody of two knights who, attempting to gain her love without success, contrive a stratagem to defame her chastity. She is thrown into prison, and the emperor

---

> Lefe frendys I shall you telle
> Of a tale that sometyme befell
> Far in unkouthe lande,
> Howe a lady had grete myschefe, &c."

[A copy from the latter has been published by Mr. Ritson. In orthography it varies considerably from the Ashmole MS., and is evidently of an earlier date.—Price.]

[1] Perhaps *ley* in the fourth line of *Sir Launfal* may mean lay in this sense. See note at the beginning of the First Dissertation.

returns unexpectedly,[1] in consequence of a vision. The tale of the two treacherous knights is believed, and she is sentenced to the flames; yet under the restriction, that if a champion can be found who shall foil the two knights in battle, her honour shall be cleared, and her life saved. A challenge is published in all parts of the world; and the Earl of Toulouse, notwithstanding the animosities which still subsist between him and the emperor, privately undertakes her quarrel. He appears at the emperor's court in the habit of a monk, and obtains permission to act as confessor to the empress in her present critical situation. In the course of the confession she protests that she was always true to the emperor, yet owns that once she gave a ring to the Earl of Toulouse. The supposed confessor pronounces her innocent of the charge brought against her; on which one of the traitorous knights affirms that the monk was suborned to publish this confession, and that he deserved to be consumed in the same fire which was prepared for the lady. The monk pretending that the honour of his religion and character was affected by this insinuation, challenges both the knights to combat: they are conquered; and the empress, after this trial, is declared innocent. He then openly discovers himself to be the Earl of Toulouse, the emperor's ancient enemy. A solemn reconciliation ensues. The earl is appointed seneschal of the emperor's domain. The emperor lives only three years, and the earl is married to the empress.

In the execution of this performance our author was obliged to be concise, as the poem was intended to be sung to the harp. Yet, when he breaks through this restraint, instead of dwelling on some of the beautiful situations which the story affords, he is diffuse in displaying trivial and unimportant circumstances. These popular poets are never so happy as when they are describing a battle or a feast.

It will not perhaps be deemed impertinent to observe that about this period the minstrels were often more amply paid than the clergy. In this age, as in more enlightened times, the people loved better to be pleased than instructed. During many of the years of the reign of Henry VI., particularly in the year 1430, at the annual feast of the fraternity of the Holy Cross at Abingdon, in Berkshire, twelve priests each received four pence for singing a dirge; and the same

---

[1] The emperor's disappointment is thus described:

" Anon to the chamber went he,
He longyd fore his wyf to se,
That was so swete a wyght:
He callyd theym that shulde her kepe,
Where is my wif: is she on slepe?
How farys that byrd so bryght?
The traytors answeryd anon,
And ye wift how she had done, &c.
The yonge knyght sir Artour,
That was her hervour, &c.
For bale his armys abrode he sprede,
And fell in swoone on his bed."

number of minstrels were rewarded each with two shillings and four pence, beside diet and horse-meat. Some of these minstrels came only from Maydenhithe, or Maidenhead, a town at no great distance in the same county.[1] In the year 1441 eight priests were hired from Coventry to assist in celebrating a yearly obit in the church of the neighbouring priory of Maxtoke; as were six minstrels, called *mimi*, belonging to the family of Lord Clinton, who lived in the adjoining castle of Maxtoke, to sing, harp, and play, in the hall of the monastery, during the extraordinary refection allowed to the monks on that anniversary. Two shillings were given to the priests, and four to the minstrels;[2] and the latter are said to have supped in *camera picta*, or the painted chamber of the convent, with the sub-prior,[3] on which occasion the chamberlain furnished eight massy tapers of wax.[4] That the gratuities allowed to priests, even if learned, for their labours, in the same age of devotion, were extremely slender, may be collected from other expenses of this priory.[5] In the same year the prior gives sixpence for a sermon to a *doctor prædicans*, or an itinerant doctor in theology of one of the mendicant orders, who went about preaching to the religious houses.

[We have mentioned Dan Robert Saltwood, monk of St. Austin's, at Canterbury, in the reigns of Henry VII. and his successor, as the person who undertook the expense of translating and publishing *The History of King Boccus and Sydracke*. This Robert Saltwood, however, besides being an encourager of letters, was a better poet than either Caumpeden or Chestre. He produced, about 1540 or 1550, a poem in seven-line stanzas, of which only one copy is supposed to remain, entitled " A comparyson bytwene. iiii. byrdes the Larke/ the Nyghtingale/ the Thrushe/ and the Cucko/ for theyr Syngynge who should be chauntoure of the quere." This title occurs over a woodcut of a branch with four birds perched upon it. On the eighteenth leaf is the colophon: " This endythth (*sic*) the comparyson of the byrdes compyled by dan Robert Saltwood monke," &c.]

We have now arrived at the reign of Edward IV., who acceded to the throne in the year 1461. But before I proceed in my series, I will employ the remainder of this section in fixing the reader's attention on an important circumstance (now operating in its full extent, and therefore purposely reserved for this period) which greatly contributed to the improvement of our literature, and consequently of our poetry: I mean the many translations of Latin books, especially classics, which the French had been making for about the two last centuries, and were still continuing to make, into their own language. In order to do this more effectually, I will collect into one view the most distinguished of these versions: not

---

[1] Hearne's *Lib. Nig. Scacc. Append.* p. 598.
[2] *Ex Computis Prioris Priorat. de Maxtock, penes me.* "Dat. sex Mimis domini Clynton cantantibus, citharisantibus, et ludentibus, in aula in dicta Pietantia, iiii. s."
[3] "Mimis cenantibus in camera picta cum suppriore eodem tempore," [the sum obliterated.]
[4] Ex comp. Camerarii, *ut supr.*
[5] Ex comp. prædict.

solicitous about those notices on this subject which have before occurred incidentally; nor scrupulous about the charge of anticipation which, to prepare the reader, I shall perhaps incur by lengthening this inquiry, for the sake of comprehension, beyond the limits of the period just assigned. In the meantime it may be pertinent to premise that, from the close communication which formerly subsisted between England and France, manuscript copies of many of these translations, elegantly written and often embellished with the most splendid illuminations and curious miniatures, were presented by the translators or their patrons to the kings of England; and that they accordingly appear at present among the royal manuscripts in the British Museum. Some of these, however, were transcribed, if not translated, by command of our kings; and others brought into England, and placed in the royal library by John, duke of Bedford, regent of France.

It is not consistent with my design to enumerate the Latin legends, rituals, monastic rules, chronicles, and historical parts of the Bible, such as the Books of Kings and of the Maccabees, which were looked upon as stories of chivalry,[1] translated by the French before the year 1200. These soon became obsolete, and are besides too deeply tinctured with the deplorable superstition and barbarity of their age to bear a recital.[2] I will therefore begin with the thirteenth century. In the year 1210 Peter Comestor's[3] *Historia Scholastica*, a sort of breviary of the Old and New Testament, accompanied with elaborate expositions from Josephus and many pagan writers, a work compiled at Paris about the year 1175, and so popular as not only to be taught in schools, but even to be publicly read in the churches with its glosses, was translated into French by Guyart des Moulins, a canon of Aire.[4] About the same time some of the old translations into French made in the eleventh century by Thibault de Vernon, canon of Rouen, were retouched; and the Latin legends of many lives of saints, particularly of St. George, of Thomas a Becket, and the martyrdom of St. Hugh, a child murdered in 12[55] by [certain Jews] at Lincoln,[5] were reduced

---

[1] As *Plusieurs Battailes des Roys d'Israel en contre les Philistiens et Assyriens*, &c. Brit. Mus. MSS. Reg. 19 D. 1, 7.

[2] I must however except their *Lapidaire*, a poem on precious stones from the Latin of Marbodeus, [as to which, see Brunet, last edit. iii. 1391,] and the *Bestiaire* [*d'Amour*, by Richard de Fournival, written in the middle of the thirteenth century, of which there was an imitation and moralization in verse. The latter and the *Lapidaire*,] however, ought to be looked upon as efforts of their early poetry, rather than translations.

[3] Or *Le Mangeur*, because he devoured the Scriptures.

[4] The French was first published [by Antoine Verard (1499), 2 vols. folio,] with woodcuts. Vossius says that the original was abridged by Gualter Hunt, an English Carmelite, about the year 1460. *Hist. Lat.* lib. iii. c. 9, p. 197, edit. 1689. It was translated into German rhymes about 1271. Sander. *Bibl. Belg.* pag. 285. There are numerous and very sumptuous MSS. of this work in the British Museum. One of them, with exquisite paintings, was written by order of Edward IV. at Bruges, 1470. MSS. Reg. 15 D. i. Another is written in 1382. *Ibid.* 19 B. xvii.

[5] See Chaucer, *Priores T.* ver. 3193. [Everything known relative to St. Hugh

into French verse. These pieces, to which I must add a metrical version of the Bible from Genesis to Hezekiah, by being written in rhyme and easy to be sung, soon became popular, and produced the desired impression on the minds of the people.¹ They were soon followed by the version of [Ægidius di Colonna] *de Regimine Principum*,² by Henri de Gauchi. Dares Phrygius, *The Seven Sages of Rome* by Herbert, Eutropius,³ and Aristotle's *Secretum Secretorum*,⁴ appeared about the same time in French. To say nothing of voluminous versions of Pandects and feudal customs,⁵ Michel de Harnes translated Turpin's *Charlemagne* in the year 1207.⁶ It was into prose, in opposition to the practice which had long prevailed of turning Latin prose into French rhymes. This piece, in compliance with an age addicted to romantic fiction, our translator undoubtedly preferred to the more rational and sober Latin historians of Charlemagne and of France, such as Gregory of Tours, Fredegaire, and Eginart. In the year 1245 the *Speculum Mundi*, a system of theology, the seven sciences, geography, and natural philosophy,⁷ was translated at the instance of the Duke of Berry and Auvergne.⁸ Among the royal MSS. is a sort of [devotional manual,] compiled in Latin by [Brother Laurence, (Frère Lorens or *Laurentius Gallus*),] the confessor of Philip III. in 1279, and translated into French;⁹ which translation [usually known under the title of *Le Somme de Vices et de Vertus*,] Queen Isabel ordered to be placed in the church of the Innocents at Paris for the use of the people.

---

has been collected together with great industry by M. Francisque Michel, and published under the following title : " Hugues de Lincoln ; Recueil de Ballades Anglo-Normandes et Ecossoises rélatives au meurtre de cet enfant," &c. 8vo. Par Silvestre, 1834.—M.]

¹ It is rather beside my purpose to speak particularly of some of the divine offices now made French, and of the church-hymns.

² See MSS. Reg. 15 E. vi. 11 ; *ibid.* 19 B. i. ; and *ibid.* 19 A. xx. " Stephanus Fortis clericus scripsit. an. 1395."

³ He was early translated into Greek at Constantinople.

⁴ Brit. Mus. MSS. Reg. 20 B. iv. 3.

⁵ See a French Justinian, &c. Brit. Mus. MSS. Reg. 20 D. ix. 2, 3. A MS. before 1300.

⁶ Caxton printed a life of *Charles the Great*, 1485. [It is a translation from the French, but the author of the original work is not known. The Early English Text Society promises us a series of the Charlemagne romances. Mr. Shelly of Plymouth has meanwhile communicated to the present work his interesting monograph on the subject. See *infrâ*, sect. v.]

⁷ One of the most eminent astronomers in this work is the poet Virgil.

I know not when *Le Livre Royall* [a version of the treatise well known in English under the title of *The Remorse of Conscience*, of which Wynkyn de Worde printed a popular metrical epitome], was made French. The Latin original was compiled at the command of Philip le Bel, king of France, in 1279. [Epilogue] to *Caxton's Engl. Translat.* 1484. [A Kentish version, called the *Ayenbite of Inwyt*, has been edited twice; for the Roxburghe Club by Mr. Stevenson, in 1855, and for the Early English Text Society by Dr. Morris, in 1866. Several MSS. of the English work exist, but only one of this dialectic version.]

⁸ See Brit. Mus. MSS. Reg. 19 A. ix. [This agrees closely with Caxton's *Mirrour of the World*, absque nota (but 1481), Blades (ii. 82-3) notices several MSS. in verse or prose, differing in certain particulars.]

⁹ Brit. Mus. MSS. Reg. 19 C. ii. [and Cotton MS., Cleop. A, v.]

The fourteenth century was much more fertile in French translation. The spirit of devotion and indeed of this species of curiosity, raised by St. Louis, after a short intermission rekindled under John II. and Charles V. I pass over the prose and metrical translations of the Latin Bible in the years 1343 and 1380 by Macè and Raoul de Presles. Under those reigns, St. Austin, Cassianus, and Gregory the Great[1] were translated into French; and they are the first of the fathers that appeared in a modern tongue. St. Gregory's *Homilies* are by an anonymous translator.[2] His *Dialogues* were probably translated by an English ecclesiastic.[3] St. Austin's *De Civitate Dei* was translated by Raoul de Presles, who acted professedly both as confessor and translator to Charles V.[4] about the year 1374. During the work he received a yearly pension of six hundred livres from that liberal monarch, who was the first founder of a royal library in France, and at whose command it was undertaken. It is accompanied with a prolix commentary, valuable only at present as preserving anecdotes of the opinions, manners and literature of the writer's age; from which I am tempted to give the following specimen, as it strongly illustrates the ancient state of the French stage, and demonstrably proves that comedy and tragedy were now known only by name in France. He observes that comedies are so denominated from a room of entertainment, or from those places, in which banquets were accustomed to be closed with singing, called in Greek *conias:* that they were like those *jeux* or plays, which the minstrel (le chanteur) exhibits in halls or other public places, at a feast: and that they were properly styled *Interludi*, as being presented between the two courses. Tragedies, he adds, were spectacles, resembling those personages which at this day we see acting in the life and passion of a martyr.[5] This shows that only the religious drama now subsisted in France. But to proceed: the *Collationes Patrum* or *Conferences* of Cassianus, was translated by John Goulain, a Carmelite monk, about 1363. Two translations of that theological romance by Boethius, the *Consolation of Philosophy*, one by the celebrated Jean de Meun, author of the *Roman de la Rose*, existed before the year 1340. Others of the early Latin Christian writers were ordered to be turned into French by Jeanne of Navarre, about 1332. But finding that the Archbishop of Rouen, who was commissioned to execute this arduous task, did not understand Latin, she employed a Mendicant friar. About the same period, and under the same patronage, the *Legenda Aurea*, written by Jacobus de Voragine, archbishop of Genoa about the year 1260, an inexhaustible repository

---

[1] Brit. Mus. MSS. Reg. 15 D. v. 1. 2.
[2] Ibid. 15 D. v. 1, 20 D. v.
[3] It is supposed that they were rendered by an Englishman, or one living in England, as the translator's name is marked by an A. And as there is a prayer in the manuscript to St. Frideswide, an Oxford saint. *Mem. Litt.* xvii. p. 735, 4to.
[4] Brit. Mus. MSS. Reg. 17 F. iii. With pictures. And 14 D. i.
[5] Ch. viii. liv. ii.

of religious fable,[1] was translated by Jehan de Vignay, a monk hospitaller.[2] The same translator gave also a version of a famous ritual entitled *Speculum Ecclesiæ*, or the *Mirror of the Church*, of *Chefs moralifed*, written by Jacobus de Caſſolis,[3] and of the *Voyage into the East*,[4] by Odoricus. Thomas Benoit, a Prior of Sainte-Genevieve, gratified the religious with a translation into a more intelligible language of some Latin liturgic pieces about the year 1330. But his chief performance was a translation into French verse of the *Rule of St. Austin*. This he undertook merely on a principle of affection and charity, for the edification of his pious brethren who did not understand Latin:

> Pour l'amour de vous, très chers freres,
> En François ai traduit ce Latin.

And in the preface he says, " Or sçai-je que *plusieurs* de vous *n'entendent pas bien* Latin auquel il fut chose neceſſaire de la rieule [regle] *entendre*." Benoit's succeſſor in the priorate of Sainte-Genevieve was not equally attentive to the discipline and piety of his monks. Instead of translating monkiſh Latin, and enforcing the salutary regulations of St. Austin, he wrote a system of rules for ballad-writing (L'Art de dictier Ballades et Rondels), the first Art of Poetry that ever appeared in France.

Among the moral books now translated, I must not omit the *Spirituelle Amitie* of John of Meun, from the Latin of Aldred [Ailred, or Ethelred, a Cistercian monk of Rievaux, an abbey in the North Riding of York. He was born in 1109, died in 1166, and was canonized in 1191. He produced a large variety of works, besides the present.][5] In the same style of mystic piety was the treatife of Consolation, written in Latin by Vincent de Beauvais, and translated in the year 1374. In the year 1340, Henri de Suson, a German dominican and a mystic doctor, wrote a most comprehensive treatise called *Horologium Sapientiæ*. This was translated into French by a monk of Saint François.[6] Even the officers of the court of Charles V. were seized with the ardour of translating religious pieces, no less than the ecclesiastics. The most elegant tract of moral Latinity translated into French was the celebrated book of our countryman, John of Salisbury, *De Nugis Curialium*. This version was made by Denis Soulechart, a learned

---

[1] In the year 1555, the learned Claude Espence was obliged to make a public recantation for calling it *Legenda Ferrea*. Thuan. *sub ann*. Laun. *Hist. Gymnas. Navarr*. pp. 704, 297.

[2] Brit. Mus. MSS. Reg. 19 B. xvii. The copy was written 1382. This version [is] the same which Caxton translated and printed [three times.] While it was printing, William Lord Arundel, [at whose command Caxton undertook it,] gave Caxton annually a buck in summer and a doe in winter.

[3] Brit. Mus. MSS. Reg. 19 C. xi. i. This version was translated into English, and printed by Caxton.

[4] *Ibid*. 19 D. i. 4. 5.

[5] [Wright's *Biographia Britannica Literaria*, Anglo-Saxon period, p. 187, *et seqq*.]

[6] [This is a different work from the *Doctrinal of Sapyence*, printed by Caxton in 1489.]

Cordelier, about the year 1360. Notwithstanding the Epistles of Abelard and Eloisa, not only from the celebrity of Abelard as a Parisian theologist, but on account of the interesting history of that unfortunate pair, must have been as commonly known, and as likely to be read in the original, as any Latin book in France, they were translated into French in this century by John of Meun, who prostituted his abilities, when he relinquished his own noble inventions, to interpret the pedantries of monks, schoolmen, and proscribed classics. I think he also translated Vegetius, who will occur again.[1] In the library of Sainte-Genevieve, there is, in a sort of system of religion, a piece called *Jerarchie*, translated from Latin into French at the command of our Queen Eleanor, in the year 1297, by a French friar.[2] I must not however forget, that amidst this profusion of treatises of religion and instruction, civil history found a place. That immense chaos of events real and fictitious, the *Historical Mirror* of Vincent de Beauvais, was translated by Jehan de Vignay above mentioned.[3] One is not surprised that the translator of the *Golden Legend* should make no better choice.

The desolation produced in France[4] by the victorious armies of the English was instantly succeeded by a flourishing state of letters. King John, having indulged his devotion and satisfied his conscience by procuring numerous versions of books written on sacred subjects, at length turned his attention to the classics. His ignorance of Latin was a fortunate circumstance, as it produced a curiosity to know the treasures of Latin literature. He employed Pierre Bercheur, Prior of Saint Eloi at Paris, an eminent theologist, to translate Livy into French;[5] notwithstanding that author had been anathematised by Pope Gregory. But so judicious a choice [may have been] dictated by Petrarch, who regarded Livy with a degree of enthusiasm, who was now resident at the court of France, and who perhaps condescended to direct and superintend the translation. The translator, in his Latin work called *Repertorium* (a sort of general dictionary, in which all things are proved to be allegorical, and reduced to a moral meaning), under the word Roma records this great attempt in the following manner: " Titum Livium, ad requi-

---

[1] There is a copy written in [1384,] Brit. Mus. MSS. Reg. 20 B. xv. Often, *ibid.* John of Meun is also said to have translated *Mirabilia Hiberniæ*.

[2] " Cette *Jerarchie* translata frere Jehan de Pentham de Latin en Françoys, à la requeste la reine d'Engleterre Alienore femme le roy Edward." There is also this note in the manuscript. " Cest livre resigna frere Jordan de Kyngestone à la commune des freres Menurs de Southampton, par la volunte du graunt frere Willame Notington [f. Northington in Hampshire,] ministre d'Engleterre... l'an. de grace M.CCC.XVII."

[3] Brit. Mus. MSS. Reg. 14 E. i.

[4] A curious picture of the distracted state of France is recorded by Petrarch. The king, with the Dauphin, returning from his captivity in England, in passing through Picardy, was obliged to make a pecuniary bargain with the numerous robbers that infested that country, to travel unmolested. *Vie de Petr.* iii. 543.

[5] See Henault. *Nouvel. Abreg. Hist. Fr.* p. 229, edit. 1752. And *Vie de Petrarque*, iii. 547.

sitionem domini Johannis inclyti Francorum regis, non sine labore et sudoribus in linguam Gallicam transtuli."[1] To this translation we must join those of Sallust, Lucan and Cæsar: all which seem to have been finished before the year 1365. This revival of a taste for Roman history [which, after all, can hardly have been very powerfully] propagated by Petrarch during his short stay in the French court, immediately produced a Latin historical compilation called *Romuleon* by an anonymous gentleman of France, who soon found it necessary to translate his work into the vernacular language. Valerius Maximus could not remain long untranslated. A version of that favourite author, begun by Simon de Hesdin, a monk, in 1364, was finished by Nicolas de Gonesse, a master in theology, 1401.[2] Under the last-mentioned reign, Ovid's *Metamorphoses moralised*[3] were translated by Guillaume de Nangis: and the same poem was translated into French verse, at the request of Jeanne de Bourbon, afterwards consort of Charles V. by Philip de Vitri, bishop of Meaux, Petrarch's friend who was living in 1361.[4] A bishop would not have undertaken this work, had he not perceived much moral doctrine couched under the pagan stories. Jean le Fevre, by command of Charles V. translated the poem *De Vetula*, falsely ascribed to Ovid.[5] Cicero's *Rhetorica* appeared in French, translated by Jean de Antioche, at the request of one Friar William, in the year 1383. About the same time, some of Aristotle's pieces were translated from Latin; his *Problems* by Evrard de Conti, physician to Charles V.; and his *Ethics* and *Politics* by Nicole d'Oresme, while canon of Rouen. This was the most learned man in France, and tutor to

---

[1] This was the translation of Livy which, with other books, the Duke of Bedford, regent of France, about 1425 sent into England to Humphrey, duke of Gloucester. The copy had been a present to the King of France. *Mem. Litt.* ii. 747, 4to. See the third *Dissertation*. In the Sorbonne library at Paris, there is a most valuable MS. of this version in two folio volumes. In the front of each book are various miniatures and pictures, most beautifully finished. Dan. Maichel, *de Bibliothec. Paris.* p. 79. There is a copy, transcribed about the time the translation was finished (Brit. Mus. MSS. Reg. 15 D. vi.): *Des Fais de Romains*. With pictures.

[2] Brit. Mus. MSS. Reg. 18 E. iii. iv. With elegant delineations, and often in the same library.

[3] [See *supra*, vol. i. p. 216.]

[4] There was a French Ovid in Duke Humphrey's library at Oxford. See *supra*. And Brit. Mus. MSS. Reg. 17 E. iv. 1. [Warton supposed that this might be the version of which Caxton executed an English prose translation, at present known only in an imperfect MS. in the Pepysian. The latter, such as it is, has been printed for the Roxburghe Club, 1819. It is to be observed that, in some old lists of Caxton's publications, this book is entered as printed in 1479; but no copy has ever come to light.]

[5] Leyserus supposes this piece to be the forgery of one Leo Protonotarius, an officer in the court at Constantinople, who writes the preface. *Hist. Poet. Med. Æv.* p. 2089. He proves the work supposititious, from its several Arabicisms and scriptural expressions, &c. Bradwardine cites many lines from it, *Advers. Pelag.* p. 33. As does Bacon, in his astrological tracts. It is condemned by Bede as heretical (in Boeth. de Trinit.) Selden intended a *Dissertation* on this forgery, *De Synedr.* iii. 16. It is in hexameters, in three books.

Charles V. who, in confequence of his inftructions, obtained a competent fkill in Latin and the rules of grammar.¹ Other Greek claffics, which had become known by being tranflated into Latin, were ftill more familiarifed, efpecially to general readers, by being turned into French. Thus the recent Latin verfion of Xenophon's *Cyropædia*, by Poggius, was tranflated into French by Vafque de Lucerie, 1370.² The *Tactics* of Vegetius, an author who frequently confounds the military practices of his own age with thofe of antiquity, appeared under the title of [*L'Art de Cheualerie felon Vegece*, &c.] by Chriftin[e de Pife].³ Petrarch's work *De Remediis utriufque Fortunæ*, a fet of Latin dialogues, was tranflated, not only by Nicole d'Orefme, but by two of the officers of the royal houfehold,⁴ in compliment to Petrarch at his leaving France.⁵ Many philofophical pieces, particularly in aftrology of which Charles V. was remarkably fond, were tranflated before the end of the fourteenth century. Among thefe, I muft not pafs over the *Quadripartitum* of Ptolemy by d'Orefme; the *Agricultura*,⁶ or *Libri ruralium Commodorum* of Peter de Crefcentiis, a phyfician of Bologna, about the year 1285, by a namelefs friar-preacher;⁷ and the book *De Proprietatibus Rerum* of Bartholomeus Glanvill, the Pliny of the monks, by John Corbichon, an Auguftine monk.⁸ I have feen a French MS. of Guido di Colonna's Trojan romance, the hand-writing of which belongs to this century.⁹

---

¹ Chriftin. *Vie Charles V.*
² Brit. Mus. MSS Reg. 17 E. v. 1; and 16 G. ix. with pictures.
³ MSS. Reg. 19 B. xviii. &c. [And compare Brunet, v. 1111.] Vegetius was early tranflated into all the modern languages. There is an Englifh one, probably by John Trevifa, as it is addreffed to his patron Lord Berkeley, A.D. 1408. MSS. Digb. 233, *Princ.* "In olde tyme it was the manere." There is a tranflation of Vegetius, written at Rhodes, "die 25 Octobris, 1459, per Johannem Newton." ad calc. Bibl. Bodl. Laud. K. 53. Chriftine's verfion was tranflated and printed by Caxton, 1489. ⁴ See Niceron, tom. 28, p. 384.
⁵ Lebeuf fays Seneca inftead of Petrarch. *Mem. Litt.* xvii. p. 752. I muft not forget to obferve, that feveral whole books in Brunetto's *Teforo* confift of tranflations from Ariftotle, Tully, and Pliny, into French. Brunetto [Latini] was a Florentine, and the mafter of Dante. He died in 1295. The *Teforo* was a fort of Encyclopedia, exhibiting a courfe of practical and theoretic philofophy, of divinity, cofmography, geography, hiftory, facred and profane, phyfics, ethics, rhetoric, and politics. It was written in French by Brunetto during his refidence in France: but [it was afterwards tranflated into Latin by Buonu Giamboni, which verfion was publifhed at Trevifo in 1474;] and it has been tranflated by others into Latin. It was the model and foundation of [Glanvill's *Proprietates Rerum*,] of Bercheur's *Repertorium*, and of many other works of the fame fpecies, which foon followed. See Brit. Mus. MSS. Reg. 17 E. i. [The original French ftill remains unprinted.]
⁶ *Des Prouffitz champeftres et ruraux.* Brit. Mus. MSS. Reg. 14 E.
⁷ In twelve books. See Jacob. Quetif. tom. i. p. 666.
⁸ Leland fays, that this tranflation is elegant; and that he faw it in Duke Humfrey's library at Oxford. *Script. Brit.* cap. ccclxviii. See Brit. Mus. MSS. Reg. 17 E. iii. With pictures. *Ibid.* 15 E. ii. Where the tranflation is affigned to the year 1362, and the writing of the MS. to 1482. With pictures.
⁹ Brit Mus. MSS. Reg. 16 F. ix. Caxton's *Godefroy of Bologne*, tranflated from the French, and printed 1481, had a Latin original. The French, a fine copy, is in Brit. Mus. MSS. Reg 17 F. v. &c.

In the fifteenth century it became fashionable among the French to polish and reform their old rude translations made two hundred years before; and to reduce many of their metrical versions into prose. At the same time, the rage of translating ecclesiastical tracts began to decrease. The latter circumstance was partly owing to the introduction of better books, and partly to the invention of printing. Instead of procuring laborious and expensive translations of the ancient fathers, the printers, who multiplied greatly towards the close of this century, found their advantage in publishing new translations of more agreeable books, or in giving ancient versions in a modern dress.[1] Yet in this century some of the more recent doctors of the church were translated. Not to mention the Epistles of St. Jerom, which Antoine Dufour, a Dominican friar, presented in French to Anne de Bretagne, consort to King Charles VIII., we find St. Anselm's *Cur Deus Homo*,[2] the *Lamentations of St. Bernard*, the *Sum of Theology* of Albertus Magnus, the *Prick of Divine Love* of St. Bonaventure, a seraphic doctor,[3] with other pieces of the kind, exhibited in the French language before the year 1480, at the petition and under the patronage of many devout duchesses. Yet in the meantime, the lives of saints and sacred history gave way to a species of narrative more entertaining and not less fabulous. Little more than Josephus, and a few *Martyrdoms*, were now translated from the Latin into French.

The truth is, the French translators of this century were chiefly employed on profane authors. At its commencement, a French

---

[1] I take this opportunity of observing, that one of these was the romance of *Sir Lancelot du Lac*, translated from the Latin by Robert de Borron, at the command of our Henry II. See *supra*, sect. 3. This new Lancelot is [substantially] the same which was printed at Paris by Antony Verard, 1494, in three vast folio volumes. Another is the romance of *Gyron le Courtois*, translated also from Latin, at the command of the same monarch, by Lucus or Luce, *chevalier du Chateau du Gast*, or *Gat*, or *Gal*, and printed by Verard as above. See Lenglet, *Bibl. Rom.* ii. p. 117. See *supra*, sect. 3.

[See on this subject the excellent work of M. Paris, *Les Manuscrits François de la Bibliothèque du Roi*, 8vo. *Par. Techener*, 1836-48, i. pp. 167-177, 209-211.—M.]

[Mr. W., says Ritson, should have proved that the romance of *Lancelot* had existed in *Latin*, before he mentioned it as a translation from that tongue. MS. note and Obs.—*Park*.]

[2] Written in 1098.

[3] He flourished in Italy, about the year 1270. The enormous magnificence of his funeral deserves notice more than any anecdote of his life; as it paints the high devotion of the times, and the attention formerly paid to theological literature. There were present Pope Gregory X., the Emperor of Greece by several Greek noblemen his proxies, Baldwin II. the Latin emperor, James, king of Arragon, the patriarchs of Constantinople and Antioch, all the cardinals, five hundred bishops and archbishops, sixty abbots, more than a thousand prelates and priests of lower rank, the ambassadors of many kings and potentates, the deputies of the Tartars and other nations, and an innumerable concourse of people of all orders and degrees. The sepulchral ceremonies were celebrated with the most consummate pomp, and the funeral oration was pronounced by a future pope. *Miræi Auctar. Script. Eccles.* p. 72, edit. Fabric. [See *supra*]

abridgment of the three first decads of Livy was produced by Henri Romain, a canon of Tournay. In the year 1416, Jean de Courci, a knight of Normandy, gave a translation of some Latin chronicle, a history of the Greeks and Romans, entitled, *Bouquassiere.* In 1403, Jean de Courteauisse, a doctor in theology at Paris, translated Seneca on the *Four Cardinal Virtues.*[1] Under the reign of King Charles VII. Jean Cossa translated the *Chronology* of Mattheus Palmerius, a learned Florentine, and a writer of Italian poetry in imitation of Dante. In the dedication to Jeanne III., queen of Jerusalem, and among other titles Countess of Provence, the translator apologises for supposing her highness to be ignorant of Latin; when at the same time he is fully convinced, that a lady endowed with so much natural grace must be perfectly acquainted with that language. "Mais pour ce que le vulgar Françoys est plus commun, j'ai pris peine y translater ladite oeuvre." Two other translations were offered to Charles VII. in the year 1445. One, of the *First Punic War* of Leonard of Arezzo, an anonymous writer, who does not choose to publish his name *à cause de sa petitesse;* and the *Stratagems* of Frontinus, often cited by John of Salisbury, and mentioned in the Epistles of Peter of Blois,[2] by Jean de Rouroy, a Parisian theologist. Under Louis XI., Sebastian Mamerot of Soissons, in the year 1466, attempted a new translation of the *Romuleon;* and he professes, that he undertook it solely with a view of improving or decorating the French language.[3]

Many French versions of classics appeared in this century. A translation of Quintus Curtius is dedicated to Charles, duke of Burgundy, in 1468.[4] Six years afterwards, the same liberal patron commanded Cæsar's *Commentaries* to be translated by Jean du Chesne.[5] Terence was made French by Guillaume Rippe, the king's secretary, in the year 1466. The following year a new translation of Ovid's *Metamorphoses* was executed by an ecclesiastic of Normandy. But Laurent Premierfait, mentioned above, translated (from the Latin), the *Oeconomics* of Aristotle, and Cicero *De Amicitia* and *De Senectute,* before the year 1420.[6] He is said also to have trans-

---

[1] It is supposititious. It was forged, about the year 560, by Martianus an archbishop of Portugal, whom Gregory of Tours calls the most eminent writer of his time. *Hist. Franc.* v. 38. It was a great favourite of the theological ages.

[2] *Epist.* 94.

[3] I am not sure whether this is not much the same as *Le Grande Histoire Cesar,* &c. Taken from Lucan, Suetonius, Orosius, &c. Written at Bruges at the command of our Edward IV. in 1479. That is, ordered to be *written* by him. A manuscript with pictures. MSS. Reg. 17, F. ii. 1. Brit. Mus. But see ibid. *Romeleon, ou des Faits des Romains,* in ten books. With pictures. MSS. Reg. 19, E. v. See also 20 C i. [Bruges seems to have been a shop for this kind of work long after printing had been discovered.—*Ashby.*]

[4] Brit. Mus. MSS. Reg. 17 F. i. With beautiful pictures.

[5] Ibid. Reg. 16, G. viii. With pictures. Another appeared by Robert Gaguin in 1485.

[6] The two latter versions were translated into English by William Botoner and John Tiptoft, earl of Worcester, and printed by Caxton, 1481. Botoner presented

lated some pieces, perhaps the *Epistles*, of Seneca. Encouraged by this example, Jean de Luxembourgh, Laurence's contemporary, translated Tully's Oration against Verres. I must not forget that Hippocrates and Galen were translated from Latin into French in the year 1429. The translator was Jean Tourtier, surgeon to the Duke of Bedford, then Regent of France; and he humbly supplicates Rauoul Palvin, confessor and physician to the duchess, and John Major, first physician to the duke, and graduate *en l'estuao d'Auxonford*,[1] and Master Roullan, physician and astronomer of the university of Paris, amicably to amend the faults of this translation, which is intended to place the science and practice of medicine on a new foundation. I presume it was from a Latin version that the *Iliad*, about this period, was translated into French metre.

Among other pieces that might be enumerated in this century, in the year 1412, Guillaume de Tignonville, provost of Paris, translated the *Dicta Philosophorum*.[c] This version was translated into English by Lord Rivers, and printed by Caxton, 1477. [The same noble author executed an English translation of a small piece by Christine de Pise, entitled *Les Prouerbes Moraux*, of which there is a copy, with other productions from her pen, in Harl. MS. 4431. The version by Lord Rivers is called *The morale prouerbes of Cristyne*, and was printed by Caxton in February, " the cold season," 1477-8.[3] This is one of the stanzas:

> There is noo thinge so riche I you enseur
> As the seruice of gode oure createur
> Litle vailleth goode exemple to see
> For him that wole not the contraire flee
> Though that the deeth to vs be lamentable,
> Hit to remembre is thinge moost conuenable.

These lines may not appear very remarkable in quality or interest, yet the original writer was unquestionably a woman of great attainments, and was regarded by the succeeding literary generation in France at least with respect. Clement Marot says of her:—

---

his manuscript copy to William of Waynflete, bishop of Winchester, in 1473. Caxton's English *Cato*, printed 1483, was from the French [of Premierfait. His version of *Æsop* came from the same source; it was printed in 1483.] Crucimanius mentions [the] version of Seneca by Premierfait, as printed at Paris in 1500. *Bibl. Gall.* p. 287. A translation of Seneca *De quatuor Virtutibus Cardinalibus*, but supposititious, is given to Premierfait, Brit. Mus. MSS. Reg. 20 A. xii. Sanders recites the *Epistles* of Seneca, translated into French by some anonymous writer, at the command of Messire Barthelemi Siginulfe, a nobleman of Naples. *Bibl. Cathedr. Tornacens.* p. 209. Pieces of Seneca have been frequently translated into French, and very early. [See Brunet, art. *Seneca*.]

[1] Oxford.
[2] Brit. Mus. MSS. Reg. 19 A. viii. Sæpius *ibid*.
[3] [Blades, ii. 47-8. The volume occupies only four leaves folio. The only original production of Lord Rivers seems to be a ballad of four stanzas, preserved by Rous (*Hist.* edit. Hearne, p. 213. See Leland, *Itin.* ed. 1745.)

"d'avoir le prix en science et en doctrine
Bien merita de Pisan la Christine
Durant ses jours."¹]

About the same time, but before 1427, Jean de Guerre translated a Latin compilation of all that was marvellous in Pliny, Solinus, and the *Otia Imperialia*, a book abounding in wonders, of our countryman Gervase of Tilbury.² The French romance, entitled *L'Assaillant*, was now translated from the Latin chronicles of the kings of Cologne: and the Latin tract *De Bonis Moribus* of Jacobus Magnus, confessor to Charles VII., about the year 1422, was made French. Rather earlier, [Lawrence] de Premierfait, translated *Boccaccio de Casibus Virorum Illustrium*.³ Nor shall I be thought to deviate too far from my detail, which is confined to Latin originals, when I mention here a book, the translation of which into French conduced in an eminent degree to circulate materials for poetry: this is Boccaccio's *Decameron*, which Premierfait also translated at the command of Jeanne of Navarre (who seems to have made no kind of conditions about suppressing the licentious stories), in the year 1414.⁴

I am not exactly informed when the *Eneid* of Virgil was translated into a sort of [prose] romance or history of *Eneas*, under the title of [*Le livre des Eneides*]. But that translation was printed at Lyons in 1483, and appears to have been finished not many years before. Among the translator's historical additions, are the description of the first foundation of Troy by Priam, and the succession of Ascanius and his descendants after the death of Turnus. He introduces a digression upon Boccaccio, for giving in his *Fall of Princes* an account of the death of Dido, different from that in the fourth book of the *Eneid*. Among his omissions, he passes over Eneas's descent into hell, as a tale manifestly forged, and not to be believed by any rational reader; as if many other parts of the translator's story were not equally fictitious and incredible.⁵

---

¹ [*History of the Venetian Republic*, 1860, iv. 198, 368-9.]
² He flourished about the year [1183].
³ This version was [translated by Lydgate, and printed in 1494, &c., as already mentioned.]
⁴ See Brit. Mus. MSS. Reg. 19 E. 1. It was printed at Paris [in 1485, &c. See Brunet, i. 1004-6. Another translation by Antoine de Maçon appeared in 1545, and others later.]
In [the second edition issued by Verard, but not in that by the same printer in 1485] of Premierfait's translation of the *Decameron*, it is said to be translated from Latin into French. But *Latin* here means *Italian*. Hence a mistake arose, that Boccaccio wrote his *Decameron* in Latin. The Italian, as I have before observed, was anciently called *Il volgare Latino*. Thus the French romance of *Meliadus de Leonnois* is said to be *translaté du Latin*, by Rusticien de Pise : edit. 1532. Thus also *Gyron le Courtois* is called a version from the Latin. M. de la Monnoye observes, "Que quand on trouve que certains vieux Romans ont été traduits de Latin en François, par Luces de Salesberies, Robert de Borron, Rusticien de Pise, ou autres, cela signifie que ç'a été d'Italien en François." *Rem. au Bibl. Fr.* du La Croix du Maine, &c. tom. ii. p. 33, edit. 1772. Premierfait's French *Decameron* is a most wretched caricature of the original.
⁵ [" C'est probablement d'après cette paraphrase anonyme que Caxton a donné

The conclusion intended to be drawn from this long digression is obvious. By means of these French translations, our countrymen, who understood French much better than Latin, became acquainted with many useful books which they would not otherwise have known. With such assistances, a commodious access to the classics was opened, and the knowledge of ancient literature facilitated and familiarised in England, at a much earlier period than is imagined; and at a time, when little more than the productions of speculative monks and irrefragable doctors could be obtained or were studied. Very few Englishmen, I will venture to pronounce, had read Livy, before the translation of Bercheur was imported by the regent Duke of Bedford. It is certain that many of the Roman poets and historians were now read in England in the original. But the Latin language was for the most part confined to a few ecclesiastics. When these authors, therefore, appeared in a language almost as intelligible as the English, they fell into the hands of illiterate and common readers, and contributed to sow the seeds of a national erudition, and to form a popular taste. Even the French versions of the religious, philosophical, historical, and allegorical compositions of those more enlightened Latin writers who flourished in the middle ages, had their use, till better books came into vogue: pregnant as they were with absurdities, they communicated instruction on various and new subjects, enlarged the field of information, and promoted the love of reading, by gratifying that growing literary curiosity which now began to want materials for the exercise of its operations. How greatly our poets in general availed themselves of these treasures, we may collect from this circumstance only: even such writers as Chaucer and Lydgate, men of education and learning, when they translate a Latin author, appear to execute their work through the medium of a French version. It is needless to pursue this history of French translation any farther. I have given my reason for introducing it at all. In the next age, a great and universal revolution in literature ensued; and the English themselves began to turn their thoughts to translation.

These French versions enabled Caxton, our first printer, to enrich the state of letters in this country with many [*comparatively*] valuable publications. He found it no difficult task, either by himself or by the help of his friends, to turn a considerable number of these pieces into English, which he printed. Ancient learning had as yet made too little progress among us to encourage this enterprising and industrious artist to publish the Roman authors in their original language: and had not the French furnished him with these materials, it is not likely that Virgil, Ovid, Cicero, and many other good writers would by the means of his press have been circulated in the English tongue, so early as the close of the fifteenth century.

It is, however, remarkable that from the year 147[2, about which

l'Eneide en anglois, imprimée en 1490." — Brunet, *Manuel*, last edit. v. 1304. Compare *Blades*, ii. 222.]

time] Caxton began to print, down to the year 1540, during which period the English press flourished greatly under the conduct of many industrious, ingenious, and even learned artists, only the very few following classics, some of which hardly deserve that name, were printed in England. These were [Cicero *De Senectute* and *De Amicitiâ*, printed by Caxton in 1481; Boethius *De Consolatione Philosophiæ*, printed by Caxton before 1479; the prose *Æsop*, also printed by Caxton; the prose *Eneid*, from the same press, in 1490; and Cicero *De Officiis*, translated by Robert Whittinton, and printed in 1534. The metrical *Æsop* from Wynkyn de Worde's press; *Terence* with the Gloss of Ascensius, 1503 and 1504, the *Bucolics* of Virgil, 1512, 1529, and 1533, and the *Seneca* of 1529 were the original Latin.] The University of Oxford, during this period, produced only the first book of Tully's *Epistles*, at the charge of Cardinal Wolsey, [if at least an edition published about 1520 be really from an Oxford press, as has been supposed]. Cambridge did not yield a single classic.

No Greek book, of any kind, had yet appeared from an English press. I believe the first Greek characters used in any work printed in England are in Linacer's translation of Galen *De Temperamentis*, printed at Cambridge in 1521. A few Greek words and abbreviatures are here and there introduced. The printer was John Siberch, a German and friend of Erasmus; he styles himself "primus utriusque linguæ in Anglia impressor." There are Greek characters in some of his other books of this date. But he printed no entire Greek book. In Linacer's treatise *De emendata Structura Latini Sermonis*, printed by Pinson in 1524, many Greek characters are intermixed. In the sixth book are seven Greek lines together. But the printer apologises for his imperfections and unskilfulness in the Greek types which, he says, were but recently cast, and not in a sufficient quantity for such a work. The passage is curious.[1] About the same period of the English press, the same embarrassments appear to have happened with regard to Hebrew types, which yet were more likely, as that language was so much less known. In the year 1524 Dr. Robert Wakefield, chaplain to Henry VIII., published his *Oratio de laudibus et utilitate trium linguarum: Arabicæ, Chaldaicæ, et Hebraicæ*, &c. The printer was Wynkyn de Worde; and the author complains that he was obliged to omit his whole third part, because the printer had no Hebrew types. Some few Hebrew and Arabic characters, however, are introduced, but extremely rude, and evidently cut in wood. They are the first of the sort used in England. This learned orientalist was instrumental in preserving, at the dissolution of monasteries, the Hebrew MSS. of Ramsey Abbey, collected by Holbech, one of the monks, together with Holbech's *Hebrew Dictionary*.[2]

---

[1] "Æquo animo feras siquæ literæ, in exemplis Hellenismi, vel tonis vel spiritibus careant. His enim non satis instructus erat typographus, videlicet recens ab eo fusis characteribus Græcis, nec parata ei copia qua ad hoc agendum opus est."

[2] Wood, *Hist. Ant. Univ. Oxon.* ii. 251. Leland, *Scriptor.* v. *Holbeccus*.

It was a circumstance favourable at least to English literature, owing indeed to the general illiteracy of the times, that our first printers were so little employed on books written in the learned languages. Almost all Caxton's books are English. The multiplication of English copies multiplied English readers, and these again produced new vernacular writers. The existence of a press induced many persons to turn authors, who were only qualified to write in their native tongue.

To some part of the reign of Henry [VI. belongs] the *Tournament of Tottenham, or the wooing, winning, and wedding of Tibbe the Reeve's Daughter there*.[1] It was published from an ancient MS. in 1631, and reduced to a more modern style, by William Bedwell, rector of Tottenham, and one of the translators of the Bible. He says it was written by Gilbert Pilkington, supposed to have been rector of the same parish, and author of an unknown tract, called *Passio Domini Jesu*. But Bedwell, without the least comprehension of the scope and spirit of the piece, imagines it to be a serious narrative of a real event, and (with as little sagacity) believes it to have been written before the year 1330. Allowing that it might originate from a real event, and that there might be some private and local abuse at the bottom, it is impossible that the poet could be serious. Undoubtedly the chief merit of this poem, although not destitute of humour, consists in the design rather than the execution. As Chaucer, in the *Rime of Sir Thopas*, travestied the romances of chivalry, the *Tournament of Tottenham* is a burlesque on the parade and fopperies of chivalry itself. In this light, it may be considered as a curiosity, and does honour to the good sense and discernment of the writer who, seeing through the folly of these fashionable exercises, was sensible at the same time that they were too popular to be attacked by the more solid weapons of reason and argument. Even on a supposition that here is an allusion to real facts and characters, and that it was intended to expose some popular story of the amours of the daughter of the Reve of Tottenham, we must acknowledge that the satire is conveyed in an ingenious mode. He has introduced a parcel of clowns and rustics, the inhabitants of Tottenham, Islington, Highgate, and Hackney (places then not quite so polished as at present),[2] who imitate all the solemnities of the bar-

---

[1] MSS. *Harl.* 5396. [One of the entries in this MS. is dated the 34th year of Henry VI. or 1456. There can be no doubt that the poem is of equal antiquity.—*Price.* The Rev. Wilhelm Bedwell, who published the *Tournament of Tottenham* from an ancient MS. in 1631, 4to. says in his epistle to the reader, " It is now seven or eight years since I came to the sight of the copy, and that by the meanes of the worthy and my much honoured good friend, M. George Withers; of whom also, now at length, I have obtained the use of the same. And because the verse was then by him (a man of so exquisite judgement in this kinde of learning) much commended, as also for the thing it seife, I thought it worth while to transcribe it and to make it public." &c.—*Park.* The MS. in question is now in the Public Library at Cambridge.]

[2] [Here Dr. Ashby remarks that Tottenham, &c. were always as near the capital, and consequently as much so then as now, comparatively. But what is more to the point, and as true as strange, the lower classes are little better than those of the same rank at a greater distance.—*Park.*]

riers. The whole is a mock parody on the challenge, the various events of the encounter, the exhibition of the prize, the devices and escutcheons, the display of arms, the triumphant procession of the conqueror, the oath before the combat, and the splendid feast which followed, with every other ceremony and circumstance which constituted the regular tournament. The reader will form an idea of the work from a short extract.[1]

> [He that berys hym best in the turnament,
> He shal be graunted the gre by the comyn assent,
> For to wynne my do3ter with du3tynesse of dent,
> And coppull my brode hen that was bro3t out of Kent,
>   And my donned cow:
>   For no spence wille I spare,
>   For no catell wille I care,
>   He shalle haue my gray mare,
>   And my spottyd sowe.
>
> Ther was mony a bolde lad theire bodys to bede,
> Than thei toke theire leue, and hamwarde thei 3ede:
> And alle the weke afterward thei graythed her wede,
> Tille hit come to the day that thei shulde do thaire dede.
>   Thei armyd theym in mattes:
>   Thei sett on theire nollys
>   Gode blake bollys,
>   For to kepe theire pollis,
>   From batteryng of battes.
>
> Thei sewed hem in schepe skynnes, for thei shuld not brest:
> And euer ilkon of hem toke a blac hatte instidde of a crest
> A baskett or a panyer be fore on thaire brest,
> And a flayle in theire honde: for to fy3t prest.
>   Forth con thei fare:
>   Ther was kid micull fors,
>   Who shulde best fend his cors:
>   He that hade no gode hors,
>   Borrowyd hym a mare.]

[In the Cambridge MS. however, of the *Tournament*, there is a sequel entitled *The Feest*. It is in the same vein of burlesque as the remainder of the poem:

> Then come in the fruture,
>   With a nobul sauoure,
>   With feterloks fried:
> And alle the cart wheles of Kent,
>   With stonys of the payment,
>   Full wel were thei tried.

Such humour is, it must be owned, somewhat dreary, and if the antiquity of the production is no longer a point of doubt, at least its merit must always remain so.]

To this period belong two persons who had the same name in common, and who have been consequently confounded[2] — two

---

[1] [The whole of the poem is republished in *Rem. of E. P. P. of Engl.* iii.]
[2] The *Myrrour of Life*, ascribed to Hampole, and the poem quoted above in the text, are one and the same. The true author is ascertained by the following lines at the end, taken from MS. Reg. 17, c. viii.:

writers known as William of Naſſyngton. One wrote a treatiſe *De Trinitate et Unitate*; the other, who was a proctor in the eccleſiaſtical court at York, tranſlated into Engliſh John de Waldenby's *Myrrour of Life*, of which there is a MS. dated 1418, in MS. Reg. 17 C. viii., the author was] an Auguſtine friar of Yorkſhire, a ſtudent in the Auguſtine convent at Oxford, the provincial of his order in England, and a ſtrenuous champion againſt the doctrines of Wickliffe.[1] [I am] tempted to tranſcribe the few following lines from Naſſyngton's prologue [to his *Mirror of Life*][2] as they convey an idea of our poet's character, record the titles of ſome old popular romances, and diſcover ancient modes of public amuſement:

> I warne you firſte at the begynnynge,
> That I will make no vayne carpynge,
> Of dedes of armes, ne of amours,
> As does mynſtrellis and geſtours,
> That maketh carpynge in many a place
> Of Octoviane and Iſenbrace,
> And of many other Geſtes,
> And namely when they come to feſtes;
> Ne of the lyf of Bevys of Hamptoune,
> That was a knyght of grete renoune:
> Ne of ſyr Gye of Warwyke, &c.

Our tranſlator in theſe verſes formally declares his intention of giving his reader no entertainment, and diſavows all concern with ſecular vanities, eſpecially thoſe unedifying tales of love and arms, which were the cuſtomary themes of other poets, and the delight of an idle age.[3] I will tranſcribe a few more dull lines:

> *Latyn* als, I trowe, canne nane
> Bot thaſe that it of ſcole hane tane,
> Some canne *frankes* and *latyn*
> That hanes vſed covrte and dwelled theryn,
> And ſom canne o *latyn* a party
> That canne *frankes* bot febely,

> "Now wille I na mare ſay;
> ȝe that have herde, I you pray
> That ȝe wald pray ſpecialy
> For Freere Johan ſaule of Waldby,
> That faſt ſtudyd day and nyght,
> And made this tale in Latyne right, &c.
> Prayes alſo wᵗ deucion
> For William ſaule of Naſſyngtone,
> That gaf hym als fulle beſyly
> Night and day to grete ſtudy
> And made this tale in Inglys tonge,
> Prayes for hyme old and ȝonge."

The poem in the Lincoln MS., A. i. 17, is quite a different work, and only conſiſts of about 440 ſhort lines. It commences:

> "O! Lord God of myghtes moſte,
> Fadere and Sone and Holy Goſte."—M.]

---

[1] Wood, *Ant. Univ. Oxon.* i. 117.
[2] See alſo MSS. Reg. 17 C. viii. p. 2.
[3] [See MSS. Bodl. 48, p. 47, a. And *ibid.* MSS. Langb. 5, p. 64.]

> And fom vnderftandes in *inglys*
> That canne nother *latyn* ne *frankys*,
> But lered and lewed alde and younge
> All vnderftandes *inglyfche* tounge
> Thare fore I halde it mafte fyker thon
> To fchewe that langage that ilk a man konne,
> And for all lewed men namely
> Thet can no maner of clergy,
> To kenne thanne what ware mafte nede.
> For clerkes canne bathe fe and rede, &c.

This poem, confifting of many thoufand verfes, begins with the fpiritual advantages of the Lord's Prayer, of its feven petitions, their effects, &c., and ends with the feven Beatitudes and their rewards. Thefe are the two concluding lines:

> To whylk blyffe he vs bryng
> That on the croffe for vs all wolde hyng.[1]

The romances of Octavian, Sir Bevis, and Sir Guy have already been difcuffed at large. That of Sir Ifembras was familiar in the time of Chaucer, and occurs in the *Rime of Sir Thopas*.[2] In [the] Garrick [collection,] there is an edition by Copland, extremely different from the manufcript copies preferved at Cambridge[3] and in the Cotton collection.[4] I believe it to be originally a French romance, yet not of very high antiquity. It is written in the ftanza of Chaucer's *Sir Thopas*. The incidents are for the moft part thofe trite expedients, which almoft conftantly form the plan of thefe metrical narratives.

I take this opportunity of remarking, that the minftrels, who in this prologue of Naffyngton are named feparately from the *geftours* or tale-tellers, were fometimes diftinguifhed from the harpers. In the year 1374, fix minftrels, accompanied by four harpers, on the anniverfary of Bifhop Alwyne performed their minftrelfies at dinner, in the hall of the convent of Saint Swithin at Winchefter; and during fupper fang the fame geft or tale in the great arched chamber of the prior; on which folemn occafion the faid chamber was hung with the arras or tapeftry of the Three Kings of Cologne.[5]

---

[1] [Lord Afhburnham has, it is faid, the beft MS. Other copies are in MS. Vernon (about 1400); MS. Simeon (fame date); and MS. Hatton 19 (in the Bodleian).]

[2] Of this tale there are fix or feven MSS. known. That in the library of Lincoln Cathedral has been included by Mr. Halliwell, in *Thornton Romances*, 1844. There is alfo an old printed edition, with a fragment of a fecond, fhowing that it paffed the prefs at leaft twice. Percy remarks (*Rel.* ed. 1812, i. 326) that Drayton, in his *Dowfabel*, "has profeffedly imitated the ftyle and metre of fome of the old metrical Romances, particularly that of *Sir Ifembras*."]

[3] MSS. Caius Coll. Clafs. A. 9. (2).

[4] Calig. A. 12, f. 128.

[5] *Regiftr. Priorat. S. Swithini Winton.* "In fefto Alwyni epifcopi ..... Et durante pietancia in aulâ conventus, fex miniftralli, cum quatuor citharifatoribus, faciebant miniftralcias fuas. Et poft cenam, in magnâ camerâ arcuatâ dom. Prioris, *cantabant* idem geftum, in quâ camerâ fufpendebatur, ut moris eft, magnum dorfale Prioris, habens picturas trium regum Colein. Veniebant autem dicti joculatores a caftello domini regis, et ex familiâ epifcopi...." The reft is much obliterated,

These minstrels and harpers belonged, partly to the royal household in Winchester castle, and partly to the Bishop of Winchester. There was an annual mass at the shrine or tomb of Bishop Alwyne in the church, which was regularly followed by a feast in the convent. It is probable, that the gest here specified was some poetical legend of the prelate, to whose memory this yearly festival was instituted, and who was a Saxon bishop of Winchester [from 1032 to 1047.][1] Although songs of chivalry were equally common, and I believe more welcome to the monks, at these solemnities. In an accompt-roll of the priory of Bicester, in Oxfordshire,[2] I find a parallel instance under the year 1432. It is in this entry. *"Dat.* sex Ministrallis de Bokyngham cantantibus in refectorio Martyrium septem dormientium *in Festo epiphanie,* iv *s."* That is, the treasurer of the monastery gave four shillings to six minstrels from Buckingham, for singing in the refectory a legend called the Martyrdom of the Seven Sleepers,[3] on the feast of the Epiphany. In the Cotton library, there is a Norman poem on this subject,[4] which was probably translated afterwards into English rhyme. The original is a Greek

---

and the date is hardly discernible. Among the Harleian manuscripts, there is an ancient song of the three kings of Cologne, in which the old story of that favourite romance is resolved into alchemy. MSS. 2407. 13. fol. Wynkyn de Worde printed this romance [at least four times between 1500 and 1533.] It is in MSS. Harl. 1704. 11. fol. 49, b. (imperf.); Coll. Trin. Dublin. V. 651. 14. [C. 16.]; MSS. More 37; and frequently in other places. Barclay, in his *Egloges* [which, however, are merely translations,] mentions this subject, a part of the nativity, painted on the walls of a church cathedral. Egl. v. signat. D. iv. ad calc. *Ship of Fools,* edit. 1570:

"And the *thre kinges,* with all their company,
Their crownes glistering bright and oriently,
With their presentes and giftes misticall,
All this behelde I in picture on the wall."

[Some additional information on this subject may be found in Halliwell's *Inventories of Ancient Tapestry, Plate,* &c. 1854.]

In an inventory of ornaments belonging to the church of Holbech, in Lincolnshire, and sold in the year 1548, we find this article. "*Item,* for the coats of the iii. kyngs of Coloyne, v *s.* iiii *d.*" I suppose these coats were for dressing persons who represented the three kings in some procession on the Nativity. Or perhaps for a Mystery on the subject, played by the parish. But in the same inventory we have, *Item,* for the apostylls [the apostles] coats, and for Harods [Herod's] coate, &c. Stukeley's *Itin. Curios.* p. 19.

[1] He is buried in the north wall of the presbytery, with an inscription.
[2] In Thesaurario Coll. Trin. Oxon. [See *supr.*]
[3] In the fourth century, being inclosed in a cave at Ephesus by the Emperor Decius, 372 years, they were afterwards found sleeping, and alive.
[4] [The poem is written in the common French hand of the thirteenth century; and the English poem mentioned in the note below is written in the reign of Henry VII. Very little dependence can be placed on Warton's knowledge of the age of MSS.—M.] MSS. Cott. *Calig.* A. ix. iii. fol. 213, b. [See *supr.*] "*Jci commence la vie* de Set dormanz."

"La uertu deu ke tut iur dure
Li tut iurz ert cereme e pure."

[This poem was written in the thirteenth century by an Anglo-Norman named Chardry. See De la Rue's *Essais sur les Trouvères,* &c., tom. iii. p. 130.—M]

legend[1] which, in the dark ages, went about in a barbarous Latin tranſlation by one Syrus;[2] or in a narrative framed from it by Gregory of Tours.[3]

The ſame era (of Henry VI.) claims the honour of a well-known poem by James I. king of Scotland, who was atrociouſly murdered at Perth in the year 1436. It is allegorical, and in the ſeven-lined ſtanza. [The title is: *The Quair, maid be king James of Scotland the Firſt, callit the king's Quair*, where the king's Quair means the king's book (Quire).] The ſubject was ſuggeſted to the poet by his own misfortunes, and the mode of compoſition by reading Boethius.

---

[1] MSS. Lambec. viii. p. 375. Photius, without naming the author, gives the ſubſtance of this Greek legend, Bibl. *Cod.* ccliii. p. 1399, edit. 1591. This ſtory was common among the Arabians. The Muſſulmans borrowed many wonderful narratives from the Chriſtians, which they embelliſhed with new fictions. They pretend that a dog, which was accidentally ſhut up in the cavern with the ſeven ſleepers, became rational. See Herbelot, *Dict. Orient.* p. 139, a. v. *Aſhab.* p. 17. In the Britiſh Muſeum there is a poem, partly in Saxon characters, *De pueritia domini noſtri Jheſu Criſti;* or, *the childhood of Criſti.* MSS. Harl. 2399. 10, fol. 47. It begins thus:

"Alle myzthty god yn Trynyte,
That bowth [bought] man on rode dere;
He geſe ows waſhe to the
A lytyl wyle that ye wyll me hyre."

Who would ſuſpect that this abſurd legend had alſo a Greek original? It was taken, I do not ſuppoſe immediately, from an apocryphal narrative aſcribed to St. Thomas the apoſtle, but really compiled by Thomas Iſraelites, and entitled, Λόγος εἰς τὰ παιδικὰ καὶ μεγαλεῖα τῦ κυρίυ καὶ σωτῆρος ἡμῶν Ἰησῦ Χριστῦ, *Liber de pueritia et miraculis domini*, &c. It is printed in part by Cotelerius, *Not. ad Patr. Apoſtol.* p. 274. Who there mentions a book of Saint Matthew the Evangeliſt, *De Infantia Salvatoris*, in which our Lord is introduced learning to read, &c. See Iren. lib. i. c. xvii. p. 104. Among other figments of this kind, in the Pſeudo-Gelaſian Decree are recited, The hiſtory and nativity of our Saviour, and of Mary and the midwife; and, The hiſtory of the infancy of our Saviour. *Jur. Can. Diſtinct.* can. 3. The latter piece is mentioned by Anaſtaſius, where he cenſures as ſuppoſititious, the puerile miracles of Chriſt. Ὀδυγ. c. xiii. p. 26.

On the ſame ſubject there is an Arabic book, probably compiled ſoon after the riſe of Mahometaniſm, tranſlated into Latin by Sikius, called *Evangelium infantiæ*, Arab. et Latin, 1697. In this piece, Chriſt is examined by the Jewiſh doctors, in aſtronomy, medicine, phyſics, and metaphyſics. Sikius ſays, that the puerile miracles of Chriſt were common among the Perſians. *Ibid.* in Not. p. 55. Fabricius cites a German poem, more than four hundred years old, founded on theſe legends. *Cod. Apocryph. Nov. Teſt.* tom. i. p. 212. Hamburg. 1703.

At the end of the Engliſh poem on this ſubject above cited, is the following rubric. "Qod dnus Johannes Arcitenens canonicus Bodminie et natus in illa." Whether this Canon of Bodmin, in Cornwall, whoſe name was perhaps Archer or Bowyer, is the poet, or only the tranſcriber, I cannot ſay. See fol. 48. In the ſame manuſcript volume, [8.] there is an old Engliſh poem to our Saviour, with this note. "Explicit *Contemplationem bonam.* Quod dnus Johannes Arcuarius canonicus Bodminie." See what is ſaid below of the *Pſeudo-Evangelium* attributed to Nichodemus.

[2] *Apud* Surium, ad 27 Jul.

[3] *Hiſtoria ſeptem Dormientium.* Paris, 1511, *ibid.* 1640. And *apud* Ruinart, p. 1270. See *Præf. Ruinart.* § 79. And Gregory himſelf, *De gloria martyrum*, cap. 95, p. 826. This piece is noticed and much commended by the old chronicler Albericus, *ad ann.* 319.

At the close he mentions Gower and Chaucer as seated on the "steppys of rhetoryke."[1] This unfortunate monarch was educated while a prisoner in England, at the command of our Henry IV.; and the poem was written during his captivity there. The Scotish historians represent him as a prodigy of erudition. He civilized the Scotish nation. Among other accomplishments, he was an admirable musician, and particularly skilled in playing on the harp.[2] Among other pieces, which I have never seen, Bale mentions his *Cantilenæ Scoticæ* and *Rhythmi Latini*.[3] It is not the plan of this work to comprehend and examine in form pieces of Scotish poetry, except such only as are of singular merit. Otherwise, our royal bard would have been considered at large, and at his proper period. I will, however, add here two stanzas of the poem contained in the Selden manuscript, which seems to be the most distinguished of his compositions:[4]

> In ver that full of vertue is and gude,
> When nature first begynneth her empryse,
> That quilham was by cruell frost and flude,
> And shoures scharp, opprest in many wyse;
> And Cynthius gynneth to aryse
> Heigh in the est a morow soft and swete
> Upwards his course to drive in Ariete:
>
> Passit hot mydday foure grees evyn
> Off lenth and brede, his angel wingis bright
> He spred uppon the ground down fro the hevyn:
> That for gladness and confort of the sight,
> And with the tikling of his hete and light
> The tender floures upinyt thanne and sprad
> And in thar nature thankit him for glad.[5]

Both these poems seem to be written on his wife Joan, daughter of the Duchess of Clarence, with whom he fell in love while a prisoner in England. Major mentions besides a *libellus artificiosus*, whether verse or prose I know not, which he wrote on this lady in

---

[1] Bibl. Bodl. MSS. Selden. Archiv. B. 24, chart, fol. [With many pieces of Chaucer.]

[2] See Lesley, *De Reb. Gest. Scot.* lib. vii. pp. 257, 266, 267, edit. 1675. The same historian says, "ita orator erat, ut ejus dictione nihil fuerit artificiosius: ita poeta, ut carmina non tam arte strinxisse, quam natura sponte fudisse videretur. Cui rei fidem faciunt carmina diversi generis, quæ in rhythmum Scotice illigavit, eo artificio," &c. *Ibid.* 267. See also Buchanan, *Rer. Scot.* lib. x. pp. 186-196. Opp. tom. i. Edinb. 1715.

[3] Bale, *Paral.* post Cent. xiv. 56, pag. 217.

[4] [*Poetic Remains of some of the Scotish Kings*, edit. Chalmers, 1824, p. 31, where, however, the spelling is modernized.]

[5] This piece is not specified by Bale, Dempster, or Mackenzie. See Bale, *ubi supr.* Dempster, *Scot. Scriptor.* ix. 714, pag. 380, edit. 1622. Mackenzie, vol. i. p. 318, Edinb. 1708, fol. John Major mentions the beginning of some of his other poems, viz. "Yas sen," &c. And "At Beltayn," &c. [Both these poems are supposed to be still existing. They will be found in Sibbald's *Chronicle of Scottish Poetry*, vol. i. pp. 55-129. There does not, however, appear to be any good authority for attributing the latter, usually called *Peblis to the Play*, to James I. The internal evidence speaks decidedly for a later æra than the reign of this distinguished monarch.—*Price.*]

England before his marriage; and which Bale entitles *Super Uxore futura*. This historian, who flourished about the year 1520, adds that our monarch's *Cantilenæ* were commonly sung by the Scot[s] as their most favourite compositions: and that he played better on the harp than the most skilful Irish or highland harper. Major does not enumerate the poem I have here cited.[1] Bishop Percy had one of James's *Cantilenæ*, in which there is much merit.

For the use of those who collect specimens of alliteration, I will add an instance in the reign of Edward III. from the *Banocburn* of Minot, all whose pieces, in some degree, are tinctured with it:

> Skottes out of Berwik and of Abirdene,
> At the Bannokburn war ye to kene;
> Thare flogh ye many fakles, als it was fene.
> And now has king Edward wroken it I wene;
> It es wroken I wene, wele wurth the while,
> War yit with the Skottes, for thai er ful of gile.
>
> Whare er ye, Skottes of faint Johnes toune?
> The boste of yowre baner es betin all doune;
> When ye bofting will bede, fir Edward es boune,
> For to kindel yow care and crak yowre crowne:
> He has crakked yowre croune, wele worth the while,
> Schame bityde the Skottes, for thai er full of gile.
>
> Skottes of Striflin war fteren and stout,
> Of God ne of gude men had thai no dout;
> Now have thai the pelers priked obout,
> Bot at the last fir Edward rifild thaire rout;
> He has rifild thaire rout, wele wurth the while,
> Bot euer er thai under bot gaudes and gile.
>
> Rughfute riueling, now kindels thi care,
> Bere-bag with thi bofte, thi biging es bare;
> Fals wretche and forfworn, whider wiltou fare?
> Bufk the unto Brig and abide thare.
> Thare wretche faltou won, and wery the while,
> Thi dwelling in Donde es done for thi gile.
>
> The Skottes gafe in burghes and betes the ftretes,
> All thife Inglis men harmes he hetes;
> Faft makes he his mone to men that he metes,
> Bot fone frendes he finds that his bale betes;
> Sune betes his bale, wele wurth the while,
> He ufes all threting with gaudes and gile.
>
> Bot many man thretes and fpekes full ill,
> That fumtyme war better to be ftane ftill;
> The Skot in his wordes has wind for to fpill,
> For at the laft Edward fall haue al his will:
> He had his will at Berwick, wele wurth the while,
> Skottes broght him the kayes, bot get for thaire gile.

A *Vifion* on vellum, perhaps of the fame age, is alliterative.[2] Thefe are specimens:

> Ryyt as the maynful mone con rys,
> Er thenne the day glem dryve al doun,
> So fodanly, on a wonder wyfe,
> I watz war of a profeffyoun.

---

[1] *Geft. Scot.* lib. vi. cap. xiv. fol. 135, edit. 1521.
[2] MSS. Cott. Nero, A. x. [Morris's *Early Allitt. Poems*, pp. 1, 33-4, 56.]

§. 24. *Alliterative Poetry.* 123

> This noble cite of ryche empreſſe
> Watʒ ſodanly full with-outen ſommoun,
> Of ſuch vergynes in the ſame gyſe
> That watʒ my bliſful an under croun,
> And coronde wern alle of the ſame faſoun,
> Depaynt in perleʒ and wedeʒ qwhyte.

Again,
> On golden gateʒ that glent as glaſſe.

Again,
> But mylde as maydeneʒ ſeme at mas.

The poem begins,
> Perle pleſaunte to princes paye,
> To clanly clos in golde ſo clere

In the ſame manuſcript is an alliterative poem without rhyme, exactly in the verſification of [Langland's *Viſion*], of equal or higher antiquity, [entitled *Cleanneſs*. The following is a ſpecimen]:

> Olde Abraham in erde oneʒ he ſytteʒ,
> Even byfore his hous dore under an oke grene,
> Bryʒt blykked the bem of the brod heven
> In the hyʒe hete therof Abraham bideʒ.

The handwriting of theſe two laſt-mentioned pieces cannot be later than Edward III.

SECTION XXV.

THE firſt poet that occurs in the reign of Edward IV. is John Harding. He was of northern extraction and educated in the family of Lord Henry Percy,[1] and at twenty-five years of age hazarded his fortunes as a volunteer at the deciſive battle of Shrewſbury, fought againſt Percy and the Scots under Lord Douglas in the year 1403. He appears to have been indefatigable in examining original records, chiefly with a deſign of aſcertaining the fealty due from the Scotiſh kings to the crown of England; and he carried from Scotland for the elucidation of this important inquiry at the hazard of his life many inſtruments which he delivered at different times to the Fifth and Sixth Henry, and to Edward IV.[2] Theſe inveſtigations ſeem to

---

[1] One William Peeris, a prieſt, and ſecretary to the fifth Earl of Northumberland, wrote in verſe, *William Peeris's diſcente of the Lord Percis.* Pr. Prol. "Cronykills and annuel books of kyngs." Brit. Muſ. MSS. Reg. 18. D. 9. Then immediately follows (10) in the ſame manuſcript, perhaps written by the ſame author, a collection of metrical proverbs painted in ſeveral chambers of Lekingfield and Wreſille, ancient ſeats of the Percy family.

[2] Henry VI. granted immunities to Harding in ſeveral patents for procuring the Scotiſh evidences. The earlieſt is dated an. reg. xviii. [1440]. There is a memorandum in the exchequer, that in 1458, John Harding of Kyme delivered to John Talbot, treaſurer of England and chancellor of the exchequer, five Scotiſh letters patent, acknowledging various homages of the kings and nobility of Scotland.

have fixed his mind on the study of our national antiquities and
history. At length he clothed his researches in rhyme, which he
dedicated under that form to Edward IV. and with the title of *The
Chronicle of England unto the reigne of king Edward the Fourth*.[1]
The copy probably presented to the king, although it exhibits at
the end the arms of Henry Percy, earl of Northumberland, most
elegantly transcribed on vellum, and adorned with superb illuminations, is preserved among Selden's MSS. in the Bodleian library.[2]
Our author is concise and compendious in his narrative of events
from Brutus to the reign of Henry IV. : he is much more minute
and diffuse in relating those affairs of which, for more than the space
of sixty years, he was a living witness, and which occurred from that
period to the reign of Edward IV. The poem seems to have been
completed about the year 1470. In his final chapter he exhorts the
king to recall his rival Henry VI. and to restore the partisans of that
unhappy prince.

This work is almost beneath criticism, and fit only for the attention
of an antiquary. Harding may be pronounced to be the most impotent of our metrical historians, especially when we recollect the
great improvements which English poetry had now received. I will
not even except Robert of Gloucester, who lived in the infancy of
taste and versification. The chronicle of this authentic and laborious
annalist has hardly those more modest graces, which could properly
recommend and adorn a detail of the British story in prose. He has
left some pieces in prose: and Winstanley says, " as his prose was
very usefull, so was his poetry as much delightfull." I am of opinion,
that both his prose and poetry are equally useful and delightful.
What can be more frigid and unanimated than these lines?

They are inclosed in a wooden box in the exchequer, kept in a large chest, under
the mark, Scotia. Harding. So says Ashmole [MSS. Ashmol. 860, p. 186] from
a register in the exchequer called the Yellow-book.

[1] Printed at London, 1543, 4to. by Grafton who has prefixed a dedication of
three leaves in verse to Thomas, Duke of Norfolk. A continuation in prose from
Edward IV. to Henry VIII. is added, probably by [Sir Thomas More. See Ellis's
Preface to edit. 1812.]

[Harding " was a most dexterous and notable forger, and obtained great rewards
from Henry VI. and Edward IV. for a number of supposititious charters of fealty
and homage from the Scotish monarchs to the kings of England, which he pretended to have obtained in Scotland at the hazard of his life, and which are still
carefully preserved in the exchequer."—*Ritson*.]

[A new edition has since been published by Sir H. Ellis, who has collated both
the Selden and Ashmole MSS., together with a very valuable one now in the
British Museum, and formerly belonging to Lord Lansdowne. The text of Sir
H. Ellis has been followed upon the present occasion. It may be right to add,
that this gentleman has suggested a possibility, that Harding was himself imposed
upon in the affair of the charters; that he was the dupe, and not the perpetrator,
of the fraud.—*Price*.]

[2] MSS. Archiv. Seld. B. 26. It is richly bound and studded. At the end is a
curious map of Scotland; together with many prose pieces by Harding of the
historical kind. The Ashmolean manuscript is entitled, *The Chronicle of John
Harding in metre from the beginning of England unto the Reign of Edward the
Fourth*. MSS. Ashmol. Oxon. 34.

> Kyng Arthure then in Aualon fo died,
> Wher he was buried in a chapell fayre,
> Whiche nowe is made and fully edified,
> The mynfter churche this daye of great repayre,
> Of Glaftenbury where nowe he hath his leyre ;
> But then it was called the blacke chapell
> Of our Lady, as chronicles can tell.
>
> Wher Geryn, erle of Chartres, then abode,
> Befyde his toumbe for whole devocion,
> Whether Launcelot de Lake came, as he rode
> Upon the chace with trompette and clarion,
> And Geryn tolde hym ther all up and downe,
> Howe Arthure was there layde in fepulture,
> For whiche with hym to byde he hight full fure.[1]

Fuller affirms our author to have "drunk as deep a draught of Helicon as any of his age." An affertion partly true: it is certain, however, that the diction and imagery of our poetic compofition would have remained in juft the fame ftate, had Harding never written.

In this reign the firft mention of the king's poet, under the appellation of *Laureate*, occurs. John Kay was appointed poet laureate to Edward IV. It is extraordinary that he fhould have left no pieces of poetry to prove his pretenfions in fome degree to this office, with which he is faid to have been invefted by the king at his return from Italy. The only compofition he has tranfmitted to pofterity is a profe Englifh tranflation of a Latin hiftory [by Gulielmus Caorfinus][2] of the Siege of Rhodes: in the dedication addreffed to King Edward, or rather in the title, he ftyles himfelf " hys humble poete laureate." Although this our laureate furnifhes us with no materials as a poet, yet his office, which here occurs for the firft time under this denomination, muft not pafs unnoticed in the annals of Englifh poetry, and will produce a fhort digreffion.

Great confufion has entered into this fubject, on account of the degrees in grammar, which included rhetoric and verfification,[3]

---

[1] Ch. lxxxiv. edit. [Ellis, p. 147.]

[2] MSS. Cotton. Vitell. D. xii. 10. [Printed by W. Caxton (*circa* 1490), folio. Warton fpeaks of an edit. of 1506. The original Latin, as ftated by him, is entitled, *Obfidio Rhodiæ Urbis* (1480). See *Handb. of E. E. Lit.* art. *Caorfinus*]. The works of this Gulielmus, which are numerous, were printed together, at Ulm, 1496, fol. with rude wooden prints. See an exact account of this writer, *Diar. Eruditor. Ital.* tom. xxi. p. 412.

[3] In the ancient ftatutes of the univerfity of Oxford, every Regent Mafter in Grammar is prohibited from reading in his faculty, unlefs he firft pafs an examination " de modo verfificandi et dictandi," &c. MSS. Bibl. Bodl. fol. membran. Arch. A. 91. [nunc. 2874.] f. 55, b. This fcholaftic cultivation of the art of Profody gave rife to many Latin fyftems of Metre about this period. Among others, Thomas Langley, a monk of Hulm in Norfolk, in the year 1430 wrote in two books *De Varietate Carminum.* Bibl. Bodl. MSS. Digb. 100. One John Seguard, a Latin poet and rhetorician of Norwich [after 1413.] wrote a piece of this kind called *Metriftenchiridion*, addreffed to Courtenay, Biſhop of Norwich, treating of the nature of metre in general, and efpecially of the common metres of the Hymns of Boecius and Oracius [Horace]. Oxon. MSS. Coll. Merton. Q. iii. 1.

anciently taken in our universities, particularly at Oxford: on which occasion a wreath of laurel was presented to the new graduate, who was afterwards usually styled "poeta laureatus."[1] These scholastic laureations, however, seem to have given rise to the appellation in question. I will give some instances at Oxford, which at the same time will explain the nature of the studies for which our academical philologists received their rewards. [On the 11th March, 1511-12,] one [Edward] Watson, a student in grammar, obtained a concession to be graduated and laureated in that science; on condition that he composed one hundred Latin verses in praise of the university, or a Latin comedy.[2] Another grammarian, [Richard Smyth,] was distinguished with the same badge, after having stipulated that, at the next public Act, he would affix the same number of hexameters on the great gates of Saint Mary's Church, that they might be seen by the whole university. This was at that period the most convenient mode of publication.[3] [In December, 1511,] one Maurice Byrchenshaw, a scholar in rhetoric, supplicated to be admitted to read lectures, that is, to take a degree in that faculty; and his petition was granted with a provision, that he should write one hundred verses on the glory of the university, and not suffer Ovid's *Art of Love* and the *Elegies* of Pamphilus[4] to be studied in his auditory.[5] [On the 3rd June, 1511,] one John Bulman, another rhetorician, having complied with the terms imposed, of explaining the first book of Tully's *Offices* and likewise the first of his *Epistles*, without any pecuniary emolument, was graduated in rhetoric; and a crown of laurel was publicly placed on his head by the hands of the chancellor of the university.[6] [Before] the year 14[90,][7] Skelton was laureated

---

[1] When any of these graduated grammarians were licensed to teach boys, they were publicly presented in the Convocation-house with a rod and ferula. Regiſtr. Univ. Oxon. G. fol. 72, a.

[2] Regiſtr. Univ. Oxon. G. fol. 143. I take this opportunity of acknowledging my obligations to the learned Mr. Swinton, keeper of the Archives at Oxford, for giving me frequent and free access to the Regiſters of that university.

[3] *Ibid.* fol. 162. [Smyth petitioned for leave to teach, May 12, 1512; and he was ordered, in January following, to proceed to his degree before Easter. Churton (*Life of Bishop Smyth*, p. 153).—*Park.*]

[4] [Byrchinshaw was admitted to his degree, Feb. 5, 1511-12, Churton, *ut supra*. —*Park.*] Ovid's suppoſititious pieces, and other verses of the lower age, were [re]printed together by Goldaſtus, 1610. Among these is, "Pamphili Mauriliani Pamphilus, five de Arte Amandi Elegiæ lxiii." This is from the same school with Ovid *De Vetula*, and by some thought to be forged by the same author.

[5] Regiſtr. Univ. Oxon. G. fol. 134, a.

[6] Regiſtr. *ut supra.* G. fol. 124, b.

[7] Caxton, in the preface to the English *Eneydos*, mentions "Mayſter John Skelton, late created poete laureate in the univerſite of Oxenford," &c. This work was printed in 1490. Churchyard mentions Skelton's academical laureation in his poem prefixed to Skelton's Works, 1568:

"Nay Skelton wore the lawrel wreath,
And paſt in ſchoels ye knoe."

And again,

"That ware the garland gay
Of lawrel leaves but laet."

at Oxford, and in the year 1493 was permitted to wear his laurel at Cambridge.¹ Robert Whittinton affords [another] instance of a rhetorical degree at Oxford. He was a secular priest, and eminent for his various treatises in grammar and for his facility in Latin poetry: having exercised his art many years, and submitting to the customary demand of an hundred verses, he was honoured with the laurel in the year 1512.² This title is prefixed to one of his grammatical systems: *Roberti Whittintoni, Lichfeldiensis, Grammatices Magistri, Protovatis Angliæ, in florentissima Oxoniensi Achademia Laureati, de Octo Partibus Orationis*.³ In his *Panegyric* to Cardinal Wolsey, he mentions his laurel,

> Suscipe lauricomi munuscula parva Roberti.⁴

With regard to the Poet laureate of the kings of England, an officer of the court remaining under that title to this day, he is undoubtedly the same that is styled the King's Versifier [in the Treasurer's Accounts for 1249 and 1251, as has been already mentioned.] But when or how that title commenced, and whether this officer was ever solemnly crowned with laurel at his first investiture, I will not pretend to determine, after the searches of the learned Selden on this question have proved unsuccessful. It seems most probable, that the barbarous and inglorious name of versifier gradually gave way to an appellation of more elegance and dignity: or rather, that at length those only were in general invited to this appointment, who had received academical sanction, and had merited a crown of laurel in the universities for their abilities in Latin composition, particularly Latin versification. Thus the king's Laureate was nothing more than "a graduated rhetorician employed in the service of the

---

¹ Regist. Univ. Cantabrig. *sub ann*. "Conceditur Johi Skelton Poetæ in partibus transmarinis atque Oxon. Laurea ornato, ut apud nos eadem decoraretur." And afterwards, an. 1504-5. "Conceditur Johi Skelton Poete Laureat. quod possit stare eodem gradu hic quo stetit Oxoniis, et quod possit uti habitu sibi concesso a Principe." The latter clause, I believe, relates to some distinction of habit, perhaps of fur or velvet, granted him by the king. Skelton is said to have been poet laureate to Henry VIII. He also styles himself "Orator regius," pp. [xiii. xx. &c.], *Works*, [1843].

² Regist. Univ. Oxon. *ut supra*. G. 173, b. 187, h. [Robert Whittington had been a scholar of rhetoric fourteen years. He was admitted to the degree of Bachelor April 15, 1513, allowed to wear a silk hood, July 3, and crowned with laurel at the act next day. Churton, *ut supra.—Park*.]

³ Lond. 1513.

⁴ In [the] "Opusculum Roberti Whittintoni in florentissima Oxoniensi achademia laureati," signat. A. iii. The Panegyrics are on Henry VIII. and Cardinal Wolsey. The Epigrams, which are long copies of verse, are addressed to Charles Brandon, duke of Suffolk, Sir Thomas More, and to Skelton, under the title *Ad lepidissimum poetam Scheltonem carmen*, &c. Some of the lines are in a very classical style, and much in the manner of the earlier Latin Italian poets. At the end of these Latin poems is a defence of the author, called *Antilycon*, &c. These pieces are in MS Oxon. MSS. Bodl. D. 3, 22. [. . . I do not trace any insertion under the title Antilycon. The splendid eulogium "in clarissimi Scheltonis Lovaniensis poetæ Epigramma" is followed by a Latin distich, and by twelve lines "In Zoilum,' which close the collection.—*Park*.]

king." That he originally wrote in Latin, appears from the ancient title Verſificator, and may be moreover collected from the two Latin poems, which [Robert] Baſton and Gulielmus [Peregrinus,] who appear to have reſpectively acted in the capacity of royal poets to Richard I. and Edward II. officially compoſed on Richard's cruſade and Edward's ſiege of Stirling caſtle.[1]

Andrew Bernard, ſucceſſively poet laureate of Henry VII. and VIII. affords a ſtill ſtronger proof that this officer was a Latin ſcholar. He was a native of Toulouſe, and an Auguſtine monk. He was not only the king's poet laureate,[2] as it is ſuppoſed, but his hiſtoriographer,[3] and preceptor in grammar to prince Arthur. He obtained many eccleſiaſtical preferments in England.[4] All the pieces now to be found, which he wrote in the character of poet laureate, are in Latin.[5] Theſe are *An Addreſs to Henry the Eighth for the moſt auſpicious beginning of the tenth year of his reign*, with an *Epithalamium on the marriage of Francis the Dauphin of France with the king's daughter*,[6] a *New Year's Gift* for the year 1515,[7] and verſes wiſhing proſperity to his majeſty's thirteenth year.[8] He has left ſome

---

[1] By the way, Baſton is called by Bale "laureatus apud Oxonienſes." Cent. iv. cap. 92.

[2] See an inſtrument *pro Poeta laureato*, dat. 1486. Rymer's *Foed*. tom. xii. p. 317. But, by the way, in this inſtrument there is no ſpecification of any thing to be done officially by Bernard. The king only grants to Andrew Bernard, *Poetæ laureato*, which we may conſtrue either "The laureated poet," or "A poet laureate [but doubtleſs more properly the former,] a ſalary of ten marks, till he can obtain ſome equivalent appointment. This, however, is only a precept to the treaſurer and chamberlains to diſburſe the ſalary, and refers to letters patent, not printed by Rymer. It is certain that Gower and Chaucer were never appointed to this office. Skelton in his [*Garland*] *of Lawrell*, ſees Gower, Chaucer, and Lydgate approach: he deſcribes their whole apparel as glittering with the richeſt precious ſtones, and then immediately adds,

"They wanted nothing but the laurell."

Afterwards, however, there is the rubric "Maiſter Chaucer laureate poete to Skelton." *Works*, edit. [1843].

[3] Apoſtolo Zeno was both poet and hiſtoriographer to his imperial majeſty. So was Dryden to James II. It is obſervable that Petrarch was laureated as poet and hiſtorian.

[4] One of theſe, the maſterſhip of Saint Leonard's hoſpital at Bedford, was given him by Biſhop Smith, one of the founders of Braſenoſe college, Oxford, in the year 1498. Regiſtr. Smith, epiſc. Lincoln. *ſub ann*.

[5] Some of Skelton's Latin poems ſeem to be written in the character of the Royal laureate, particularly [two ſubſcribed reſpectively] *Hæc Laureatus Skeltonus, orator reginæ, ſuper triumphali*, [and] *Per Skeltonida Laureatum, oratorem regium*. *Works* [by Dyce, i. 190-1]. Hardly any of his Engliſh pieces, which are numerous, appear to belong to that character. With regard to the *Orator Regius*, I find one John Mallard in that office to Henry VIII. and his epiſtolary ſecretary. He has left *a Latin elegiac paraphraſe on the Lord's Prayer* (MSS. Bibl. Reg. 7 D. xiii.) dedicated to that king. *Le premier livre de la coſmographie*, in verſe, *ibid*. 20 B. xii. And a *Pſalter*, beautifully written by himſelf for the uſe of the king. In the margin, are ſhort notes in the handwriting, and two exquiſite miniatures, of Henry VIII. *Ibid*. 2 A. xvi.

[6] MS. olim penes Thom. Martin de Palgrave.

[7] MSS. Coll. Nov. Oxon. 287.

[8] Brit. Muſ. MSS. Reg. 12 A. x. The copy preſented. On paper. There is a wretched falſe quantity in the firſt line,

"Indue, honor, cultus, et *adole* munera flammis."

Latin hymns:[1] and many of his Latin prose pieces, which he wrote in the quality of historiographer to both monarchs, are remaining.[2]

I am of opinion that it was not customary for the royal laureate to write in English, till the reformation of religion had begun to diminish the veneration for the Latin language: or rather, till the love of novelty and a better sense of things had banished the narrow pedantries of monastic erudition, and taught us to cultivate our native tongue. In the meantime it is to be wished that another change might at least be suffered to take place in the execution of this institution, which is confessedly Gothic, and unaccommodated to modern manners. I mean, that the more than annual return of a composition on a trite argument would be no longer required. I am conscious I say this at a time when the best of kings affords the most just and copious theme for panegyric; but I speak it at a time when the department is honourably filled by a poet of taste and genius, which are idly wasted on the most splendid subjects, when imposed by constraint, and perpetually repeated.[3]

To what is here incidentally collected on an article more curious than important, I add an observation, which shews that the practice of other nations in this respect altogether corresponded with that of our own. When we read of the laureated poets of Italy and Germany, we are to remember, that they most commonly received this honour from the state or some university; seldom, at least not immediately, from the prince: and if we find any of these professedly employed in the department of a court-poet, that they were not, in consequence of that peculiar situation, styled poets laureate. The distinction, at least in general, was previously conferred.[4] The Ser-

---

[1] And a Latin life of Saint Andrew. MSS. Cotton. Domitian. A. xviii. 15.

[2] A chronicle of the life and achievements of Henry VII. to the taking of Perkin Warbek, MSS. Cotton. Domitian. A. xviii. 15. Other historical commentaries on the reign of that king. Ibid. *Jul.* A. 4. *Jul.* A. 3. [Published in *Chronicles and Memorials of Great Britain*, 1858.—Rye. See *Archæologia*, xxvii. pp. 154, 192.—Madden.]

[3] [The birth-day of William III. in 1694 appears to have been officially celebrated by Tate, whom Rowe succeeded in the laureateship; and from the year 1718 a regular series may almost be traced of birth-day and new-year odes. Warton gave an historical dignity and a splendour of poetical diction to those he composed, which would hardly leave a reader to conceive that the subjects were " imposed by constraint." His predecessor Whitehead must strongly have felt the irksome force of this constraint, when he lamented, in his pathetic apology for all laureates, that—

> " His muse, *obliged* by sack and pension,
> Without a subject, or invention,
> Must certain words in order set
> As innocent as a gazette;
> Must some half-meaning half disguise,
> And utter neither truth nor lies."
>   *Park.*]

[4] The reader who requires a full and particular information concerning the first origin of the laureation of poets, and the solemnities with which this ceremony was performed in Italy and Germany, is referred to Selden's *Tit. Hon.* Op. tom. p. 457, seq. *Vie de Petrarque*, tom. iii. *Notes, &c.* p. 1. *Not. quat.* And to a memoir

jeant of the King's Minſtrels occurs under this reign, and in a manner which ſhews the confidential character of this officer, and his facility of acceſs to the king at all hours and on all occaſions. "And as he [k. Edward IV.] was in the north contray in the moneth of Septembre, as he laye in his bedde, one namid Alexander Carliſle, that was *ſariaunt of the mynſtrallis,* cam to him in grete haſte, and bade him aryſe, for he hadde enemys cummyng," &c.¹

John Scogan is commonly ſuppoſed to have been a cotemporary of Chaucer, but this miſtake [has ariſen from confounding him with *Henry* Scogan, who appears to have been actually coeval with the author of the *Canterbury Tales,* and who has left one or two pieces, including *A Moral Balade,* inſerted in the old editions of Chaucer. John Scogan² was educated [it is ſaid, though on very ſlender authority,] at Oriel college in Oxford: and being an excellent mimic, and of great pleaſantry in converſation, became the favourite buffoon of the court of Edward IV., in which he paſſed the greateſt part of his life. Bale inaccurately calls Scogan the Joculator of Edward IV.: by which word he ſeems ſimply to underſtand the king's Joker, for he certainly could not mean that Scogan was his majeſty's minſtrel.³ [Under the name of] Andrew Borde, a phyſician and author in the reign of Henry VIII., was publiſhed [a ſilly book called] *Scogin's Jeſts,*⁴ which are without humour and invention, and give us no very favourable idea of the delicacy of the king and courtiers, who could be exhilarated by the merriments of ſuch a writer. [In the unique quarto volume at Cambridge with ſome minor pieces by Chaucer and Lydgate, all from Caxton's preſs, occurs: "Here after foloweth a tretyſe whiche John Skogan ſente vnto the lordes and gentilmen of the kinges hows exhortyng them to loſe no tyme in theyr yougthe, but to vſe vertues;" but this was, in all probability, by *Henry,* not John, Scogan or Skogan.]⁵ Bale men-

---

of M. l'Abbè du Reſnel, *Mem. Lit.* x. 507, 4to. I will only add the form of the creation of three poets laureate by the chancellor of the univerſity of Straſburgh, in the year 1621. "I create you, being placed in a chair of ſtate, crowned with laurel and ivy, and wearing a ring of gold, and the ſame do pronounce and conſtitute, Poets Laureate, in the name of the holy Trinity, the father, ſon, and holy Ghoſt. Amen."

¹ *A Remarkable Fragment,* &c. [an. ix. Edward IV.] ad calc. Sportti *Chron.* edit. Hearne. Compare Percy's *Eſſ. Minſtr.* p. 56. Anſtis, *Ord. Gart.* ii. 303.

² See Holinſh. *Chron.* iii. f. 710, and MSS. Fairfax. xvi. [See alſo Ritſon's *Bibl. Poet.* art. *Scogan.*]

³ *Script.* xi. 70.

⁴ It is from theſe pieces we learn that he was of Oriel college: for he ſpeaks of retiring, with that ſociety, to the hoſpital of Saint Bartholomew, while the plague was at Oxford. Theſe *Jeſts* are [78 in number in the edit. of 1626.] *Pr. Pref.* [edit. 1626:] "There is nothing beſides." *Pr.* "On a time in Lent." [The earlieſt impreſſion now known is that of 1613, 8vo.] They were reprinted [with omiſſions] about the reſtoration, [but one of the genuine editions (1626) is republiſhed in *Old Engliſh Jeſt-Books,* ii. That of 1613 (in the Bodleian) varies from the later one—a fact of which I was not aware when I edited the ſeries juſt named.]

⁵ The little piece, [correctly] printed as Chaucer's [Urr. ed. p. 548], called *Flee*

tions his *Comedies*,¹ which certainly mean nothing dramatic, and are perhaps only his *Jests* above mentioned. He seems to have flourished about the year 1480.

Two didactic poets on chemistry appeared in this reign, [Thomas] Norton and George Ripley. Norton was a native of Bristol,² and the most skilful alchemist of his age.³ His poem is called the *Ordinal*, or a manual of the chemical art.⁴ It was presented to Nevil archbishop of York, a great patron of the hermetic philosophers;⁵ who had lately grown so numerous in England, as to occasion an act of parliament against the transmutation of metals. Norton's reason for treating his subject in English rhyme, was to circulate the principles of a science of the most consummate utility among the unlearned.⁶ This poem is totally void of every poetical elegance. The only wonder which it relates, belonging to an art so fertile in striking inventions, and contributing to enrich the store-house of Arabian romance with so many magnificent imageries, is that of an alchemist, who projected a bridge of gold over the River Thames near London, crowned with pinnacles of gold, which being studded with carbuncles, diffused a blaze of light in the dark.⁷ I will add a few lines only, as a specimen of his versification:

> Wherefore he would set up in hist
> That bridge, for a wonderfull sigt,
> With pinnacles guilt, shininge as goulde,
> A glorious thing for men to beholde.
> Then he remembered of the newe,
> Howe greater fame shulde him pursewe,
> If he mought make that bridge so brighte,
> That it mought shine alsoe by night:
> And so continewe and not breake,
> Then all the londe of him would speake, &c.⁸

Norton's heroes in the occult sciences are Bacon, Albertus Magnus, and Raymond Lully, to whose specious promises of supplying the coinage of England with inexhaustible mines of philosophical gold Edward III. became an illustrious dupe.⁹

George Ripley, Norton's cotemporary, was accomplished in many parts of erudition, and still maintains his reputation as a learned

---

from the Presse, is [wrongly] given to Scogan, and called *Proverbium Joannis Skogan*, MSS. C.C.C. Oxon. 203. [See *supr.* ii. 384.]

¹ xi. 70.
² He speaks of the wife of William Canning, five times mayor of Bristol, and the founder of Saint Mary of Radcliffe church there. *Ordinal*, p. 34.
³ Printed by Ashmole, in his *Theatrum Chemicum*, 1652, p. 6. It was finished A.D. 1477. *Ordin.* p. 106. It was translated into Latin by Michael Maier, M.D. 1618. Norton wrote other chemical pieces.
⁴ See *Ordin.* pp. 9, 10. Norton declares, that he learned his art in forty days, at twenty-eight years of age. *Ibid.* pp. 33, 88.
⁵ Ashmole, *ubi supr.* p. 455, *Notes.* ⁶ Pag. 106.
⁷ *Ibid.* ⁸ *Ibid.*
⁹ Ashmol. *ubi supr* pp. 443, 467, and Camden's *Rem.* p. 242, edit. 1674. By the way, Raymond Lully is said to have died at eighty years of age, in the year 1315. Whart. *App. Cave*, cap. p. 6.

chemift of the lower ages. He was a canon regular of the monaftery of Bridlington in Yorkfhire, and a great traveller,[1] and ftudied both in France and Italy. At his return from abroad, Innocent VIII. abfolved him from the obfervance of the rules of his order, that he might profecute his ftudies with more convenience and freedom. But, his convent not concurring with this very liberal indulgence, he turned Carmelite at Saint Botolph's in Lincolnfhire, and died an anchorite in that fraternity in the year 1490.[2] His chemical poems are nothing more than the doctrines of alchemy clothed in plain language, and a very rugged verfification. The capital performance is *The Compound of Alchemy*, written in the year 1471.[3] It is in the octave metre, and dedicated to Edward IV.[4] Ripley has left a few other compofitions on his favourite fcience, printed by Afhmole, who was an enthufiaft in this abufed fpecies of philofophy.[5] One of them, the *Medulla*, written in 1476, is dedicated to Archbifhop Nevil.[6] Thefe pieces have no other merit than that of ferving to develope the hiftory of chemiftry in England. They certainly contributed nothing to the ftate of our poetry.

It will be fufficient to throw three of the obfcurer rhymers of this period together. Ofbern Bokenham wrote or tranflated metrical lives of the faints, about 1445, [printed for the Roxburghe Club, 1835.] Gilbert Banefter wrote in Englifh verfe the *Miracle of faint Thomas*, in the year 1467.[7] Of the fame date [(if not earlier),

---

[1] Afhmole fays that Ripley, during his long ftay at Rhodes, gave the knights of Malta 100,000*l.* annually towards maintaining the war againft the Turks. *Ubi fupr.* p. 458. Afhmole could not have made this incredible affertion, without fuppofing a circumftance equally incredible, that Ripley was in actual poffeffion of the philofopher's ftone.

[2] Afhmol. p. 455, *feq.* Bale, viii. 49. Pits, p. 677.

[3] Afhmol. *Theatr. Chem.* p. 193. It was firft printed in 1591, 4to. Reprinted by Afhmole, *Theatr. Chem.* ut fupr. p. 107. It has been thrice tranflated into Latin, Afhm. *ut fupr.* p. 465. See *ibid.* pp. 108, 110, 122. Moft of Ripley's Latin works were printed [at Frankfort in 1614.]

[4] He mentions the abbey church at Weftminfter as unfinifhed. Pag. 154, ft. 27, P. 156, and ft. 34.

[5] Afhmole conjectures that an Englifh chemical piece in the octave ftanza, which he has printed, called *Hermes's Bird*, no unpoetical fiction, was tranflated from Raymond Lully by Cremer, abbot of Weftminfter, a great chemift; and adds that Cremer brought Lully into England, and introduced him to the notice of Edward III. about the year 1334. Afhmol. *ubi fupra*, pp. 213, 467. [It was tranflated by Lydgate from a French Fabliau. See Way's Fabliaux, vol. i. It had been previoufly printed by Caxton, De Worde, &c., under the title of the *Chorle and the Byrde.—Price.*] Afhmole mentions a curious picture of the grand Myfteries of the Philofopher's Stone, which Abbot Cremer ordered to be painted in Weftminfter Abbey, upon an arch where the waxen kings and queens are placed; but that it was obliterated with a plafterer's brufh by the Puritans in Oliver's time. He alfo mentions a large and beautiful window, behind the pulpit in the neighbouring church of Saint Margaret, painted with the fame fubject, and deftroyed by the fame ignorant zealots, who miftook thefe innocent hieroglyphics for fome ftory in a popifh legend. Afhmol. *ibid.* 211, 466, 467. Compare Widmore's *Hift. Weftminfter-Abbey*, p. 174, *feq.* edit. 1751.

[6] Afhmol. p. 389. See alfo p. 374, *feq.*

[7] CCCC. MSS. Q. viii. Lel. *Collectan.* tom. i. (p. ii.) pag. 510, edit. 1770.

in its pristine shape, is perhaps the *King and the Tanner of Tamworth*,[1] which is called in the original draft the *King and the Barker* (or Tanner).] Hearne affirms that in this piece there are some " romantic assertions; otherwise 'tis a book of value, and more authority is to be given to it than is given to poetical books of late years."[2]

SECTION XXVI.

THE subsequent reigns of Richard III., Edward V., and Henry VII., abounded in obscure versifiers.

[Two mutilated poems occur] among the Cotton MSS. in the British Museum, [one of which] contains a satire on the nuns who, not less from the nature of their establishment than from the usual degeneracy which attends all institutions, had at length lost their original purity, seems to belong to this period.[3] It is without wit, and almost without numbers. [The other] was written, [or rather, perhaps, transcribed,] by one Bertram [Waton],[4] whose name now first appears in the catalogue of English poets, and whose life I calmly resign to the researches of some more laborious and patient antiquary.

About the year [1470] Benedict Burgh, a Master of Arts of Oxford, among other promotions in the church, archdeacon of Colchester, prebendary of Saint Paul's, canon of Saint Stephen's Chapel at Westminster,[5] [and vicar of Malden in Essex,] translated [Dionysius] Cato's *Disticha Moralia* into the royal stanza for the use of his pupil Viscount Bourchier, son of the Earl of Essex.[6] Encouraged

---

[1] [*Remains of the Early Pop. Poetr. of Engl.* i.]
[2] Edit. 1770 of Leland's *Collect.* ii. 103.
[3] Disadvantageous suspicions against the chastity of the female religious were pretended in earlier times. About the year 1250 [Robert Grosseteste,] bishop of Lincoln, visited the nunneries of his diocese; on which occasion, says the continuator of Matthew Paris, " ad domos religiosarum veniens, fecit exprimi mamillas earundem, ut sic physice, si esset inter eas corruptela, experiretur." Matt. Paris. *Hist.* p. 789:—*Henricus* iii. edit. Tig. 1589, fol. An anecdote, which the historian relates with indignation; not on account of the nuns, but of the bishop.
[4] [Sir F. Madden first pointed out that Warton had confounded the fragments of two poems together. The first, he says, contains the invective against nunneries; the other, Waton's copy of the indulgences granted to the monasteries at Rome. Of the latter, of which Waton is probably no more than the copyist, there is another text in Lambeth MS. 306, printed in Mr. Furnivall's *Political, Religious and Love Poems*, 1866, p. 113, *et seq.*; and a third, earlier and better, in Vernon MS., printed by the same gentleman in 1867.]
[5] See Newcourt, *Repertor.* i. 90, ii. 517. The university sealed his letters testimonial, Jul. 3, 1433. Registr. Univ. Oxon. T. f. 27, b. He died 1483.
[6] Gascoigne says that " Rythme royall is a verse of tenne sillables, and seuen such verses make a staffe," &c. *Instructions for verse*, &c., [1575 Works, by Hazlitt, i. 506.] Burgh's stanza is here called "balade royall;" by which, I believe, is commonly signified the octave stanza. All those pieces in Chaucer, called " Cer-

by the example and authority of so venerable an ecclesiastic, Caxton [not only issued three editions of Burgh's English version, but in 1483 translated and published the large French gloss, a folio volume of nearly 200 pages, accompanied by woodcuts.] He calls, in his preface, the measure used by Burgh the Balad Royal. Caxton's translation, which superseded Burgh's work, and with which it [should not be] confounded, is divided into four books, which comprehend seventy-two heads.

In the British Museum there is a poem entitled *A Christemasse Game made by maister Benet howe God Almyghty seyde to his apostelys and echeon of them were baptiste and none knew of othir.* The piece consists of twelve stanzas, an apostle being assigned to each stanza. Probably "maister Benet" is Benedict Burgh. This is St. Paul's stanza:

> Doctour of gentiles, a perfite Paule,
> By grace convertid from thy grete erroure,
> And cruelte, changed to Paule from Saule,
> Of fayth and trouth most perfyte prechoure,
> Slayne at Rome undir thilke emperoure
> Cursyd Nero. Paule, syt down in thy place
> To the ordayned by purveaunce of grace.¹

I do not mean to affront my readers when I inform them without any apology that the Latin original of this piece was not written by Cato the censor, nor by Cato of Utica,² although it is perfectly in the character of the former, and Aulus Gellius has quoted Cato's poem *de Moribus*.³ Nor have I the gravity of the learned Box-

---

taine Ballads," are in this measure. In Chaucer's *Legend of good Women*, written in long verse, a song of three octave stanzas is introduced; beginning, "Hide Absolon thy gilte tressis clere," ver. 249. Afterwards Cupid says, ver. 537:

> "—— A ful grete necligence
> Was yt to the, that ilke tyme thou made,
> Hyd Absolon thy tresses in balade."

In the British Museum there is "a Kalandre in Englysshe, made in Balade by Dann John Lydgate monke of Bury;" that is, in this stanza. MSS. Harl. 1706, 2, fol. 10, b. The reader will observe that, whether there are eight or seven lines, I have called it the octave stanza. Lydgate has, most commonly, only seven lines, as in his poem on Guy, earl of Warwick, MSS. Laud. D. 31, fol. 64, "Here ginneth the lyff of Guy of Warwyk." [Pr. From Cristes birth compleat nine 100 yere.] He is speaking of Guy's combat with the Danish giant Colbrand, at Winchester:

> "Without the gate remembered as I rede,
> The place callyd of antiquytye
> In Inglysh tonge named hyde mede,
> Or ellis denmarch nat far from the cyte:
> Meeting to gedre, there men myght see
> Terryble strokys, lyk the dent of thonder;
> Sparklys owt of thar harnyss," &c.

¹ Harl. MS. 7333. [The Harl. MS. 1706 contains "Aristotle's A, B, C," made by this mayster Benet.—*Ritson*. Burgh's *Cato* is very common in MSS. There are at least seven copies of it in the British Museum: Arundel MS. 168, and Harleian MSS. 116, 172, 271, 2251, 4733, 7333.—*Brock*.]

² See [B. d'Argonne, *Melanges*,] tom. i. p. 56.

³ *Noct. Att* xi. 2.

hornius, who in a prolix and elaborate differtation has endeavoured to demonftrate that thefe diftichs are undoubtedly fuppofititious, and that they could not poffibly be written by the very venerable Roman, whofe name they bear. [In the early editions the title is fimply] *Difticha de Moribus*, which [diftiches] are diftributed into four books.

[A needlefs diftinction has been made fometimes between *Parvus* and *Magnus Cato*, names ufed in the later manufcripts to diftinguifh between a fet of fhort precepts in profe and the diftichs which follow them. The former appear in the beft editions under the title of *Breves Sententiæ*, and are found in the oldeft known MS. of Cato, written about A. D. 900, preferved at Zurich, and printed in Dr. Zarncke's work, *Der deutfche Cato*. It is, moreover, a miftake to confound *Parvus Cato* with a diftinct poem entitled *Facetus*, the author of which (fometimes, but perhaps incorrectly, faid to be Johannes de Garlandia) tells us in his opening lines:

> Cum nihil vtilius humanæ credo faluti
> Quam rerum nouiffe modos & moribus vti;
> Quod minus exequitur morofi dogma Catonis
> *Supplebo* pro poffe meo monitu rationis.

As to the writer of *Facetus*, a commentary on the work in Arundel MS. 243 informs us that he was " vnus religiofus nomine Iohannes qui, videns homines a via morum et virtutum declinare et vicijs inherere, compofuit hunc librum de moribus et virtutibus, volens eos in via morum et virtutum conferuare."]

This work has been abfurdly attributed by fome critics to Seneca, and by others to Aufonius.[1] It is, however, more ancient than the time of the Emperor Valentinian III. who died in 455.[2] On the other hand, it was written after the appearance of Lucan's *Pharfalia*, as the author, at the beginning of the fecond book, commends Virgil, Macer,[3] Ovid, and Lucan. The name of Cato probably became prefixed to thefe diftichs, in a lower age, by the officious ignorance of tranfcribers, and from the acquiefcence of readers equally ignorant, as Marcus Cato had written a fet of moral diftichs. Whoever was the author, this metrical fyftem of ethics had attained the higheft degree of eftimation in the barbarous ages. [There is a paraphrafe in Anglo-Saxon profe of many of Cato's diftichs in the Cotton MS. Julius A II. and a later (or femi-Saxon) copy of the fame in Cotton MS. Vefpafian, D. XIV. In the Vernon MS. in

---

[1] It was printed under the name of Aufonius, Roftoch. 1572. 8vo.

[2] *Ex Epiftol.* Vindiciani Medici, ad Valent. They are mentioned by Notkerus, who flourifhed in the tenth century, among the *Metrorum, Hymnorum, Epigrammatumque conditores*. Cap. vi. *De Illuftrib. Vir.* &c., printed by Fabric. *M. Lat.* v. p. 904.

[3] The poem *De Virtutibus Herbarum*, under the name of Macer, now extant, was written by Odo or Odobonus, a phyfician of the dark ages. It was tranflated into Englifh by John Lelarmoner, or Lelamar, mafter of Hereford fchool, about the year 1373. MSS. Sloane. 29. *Princ.* "Apium, Ache is hote and drie." There is *Macer's Herbal, ibid.* 43. [Of this there were at leaft two printed editions. In one of them it is called *Macers Herball Practyfyd by Doctor Lynacro.* Both were from the prefs of R. Wyer.]

the Bodleian library there is a triglot Cato in Latin, French, and English. The French text is a somewhat corrupt copy of Everard's translation, the English an imitation of Everard. This version seems never to have been completed, as blanks are left in the MS. where several of the stanzas should stand; similar blanks occur at the same spots in another copy (Additional MS. 22,283). There is a fragment of another early English translation in Fairfax MS. 14.[1]] Among Langbaine's MS. bequeathed to the University of Oxford by Antony Wood, it is accompanied by a Saxon paraphrase.[2] John of Salisbury, in his *Polycraticon*, mentions it as the favourite and established manual in the education of boys.[3] To enumerate no others,

---

[1] [Mr. Brock's addition. See Blades's *Life and Typography of William Caxton*, i. 52, *et seq.* and 278.]

[2] Cod. [2. old number 8615.]

[3] *Polycrat.* vii. 9, p. 373, edit. Lugd. Bat. 1595. It is cited, *ibid.* pp. 116, 321, 512. In the *Art of Versification*, a Latin poem, written by Everhardus Bethuniensis, about the year 1212, there is a curious passage, in which all the classics of that age are recited; or the best authors then in vogue, and whom he recommends to be taught to youth. [Leyser. *Poet. Med. Æv.* p. 825.] They are, Cato the moralist. Theodolus, the author of a leonine eclogue, a dialogue between Truth and Falsehood, written in the 10th century, printed among the *Octo Morales*, and by Goldastus, *Man. Bibl.* 1620. MSS. Harl. 3093. 4. [This piece, sometimes inaccurately ascribed to the press of] Wynkyn de Worde, was printed under the title of *Theodoli liber, cum commento*, 1515. It was from one of these *Eclogues*, beginning *Æthiopum terras*, that Field, master of Fotheringay College about the year 1480, set the verses of the book called *Æthiopum terras* in the glass window with figures very neatly. Leland. *Itin.* i. fol. 5. [p. 7, edit. 1745.] This seems to have been in a window of the new and beautiful cloister, built about that time. Flavius Avianus, a writer of Latin fables, or apologues. Æsop, or the Latin fabulist, printed among the *Octo Morales*, Lugd. Bat. 1505. Maximianus, whose six elegies, written about the seventh century, pass under the name of Gallus. Chaucer cites this writer, and in a manner which shows his elegies had not then acquired the name of Gallus. *Court of L.* v. 798: "Maximinian truely thus doeth he write." Pamphilus Maurilianus, author of the hexametrical poem *De Vetula*, and the elegies *De Arte amandi*, entitled *Pamphilus*, published by Goldastus, *Cataleêt. Ovid.* 1610. Dares Phrygius, on the destruction of Troy. Macer. Marbodeus [or Marbodus Gallus, author of *Hymns, Epistles*, and a treatise *De Gemmis*, printed together in 1524. See Brunet, iii. 1391.] Petrus de Riga, canon of Rheims, whose *Aurora*, or the *History of the Bible allegorised*, in Latin verses, some of which are in rhyme, was never printed entire. He has left also *Speculum Ecclesiæ*, with other pieces, in Latin poetry. He flourished about the year 1130. Sedulius. Prosper. Arator. Prudentius. Boethius. Alanus, author of the *Anticlaudian*, a poem in nine books, occasioned by the scepticism of Claudian. Virgil, Horace, Ovid, Lucan, Statius, Juvenal, and Persius. John [de] Hauteville, an Englishman, who wrote the *Architrenius* in the twelfth century, a Latin hexameter poem in nine books. Philip Gualtier, of Chatillon, who wrote, about the same period, the *Alexandreis*, an heroic poem on Alexander the Great. Solymarius or Gunther, a German Latin poet, author of the *Solymarium* or *Crusade*. Galfridus, our countryman, whose *Nova Poetria* was in higher celebrity than Horace's *Art of Poetry*. Matthæus of Vendome who, in the year 1170, paraphrased the *Book of Tobit* into Latin elegiacs from the Latin bible of Saint Jerom, under the title of the *Tobiad*, sometimes called the *Thebaid*, and first printed among the *Octo Morales*. Alexander [Gallus or] de Villa Dei, whose *Doctrinale* or Grammar in Leonine verse superseded Priscian about the year 1200. It was first printed [with the types of Johan de Spira about 1470, and] by Wynkyn de Worde, 1503. He was a French friar-minor, and also wrote the *Arguments of the chapters of all the books of either Testament*, in 212 hexameters. With some other forgotten pieces.

it is much applauded by Isidore the old etymologist,[1] Alcuin,[2] and Abelard:[3] and we must acknowledge that the writer, exclusively of the utility of his precepts, possesses the merit of a nervous and elegant brevity. It is [again and again] quoted by Chaucer. In the *Merchant's Tale*, having quoted Seneca to prove that no blessing is equal to an humble wife, he adds Cato's precept of prudently bearing a scolding wife with patience[4] [and in the *Nun's Priest's Tale* Pertelot appeals to Cato to disprove the significance of dreams]. Chaucer constantly [but mistakenly refers to Facetus under the name of] Catoun, which [however] shows that he was more familiar in French than in Latin. It was translated into Greek at Constantinople by Maximus Planudes, who has the merit of having familiarized to his countrymen many Latin classics of the lower empire by metaphrastic versions:[5] and at the restoration of learning in Europe, illustrated by Erasmus with a commentary which is much extolled by Luther.[6] There are [several] French translations.[7] That of Mathurine Corderoy is dedicated to Robert Stevens. In the British Museum there is a French translation by Helis de Guincestre or Winchester, made perhaps at the time when our countrymen affected to write more in French than in English.[8] Caxton in

---

Marcianus Capella, whose poem on the *Marriage of Mercury with Philology* rivalled Boethius. [See *supra*.] Joannes de Garlandia, an Englishman, a poet and grammarian, who studied at Paris about the year 1200. The most eminent of his numerous Latin poems, which crowd our libraries, seem to be his *Epithalamium on the Virgin Mary* in ten books of elegiacs (MSS. Cotton. Claud. A. x.) and *De Triumphis Ecclesiæ*, in eight books, which contains much English history. (MS. *ibid.*) Some of his pieces, both in prose and verse, have been printed. [But see Brunet, in v. Garlandia.] Bernardus Carnotensis or Sylvester, much applauded by John of Salisbury, who styles him the most perfect Platonic of that age. *Metallog.* iv. c. 35. His *Megacosm* and *Microcosm*, a work consisting both of verse and prose, is frequently cited by the barbarous writers. He is imitated by Chaucer, *Man of L. Tale*, v. 4617. "In sterres many a winter," &c. Physiologus or Theobaldus Episcopus, who wrote in Latin verse *De Naturis xii. animalium*, MSS. Harl. 3093. 5. He is there called Italicus. There is also a Magister Florinus, styled also *Physiologus*, on the same subject. Chaucer quotes Physiologus. "For Phisiologus says sikerly." *Nonnes Pr. Tale*, v. 15,277. Sidonius, who wrote a metrical dialogue between a Jew and a Christian on both the Testaments, and a Sidonius, perhaps the same, *regis qui fingit prælia*. To these our author adds his own *Grecismus*, or a poem in hexameters on rhetoric and grammar which, as Du Cange [*Præf. Lat. Gloss.* sect. xlv.] observes, was anciently a common manual in the seminaries of France, and, I suppose, of England.

[1] *Etymol.* v. *Officiperda*.   [2] *Contra Elipand.* lib. ii. p. 949.
[3] Lib. i. *Theol. Christ.* p. 1183.   [4] v. 9251.
[5] It occurs often among the Baroccian MSS. (Bibl. Bodl. viz. 64, 71. bis. 95, 111, 194). The first edition of Cato, soon followed by many others [is without a date, but *circa* 1467. See Brunet, i. 1666. It was printed (at Strasburgh) in 1475.] The most complete edition is that of Christ. Daumius. Cygn. 1672, 8vo.: containing the Greek metaphrases of Maximus Planudes, Joseph Scaliger, Matthew Zuber and John Mylius; a German version by Martinus Apicius, with annotations and other accessions. It was before translated into German rhymes by Abraham Morterius, of Weissenburgh. Francof. 1590. 8vo.
[6] *Colloq. Mensal.* c. 37.
[7] One [attributed to] Pierre Grosnet, *Les mots dores de Cathon.* Paris, [1530.]
[8] MSS. Harl. 4388. This MS. is older than 1400. [Brunet (last edit. i. 1669) cites several French editions of the French Gloss on Cato; but in 1548 appeared a

the preface to his aforesaid translation, affirms that Poggius Florentinus [or Poggio Bracciolini,] whose library was furnished with the most valuable authors, esteemed *Cathon glosed*, that is, Cato with notes, to be the best book in his collection.[1] The glossarist I take to be Philip de Pergamo, a prior at Padua, who wrote a most elaborate *Moralisation on Cato*, under the title of *Speculum Regiminis*, so early as the year 1380.[2] In the same preface, Caxton observes that it is "the beste book for to be taught to yonge children in scole." But he supposes the author to be Marcus Cato, whom he duly celebrates with the two Scipios and other "noble Romaynes."[3] Burgh's performance is too jejune for transcription; and (I suspect) would not have afforded a single splendid extract, had even the Latin possessed any sparks of poetry. It is indeed true, that the only critical excellence of the original, which consists of a terse con-

---

translation of the Latin work into French verse with certain additions.] See MSS. Ashmol. 789. 2, [and consult Brunet *ut supr.*]

In Bennet College library there is a copy of the French *Cato* by Helis of Winchester, MSS. ccccv. 24, fol. 317. It is entitled and begins thus — *Les Distiches Morales de Caton mises en vers par* Helis de Guyncestre.

"Ki vout saver la faitement
Ki Catun a sun fi₃ a prent,
Si en Latin nel set entendre,
Ici le pot en rumain₃* aprendre,
Cum Helis de Guyncestre
Ki deu met a se destre
La translate si fatemente."

The transcript is of the 14th century. Compare Verdier, *Bibl. Franc.* tom. iii. p. 288, edit. 1772. In the [*Paralipomena*] of Anonymus Salernitanus, written about the year 900, the writer mentions a description in Latin verse of the palace of the city of Salerno, but laments that it was rendered illegible through length of time: "Nam si unam paginam fuissemus nacti, comparare illos [versus] profecto potuissemus Maroni in voluminibus, Catonique, sive profecto aliis Sophistis." cap. xxviii. Muratori, *Scriptor. Rer. Ital.* vol. ii.

[1] Many of the glossed manuscripts, so common in the libraries, were the copies with which pupils in the University attended their readers or lecturers, from whose mouths paraphrastic notes were interlined or written in the margin, by the more diligent hearers. In a Latin translation of some of Aristotle's philosophical works, once belonging to Rochester priory, and transcribed about the year 1350, one Henry de Rewham is said to be the writer, and to have glossed the book, during the time he heard it explained by a public reader in the schools of Oxford. "Et audivit in scholis Oxonie, et emendavit et glosavit audiendo." MSS. Reg. 12, G. ii. In the meantime, I am of opinion that the word *reader* originally took its rise from a paucity of books: when there was only one book to be had, which a professor or lecturer recited to a large audience.

[2] Printed August, 1475. In Exeter College library there is *Cato Moralisatus*, MSS. 37. [837.] And again at All Souls, MSS. 9. [1410.] Compare MSS. More, 35. [9221.] And Bibl. Coll. Trin. Dublin. 651. 14. And MSS. Harl. 6294.

[3] [A sufficiently copious account of all the early English printed works on this subject will be found in the *Handb. of E. E. Lit.* under Cato; but the reader may also consult Herbert's *Ames* and Blades's monograph on Caxton.] The *Proverbia Catonis* are a different work from [this], written in hexameters, by Marbodeus, Opp. Hildebert. p. 1634. Paris 1708. fol.

---

* in romance, *i.e.* in French.

ciseness of sentences, although not always expressed in the purest latinity, will not easily bear to be transfused.[1]

About the year 1481, Juliana Barnes, more properly Berners, sister of Richard, lord Berners, and Prioress of the Nunnery of Sopewell, wrote three English tracts on *Hawking, Hunting,* and *Armory* or *Heraldry,* which were soon afterwards printed in the neighbouring monastery[2] of Saint Alban's.[3] From an abbess disposed to turn author, we might more reasonably have expected a manual of meditations for the closet, or select rules for making salves or distilling strong waters. But the diversions of the field were not thought inconsistent with the character of a religious lady of this

---

[1] There is a translation of the *Wyz Cato* and *Æsop's Fables* into English dogrell, [and on the phonetic principle] by William Bulloker, 1585. [See *inf.* sect. 55.]

[2] There was a strong connection between the two monasteries. In that of Saint Alban's a monk was annually appointed, with the title of Custos monialium de Sopewelle. Registr. Abbat. Wallingford, [*sub ann.* 1480] MSS. Bibl. Bodl. MSS. Tanner.

[3] 1486. fol. Again, by W. de Worde, 1496 [folio, and n. d.] 4to. The barbarism of the times strongly appears in the indelicate expressions which she often uses; and which are equally incompatible with her sex and profession. [The entire work was reprinted from the edit. of 1496 by Haslewood, 1810, and Dallaway, in his *Heraldry,* 1793, gave the section on *Blason* from the edition of 1486. The division relating to *Angling* was also reprinted separately in 1827.] The poem begins thus. I transcribe from a good MS. (MSS. Rawlins. Bibl. Bodl.):

> "Mi dere sones, where ye fare, by frith or by fell,*
> Take good hede in his tyme how Tristrem † wol tell;
> How many maner bestes of venery there were,
> Listenes now to our Dame, and ye shullen here.
> Fowre maner bestes of venery there are,
> The first of hem is a hart, the second is an hare;
> The boor is one of tho,
> The wolff, and no mo.
> And wherefo ye comen in play ‡ or in place,
> Now shal I tel you which ben bestes of chace:
> One of the a buck, another a doo,
> The Fox and the marteryn, and the wilde roo:
> And ye shall, my dere sones, other bestes all,
> Where so ye hem finde, rascall hem call,
> In frith or in fell,
> Or in Forrest, y yow tell.
> And to speke of the hert, if ye wil hit lere,
> Ye shall call him a calfe at the first yere;
> The second yere a broket, so shall he be,
> The third yere a spayard, lerneth this at me;
> The .iiii. yere calles hem a stagge, be any way
> The first yere a grete stagge, my dame bade you say."

[A full account of the various editions of this interesting and valuable publication is given in the *Handb. of E. E. Lit.,* and need scarcely be reproduced here. The edition of 1586, mentioned by Dibdin, whom it incautiously followed, is a different work. The latest issue of the *Book of St. Albans* was in 1614, when Gervase Markham's alteration of the original text was printed with further changes, and adaptations to the more modern practice, under the title of *A Jewell for Gentrie.*]

---

* See Gascoigne, ii. 345.]
† See Haslewood's edit. *Introd.* and Gascoigne's *Works,* ii. 306.] ‡ plain.

eminent rank, who refembled an abbot in refpect of exercifing an extenfive manorial jurifdiction; and who hawked and hunted in common with other ladies of diftinction.[1] This work, however, is here mentioned, becaufe the fecond of thefe treatifes is written in rhyme.[2] It is fpoken in her own perfon; in which, being otherwife a woman of authority, fhe affumes the title of dame. I fufpect the whole to be a tranflation from the French and Latin.[3]

Henry Bradfhaw has rather larger pretenfions to poetical fame, although fcarcely deferving the name of an original writer in any refpect. He was a native of Chefter, educated at Gloucefter College in Oxford, and at length a Benedictine monk of Saint Werburgh's Abbey in his native place.[4] Before the year 1500, he wrote the *Life of Saint Werburgh*, a daughter of a king of the Mercians, in Englifh verfe.[5] This poem, befide the devout deeds and paffion of the poet's patronefs-faint, comprehends a variety of other fubjects;

---

[1] At the magnificent marriage of the princefs Margaret with James IV. king of Scotland, in 1503, his majefty fends the new queen, "a grett tame hart, for to have a corfe." Leland. *Coll. Append.* iii. 280, edit. 1770.

[2] This part is tranflated or abftracted from Upton's book *De re militari, et factis illuftribus*, written about 1441. See the fourth book *De infignibus Anglorum nobilium*. Edit. Bifs. 1654. It begins with the following curious piece of facred heraldry. "Of the offspring of the gentilman Jafeth, come Habraham, Moyfes, Aron and the profettys, and alfo the kyng of the right lyne of Mary, of whom that gentilman Jhefus was borne, very god and man: after his manhode kynge of the land of Jude and of Jues, gentilman by is moder Mary, prynce of Cote armure," &c. Nicholas Upton, above mentioned, was a fellow of New College Oxford about 1430. He had many dignities in the church. He was patronifed by Humphrey duke of Gloucefter, to whom he dedicates his book. This I ought to have remarked before. [See *fupr.* fect. xx.]

[3] [I can, however, hardly underftand how fhe could get the technical Englifh terms, as I can hardly believe one in her fituation followed the chafe, and converfed with huntfmen enough for the purpofe. I think that thefe Religious tranflated the French or Latin books on hunting, war, &c., to pleafe their friends, who were profeffed ftatefmen and warriors, and that they furnifhed them the terms of art.— *Afhby*.] [4] *Athen. Oxon.* i. p. 9. Pits, 690.

[5] He declares, that he does not mean to rival Chaucer, Lydgate, fententious, pregnant Barklay, and inventive Skelton. The two laft were his cotemporaries. L. ii. c. 24. [Bradfhaw feems rather to fay, that as his book was compiled for unlearned readers, it ought to fubmit itfelf with deference to the judgment of learned poets. But as the paffage is interefting, I will prefent it, with the context. It occurs in a brief conclufion to the work by the tranflator:

> "Go forth, litell boke, Jefu be thy fpede,
> And faue the alway from myfrepoityng,
> Whiche art compiled for no clerke in dede,
> But for marchaunt men hauyng litell lernyng,
> And that rude people therby may haue knowyng,
> Of this holy virgin and redolent rofe,
> Which hath ben kept full longe tyme in clofe.
>
> To all auncient poetes, litell boke, fubmytte the,
> Whilom flouryng in eloquence facundious,
> And to all other whiche prefent nowe be,
> Fyrft to maifter Chaucer and Ludgate fentencious,
> Alfo to preignaunt Barkley nowe beyng religious,
> To inuentiue Skelton and poet laureate,
> Praye them all of pardon both erly and late."—*Park*.]

as a description of the kingdom of the Mercians,¹ the lives of Saint Etheldred and Saint Sexburgh,² the foundation of the city of Chester,³ and a chronicle of our kings.⁴ It is collected from Bede, Alfred

---

¹ Lib. i. c. ii.   ² Lib. i. cap. xviii, xix.   ³ Lib. i. cap. iii.
⁴ Lib. ii. cap. xv. The practice of writing metrical *Chronicles of the kings of England* grew very fashionable in this century. See *supr.* Many of these are evidently composed for the harp: but they are mostly mere genealogical deductions. Hearne has printed from the Heralds office a *Petegree* of our kings from William the conqueror to Henry VI., written in 1448. [*Appendix* to Rob. Gloucester, vol. ii p. 585, see p. 588.] This is a specimen:

> "Then regnyd Harry nought full wyfe,
> The sone of Mold [Maud] the emperefe.
> In his tyme then Seynt Thomas
> At Caunterbury marteryd was.
> He held Rosomund the shen,
> Gret sorwe hit was for the quen:
> At Wodestoke for hure he made a toure,
> That is called Rosemoundes boure.—
> And sithen regnyd his sone Richard,
> A man that was neuer a ferd:
> He werred ofte tyme and wyse
> Worthily vpon godis enemyse.
> And sithen he was shoten, alas!
> Atte castelle Gailard there he was.
> Att Foonte Euerard he lithe there:
> He regnyd almost .x. yere.—
> In Johne is tyme, as y vnderstond,
> Was enterdyted alle Engelond:
> He was fulle wrothe and grym,
> For prestus wold nought synge before hym," &c.

Lydgate has left the best chronicle of the kind, and most approaching to poetry. *The regnynge of kyngys after the conquest by the monk of Bury.* MSS. Fairf. Bibl. Bodl. 16; [MSS. Ashmol. 59. ii. MSS. Harl. 2251. 3; and a beautiful copy, with pictures of the kings, MSS. Cotton. *Julius.* E. 5. Printed by W. de Worde in 1530.] This is one of the stanzas. [MSS. Bodl. B. 3. 1999. 6.]

RICARDUS PRIMUS.

> "Rychard the next by successyon,
> First of that name, strong, hardy, and notable,
> Was crouned kynge, called Cur de lyon,
> With Saryzonys hedys served atte table:
> Sleyn at Galard by death full lamentable:
> The space regned fully ix. yere;
> His hert buryed in Roon atte highe autere."

Compare MSS. Harl. 372. 5. There was partly a political view in these deductions: to ascertain the right of our kings to the crowns of France, Castile, Leon, and the duchy of Normandy. See MSS. Harl. 326. 2.—116. 11. fol. 142. I know not whether it be worth observing, that about this time a practice prevailed of constructing long parchment-rolls in Latin, of the pedigree of our kings. Of this kind is the *Pedigree of British kings from Adam to Henry the Sixth*, written about the year 1450, by Roger Alban, a Carmelite friar of London. It begins, "Confiderans chronicorum prolixitatem." The original copy, presented to Henry VI., by the compiler, is now in Queen's College library at Oxford. MSS. [22.] B. 5. 3. There are two copies in Winchester College library, and another in the Bodleian. Among Bishop More's MSS. there is a parchment-roll of the pedigree of our kings from Ethelred to Henry IV. in French, with pictures of the several monarchs, MSS. 495; and in the same collection, a pedigree from Harold to Henry IV. with elegant illuminations, MSS. 479. In the same rage of

of Beverley, Malmesbury, Girardus Cambrensis, Higden's *Polychronicon*, and the passionaries of the female saints, Werburgh, Etheldred and Sexburgh, which were kept for public edification in the choir of the church of our poet's monastery:

> For as declareth the true Passionary,
> A boke where her holie lyfe wrytten is,
> Which boke remayneth in Chester monastery.[1]

And again,

> I folow the legend and true hystory
> After an humble stile, and from it lytell vary.

And in the prologue,[2]

> Untoo this rude worke myne auctors these,
> Fyrst the true Legends, and the venerable Bede,
> Mayster Alfrydus, and Wyllyam Malmusbury,
> Gyrard, Polychronicon, and other mo indeed.

Bradshaw is not so fond of relating visions and miracles as his argument seems to promise. Although concerned with three saints, he deals more in plain facts than in the fictions of religious romance; and on the whole his performance is rather historical than legendary. This is remarkable in an age when it was the fashion to turn history into legend. Even scripture-history was turned into romance. The story of Esther and Ahasuerus, or of Amon or Hamon, and Mardocheus or Mordecai, was formed into a fabulous poem:[3]

> OF AMON and MORDOCHEUS.
> Mony wynter witerly
> Or Crist weore boren of vre ladi,
> A rich kynge, hiȝte Ahasfwere,
> That stif was on stede and stere;
> Mighti kynge he was, i wis,
> He livede muchel in weolye ant blis,
> His blisse may i nat telle ȝou,
> How lange hit weore to schewe hit nou;
> But thing that tovcheth to vre matere
> I wol ȝou telle, ȝif ȝe wol here.
> The kyng lovede a knight so wele,
> That he commaunded men should knele
> Bifore him, in vche a streete,
> Over all ther men miȝte him meete;
> Amon was the kniȝtes nome,
> On him fell muchel worldus schome,
> For in this ilke kynges lande
> Was moche folke of Jewes wonande,
> Of heore kynd the kyng hym tok
> A qwene to wyve, as telleth the bok, &c.

---

genealogising, Alban above mentioned framed the Descent of Jesus Christ, from Adam through the Levitical and regal tribes, the Jewish patriarchs, judges, kings, prophets and priests. The original roll, as it seems, on vellum, beautifully illuminated, is in MSS. More, *ut supr.* 495. But this was partly copied from Peter of Poiétou, a disciple of Lombard about 1170 who, for the benefit of the poorer clergy, was the first that found out the method of forming, and reducing into parchment-rolls, *Historical Trees* of the Old Testament. Alberic. in *Chron.* p. 441. See MSS. Denb. 1627. 1. Rot.

[1] Lib. i. c. vii. signat. C. ii.   [2] Lib. i. signat. A iiii.
[3] MS. Vernon, *ut supr.* fol. 213.

In the British Museum, there is a long commentitious narrative of the *Creation of Adam and Eve, their Sufferings and Repentance, Death and Burial*.[1] This is from a Latin piece on the same subject.[2] In the English, Peter Comestor, the "maister" of stories, author of the *Historia Scholastica*, who flourished about the year 1170, is quoted.[3] But he is not mentioned in the Latin at fol. 49. [In the library of Winchester Cathedral, is a MS. about 1320, containing *Expulsio Ade* [Adam] *de Paradisis, et quo modo crevit crux Christi, et quomodo miracula facta sunt per lignum*. It is a 4to book of several hundred pages. It contains a notice of all the popes and emperors, &c.]

In Chaucer's *Miller's Tale*, v. 3538, we have this passage:

> Hast thou not herd, quod Nicholas also,
> The sorwe of Noe with his felawship,
> Or that he might get his wif to ship?

I know not whether this anecdote about Noah is in any similar suppositititious book of Genesis. It occurs, however, in the *Chester Whitsun Plays*, where the authors, according to the established indulgence allowed to dramatic poets, perhaps thought themselves at liberty to enlarge on the sacred story.[4] This altercation between Noah and his wife takes up almost the whole third pageant of these interludes. Noah, having reproached his wife for her usual frowardness of temper, at last conjures her to come on board the ark, for fear of drowning. His wife insists on his sailing without her, and swears by Christ and St. John, that she will not embark till some of her old female companions are ready to go with her. She adds, that if he is in such a hurry, he may sail alone, and fetch himself a new wife. At length Shem, with the help of his brothers, forces her into the vessel; and while Noah very cordially welcomes her on board, she gives him a box on the ear.[5]

Bradshaw's fabulous origin of Chester is not so much to be imputed to his own want of veracity, as to the authority of his voucher Ranulph Higden, a celebrated chronicler, his countryman, and a monk of his own abbey.

As to Bradshaw's history of the foundation of Chester, it may be classed with [the anonymous poem of four leaves only printed by R. Pynson about 1500, entitled *The Foundation of the Chapel of Walsingham* (conjecturally, as in the only known copy the first leaf is missing, and this is the subject). The narrative commences thus:

> Of this chapell se here the fundacyon,
> Bylded the yere of crystes incarnacyon,
> A thousande complete lyxty and one,
> The tyme of sent edward kyng of this region.

Of the same class is the *Foundation of the Abbey of Gloucester* in twenty-two stanzas, printed by Hearne, and written in 1534 by the

---

[1] MSS. Harl. 1704. 5. fol. 18.   [2] *Ibid.* 495. 12. fol. 43. imperf.
[3] fol. 26.   [4] MSS. Harl. 2013.
[5] [In *Notes and Queries* for April 9, 1870, occurs a short paper on the Anglo-Norman Morality of Adam.]

laſt abbot, William Malverne. Bradſhaw's piece is mentioned by Harpsfield.[1]

He [Bradſhaw] ſuppoſes that Cheſter, called by the ancient Britons Cair-Lleon, or the city of Legions, was founded by Leon Gaur, a giant, corrupted from *Leon Vaur*, or the great legion:

> The founder of this citie, as ſayth Polychronicon,
> Was Leon Gaur, a myghte ſtronge gyaunt,
> Which buildid caves and dongeons manie a one,
> No goodlie buildyng, ne proper, ne pleaſant.

He adds with an equal attention to etymology:

> But kinge Leir a Britan fine and valiaunt,
> Was founder of Cheſter by pleaſaunt buildyng,
> And was named Guar Leir by the kyng.[2]

But a greater degree of credulity would perhaps have afforded him a better claim to the character of a poet: and, at leaſt, we ſhould have conceived a more advantageous opinion of his imagination, had he been leſs frugal of thoſe traditionary fables, in which ignorance and ſuperſtition had clothed every part of his argument. This piece was firſt printed in 1521.[3]

[The following is one of the introductory chapters, and is headed: *A deſcrypcyon of the Geanealogy of ſaynt Werburge, and how ſhe deſcended of foure kynges of this lande & of the royall blode of Fraunce.* The genealogy is traced with much hiſtorical accuracy, and this portion of the performance may perhaps be partly original:]

> This noble pryncess, the doughter of Syon,
> The floure of vertu, and vyrgyn gloryous,
> Bleſſed Saynt Werburge, full of deuocyon,
> Deſcended by auncetry, and tytle famous,
> Of foure myghty kynges, noble and vyctoryous,
> Reynynge in his lande, by true ſucceſſyon,
> As her lyfe hiſtoryall, maketh declaracyon.
>   The yere of our lorde, frome the natyuyte
> Fyue hundreth. xiiii. and alſo iiii. ſcore,
> Whan Auſtyn was ſende from ſaynt Gregorye,
> To conuert this regyon unto our ſauyoure
> The noble kyng Cryda than reygned with honoure
> Vpon the mercyens, whiche kynge was father
> Vnto kynge Wybba and Quadriburge his ſyſter.
>   This Wybba gate Penda, kynge of mercyens,
> Whiche Penda ſubdued fyue kynges of this regyon
> Reygnỹge thyrty yere, in worſhyp and reuerens
> Was grauntfather to Werburge, by lynyall ſucceſſyon
> By his quene Kyneſwith, had a noble generacyon
> Fyue valeant prynces, Penda and kynge Wulfer,
> Kynge Ethelred, ſaint Marceyl, ſaynt Marwalde, 1 fere.[4]

---

[1] MSS. Harl. 539. 14, fol. 111. *Hiſt. Eccles. Angl.* p. 264. Princip. "In ſundrie fayer volumes of antiquitie."

[2] Lib. ii. c. iii.

[3] In [4to.] With a wooden cut of the Saint. Princip. "Whā Phebus had roūe his cours ī Sagittari." At the beginning is [*The prologe of J. T.*, &c., including an acroſtic on the tranſlator Bradſhaw's name, and at the end are three Ballads.]

[4] [*The Holy Lyfe and Hiſtory of Saynt Werburge*, &c. Edited by Edward Hawkins, Eſq. Chetham Society, 1848].

The most splendid passage of this poem is the following description of the feast made by King Wulfer in the hall of the abbey of Ely, when his daughter Werburgh was admitted to the veil in that monastery. Among other curious anecdotes of ancient manners, the subjects of the tapestry, with which the hall was hung, and of the songs sung by the minstrels, on this solemn occasion, are given at large. The heading of the chapter is: "Of the great solempnyte kynge Wulfer made at the ghostly maryage of saynt Werburge his doughter, to al his louers, cosyns, and frendes."[1]

> Kynge Wulfer her father/ at this ghostly spousage
> Prepared great tryumphes/ and solemptnyte
> Made a royall feest/ as custome is of maryage
> Sende for his frendes/ after good humanyte
> Kepte a noble housholde/ shewed great lyberalyte
> Both to ryche and poore/ that to this feest wolde come
> No man was denyed/ every man was well come.
>
> Her uncles and auntes/ were present there all
> Ethelred and Merwalde/ and Mercelly also
> Thre blessed kynges/ whome sayntes we do call
> Saint kenefwyd/ saint keneburg/ theyr systers both two
> And of her noble lygnage/ many other mo
> Were redy that seaion/ with reuerence and honour
> At this noble tryumphe/ to do all theyr deuour.
>
> Tho kynges mette them/ with theyr company,
> Egbryct kynge of kent/ brother to the quene
> The seconde was Aldulphe kynge of the eest party
> Brother to saynt Audry/ wyfe and mayde serene
> With dyuers of theyr progeny/ and nobles as I wene
> Dukes/ erles/ barons/ and lordes ferre and nere
> In theyr best aray/ were present all in fere.[2]
>
> It were full tedyous/ to make descrypcyon
> Of the great tryumphes/ and solempne royalte
> Belongynge to the feest/ the honour and prouysyon,
> By playne declaracyon/ vpon euery partye
> But the sothe to say/ withouten ambyguyte
> All herbes and floures/ fragraunt fayre and swete
> Were strawed in halles/ and layd vnder theyr fete.
>
> Clothes of golde and arras/ were hanged in the hall
> Depaynted with pyctures/ and hystoryes manyfolde
> Well wrought and craftely/ with precyous stones all
> Glyterynge as Phebus/ and the beten golde
> Lyke an erthly paradyse/ pleasaunt to beholde
> As for the sayd moynes[3]/ was not them amonge
> But prayenge in her cell/ as done all nouice yonge.
>
> The story of Adam/ there was goodly wrought
> And of his wyfe Eue/ bytwene them the serpent
> How they were deceyued/ and to theyr peynes brought
> There was Cayn and Abell/ offerynge theyr present
> The sacryfyce of Abell/ accepte full euydent
> Tuball and Tubalcain/ were purtrayed in that place
> The inuentours of musyke/ and craftes by great grace.
>
> Noe and his shyppe/ was made there curyously
> Sendynge forth a rauen/ whiche neuer came agayne;

---

[1] [Edit. 1848, cap. xvi. p. 58.]
[2] together.
[3] nun, i. e. The Lady Werburg.

And how the doue retourned/ with a braunche haftely
A **token** of conforte and peace/ to man certayne
Abraham there was/ ftandynge vpon the mount playne
To offer in facryfyce/ Ifaac his dere fone,
And how the fhepe for hym/ was offered in oblacyon.

The twelue fones of Jacob/ **there were** in purtrayture
And how into Egypt/ yonge Jefeph **was** folde
There was impryfoned/ by a falfe **coniectour**
After **in** all Egypt/ was ruler (as is **tolde**).
There was in pycture/ Moyfes **wyfe and bolde**
Our lorde apperynge in bufhe flammynge as fyre
And nothynge therof brent/ lefe/ tree/ nor fpyre.[1]

The ten plages of Egypt/ were well emboft
The chyldren of Ifrael/ paffynge the reed fee
Kynge Pharoo drowned/ with all his proude hooft
And how the two tables/ at the mounte of Synaye
Were gyuen to Moyfes/ and how foone to ydolatry
The people were prone/ and punyfshed were therfore,
How Datan and Abyron/ for pryde were loft full youre.[2]

Duke Jofue was ioyned/ after them in pycture,
Ledynge the Ifrehelytes/ to the lande of promyffyon
And how the faid lande/ was diuyded by mefure
To the people of god/ by equall fundry porcyon
The Judges and byfshops/ were there euerychone
Theyr noble actes/ and tryumphes Marcyall
Frefshly were browdred/ in thefe clothes royall.

Nexte to hye borde/ appered fayre and bryght
Kynge Saull and Dauyd/ and prudent Salomon,
Roboas fuccedynge/ whiche foone loft his myght
The good kynge Efechyas/ and his generacyon
And fo to the Machabees/ and dyuers other nacyon
All thefe fayd ftoryes/ fo rychely done and wrought
Belōgyng to kyng Wulfer/ agayn y[t] tyme were brought.[3]

But ouer the hye deffe[4]/ in the pryncypall place
Where the fayd thre kynges/ fate crowned all
The beft hallynge[5] hanged/ as reafon was
Wherin were wrought/ the .ix. ordres angelycall
Dyuyded in thre Jerarchyfes/ not ceffynge to call
Sanctus/ fanctus/ fanctus/ bleffed be the trynyte
Dominus Deus fabaoth/ thre perfones in one deyte

Nexte in ordre fuynge[6]/ fette in goodly purtrayture
Was our bleffed lady/ floure of femynyte
With the twelue apoftles/ echeone in his fygure
And the foure euangelyftes/ wrought mooft curyoufly
Alfo the dyfcyples/ of chryft in theyr degre
Prechynge and techynge/ vnto euery nacyon
The faythtes[7] of holy chyrche/ for their faluacyon.

Martyrs than folowed/ ryght manyfeftly
The holy innocentes/ whome Herode had flayne,
Bleffed faynt Stephan/ the prothomartyr truly
Saynt Laurēce/ faynt Vyncēt/ fufferynge great payne
With many other mo/ than here ben now certayne

---

[1] twig, branch.   [2] burnt.
[3] All this tapeftry, belonging to King Wulfer, was brought to Ely monaftery on this occafion.
[4] feat; [*vid. fupr.*]   [5] tapeftry.   [6] following.   [7] feats; facts.

Of whiche sayd martyrs/ exsample we may take
Pacyence to obserue/ in herte for chrystes sake.

Confessours approched/ ryght conuenyent,
Freshely enbrodred/ in ryche tyshewe and fyne;
Saynt Nycholas/ saynt Benedycte/ and his couente
Saynt Jerom/ Basylyus/ and saynt Augustyne
Gregory the great doctour/ Ambrose and saynt Martyne
All these were sette/ in goodly purtrayture
Them to beholde/ was a heuenly pleasure.

Vyrgyns them folowed/ crowned with the lyly
Amonge whome our lady/ chefe presydent was
Some crowned with rooses/ for theyr great vyctory
Saynt Katheryne/ saynt Margerete/ saynt Agathas
Saynt Cycyly/ saynt Agnes/ and saynt Charytas
Saynt Lucye/ saynt Wenefryde/ and saynt Apolyn
All these were brothered/[1] the clothes of golde within.

Upon the other syde of the hall sette were
Noble auncyent storyes/ & how the stronge Sampson
Subdued his enemyes by his myghty power
Of Hector of Troy/ slayne by fals treason
Of noble Arthur/ kynge of this regyon
With many other mo/ whiche it is to longe
Playnly to expresse/ this tyme you amonge.

The tables were couered with clothes of Dyaper
Rychely enlarged/ with syluer and with golde
The cupborde with plate/ shynynge fayre and clere
Marshalles theyr offyces/ fulfylled manyfolde
Of myghty wyne plenty/ bothe newe and olde
All maner kynde/ of meetes delycate
(Whan grace was sayd) to them was preparate.

To this noble feest/ there was suche ordynaunce
That nothynge wanted/ that goten myght be
On see and on lande/ but there was habundaunce
Of all maner pleasures/ to be had for monye
The bordes all charged/ full of meet plente
And dyuers subtyltes/[2] prepared sothly were
With cordyall spyces/ theyr ghestes for to chere.

The Joyfull wordes/ and swete communycacyon
Spoken at the table/ it were harde to tell
Eche man at lyberte/ without interrupcyon
Bothe sadnes and myrthes/ also pryue counsell
Some adulacyon/ some the truthe dyd tell
But the great astates/[3] spake of theyr regyons
Knyghtes of theyr chyualry/ of craftes the comons.

Certayne at eche cours/ of seruice in the hall
Trumpettes blewe vp/ shalmes and claryons
Shewynge theyr melody with/ toynes [4] musycall
Dyuers other mynstrelles/ in crafty proporcyons
Made swete concordaunce/ and lusty dyuysyons
An heuenly pleasure/ suche armony to here
Reioysynge the hertes/ of the audyence full clere.

A synguler mynstrell/ all other ferre passynge
Toyned [5] his instrument/ in pleasaunte armony

---

[1] embroidered. [2] dishes of curious cookery, so called. [3] kings.
[4] tunes. [5] tuned.

And fange mooſt ſwetely/ the company gladynge
Of myghty conquerours/ the famous vyctory
Wherwith was rauyſshed/ theyr ſpyrytes and memory
Specyally he ſange/ of the great Alexandere
Of his tryumphes and honours/ endurynge .xii. yere.

Solemply he ſonge/ the ſtate of the Romans
Ruled vnder kynges/ by polycy and wyſedome
Of theyr hye iuſtyce/ and ryghtfull ordynauns
Dayly encreaſynge/ in worſhyp and renowne
Tyll Tarquyne ye proude kynge/ with ye great cöfuſyon
Oppreſſed dame Lucrece/ the wyfe of Colatyne
Kynges neuer reygned in Rome/ ſyth that tyme.

Alſo how the Romayns/ vnder thre dyctatours
Gouerned all regyons/ of the worlde ryght wyſely
Tyll Julyus Ceſar/ excellynge all conquerours
Subdued Pompeius/ and toke the hole monarchy
And the rule of Rome/ to hymſelfe manfully
But Caſſius Brutus/ the fals conſpyratour
Cauſed to be ſlayne/ the ſayd noble emperour.

After the ſayd Julyus/ ſucceded his ſyſter ſone
Called Octuyanus/ in the imperyall ſee
And by his precepte/ was made deſcrypcyon
To euery regyon/ lande/ ſhyre/[1] and cytee
A trybute to pay/ vnto his dygnyte
That tyme was/ vnyuerſall peas and honour
In whiche tyme was borne/ our bleſſed ſavyoure.

All theſe hyſtoryes/ noble and auncyent
Reioyſynge the audyence/ he ſange with pleaſuer
And many other mo of the newe teſtament
Pleaſaunt and profytable/ for theyr ſoules cure
Whiche be omytted/ now not put in vre
The mynyſters were redy/ theyr offyce to fulfyll
To take vp the tables/ at theyr lordes wyll.

Whan this noble feeſt/ and great ſolempnyte
Dayly endurynge/ a longe tyme and ſpace
Was royally ended/ with honour and royalte
Eche kynge at other/ lyſence taken hace
And ſo departed from thens/ to theyr place
Kynge Wulfer retourned/ with worſhyp and renowne
Frome the houſe of Ely to his owne manſyon.

If there be any merit of imagination or invention, to which the poet has a claim in this deſcription, it altogether conſiſts in the application. The circumſtances themſelves are faithfully copied by Bradſhaw, from what his own age actually preſented. In this reſpect, I mean as a picture of ancient life, the paſſage is intereſting; and for no other reaſon. The verſification is infinitely inferior to Lydgate's worſt manner.

Bradſhaw [died on the 15th May, 1513, and] was buried in the cathedral church, to which his convent was annexed.[c] Bale, a

---

[1] This puts one in mind of the *Sheriffs*, in our tranſlation of the Bible, among the officers of the kingdom of Babylon, *Dan.* iii. 2.

[2] *Ath. Oxon.* i. 9, [and Wright's *Biog. Brit. Lit.* Anglo-Saxon period, 518-19. The *year* is aſcertained by one of the laudatory "balades" affixed, which ſpeaks of Bradſhaw :

violent reformer, obferves that our poet was a perfon remarkably pious for the times in which he flourifhed.¹ This is an indirect fatire on the monks, and on the period which preceded the Reformation. I believe it will readily be granted, that our author had more piety than poetry. His Prologue contains the following humble profeffions of his inability to treat lofty fubjects, and to pleafe light readers:

> To defcrybe hye hyftoryes/ I dare not be fo bolde
> Syth it is a mater/ for clerkes conuenyent
> As of the .vii. aeges/ and of our parentes olde
> Or of the iiii. empyres whylom mooft excellent
> Knowynge my lernynge therto infufficient
> As for bawdy balades you fhall haue none of me
> To excyte lyght hertes to pleafure and vanyte.²

A great tranflator of the lives of the Saxon faints from the Saxon, in which language only they were then extant, into Latin, was [Gotfelin or] Gofcelinus, a monk of [the monaftery of St. Bertin], who paffed from France into England with Hereman [afterwards] bifhop of Salifbury, [in] 1058.³ As the Saxon language was at this time but little underftood, thefe tranflations opened a new and ample treafure of religious hiftory: nor were they acquifitions only to the religion, but to the literature, of that era. Among the reft were the Lives of Saint Werburgh,⁴ Saint Etheldred,⁵ and Saint Sexburgh,⁶ moft probably the legends, which were Bradfhaw's originals. Ufher obferves, that Gofcelinus alfo tranflated into Latin the ancient Catalogue of the Saxon faints buried in England.⁷ In the Regifter of Ely it is recorded, that he was the moft eloquent writer of his age; and that he circulated all over England, the lives, miracles and gefts of

---

"Now departed from this temporall lyght,
The prefent yere of this Tranflacion
M. D. XIII. of Chriftis incarnacion."

Sign. f ii b.—*Park*.]
¹ Cent. ix. Numb. 17.
[² Edit. 1848, p. 4. Bradfhaw alfo wrote the *Life of Saynt Radegunde*, in 7-line ftanzas, printed by Pynfon, without date in 4to.]
³ W. Malmefbur. lib. iv. *ubi infr*.—Gofcelin. in *Præfat. ad Vit. S. Auguftini*. See Mabillon, *Act. Ben. Sæc*. i. p. 499 [and Le Neve, *Fafti Eccl. Anglic*. ii. 594, edit. Hardy.]
⁴ *Act. Sanctor*. Bolland. tom. i. Februar. p. 386. A part in Leland, *Coll*. ii. 154. Compare MSS. C.C.C. Cant. J. xiii. [which contains, however, only fo much as related to St. Auguftine and his companions. The moft important MS. of Gotfelin's *Lives of Saints* in Latin is MS. Cotton. Vefp. B. xx. nearly coeval with the author. See alfo *ibid*. Claudius, A, v. and Harl. MS. 105, where the feries of lives is called *Ecclefiafticæ Hiftoriæ Libri* viii.]
⁵ Regiftr. Eliens. *ut infra*.
⁶ See Leland, *Coll*. iii. p. 152. Compare the Lives of SS. Etheldred, Werburgh, and Sexburgh, at the end of the *Hiftoria aurea* of John of Tynemouth, MS. Lambeth, 12. I know not whether they make a part of his famous *Sanctilogium* [or *Nova Legenda Angliæ*, attributed to Capgrave. See a lift of the contents in *Catal. Cotton. MSS*. pp. 76-7.] He flourifhed about the year 1380.
⁷ *Antiquit. Brit*. c. ii. p. 15. See Leland's *Coll*. iii. 86 *feq*. And Hickes, *Thefaur*. laft vol. pp. 86, 146, 208.

the faints of both fexes, which he reduced into profe-hiftories.[1] The words of the Latin deferve our attention. "In hiftoriis in *profa* dictando mutavit." Hence we may perhaps infer, that they were not before in profe, and that he took them from old metrical legends: this is a prefumptive proof, that the lives of the faints were at firft extant in verfe. The paffion for verfifying everything was carried to fuch a height in the middle ages, that before the year 1300, Juftinian's Inftitutes and the code of French jurifprudence were tranflated into French rhymes. There is a very ancient edition of this work, without date, place, or typographer, faid to be corrected *par plufieurs docteurs* and *fouverains legiftes*, in which are thefe lines:—

> J'ay par pareffe demouré
> Trop longuement a commencer
> Pour Inftitutes *romancer*.[2]

In the fame light we are to underftand the words which immediately follow in the Regifter: "Hic fcripfit *Profam* fanctæ Etheldredæ;" which is extant in this Ely regifter, and contains 54 heads; where the *profe* of St. Etheldred is oppofed to her *poetical* legend. Thefe improved profe-narratives were often turned back again into verfe, even fo late as in the age before us: to which (among others I could mention) we may refer the legend of St. Euftathius:—

> Seynt *Euftace*, a nobull kniȝte,
> Of hethen law he was;
> And ere than he cryftened was
> Mene callyd him *Placidas*.
> He was with *Trajan* themperor, &c.[3]

By *mutavit dictando* we are to underftand, that he *tranflated* or *reformed*, or, in the moft general fenfe, *wrote anew in Latin*, thefe antiquated lives. His principal objects were the more recent faints, efpecially thofe of this ifland. Malmefbury fays, "Innumeras *Sanctorum Vitas Recentium ftylo extulit*, veterum vel amiffas, vel *informiter editas*, comptius renovavit."[4] In this refpect, the labours of Gotfelin partly refembled thofe of Symeon Métaphraftes, a celebrated Conftantinopolitan writer of the tenth century, who obtained the diftinguifhed appellation of the *Metaphraft* becaufe, at the command and under the aufpices of Conftantine Porphyrogenita, he modernifed the more ancient narratives of the miracles and martyrdoms of the moft eminent eaftern and weftern faints for the ufe of the Greek church: or rather digefted from detached, imperfect, or obfolete books on the fubject a new and more commodious body of facred biography.

Concerning legend-makers, there is a curious ftory in [Richard

---

[1] Cap. x. *Vit. Ethel.*
[2] See Menage, *Obs. fur la Lang. Fr.* partie prem. ch. 3. Verdier and La Croix, iii. 428, iv. 160, 554, 560. *Bibl. Fr.* edit. 1773.
[3] MSS. Cotton, Calig. A. 2. A Latin legend on this faint is in MS. Harl. 2316, 42.
[4] *Hift. Angl.* lib. iv. p. 130.

§ 26. A curious Anecdote of Legend-making.

James's *Iter Lancastrense*.][1] Gilbert de Stone, a learned ecclesiastic, who flourished about the year 1380, was solicited by the monks of Holywell in Flintshire to write the life of their patron saint. Stone, applying to these monks for materials, was answered that they had none in their monastery. Upon which he declared, that he could execute the work just as easily without any materials at all: and that he would write them a most excellent legend, after the *manner* of the legend of Thomas à Becket. He has the character of an elegant Latin writer, and seems to have done the same piece of service, perhaps in the same way, to other religious houses. From his *Epistles* it appears that he wrote the *Life of St. Wolfade*, patron of the priory of canons regular of his native town of Stone in Staffordshire, which he dedicated to the prior, William de Madely.[2] He was Latin secretary to several bishops, and could possibly write a legend or a letter with equal facility. His epistles are 123 in number. The first of them in which he is styled "chancellor to the Bishop of Winchester," is to the Archbishop of Canterbury.[3] This Bishop of Winchester must have been William of Wykeham.

The most extraordinary composition of this kind, if we consider, among other circumstances, that it was compiled at a time when knowledge and literature had made some progress, and when mankind were so much less disposed to believe or to invent miracles, more especially when the subject was quite recent, is the *Legend of King Henry the Sixth*. It is entitled, *De Miraculis beatissimi illius Militis Christi, Henrici sexti*, &c. That it might properly rank with other legends, it was translated from an English copy into Latin by one Johannes, styled *Pauperculus*, a monk, about [1490], at the command of John Morgan, dean of Windsor, afterwards [in 1496] Bishop of St. David's. It is divided into two books: to both of which prefaces are prefixed, containing proofs of the miracles wrought by this pious monarch. At the beginning there is a hymn with a prayer addressed to the royal saint[4]:—

> Salve, miles preciose,
> Rex Henrice generose, &c.

Henry could not have been a complete saint without his legend.[5] What shall we think of the judgment and abilities of the dignified ecclesiastic, who could seriously patronise so ridiculous a narrative?

Among the many striking contrasts between the manners and characters of ancient and modern life, which these annals present, we must not be surprised to find a mercer, a sheriff, and an alderman of London, descending from his important occupations to write verses. This is Robert Fabyan, who yet is generally better known as an

---

[1] MSS. James, xxxi. p. 6 (Bibl. Bodl.) [The *Iter* was edited by Mr. Corser for the Chetham Society, 1845.]
[2] *Epist*. iii. dat. 1399. MSS. Bibl. Bodl. Sup. D i. Art. 123.
[3] [MSS. Cotton. Vitell. E. x, 17.]
[4] Fol. 72.
[5] MSS. Harl. 423, 7. And MSS. Reg. 13 C. 8.

historian than as a poet. He was esteemed not only the most facetious, but the most learned, of all the mercers, sheriffs and aldermen of his time: and no layman of that age is said to have been better skilled in the Latin language. [He was the son of John Fabyan, and is supposed to have been a native of Essex. His will was proved in the Prerogative Court of Canterbury, July 12, 1513 (though dated July 11 in the previous year), and Bale says that he died Feb. 28, 1512-13.[1] Very little is known of his personal history. He was sheriff of London in 1493]. In his *Chronicle* or *Concordance of Histories* from Brutus to the year 1485, it is his usual practice, at the division of the books [and elsewhere] to insert metrical prologues and other pieces in verse. The best of his metres is the *Complaint* of Edward II. who, like the personages in Boccaccio's *Fall of Princes*, is very dramatically introduced, reciting his own misfortunes.[2] But this soliloquy is nothing more than a translation from a short and a very poor Latin poem attributed to that monarch, but probably written by William of Wyrcester, which is preserved among the MSS. of the College of Arms, and entitled, *Lamentatio gloriosi regis Edvardi de Karnarvon quam edidit tempore suæ incarcerationis*. Our author's transitions from prose to verse, in the course of a prolix narrative, seem to be made with much ease; and when he begins to versify, the historian disappears only by the addition of rhyme and stanza. In the first edition of his *Chronicle*, by way of epilogues to his seven books, he has given us *The Seven Joys of the Blessed Virgin in English Rime*; and under 1325 there is a poem to the virgin, and another on one Badby a Lollard under the year 1409.[3] These are [in part omitted and in part altered in Reynes's and Kingston's editions, but inserted entire in Rastell's]. He has likewise left a panegyric on the city of London; but despairs of doing justice to so noble a subject for verse, even if he had the eloquence of Tully, the morality of Seneca, and the harmony of that *faire Lady* Calliope.[4] The reader will thank me for citing only one stanza from King Edward's *Complaint*:—

> Whan Saturne with his colde isy face,
> The grounde with his frostys turnyth the grene to whyte,
> The tyme of wynter which trees doth deface
> And causyth all verdure to avoyde quyte:
> Then fortune, whiche sharpe was with stormys not alyte,

---

[1] [Edit. 1811, Preface, iii., where his will is printed entire.]

[2] [Page 431, edit. 1811.] See Hearne's *Lib. Nig. Scacc.* p. 425. And *Præfat.* p. xxxviii. Fabyan says, "They are reported to be his own makynge, in the tyme of his emprysonment."—*Ibid.* By the way, there is a passage in this chronicler which points out the true reading of a controverted passage in Shakespeare, "Also children were christened thorough all the land, and menne *houseled and aneled*, excepte suche," &c. tom. ii. p. 30, coll. 2. Another proof which ascertains this reading of the controverted passage in *Hamlet*, occurs in the romance of *Morte Arthur*. When Sir Lancelot was dying, "whan he was *howseled* and *eneled*, and had *all that a crysten man ought to have*, he praid the bishop, that his felowes might beare his bodie unto Joyous Garde," &c. B. xxi. cap. xii.

[3] Edit. Lond. 1516, fol.

[4] Fol. 2, tom. ii. *ut supr.*

> Hath me affautyd with hir frowarde wyll,
> And me beclypped with daungeours right yll.[1]

As an hiftorian, our author is the dulleft of compilers. He is equally attentive to the fucceffion of the mayors of London and of the monarchs of England: and feems to have thought the dinners at Guildhall and the pageantries of the city companies more interefting tranfactions than our victories in France and our ftruggles for public liberty at home. One of Fabyan's hiftorical anecdotes, under the important reign of Henry V., is that a new weathercock was placed on the crofs of Saint Paul's fteeple. It is faid that Cardinal Wolfey commanded many copies of this chronicle to be committed to the flames, becaufe it made too ample a difcovery of the exceffive revenues of the clergy. The earlier chapters of thefe childifh annals faithfully record all thofe fabulous traditions, which generally fupply the place of hiftoric monuments in defcribing the origin of a great nation.

Another poet of this period is John [Watton], a prieft. He wrote a Latin theological tract entitled *Speculum Chriftiani*, which is a fort of paraphrafe on the decalogue and the creed.[2] But it is interfperfed with a great number of wretched Englifh rhymes: among which is the following hymn to the Virgin Mary:[3]

> Mary Moder, wel thu be;
> Mary Moder thenk on me:
> Mayden and moder was never non
> Togedir, lady, fave thu allon.[4]

---

[1] In the Britifh Mufeum there is a poem [by Sir Francis Hubert, knight,] on this fubject, and in the fame ftanza. MSS. Harl. 2393, 4to. 1. [Printed furreptitioufly in 1628, again in 1629 and 1631 from a genuine text, and fourthly in 1721. Sir F. Madden thinks the Harl. MS. may be autograph.] The ghoft of Edward II., as here, is introduced fpeaking. It is addreffed to Queen Elizabeth, as appears (among other paffages) from ft. 92, 242, 243, 305. It begins thus:
> "Whie fhould a wafted fpirit fpent in woe
> Difclofe the wounds receyved within his breft?"

It is imperfect, having only 352 ftanzas. Then follows the fame poem, with many alterations, additions, and omiffions. This is addreffed to James I., as appears from ftanza 6, 259, 260, 326, &c. It contains 581 ftanzas. There is another copy in the fame library, Num. 558. At the end the poet calls himfelf Infortunio. It begins thus:—
> I fing thy fad difafter, fatal king,
> Carnarvon Edward, fecond of that name.

The poem on this fubject in the addition to the *Mirror of Magiftrates* by [Richard] Niccols, is a different compofition, [and is called]: *A Winter Night's Vifion*. [Edit.] 1610, p. 702. Thefe two manufcript poems deferve no further mention: nor would they have been mentioned at all, but from their reference to the text, and on account of their fubject. Compare MSS. Harl. 2251, 119. fol. 254. An unfinifhed poem on Edward II., perhaps by Lydgate. Princ. *Beholde this greate prince Edward the Secunde.*

[2] MSS. C.C.C. Oxon. 155. MSS. Laud. G. 12, MSS. Thorefb. 530. There is an abridgment of this work, [MSS. Harl. 2250. 20.] with the date 1477. This is rather beyond the period with which we are at prefent engaged.

[3] Compare a hymn to the Holy Virgin, *fupra*.

[4] Thefe four lines are in the exordium of a prayer to the virgin, MSS. Harl. 2382. (4to) 3. fol. 86, b.

> Swete lady, mayden clene,
> Schilde me fro ille, fchame, and tene,
> And out of dette, for charitee, &c.[1]

[In this work is a ftory taken from the *Gefta Romanorum*.][2]

Matthew Paris relates that Godrich, a hermit about the year 1150, who lived in a folitary wild on the banks of the river Wear near Durham, had a vifion in his oratory of the Virgin Mary, who taught him this fong:

> Sainte Marie [clane] virgine,
> Moder Jhefu Criftes Nazarene,
> Onfo, fchild, help thir Godric
> Onfang, bring hegilich with the in godes riche.
> Sainte Marie, Chriftes bur.
> Maidens clenhad, moderes flur,
> Dilie min finne, rix in min mod,
> Bring me to winne with the felid god.[3]

In [Harl. MS. 2253, of the time of Edward I. or Edward II., from which fome extracts have been given in a preceding fection,] many very ancient hymns to the Holy Virgin occur. Thefe are fpecimens:[4]

> Bleffed be þou levedy, ful of heovene bliffe,
> Swete flur of paradys, moder of mildeneffe,
> Preye Jhefu þy fone þat he me rede and wyffe
> So my wey forte gon, þat he me never myffe.[5]

> As y me rod þis ender day,
> By grene wode to feche play,
> Mid herte y þohte al on a May
>   Sweteft of alle þinge!
> Lyþe, and ich ou telle may al of þat fuete þinge.[6]

> Mayden moder milde, *oiez cel oreyfoun*,
> From fhome þou me fhilde, *e di ly mal feloun*,
> For love of thine childe, *me menez de trefoun*,
> Ich wes wod and wilde, *ore fu en prifoun*.[7]

In the library of Mr. Farmer, of Tufmore in Oxfordfhire, [was] a collection of hymns and antiphones, paraphrafed into Englifh by William Herbert, a Francifcan friar and a famous preacher about the year 1330. Thefe, with fome other of his pieces in autograph contained in the fame library, are unmentioned by Bale[8] and Pits,[9] Pierre de Corbian, a troubadour, has left a hymn or prayer to the Holy Virgin which, he fays, he chofe to compofe in the romance-language, becaufe he could write it more *intelligibly* than Latin. Another troubadour, a mendicant friar of the thirteenth century, had worked himfelf up into fuch a pitch of enthufiafm concerning the Holy Virgin, that he became deeply *in love* with her. It is partly

---

[1] Printed by William Machlinia [about 1480, in 4to.]
[2] [Sir F. Madden's information. Edit. 1838, No. 37.*]
[3] Matt. Paris, *Hift. Angl.* [*Henric.* ii.] p. 115, edit. 1589. [The prefent text has been taken from Mr. Ritfon's *Bibliographia Poetica*.—Price.]
[4] *Ibid.* 66, fol. 80, b.
[5] *Ibid.* 67, fol 81, b.
[6] *Ibid.* 69, fol. 83. In French and Englifh.
[7] See alfo *ibid.* 49, fol. 75; 57, fol. 78; and 372, 7, fol. 55.
[8] *Ibid.* v. 31.   [9] *Ibid.* p. 428.

owing, as I have already hinted, to the gallantry of the dark ages, in which the female sex was treated with so romantic a respect, that the Virgin Mary received such exaggerated honours, and was so distinguished an object of adoration in the devotion of those times.

Caxton, the celebrated printer, was likewise a poet; [see] the rhyming introductions and epilogues with which he frequently decorates his books.

Among the anonymous pieces of poetry belonging to this period, which are very numerous, the most conspicuous is the *Calendar of Shepherds*. It seems to have been translated into English about the year 1480, [or perhaps somewhat later,] from a French book entitled *Kalendrier des Bergers*. It was printed [at Paris in 1503, folio, and having been re-translated or revised throughout by Robert Copland, was again printed before 1506. There are many later impressions from the presses of De Worde, Pynson, and other typographers.][1] This piece was calculated for the purposes of a perpetual almanack, and seems to have been the universal magazine of every article of salutary and useful knowledge. It is a medley of verse and prose, and contains, among many other curious particulars, the saints of the whole year, the moveable feasts, the signs of the zodiac, the properties of the twelve months, rules for blood-letting, a collection of proverbs, a system of ethics, politics, divinity, physiognomy, medicine, astrology, and geography. Pieces of this sort were not uncommon. In the British Museum there is an astrological poem, teaching when to buy and sell, to let blood, to build, to go to sea, the fortune of children, the interpretation of dreams, with other like important particulars, from the day of the moon's age.[2] In the principal letter the author is represented in a studious posture. The manuscript, having [the usual] Saxon letters intermixed, begins thus:

> He that wol herkyn of wit
> That ys witnest in holy wryt,
> Lystenyth to me a stonde,
> Of a story y schal yow telle,
> What tyme ys good to byen and to sylle,
> In bok as hyt ys y-fownde.

The reader who is curious to know the state of quackery, astrology, fortune-telling, midwifery, and other occult sciences about the year 1420, may consult the works of one John Crophill, who practised in Suffolk.[3] This *cunning-man* was likewise a poet, and has left in the same manuscript some poetry spoken at an entertainment of *Frere Thomas* and five ladies of quality, whose names are mentioned, at which two great bowls or goblets, called *Mercy* and *Charity*, were briskly circulated.[4]

---

[1] I have an edition printed by John Waley, without date, 4to. In the prologue it is said, "This book was first corruptly printed in France, and after that at the cost and charges of Richard Pinson, newly translated and reprinted, although not so faithfully as the original copy required," &c. [See Herbert's *Ames*, i. 210-12.]
[2] MSS. Harl. 2329. 3, fol. 31.
[3] MSS. Harl. 1735. 4to. 3 *seq*. [See fol. 29. 36.]
[4] *Ibid.* fol. 48.

Among other authors, *Cathon the great clarke*,[1] *Solomon*, *Ptolomeus the prince of astronomy*, and Aristotle's *Epistle to Alexander*, are quoted [in this calendar.][2] Every month is introduced respectively speaking, in a stanza of *balad royal*, its own panegyric. This is the speech of May:[3]

> Of all monthes in the yeare I am kinge,
> Flourishing in beauty excellently;
> For, in my time, in vertue is all thinge,
> Fieldes and medes sprede most beautiously,
> And birdes singe with sweete harmony;
> Rejoysing lovers with hot love endewed,
> With fragrant flowers all about renewed.

In the theological part, the terrors and certainty of death are described by the introduction of Death, seated on the pale horse of the Apocalypse, and speaking thus:[4]

> Upon this horse blacke and hideous
> Death I am, that fiercely doth sitte:
> There is no faireneffe, but fight tedious,
> All gay colours I do hitte.
> My horse runneth by dales and hilles,
> And many he smiteth dead and killes.
> In my trap I take some by every way,
> By towns [and] castles I take my rent.
> I will not respite one an houre of a daye,
> Before me they must needes be present.
> I flea all with my mortall knife,
> And of duety I take the life.
> Hell knoweth well my killing,
> I sleepe never, but wake and warke;
> It[5] followeth me ever running,
> With my darte I flea weake and starke:
> A great number it hath of me,
> Paradyse hath not the fourth parte, &c.

In the eighth chapter of our calendar are described the seven visions, or the punishments in hell of the seven deadly sins, which Lazarus saw between his death and resurrection. These punishments are imagined with great strength of fancy, and accompanied with wooden cuts[6] boldly touched, and which the printer probably procured from some German engraver in the infancy of the art.[7] The proud are bound by hooks of iron to vast wheels, like mills, placed between craggy precipices, which are incessantly whirling with the most violent impetuosity, and sound like thunder. The envious are

---

[1] Epilogue.   [2] Cap. 42.   [3] Cap. 2.
[4] Cap. xix. [Mr. Ashby asks, how can a black and a pale horse be one and the same? Groseley and Comines both make the same mistake, owing to the likeness of *blanc* and *black*. MS. note.—*Park*. May not a horse be black and pale too?]
[5] That is, hell.
[6] [Herbert remarks here, that W. de Worde's edition being but a small quarto, could not admit of the more elegant drawings to the folio edition in 1503, which were exactly copied in 1656.—*Park*. But the cuts described here by Park, as in the folio of 1656, were also in those of 1556, 1559, &c.]
[7] Compare the torments of Dante's Hell. *Inf.* Cant. v. vi. *seq.*

plunged into a lake half frozen, from which as they attempt to emerge
for ease, their naked limbs are instantly smitten with a blast of such
intolerable keenness, that they are compelled to dive again into the
lake. To the wrathful is assigned a gloomy cavern, in which their
bodies are butchered, and their limbs mangled, by demons with
various weapons. The slothful are tormented in a horrible hall dark
and tenebrous, swarming with innumerable flying serpents of various
shapes and sizes, which sting to the heart. This, I think, is the hell
of the Gothic Edda. The covetous are dipped in caldrons filled
with boiling metals. The gluttonous are placed in a vale near a
loathsome pool, abounding with venomous creatures, on whose banks
tables are spread, from which they are perpetually crammed with
toads by devils. Concupiscence is punished in a field full of immense
pits or wells, overflowing with fire and sulphur. This visionary scene
of the infernal punishments seems to be borrowed from a legend related by Matthew Paris, under the reign of King John: in which
the soul of one Turkhill, a native of Tidstude in Essex, is conveyed
by St. Julian from his body, when laid asleep, into hell and heaven.
In hell he has a sight of the torments of the damned, which are
presented under the form and name of the infernal pageants, and
greatly resemble the fictions I have just described. Among the tormented is a knight, who had passed his life in shedding much innocent blood at tilts and tournaments. He is introduced, completely
armed on horseback, and couches his lance against the demon, who
is commissioned to seize and to drag him to his eternal destiny.
There is likewise a priest who never said mass, and a baron of the
exchequer who took bribes. Turkhill is then conducted into the
mansions of the blessed, which are painted with strong oriental
colouring: and in Paradise, a garden replenished with the most
delicious fruits and the most exquisite variety of trees, plants and
flowers, he sees Adam, a personage of gigantic proportion but the
most beautiful symmetry, reclining on the side of a fountain which
sent forth four streams of different water and colour, and under the
shade of a tree of immense size and height, laden with fruits of every
kind, and breathing the richest odours. Afterwards St. Julian conveys the soul of Turkhill back to his body; and when awakened, he
relates this vision to his parish priest.[1] There is a story of a similar
cast in Bede,[2] which I have mentioned before.

---

[1] Matt. Paris. *Hist.* p. 206, *seq.* Edit. Tig. Much the same sort of fable is
related, *ibid.* p. 178, *seq.* There is an old poem on this subject called *Owayne
Miles*, MSS. *Cott. Calig.* A. 12, f. 90. [Another copy of *Owain Miles* is in the
Auchinleck MS., and has been printed by Laing, 1837. See also the well-known
Visions of Tundale, which involve a similar superstition. An English translation is
in the Auchinleck MS. and has been (not very carefully) edited by Turnbull. Mr.
Wright's monograph on *St. Patrick's Purgatory*, 1842, should also be consulted.
Warton himself says:] See also the legend of St. Patrick's cave, Matt. Paris, p.
843; and MSS. Harl. 2385. 82. *De quodam ducto videre penas Inferni*, fol. 56, b.
[2] See [*supra*, vol. i p. 203]. The Dead Man's Song there mentioned seems to
be more immediately taken from this fiction as it stands in our *Shepherd's Kalender*.
It is entitled, *The Dead Man's Song*, whose dwelling was near Basinghall in

As the ideas of magnificence and elegance were enlarged, the public pageants of this period were much improved: and (beginning now to be celebrated with new splendour) received among other advantages the addition of *speaking personages*. These spectacles, thus furnished with speakers characteristically habited, and accompanied with proper scenery, co-operated with the *Mysteries*, of whose nature they partook at first, in introducing the drama. It was customary to prepare these shows at the reception of a prince, or any other solemnity of a similar kind; and they were presented on moveable theatres or occasional stages, erected in the streets. The speeches were in verse; and as the procession moved forward the speakers, who constantly bore some allusion to the ceremony, either conversed together in the form of a dialogue, or addressed the noble person whose presence occasioned the celebrity. Speakers seem to have been admitted into our pageants about the reign of Henry VI.

In the year 1432, when Henry VI., after his coronation at Paris, made a triumphal entry into London, many stanzas, very probably written by Lydgate, were addressed to his majesty, amidst a series of the most splendid allegorical spectacles, by a giant representing religious fortitude, Enoch and Eli, the holy Trinity, two Judges and eight "Serjeants of the coife, dame Clennesse," Mercy, Truth, and other personages of a like nature.[2]

In the year 1456, when Margaret, wife of Henry VI., with her little son Edward, came to Coventry on the Feast of the Exaltation of the Holy Cross, she was received with the presentation of pageants, in one of which Edward the Confessor, Saint John the Evangelist, and Saint Margaret, each speak to the queen and the prince in verse.[3] In the next reign, in the year 1474, another Prince Edward, son of

---

London. Wood's *Ballads* [and other copies exist in the various collections.] It begins thus:

"Sore sicke, dear friends, long tyme I was,
And weakly laid in bed," &c.

These highly painted infernal punishments and joys of Paradise are not the invention of the author of the *Kalendrier*. They are taken both from M. Paris and from Henry of Saltry's Description of St. Patrick's *Purgatory*, written in 1140, and printed by Messingham in his *Florilegium Insulæ Sanctorum*, &c. Paris, 1624, fol. cap. vi. &c. p. 101. See *Bibl.* Bodl. MSS. 550. [See *infra*, p. 128.] Messingham has connected the two accounts of M. Paris and H. de Saltry with some interpolations of his own. This adventure appears in various MSS. No subject could have better suited the devotion and the credulity of the dark ages.

[2] Fabyan, *ubi supr.* fol. 382, *seq.*

[3] Leet-book of the city of Coventry. MS. fol. 168. Stow says that at the reception of this queen in London in the year 1445, several pageants were exhibited at Paul's-gate, with verses written by Lydgate, on the following lemmata. "Ingredimini et replete terram. Non amplius irascar super terram. Madam Grace chancellor de dieu. Five wise and five foolish virgins. Of saint Margaret," &c. *Chronicle*, pag. 385, edit. Howes. I know not whether these poems were spoken, or only affixed to the pageants. Fabyan says that in those pageants there was "resemblance of dyvirse olde hystoryes." I suppose tapestry. *Cron.* tom. ii. fol. 398, edit. 1533. See the ceremonies at the coronation of Henry VI. in 1430. Fab. *ibid.* fol. 378.

Edward IV., visited Coventry, and was honoured with the same species of show: he was first welcomed in an octave stanza by Edward the Confessor, and afterwards addressed by St. George, completely armed: a king's daughter holding a lamb, and supplicating his assistance to protect her from a terrible dragon, the lady's father and mother standing in a tower above, the conduit on which the champion was placed "renning wine in four places, and minstralcy of organ playing."[1] Undoubtedly the Franciscan Friars of Coventry, whose sacred interludes, presented on Corpus Christi day in that city and at other places, make so conspicuous a figure in the history of the English drama, were employed in the management of these devises; and that the Coventry men were famous for the arts of exhibition, appears from the share they took in the gallant entertainment of Queen Elizabeth at Kenilworth Castle, before whom they played their old storial show. The friars themselves were [originally] the actors. But this practice being productive of some enormities, and the laity growing as wise as the clergy, at least as well qualified to act plays, there was an injunction in the *Mexican Council*, ratified at Rome in the year 1589, to prohibit all clerks from playing in the Mysteries, even on Corpus Christi Day. "Neque in Comœdiis personam agant, etiam in festo Corporis Christi."[2]

At length personages of another cast were added; and this species of spectacle, about the period with which we are concerned, was enlivened by the admission of new characters, drawn either from profane history or from profane allegory, in the application of which some degree of learning and invention appeared. Profane allegory, however, had been applied in pageants somewhat earlier. In the pageants above mentioned, presented to Henry VI., the seven liberal sciences personified are introduced in a "tabernacle of curious worke," from which their queen, "dame Sapience," speaks verses. At entering the city she is met and saluted in metre by three ladies "richly cladde in golde and silkes," with coronets, who suddenly issue from a stately tower hung with the most splendid arras. These are the dames: Nature, Grace, and Fortune.[3] But this is a rare instance so early.

I have observed in a former work, and it is a topic which will again be considered in its proper place, that the frequent and familiar use of allegoric personifications in the public pageants—I mean the general use of them—greatly contributed to form the school of Spenser.[4] But moreover, from what is here said, it seems probable that the Pageants, which being shown on civil occasions, derived great part of their decorations and actors from historical fact, and consequently made profane characters the subject of public exhibition,

---

[1] Fab. *ib.* fol. 221.
[2] *Sacrosanct. Concil.* fol. per Labb. tom. xv. p. 1268, edit. 1672.
[3] Fabyan, *ut supr.* fol. 382, *seq.* [Mr. Collier seems to differ from Warton here, and to consider his account of the origin of the Moralities incorrect. *Hist. of Dram. Poet.* iii. 260-1.]
[4] See *Obs. Fairy Queen*, ii. 90.

dictated ideas of a regular drama much sooner than the Mysteries, which being confined to Scripture stories, or rather the legendary miracles of sainted martyrs, and the no less ideal personifications of the Christian virtues, were not calculated to make so quick and easy a transition to the representations of real life and rational action.

In the year 1501, when the Princess Catharine of Spain came to London to be married to Prince Arthur, her procession through the city was very magnificent. The pageants, in which the principal actors or speakers were not only God the Father, St. Catharine, and St. Ursula, but King Alphonsus the astronomer and an ancestor of the princess, a Senator, an Angel, Job, Boethius, Nobility, and Virtue, were numerous, and superbly furnished. These personages sustained a sort of action, at least of dialogue. The lady was compared to Hesperus, and the prince to Arcturus; and Alphonsus, from his skill in the stars, was introduced to be the fortune-teller of the match.[1] These machineries were contrived and directed by an ecclesiastic of great eminence, Bishop Fox who, says Bacon, "was not only a grave counsellor for war or peace, but also a good surveyor of works and a good master of ceremonies, and anything else that was fit for the active part belonging to the service of court or state of a great king." It is probable that this prelate's dexterity and address in the conduct of a court rareeshow procured him more interest than the gravity of his counsels and the depth of his political knowledge; at least his employment in this business presents a striking picture of the importance of those popular talents which, even in an age of blind devotion and in the reign of a superstitious monarch, were instrumental in paving the way to the most opulent dignities of the church. "Whosoever," adds the same penetrating historian, "had these toys in compiling, they were not altogether pedantical."[2] About the year 1487, Henry VII. went a progress into the north, and at every place of distinction was received with a pageant, in which he was saluted in a poetical oration not always religious, as at York by Ebranck, a British king and the founder of the city, as well as by the Holy Virgin and King David; at Worcester by Henry VI. his uncle; at Hereford by St. George and King Ethelbert, at entering the cathedral there; at Bristol, by King Bremmius, Prudence, and Justice. The two latter characters were personated by young girls.[3]

In the mean time it is to be granted, that profane characters were personated in our pageants before the close of the fourteenth century. Stow relates that in the year 1377, for the entertainment of the young Prince Richard, son of Edward the Black Prince, one hundred and thirty citizens rode disguised from Newgate to Kennington where the court resided, attended by an innumerable multitude of waxen torches and various instruments of music, in the

---

[1] *Chron.* MS.
[2] Bacon's *Henry the Seventh* (*Compl. Hist. Eng.* vol. i. p. 628).
[3] From a MS. in the Cotton library, printed in Leland's *Collectan ad calc.* vol. iii. p. 185.

evening of the Sunday preceding Candlemas-day. In the first rank were forty-eight, habited like esquires, with visors, and in the second the same number, in the character of knights. "Then followed one richly arrayed like an Emperor, and after him, at some distance, one stately-tyred like a Pope, whom followed twenty-four Cardinalls, and after them eyght or tenne with blacke visors not amiable, as if they had been Legates from some forrain princes." But this parade was nothing more than a dumb show, unaccompanied by any kind of interlocution. This appears from what follows. For our chronicler adds that, when they entered the hall of the palace, they were met by the prince, the queen, and the lords, "whom the said mummers did salute, *shewing by a pair of dice their desire to play with the prince,*" which they managed with so much complaisance and skill, that the prince won of them a bowl, a cup, and a ring of gold, and the queen and lords, each a ring of gold. Afterwards, having been feasted with a sumptuous banquet, they had the honour of dancing with the young prince and the nobility; and so the ceremony was concluded.[1] Matthew Paris informs us that at the magnificent marriage of Henry III. with Eleanor of Provence in 1236 certain strange pageants and wonderful devices were displayed in the city of London; and that the number of Histriones on this occasion was infinite.[2] But the word *histrio*, in the Latin writers of the barbarous ages, generally comprehends the numerous tribe of mimics, jugglers, dancers, tumblers, musicians, minstrels, and the like public practitioners of the recreative arts, with which those ages abounded: nor do I recollect a single instance in which it precisely bears the restrained modern interpretation.

The most splendid spectacle of this sort which occurs in history, at least so early as the fourteenth century, is described by Froissart, who was one of the spectators. It was one of the shows at the magnificent entrance of Queen Isabel into Paris in 1389. The story is from the Crusade against Saladin. I will give the passage: "Than after, under the mynster of the Trinyte, in the strete,

---

[1] Stow's *Surv. Lond.* p. 71, edit. 1599. It will perhaps be said, that this show was not properly a pageant but a mummery. But these are frivolous distinctions: and, taken in a general view, this account preserves a curious specimen of early personation, and proves at least that the practice was not then in its infancy.

[2] I will cite the passage more at large, and in the words of the original. "Convenerunt autem vocata ad convivium nuptiale tanta nobilium multitudo utriusque sexus, tanta religioforum numerositas, tanta plebium populositas, tanta histrionum *Varietas*, quod vix eos civitas Londoniarum sinu suo capaci comprehenderet. Ornata est igitur civitas tota olosericis, et vexillis, coronis, et palliis, cereis et lampadibus, et quibusdam *prodigiosis ingeniis et portentis,*" &c. *Hist.* p. 406, edit. 1589, *sub* Henrico III. Here, by the way, the expression "*Varietas* histrionum" plainly implies the comprehensive and general meaning of the word histrio; and the multifarious performances of that order of men. [" Among the regulations under A.D. 1258, we meet with the following remarkable expression! ' Histrionibus potest dari cibus, quia pauperes sunt, non quia histriones; et eorum ludi non videantur, vel audiantur, vel permittantur fieri coram Abbate et Monachis.' Here the words *histriones* and *ludi* would seem distinctly to point out the nature of the performance."—*Collier.*]

there was a ſtage, and therupon a caſtell. And along on the ſtage there was ordeyned the Paſſe of Kyng Salhadyn, and all their dedes in Perſonages: the criſten men on the one parte, and the Sarazins on the other parte. And there was, in Perſonages, all the lordes of name that of olde tyme hadde ben armed, and had done any feates of armes at the Paſſe of Salhadyne, and were armed with ſuche armure as they than uſed. And thanne, a lyttel above them, there was in Perſonages the Frenche kynge and the twelve Peeres of Fraunce armed, with the blaſon of their armes. And whan the Frenche queues lytter was come before this ſtage, ſhe reſted there a ſeaſon. Thenne the Perſonages on the ſtage of Kynge Rychard departed fro his company, and wente to the Frenche kynge, and demaunded lycence to go and aſſayle the Sarazins; and the kynge gave hym [them] leave. Thanne kynge Rycharde retourned to his twelve companyons. Thanne they all ſette them in order, and incontynente wente and aſſayled Salhadyne and the Sarazins. Then in ſporte there ſeemed a great bataile, and it endured a good ſpace. This pageaunt was well regarded."[1] By the two kings, he means Philip of France and our Richard I. who were jointly engaged in this expedition. It is obſervable, that the ſuperiority is here given to the King of France.

I cannot omit the opportunity of adding a ſtriking inſtance of the extraordinary freedom of ſpeech, permitted to the minſtrels at the moſt ſolemn celebrities. About 1250, Henry III. paſſing ſome time in France, held a moſt magnificent feaſt in the great hall of the knights-templars at Paris: at which, beſide his own ſuite, were preſent the kings of France and Navarre, and all the nobility of France. The walls of the hall were hung all over with ſhields, among which was that of our Richard I. Juſt before the feaſt began, a joculator or minſtrel accoſted King Henry thus: "My lord, why did you invite ſo many Frenchmen to feaſt with you in this hall? Behold, there is the ſhield of Richard, the magnanimous king of England!—All the Frenchmen preſent will eat their dinner in fear and trembling!"[2] Whether this was a preconcerted compliment, previouſly ſuggeſted by the King of France, or not, it is equally a proof of the familiarity with which the minſtrels were allowed to addreſs the moſt eminent perſonages.

There is a paſſage in John of Saliſbury much to our purpoſe, which I am obliged to give in Latin.[3] Here Gignadii, a word unexplained

---

[1] *Chron.* tom. ii. c. 56, fol. clxxii. col. i. Lord Berners's tranſl. 1523.
[2] Matt. Paris. p. 871, *ſub* Henr. III. edit. 1589.
[3] "At eam [deſidiam] noſtris prorogant hiſtriones. Admiſſa ſunt ergo Spectacula, et infinita lenocinia vanitatis.—Hinc *mimi, ſalii vel ſaliares, balatrones, æmiliani, gladiatores, paleſtritæ, gignadii, præſtigiatores* malefici quoque multi, et tota joculatorum ſcena proćedit. Quorum adeo error invaluit, ut a *præclaris domibus* non arceantur etiam illi, qui *obſcœnis partibus corporis, oculis* omnium eam ingerunt *turpitudinem*, quam erubeſcet videre vel cynicus. Quodque magis mirere, nec tunc ejiciuntur, quando tumultuantes inferius *crebro ſonitu aerem fœdant, et turpiter incluſum turpius produnt.* Veruntamen quid in ſingulis poſſit aut deceat, animus

by Du Cange, signifies wrestlers or the performers of athletic exercises: for *gignasium* was used for *gymnasium* in the barbarous Latinity. By *apologos*, we are perhaps to understand an allegorical story or fable, such as were common in the Provençal poetry, and by *narrationes*, tales of chivalry: both which were recited at festivals by these histriones. *Spectacula* I need not explain: but here seems to be pointed out the whole system of ancient exhibition or entertainment. I must add another pertinent passage from this writer, whom the reader will recollect to have flourished about the year 1140.[1]

With regard to Apologi, mentioned below, I have farther to observe that the Latin metrical apologues of the dark ages are probably translations from the Provençal poetry. Of this kind is Wircker's *Speculum Stultorum*, or *Burnell's Ass* and the *Asinus Pœnitentiarius*, in which an ass, wolf and fox are introduced, confessing their sins, &c.[2] In the British Museum there is an ancient thin folio volume on vellum, containing upwards of two hundred short moral tales in Latin prose, which I also class under the apologi here mentioned by John of Salisbury. Some are legendary, others romantic, and others allegorical. Many of them I believe to be translations from the Provençal poetry. Several of the *Æsopian* fables are intermixed. In this collection is Parnell's *Hermit*,[3] and a tale in Fontaine of the king's son who never saw a woman.[4] The stories seem to have been collected by an Englishman, at least in England, for there is the tale of one Godfrey, a priest of Sussex.[5] The story of Parnell's *Hermit* is in *Gesta Romanorum*.[6]

As our thoughts are here incidentally turned to the rudiments of the English stage, I must not omit an anecdote with regard to the mode of playing the Mysteries at this period, which yet is perhaps of much higher antiquity. In 1487, while Henry VII. kept his residence at the castle at Winchester, on occasion of the birth of Prince Arthur, on a Sunday during the time of dinner he was entertained with a religious drama called *Christi Descensus ad Inferos*, or *Christ's descent into hell*.[7] It was represented by the Pueri Eleemosynarii or choir-boys of Hyde Abbey and St. Swithin's Priory, two large monasteries at Winchester. This is the only proof I have ever seen of choir-boys acting in the old Mysteries, nor do I recollect any other instance of a royal dinner, even on a festival, accom-

---

sapientis advertit, nec apologos refugit, aut narrationes, aut quæcunque spectacula, dum virtutis," &c. *Polycrat*. lib. i. cap. viii. p. 28, edit. 1595.

[1] "Non facile tamen crediderim ad hoc quemquam impelli posse litteratorem, ut histrionem profiteatur.—Gestus siquidem exprimunt, rerum utilitate deducta." Ibid. lib. viii. cap. xii, p. 514. Compare *Fragm. Antiquitatis*, 1815, p. 79, [where, however, I can discover nothing to the purpose.]

[2] See Matt. Flacius, *Catal. Test. Verit*. p. 903, edit. 1556.

[3] De Angelo et Heremita Peregrinum occisum sepelientibus, *Rubr*. 32, fol. 7.

[4] *Rubr*. 8, fol. 2.

[5] *Rubr*. 40, fol. 8. MSS. Harl. 463.

[6] MSS. Harl. 2270, ch. lxxxx. [Several of these are included in Mr. Wright's *Latin Stories, A Contribution to the History of Fiction During the Middle Ages*, 1842.]

[7] *Registr. Priorat. S. Swithin. Winton*. MS. *ut supr*.

panied by this species of diversion.¹ The story of this interlude, in which the chief characters were Christ, Adam, Eve, Abraham, and John the Baptist, was not uncommon in the ancient religious drama, and I believe made a part of what is called the *Ludus Paschalis*, or *Easter Play*.² It occurs in the Coventry plays acted on Corpus Christi day,³ and in the Whitsun-plays at Chester, where it is called the *Harrowing of Hell*.⁴ The representation is Christ entering hell triumphantly, delivering our first parents and the most sacred characters of the Old and New Testaments from the dominion of Satan, and conveying them into Paradise.⁵ There is an ancient dramatic poem on the same subject among the Harleian MSS., containing our Saviour's dialogues in hell with Sathanas, the Janitor or porter of hell, Adam, Eve, Habraham, David, Johan *Baptist*, and Moyses. It begins,

> Alle herkneþ to me nou :
> A strif wolle y tellen ou
> Of Jhesu ant of Sathan
> þo Jhesu wes to helle y-gan.⁶

The composers of the *Mysteries* did not think the plain and probable events of the New Testament sufficiently marvellous for an audience who wanted only to be surprised. They frequently selected their materials from books which had more of the air of romance. The subject of the *Mysteries* just mentioned was borrowed from the Gospel of Nicodemus :⁷ a book which, together with the numerous

---

¹ Except, that on the first Sunday of the magnificent marriage of James of Scotland with the Princess Margaret of England, daughter of Henry VII. celebrated at Edinburgh with high splendour, "after dynnar a Moralite was played by the said Master Inglyshe and hys companyons in the presence of the kyng and qwene." On one of the preceding days, "After soupper the kynge and qwene beyng togader in hyr grett chamber, John Inglysh and his companyons *plaid*." This was in 1503. Leland, *Coll*. iii. pp. 300, 299. *Append*. edit. 1770.

² The Italians pretend that they have a Ludus Paschalis as old as the twelfth century. *Teatro Italiano*, 1723, tom. i. See *Istoria del Teatro*, &c. prefixed, p. ii.

³ [*Ludus Coventriæ*, 1841, p. 329.] " Nunc dormiunt milites, et veniet anima Christi de inferno cum Adam et Eva, Abraham, Joh. Baptiste, et aliis."

⁴ [*Chester Mysteries*, ed. Wright, ii. 71. This was the Cooks' Play.]

⁵ [" This legend, so very popular in the middle ages, was taken .... from the apocryphal gospel of Nicodemus. It enters into the French Mystery of the Resurrection. It forms a separate play in the Townley series (under the title of *Extractio Animarum ab Inferno*)."—Wright.]

⁶ [Copies are in Harl. MS. 2258, Digby MS. 86, and the Auchinleck MS. The last was printed with *Owain Miles*, &c. 1837, 8vo., but it is incomplete. The Digby and Harl. MSS. have also been published, the latter by Mr. Halliwell, 1840, 8vo.] There is a poem on this subject, MS. Bodl. 1687 :

> " How Jesu Crist harowed helle
> Of hardi gestes ich wille telle."

[See *supr*. vol. i.]

⁷ In Latin. A Saxon translation, from a MS. at Cambridge, coeval with the Conquest, was printed by Thwaites, 1699. In an English translation [printed in 1509] by Wynkyn de Worde, the prologue says, " Nichodemus, which was a worthy

apocryphal narratives, containing infinite innovations of the evangelical history, and forged at Constantinople by the early writers of the Greek church, gave birth to an endless variety of legends concerning the life of Christ and his apostles;[1] and which, in the barbarous ages, was better esteemed than the genuine Gospel, on account of its improbabilities and absurdities.

But whatever was the source of these exhibitions, they were thought to contribute so much to the information and instruction of the people on the most important subjects of religion, that one of the Popes granted a pardon of one thousand days to every person who resorted peaceably to the plays performed in the Whitsun week at Chester, beginning with the creation and ending with the general judgment; and this indulgence was seconded by the bishop of the diocese, who granted forty days of pardon: the pope at the same time denouncing the sentence of damnation on all those incorrigible sinners, who presumed to disturb or interrupt the due celebration of these pious sports.[2] It is certain that they had their use, not only in teaching the great truths of Scripture to men who could not read the Bible, but in abolishing the barbarous attachment to military games, and the bloody contentions of the tournament, which had so long prevailed as the sole species of

---

prynce, dydde wryte thys blessyd storye in Hebrewe. And Theodosius, the emperour, dyde it translate out of Hebrew into Latin, and bysshoppe Turpyn dyde translate it out of Latin into Frensshe." See a very old French version, MSS. Harl. 2253, 3, fol. 33, b. There is a translation into English verse, about the fourteenth century. MSS. Harl. 4196, 1, fol. 206. See also, 149, 5, fol. 254, b. And MSS. Coll. Sion. 17. The title of the original is, *Nicodemi Discipuli de Jesu Christi passione et resurrectione Evangelium*. Sometimes it is entitled *Gesta Salvatoris nostri Jesu Christi*. Our lord's Descent into hell is by far the best invented part of the work. Edit. apud *Orthodox Patr.* Basil. 1569, pag. 653, *seq.* The old Latin title to the pageant of this story in the Chester plays is: *De Descensu ad inferna, et de his que ibidem fiebant secundum Evangeliam Nicodemi.* [p. 71, *ut supr.*] Hence the first line in the old interlude, called *Hyckescorner* [circâ 1510], is illustrated.

" Now Jesu the gentyll that brought Adam from hell."

There is a Greek homily on St. John's Descent into hell, by Eusebius Alexandrinus. They had a notion that St. John was our Saviour's precursor, not only in this world, but in Hades. See Allat. *de libr. eccles. Græcor.* p. 303, *seq.* Compare the Legend of Nicodemus, Christ's descent into hell, Pilate's exile, &c. MSS. Bodl. B. 5, 2021, 4, *seq.*

[1] In the MS. Register of St. Swithin's Priory at Winchester, it is recorded that Leofric, bishop of [Devonshire and Cornwall] about 1150, gave to the convent a book called *Gesta Beatissimi Apostoli Petri cum Glosa.* This is probably one of these commentitious histories. By the way, the same Leofric was a great benefactor in books to his church at Exeter. Among others, he gave *Boetii Liber Anglicus* and *Magnus Liber Anglicus omnino metrice descriptus*. What was this translation of Boethius, I know not, unless it is Alfred's. The other piece, the *great book of English* [was no doubt the celebrated *Codex Exoniensis*, edited by Thorpe in 1842. See Wright's *Biog. Brit. Lit.* A.-S. period, 38-9.] The grant is in Saxon, and, if not genuine, must be of high antiquity Dugdale's *Monast.* tom. i. p. 222. I have given Dugdale's Latin translation. The Saxon words are, " Boeþeɼ boc on enᵹliɼc. —Anꝺ i mycel enᵹliɼc boc be ᵹehƿilcum þinᵹum on leoð hƿan ᵹeƿohte." The Saxon text speaks neither of prose nor verse. [Dugdale has confounded leoɼ, populus, with leoð, carmen.—Price.]

[2] MSS. Harl. 2124, 2013.

popular amufement. Rude and even ridiculous as they were, they foftened the manners of the people, by diverting the public attention to fpectacles in which the mind was concerned, and by creating a regard for other arts than thofe of bodily ftrength and favage valour.

[This feems a more fuitable place than was originally felected for mentioning a few of the mifcellaneous poetical compofitions of the reign of Henry VII. They may as well be taken in the order in which they have been hitherto thrown together in a foot note. A tranflation of the *Caftle of Labour* was made from the French of Pierre Gringoire by Alexander Barclay, and printed by Pynfon without date, and by W. de Worde in 1506. Which of thefe was the prior is uncertain: that from the prefs of Pynfon has fome good woodcuts. The colophon fays in both cafes: " Thus endeth the caftell of labour wherein is rycheffe vertue and honour."

It is of fome length, and an allegory in which Lady Reafon conquers Defpair, Poverty, and other evils, which attend a poor man lately married. The Prologue begins, " Ye mortal people that defire to obtayne." The poem begins, " In mufyng an evenynge with me was none." It is in feven-lined ftanzas. The French poem by [Pierre Gringoire was firft printed in 1499, and entitled *Le Chateau de Labour*. It became popular, and was frequently republifhed.] Our higheft efforts of poetry at this period were tranflations from the French. This piece of Gringoire] was alfo tranflated into Englifh rhymes by one Dane or dominus James: the fame perhaps who made the verfion of the *Orchard of Syon:* " Prynted at the coft of mafter Richard Sutton efquyre," Stewarde of the monafterie of Syon, by Wynkyn de Worde, 1529, folio, with fine Gothic cuts in wood. This Mafter Richard Sutton, fteward of the opulent monaftery of Sion near London, was one of the founders of Brafenofe college in Oxford, [and perhaps father of Thomas Sutton, founder of the Charter-Houfe.]

In 1509, W. de Worde printed *The Parlyament of Deuylles*; it was republifhed by Richard Fakes and Julian Notary, in both cafes without date. There is an early MS. of it at Lambeth, which has been printed for the Early Englifh Text Society. De Worde's edition commences: " As Mary was great with Gabriel." The poem occupies eight quarto leaves in the old printed copies.

Of the *Hyftorye of Jacob and his Twelve Sones*, in verfe, there have been at leaft four early impreffions, all without date, fo far as can be afcertained. The firft was from the prefs of W. de Worde about 1504, and the lateft from that of John Allde about 1570. The edition by Allde has been reprinted. It would not be very furprifing, perhaps, to find even a later edition than that iffued by John Allde: for the book is mentioned in the inventory of the ftock of John Fofter, bookfeller of York, fo late as 1616, and as a rule Fofter appears to have confined himfelf to recent publications.[1] It is a doggrel poem in feven-line ftanzas, on fourteen leaves, and begins:

---

[1] [Davies, *Memoir of the York Prefs*, 1868.]

>All yong and olde that lift for to here
>Of deeds doon in old time
>By the holy Patriarks that there were
>Which defcendid of olde Adams line,
>Often the fun of grace on them did fhine,
>For to read this Story it wil doo you much good,
>Of Abram's Sonne, that was fith Noes flood.
>
>Vnto one Rebecca this Ifaac was maried,
>Of age (the Bible faith) he was .xl. year,
>Indeed his maidenhed fo long with him taried,
>And yet in long time his wife no child did here,
>Then to our Lord God he made his prayer
>For to fend him frute this world to multiply,
>And then his wife conceived, as Scriptur doth fpecifie.

About the fame time W. de Worde iffued a *Lytel Treatyfe called the Dyfputacyon, or Complaynte of the Herte thorughe perced with the lokynge of the Eye*, a tranflation of *Le Debat du Cuer et de l'Oeil*, which is printed from a MS. in the Bibliothèque Imperiale in the Appendices to Mr. Wright's edition of the Poems afcribed to Walter Mapes, or from the Latin *Difputatio inter cor et Oculum*, of which there is a copy among the Digby MSS. This feems to be a kindred compofition to the *Debat du Corps et de l'Ame* attached to *La Grande Danfe Machabre*, 1486. The French commences:

>En May la premiere fepmaine —

Of the Englifh verfion, the firft ftanza runs thus:

>In the fyrft weke of the feafon of Maye,
>Whan that the wodes be covered in grene,
>In which the nyghtyngale lyft for to playe
>To fhewe his voys among the thornes kene,
>Them to rejoyce which loves fervaunts bene,
>Which fro all comforte thynke them faft behynd;
>My pleafyr was, as it was after fene,
>For my difport to chafe the harte and hynde.

A highly curious production from Pynfon's prefs in 1520 was *The lyfe of Jofeph of Armathia*, which is not in the Golden Legend, and which is a poetical narrative of Jofeph of Arimathea's adventures in Somerfetfhire, his Travels about Glaftonbury, and his afcent of what is called in the poem (as it is now) *Weary-all Hill*. The ftory is in the octave ftanza, and is contained on ten leaves. But of this tract there are earlier copies in MS. Another biography, but of a different ftamp, is the *Lyfe of Petronylla*, printed by Pynfon without date. It is alfo in verfe, and begins thus on the fecond of the four leaves, of which it confifts:

>The parfite lyfe to put in remembraunce
>Of a virgyn mooft gracious and entere
>Which in all vertu had foveryn fuffyfaunce,
>Called Petronilla petyrs doughter dere.
>Benygne of porte, humble of face and chere,
>All other maydyns excelled in faireneffe,
>And as her legende playnly doth us lere,
>Though fhe were fayre more commended for mekenefs.

The *A. B. C. of Ariſtotle*[1] confiſts of proverbial verſes in the alliterative manner, viz.

> Woſo wil be wiſe and worſhip defireth,
> Lett him lerne one letter, and loke on another, &c.

There are alſo ſome ſatirical ballads written by Frere Michael Kildare, chiefly on the Religious orders, Saints, the White Friars of Drogheda, the vanity of riches, &c. &c. A divine poem on death, &c.[2] He has left a Latin poem in rhyme on the abbot and prior of Glouceſter,[3] and burleſque pieces on ſome of the divine offices.[4] Hither we may alſo refer a few pieces written by one Whyting, not mentioned in Tanner.[5] Undoubtedly many other poems of this period both printed and MSS. have eſcaped my enquiries. Among Rawlinſon's MSS. there is a poem of conſiderable length on the antiquity of the Stanley family, beginning thus,

> I entende with true reporte to praiſe
> The valiaunte actes of the ſtoute Standelais,
> From whence they came, &c.

It comes down no lower than Thomas Earl of Derby, who was executed in the reign of Henry VII. This induced me to think at firſt, that the piece was written about that time. But the writer mentions Henry VIII. and the ſuppreſſion of monaſteries. [To theſe compoſitions may be added *The moſt pleaſant Song of Lady Beſſy*, an important hiſtorical poem upon the proceedings of Elizabeth of York, afterwards Queen of England, from Chriſtmas, 1484, to the Battle of Boſworth-field. Two MSS. of it are known, one Harl. Coll. 367, and the other in private hands.[6] It cannot be ſaid that either of the copies is of any particular antiquity or philological value; but in a literary point of view the poem is intereſting and valuable. The ſuppoſed author is Humphrey Brereton, the Lady's ſquire, and a dependent of the Stanleys.

We muſt not overlook another piece ſomewhat of the ſame nature, alleged to have been written by Robert Boſtock, entitled *The Earles of Cheſter*, of which there is a copy among Cole's collections, and a ſecond in the recently edited Percy MS. It is a mere biographical chronicle in ſtanzas, and has no pretenſions to poetical merit.]

I will only add part of a Will in verſe, dated 1477:[7]

> Fleſhly luſtes and feſtes,
> And furures of divers beſtes,
> (A fend was hem fonde;)
> Hole clothe caſt on ſhredys,
> And wymen with thare hye hedys,
> Have almoſt loſt thys londe!

To the reign of Henry VI. we may alſo refer a poem written by

---

[1] MSS. Harl. 1304, 4, again, ibid. 541, 19, fol. 213. [Compare ibid. 913, 10, fol. 15, b. 11, fol. 15 b.]
[2] MSS. Harl. 913; 3, fol. 7; 4, fol. 9; 5, fol. 10; 13, fol. 16.
[3] Ibid. 5, fol. 10.   [4] Ibid. 6, fol. 12; 7, fol. 13 b.
[5] MSS Harl. 541, 14, fol. 207, ſeq.
[6] [Both are printed by Mr. Halliwell in his *Palatine Anthology*, 1850.]
[7] MSS. Langb. Bibl. Bodl. vi. fol. 176. [M. 13. Th.]

one Richard Sellyng, whose name is not in any of our biographies.[1] It is entitled and begins thus, " Evidens to be ware and gode covnsayle made now late by that honovrable squier Richard Sellyng:

> Loo this is but a symple tragedie,
> Ne thing lyche un to hem of Lumbardye,
> Which that Storax wrote unto Pompeie,
> Sellyng maketh this in his manere,
> And to John Shirley now sent it is
> For to amende where it is amisse.

He calls himself an old man. Of this honourable squire I can give no further account. John Shirley, here mentioned, lived about the year 1440. He was a gentleman of good family, and a great traveller. He collected, and transcribed in several volumes which John Stow had seen, many pieces of Chaucer, Lydgate, and other English poets. [Among the Ashmole MSS. now in the Bodleian library], occurs: *A boke cleped the Abstracte Brevyare compyled of divers balades, roundels, virilays, tragedyes, envoys, complaints, moralities, storyes, practysed, and eke devysed and ymagined, as it sheweth here followyng, collected by John Shirley.*[2] In Thoresby's library was a MS. once belonging to the college of Selby, *A most pyteous cronycle of thorribil dethe of James Stewarde, late kynge of Scotys, nought long agone prisoner yn Englande yn the tymes of the kynges Henry the Fifte and Henry the Sixte, translated out of Latine into oure mothers Englishe tong bi your simple subject John Shirley.*[3] Also, *The boke clepyd Les bones meures translated out of French by your humble serviture John Shirley of London*, MCCCCXL, comprised in V. partes. The firste partie spekith of remedie that is agaynst the sevyn deadly sins. 2. The estate of holy church. 3. Of prynces and lordes temporall. 4. Of comone people. 5. Of deth and universal dome. Also, his Translation of the Sanctum Sanctorum, &c.[4] A preserver of Chaucer's and Lydgate's works deserved these notices. Ames, the industrious author of the *History of Printing*, had in his possession a folio volume of English Ballads in manuscript, composed or collected by one John Lucas about the year 1450.

SECTION XXVII.

THE only writer deserving the name of a poet in the reign of Henry VII. is Stephen Hawes. He was patronised by that monarch, who possessed some tincture of literature, and is said by Bacon to have confuted a Lollard in a public disputation at Canterbury.[5]

Hawes flourished about the close of the fifteenth century, and was

---

[1] MSS. Harl. f. 38, a.   [2] MSS. 89, ii. [But see Ritson (*Bibl. Poet.* 101).]
[3] [This has been printed.—F.]
[4] *Ducat. Leod.* p. 530. [Add. MS. Br. Mus. 5467.]
[5] *Life of Henry VII.* p. 628, edit. *ut supr.* One Hodgkins, a fellow of King's College in Cambridge, and vicar of Ringwood in Hants, was eminently skilled in the mathematics; and on that account Henry VII. frequently condescended to visit him at his house at Ringwood. Hatcher. MS. *Catal. Præpos. et Soc. Coll. Regal. Cant.*

a native of Suffolk.[1] After an academical education at Oxford, he travelled much in France, and became a complete master of the French and Italian poetry. His polite accomplishments quickly procured him an establishment in the household of the king who, struck with the liveliness of his conversation, and because he could repeat by memory most of the old English poets, especially Lydgate, made him groom of the privy chamber.[2] His facility in the French tongue was a qualification which might strongly recommend him to the favour of Henry VII. who was fond of studying the best French books then in vogue.[3]

Hawes has left many poems, which are now but imperfectly known, and scarcely remembered. These are, the *Conversion of Swearers*,[3] in octave stanzas, with Latin lemmata, printed in 1509 [and afterwards]. *A Joyful Meditation to all England of the Coronation of our most natural sovereign Lord King Henry the Eighth* [1509]. These coronation-carols were customary. There is one by Lydgate.[4] *The [Comfort] of Lovers. The Example of Virtue. The Delight of the Soul. Of the Prince's Marriage. The Alphabet of Birds.* [Of the two last pieces we know nothing. Perhaps the *Alphabet of Birds* may be the *Armonye of Byrdes*, a well known poem, but not by Hawes, and by possibility the piece *Of the Pryncees Marriage* may simply be a mistake by Wood for the *Joyfull Medytacyon.* Of the *Example of Virtue* W. de Worde issued two editions, one without date, but about 1512, and the other in 1530. The former possesses the following explanatory colophon: "This boke called the example of vertue was made and compyled by Stephyn Hawys one of the gromes of the moost honorable chamber of oure souerayne lorde kynge Henry the .vii. the .xix. yere of his moost noble reygne, and by hym presented to our sayd souerayne lorde chapytred and marked after this table here before sette." The latest edition of the *Conversyon of Swerers* was printed by William Copland in 1551. *The Comfort of Lovers* is described as a poem on eighteen leaves from the press of Wynkyn de Worde, but we have never met with a copy.]

Hawes's capital performance is a poem entitled *The Pastime of Pleasure; or the History of Graunde Amour and La Bell Pucel: conteining the knowledge of the seven Sciences, and the course of mans life in this worlde. Invented by Stephen Hawes, grome of kyng Henry the Seventh his chamber.*[5] It is dedicated to the kyng, and was finished at the beginning of the year 1506.

---

[1] Wood, *Ath. Oxon.* i. 5.

[2] Bale says, that he was called by the king, "ab interiori camera ad privatum cubiculum." Cent. viii.

[3] Bacon, *ut supr.* p. 637. [Several illustrations of Henry's love of books might be produced from records of the period. See *Excerpta Historica*, 1833, where selections are given from his *Privy Purse Expenses*. But he was not peculiar in this respect. Mr. Rye, of the British Museum, in a MS. note to his copy of Warton, notices an entry of a payment of £1. to Hampton of Worcester for making ballads.]

[4] *A Ballad presented to Henry the Sixth the day of his coronation*. Princ. "Most noble prince of crysten princes all." MSS. Ashmol. 59, ii.

[5] By Wynkyn de Worde, in 1517, with woodcuts. [It was reprinted in 1554 and 1555, and has been republished by the Percy Society, 1845.] See a poem called

The *Pastime of Pleasure* is almost the only effort of imagination and invention which had yet appeared in our poetry since Chaucer. This poem contains no common touches of romantic and allegoric fiction. The personifications are often happily sustained, and indicate the writer's familiarity with the Provençal school. The model of his versification and phraseology is that improved harmony of numbers, and facility of diction, with which his predecessor Lydgate adorned our octave stanza. But Hawes has added new graces to Lydgate's manner. Antony Wood, with the zeal of a true antiquary, laments that "such is the fate of poetry, that this book, which in the times of Henry VII. and VIII. was taken into the hands of all ingenious men, is now thought but worthy of a ballad-monger's stall!" The truth is, such is the good fortune of poetry, and such the improvement of taste, that much better books have become fashionable. It must indeed be acknowledged, that this poem has been unjustly neglected: and on that account an apology will be less necessary for giving the reader a circumstantial analysis of its substance and design.

Graunde Amoure, the hero of the poem, who speaks in his own person, is represented walking in a delicious meadow. There is something dramatic in this circumstance. Raimond Vidal de Besaudin, a troubadour of Provence, who flourished about the year 1200, has given the following dramatic form to one of his *contes* or tales. One day, says the troubadour, Alphonsus, King of Castille, whose court was famous for good cheer, magnificence, loyalty, valour, the practice of arms and the management of horses, held a solemn assembly of minstrels and knights. When the hall was quite full, came his Queen Eleanor, covered with a veil, and disguised in a close robe bordered with silver, adorned with the blazon of a golden lion; who making obeysance, seated herself at some distance from the king. At this instant, a minstrel advancing to the king addressed him thus: "O king, emperor of valour, I come to supplicate you to give me audience." The king, under pain of disgrace, ordered that no person should interrupt the minstrel in what he should say. The minstrel had travelled from his own country to recite an adventure which had happened to a baron of Arragon, not unknown to King Alphonsus; and he now proceeds to tell no unaffecting story concerning a jealous husband. At the close, the minstrel humbly requests the king and queen to banish all jealous husbands from their dominions. The king replied, "Minstrel, your tale is pleasant and gentle, and you shall be rewarded. But to show you still further how much you have entertained me, I command that henceforth your tale shall be called Le Jaloux Chatie." Our trou-

---

a *Dialogue between a Lover and a Jay*, by Thomas Feylde [twice] printed by Wynkyn de Worde, in 4to. Princ. Prol. "Thoughe laureate poetes in old antiquite." [Mr. Heber has enabled me to produce an allusion by Feylde to Hawes:

"Yonge Steven Hawes, whose soule God pardon
  Treated of love so clerkely and well,
To rede his workes is myne affeccyon,
  Which he compyled of La Bell Pusell."—*Park.*]

badour's tale is greatly enlivened by thefe accompaniments, and by being thrown into the mouth of a minftrel.

In the meadow, the hero difcovers a path which conducts him to a glorious image, both whofe hands are ftretched out and pointing to two highways; one of which is the path of Contemplation, the other of Active Life, leading to the Tower of Beauty. He choofes the laft-mentioned path, yet is often tempted to turn afide into a variety of bye-paths, which feemed more pleafant; but proceeding directly forward, he fees afar off another image, on whofe breaft is written, "This is the road to the Tower of Doctrine, he that would arrive there muft avoid floth," &c. The evening being far advanced, he fits down at the feet of the image, and falls into a profound fleep; when, towards the morning, he is fuddenly awakened by the loud blaft of a horn. He looks forward through a valley, and perceives a beautiful lady on a palfrey, fwift as the wind, riding towards him, encircled with tongues of fire.[1] Her name was Fame, and with her ran two milk-white greyhounds, on whofe golden collars were infcribed in diamond letters Grace and Governaunce.[2]

Greyhounds were anciently almoft as great favourites as hawks. Our forefathers reduced hunting to a fcience; and have left large treatifes on this fpecies of diverfion, which was fo connected with their ftate of life and manners. The moft curious one I know was among the manufcripts of Mr. Farmer, of Tufmore in Oxfordfhire. It was entitled, *Le Art de Venerie, le quel maiftre Guillaume Twici venour le roy d' Angleterre fift en fon temps per aprandre autres.* This mafter William Twici was grand huntfman to Edward II. In the Cotton library this book occurs in Englifh under the names of William Twety and John Giffard, moft probably a tranflation from the French copy, with the title of *a book of Venerie dialogue wife*.[3] The lefs ancient tract on this fubject, called the *Maiftre of the Game*, written for the inftruction of Prince Henry, afterwards Henry V., is much more common.[4] I believe the *maiftre veneur* has been long abolifhed in England, but the royal falconer ftill remains. The latter was an officer of high dignity in the Grecian court of Conftantinople, at an early period, under the ftyle of πρωτοιερακαριος.[5] Phrenzes fays, that the Emperor Andronicus Palæologus the younger kept more than one thoufand four hundred hawks, with almoft as many men to take care of them.[6]

About the year 750, Winifrid or Boniface, a native of England and archbifhop of Mons, acquaints Ethelbald, a king of Kent, that he has fent him one hawk, two falcons, and two fhields. Hedilbert, a king of the Mercians, requefts the fame archbifhop

---

[1] In Shakefpeare, Rumour is painted full of tongues. This was from the Pageants.
[2] See *fupr*.
[3] Princ. "Twety now will we beginnen." MSS. Cotton. Vefpas. B. xii.
[4] MSS. Digb. 182. Bibl. Bodl.
[5] Pachym. lib. i. c. 8, x. 15, Codin. cap. ii.
[6] Lib. i. c. 10.

Winifrid to send him two falcons which have been trained to kill cranes.¹ Falconry, or a right to sport with falcons, is mentioned so early as the year 986.² A charter of Kenulf, King of the Mercians, granted to the abbey of Abingdon, and dated 821, prohibits all persons carrying hawks or falcons to trespass on the lands of the monks.³ Julius Fermicus, who wrote about the year 355, is the first Latin author who mentions hawking, or has even used the word falco.⁴ Hawking is often mentioned in the capitularies of the eighth and ninth centuries. The grand fauconnier of France was an officer of great eminence. His salary was 4000 florins; he was attended by a retinue of fifty gentlemen and fifty assistant falconers, and allowed to keep three hundred hawks. He licensed every vendor of falcons in France, and received a tribute for every bird that was sold in that kingdom, even within the verge of the court. The King of France never rode out on any occasion without this officer.

An ingenious French writer insinuates, that the passion for hunting, which at this day subsists as a favourite and fashionable species of diversion in the most civilised countries of Europe, is a strong indication of our gothic origin, and is one of the savage habits, yet unreformed, of our northern ancestors. Perhaps there is too much refinement in this remark. The pleasures of the chace seem to have been implanted by nature; and under due regulation, if pursued as a matter of mere relaxation and not of employment, are by no means incompatible with the modes of polished life.

[To return: the palfrey of Fame] is Pegasus; and the burning tongues denote her office of consigning the names of illustrious personages to posterity; among which she mentions a lady of matchless accomplishments, named La Bell Pucell, who lives within a tower seated in a delightful island; but which no person can enter without surmounting many dangers. She then informs our hero that, before he engages in this enterprise, he must go to the Tower of Doctrine, in which he will see the seven sciences; and that there, in the turret or chamber of music, he will have the first sight of La Bell Pucell.

[Brunetto Latini, in his *Tesoro*, gives the following account of his own system of erudition, which may not be inapplicable here. He means to show himself a profound and universal scholar; and professes to understand the seven liberal arts, grammar, the Latin language, logic, the Decretals of Gratian, music according to Boethius and Guy Aretin, arithmetic, geography, astronomy, the ecclesiastic computation, medicine, pharmacy, surgery, necromancy, geomancy, magic, divination, and mythology, better than Ovid and Thales le Menteur: the histories of Thebes, Troy, Rome, Romulus, Cæsar, Pompey, Augustus, Nero, Vespasian, Titus who took Jerusalem, the

---

¹ See *Epistol.* Winifrid [Bonifac.] Mogunt. 1605. 1629. And in Bibl. Patr. tom. vi. and tom. xiii. p. 70.
² Chart. Ottonis iii. Imperator *ann.* 986. *apud* Ughell. *De Episcop. Januens.*
³ Dugd. *Monast.* i. p. 100.
⁴ Mathes. lib. v. c. 7, vii. c. 4.

Twelve Cæsars down to Constantine: the history of Greece; and that of Alexander, who dying distributed his acquisitions among his twelve peers; the history of France, containing the transactions of Clovis, converted by St. Remi; Charles Martel, who established tenths; King Pepin, Charlemagne and Roland, and the good King Louis. To these he adds the history of England, which comprehends the arrival of Brutus in England, and his conquest of the giant Corineus, the prophecies of Merlin, the redoubted death of Arthur, the adventures of Gawaine, and the amours of Tristram and Bel Isould. Amidst this profusion of fabulous history, which our author seems to think real, the history of the Bible is introduced; this he traces from the patriarchs down to the day of judgment. At the close of the whole, he gives us some more of his fashionable accomplishments, and says that he is skilled in the plain chant, in singing to the lute, in making canzonetts, pastorals, amorous and pleasant poesies, and in dancing: that he is beloved by ecclesiastics, knights, ladies, citizens, minstrels, squires, &c.[1]

Fame departs, but leaves with him her two greyhounds. Graunde Amoure now arrives at the tower, or rather castle, of Doctrine framed of fine copper, and situated on a craggy rock: it shone so brightly that he could distinctly discern the form of the building; till at length, the sky being covered with clouds, he more visibly perceives its walls decorated with figures of beasts in gold, and its lofty turrets crowned with golden images. He says that the little turrets had, for weathercocks or fans, images of gold which, moving with the wind, played a tune. So, [in the poem called *Chaucer's Dream*:]

> For every yate of fine golde
> A thousand fanes, aie turning,
> Entuned had, and briddes singing,
> Divers, and on each fane a paire,
> With open mouth again *here*;
> And of a sute were all the toures,
> * * *
> With many a small turret hie.[2]

Again, in the Castle of Pleasant Regard, the fans on the high towers are mentioned as a circumstance of pleasure and beauty:

> The towris hie full pleasant shall ye finde,
> With phanis freshe, turning with everie winde.

And our author Hawes, again,[3]

> Aloft the towres the golden fanes goode
> Dyde with the wynde make full sweete armony
> Them for to heare it was great melody.

Hawes here paints from the life. An excessive agglomeration of turrets, with their fans, is one of the characteristic marks of the florid mode of architecture, which was now almost at its height, as

---

[1] [See *supra*, i. 147, and *infr.* iv. 179.]
[2] [Morris's *Chaucer*, vol. v. p. 88, v. 76.]
[3] Ch. xxxviii. *The Assembly of Ladies*, v. 160 [printed improperly by Urry in 1721 among Chaucer's works.]

may be seen in the old views of the palaces of Nonesuch and Richmond.

Graunde Amoure is admitted to the Tower by Countenance the portress, who leads him into a court, where he drinks water of a most transcendent fragrance from a magnificent fountain, whence flow four rivers, clearer than Nilus, Ganges, Tigris, or Euphrates.

The crusades made the eastern rivers more famous among the Europeans than any of their own. Arnaud Daniel, a troubadour of the thirteenth century, declares he had rather please his mistress than possess all the dominions which are washed by Hebrus, Meander and Tigris.[1] The compliment would have been equally exaggerated, if he had alluded to some of the rivers of his own country.

He next enters the hall framed of jasper, its windows crystal, and its roof overspread with a golden vine, whose grapes are represented by rubies;[2] the floor is paved with beryl, and the walls hung with rich tapestry, on which our hero's future expedition to the Tower of La Bell Pucell was gloriously wrought. In the eleventh book of Boccaccio's *Theseid*, after Arcite is dead, Palamon builds a superb temple in honour of him, in which his whole history is painted. The description of this painting is a recapitulatory abridgment of the preceding part of the poem. Hawes's tapestry is less judiciously placed in the beginning of the piece, because it precludes expectation by forestalling all the future incidents.

The marshal of the castle of La Bell Pucell is Reason, the sewer Observance, the cook Temperance, the high-steward Liberality, &c. He then explains to Doctrine his name and intended adventure; and she entertains him at a solemn feast. He visits her seven daughters, who reside in the castle. First he is conducted to Grammar, who delivers a learned harangue on the utility of her science: next to Logic, who dismisses him with a grave exhortation: then to Rhetoric who, crowned with laurel and seated in a stately chamber strewed with flowers and adorned with the clear mirrors of speculation, explains her five parts in a laboured oration. Graunde Amoure resolves to pursue their lessons with vigour, and animates himself, in this difficult task, with the examples of Gower, Chaucer, and Lydgate, who are panegyrised with great propriety.

He recites some of the pieces of the two latter. Chaucer, he says, wrote the *Book of Fame* "on hys own invencion." *The Tragedies of the xix ladies*, he wrote "a translacyon." *The Canterbury Tales*, he calls "upon hys ymaginacyon, some of which are vertuous, others glad and merry." *The pytous dolour of Troylus and Cressida*, "and many other bokes."

---

[1] *Hist. Troub.* ii. p. 485.
[2] From Sir John Mandeville's *Travels*. "In the hall, is a vine made of *gold*, that goeth all aboute the hall: and it hath many bunches of grapes, some are white, &c. All the *red* are of *rubies*," &c. ch. lxvii. Paulus Silentiarius, in his description of the church of S. Sophia at Constantinople, mentions such an ornament, ii. 235:

Κλημασι χρυσοκομοισι περιδρομος αμπελος ερπει, &c.
Palmitibus auricomis circumcurrens vitis serpit.

Among Lydgate's works, he recites the *Life of our Lady. Saint Edmund's Life. The Fall of Princes. The three Reasons. The Chorle and the Bird. The Troy Book. Virtue and Vice.*[1] *The Temple of Glass. The [Interpretacion of the Names] of Gods and Goddesses.*

The poem of the *Chorle and the Bird* our author calls a "pamflete." Lydgate himself says that he tranflated this tale from a "pamflete in Frenfche," ft. 5. The fable on which it is founded is told by Petrus Alphonfus, a writer of the twelfth century, in his tract *De Clericali Difciplina*, [printed in 1825 and 1827.[2]]

Our author, in his recital of Chaucer's pieces, calls the *Legend of good Women* "tragedies." Anciently a serious narrative in verfe was called a tragedy; and it is obfervable, that he mentions "xix. ladyes" belonging to this legend. Only *nine* appear at prefent. Nineteen was the number intended, as we may collect from Lydgate's *Fall of Princes*,[3] where eight more ladies than are in the prefent legend are mentioned. This piece is called the *legendis of ix good women*.[4] Chaucer himfelf fays, "I fawe cominge of ladyes nineteen in royall habit."[5]

Our hero is afterwards admitted to Arithmetic, who wears a golden "wede,"[6] and (laft of all) is led to the Tower of Mufic, which was compofed of cryftal, in eager expectation of obtaining a view of La Bell Pucell, according to Fame's prediction. In the [*Teforo* of Latini] cited at large above, Mufic, according to Boethius and Guy Aretin, is one of the feven liberal fciences. At Oxford, the graduates in mufic, which ftill remains there as an academical fcience, are at this day required to fhew their proficiency in Boethius *De Mufica*. In a pageant, at the coronation of Edward VI., Mufic perfonified appears among the feven fciences.[7] Mufic was playing on an organ before a folemn affembly, in the midft of which at length he difcovers La Bell Pucell, is inftantly captivated with her beauty, and almoft as foon tells her his name, and difclofes his paffion. In the defcription of her perfon, which is very elegant, and confifts of three ftanzas, there is this circumftance, "She gartered wel her hofe."[8] She is more beautiful than Helen, Proferpine, Creffida, Queen Hyppolita, Medea, Dido, Polyxena, Alcmena, Menalippa or even fair

---

[1] MSS. Harl. 2251, 63, fol. 95.   [2] [Compare p. 132, *fupr.* note 5.]
[3] Prol. and *ibid.* l. i. c. 6. Compare *Man of L. T.* Prol. v. 60.
[4] MSS. Fairf. xvi.
[5] ver. 383. Compare *Pars. T.* Urr. p. 214, col. 1. [An additional argument, for believing that the number intended was nineteen, may be drawn from the *Court of Love*, ver. 108, where, fpeaking of Alcefte, Chaucer fays:

"To whom obeyed the ladies gode nineteen."—*Tyrwhitt.*

See alfo the note on ver. 4481 of the *Canterbury Tales.*—Price.]
[6] The walls of her chamber are painted in gold with the three fundamental rules of arithmetic.
[7] Leland, *Coll. Append.* iii. 317, edit. 1770.
[8] ch. xxx. Chaucer has this circumftance in defcribing the Wife of Bath, *Prol.* ver. 458:

"Hire hofen weren of fine fcarlet rede
Full *ftraite yteyed.*"

Rosamund. The solemnity being finished, Music and La Bell Pucell go forth into a stately temple, whither they are followed by our hero. Here Music seats herself amidst a concert of all kinds of instruments. She explains the principles of harmony. A dance is played,¹ and Graunde Amoure dances with La Bell Pucell. That is, tabours, trumpets, pipes, sackbuts, organs, recorders, harps, lutes, "croudds, tymphans," [? symphans] dulcimers, "claricimbales, rebeckes, clarychordes."² At the marriage of James of Scotland with the Princess Margaret, in the year 1503, " the king began before hyr to play of the clarychordes and after of the lute. And uppon the said clarychorde sir Edward Stanley played a ballade and sange therewith." Again, the king and queen being together, "after she played upon the clarychorde and after of the lute, he beinge uppon his knee allwaies bareheaded."³ In Lydgate's poem, entitled *Reason and Sensuallite,* various instruments and sorts of music are recited:⁴—

> Of al maner mynstralcye
> That any man kan specifye:
> For there were rotys of Almayne,
> And eke of Arragon and Spayne:
> Songes, stampes, and eke daunces,
> Divers plente of plesaunces;
> And many unkouth notys newe
> Of swiche folke as lovid trewe;
> And instrumentys that dyd excelle,
> Many moo than I kan telle:
> Harpys, fythales, and eke rotys,
> Well according with her notys,
> Lutys, ribibles, and geternes,
> More for estatys than tavernes;
> Orguys, cytolis, monacordys.
> There were trumpes, and trumpettes,
> Lowde shallys and doucettes.

Here "geterne" is a guitar which, with "cytolis," has its origin in *cithara.* "Fythales" is fiddles. "Shallys," I believe, should be shalmies, or shawms. "Orguys" is organs. By "estatys" he means [royal or noble] assemblies.

Graunde Amoure retires, deeply in love. He is met by Counsel, who consoles and conducts him to his repose in a stately chamber of the castle. In the morning, Counsel and our hero both together visit La Bell Pucell. At the gate of the garden of the castle they are informed by the portress Courtesy, that the lady was sitting alone in an arbour, weaving a garland of various flowers. The garden is

---

¹ Music commands her minstrels to play the dance, which was called "Mamours the swete." So at the royal marriage just mentioned, "The mynstrelles begonne to play a basse dance, &c. After this done, they plaid a rownde, the which was daunced by the lorde Grey ledyinge the said queene.—After the dinner incontynent the mynstrelles of the chammer [chamber] began to play and then daunced the quene," &c. Leland, *Append. ubi supr.* p. 284, *seq.*
² Cap. xvi. ³ Leland, *Coll. Append.* iii. pp. 284, 285, edit. 1770.
⁴ MSS. Fairfax, xvi. Bibl. Bodl. [Pr. "To all folkys virtuous."] "Here reherfyth the auctor the mynstraleys that were in the gardyn." [See Ritson's *Bibl. Poet.* p. 69, note †.]

described as very delicious, and they find the lady in the arbour near a stately fountain, "among the flowers of aromatic fume." After a long dialogue, in which for some time she seems to reject his suit, at last she resigns her heart; but withal acquaints her lover, that he has many monsters to encounter and many dangers to conquer, before he can obtain her. He replies, that he is well acquainted with these difficulties, and declares that, after having received instructions from Astronomy, he will go to the Tower of Chivalry, in order to be more completely qualified to succeed in this hazardous enterprise. They take leave with tears, and the lady is received into a ship, which is to carry her into the island, where her tower stood. Counsel consoles Amoure,[1] and leaves him to attend other desponding lovers. Our hero bids adieu in pathetic terms to the Tower of Music, where he first saw Pucell. Next he proceeds to the Tower of Geometry, which is wonderfully built and adorned. From thence he seeks Astronomy, who resides in a gorgeous pavilion pitched in a fragrant and flowery meadow: she delivers a prolix lecture on the several operations of the mind, and parts of the body.[2] He then, accompanied with his greyhounds, enters an extensive plain overspread with flowers; and looking forward, sees a flaming star over a tower. Going forward, he perceives that this tower stands on a rough precipice of steel, decorated with beasts of various figures. As he advances towards it, he comes to a mighty fortress, at the gate of which were hanging a shield and helmet, with a marvellous horn. He blows the horn with a blast that shook the tower, when a knight appears: who, asking his business, is answered that his name is Graunde Amoure, and that he was just arrived from the tower of Doctrine. He is welcomed by the knight, and admitted. This is the castle of Chivalry. The next morning he is conducted by the porter Stedfastness into the base court, where stood a tower of prodigious height, made of jasper: on its summit were four images of armed knights on horses of steel which, on moving a secret spring, could represent a turney. Near this tower was an ancient temple of Mars: within it was his statue or picture of gold, with the figure of Fortune on her wheel: and the walls were painted with the siege of Troy. This

---

[1] Counsel mentions the examples of Troilus and Cressida, and of Ponthus and Sidonia. Of the latter faithful pair, there is an old French romance [of which the earliest edition seems to want the title-page in the only copy traceable (see Brunet, last edit. iv. 810); but it was frequently republished under the title of] *Le Roman du noble roy Ponthus filz du roy de galice et la belle sidoine fille du roy de bretagne.* It is in the royal library at Paris, MS. fol. (see Lengl. *Bibl. Rom.* ii. 250), and among the king's MSS. in the British Museum there is *Le Livre du roy Ponthus.* 15 E. vi. 6. I think there are some elegant miniatures in this MS. Our author calls him "the famous knyght yclypped Ponthus, whych loved Sydonye," cap. xvi. *King Ponthus* was first printed by Wynkyn de Worde, *The Noble Hystory of Ponthus and Galyce, and of lytell Brytayne.* With woodcuts, 1511, 4to. [It is another reading of the Legend or Gest of *King Horn*, as to which see *supr.* i. sect. i.]

[2] In a woodcut Ptolemy the astronomer is here introduced, with a quadrant; and Plato, the "conynge and famous clerke," is cited.

was a common subject of tapestry, as I have before observed: but as it was the most favourite martial subject of the dark ages, is here introduced with peculiar propriety. The general popularity of the story made it a subject for painted glass, as in [the poem entitled] *Chaucer's Dream:*[1]

> and with glas
> Were al the windowes wel yglased
> Ful clere, and nat an hole ycrased.
> That to beholde it was grete joy;
> For wholly all the story of Troy
> Was in the glasinge ywrought thus,
> Of Hector, and king Priamus,
> Achilles, &c.

In our author's description of the palace of Pucell, "there was enameled with figures curious *the syege of Troy.*"[2]

Our hero now supplicates Mars, that he may be enabled to subdue the monsters which obstruct his passage to the Tower of Pucell. Mars promises him assistance; but advises him first to invoke Venus in her temple. Fortune reproves Mars for presuming to promise assistance, and declares that all human glory is in the power of herself alone. Amoure is then led by Minerva through the sumptuous hall of the castle, which is painted with the *Siege of Thebes,* and where many knights are playing at chess, to king Melyzus,[3] the inventor of tilts and tournaments, who dubs him a knight. He leaves the castle of Chivalry, and on the road meets a person, habited like a fool, named Godfrey Gobilive, who enters into a long discourse on the falsehood of women:

> His father is *Davy Drunken nole,*
> Who never dranke but in a fayre *blacke boule.*

Here he seems to allude to Lydgate's poem, called *Of Jack Wat that could pull the lining out of a black boll.*[4] One *Jack Hare* is the same sort of ludicrous character, who is thus described in Lydgate's *Tale of froward Maymonde.*[5]

> A froward knave pleynly to descryve,
> And a sloggard shortely to declare,
> A precious knave that castith hym never to thryve.
> His mouth weel weet, his slevis rijt thredbare;
> A turnebroche [turn-spit], a boy for hogge of ware,
> With louring face noddyng and slumberyng,
> Of new cryftened, and called Jakke Hare,
> Whiche of a *boll* can *plukke out the lynyng.*

---

[1] V. 322.

[2] Cap. xxxviii. sign. A iii, edit. 1555. The arras was the "syege of Thebes." Ibid. In the Temple of Mars was also "the sege of Thebes depaynted fayre and clere" on the walls, cap. xxvii. sign. Q iii. [See *supr.*]

[3] A fabulous king of Thrace who, I think, is mentioned in Caxton's *Recuyell of the Hystoryes of Troy,* printed [between 1471 and 1474.] Our author appeals to this romance, which he calls the *Recule of Troye,* as an authentic voucher for the truth of the labours of Hercules, ch. i. By the way, Boccaccio's *Genealogy of the Gods* is quoted in this romance of Troy, B. ii. ch. xix.

[4] MS. Ashmol. Bodl. 59. ii; MSS. Harl. 2251. 12, fol. 14.

[5] MSS. Laud. D. 31. Bodl.

These two pieces of Lydgate [are] the same.¹

He relates how Ariſtotle, *for all his clergy*, was ſo infatuated with love, that he ſuffered the lady, who only laughed at his paſſion, to bridle and ride him about his chamber.² Then follows a long and ridiculous ſtory about Virgil the poet [transformed into a necromancer, as appears in the romance of *Virgilius*,] in the dark ages, who is deceived by the tricks of a lady at the court of Rome; on whom, however, her paramour takes ample revenge by means of his ſkill in muſic, ch. xxix. [Similar honours have been conferred upon Horace in the neighbourhood of Paleſtrina, where he is ſtill revered by the people as a powerful and benevolent wizard.] This fiction is alſo alluded to by Gower, and added to that of Ariſtotle's, among his examples of the power of love over the wiſeſt men:³

> And eke Virgile of aqueintaunce
> I ſigh [ſaw] where he the maiden praid
> Which was the doughter, as men ſaid,
> Of themperour whilom of Rome.⁴

Graunde Amoure and his companion go together into the temple of Venus, who was now holding a ſolemn aſſembly or court for the redreſs of lovers. Here he meets with Sapience, who draws up a ſupplication for him, which he preſents to Venus. Venus, after having exhorted him to be conſtant, writes a letter to Pucell, which ſhe ſends by Cupid. After offering a turtle, he departs with Godfrey Gobilive, who is overtaken by a lady on a palfrey, with a knotted whip in her hand, which ſhe frequently exerciſes on Godfrey.⁵ Amoure aſks her name which, ſhe anſwers, is Correction; that ſhe lived in the Tower of Chaſtity, and that he who aſſumed the name of Godfrey Gobilive was Falſe Report, who had juſt eſcaped from her priſon, and diſguiſed himſelf in a fool's coat. She invites Amoure to her Tower, where they are admitted by Dame Meaſure; and led into a hall with a golden roof, in the midſt of which was a carbuncle of a prodigious ſize, which illuminated the room.⁶ They are next

---

¹ [See Ritſon's *Bibl. Poet.* p. 72.]
² This ſtory is in Gower, *Conf. Amant.* lib. viii. [edit. 1857, iii. 366.] See *ſupr.* vol ii.

> "I ſigh there Ariſtotle alſo
> Whom that the quene of Grece alſo
> Hath bridled," &c.

³ *Ubi ſupr.*
⁴ *Virgil's Life* is mentioned by Laneham among other romantic pieces, *Killinw. Caſtle*, p. 34, edit. 1575.
⁵ In another place he is called *Folly*, and ſaid to ride on a mare. When chivalry was at its height in France, it was a diſgrace to any perſon, not below the degree of a gentleman, *to ride a mare*.
⁶ From Chaucer, *Rom. Roſe*, v. 1119. [edit. Morris.] Richeſſe is crowned with the coſtlieſt gems:

> "But alle byfore ful ſottilly
> A fyn charboncle ſette ſaugh I.
> The ſtoon ſo clere was and ſo bright,
> That, alſo ſoone as it was nyght,
> Men myghte ſeen to go for nede

introduced to a fair chamber; where they are welcomed by many famous women of antiquity, Helen, *quene* Proserpine, the *lady Meduse*, Penthesilea, &c. The next morning, Correction shews our hero a marvellous dungeon, of which Shamefastness is the keeper; and here False Report is severely punished. He now continues his expedition, and near a fountain observes a shield and a horn hanging. On the shield was a lion rampant of gold in a silver field, with an inscription importing that this was the way to La Bell Pucell's habitation, and that whoever blows the horn will be assaulted by a most formidable giant. He sounds the horn: when instantly the giant appeared, twelve feet high, armed in brass, with three heads on each of which was a streamer, with the inscriptions *Falsehood, Imagination, Perjury*. After an obstinate combat, he cuts off the giant's three heads with his sword *Claraprudence*. He next meets three fair ladies, Vanity, Good-operation, Fidelity. They conduct him to their castle with music; where, being admitted by the portress Observance, he is healed of his wounds by them. He proceeds and meets Perseverance, who acquaints him that Pucell continued still to love: that, after she had read Venus's letter, Strangeness and Disdain came to her, to dissuade her from loving him; but that soon after Peace and Mercy[1] arrived, who soon undid all that Disdain and Strangeness had said, advising her to send Perseverance to him with a shield. This shield Perseverance now presents, and invites him to repose that night with her cousin Comfort, who lived in a moated manor-place under the side of a neighbouring wood. There is a description of a magnificent *manor-place*, curious for its antiquity, in an old poem, written [in the fourteenth century], entitled a *Disputation bytwene a Crysten man and a Jewe*, perhaps translated from the French:[2]

> Forth heo[3] wenten on the Feld
> To an hul[4] thei bi held,
> The eorthe clevet[5] as a scheld,[6]
> On the grownde grene:
>
> A myle or two, in lengthe and brede.
> Sich lyght tho sprange oute of the stone."

But this is not uncommon in romance, and is an Arabian idea. See *supr.* vol. ii. In the *History of the Seven Champions*, a book compiled in the reign of [Elizabeth] by Richard Johnson, and containing some of the most capital fictions of the old Arabian romance, in the adventure of the *Enchanted Fountain*, the knights entering a dark hall, "tooke off their gauntletts from their left hands whereon they wore *marvellous great and fine diamonds*, that gave so *much light*, that they might *plainly see* all things that were in the hall, the which was very great and wide, and upon the walls were painted the figures of many furious fiends," &c. Sec. P. ch. ix. And in Mandeville's *Travels*, "The emperour hath in his chamber a pillar of gold, in which is a ruby and carbuncle a foot long, which lighteth all his chamber by night," &c. ch. lxxii.

[1] Mercy is no uncommon divinity in the love-system of the troubadours. See Millot's *Hist. Litt. des Troubad.* tom. i. p. 181, Par. 1774.

[2] MS. Vernon, fol. 301, *ut supr.* [See Carpentier's *Suppl.* du Cange, *Lat. Gloss.* V. *Radimere*.]

[3] they.   [4] hill.   [5] cleaved.   [6] shield.

Some fonde thei on ſtiʒ,¹
Thei went theron radly ;²
The criſten mon hedde farly³
    What hit miʒte mene.

Aftir that ſtiʒ lay a ſtrete,
Clere i-pavet with gete,⁴
Thei fond a Maner that was mete
    With murthes ful ſchene :
Wel corven and wroʒt
With halles heiʒe uppon loft,⁵
To a place weore thei bouʒt
    As paradys the clene.⁶

Ther was foulen⁷ ſong,
Much murthes among,
Hoſe lenge wolde longe
    Ful luitell hym thouʒt :
On vehe a ſyde of the halle,
Pourpell, pelure, and palle ;⁸
Wyndowes in the walle
    Was wonderli i-wrouʒt :⁹

There was doſers¹⁰ on the dees,¹¹
Hoſe the cheefe wolde ches¹²
That never richere was,
    In no ſale¹³ ſouʒt :
Both the mot and the mold
Schone al on red golde :
The criſtene mon hadde ferli of that folde,¹⁴
    That hider was brouʒt.

There was erbes¹⁵ growen grene,
Spices ſpringynge bi twene,
Such hadde I not ſene,
    For ſothe as I ſay :
The thruſtell¹⁶ ſonge full ſhrille,
He newed notes at his wille ;
Faire fflowers to fille,
    Fine in that Fay :

And al the rounde table good,
Hou Arthur in eorthe ʒod,¹⁷
Sum ſate and ſum ſtod,
    O the grounde grey :

---

¹ road, way, cavern aſcent.   ² readily, eaſily.
³ [had wonder. *Ritſon.*]   ⁴ paved with [jet. *Ritſon.*]
⁵ with halls built high.   ⁶ bright, or pleaſant, as Paradiſe.
⁷ fowls, birds.   ⁸ [The hall was hung with purple, &c.—*Price.*]
⁹ wonderfully wrought.
¹⁰ *doſſer* is a baſket carried on the back. Lat. *dorſarium*. Chaucer's *H. F.* iii. 850. "Or elſe hutchis or *doſſers.*" We muſt here underſtand proviſions.
¹¹ *dees* is here the *table*.   ¹² whoever would chuſe the beſt.
¹³ hall. Lat. *ſala*.   ¹⁴ [ground.]
¹⁵ An Herbary, for furniſhing domeſtic medicines, always made a part of our ancient gardens. In Hawes's poem, now before us, in the delicious gardens of the caſtle of Muſic, "Amiddes the garden there was an *herber* fayre and quadrante," ch. xviii. [But whatever *Herbary* may be underſtood to mean, *Herber*, in our old poetry, undoubtedly ſignifies arbour, or rather a houſe or *bower*, fitted up in the garden. Roſamond's Bower was an arbour in this ſenſe.]
¹⁶ thruſh.   ¹⁷ *yod*, went ; walked *on earth*.

> Hit was a wonder fiȝt
> As thei were quik men¹ diȝt
> To fe hou they play.²

Together with some of his expressions, I do not always understand Hawes's context and transitions, which have great abruptness. In what he says of King Arthur, I suppose he means that King Arthur's round table, and his knights turneying, were painted on the walls of the hall.³

[At the house of Comfort, Grande Amoure] is ushered into a "chamber precious," perfumed with the richest odours. Next morning, guided by Perseverance and Comfort, he goes forward and sees a castle, nobly fortified and walled with jet. Before it was a giant with seven heads, and upon the trees about him were hanging many shields of knights, whom he had conquered. On his seven heads were seven helmets crowned with seven streamers, on which were inscribed Dissimulation, Delay, Discomfort, Variance, Envy, Detraction, Doubleness. After a bloody battle, he kills the giant, and is saluted by the five ladies, Steadfastness, Amorous Purveyance, Joy after Sorrow, Pleasance, Good Report, Amity, Continuance, all riding from the castle on white palfreys. These ladies inform Amoure, that they had been exiled from La Bell Pucell by Disdain, and besieged in this castle, for one whole year, by the giant whom he had just slain. They attend him on his journey, and travel through a dreary wilderness, full of wild beasts: at length they discern, at a vast distance, a glorious region, where stood a stately palace beyond a tempestuous ocean. "That (says Perseverance) is the palace of Pucelle." They then discover in the island before them an horrible fiend, roaring like thunder, and breathing flame, which my author strongly paints:

> The fyre was greet, it made the yland lyght.

Perseverance tells our hero that this monster was framed by the two witches Strangeness and Disdain, to punish La Bell Pucell for having banished them from her presence. His body was composed of the seven metals, and within it a demon was inclosed. They now enter a neighbouring temple of Pallas, who shews Amoure in a trance the secret formation of this monster, and gives him a box of wonderful ointment. They walk on the sea-shore, and espy two ladies rowing towards them; who land, and having told Amoure that they are sent by Patience to enquire his name, receive him and his company into the ship Perfectness. They arrive in the island; and Amoure discovers near a rock the monster, whom he now examines more distinctly. The face of the monster resembled a virgin's, and was of gold; his neck of silver; his breast of steel; his fore-legs, armed with strong talons, of laten; his back of copper; his tail of

---

¹ as if they were living men. ² to see their sports, tournaments, &c.
³ [Arthur and his knights appear rather to be the inhabitants of this marvellous spot. Some were engaged in sports, whilst others either "sat or stood upon the gray ground" observing them.—*Price*.]

lead, &c. Amoure, in imitation of Jason, anoints his sword and armour with the unguent of Pallas which, at the first onset, preserves him from the voluminous torrent of fire and smoke issuing from the monster's mouth. At length he is killed, and from his body flew out a foule ethiope or black spirit, accompanied by such a smoke that all the island was darkened, and loud thunder-claps ensued. When this spirit had entirely vanished, the air grew serene; and our hero now plainly beheld the magnificent castle of La Pucell, walled with silver, and " many a story upon the wall enameled royally." I know not from what romantic history of the Crusades Richard Johnson took the description of the stately house of the courteous Jew at Damascus, built for entertaining Christian pilgrims, in which " the walls were painted with as many stories as there were years since the creation of the world."[1] The word *enamelled* is probably used in the same sense as in Stow.[2] "The great bell-tower [of the priory of S. John in Clerkenwell], a most curious piece of workmanshippe, graven, guilt, and inameled, to the great beautifying of the citie, and passinge all other that I have seene," &c. So again our author Hawes:[3]

> where the tower doth stande
> Made all of golde, enameled aboute
> Wyth noble storyes.

Our hero rejoins his company; and entering the gates of the castle, is solemnly received by Peace, Mercy, Justice, Reason, Grace, and Memory. He is then led by the portress Countenance into the base court where, into a conduit of gold, dragons spouted water of the richest odour. The gravel of the court is like gold, and the hall and chambers are most superbly decorated. Amoure and La Pucell sit down and converse together. Venus intervenes, attended by Cupid clothed in a blue mantle embroidered with golden hearts pierced with arrows, which he throws about the lovers, declaring that they should soon be joined in marriage. A sudden transition is here made from the pagan to the Christian theology. The next morning they are married, according to the catholic ritual, by *Lex Ecclesiæ*; and in the wooden print prefixed to this chapter, the lovers are represented as joining hands at the western portal of a great church, a part of the ceremonial of ancient marriages.[4] A solemn feast is then held in honour of the nuptials, which are described thus:[5]

> Why should I tary by long continuance
> Of the feast, &c.

In the same manner Chaucer passes over the particularities of Cambuscan's feast.[6] Matthew Paris, in describing the magnificent mar-

---

[1] See. P. ch. iv.　　[2] *Survey*, p. 359, edit. 1599.
[3] Cap. ii.
[4] For this custom, see the romance of *Appolyne* [*of Thyre,*] ch. xxxiii.
[5] Cap. xxix.
[6] *Squ. T.* v. 83. And of Theseus's feast, *Kn. T.* v. 2199. See also *Man of L. T.* v. 704, and Spenser's *Fairy Qu.* v. iii. 3.

riage and coronation of Queen Eleanor in 1236, uses exactly the same formulary, and on a similar subject.[1] Compare another feast described in the same chronicle, much after the same manner; and which, the writer adds, was more splendid than any feast celebrated in the time of Ahasuerus, King Arthur, or Charlemagne.[2]

Here the poem should have ended. But the poet has thought it necessary to extend his allegory to the death and burial of his hero. Graund Amoure, having lived in consummate happiness with his amiable bride for many years, saw one morning an old man enter his chamber, carrying a staff, with which he strikes Amoure's breast, saying, "Obey," &c. His name is Old Age. Not long after came Policy or Cunning and Avarice. Amoure now begins to abandon his triumphal shows and splendid carousals, and to be intent on amassing riches. At last arrived Death, who peremptorily announces, that he must prepare to quit his wealth and the world. After this fatal admonition, came Contrition and Conscience, and he dies. His body is interred by Mercy and Charity; and while his epitaph is written by Remembrance, Fame appears; promising that she will enroll his name with those of Hector, Joshua, Judas Maccabeus, King David, Alexander the Great, Julius Cæsar, Arthur, Charlemagne,[3] and Godfrey of Boulogne.[4] The chief reason for ranking King David among the knights of romance was, as I have already hinted, because he killed the giant Goliah; an achievement here mentioned by Hawes. Of Arthur and his knights he says, that their exploits are recorded "in royall bokes and jestes hystoryall."[5] Sir Thomas [Malory] had now just published his *Morte Arthur*, a narrative digested from various French romances on Arthur's story. [Some] printed copy of this favourite volume, which first appeared in 1485 from Caxton's press, must have been known to our poet

---

[1] "Quid in ecclesia seriem enarrem deo, ut decuit, reverenter ministrantium? Quid in mensa dapium et diversorum libaminum describam fertilitatem redundantem? Venationis [venison] abundantiam? Piscium varietatem? Joculatorum voluptatem? Ministrantium venustatem," &c. *Hist. Angl.* sub Hen. iii. p. 406, edit. 1589.

[2] *Ibid.* p. 871.

[3] With his "douseperes" or twelve peers, among which he mentions Rowland and Oliver.

[4] These are the Nine Worthies: to whom Shakespeare alludes in *Love's Lab. Lost.* "Here is like to be a good presence of Worthies. He presents Hector of Troy: The swain, Pompey the Great: The parish-curate, Alexander: Armado's page, Hercules: The pedant, Judas Maccabeus," &c. Act v. Sc. [ii, Dyce's edit. 1868, ii. 226]. Elias Cairels, a troubadour of Perigord, about the year 1240, wishes for the wisdom of Solomon, the courtesy of Roland, the puissance of Alexander, the strength of Samson, the friendly attachment of Sir Tristram, the "chevalerie" of Sir Gawaine, and the learning of Merlin. Though not immediately connected with the present purpose, I cannot resist the temptation of transcribing the remainder of our troubadour's idea of complete happiness in this world. His ambition can be gratified by nothing less than by possessing "Une si parfaite loyauté, que nul chevalier et nul jougleur n'aient rien à reprendre en lui; une maitresse jeune, jolie, et decente; mille cavaliers bien en ordre pour le suivre par tout," &c. Millot, *Hist. Litt. des Troubad.* tom. i. p. 388. [See *supr.* vol. ii.]

[5] Cap. xliii.

Hawes. By the way, in panegyrifing Chaucer, Hawes mentions it as a circumftance of diftinction, that his works were printed:[1]

<blockquote>
Whofe name
In printed bokes doth remayne in fame.
</blockquote>

This was natural at the beginning of the typographic art. Many of Chaucer's poems had been now [1506] recently printed by Caxton. With regard to [Malory's] book, much, if not moft of it, I believe, is taken from the great French romance of *Lancelot*, tranflated from Latin into French at the command of [Henry II.][2] It appears, however, that Henry III. alfo paid great attention to thefe compofitions from the following curious anecdote, which throws new light on the monarch's character:—Arnaud Daniel, a troubadour, highly celebrated by Dante and Petrarch, about 1240 made a voyage into England, where (in the court of Henry III.) he met a minftrel, who challenged him at difficult rhymes. The challenge was accepted, a confiderable wager was laid, and the rival bards were fhut up in feparate chambers of the palace. The king, who appears to have much interefted himfelf in the difpute, allowed them ten days for compofing, and five more for learning to fing, their refpective pieces: after which each was to exhibit his performance in the prefence of his majefty. The third day, the Englifh minftrel announced that he was ready. The troubadour declared he had not written a line; but that he had tried, and could not as yet put two words together. The following evening he overheard the minftrel practifing his chanfon to himfelf. The next day he had the good fortune to hear the fame again, and learned the air and words. At the day appointed they both appeared before the king. Arnaud defired to fing firft. The minftrel, in a fit of the greateft furprife and aftonifhment, fuddenly cried out "C'eft ma chanfon, This is my fong." The king faid it was impoffible. The minftrel ftill infifted upon it; and Arnaud, being clofely preffed, ingenuoufly told the whole affair. The king was much entertained with this adventure; and, ordering the wager to be withdrawn, loaded them with rich prefents. But he afterwards obliged Arnaud to give a chanfon of his own compofition.[3] In the meantime Henry II. equally encouraged thefe pieces; for Walter Mapes, archdeacon of Oxford, tranflated from Latin into French the popular romance of *Saint Graal*, at the inftance of Henry II. to whom he was chaplain, about 1190.[4] Benoit [de Sainte Maur (or More) already mentioned] was alfo patronifed by this monarch, at whofe command he compiled his metrical Chronicle of the Dukes of Normandy, in which are cited Ifidor Hifpanfis, Pliny, and Saint Auftin.[5]

---

[1] Cap. xiiii.

[2] [The Englifh verfion in Benet College library is the *Hiftory of the Holy Graal* (or the romance of *Jofeph of Arimathea*), edited by me for the Roxburghe Club, followed by part of the *Romance of Merlin*.—F.]

[3] Millot, *ut fupr.* tom. ii. p. 491.

[4] See MSS. Reg. 20 D. iii. a [MS. written in the thirteenth century].

[5] MSS. Harl. 1717, 1, on vellum. See fol. 85, 163, 192, 236. This old French

Afterwards (to return from this digression) Time and Eternity, clothed in white vestments and crowned with a triple diadem of gold, enter the temple, and pronounce an exhortation. Last follows an epilogue, in which the poet apologises for his hardiness in attempting to feign and devise this fable.

The reader readily perceives, that this poetical apologue is intended to shadow the education of a complete gentleman; or rather, to point out those accomplishments which constitute the character of true gallantry, and most justly deserve the reward of beauty. It is not pretended, that the personifications display that force of colouring and distinctness of delineation, which animate the ideal portraits of Jean de Meun. But we must acknowledge, that Hawes has shown no inconsiderable share of imagination, if not in inventing romantic action, at least in applying and enriching the general incidents of the Gothic fable. In the creation of allegoric imagery he has exceeded Lydgate. That he is greatly superior to many of his immediate predecessors and cotemporaries in harmonious versification and clear expression, will appear from the following stanza:

> Besydes this gyaunt, upon every tree
> I did see hang many a goodly shelde
> Of noble knyghtes, that were of hye degre,
> Whiche he had slayne and murdred in the fielde:
> From farre this gyaunt I ryght well behelde;
> And towarde hym as I rode my waye,
> On his first head I sawe a banner gay.[1]

To this poem a dedication of eight octave stanzas is prefixed, addressed to King Henry VII.: in which our author professes to follow the manner of his "maister" Lydgate:

> To folowe the trace and all the perfitness
> Of my maister Lydgate with due exercise,
> Suche fayned tales I do fynde[2] and devyse:
> For under a coloure a truthe may aryse,
> As was the guyse, in olde antiquitie,
> Of the poetes olde a tale to surmyse,
> To cloke the truthe.

In the course of the poem he complains that, since Lydgate, "the most dulcet sprynge of famous rhetoryke," that species of poetry, which deals in fiction and allegoric fable, had been entirely lost and neglected. He allows, that some of Lydgate's successors had been skilful versifiers in the ballad royal or octave stanza, which Lydgate carried to such perfection: but adds this remarkable restriction:

> They fayne no fables pleasaunt and covert:—
> Makynge balades of fervent amyte,
> As gestes and tryfles.[3]

---

poem is full of fabulous and romantic matter, and seems to be partly translated from a Latin Chronicle, [edited by M. Francisque Michel, Paris, 1836-44, 3 vols. 4to.] *De Moribus et Actis primorum Normanniæ Ducum*, written about 1000, by Dudo, dean of St. Quintin's, and first printed among Du Chesne's *Scriptor. Norman.* p. 49, edit. 1619. Maister Benoit ends with our Henry I., Dudo with the year 996.

[1] Ch. xxxv. [repr. of ed. 1555, 1845, p. 179].   [2] invent.
[3] Ch. xiv. So Barclay, in the *Ship of Fooles*, finished in 1508, fol. 18, a. edit.

These lines, in a small compass, display the general state of poetry which now prevailed.

[We venture to lay before the reader, before leaving Hawes, specimens of his two other performances already mentioned, *The Conversyon of Swerers* and *A Joyfull Medytacyon*. The following is a stanza from the Prologue of the *Conversyon of Swerers*:

> I lytell or nought expert in poetrye,
> Remembrynge my youth so lyght and frayle
> Purpose to compyle here full breuyatly
> A lytell treatyse wofull to bewayle
> The cruell swerers whiche do god assayle
> On every syde his swete body to tere
> With terryble othes as often as they swere.

This is neither better nor worse than the rest, which is a production altogether destitute of pathos, imagery, or invention of any kind. The *Joyfull Medytacyon* is a very superior piece, and contains some pretty and even elegant passages. Take a stanza from the Prologue, addressed to Henry VIII.:

> Amyddes the medowe of flora the quene
> Of the goddes elycon, is the sprynge or well
> And by it groweth a fayre laurell grene
> Of whiche the poetes do ofte write and tell;
> Besyde this olyue I dyde neuer dwell
> To tast the water whiche is aromatyke
> For to cause me wryte with lusty rethoryke.]

Coeval with Hawes was William Walter, a retainer to Sir Henry Marney, chancellor of the Duchy of Lancaster: an unknown and obscure writer whom I should not have named, but that he versified, in the octave stanza, Boccaccio's story, so beautifully paraphrased by Dryden, of *Sigismonda and Guiscardo*. This poem was printed by Wynkyn de Worde [1532].[1] It is in two books. He also wrote a dialogue in verse, called the *Spectacle of Lovers*: [a lytell contravers dyalogue bytwene love and councell, printed by W. de Worde, without date. To this poem there is a prologue by Robert Copland.[2] Walter is likewise the author of *The History of Titus and Gesippus, transflated out of latyn into englysshe by Wyllyam Walter*, &c.]

About the year [1500], Henry Medwall, chaplain to Morton, Archbishop of Canterbury, composed an interlude called *Nature*. It is not improbable, that it was played before the archbishop. It was

---

1570. He is speaking of the profane and improper conversation of priests in the choir:

> "And all of fables and jestes of Robin Hood,
> Or other trifles."

[1] [A later translation appeared in 1597, under the title of *The tragedy of Guistard and Sismond*, among] *Certaine worthye Manuscript Poems of great Antiquitie, Reserued long in the studie of a Northfolke Gentleman, & now first published by J. S.* [The *Stately Tragedy* is a totally different translation from that of Walter. In MS. Add. 12,124, Brit. Mus. is a much earlier translation in verse of the story of Guiscard and Sigismond, by Gilbert Banestre, a poet of the fourteenth century.—Madden.]

[2] Begins the Prologue, "Forasmuche as ydelness is rote of all vices."

the business of chaplains in great houses to compose interludes for the family. This piece was printed by [John Rastell, about 1510], and entitled, *Nature, a goodly interlude of Nature, copylyd by mayster Henry Medwall, chapleyn to the ryght reuerent father in god Johan Morton somtyme Cardynall and archebyshop of Canterbury.*[1] [The date of the original composition of the interlude of *Nature* is very uncertain; but it appears that it was performed (probably as a revival) at Christmas, 1514-15, before the king at Richmond, by "Inglyshe and oothers of the Kynges pleyers," but that it proved tedious owing to its length, and that "the kyng departyd befor the end to hys chambre."][2]

In the year 1497, Laurence Wade, a Benedictine monk of Canterbury,[3] translated into English rhymes *The Life of Thomas a Beckett*, written about the year 1180 in Latin[4] by Herbert Bosham. The MS., which will not bear a citation, is preserved in Benet college in Cambridge.[5] The original had been translated into French verse by Peter Langtoft.[6] Bosham was Becket's secretary, and was present at his martyrdom.

SECTION XXVIII.

PLACE Alexander Barclay within the year 1500, as his *Ship of Fools* appears to have been projected about that period. He was educated, [it has been said,] at Oriel College in Oxford, accomplished his academical studies by travelling, and was appointed one of the priests or prebendaries of the college of Saint Mary Ottery in Devonshire. He seems to have spent some time at Cambridge,[7]

>And once in Cambridge I heard a scoller say,
>(One of the same which go in copes gay).[8]

The chief patron of his studies appears to have been Thomas Cornish, provost of Oriel College, and Suffragan Bishop of Tyne in the diocese of Bath and Wells, to whom he dedicates, in a handsome Latin epistle, his *Ship of Fools.* But in the poem he mentions

---

[1] [The same to whom Sir Thomas More was a page in his youth. Perhaps some of the dramatic or *quasi*-dramatic compositions, which we are at present obliged to regard as anonymous, and which were chiefly printed by John Rastell, More's relative by marriage, were written by the future Chancellor.]

[2] [Collier's *Hist. of Dram. Poet.* i. 65.]

[3] Professed in the year 1467. *Catal. Mon. Cant.* inter MSS. C. C. C. C. (N. 7).

[4] *Vita et Res Gestæ Thomæ Episcopi Cantuariensis,* published in the *Quadrilogus*, 1495.

[5] MSS. Coll. C. C. Cant. CCCXCVII. 1. Beginn. Prol. "O ye vertuous soverayns spirituall and temporall."

[6] Pits. p. 890, *Append.*

[7] [There seems to be no sufficient evidence that Barclay was educated at Oriel College.]

[8] *Eglog.* i. signat. A 4, *verso.*

My *Maister Kyrkham*, calling himself " his true servitour, his chaplayne, and bede man."[1] Some biographers suppose Barclay to have been a native of Scotland. It is certain that he has a long and laboured encomium on James IV., king of Scotland, whom he compliments for his bravery, prudence, and other eminent virtues. One of the stanzas of this panegyric is an acrostic on Jacobus.[2] Afterwards he became a Benedictine monk of Ely monastery;[3] and at length took the habit of the Franciscans at Canterbury.[4] He temporised with the changes of religion; for he possessed some church-preferments in the reign of Edward VI. He was instituted to Much Badew in Essex, in 1546. And to Wokey in Somersetshire, the same year.[5] He had also the church of All Saints in Lombard Street, London, on the presentation of the dean and chapter of Canterbury, which was vacant by his death, Aug. 24, 1552.[6]

He frequently mentions Croydon in his *Egloges*. He was buried in Croydon church:[7]

> And as in Croidon I heard the Collier preache.

Again:[8]

> While I in youth in Croidon towne did dwell.

Again:[9]

> He hath no felowe betwene this and Croydon
> Save the proude plowman (Gnoto) of Chorlington.

He mentions the collier again:[10]

> Such maner riches (the Collyer tell thee can).

Also [alluding to Bishop Alcock]:[11]

> As the riche shepheard which woned in Mortlake.

He died, very old, at Croydon in 1552. [It seems pretty certain that he was of Scotish extraction; for Bullein the physician, who was his contemporary, expressly tells us, that he was born "beyond the cold river of Tweed."]

Barclay's principal work is the *Ship of Fools*, above mentioned. About the year [1494][12] Sebastian Brandt, a learned civilian of Basle and an eminent philologist, had published a satire in German with this title.[13] The design was to ridicule the reigning vices and follies

---

[1] Fol. 152, b, edit. 1570. [2] Fol. 206, a.
[3] In the title to his translation from Mancinus, called the *Mirrour of Good Manners*.
[4] MS. Bale, Sloan. f. 68.
[5] Newcourt, Rep. i. 254, and *Registr. Wellens*. [6] Newc. Ibid.
[7] [*Eglog*. i. sign. A 4, *verso*.] [8] [Sign. A ij, *verso*.]
[9] [Sign. A 4, *verso*.] [10] [Ibid.] [11] [Sign. A iij, *recto*.]
[12] [The German bibliographers speak of an edition printed at Basle, without date, as the earliest known to them, though others maintain the Strasburg edition of 1494 to be the first of the German original. See Brunet, last edit. in v.—*Price*.]
[13] I presume this is the same Sebastian Brandt, to whom Thomas Acuparius, poet laureate, dedicates a volume of Poggius, *Argentorat*. 1513, fol. He is here styled, "Juris utriusque doctor, et S. P. Q. Argentinensis cancellarius." The dedication is dated 1511. See Hendreich. *Pandect*. p. 703.—[Brandt was a doctor of laws, an imperial counsellor, and Syndic to the Senate of Strasburgh.—*Price*.]

of every rank and profession, under the allegory of a ship freighted with fools of all kinds, but without any variety of incident or artificiality of fable; yet although the poem is destitute of plot, and the voyage of adventures, a composition of such a nature became extremely popular. It was translated into French[1] [verse by Pierre Riviere, whose work appeared at Paris in 1497, and thence into French prose by Jean Drouyn, the latter printed in 1498; but in the preceding year (1497) had been published a translation] into tolerable Latin verse by James Locher,[2] a German, and a scholar of the inventor Brandt.[3] From the original and the two translations Barclay formed a large English poem in the ballad or octave stanza, with considerable additions gleaned from the follies of his countrymen. It was printed in 1509 by Pinson, whose name occurs in the poem:

> How be it the charge Pynson has on me laide
> With many fooles our Nauy not to charge.[4]

It was finished in 1508 in the college of Saint Mary Ottery, as appears by the title: *The Shyp of Folys of the Worlde*. *This present boke named the shyp of folys of the worlde was translated in the college of saynt mary Otery, in the counte of Deuonshyre oute of Laten, Frenche, and Doche into Englishe tonge, by Alexander Barclay preste and at that tyme chaplen in the sayde college, translated the yere of our Lord-God, M.CCCCC.VIII.*[5] Our author's stanza is verbose, prosaic and tedious: and for many pages together his poetry is little better than a trite homily in verse. The title promises much character and pleasantry: but we shall be disappointed, if we expect to find the foibles of the crew of our ship touched by the hand of the author of the *Canterbury Tales*, or exposed in the rough yet strong satire of Langland. He sometimes has a stroke of humour: as in the following stanza, where he wishes to take on board the eight secondaries or minor canons of his college. *Alexander Barclay ad fatuos, vt dent locum octo*

---

[1] By Joce Bade. Paris, 1497. In verse. From which the French prose translation was made the next year.

[2] In the colophon, it is said to have been *jampridem traducta* from the German original by Locher; and that this Latin translation was revised by the inventor Brandt, with the addition of many new Fools. A second edition of Locher's Latin was printed at Paris in 1498, 4to. In the royal library at Paris there is a curious copy of Barclay's English *Ship of Folys* by Pinson on vellum, a rarity not, I believe, to be found in England.

[3] See *The Prologue*.

[4] Fol. 38, *verso*. In another place he complains that some of his *wordes* are *amis*, on account of the "printers not perfect in science." And adds, that

> "The Printers in'their busynes
> Do all their workes speedely and in haste—"

fol. 258, b, [edit. 1570].

[5] In folio. A second edition, from which I cite, was printed with his other works in the year 1570, also in folio, with curious wooden cuts, taken from Pynson's impression, viz. *The Ship of Fooles, wherin is shewed the folly of all States, with diuers other workes adioyned vnto the same*, &c. This has both Latin and English. [In all the former editions, the extracts from Barclay are (as usual) inaccurate, and the references often erroneous.]

secundariis beatæ Mariæ de Oterei, qui quidem prima huius ratis transtra merentur.[1]

>   Softe,[1] fooles, softe, a little flacke your pace,
>   Till I haue fpace you to' order by degree,
>   I haue eyght neyghbours, that firſt ſhall haue a place
>   Within this my ſhip, for they moſt worthy be;
>   They may their learning receyue coſtles and free,
>   Their walles abutting and ioyning to the ſcholes;[2]
>   Nothing they can,[3] yet nought will they learne nor ſee,
>   Therfore ſhall they guide this our ſhip of fooles.

The ignorance of the Engliſh clergy is one of the chief objects of his animadverſion. He ſays:[4]

>   For if one can flatter, and beare a Hauke on his fiſt,
>   He ſhalbe made Parſon of Honington or of Cliſt.

Theſe were rich benefices in the neighbourhood of Saint Mary Ottery. He diſclaims the profane and petty tales of the times:

>   I write no jeſte ne tale of Robin Hood,[5]
>   Nor ſowe no ſparkles, ne ſede of viciouſnes;
>   Wiſe men loue vertue, wilde people wantonnes,
>   It longeth not my ſcience nor cuning,
>   For Philip the ſparrow the dirige to ſing.

The laſt line is a ridicule on his cotemporary Skelton, who wrote *The Booke of Philip Sparrow*, or a Dirge

>   For the ſowle of Philip Sparowe
>   That was late flayne at Carow, &c.[6]

[Or rather perhaps it may be an alluſion to the latent meaning of the phraſe, for probably Skelton in his poem, and certainly Gaſcoigne in his *Praiſe of Phillip Sparrowe*, intended *an erotic allegory*.][7] In another place, he thus cenſures the faſhionable reading of his age, much in the tone of his predeceſſor Hawes:

>   Nor godly ſcripture is not worth an hawe;
>   But tales are loued, ground of ribaudry,
>   And many are ſo blinded with their foly,
>   That no ſcripture thinke they ſo true nor good
>   As is a fooliſhe ieſt of Robin Hood.[8]

As a ſpecimen of his general manner, I inſert his character of the Student or Bookworm: whom he ſuppoſes to be the Firſt Fool in the veſſel:[9]

That in this Ship the chief place I gouerne,	Primus in excelſa teneo quod naue rudentes,
By this wide Sea with fools wandering,	Stultiuagoſq; ſequor comites per flumina vaſta:

---

[1] fol. 68.
[2] To the collegiate church of Saint Mary Ottery a ſchool was annexed by the munificent founder, Grandiſon, biſhop of Exeter. This college was founded in the year 1337.
[3] know. [4] Fol. 2.
[5] Fol. 23. [6] [Skelton's works, edit. Dyce, i. 51.]
[7] [Gaſcoigne's works, by Hazlitt, i. 488-9. See a paſſage, moreover, in Skelton's *Magnyfycence*, (Works, by Dyce, i. 276.)]
[8] Fol. 23.
[9] I add the Latin from which he tranſlates, that the reader may judge how much is our poet's own, fol. 1. a.

The cause is plaine and easy to discerne,
Still am I busy bookes assembling,
For to haue plentie it is a pleasaunt thing
In my conceyt, and to haue them ay in
    hande:
But what they meane do I not vnder-
    stande.

But yet I haue them in great reuerence
And honoure, sauing them from filth
    and ordure;
By often brushing and moch diligence,
Full goodly bounde in pleasaunt couer-
    ture
Of Damas, Sattin, or els of Veluet pure:[1]
I keepe them sure, fearing least they
    should be lost,
For in them is the cunning wherein I
    me boast.

But if it fortune that any learned man
Within my house fall to disputation,
I drawe the curtaynes to shewe my bokes
    then,
That they of my cunning should make
    probation:
I loue not to fall in altercation:
And while the commen, my bookes I
    turne & winde,
For all is in them, and nothing in my
    minde.

Ptolomeus[2] the riche caused longe agone
Ouer all the worlde good bookes to be
    sought,
Done was his commaundement anone:
                *   *   *   *

Lo in likewise of bookes I haue store,
But fewe I reade, and fewer vnderstande,
I folowe not their doctrine nor their lore,
It is ynough to beare a booke in hande:
It were too muche to be in suche a bande;
For to be bound to loke within the booke,
I am content on the fayre couering to
    looke.——

Eche is not lettred that nowe is made a
    lorde,
Nor eche a Clerke that hath a benefice:
They are not all lawyers that plees do
    recorde,
All that are promoted are not fully wise,
On suche chaunce nowe fortune throwes
    her dice,

Non ratione vacat certa, sensuq; la-
    tenti:
Congestis etenim stultus confido libellis;
Spem quoq; nec paruam, collecta vo-
    lumina præbent,
Calleo nec verbum, nec libri sentio men-
    tem:
Attamen in magno per me seruantur
    honore,
Pulueris & cariem plumatis tergo fla-
    bellis.

Ast vbi doctrinæ certamen voluitur, in-
    quam,
Ædibus in nostris librorum culta su-
    pellex
Eminet, & chartis viuo contentus opertis:
Quas video ignorans, iuuat & me copia
    sola.

Constituit quondam diues Ptolomeus,
    haberet
Vt libros toto quæsitos undiq; mundo,
Quos grandes rerum thesauros esse pu-
    tabat:

Non tamen archanæ legis documenta
    tenebat,
Quis fine non poterat vitæ disponere
    cursum.
En pariter teneo numerosa volumina,
    tardus
Pauca lego, viridi contentus tegmine
    libri.

Cur vellem studio sensus turbare fre-
    quenti,
Aut tam sollicitis animum confundere
    rebus?
Qui studet, assiduo motu fit stultus &
    amens.

---

[1] Students and monks were anciently the binders of books. In the first page of a MS. Life of Concubranus this note occurs, "Ex conjunctione dompni Wyllelmi Edys monasterii B. Mariæ S. Modwenæ virginis de Burton super Trent monachi, dum esset studens Oxoniæ, A. D. MDXVII." See MSS. Cotton. Cleopatr. ii., and MSS. Coll. Oriel. N. vi. 3, et 7, Art. The word conjunctio=ligatura. The book is much older than this entry.

[2] Ptolomeus Philadelphus, for whom he quotes Josephus, lib. xii.

That though one knowe but the yrifhe
    game,[1]
Yet would he haue a gentlemans name.
So in like wife I am in fuche eafe,
Though I nought can, I woulde be
    called wife:
Alfo I may fet another in my place,
Which may for me my bookes exercife;
Or els I fhall enfue the common guife,
And fay *concedo* to euery argument
Leaft by much fpeeche my latin fhould
    be fpent.[2]

Seu ftudeam, feu non, dominus tamen
    effe vocabor;
Et poffum ftudio focium difponere
    noftro,
Qui pro me fapiat, doctafq; examinet
    artes:
At fi cum doctis verfor, concedere
    malo
Omnia, ne cogar fors verba latina pro-
    fari.

In one part of the poem the apologue of Prodicus, of Hercules meeting Virtue and Pleafure, is introduced. In the fpeech of Pleafure our author changes his metre, and breaks forth into a lyrical ftrain, not totally void of elegance and delicacy, and in a rhythmical arrangement adopted by Gray:

All my vefture is of golde pure,
My gay Chaplet with ftones fet,
With couerture of fine afure,
In filuer net my heare vp knet,
Softe filke betwene, leaft it might fret;
My purple pall ouercouereth all,
Cleare as Chriftall, no thing egall.—

With harpe in hande alway I ftande,
Paffing eche houre in fwete pleafour;
A wanton bande of euery lande,
Are in my towre me to honour,
Some of valour, fome bare and poore;
Kinges in their pride fit by my fide:
Euery frefhe floure, of fwete odoure,
To them I prouide, that with me bide.—

Who euer they be that folowe me,
And gladly flee to my ftandarde,
They fhall be free, not ficke, nor fee
Aduerfitie nor paynes harde.

No poynt of payne fhall he fuftayne,
But ioy fouerayne, while he is here;
No froft ne rayne there fhall diftayne
His face by payne, ne hurt his chere.

He fhall his head caft to no drede
To get the mede[3] and lawde of warre;
Nor yet have nede for to take hede,
How battayles fpede, but ftande a farre.

Nor yet be bounde to care the founde
Of man or grounde, or trompet fhrill,
Strokes that redound fhall not confounde,
Nor his minde wounde, but if he will, &c.[4]

All ancient fatirical writings, even thofe of an inferior caft, have their merit, and deferve attention, as they tranfmit pictures of familiar manners, and preferve popular cuftoms. In this light, at leaft,

---

[1] [See *Popular Antiquities of Great Britain*, 1870, ii. 315.]   [2] fol. 2.
[3] *meed*; reward.   [4] fol. 241-2.

Barclay's *Ship of Fools*, which is a general satire on the times, will be found entertaining. Nor must it be denied that his language is more cultivated than that of many of his cotemporaries, and that he contributed his share to the improvement of the English phraseology. His author, Sebastian Brandt, appears to have been a man of universal erudition; and his work, for the most part, is a tissue of citations from the ancient poets and historians.

[In 1517, Henry Watson, the compiler of the old romance of *Valentine and Orson*, produced a prose version of Locher's Latin, and it came from the press of Wynkyn de Worde in 1518. The translator says "that this booke hathe ben made in Almayne language/ and out of Almayne it was translated into Latyne by mayster Jaques Locher/ and out of Latyn in to rethoryke Frensshe." He further informs us that he thought that a prose version would be more acceptable than a metrical one, and that he had executed the task at the request of his worshipful master Wynken de Worde, through the "enticement" and exhortation of the Countess of Richmond and Derby.]

Barclay's other pieces are the *Mirror of Good Manners*, and five *Eclogues*. He also wrote: 1. *The figure of our Mother holy church oppressed by the French king*, [known at present only from Maunsell's *Catalogue*.] 2. *Against Skelton*, [which is mentioned by Bale, but is not otherwise traceable.[1]] 3. *The Lives of St. Catharine, St. Margaret, and St. Etheldred*. 4. *The Life of S. George*, from Mantuan: dedicated to N. West, bishop of Ely, and written while our author was a monk of Ely. 5. [*The Introductory to wryte and pronoynce French*, which will occur again.] 6. *The famous cronycle of the warre which/ the Romaynes had agaynst Jugurth vsurper of the kyngdome of Numidy: which cronycle is compyled in latyn by the renowed Sallust*. And *translated into englysshe by Syr Alexander Barclay, preest at comaundment of the right hye and mighty prince: Thomas duke of Northfolke*. The Latin and English are printed together. The Latin is dedicated to Vesey, bishop of Exeter, and dated "ex Cellula Hatfeld regis [*i.e.* King's Hatfield, Hertfordshire] iii. id. Novemb." A new edition, without the Latin and the two dedications, was printed in 1557. 7. *Orationes variæ*. 8. *De fide Orthodoxa*.

The *Mirror* is a translation from a Latin elegiac poem, written in the year 1516 by Dominicus Mancinus, *De quatuor Virtutibus*. It is in the ballad stanza.[2] Our translator, as appears by the address prefixed, had been requested by Sir Giles Alyngton to abridge or modernize Gower's *Confessio Amantis*. But the poet declined this undertaking as unsuitable to his age, infirmities and profession, and chose rather to oblige his patron with a grave system of ethics. It is

---

[1] ["Bale mentions, among the writings of Alexander Barclay, a piece 'against Skelton.' It has not come down to us, but the extant works of Barclay bear testimony to the hearty dislike with which he regarded our author."—*Dyce*.]

[2] [It was printed separately by R. Pynson, without date, folio, and is included in the ed. of the *Ship of Fools*, 1570.]

certain that he made a prudent choice. The performance shows how little qualified he was to correct Gower. [He was not, however, the only renderer into our English tongue of the treatise on the Virtues; for W. de Worde printed, in or about 1518, a different translation with the original Latin of Mancinus. Of a still later version we shall speak in another place.]

Our author's *Eclogues*, I believe, are the first that appeared in the English language.[1] They are, like Petrarch's and Mantuan's,[2] of the moral and satirical kind, and contain but few touches of rural description and bucolic imagery. They seem to have been written about the year 1514.[3] The three first are paraphrased, with very large additions, from the *Miseriæ Curialium* of Eneas Sylvius,[4] and treat of the *Miseryes of Courtiers and Courtes of all princes in generall*. The fourth (in which is introduced a long poem in stanzas, called the *Towre of vertue and honour*)[5] treats *of the behaviour of Riche men agaynst Poetes*. The fifth, *of the disputation of Citizens and men of the Countrey*. These pastorals, if they deserve the name, contain many allusions to the times. The poet is prolix in his praises of Alcock, bishop of Ely, and founder of Jesus College in Cambridge. This very learned and munificent prelate deservedly possessed some of the highest dignities in church and state. He was appointed Bishop of Ely in 1486. He died at Wisbeach in 1501.[6] Rosse says that he was tutor to Prince Edward, afterwards Edward V., but was removed by the king's uncle, Richard. Rosse, I think, is the only historian who records this anecdote."[7]

> Yes since his dayes a cocke was in the fen,[8]
> I knowe his voyce among a thousande men:
> He taught, he preached, he mended euery wrong;
> But, Coridon, alas no good thing bideth long.

---

[1] [The first four were printed by R. Pynson, without date, 4to, with woodcuts; the fifth, *Of the Cytezen and Vplondishman*, came from W. de Worde's press, also without date, 4to. There are later editions.]

[2] Whom he mentions, speaking of Egloges. *Eglog.* 1, Prol.

> "And in like maner nowe lately in our dayes,
> Hath other Poetes attempted the same wayes:
> As the moste famous Baptist Mantuan
> The best of that sort since Poetes first began,
> And Frauncis Petrarke also in Italy," &c.

[3] Because he praises "noble Henry which now departed late." Afterwards he falls into a long panegyric on his successor Henry VIII. *Eglog.* i. As he does in the *Ship of Fooles*, fol. 205, a, where he says:

> "This noble prince beginneth vertuously
> By iustice and pitie his realme to maynteyne."

He then wishes he may retake Jerusalem from the Turks, and compares him to Hercules, Achilles, &c.

[4] That is, Pius II., who died in 1464. This piece is among his *Epistles*, some of which are called tracts. *Epist.* clvi.

[5] It is properly an Elegy on the death of the Duke of Norfolk, lord high admiral.

[6] See Whart. *Angl. Sacr.* i. 675, 801, 381.

[7] *Hist. Reg. Angl.* p. 212, edit. Hearn.

[8] The isle of Ely.

> He all was a cocke,[1] he wakened vs from flepe,
> And while we flumbred, he did our foldes kepe.
> No cur, no foxes, nor butchers dogges wood,
> Coulde hurte our fouldes, his watching was fo good.
> The hungry wolues, which that time did abounde,
> What time he crowed,[2] abafhed at the founde.
> This cocke was no more abafhed of the foxe,
> Than is a lion abafhed of an oxe.
> When he went, faded the floure of al the fen;
> I boldly dare fweare this cocke trode neuer hen![3]

Alcock, while living, erected a beautiful fepulchral chapel in his cathedral, ftill remaining, but defaced. To which the fhepherd alludes in the lines that follow:

> This was a father of thinges paftorall,
> And that well fheweth his Church cathedrall.
> There was I lately about the middell of May;
> Coridon, his Church is twenty fith more gay
> Then all the Churches betwene the fame and Kent;
> There fawe I his tome and Chapell excellent.—
> Our parifhe Church is but a dongeon
> To that gay Churche in comparifon.—
> When I fawe his figure lye in the Chapell fide, &c.[4]

In another place he thus reprefents the general lamentation for the

---

[1] Alcock.

[2] Among Wren's MSS. Collections (Regiftr. parv. Confiftorii Elienfis, called the *Black Book*) the following curious memorial, concerning a long fermon preached by Alcock at Saint Mary's in Cambridge, occurs: "1. Alcock, divina gratia epifcopus Elienfis, prima die dominica, 1488, bonum et blandum fermonem prædicavit in ecclefia B. Mariæ Cantabrig. qui incepit in hora prima poft meridiem et duravit in horam tertiam et ultra." He fometimes, and even in the epifcopal character, condefcended to fport with his own name. He publifhed an addrefs to the clergy affembled at Barnwell, under the title of *Galli cantus ad confratres fuos curatos in fynodo apud Barnwell*, 25 Sept. 1498; to which is annexed his Conftitution for celebrating certain feafts in his diocefe, printed by Pinfon, 1498. In the beginning is the figure of the bifhop preaching to his clergy, with two cocks on each fide; and there is a cock in the firft page. By the way, Alcock wrote many other pieces. *The Hill of Perfection*, from the Latin, 1497, 4to; again, 1501, 4to. *Spoufage of a Virgin to Chrift*, 1486. *Homeliæ vulgares*. *Meditationes piæ*. A fragment of a [tranflation of] the *Seven Penitential Pfalms*, in Englifh verfe, is fuppofed to be by Bifhop Alcock, MSS. Harl. 1704, 4, fol. 13. [But Sir F. Madden has pointed out to the prefent editor that this is the fame which is found in MS. Sloane 1853, and MS. Trin. Coll. Camb. R. 3.20, and is affigned to Thomas Brampton. It was edited for the Percy Society by Mr. W. H. Black in 1842. Warton alfo wrongly attributed to Alcock the *Abbaye of the Holy Ghoft*, a copy of which is in the Vernon MS. written before he was born. Sir F. Madden remarks: Another copy of the piece is in the Thornton MS. in the library of Lincoln Cathedral, A. 1. 17, of the middle of the fifteenth century. Mr. Furnivall notes incidentally: "The Porkington MS. No. 20, belonging to Mr. Ormfby Gore, contains a tranflation of the *Seven Penitential Pfalms*, beginning,

> 'Lord, in thyn yre vp take me nouyt,
> And in thyn yre blame not me—'

This MS. may be about A. D. 1400. MS. No. 19, in the fame collection, a tranflation in profe of the *Horologium Sapientiæ*, is dated May 31, 1419."]

[3] [Sign. A iij, *recto*. The *butchers dogges wood* may be an oblique allufion to Wolfey.]

[4] *Eglog.* i. fignat. A iij, *recto*.

death of this worthy prelate: and he rises above himself in describing the sympathy of the towers, arches, vaults, and images of Ely Monastery:

> The pretie palace by him made in the fen,[1]
> The maides, widowes, the wiues, and the men,
> With deadly dolour were pearsed to the hearte,
> When death constrayned this shepheard to departe.
> Corne, grasse, and fieldes, mourned for wo and payne,
> For oft his prayer for them obtayned rayne.
> The pleasaunt floures for wo faded eche one.—
> The okes, elmes, and euery sorte of dere[2]
> Shronke vnder shadowes, abating all their chere.
> The mightie walles of Ely monastery,
> The stones, rockes, and towres semblably,
> The marble pillers and images echeone,
> Swet all for sorowe, when this good cocke was gone, &c.[3]

It should be remembered that these pastorals were probably written while our poet was a monk of Ely; and although Alcock was then dead, yet the memory of his munificence and piety was recent in the monastery.[4]

Speaking of the dignity and antiquity of shepherds, and particularly of Christ at his birth being first seen by shepherds, he seems to describe some large and splendid picture of the Nativity painted on the walls of Ely cathedral:

> I sawe them my selfe well paynted on the wall,
> Late gasing upon our Churche Cathedrall:
> I sawe great wethers in picture and small lambes,
> Daunsing, some sleeping, some sucking of their dams,
> And some on the grounde me semed lying still:
> Then sawe I horsemen at pendant of an hill.[5]

---

[1] He rebuilt, or greatly improved, the episcopal palace at Ely.

[2] beasts, quadrupeds of all kinds. So in the romance of *Syr Bevis*, signat. F iij:

> "Rattes and myce and such smal dere
> Was his meate that seven yere."

Whence Shakespeare took, as Dr. Percy has observed, the well-known distich of the madman in *King Lear*, act iii. sc. 4:

> "But mice and rats, and such small deer
> Have been Tom's food for seven long year."

[Dyce's edit. 1868, vii. 302.] It cannot now be doubted, that Shakespeare in this passage wrote *deer*, instead of *geer* or *cheer*, which have been conjecturally substituted by his commentators.

[3] *Egl.* iii.

[4] He also compliments Alcock's predecessor, Morton, afterwards archbishop of Canterbury: not without an allusion to his troubles, and restoration to favour, under Richard III, and Henry VII. *Egl.* iii. [sign. C ij, *verso*.]

> "And shepheard Morton, when he durst not appeare,
> Howe his olde servauntes were carefull of his chere;
> In payne and pleasour they kept fidelitie,
> Till grace agayne gaue him aucthoritie, &c."

And again, *Egl.* iiii. [sign. C v, *recto*]:

> "Micene [Mecænas] and Morton be dead and gone certayne."

The *Dean of Powles*, I suppose Dean Colet, is celebrated as a preacher, *ibid.* As is, "The olde friar that wonned in Greenwich." *Egl.* v.

[5] *Egl.* v. [sign. D iv, *recto*. A portion of this passage has already been cited (p. 119, *supr.*), and has therefore not been repeated.]

Virgil's poems are thus characterised in some of the best-turned lines we find in these pastorals:

> He songe of fieldes and tilling of the grounde,
> Of shepe and oxen, and battayle did he sounde;
> So shrill he sounded in termes eloquent
> I trowe his tunes went to the firmament.[1]

He gives us the following idea of the sports, spectacles and pleasures of his age:

> Some men deliteth beholding men to fight,
> Or goodly knightes in pleasaunt apparayle,
> Or sturdie souldiers in bright harnes and male.[2]—
> Some glad is to see these Ladies beauteous,
> Goodly appoynted in clothing sumpteous:
> A number of people appoynted in like wise[3]
> In costly clothing after the newest gise;
> Sportes, disgising,[4] fayre coursers mount and praunce,
> Or goodly ladies and knightes sing and daunce:
> To see fayre houses and curious picture[s],
> Or pleasaunt hanging[5] or sumpteous vesture,
> Of silke, of purpure, or golde moste orient,
> And other clothing diuers and excellent:
> Hye curious buildinges or palaces royall,
> Or Chapels, temples fayre and substanciall,
> Images grauen or vaultes curious;[6]
> Gardeyns and medowes, or place[7] delicious,
> Forestes and parkes well furnished with dere,
> Cold pleasaunt streames or welles fayre and clere,
> Curious cundites, &c.[8]

I shall here throw together some traits in these Eclogues of the common customs and manners of the times. A shepherd, after mentioning his skill in shooting birds with a bow, says:

> No shepheard throweth the axeltree so farre.[9]

A gallant is thus described:

> For women vse to loue them moste of all,
> Which boldly bosteth, or that can sing and iet;
> Whiche hath the maistrey ofte time in tournament,
> Or that can gambauld, or daunce feat and gent.[10]

The following sorts of wine are recited:

> As Muscadell, Caprike, Romney, and Maluesy,
> From Gene brought, from Grece or Hungary.[11]

As are the dainties of the table. A shepherd at court must not think to eat

> Swanne, nor heron,
> Curlewe, nor crane.[12]

---

[1] *Egl.* iv. [sign. C iv, *verso*, col. 2.]
[2] armour and coats of mail.
[3] apparelled in uniform.
[4] masques, &c.
[5] tapestry.
[6] roofs, curiously vaulted.
[7] houses, seats.
[8] *Egl.* ii. [sign. B i, *recto*, col. 1.]
[9] *Ibid.* [sign. A ij, *recto*, col. 2, edit. *ut supr.*]
[10] *Ibid.* ii. [sign. B ij, *recto*, col. 1.]
[11] *Ibid.* i; [sign. B iii, *recto*, col. 1.]
[12] *Ibid.*

Again :

> What fishe is of sauor swete and delicious,—
> Rosted or sodden in swete hearbes or wine ;
> Or fried in oyle, moste saporous and fine.—
> The pasties of a hart.
> The crane, the sesant, the pecocke and curlewe,
> The partriche, plouer, bitter, and heronsewe—
> Seasoned so well in licour redolent,
> That the hall is full of pleasaunt smell and sent.[1]

At a feast at court :

> Slowe be the seruers in seruing in alway,
> But swift be they after, taking thy meate away :
> A speciall custome is vsed them amonge,
> No good dish to suffer on borde to be longe
> If the dishe be pleasaunt, eyther fleshe or fishe,
> Ten handes at once swarme in the dishe :
> And if it be flesh, ten kniues shall thou see
> Mangling the flesh, and in the platter flee :
> To put there thy handes is perill without fayle,
> Without a gauntlet or els a gloue of mayle.[2]

The two last lines remind us of a saying of Quin, who declared it was not safe to sit down to a turtle-feast in one of the city-halls, without a basket-hilted knife and fork. Not that I suppose Quin borrowed his *bons-mots* from black-letter books.

The following lines point out some of the festive tales of our ancestors :

> Yet would I gladly heare some mery fit
> Of mayde Marian, or els of Robin hood ;
> Or Bentleyes ale which chafeth well the blood,
> Of perre of Norwich, or sauce of Wilberton,
> Or buckish Joly well-stuffed as a ton.[3]

He mentions " Bentley's Ale," which " maketh me to winke ; "[4] and some of our ancient domestic pastimes and amusements are recorded :

> Then is it pleasure the yonge maydens amonge
> To watche by the fire the winters nightes long :—
> And in the ashes some playes for to marke,
> To couer wardens [pears] for fault of other warke :
> To toste white sheuers, and to make prophitroles ;
> And aftir talking oft time to fill the bowles, &c.[5]

He mentions some musical instruments :

> Methinkes no mirth is scant,
> Where no rejoysing of minstrelsie doth want :
> The bagpipe or fiddle to us is delectable, &c.[6]

And the mercantile commodities of different countries and cities :

> Englande hath cloth, Burdeux hath store of wine,
> Cornewall hath tinne, and lymster wools fine.
> London hath scarlet, and Bristowe pleasaunt red, &c.[7]

---

[1] *Ibid.* [edit. *ut supr.* sign. B iii, *verso*.]
[2] *Ibid.* [sign. B iv, col. 2.]
[3] *Ibid.* iv. [sign. C vi, *recto*, col. 1.]
[4] *Ibid.* ii.
[5] *Ibid.* iv. [sign. C iv, *verso*, col. 2.]
[6] *Ibid.* ii.
[7] *Ibid.* iv. [sign. C iv, *verso*.]

Of songs at feasts:

> When your fat dishes smoke hote vpon your table,
> Then lavde ye songes and balades magnifie,
> If they be mery, or written craftely,
> Ye clappe your handes and to the making harke,
> And one say to other, lo here a proper warke.¹

He says that minstrels and singers are highly favoured at court, especially those of the French *gise*.² Also jugglers and pipers.³

We have before seen, that our author and Skelton were rivals. He alludes to Skelton, who had been laureated at Oxford, in the following lines:

> Then is he decked as Poete laureate,
> When stinking Thais made him her graduate:—
> If they have smelled the artes triuiall,
> They count them Poetes hye and heroicall.⁴

The *Tower of Vertue and Honour*, introduced as a song of one of the shepherds into these pastorals, exhibits no very masterly strokes of a sublime and inventive fancy. It has much of the trite imagery usually applied in the fabrication of these ideal edifices. It, however, shows our author in a new walk of poetry. This magnificent tower or castle is built on inaccessible cliffs of flint: the walls are of gold, bright as the sun, and decorated with "olde historyes and pictures manyfolde:" the turrets are beautifully shaped. Among its heroic inhabitants are Henry VIII., Howard, Duke of Norfolk, and the Earl of Shrewsbury. Labour is the porter at the gate, and Virtue governs the house. Labour is thus pictured, with some degree of spirit

> Fearfull is labour without fauour at all,
>   Dreadful of visage, a monster intreatable,
> Like Cerberus lying at gates infernall;
>   To some men his looke is halfe intollerable,
> His shoulders large, for burthen strong and able,
>   His bodie bristled, his necke mightie and stiffe;
> By sturdie senewes, his ioyntes stronge and stable,
>   Like marble stones his handes be as stiffe.
>
> Here must man vanquishe the dragon of Cadmus,
>   Against the Chimer here stoutly must he fight,
> Here must he vanquish the fearefull Pegasus,
>   For the golden flece here must he shewe his might:
> If labour gaynsay, he can nothing be right,
>   This monster labour oft chaungeth his figure,
> Sometime an oxe, a bore, or lion wight,
>   Playnely he seemeth, thus changeth his nature.
> Like as Protheus ofte chaunged his stature.
>   *   *   *   *
>
> Under his browes he dreadfully doth loure
>   With glittering eyen, and side-dependaunt beard,
> For thirst and hunger alway his chere is foure,
>   His horned forehead doth make faynt heartes feard.

---

¹ *Elg.* iv. [sign. C iv, *verso*.]   ² *Ibid.* ii.   ³ *Ibid.* iv.
⁴ *Ibid.* iv. [sign. C v, *verso*, col. 2.]

> Alway he drinketh, and yet alway is drye,
> The fweat diftilling with droppes aboundaunt, &c.

The poet adds that, when the noble Howard had long boldly contended with this hideous monfter, had broken the bars and doors of the caftle, had bound the porter, and was now preparing to afcend the tower of Virtue and Honour, Fortune and Death appeared, and interrupted his progrefs.[1]

The earlieft modern Latin Bucolics are thofe of Petrarch, in number twelve, written about 1350.[2] The Eclogues of Mantuan, our author's model, appeared about 1400, and were followed by many others. Their number multiplied fo foon, that a collection of thirty-eight modern bucolic poets in Latin was printed at Bafle in 1546.[3] Thefe writers judged this indirect and difguifed mode of dialogue, confifting of fimple characters which fpoke freely and plainly, the moft fafe and convenient vehicle for abufing the corruptions of the church.

[It may perhaps be added here, that this was the character of the Paftoral fchool of poetry long before Petrarch's time, for the Eclogues of Virgil are, in feveral inftances, mere apologues, and fo it was, later on, with thofe of Browne, author of the *Shepheards Pipe*. The political verfes printed by Bentley, in his *Excerpta Hiftorica*, 1833, are equally in the nature of apologues, and paint real perfons and events under feigned names. The fame obfervation applies to the *Parlyament of Byrdes*, Drayton's *Owl*, and other pieces which might be fpecified.]

Mantuan became fo popular, as to acquire the eftimation of a claffic, and to be taught in fchools. Nothing better proves the reputation in which this writer was held, than a fpeech of Shakefpeare's pedant, the pedagogue Holofernes:

> Faufte precor, gelida quando
> Pecus omne fub umbrâ,[4]

and fo forth. Ah, good old Mantuan! I may fpeak of thee, as the traveller doth of Venice,

> Vinegia, Vinegia chi non te vede,
> Ei non te pregia.

Old Mantuan! Old Mantuan! Who underftandeth thee not loves thee not."[5] But although Barclay copies Mantuan, the recent and feparate publication in England of Virgil's bucolics by Wynkyn de Worde[6] might partly fuggeft the new idea of this kind of poetry.

With what avidity the Italian and French poets, in their refpective

---

[1] *Egl.* iv.   [2] *Bucolicorum Eclogæ* xii.
[3] [*Bucolicorum auctores* xxxviii. *quotquot à Virgilii ætate,* &c. See Brunet, laft edit. i. 1373.]
[4] One of Mantuan's lines. Farnaby, in his Preface to Martial, fays that *Faufte precor gelida* was too often preferred to *Arma virumque cano*. Mantuan was three times printed in England before the year 1600. [See Herbert's edit. of Ames for the full and correct titles, ii. 941, 1268.]
[5] *Love's Lab. L.* act iv. fc. 3 [edit. *ut fupr.* ii. 195.]
[6] [W. de Worde appears to have printed this pretty often; but fome of the editions cited by Ames and others are doubtful.]

languages, entered into this species of composition, when the rage of Latin versification had subsided, and for the purposes above mentioned, is an inquiry reserved for a future period. I shall only add here, that before the close of the fifteenth century, Virgil's bucolics were translated into Italian [1] by Bernardo Pulci, Fossa de Cremona, [Hieronimo] Benivieni, and [Jacopo] Fiorino [de] Buoninsegni.

[We must not neglect to notice the work, which of all those which have come down to us from Barclay's pen, is best entitled, perhaps, to the merit of originality. This book was called *The Introductory to wryte and pronounce French compyled by Alexander Barclay compendiously at the commaūdemēt of the ryght hye excellent and myghty prynce Thomas duke of Northfolke*. The particulars, which precede, are above a shield of arms, exhibiting a lion rampant holding another shield with a lion on it, and beneath the woodcut occurs: "R. Coplande to the whyte lyone, Ballade [in French]." This educational treatise was printed by Copland in 1521, and occupies only 30 folio pages. It is the tract to which Palsgrave refers in his *Eclaircissement de la Langue Françoise*, 1530.[2]

Barclay was employed by Henry VIII. to compose the impresses, or some of them, which were used at the *Field of Cloth of Gold* in 1520.[3] Barclay translated the Eclogues of Æneas Sylvius into English; but it does not appear who was the renderer into our language of that writer's somewhat tragical story of *Lucrece and Eurialus*, which went through at least three editions between 1549 and 1567, and which affords a curious glimpse of the state of Italian manners and morals in the fifteenth century.

Another writer, belonging to this period, was George Cavendish, gentleman-usher to Cardinal Wolsey, author of his Life, and also of certain Metrical Visions, somewhat on the plan of the *Mirror for Magistrates*. Of the latter some specimens are furnished elsewhere:[4] they are not remarkable for poetical elegance. Cavendish's *Life of Wolsey* itself is a work too well known to require further notice.]

---

[1] Viz. La Bucolica di Virgilio per el clarissimo poeta frate Evangelista Fossa de Cremona. Venezia, 1494, 4to. But thirteen years earlier we find *la Bucolica* di Virgilio *tradotta da Bernardo Pulci con le bucoliche di Fr. de arsochis*, &c. Firenze, 1481. A dedication is prefixed, by which it appears that Buoninsegni wrote a *Piscatory Eclogue*, the first ever written in Italy, in the year 1468.

[2] ["John Palsgrave," notes Warton himself, "a polite scholar and an eminent preceptor of the French language about the reign of Henry VIII., and one of the first who published in English a grammar or system of rules for teaching that language."]

[3] [Ellis, *Orig. Lett.* 1st S. i. 163.]

[4] [*Letters of Royal and Illustr. Ladies*, iii. 91, 273.]

SECTION XXIX.

T is not the plan of this work to comprehend the Scotish poetry. But when I confider the clofe and national connection between England and Scotland in the progrefs of manners and literature, I am fenfible I fhould be guilty of a partial and defective reprefentation of the poetry of the former, were I to omit in my feries a few Scotifh writers, who have adorned the prefent period with a degree of fentiment and fpirit, a command of phrafeology, and a fertility of imagination, not to be found in any Englifh poet fince Chaucer and Lydgate: more efpecially as they have left ftriking fpecimens of allegorical invention, a fpecies of compofition which appears to have been for fome time almoft totally extinguifhed in England.

The firft I fhall mention is William Dunbar, a native of Salton in Eaft Lothian, about the year [1460].[1] His moft celebrated poems are *The Thiftle and the Rofe* and *The Golden Terge.*

The *Thiftle and the Rofe* was occafioned by the marriage of James IV., King of Scotland, with Margaret Tudor, eldeft daughter of Henry VII., King of England: an event, in which the whole future political ftate of both nations was vitally interefted, and which ultimately produced the union of the two crowns and kingdoms. It was finifhed on the ninth day of May in the year 1503, nearly three months before the arrival of the queen in Scotland: whofe progrefs from Richmond to Edinburgh was attended with a greater magnificence of parade, proceffions, and fpectacles, than I ever remember to have feen on any fimilar occafion.[2] It is worthy of particular notice, that during this expedition there was in the magnificent fuite of the princefs a company of players, under the direction of one John Inglifh, who is fometimes called Johannes. "Amonge the faide lordes and the qweene was in order, Johannes and his companye, the minftrells of muficke," &c.[3] In the midft of a moft fplendid proceffion, the princefs rode on horfe-back behind the king into the city of Edinburgh.[4] Afterwards the ceremonies of this ftately marriage are defcribed; which yet is not equal, in magnificence and expenfe, to that of Richard II. with Ifabel of France at Calais in 1397. This laft-mentioned marriage is re-

---

[1] ["William Dunbar was born about the middle of the fifteenth century. The precife date of his birth has not been afcertained, but, from circumftances to be afterwards ftated, we may with certainty place it not later than the year 1460."—Laing. It may be added that all the extracts from Dunbar, derived by Warton and his editors from inferior texts, have been collated with Mr. Laing's ed. 1834, 2 vols. 8vo.]

[2] See a memoir, cited above, in Leland's *Coll.* tom. iii. *Append.* edit. 1770, p. 265.

[3] P. 267. See alfo, pp. 299, 300, 280, 289.   [4] P. 287.

corded with the moſt minute circumſtances, the dreſſes of the king and the new queen, the names of the French and Engliſh nobility who attended, the preſents, one of which is a collar of gold ſtudded with jewels and worth three thouſand pounds, given on both ſides, the banquets, entertainments, and a variety of other curious particulars, in five large vellum pages, in an ancient Regiſter of Merton priory in Surrey, in old French.¹ Froiſſart, who is moſt commonly prolix in deſcribing pompous ceremonies, might have greatly enriched his account of the ſame royal wedding from this valuable and authentic record.²

It may be pertinent to premiſe, that Margaret was a ſingular patroneſs of the Scotiſh poetry, now beginning to flouriſh. Her bounty is thus celebrated by Stewart of Lorne, in a Scotiſh poem, called *Lerges of this New ʒeir Day*, written in the year 1527:

> Grit God relief³ Margaret our quene!
> For and ſcho war as ſcho hes bene⁴
>   Scho wald be lerger of luſray⁵
> Then all the laif that I of mene,⁶
>   For lerges⁷ of this new-yeir day.⁸

Dunbar's *Thiſtle and Roſe* is opened with the following ſtanzas, which are remarkable for their deſcriptive and picturesque beauties:

> Quhen⁹ Merch wes with variand windis paſt,
> And Appryll had with hir ſilver ſchouris
> Tane leif¹⁰ at Nature, with ane orient blaſt,
> And luſty May, that muddir¹¹ is of flouris,
> Had maid the birdis to begyn thair houris,¹²
> Amang the tendir odouris reid and quhyt,
> Quhois armony to heir it wes delyt:

> In bed at morrow ſleiping as I lay,
> Me thocht Aurora, with hir criſtall ene

---

¹ MSS. Laud, E. 54, fol. 105, b. Bibl. Bodl. Oxon.
² See his *Cron.* tom. iv. p. 226, ch. 78. B. *penult*. Paris, 1574. Or lord Berners's Tranſlation, vol. ii. f. 275, cap. ccxvi. edit. 1523.
³ great God help, &c.   ⁴ If ſhe continues to do as ſhe has done.
⁵ bounty. Fr. l'Offre.   ⁶ any other I could ſpeak of.
⁷ largeſs, bounty.   ⁸ St. x.   ⁹ when. *Qu* has the force of *w*.
¹⁰ taken leave.   ¹¹ mother.
¹² Mattin oriſons. From *Horæ* in the miſſal. So again in the *Golden Terge*, St. ii. Where he alſo calls the birds the "chapel-clarkes" of Venus, St. iii. In the *Court of Love*, Chaucer introduces the birds ſinging a maſs in honour of May. Morris's *Chaucer*, vol. iv. p. 47, v. 1352, *ſeq*.

> "On May day, when the larke began to ryſe,
> To matens wente the luſty nightingale."

He begins the ſervice with *Domine labia*. The eagle ſings the *Venite*. The popinjay *Cæli enarrant*. The peacock *Dominus regnavit*. The owl *Benedicite*. The *Te Deum* is converted into *Te Deum Amoris*, and ſung by the thruſh, &c. &c. Skelton, in the *Book of Philip Sparrow*, ridicules the miſſal, in ſuppoſing various parts of it to be ſung by birds. Much the ſame ſort of fiction occurs in [*the Armonye of Byrdes*, a poem printed *circâ* 1550, and in] Sir David Lindſay's *Complaynt of the Papyngo*, edit. *ut infr*. ſignat. B iii:

> "Suppoſe the geis and hennis ſuld cry alarum,
> And we ſall ſerve *ſecundum uſum Sarum*," &c.

> In at the window lukit¹ by the day,
> And halfit² me with vifage paill and grene;
> On quhois hand a lark fang, fro the fplene,³
> "Awalk, luvaris,⁴ out of your flomering,⁵
> Se how the lufty morrow dois up fpring!"
>
> Me thocht frefche May befoir my bed up ftude,
> In weid⁶ depaynt of mony diverfs hew,
> Sober, benyng, and full of manfuetude,
> In brycht atteir of flouris forgit new,⁷
> Hevinly of color, quhyt, reid, broun, and blew,
> Balmit in dew, and gilt with Phebus' bemys;
> Quhyll al the houfe illumynit of hir lemys.⁸

May then rebukes the poet for **not** rifing early, according to his annual cuftom, to celebrate the **approach of** the fpring; efpecially as the lark has now **announced the dawn** of day, and his heart in former years had always

> ——— glaid and blifsful bene
> Sangis⁹ to mak undir the levis grene.¹⁰

The poet replies, that the fpring of the prefent year was unpromifing and ungenial; unattended with the ufual fong of birds and ferenity of fky: and that ftorms and fhowers, and the loud blafts of the horn of lord Eolus, had ufurped her mild dominion, and hitherto prevented him from wandering at leifure under the vernal branches. May rejects his excufe, and with a fmile of majefty commands him to arife, and to perform his annual homage to the flowers, the birds, and the fun. They both enter a delicious garden, filled with the richeft colours and odours. The fun fuddenly appears in all his glory, and is thus defcribed in the luminous language of Lydgate:

> The purpour fone, with tendir bemys reid,
> In orient bricht as angell did appeir,
> Throw goldin fkyis putting up his heid,
> Quhois gilt treffis fchone fo wondir cleir,
> That all the world tuke comfort fer and neir.¹¹

Immediately the birds, like the morning-ftars, finging together, hail the unufual appearance of the fun-fhine:

> And, as the blifsful foune of cherarchy,¹²
> The fowlis fong throw confort of the licht;

---

¹ looked. ² hailed. ³ with good will. ⁴ lovers.
⁵ flumbering. ⁶ attire.
⁷ From Chaucer, *Miller's Tale*, vol. ii. p. 100, v. 69, Morris.
  "For brighter was the fchynyng of hir hewe,
  Than in the Tour the noble i-forged newe."
⁸ brightnefs. ⁹ fongs.
¹⁰ St. iv. See Chaucer's *Knight's Tale*, vol. ii. p. 33, v. 183, Morris.
  "Sche was arifen, and al redy dight;
  For May wole have no floggardye a nyght.
  The feifoun priketh every gentil herte,
  And maketh him out of his fleepe fterte,
  And feith, 'Arys, and do thin obfervance,'" &c.
¹¹ St. viii.
¹² The hierarchy. See *Job*, ch. xxxviii. v. 7. The morning-ftars finging together.

> The birdis did with oppin vocis cry,
> O luvaris fo, "Away thow dully nycht,
> And welcum day that confortis every wicht.
> Haill May, haill Flora, haill Aurora fchene,
> Haill princes Nature, haill Venus luvis quene."[1]

Nature is then introduced, iffuing her interdict, that the progrefs of the fpring fhould be no longer interrupted, and that Neptune and Eolus fhould ceafe from difturbing the waters and air:

> Dame Nature gaif an inhibitioun thair,
> To ferfs Neptunus, and Eolus the bawld,[2]
> Nocht to perturb the wattir nor the air;
> And that no fchouris[3] [fnell] and no blaftis cawld
> Effray fuld[4] flouris, nor fowlis on the fald;
> Scho bad eik Juno goddes of the fky
> That fcho the hevin fuld keip amene and dry.[5]

This preparation and fufpence are judicious and ingenious; as they give dignity to the fubject of the poem, awaken our curiofity, and introduce many poetical circumftances. Nature immediately commands every bird, beaft, and flower, to appear in her prefence; and, as they had been ufed to do every May-morning, to acknowledge her univerfal fovereignty. She fends the roe to bring the beafts, the fwallow to collect the birds, and the yarrow[6] to fummon the flowers. They are affembled before her in an inftant. The lion advances firft, whofe figure is drawn with great force and expreffion:

> This awfull beift full terrible of cheir,
> Perfing of luke, and ftout of countenance,
> Rycht ftrong of corpis, of faffoun fair, but feir,[7]
> Lufty of fchaip, lycht of deliverance,
> Reid of his cullour as the ruby glance,
> On feild of gold he ftude full mychtely
> With floure de lycis firculit[8] luftely.[9]

This is an elegant and ingenious mode of blazoning the Scotifh arms, which are a lion with a border or treffure, adorned with flower de luces. We fhould remember, that heraldry was now a fcience of high importance and efteem. Nature, lifting up his *cluvis cleir* or fhining claws, and fuffering him to reft on her knee, crowns him with a radiant diadem of precious ftones, and creates him the king of beafts: at the fame time fhe enjoins him to exercife juftice with mercy, and not to fuffer his fubjects of the fmalleft fize or degree to be oppreffed by thofe of fuperior ftrength and dignity. This part of Nature's charge to the lion is clofed with the following beautiful ftroke, which indicates the moral tendernefs of the poet's heart:

---

[1] St. ix. [2] bold. [3] read *Scho u-ris.*
[4] fhould [affright.] [5] St. x.
[6] The yarrow is *Achillea* or Millefolium, commonly called *Sneefwort*. There is no reafon for felecting this plant to go on a meffage to the flowers; but that its name has been fuppofed to be derived from *Arrow*, being held a remedy for healing wounds inflicted by that weapon. The poet, to apologife for his boldnefs in perfonifying a plant, has added, "full craftely conjurit fcho." St. xii.
[7] fierce. [8] encircled. [9] St. xiv.

> And lat no bowgle with his busteous¹ hornis
> The meik pluch-ox² oppress for all his pryd,
> Bot in the yok go peciable him besyd.³

She next crowns the eagle king of fowls: and sharpening his talons like darts of steel, orders him to govern great and small, the wren or the peacock, with an uniform and equal impartiality. I need not point out to my reader the political lessons couched under these commands. Nature now calls the flowers; and observing the thistle to be surrounded with a bush of spears, and therefore qualified for war, gives him a crown of rubies, and says, "In field go forth and fend the laif."⁴ The poet continues elegantly to picture other parts of the royal arms; in ordering the thistle, who is now king of vegetables, to prefer all herbs or flowers of rare virtue and rich odour: nor ever to permit the nettle to associate with the fleur de lis, nor any ignoble weed to be ranked in competition with the lily. In the next stanza, where Nature directs the thistle to honour the rose above all other flowers, exclusively of the heraldic meaning our author with much address insinuates to King James IV. an exhortation to conjugal fidelity, drawn from the high birth, beauty, and amiable accomplishments of the royal bride, the Princess Margaret. Among the pageants exhibited at Edinburgh in honour of the nuptials, she was complimented with the following curious mixture of classical and scriptural history. "Ny to that cross was a scarfawst [scaffold] made, where was represented Paris and the three Deesses, with Mercure that gaff hym the apyll of gold for to gyffe to the most fayre of the Thre, which he gave to Venus. In the scarfawst was also represented the Salutacion of Gabriell to the Virgyne in saying *Ave gratia*, and sens after [next,] the sollempnizacion of the very maryage betwix the said Vierge and Joseph."⁵

> Nor hald non udir flour in sic denty⁶
> As the fresche Rois, of cullour reid and quhyt;
> For gife thow dois,⁷ hurt is thyne honesty,
> Confiddering that no flour is so perfyt,
> So full of vertew, plesans, and delyt,
> So ful of blisful angeilike bewty,
> Imperiall birth, honour, and dignite.⁸

Nature then addresses the rose whom she calls, "O lusty daughter most benyng," and whose lineage she exalts above that of the lily. This was a preference of Tudor to Valois. She crowns the rose with *clarefied* gems, the lustre of which illumines all the land. The rose is hailed queen by the flowers. Last, her praises are sung by the universal chorus of birds, the sound of which awakens the poet from his delightful dream. The fairy scene has vanished, and he calls to the muse to perpetuate in verse the wonders of the splendid vision.

Although much fine invention and sublime fabling are displayed in

---

¹ boisterous, strong. ² plough-ox. ³ St. xvi. ⁴ defend the rest.
⁵ Leland, *Coll.* iii. Append p. 289, *ut supr.* Not to mention the great impropriety, which they did not perceive, of applying such a part of scripture.
⁶ *dainty*, price. ⁷ if thou doest. ⁸ St. xxi.

the allegorical visions of our old poets, yet this mode of composition, by dealing only in imaginary personages, and by excluding real characters and human actions, necessarily fails in that chief source of entertainment which we seek in ancient poetry, the representation of ancient manners.

Another general observation, immediately resulting from the subject of this poem, may be here added, which illustrates the present and future state of the Scotish poetry. The marriage of a princess of England with a king of Scotland, from the new communication and intercourse opened between the two courts and kingdoms by such a connection, must have greatly contributed to polish the rude manners, and to improve the language, literature, and arts, of Scotland.

The design of Dunbar's *Golden Targe* is to shew the gradual and imperceptible influence of love, when too far indulged, over reason. The discerning reader will observe, that the cast of this poem is tinctured with the morality and imagery of [Chaucer's] *Romaunt of the Rose*, and the [poem called the *Flower and the Leaf*.][1]

The poet walks forth at the dawn of a bright day. The effects of the rising sun on a vernal landscape, with its accompaniments, are thus delineated in the manner of Lydgate, yet with more strength, distinctness, and exuberance of ornament:

> Bryght as the stern of day begouth to schyne,
> Quhen gone to bed war Vesper and Lucyne,
> I raise, and by a rosere[2] did me rest:
> Up sprang the goldyn candill matutyne,
> With cleir depurit[3] bemes cristallyne,
> Glading the mery foulis in thair nest :
> Or Phebus wes in purpur cape[4] revest,
> Up raise the lark, the hevenis menstrale fyne,[5]
> In May in till a morow myrthfullest.
>
> Full angellike thir birdis sang thair houris,
> Within their courtyns[6] grene, in to thair bouris
> Apparalit quhite and reyd wyth blomes suete :
> Anamalit wes the feyld wyth all colouris,
> The perly droppis schuke in silvir schouris,[7]
> Quhill all in balme did branch and levis flete
> To part fra Phebus, did Aurora grete,

---

[1] ["*The Golden Targe* is moral, and so are many of his smaller pieces; but humour, description, allegory, great poetical genius, and a vast wealth of words, all unite to form the complexion of Dunbar's poetry."—*Pinkerton.* "Mr. Warton, who has bestowed great commendations on Dunbar, observes that his genius is 'peculiarly of a moral and didactic cast ;' and it is certainly in such pieces that he is most confessedly superior to all who preceded, and to nearly all who have followed him ; but his satires, his allegorical and descriptive poetry, and his tales, are all admirable, and full of fancy and originality."—*G. Ellis.*]

[2] rose-tree.   [3] purified.

[4] cape. Ere Phebus was dressed in his purple robe.

[5] then. [The printed copies read *fyne*, instead of *syne*, as originally given by Warton.—*Price.*]

[6] curtains.

[7] The pearled drops fell from the trees like silver showers.

Hir criſtall teiris I ſaw hyng on the flouris,
Quhilk he for luſe all drank up with his hete.

For mirth of May, wyth ſkippis and wyth hoppis,
The birdis ſang upon the tender croppis,[1]
With curious notis, as Venus chapell clerkis:
The roſis yong, new ſpreding of thair knoppis,[2]
War ponderit[3] brycht with hevinly berial droppis,
Throu bemes reid, birnyng as ruby ſperkis;
The ſkyes rang for ſchoutyng of the larkis,
The purpur hevin oure ſkailit in ſilvir floppis[4]
Ouregilt the treis, branchis, leivis and barkis.

Doun throu the ryce[5] a rivyr ran wyth ſtremys
So luſtily agayn the lykand[6] lemys,
That all the lake as lamp did leme of licht,
Quhilk ſchadouit all about wyth twynkling glemis;[7]
The bewis[8] baithit war in ſecund bemis,
Throu the reflex of Phebus viſage brycht
On every ſide the hegeis raiſe on hicht:[9]
The bank was grene, the broke wes ful of bremys,
The ſtanneris cleir as ſternis in froſty nycht.

The criſtall air, the ſapher firmament,
The ruby ſkyes of the orient,
Keſt[10] berial bemes on emerant bewis grene,
The roſy garth,[11] depaynt and redolent,
With purpur, azure, gold, and goulis[12] gent,
Arayed wes by dame Flora the quene,
So nobily, that joy wes for to ſene:
The roch,[13] agayn the ryvir reſplendent,
As low enlumynit all the leves ſchene.[14]

---

[1] branches.   [2] knobs; buds.
[3] beſprinkled. An heraldic term. See *Obſervations on the Fairy Queen*, ii. p. 158, *ſeq*.
[4] covered with ſtreaks, *ſlips*, of ſilver.
[5] through the buſhes, the trees. Rice, or *Ris*, is properly a long branch. This word is ſtill uſed in the weſt of England. Chaucer, *Miller's Tale*, v. 137:

    "And therupon he had a gay ſurplys,
    As whyt as is the bloſme upon the rys."

So Alexander Scot:

    "Welcum oure rubent rois vpoun þe *ryce*."

[A. Scot's poems, edit. Laing, p. 5.] So alſo Lydgate, in his poem called *London Lickpenny* (MSS. Harl. 367):

    "Hot peſcode own [one] began to crye,
    Straberys rype, and cherryes in the ryſe."

That is, as he paſſed through London ſtreets, they cried, hot peas, ripe ſtrawberries, and cherries on a bough or twig.

[6] pleaſant.
[7] The water blazed like a lamp, and threw about it ſhadowy gleams of twinkling light.
[8] boughs.   [9] the high-raiſed edges, or bank.
[10] caſt.   [11] garden.
[12] gules. The heraldic term for red.
[13] The rock, glittering with the reflection of the river, illuminated as with fire all the bright leaves. *Low* is flame.
[14] Compare Chaucer's Morning in the *Knight's Tale*, v. 633 (edit. Morris):

    "The buſy larke, meſſager of *day*,
    Salueth in hire ſong the morwe gray;

Our author, lulled by the music of the birds and the murmuring of the water, falls asleep on the flowers, which he calls "Flora's mantill." In a vision, he sees a ship approach, whose sails are like the "blossom upon the spray," and whose masts are of gold bright as the "star of day."[1] She glides swiftly through a crystal bay; and lands in the blooming meadows, among the green rushes and reeds, an hundred ladies clad in rich but loose attire. They are clothed in green kirtles; their golden tresses, tied only with glittering threads, flow to the ground; and their snowy bosoms are unveiled:

> Als fresche as flouris that in May up spredis
> In kirtillis grene, withoutyn kell[2] or bandis:
> Thair brycht hairis hang gletering on the strandis
> In tressis clere, wyppit[3] with goldyn thredis;
> With pappis[4] quhite, and mydlis small as wandis.[5]

In this brilliant assembly, the poet sees Nature, dame Venus quene, the fresche Aurora, May, "lady Flora schene," Juno, Latona, Proserpine, Diana "goddess of the chase and woodis grene," lady Clio, Minerva, Fortune, and Lucina. These "michty quenes" are crowned with diadems, glittering like the morning-star. They enter a garden. May, the queen of mirthful months, is supported between her sisters April and June: as she walks up and down the garden, the birds begin to sing, and Nature gives her a gorgeous robe adorned with every colour under heaven:

> Thare saw I Nature present hir[6] a goun
> Rich to behald, and nobil of renoun,
> Off eviry hew undir the hevin that bene
> Depaynt, and braid[7] be gude proporcoun.[8]

The vegetable tribes then do their obeisance to Nature in these polished and elegant verses:

> And eviry blome on branch, and eke on bonk,
> Opnyt, and spred thair balmy levis donk,

> And fyry Phebus ryseth up so bright,
> That al the orient laugheth of the light,
> And with his stremes dryeth in the greves
> The silver dropes, hongyng on the leeves."

It is seldom that we find Chaucer indulging his genius to an absurd excess in florid descriptions. The same cannot be said of Lydgate.

[1] In our old poetry and the romances, we frequently read of ships superbly decorated. This was taken from real life. [In the description of the Venetian ships which conveyed the crusaders to Constantinople in 1202 we meet with similar particulars.] Froissart, speaking of the French fleet in 1387, prepared for the invasion of England under the reign of Richard II. says, that the ships were painted with the arms of the commanders, and gilt, with banners, pennons, and standards of silk: and that the masts were painted from top to bottom, glittering with gold. The ship of Lord Guy of Tremoyll was so sumptuously garnished, that the painting and colours cost 2000 French franks, more than 222 pounds of English currency at that time. See Grafton's *Chron.* p. 364. At his second expedition into France, in 1417, Henry V. was in a ship, whose sails were of purple silk most richly embroidered with gold. Speed's *Chron.* B. ix, p. 636, edit. 1611. Many other instances might be brought from ancient miniatures and illuminations.

[2] caul. [3] bound. [4] paps. [5] St. vii.
[6] to her. [7] broad. [8] St. x.

> Full low enclynyng to thair Quene fo clere,
> Quham of thair nobill norifing thay thonk.¹

Immediately another court, or group, appears. Here Cupid the king prefides:

> —wyth bow in hand ybent,
> And dredefull arowis grundyn fcharp and square.
> Thare faw I Mars the god armypotent
> Aufull and fterne, ftrong and corpolent.
> Thare faw I crabbit² Saturn, ald and haire,³
> His luke wes lyk for to perturb the air.
> Thair wes Mercurius, wife and eloquent,
> Of rethorike that fand⁴ the ftouris faire.⁵

Thefe are attended by other pagan divinities, Janus, Priapus, Eolus, Bacchus the "glader of the table," and Pluto. They are all arrayed in green; and, finging amorous ditties to the harp and lute, invite the ladies to dance. The poet quits his ambufh under the trees, and prefling forward to gain a more perfect view of this tempting fpectacle, is efpied by Venus. She bids her "keen archers" arreft the intruder. Her attendants, a group of fair ladies, inftantly drop their green mantles, and each difcovers a huge bow. They form themfelves in battle-array, and advance againft the poet·

> And firft of all, with bow in hand ybent,
> Come dame Beautee, rycht as fcho wald me fchent;
> Syne folowit all hir damofells yfere,
> With mony diverfe aufull inftrument:⁶
> Unto the pres Fair Having⁷ wyth her went;
> Fyne⁸ Portrature, Plefance, and lufty Chere.
> Than come Refoun, with fchelde of gold fo clere,
> In plate and maille, as Mars armypotent,
> Defendit me this noble⁹ chevallere.¹⁰

Beauty is affifted by tender Youth with her "virgins ying," green Innocence, Modefty, and Obedience: but their refiftance was but feeble againft the golden target of Reafon. Womanhood then leads on Patience, Difcretion, Stedfaftnefs, Benign Look, Mild Cheer, and Honeft Bufinefs:

> Bot Refon bure the Targe with fik conftance,
> Thair fcharp affayes might do no dures¹¹
> To me for all thair aufull ordynance.¹²

The attack is renewed by Dignity, Renown, Riches, Nobility, and Honour. Thefe, after difplaying their high banner, and fhooting a cloud of arrows, are foon obliged to retreat. Venus, perceiving the rout, orders Diffemblance to make an attempt to pierce the golden fhield. Diffemblance or Diffimulation choofes for her archers, Prefence, Fair Calling, and Cherifhing. Thefe bring back Beauty to the charge. A new and obftinate conflict enfues:

> Thik was the fchote of grundyn dartis kene,
> But Refoun, with the Scheld of Gold fo fchene,

---

¹ St. xi. ² crabbed. ³ hoar. ⁴ found. ⁵ St. xiii.
⁶ formidable weapons. ⁷ behaviour. ⁸ [after.] ⁹ warrior.
¹⁰ St. xvii. ¹¹ injury. ¹² weapons. St. xix.

> Warly[1] defendit quho fo evir affayit:
> The aufull ftour he manly did fuftene.[2]

At length Prefence, by whom the poet underftands that irrefiftible incentive accruing to the paffion of love by fociety, by being often admitted to the company of the beloved object, throws a magical powder into the eyes of Reafon; who is fuddenly deprived of all his powers, and reels like a drunken man. Immediately the poet receives a deadly wound, and is taken prifoner by Beauty; who now affumes a more engaging air, as the clear eye of Reafon is growing dim by intoxication. Diffimulation then tries all her arts on the poet: Fair Calling fmiles upon him: Cherifhing foothes him with foft fpeeches: New Acquaintance embraces him awhile, but foon takes her leave, and is never feen afterwards. At laft Danger delivers him to the cuftody of Grief.

By this time, "God Eolus his bugle blew." The leaves are torn with the blaft: in a moment the pageant difappears, and nothing remains but the foreft, the birds, the banks, and the brook.[3] In the twinkling of an eye, they return to the fhip: and unfurling the fails, and ftemming the fea with a rapid courfe, celebrate their triumph with a difcharge of ordnance. This was now a new topic for poetical defcription. The fmoke rifes to the firmament, and the roar is re-echoed by the rocks, with a found as if the rainbow had been broken:

> And as I did awake of my fueving,[4]
> The joyfull birdis merily did fyng
> For myrth of Phebus tendir bemes fchene.
> Suete war the vapouris, foft the morowing,
> Halefum the vale[5] depaynt wyth flouris ying,
> The air attemperit fobir and amene:
> In quhite and reid was all the field befene,
> Throu Naturis nobil frefch anamalyng
> In mirthfull Maye of eviry moneth Quene.[6]

Our author then breaks out into a laboured encomium on Chaucer, Gower, and Lydgate. This I choofe to recite at large, as it fhews the peculiar diftinction anciently paid to thofe fathers of verfe, and the high ideas which now prevailed, even in Scotland, of the improvements introduced by their writings into the Britifh poetry, language, and literature:[7]

> O reverend Chaucere, rofe of rethoris all,
> As in oure tong ane flour imperial[8]
> That raife in Britane evir, quho reidis rycht,[9]
> Thou beris of Makaris[10] the tryumph ryall,
> Thy frefch anamilit termes celicall:
> This matir coud illumynit have full brycht,[11]

---

[1] warily. [2] St. xxiii. [3] St. xxvi.
[4] dream. [5] vale. [6] St. xxviii.
[7] Other inftances occur in the elder Scotifh poets.
[8] one flower.
[9] Ever rofe, or fprung, in Britain, whofo reads right.
[10] Thou bearest of poets.
[11] This fubject would have appeared to fome advantage, had not, &c.

> Was thou noucht of our Inglifch all the lycht,
> Surmounting eviry tong terreftriall
> Alls fer as Mayes morow dois mydnycht.
>
> O morall Gower, and Lydgate laureate,
> Your fugarit[1] lippis,[2] and tongis aureate,
> Bene to oure eiris[3] caufe of grete delyte,
> Your angel mouthis moft mellifluate
> Our rude langage hes clere illumynate,
> And faire oure-gilt our fpeche, that imperfyte
> Stude, or your goldyn pennis fchupe to write,[4]
> This Ile befoir wes bare and defolate[5]
> Of rethorike, or lufty frefch endyte.[6]

This panegyric, and the poem, is clofed with an apology, couched in elegant metaphors, for his own comparative humility of ftyle. He addreffes the poem, which he calls a "litill quair:"

> I knaw quhat thou of rethorike hes fpent;
> Off all hir lufty rofis redolent
> Is nane in to thy gerland fett on hicht;[7]
> Efchame[8] thar of, and draw the out of ficht!
> Rude is thy wede[9] difteynit, bare, and rent,
> Wele aucht thou be aferit of the licht![10]

Dunbar's *Dance of the Seven Deadly Sins* has very great merit in the comic ftyle of painting. It exhibits a group of figures touched with the capricious but fpirited pencil of Callot.[11] On the eve of Lent, a general day of confeffion, the poet in a dream fees a difplay of heaven and hell. Mahomet,[12] or the devil, commands a dance to be performed by a felect party of fiends; particularly by thofe, who in the other world had never made confeffion to the prieft, and had confequently never received abfolution. Immediately the feven deadly fins appear, and prefent a mafk or mummery with the neweft gambols juft imported from France.[13] The firft is Pride, who properly takes place of all the reft, as by that fin fell the angels. He is defcribed in the fafhionable and gallant drefs of thofe times: in a bonnet and gown, his hair thrown back, his cap awry, and his gown affectedly flowing to his feet in large folds:

---

[1] fugared.   [2] lips.   [3] to our ears.
[4] Ere your golden pens were fhaped to write.
[5] bare and defolate.   [6] elegant compofition. St. xxx.
[7] No frefh and fragrant rofes of rhetoric are placed on high in thy garland.
[8] be afhamed.   [9] weed, drefs.   [10] St. xxxi.
[11] [Warton feems here to have adopted the opinion of Dalrymple. "I do not recollect ever to have feen the *Seven Deadly Sins* painted by a more mafterly pencil than that of Dunbar. His defigns certainly excel the explanatory peacocks and ferpents of Callot."—*Lord Hailes* (Dalrymple), 1770.]
[12] Mahon. Sometimes written Mahoun or Mahound. See Matt. Paris, p. 289. ad ann. 1236; and Du Cange, *Lat. Glofs.* v. *Mahum.* The Chriftians in the crufades were accuftomed to hear the Saracens fwear by their prophet Mahomet: which thence became in Europe another name for the devil.
[13] The original is *garmountis*. In the memoir, cited above, concerning the progrefs of the Princefs Margaret into Scotland, we have the following paffage. "The lord of Northumberland made his *devoir*, at the departynge, of *gambades* and *lepps*, [leaps,] as did likewife the Lord Scrop the father, and many others that retorned agayne, in *takyng their congie.*"

> Lat fe, quoth he,[1] now quha begynnis.
> With that the fowll Sevin Deidly Synnis
> > Begowth to leip at anis.[2]
> And firſt of all in Dance was Pryd,
> With hair wyld bak, and bonet on fyd,
> > Lyk to mak vaiſtie wanis;
> And round abowt him as a quheill,[3]
> Hang all in rumpillis[4] to the heill,
> > His kethat[5] for the nanis.[6]
> Mony prowd trumpour[7] with him trippit,
> Throw ſkaldand[8] fyre ay as thay ſkippit
> > They girnd with hyddouſs[9] granis.[10]

Several holy harlots [had been previouſly introduced], attended by monks, who made great ſport for the devils:[11]

> Heilie Harlottis in hawtane wyiſs,[12]
> Come in with mony ſindrie gyiſs,[13]
> > Bot yit luche nevir[14] Mahoun:
> Quhill prieſtis come in with bair ſchevin[15] nekkis,
> Than all the Feyndis lewche[16] and maid gekkis,[17]
> > Blak-belly and Bawſy-Broun.

Black-belly and *Bawſy-brown* are the names of popular ſpirits in Scotland. The latter is perhaps our *Robin Goodfellow*, known in Scotland by the name of *Brownie*. ["In Bannatyne's MS." obſerves Dalrymple, "among other ſpirits there occurs,

> Browny als that can play kow
> Behind the claith with mony mow."]

Anger is drawn with great force, and his accompaniments are boldly feigned. His hand is always upon his knife, and he is followed in pairs by boaſters, threateners, and quarrelſome perſons, all armed for battle, and perpetually wounding one another:[18]

> Then Yre come in with ſturt[19] and ſtryfe;
> His hand wes ay upoun his knyfe,
> > He brandeiſt lyk a beir:
> Boſtaris, braggaris, and barganeris,
> Eftir hym paſſit into pairis,
> > All bodin in feir of weir:[20]

---

[1] Mahomet.   [2] began to dance at once.   [3] wheel.
[4] rumples.   [5] caſaque, caſſock.   [6] nonce, deſignedly.
[7] Deceivers. [Mr. Laing, after citing the opinions of Dalrymple and Tyrwhitt, both of whom certainly ſeem to have miſtaken the ſenſe here, obſerves: "The word, however, no doubt means *deceiver;* and in this ſenſe it occurs in the poem on Diſcretion in Giving (p. 169 [of Mr. L.'s ed.]):

> 'Sum gevis to trumpouris and to ſchrewis.'"

[8] ſcalding.   [9] they grinned hideouſly.
[10] St. ii.   [11] St. iii.   [12] haughty guiſe.   [13] [a maſk.]
[14] never laughed.   [15] while prieſts came with bare-ſhaven.
[16] laughed.   [17] ſigns of deriſion.   [18] St. iv.   [19] diſturbance; affray.
[20] Literally, "All arrayed in feature of war." *Bodin*, and *feir of war*, are in the [Scotiſh] ſtatute book. Sir David Lindſay thus ſpeaks of the ſtate of Scotland during the minority of James V. *Complaynt of the Papyngo*, ſignat. B iii, edit. *ut infr.:*

> "Oppreſſioun did ſa loud his bougill blaw,
> That none durſt ride but into *feir of weir.*"

That is, *without being armed for battle.*

> In jakkis and fcryppis, and bonettis of fteill,[1]
> Thair leggis wer cheyneit to the heill,[2]
>   Frawart wes thair affeir;[3]
> Sum upoun uder with brandis beft,[4]
> Sum jagit utheris to the heft[5]
>   With knyvis that fcherp cowd fcheir.[6]

Envy is equal to the reft. Under this Sin our author takes occafion to lament with an honeft indignation, that the courts of princes fhould ftill give admittance and encouragement to the whifperers of idle and injurious reports:[7]

> Nixt in the dance followit Invy,
> Fild full of feid[8] and fellony,
>   Hid malyce and difpyte;
> For pryvie hatreut[9] that tratour trynilit;[10]
> Him followit mony freik diffymlit,[11]
>   With feyneit wordis quhyte:
>
> And flattereris in to menis facis,
> And back-byttaris[12] in fecreit placis,
>   To ley[13] that had delyte.
> With rownaris[14] of fals lefingis:[15]
> Allace! that courtis of noble kingis
>   Of thame can nevir be quyte![16]

Avarice is ufhered in by a troop of extortioners and other mifcreants, patronifed by the magician Warloch,[17] or the demon of the covetous; who vomit on each other torrents of melted gold, blazing like wild-fire; and as they are emptied at every difcharge, the devils replenifh their throats with frefh fupplies of the fame liquefied metal.[18]

Sloth does not join the dance till he is called twice: and his companions are fo flow of motion, that they cannot keep up with the reft, unlefs they are roufed from their lethargy by being fometimes warmed with a glimpfe of hell-fire:[19]

> Syne Sweirnes, at the fecound bidding,
> Come lyk a fow out of a midding,[20]
>   Full flepy wes his grunyie.[21]

---

[1] In fhort jackets, plates or flips, and bonnets of fteel. Short coats of mail and helmets.
[2] Their legs armed with iron, perhaps iron network, down to the heel.
[3] Their look was *froward*, fierce. *Feir* is feature.
[4] Some ftruck others, their companions, with fwords,
[5] Wounded others to the haft.
[6] cut fharp. [7] St. v. [8] enmity. [9] hatred. [10] trembled.
[11] diffembling gallant. [12] backbiters. [13] lye
[14] Rounders, whifperers. To *round in the ear*, or fimply to *round*, was to whifper in the ear.
[15] falfities. [16] free.
[17] [The original reads:
> "Next him in Dans come Cuvatyce—
> Catyvis, wrechis, and ockeraris,—
>   All with that *warlo* went."

Where *warlo* means a wicked perfon. A.-S. wær-loga, *iniquus.—Price.*]
[18] St. vi. [19] St. vii. [20] dunghill. [21] [grunt.]

S. 29.   "*Dance of the Seven Deadly Sins.*"   217

> Mony fweir bumbard belly-huddroun,[1]
> Mony flute daw and flepy duddroun,[2]
>   Him fervit ay with founyie[3]
> He drew thame furth in till a chenyie,[4]
> And Belliall, with a brydill reynie,[5]
>   Evir lafcht thame on the funyie.[6]
> In Dance thay war fo flaw of feit
> They gaif thame in the fyre a heit
>   And maid them quicker of counyie.[7]

Luft enters, neighing like a horfe,[8] and is led by Idlenefs. When his affociates mingle in the dance, their vifages burn red like the turquoife-ftone.[9] The remainder of the ftanza, although highly characteriftical, is too obfcene to be tranfcribed. But this gave no offence. Their manners were too indelicate to be fhocked at any indecency. I do not mean that thefe manners had loft their delicacy, but that they had not yet acquired the fenfibility arifing from civilization. In one of the Scotifh interludes of this age, written by a fafhionable court-poet, among other ridiculous obfcenities, the trying on of a Spanifh padlock in public makes a part of theatrical reprefentation.

Gluttony brings up the rear; whofe infatiable rout are inceffantly calling out for meat and drink; and although they are drenched by the devils with draughts of melted lead, they ftill afk for more:

> Than the fowll monftir Gluttony,
> Off wame[10] unfafiable and gredy,
>   To Dance he did him drefs:
> Him followit mony fowll drunckart,
> With can and collep, cop[11] and quart,
>   In furffet and excefs.
> Full mony a waiftlefs wally-drag[12],
> With wamis[13] unweildable did furth wag,
>   In creifche[14] that did increfs:
> *Drink* ay thay cryit with mony a gaip;[15]
> The Feyndis gaif thame hait feid to laip,[16]
>   Their leweray[17] wes na lefs.[18]

At this infernal dance no minftrels played. No gleeman or minftrel ever went to hell; except one who committed murder, and was admitted to an inheritance in hell " by brief of richt," that is, *per breve de recto*.[19] This circumftance feems an allufion to fome real fact.

The concluding ftanza is entirely a fatire on the Highlanders. Dunbar, as I have already obferved, was born in Lothian, a county of the Saxons.[20] The mutual antipathy between the Scotifh Saxons and the Highlanders was exceffive, and is not yet quite eradicated. Mahoun or Mahomet, having a defire to fee a highland pageant, a

---

[1] glutton.   [2] fluggard.   [3] attended on him with care.
[4] into a chain.   [5] a bridle rein; a thong of leather.
[6] lafhed them on the loins.   [7] apprehenfion.
[8] "Berand like a bagit horfe." The French *baguette* need not be explained.
[9] St. viii.   [10] belly.   [11] cup.   [12] fot.
[13] bellies.   [14] fat.   [15] gape.   [16] hot lead to drink, to lap.
[17] defire, appetite.   [18] St. ix.   [19] St. x.
[[20] This is little more than a paraphrafe of what Dalrymple fays. See Mr. Laing's *Dunbar*, ii. 263.]

fiend is commissioned to fetch Macfadyan; an unmeaning name, chosen for its harshness. As soon as the infernal messenger begins to publish his summons, he gathers about him a prodigious crowd of "Ersche men;" who soon took up great room in hell. These loquacious termagants began to chatter like rooks and ravens, in their own barbarous language: and the devil is so stunned with their horrid yell, that he throws them down to his deepest abyss, and smothers them with smoke:

> Than cryd Mahoun for a Heleand Padyane,
> Syne ran a Feynd to feche Makfadyane
>   Far northwart in a nuke:[1]
> Be he the Correnoth had done schout,[2]
> Ersche men so gadderit him abowt,
>   In Hell grit roume thay tuke:
> Thae tarmegantis[3] with tag and tatter
> Full lowd in Ersche begowth to clatter,
>   And rowp lyk revin and ruke.[4]
> The Devill sa devit[5] wes with thair yell
> That in the depest pot of hell
>   He smorit thame with smuke.[6]

I have been prolix in my citations and explanations of this poem, because I am of opinion, that the imagination of Dunbar is not less suited to satirical than to sublime allegory; and that he is the first poet who has appeared with any degree of spirit in this way of writing since Langland. His *Thistle and Rose* and *Golden Targe* are generally and justly mentioned as his capital works: but the natural complexion of his genius is of the moral and didactic cast. The measure of this poem is partly that of *Sir Thopas* in Chaucer: and hence we may gather, by the way, that *Sir Thopas* was anciently viewed in the light of a ludicrous composition. It is certain that the pageants and interludes of Dunbar's age must have quickened his invention to form those grotesque groups. The exhibition of moralities was now in high vogue among the Scots. [Two pageants, *The Salutation of Gabriel* and *The Marriage of the Virgin* were exhibited at Edinburgh] at the marriage of James IV. and the princess Margaret.[7] Mummeries, which they call *Gysarts*, and which are composed of moral personifications, are still known in Scotland: and even till the beginning of [the last] century, especially among the festivities of Christmas, itinerant maskers were admitted into the houses of the Scotish nobility.[8]

---

[1] nook.
[2] ["As soon as he had made the cry of distress, or what in old French is called *a l'aide*. So in the ballad of the battle of Harlaw: 'Cryand the *Corynoch* on hie.' The glossary subjoined to the *Evergreen* says, that it means a Highland *tune*: that is, it may be either a strain of victory, or a dirge."—*Hailes* (or *Dalrymple*.)]
[3] [I suspect that Dunbar meant another word than termagant, or "heathenish crew." There is a species of wild fowl well known in the Highlands of Scotland, which our statute-book calls *termigant*. Dunbar may have likened the Highlanders to a flock of their country birds.—*Laing*. Termagant, a devil or Pagan god, as Mahomed was.—F. *Termigant* may be another form of *ptarmigan*.]
[4] chattered hoarsely.   [5] deafened.   [6] St. xi.
[7] *Memoir*, ut supra, p. 300, [and *supr*. ii. 224, Note.]
[8] [An account of all the *printed* editions of Dunbar's works will be found in the

SECTION XXX.

NOTHER of the distinguished luminaries, that marked the restoration of letters in Scotland at the commencement of the sixteenth century, not only by a general eminence in elegant erudition, but by a cultivation of the vernacular poetry of his country, is Gawen Douglas. He was descended from a noble family, and born in the year 1475.[1] According to the practice of that age, especially in Scotland, his education perhaps commenced in a grammar-school of one of the monasteries: there is undoubted proof, that it was finished at the University of Paris. It is probable, as he was intended for the sacred function, that he was sent to Paris for the purpose of studying the canon law: in consequence of a decree promulged by James I., which tended in some degree to reform the illiteracy of the clergy, as it enjoined that no ecclesiastic of Scotland should be preferred to a prebend of any value without a competent skill in that science.[2] Among other high promotions in the church, which his very singular accomplishments obtained, he was provost of the collegiate church of St. Giles at Edinburgh, abbot of the opulent convent of Abberbrothrock, and Bishop of Dunkeld. He appears also to have been nominated by the Queen Regent to the archbishopric, either of Glasgow or of St. Andrew's: but the appointment was repudiated by the pope.[3] In 1513, to avoid the persecutions of the Duke of Albany, he fled from Scotland into England, and was most graciously received by Henry VIII. who, in consideration of his literary merit, allowed him a liberal pension.[4] In England he contracted a friendship with Polydore Vergil, one of the classical scholars of Henry's court.[5] He died of the plague in London, and was buried in the Savoy church, in the year 1521.[6]

In his early years he translated Ovid's *Art of Love* (the favourite Latin system of the science of gallantry) into Scotish metre: which is now lost.[7] In the year 1513, and in the space of sixteen months,[8]

Handb. of E. E. Lit. in voce; of the MSS. Mr. Laing furnishes a list. There can be no doubt that Chepman and Millar, the proto-typographers of Scotland, published other pieces by Dunbar, not now known to exist. It is most singular that between 1508 and the appearance of Ramsay's *Evergreen* nothing of his should have been printed.]

[1] Hume, *Hist. Dougl.* p. 219.   [2] Lesl. *De Reb. Gest. Scot.* lib. ix.
[3] Thynne, *Continuat. Hist. Scot.* 455.
[4] Holinsh. *Scot.* 307.—iii. 872.   [5] Bale, xiv. 58.
[6] Weever, *Fun. Mon.* p. 446, and Stillingfl. *Orig. Brit.* p. 54.
[7] See edit. 1710, p. 483, *Epistle* or *Epilogue* to Lord Sinclair. The editor's name is [Thomas Ruddiman] a Scotchman. This translation was first printed at London, 1553. 4to. [But the best text is that of Edinb. 1839, 2 vols. 4to, taken from Gale's MS. in Trinity College, Cambridge. With that the extracts made by Warton have been collated. This MS. includes, at the end, an imperfect comment by the translator, not found elsewhere.]
[8] Lesl. *De Reb. Gest. Scot.* lib. ix. p. 379. Rom. 1675.

he tranflated into Scotifh heroics the *Eneid* of Virgil, with the additional thirteenth book by Mapheus Vegius, at the requeft of his noble patron Henry Earl of Sinclair.[1] But it was projected fo early as the year 1501. For, in one of his poems written that year,[2] he promifes to Venus a tranflation of Virgil, in atonement for a ballad he had publifhed againft her court: and when the work was finifhed, he tells Lord Sinclair that he had now made his peace with Venus, by tranflating the poem which celebrated the actions of her fon Eneas.[3] No metrical verfion of a claffic had yet appeared in Englifh; [for even that] of Boethius, who fcarcely deferves the appellation, [was not executed till a later date]. Virgil was hitherto commonly known only by Caxton's romance on the fubject of the Eneid which, our author fays, no more refembles Virgil, than the devil is like Saint Auftin.[4]

This tranflation is executed with equal fpirit and fidelity, and is a proof that the Lowland Scotifh and Englifh languages were now nearly the fame. I mean the ftyle of compofition; more efpecially in the glaring affectation of anglicifing Latin words. The feveral books are introduced with metrical prologues, which are often poetical, and fhow that Douglas's proper walk was original poetry. In the prologue to the fixth book, he wifhes for the Sibyl's golden bough, to enable him to follow his mafter Virgil through the dark and dangerous labyrinth of the infernal regions.[5] But the moft confpicuous of thefe prologues is a defcription of May [which occurs in that to the twelfth book,] and the greater part of which I will infert:[6]

>   As frefch Aurore, to myghty Tithone fpows,
>   Ifchit[7] of hir fafron bed, and evir[8] hous,
>   In crammyfyn[9] cled and granyt violat,
>   With fangwyne cape, the felvage[10] purpurat,
>   Onfchet[11] the wyndois of hir large hall,
>   Spred all with rofys, and full of balm ryall.
>   And eik the hevynly portis criftallyne
>   Vpwarpis braid, the warld to illumyn.
>   The twynklyng ftremowris[12] of the orient
>   Sched purpour fprangis with gold and afure ment.[13]
>   Peffaud the fabill barmkyn nocturnall,
>   Bet doun the fkyis clowdy mantill wall:
>   Eous the fteid, with ruby hamys red,
>   Abuf the fey lyftis furth hys hed

---

[1] *Epil.* ut fupr.
[2] The *Palice of Honour*, ad calcem.   [3] *Epil.* ut fupr.
[4] *Prologue to the Tranflation*, p. 5. The manufcript notes written in the margin of a copy of the old quarto edition of this tranflation by Patrick Junius, which Bifhop Nicolfon (*Hift. Libr.* p. 99) declares to be excellent, are of no confequence, Bibl. Bodl. *Archiv. Seld.* B. 54, 4to. The fame may be faid of Junius's Index of obfolete words in this tranflation, Cod. MSS. Jun. 114. (5225.) See alfo *Diverfe Scotch words*, &c. MS. *Afhm.* 846. 13.
[5] In the *Prologue* to the eighth book, the alliterative manner of Langland is adopted.
[6] Pag. 400.   [7] iffued.   [8] ivory.   [9] crimfon.
[10] edge.   [11] unfhut, *i.e.* opened.   [12] ftreamers.
[13] ftreaks, mingled with, &c.

His Translation of Virgil.

Of cullour foyr, and fum deill brovn as berry,
Forto alichtyn and glaid our emyſpery,
The flambe owtbraſtyng at his noys thyrlys;
Quhill ſchortly, with the bleſand¹ torch of day,
Abilȝeit² in hys lemand³ freſch array,
Furth of hys palyce ryall iſchit Phebus,
With goldyn crovn and viſſage gloryus,
Cryſp haris,⁴ brycht as chriſolite or topace;
For quhais hew⁵ mycht nane behald hys face:
The fyry ſparkis braſtyng from hys eyn,
To purge the ayr, and gylt the tendyr greyn.
The aureat fanis⁶ of his trone ſouerane
With glytrand glans ourſpred the occiane;⁷
The large fludis, lemand all of lycht,
Bot with a blenk⁸ of hys ſupernale ſycht,
Forto behald, it was a glor to ſe
The ſtablit⁹ wyndis, and the cawmyt ſee,
The ſoft ſeſſom,¹⁰ the firmament ſereyn;
The lowne illumynat ayr,¹¹ and fyrth¹² ameyn:
The ſiluer ſcalyt fyſchis on the greit,¹³
Ourthwort¹⁴ cleir ſtremys ſprynkland¹⁵ for the heyt,
With fynnys ſchynand brovn as ſynopar,¹⁶
And chyſſell talys,¹⁷ ſtowrand heir and thar:¹⁸
The new cullour alychtnyng¹⁹ all the landis,
Forgane the ſtannyris ſchane,²⁰ the beriall ſtrandis:
Quhil the reflex of the diurnal bemys
The beyne bonkis²¹ keſt ful of variant glemys:
And luſty Flora dyd hyr blomys ſpreid
Vnder the feit of Phebus fulȝart²² ſteid,
The ſwardit ſoyll enbrovd with ſelcouth hewys,²³
Wod and foreſt obumbrat with thar bewys,²⁴
Quhois bliſfull branſchis, porturat²⁵ on the grund,
With ſchaddoys ſchene ſchew rockis rubicund:
Towris, turettis, kyrnellis,²⁶ pynnaclys hie,
Of kyrkis, caſtellis, and ilke fair cite,
Stude payntit, euery fyall,²⁷ fayn, and ſtage,²⁸
Apon the plane grund by thar awyn vmbrage.²⁹
Of Eolus north blaſtis havand³⁰ no dreid
The fulȝe ſpred hir braid boſum on breid.³¹
The cornys croppis, and the beris newbrerd,³²
With glaidſum garmont reveſtyng the erd.³³

---

¹ blazing. ² Fr. habillé; clothed.
³ luminous. ⁴ curled locks. ⁵ whoſe exceſſive brightneſs.
⁶ vanes of gold. ⁷ ocean. ⁸ only with one glance.
⁹ ſettled, calmed. ¹⁰ ſeaſon. ¹¹ air without wind, &c.
¹² frith. ¹³ ſand, gravel. ¹⁴ athwart, acroſs, through.
¹⁵ gliding ſwiftly, with a tremulous motion, or vibration of their tails.
¹⁶ cinnabar. ¹⁷ tails ſhaped like chiſſels.
¹⁸ ſwimming ſwiftly, darting haſtily. ¹⁹ illuminating.
²⁰ over, upon, over-againſt, the bright gravel, or ſmall ſtones, thrown out on the banks of rivers. Hence the ſtrands were all of beryl.
²¹ pleaſant banks. ²² brilliant, glittering.
²³ Bladed with graſs, and embroidered with ſtrange colours.
²⁴ boughs. ²⁵ portrayed, painted, reflected. ²⁶ battlements.
²⁷ round tower. ²⁸ fiery. ²⁹ their own ſhadow.
³⁰ having.
³¹ The ſoil, the country, ſpread abroad her expanſive boſoms.
³² new-ſprung barley. ³³ earth.

The variand veſtur of the venuſt vaill
Schrowdis the ſcherald fur,[1] and euery faill[2]
Ourfret[3] with fulȝeis[4] and figuris ful diuers,
The pray[5] byſprent with ſpryngand ſprowtis diſpers,
For callour humour on the dewy nyht,
Rendryng ſum place the gers pilis thar hycht,
Als far as catal the lang ſymmyris day
Had in thar paſtur eyt and knyp away:
And blisfull bloſſummys in the blomyt ȝard
Submittis thar hedys in the ȝong ſonnys falfgard:
Iue levis[6] rank ourſpred the barmkyn[7] wall,
The blomyt hauthorn cled hys pykis all,
Furth of freſch burgionys[8] the wyne grapis[9] ȝing
Endlang the treilȝeis[10] dyd on twyſtis hyng,
The loukit[11] buttouns on the gemyt treis
Ourſpredand leyuis of naturis tapeſtreis.
Soft greſy verdour eſtir balmy ſchowris,
On curland ſtalkis ſmylyng to thar flowris:
Behaldand thame ſa mony diuers hew
Sum pers,[12] ſum paill, ſum burnet, and ſum blew,
Sum greyce, ſum gowlys, ſum purpour, ſum ſangwane,
Blanchit or brovne, fawch ȝallow mony ane,
Sum heuynly culloryt in celeſtiall gre,
Sum watry[13] hewit as the haw wally[14] ſee
And ſum depart in freklys red and quhite,
Sum brycht as gold with aureat leuys lyte.
The daſy dyd on breid[15] hir crownell ſmaill,
And euery flour onlappit in the daill,
In battill gyrs[16] burgionys, the banwart wild,
The clauir, catcluke, and the cammamyld;
The flour delys furthſpred hys heuynly hew,
Floure dammes, and columby blauk and blew,
Seir downys ſmaill on dent de lyon[17] ſprang,
The ȝyng greyn[18] blomyt ſtrabery levis amang,
Gymp gerraflouris[19] thar royn leuis onſchet,
Freſch prymros, and the purpour violet,
The roys knoppys, tutand furth thar hed,
Gan chyp, and kyth thar vermel lyppis red,
Cryſp ſcarlet leuis ſum ſcheddand baith atanis,
Keſt[21] fragrant ſmell amyd from goldyn granys,[20]

---

[1] furrow. [2] turf.
[3] It is evident our author intends to deſcribe two diſtinct things, viz. corn-fields and meadows or paſture lands: the former in the three firſt lines; *the varyant veſture*, &c. is plainly arable, and the *fulȝeis and figuris ful diuers*, are the various leaves and flowers of the weeds growing among the corn, and making a piece of embroidery. And here the deſcription of corn-fields ends: and that of paſture-lands begins at, *The pray byſprent*, &c. Pray [in the edition of 1839, corruptly] *ſpray*, is formed, through the French, from the Lat. *Pratum*, and *Spryngand Sproutis*, riſing ſprings, from the Ital. *ſpruzzure, ſpruzzolare, aſpergere*.
[4] leaves.   [5] mead.   [6] ivy-leaves.   [7] rampart.
[8] ſprigs.   [9] young.   [10] trelliſſes; eſpaliers for vines.
[11] locked, encloſed, gemmed.   [12] red.   [13] watchet.
[14] blue and wavy.   [15] unbraid.   [16] graſs embattelled.
[17] dandelion.   [18] young weeds.
[19] Gilliflowers. Gariophilum, Lat. Καρυοφυλλον, Gr. The Scotiſh word is nearer the original. Probably the poet wrote *thar awin*. See ver. 72, *thare awin umbrage*.   [20] ſeeds.
[21] It is obſervable, that our Poet never once mentions the ſcent of flowers till he

Heuynly lylleis, with lokrand toppys quhyte,
Oppynnit and fchew thar creiftis redymyte,[1]
The balmy vapour from thar filkyn croppys
Diftilland hailfum fugurat hunny droppys,
And fyluer fchakaris[2] gan fra leuys hing,
With cryftal fprayngis on the verdour fing
The plane pulderit with femyl fettis fovnd,
Bedyit full of dewy peirlys rovnd ;
So that ilk burgiou, fyon, herb, or flour,
Wolx all embalmyt of the frefch liquor,
And bathit hait dyd in dulce humouris fleyt,
Quharof the byis wrocht thar hunny fweit.
Swannys[3] fwouchis throw owt the ryfp[4] and redis,
Our al thir lowys[5] and the fludis gray,
Seirfand by kynd a place quhar thai fuld lay ;
Phebus red fowle hys corale creift can fteir,
Oft ftrekyng furth hys hekkill crawand cleir
Amyd the wortis, and the rutys gent,
Pykland hys meyt in alleis quhar he went,
Hys wifis Toppa and Partolet hym by,
As byrd al tyme that hantis bigamy ;
The pantyt povn[6] pafand with plomys gym,
Keft vp his taill a provd plefand quheil rym,[7]
Yfchrowdyt in hys fedramme brycht and fcheyn,
Schapand the prent of Argus hundreth eyn ;
Amang the bronys[8] of the olyue twiftis,
Scir fmaill fowlys, wirkand crafty neftis,
Endlang the heggeis thyk, and on rank akis[9]
Ilk byrd reiofyng with thar myrthfull makis :
In corneris and cleir fenyftaris of glas
Full biffely Aragne weuand was,
To knyt hir nettis and hir wobbys fle,
Tharwith to caucht the myghe[10] or litill fle :
Vnder the bewyis beyir in lufty valys,

---

comes to the rofe, and never at all the fcent of any particular flower, except the rofe, not even of the lily; for I take it, the words, *from thar fylkyn croppys*, are meant to defcribe the flowers in general; and *the balmy vapour* to be the fame with the *frefch liquor*, and *the dulce humouris quharof the bis wrocht thar hunny fweit*, an exhalation diftinct from that which caufes the fcent. Afterwards *redolent odour*, is general ; for he certainly means to clofe his defcription of the vegetable world by one univerfal cloud of fragrance from all nature.

[1] [Encircled, bound,] from *Redimitus*, Lat.
[2] fhakers.
[3] That Milton had his eye upon this paffage is plain, from his defcribing the fwan, the cock, and peacock, in this order, and with feveral of the attributes that our author has given them. See *Parad. L.* vii. 438, *feq.*

"The Swan with arched neck
Between her white wings, mantling proudly, rows
Her ftate with oary feet ; yet oft they quit
The dank, and, rifing on ftiff pennons, tower
The mid aereal fky : others on ground
Walk'd firm : the crefted Cock, whofe clarion founds
The filent hours, and th' Other, whofe gay train
Adorns him, color'd with the florid hue
Of rainbows and ftarry eyes."

[4] ruftling.   [5] lakes.   [6] peacock.   [7] wheel-rim.
[8] branches.   [9] oaks.   [10] gnat.

Within fermans and parkis cloys of palys,
The bustuus bukkis rakis furth on raw,
Heyrdis of hertis throw the thyk wod schaw,
The ȝong fownys followand the dun days,[1]
Kyddis skippand throw ronnys eftir rays,[2]
In yssouris[3] and on leys litill lammys
Full tayt and tryg socht bletand to thar dammys.
On salt stremys wolx Doryda and Thetis,
By rynnand strandis, Nymphis and Naedes,
Sik as we clepe wenschis and damysellis,
In gresy grauy wandrand by spryng wellis,
Of bloomyt branchis and flowris quhite and red
Plettand thar lusty chaplettis for thar hed:
Sum sang ring sangis, dansys, ledis, and rovndis,
With vocis schill, quhill all the daill resovndis.
Dame naturis menstralis on that other part,
Thar blisfull bay entonyng euery art,
To beyt thir amorus of thar nychtis baill,
The merly, the mauys, and the nychtyngale,
With mery notis myrthfully furth brest,
Enforcying thame quha mycht do clynk it best:
The cowschet[4] crowdis and pyrkis on the rys,
The styrlyng changis diuers steuynnys nys,[5]
The sparrow chyrmys in the wallis clyft,
Goldispynk and lintquhyte fordynnand the lyft,[6]
The gukgo galys,[7] and so quytteris the quaill
Quhill ryveris rerdit,[8] schawis, and euery vaill,
And tender twystis trymlyt on the treis,
For byrdis sang, and bemyng of the beys,
In wrablis dulce of heuynly armonyis,
The larkis, lowd releschand[9] in the skyis,
Louys thar lege[10] with tonys curius;
Baith to dame Natur, and the fresch Venus,
Rendryng hie lawdis in thare obseruance,
Quhais suguryt throtis[11] maid glaid hartis dans,
And al smail sowlis syngis on the spray;
    Welcum the lord of lycht, and lamp of day,
Welcum fostyr of tendir herbys grene,
Welcum quyknar of sluryst flowris scheyn,
Welcum support of euery rute and vayn,
Welcum consort of alkynd fruyt and grayn,

---

[1] does.   [2] roes.   [3] leasowes.   [4] dove.
[5] fine tunes.   [6] firmament.
[7] Cries. So Chaucer of the nightingale. *Court of Love*, v. 1356.

"But *domine labia* gan he crie and *gale*."

So the Friar is said to gale, *Wife of B. Prol.* v. 832. In Chaucer's *Cuckowe and Nightingale*, the latter is said to *grede*, v. 135.

"And grede for that skillle, ocy ocy, I grede."

That is, *I cry*. Ital. *Gridare*. The word is used with more propriety in [the] *Gest of Alexander*, written in 1312, fol. 55, col. 2. [See *supr.* ii. 205, *et seq.*]

"Averil is meory, and longith the day,
Ladies loven solas and play,
Swaynes justis, knyȝtis turnay,
Syngith the nyȝtyngale, *gredeth* the Jay."

[8] resounded.
[9] mounting.   [10] praised their Lady Nature.   [11] sugared throats.

§. 30.   *Remarks on the Work.*   225

> Welcum the byrdis beild ¹ apon the brer,
> Welcum mayster and rewlar of the yer,
> Welcum wailfar of husbandis at the plewys,²
> Welcum reparar of woddis, treis, and bewys,
> Welcum depayntar of the blomyt medis,
> Welcum the lyfe of euery thyng that spredis,
> Welcum storour ³ of alkynd bestiall,
> Welcum be thy brycht bemys gladyng all.⁴

The poetical beauties of this specimen will be relished by every reader who is fond of lively touches of fancy and rural imagery. In the [*Life of Alexander*, just quoted,] Autumn is touched with these circumstances : ⁵

> In tyme of hervest merry it is ynou},
> Peres and apples hongeth on bou},
> The hayward bloweth his horne,
> In everych felde ripe is corne,
> The grapes hongen on the vyne,
> Swete is trewe love and fyne ;
> King Alisaunder a morowe arist,
> The sonne dryveth away the mist,
> Forth he went farre into Ynde
> Moo mervayles for to fynde.

But the verses of Douglas will have another merit with those critics who love to contemplate the progress of composition, and to mark the original workings of genuine nature ; as they are the effusion of a mind not overlaid by the descriptions of other poets, but operating by its own force and bias in the delineation of a vernal landscape, on such objects as really occurred. On this account, they deserve to be better understood : and I have therefore translated them into plain modern English prose. In the meantime, this experiment will serve to prove their native excellence. Divested of poetic numbers and expression, they still retain their poetry ; and (to use the comparison of an elegant writer on a like occasion) appear like Ulysses still a king and conqueror, although disguised like a peasant, and lodged in the cottage of the herdsman Eumaeus.

" Fresh Aurora, the wife of Tithonus, issued from her saffron bed, and ivory house. She was cloathed in a robe of crimson and violet-colour ; the cape vermilion, and the border purple : she opened the windows of her ample hall, overspread with roses, and filled with balm, or nard. At the same time, the crystal gates of heaven were thrown open, to illumine the world. The glittering streamers of the orient diffused purple streaks mingled with gold and azure. The steeds of the sun, in red harness of rubies, of colour brown as the berry, lifted their heads above the sea, to glad our hemisphere : the flames burst from their nostrils : while shortly, apparelled in his luminous array, Phebus, bearing the blazing torch of day, issued from his royal palace ; with a golden crown, glorious visage, curled

---

¹ who build.   ² ploughs.   ³ restorer.
⁴ [*Prologue to the Twelfth Book*, edit. 1839. This is a very superior text to that furnished in all the preceding editions of Warton.]
⁵ Fol. 95, col. 2.

locks bright as the chryfolite or topaz, and with a radiance intolerable. The fiery fparks, burfting from his eyes, purged the air, and gilded the new verdure. The golden vanes of his throne covered the ocean with a glittering glance, and the broad waters were all in a blaze, at the firft glimpfe of his appearance. It was glorious to fee the winds appeafed, the fea becalmed, the foft feafon, the ferene firmament, the ftill air, and the beauty of the watery fcene. The filver-fcaled fifhes, on the gravel, gliding haftily, as it were from the heat or fun, through clear ftreams, with fins fhining brown as cinnabar, and chiffel-tails, darted here and there. The new luftre, enlightening all the land, beamed on the fmall pebbles on the fides of rivers, and on the ftrands, which looked like beryl: while the reflection of the rays played on the banks in variegated gleams; and Flora threw forth her blooms under the feet of the fun's brilliant horfes. The bladed foil was embroidered with various hues. Both wood and foreft were darkened with boughs; which, reflected from the ground, gave a fhadowy luftre to the red rocks. Towers, turrets, battlements, and high pinnacles, of churches, caftles, and every fair city, feemed to be painted; and, together with every baftion and ftory, expreffed their own fhape on the plains. The glebe, fearlefs of the northern blafts, fpread her broad bofom. The corn-crops, and the new-fprung barley, reclothed the earth with a gladfome garment. The variegated vefture of the valley covered the cloven furrow; and the barley-lands were diverfified with flowery weeds. The meadow was befprinkled with rivulets: and the frefh moifture of the dewy night reftored the herbage which the cattle had cropped in the day. The bloffoms in the blowing garden trufted their heads to the protection of the young fun. Rank ivy-leaves overfpread the wall of the rampart. The blooming hawthorn clothed all his thorns in flowers. The budding clufters of the tender grapes hung end-long, by their tendrils, from the trellifes. The gems of the trees unlocking, expanded themfelves into the foliage of Nature's tapeftry. There was a foft verdure after balmy fhowers. The flowers fmiled in various colours on the bending ftalks. Some red, &c. Others, watchet, like the blue and wavy fea; fpeckled with red and white; or, bright as gold. The daify unbraided her little coronet. The grafs ftood embattelled, with banewort, &c. The feeded down flew from the dandelion. Young weeds appeared among the leaves of the ftrawberries. Gay gilliflowers, &c. The rofe buds, putting forth, offered their 'red vernal lips' to be kiffed; and diffufed fragrance from the crifp fcarlet that furrounded their golden feeds. Lilies, with white curling tops, fhewed their crefts open. The odorous vapour moiftened the filver webs that hung from the leaves. The plain was powdered with round dewy pearls. From every bud, fcyon, herb, and flower, bathed in liquid fragrance, the bee fucked fweet honey. The fwans clamoured amid the ruftling reeds; and fearched all the lakes and gray rivers where to build their nefts. The red bird of the fun lifted his coral creft, crowing clear among the plants and 'rutis gent,' picking his food from every path, and attended by his wives

Toppa and Tartlet. The painted peacock with gaudy plumes, unfolded his tail like a bright wheel, inshrouded in his shining feathers, resembling the marks of the hundred eyes of Argus. Among the boughs of the twisted olive, the small birds framed their artful nests, or along the thick hedges or rejoiced with their merry mates on the tall oaks. In the secret nook, or in the clear windows of glass, the spider full busily wove her sly net, to ensnare the little gnat or fly. Under the boughs that screen the valley, or within the pale-inclosed park, the nimble deer trooped in ranks, the harts wandered through the thick woody shaws, and the young fawns followed the dappled does. Kids skipped through the briers after the roes; and in the pastures and leas, the lambs, 'full tight and trig,' bleated to their dams. Doris and Thetis walked on the salt ocean; and Nymphs and Naiads, wandering by spring-wells in the grassy groves, plaited lusty chaplets for their hair, of blooming branches, or of flowers red and white. They sung, and danced, &c. Meantime, Dame Nature's minstrels raise their amorous notes, the ring-dove coos and pitches on the tall copse, the starling whistles her varied descant, the sparrow chirps in the clefted wall; the goldfinch and linnet filled the skies, the cuckow cried, the quail twittered; while rivers, shaws, and every dale resounded; and the tender branches trembled on the trees, at the song of the birds, and the buzzing of the bees," &c.

This landscape may be finely contrasted with the description of *Winter* from the Prologue to the seventh book,[1] a part of which I will give in literal prose:

"The fern withered on the miry fallows: the brown moors assumed a barren mossy hue: banks, sides of the hills, and bottoms, grew white and bare: the cattle looked hoary from the dank weather: the wind made the red weed waver on the dike: From crags and the foreheads of the yellow rocks hung great icicles, in length like a spear: the soil was dusky and grey, bereft of flowers, herbs, and grass: in every holt and forest, the woods were stripped of their array. Boreas blew his bugle horn so loud, that the solitary deer withdrew to the dales: the small birds flocked to the thick briers, shunning the tempestuous blast, and changing their loud notes to chirping: the cataracts roared, and every linden-tree whistled and brayed to the founding of the wind. The poor labourers 'went wet and weary, draggled in the fen.' The sheep and shepherds lurked under the hanging banks, or wild broom. Warm from the chimney-side, and refreshed with generous cheer, I stole to my bed, and laid down to sleep; when I saw the moon shed through the windows her twinkling glances, and watery light: I heard the horned bird, the night-owl, shrieking horribly with crooked bill from her cavern: I heard the wild-geese, with screaming cries, fly over the city through the silent night. I was soon lulled asleep; till the cock clapping his wings crowed thrice, and the day peeped. I waked and saw the moon disappear, and heard the jack-daws cackle on the

---

[1] P. 200, edit. 1710.

roof of the houfe. The cranes, prognofticating tempefts, in a firm phalanx, pierced the air with voices founding like a trumpet. The kite, perched on an old tree, faft by my chamber, cried lamentably, a fign of the dawning day. I rofe, and half-opening my window, perceived the morning, livid, wan, and hoary; the air overwhelmed with vapour and cloud; the ground ftiff, grey, and rough; the branches rattling; the fides of the hills looking black and hard with the driving blafts; the dew-drops congealed on the ftubble and rind of trees; the fharp hailftones, deadly-cold, 'hopping' on the thatch and the neighbouring caufeway," &c.

Bale, whofe titles of Englifh books are often obfcured by being put into Latin, recites among Gawin Douglas's poetical works his *Narrationes aureæ* and *Comœdiæ aliquot facræ*.[1] Of his *Narrationes aureæ* our author feems to fpeak in the *Epilogue to Virgil*, addreffed to his patron Lord Sinclair:[2]

> I have alfo a ftrange command [comment] compyld,
> To expone ftrange hyftoryes and termes wild.

Perhaps thefe tales were the fictions of ancient mythology. Whether the *Comœdiæ* were facred interludes or Myfteries for the ftage, or only facred narratives, I cannot determine. [One] of his original poems is the *Palace of Honour*, a moral vifion, written in the year 1501, planned on the defign of the Table of Cebes, and imitated in the elegant Latin dialogue *De Tranquillitate Animi* of his countryman Florence Wilfon (or Florentius Volufenus).[3] It was firft printed at London in 1553, [with his verfion of the *Æneid*, but at prefent is rarely found bound up with the latter. The printer of the later edition of 1579, at Edinburgh, fpeaks of the book as having been publifhed in Scotland before, and there is a ftrong prefumption that the London edition of 1553 is merely a reprint of one of thefe loft Scotifh impreffions. The earlier quarto (of 1553) is valuable as containing marginal notes, which were omitted in that of 1579.][4] The object of this allegory is to fhow the inftability and infufficiency of worldly pomp, and to prove that a conftant and undeviating habit of virtue is the only way to true Honour and Happinefs, who refide in a magnificent palace fituated on the fummit of a high and inacceffible mountain. The allegory is illuftrated by a variety of examples of illuftrious perfonages: not only of thofe who, by a regular perfeverance in honourable deeds, gained admittance into this fplendid habitation, but of thofe who were excluded from it by debafing the

---

[1] xiv. 58. [2] *Ut fupr.* p. 483.
[3] Lugd. 1543, 4to.
[4] Again, Edinb. 1579, 4to., "When pale Aurora with face lamentable." [Mr. Pinkerton has fince publifhed another allegorical poem by Douglas, called *King Hart.* Vide *Ancient Scottifh Poems,* 1786.—*Price.* See alfo a Dialogue concerning a theological fubject to be debated between *duos famatos viros,* G. Douglas, Provoft of St. Giles, and mafter David Cranftoun, bachelor of divinity, prefixed to John Major's *Commentarii in prim. Sentent.* Paris, 1519. [The *Palace of Honour* has been reprinted for the Bannatyne Club, 1827, from a collation of the quartos of 1553 and 1579.]

dignity of their eminent stations with a vicious and unmanly behaviour. It is addressed, as an apologue for the conduct of a king, to James IV. is adorned with many pleasing incidents and adventures, and abounds with genius and learning.

SECTION XXXI.

ITH Dunbar and Douglas I join Sir David Lyndsay, although perhaps in strictness he should not be placed so early as the close of the fifteenth century. He appears to have been employed in several offices about the person of James V., from the infancy of that monarch, by whom he was much beloved; and at length, on account of his singular skill in heraldry, a science then in high estimation and among the most polite accomplishments, he was knighted and appointed Lion King-at-arms of the kingdom of Scotland. Notwithstanding these situations, he was an excellent scholar.[1]

Lyndsay's principal performances are *The Dream* and *The Monarch*. In the address to James V, prefixed to the *Dream*, he thus, with much tenderness and elegance, speaks of the attention he paid to his majesty, when a child:

> Quhen thou wes young, I bure the in myne arme
> Full tenderlye, till thow begouth to gang;[2]
> And in thy bed oft happit the full warme,
> With lute in hand fyne[3] softlye to the sang.

He adds that he often entertained the young prince with various dances and gesticulations, and by dressing himself in feigned characters, as in an interlude.[4] A new proof that theatrical diversions were now common in Scotland.

---

[1] [The 4to edit. of 1568 may be considered as the *editio princeps* of the *Works* of Lyndsay. Copies are at Mostyn and Britwell. But for a tolerably copious account of all the impressions, both anterior to 1568 and subsequent to it, see *Handb. of E. E. Lit.* in v. The last edition is by Mr. G. Chalmers, 3 vols. 8vo., London, 1806, by which the present text has been corrected.—*Price.* But the Early English Text Society has now issued a reprint of the *Monarke*, called in the old printed copies *A Dialogue between Experience and a Courtier*, and of the *Minor Poems*, from the second edition by John Skot, and Mr. Laing's long-promised edition of the whole Works is believed to be in a very forward state. This was written in 1869; but the said edition is not yet forthcoming (1871).]

[2] began to walk.   [3] then.

[4] So also his *Complaynt to the Kingis Grace*. Signat. E iii:

> "As ane chapman beris his pack,
> I bure thy grace upon my back;
> And sumtymes stridlingis on my nek,
> Dansand with mony bend and bek,
> And ay quhen thow come fra the scule,
> Than I behuffit to play the fule.
> I wat thou luffit me better than
> Nor now sum wyfe dois hir gude man."

> Sumtyme in danfing feirelie I flang,
> And fumtyme playand farfis¹ on the flure,—
> * * * *
> And fumtyme lyke ane feind² transfigurate,
> And fumtyme lyke the griflie gaift of Gy,³
> In divers formis oftymes disfigurate,
> And fumtyme difgyfit full plefandlye.⁴

He adds:

> So fen thy birth I have continuallye
> Bene occupyit, and ay to thy plefour,
> And fumtyme Sewar, Coppar, and Carvour.

That is, fewer, and cupper or butler. He then calls himfelf the king's "fecreit Thefaurar" and "chief Cubicular." Afterwards he enumerates fome of his own Works:

> I have at lenth the ftoreis done difcryve
> Of Hector, Arthur, and gentill Julius,
> Of Alexander and worthy Pompeius.
>
> Of Jafon and Medea, al at lenth,
> Of Hercules the actis honorabill,
> And of Sampfon the fupernaturall ftrenth,
> And of leill luffaris [lovers] ftories amiabill :
> And oftymes have I feinyeit mony fabill,
> Of Troylus the forrow and the joy,
> And feiges all of Tyre, Thebes, and Troy.
> The prophecyis of Rymour, Beid, and Marling,
> And of mony uther plefand ftorye,
> Of the reid Etin and the gyir carling.⁵

In the Prologue to the *Dream* our author difcovers ftrong talents for high defcription and rich imagery. In a morning of the month of January the poet quits the copfe and the bank, now deftitute of verdure and flowers, and walks towards the fea-beach. The dawn of day is expreffed by a beautiful and brilliant metaphor :

---

¹ playing farces, frolics. ² in the fhape of a fiend.
³ [The ghoft of Guy of Aloft. It will be perhaps fufficient to refer the reader to Dyce's *Skelton*, ii. 185.]
⁴ Difguifed, mafked, to make fport. Signat. D i.
⁵ As to the prophecies of Thomas the Rhymer, venerable Bede, and Merlin, [fee *fupr.* vol. ii. 87, and MSS. Afhm. 337, 6.] Thomas the Rhymer, or Thomas Leirmouth of Erceldoun, feems to have written a poem on Sir Triftram, [of which the original caft has not come down to us; at leaft no copy is at prefent known.] Rob. de Brunne fays this ftory would exceed all others :

> "If men yt fayd as made Thomas."

That is, "If men recited it according to the original compofition of Thomas Erceldoun, or the Rhymer." See Langtoft's *Chron. Append. Pref.* p. 100, vol. i. edit. 1725. He flourifhed about 1280. [The "tayle" of the red Etin is mentioned in *The Complaynt of Scotland*, as a popular ftory of a giant with three heads. —*Chalmers.* The Gyir-carling is Hecate, or the mother-witch of the Scotifh peafants.—*Dr. Jamiefon.*] Many of Lyndfay's Interludes are among Lord Hyndford's MSS. of Scotifh poetry, and are exceedingly obfcene. One of Lyndfay's *Moralities*, called *Ane Satyre of the three Eftaits in commendation of vertew and vytuperation of vyce*, was printed at Edinburgh, 1602. This piece, which is entirely in rhyme, and confifts of a variety of meafures, muft have taken up four hours in the reprefentation. [Whether fo or not, it was performed at Linlithgow in 1540. See Ellis's *Orig. Letters*, 3rd S. iii. 280.]

> Be this fair Titan with his lemis licht
> Over all the land had spred his baner bricht.

In his walk, musing on the desolations of the winter and the distance of spring, he meets Flora disguised in a sable robe :[1]

> I met dame Flora in dule weid disgysit,[2]
> Quhilk into May was dulce and delectabill,
> With stalwart[3] stormis hir sweitnes wes suppryfit,
> Hir hevinly hewis war turnit into sabill,
> Quhilkis umquhyle[4] war to luffaris amiabill.
> Fled from the frost the tender flouris I saw
> Under dame Naturis mantill lurkyng law.[5]

The birds are then represented, flocking round Nature, complaining of the severity of the season, and calling for the genial warmth of summer. The expostulation of the lark with Aurora, the sun, and the months, is conceived and conducted in the true spirit of poetry:

> Allace, Aurore, the sillie lark can cry,
> Quhare hes thow left thy halmy liquour sweit,
> That us rejosit, we mounting in the sky?
> Thy silver droppis ar turnit into sleit!
> O fair Phebus, quhare is thy hailsum heit?
>   *   *   *   *   *
> Quhare art thow, May, with June thy sister schene,
> Weill bordourit with dasyis of delyte?
> And gentill Julie, with thy mantill grene
> Enamilit with rosis reid and whyte?

The poet ascends the cliffs on the sea-shore, and entering a cavern, "high in the crags," sits down to "register in rhyme some mery mater of antiquitie." He compares the fluctuation of the sea with the instability of human affairs;' and at length, being comfortably shrouded from the falling sleet by the closeness of his cavern, is lulled asleep by the whistling of the winds among the rocks, and the beating of the tide. He then has the following vision.

He sees a lady of great beauty and benignity of aspect; who says, she comes to sooth his melancholy by showing him some new spectacles. Her name is Remembrance. Instantaneously she carries him into the centre of the earth. Hell is here laid open;[6] which is filled with popes, cardinals, abbots, archbishops, in their pontifical attire, and ecclesiastics of every degree. In explaining the causes of their punishments, a long satire on the clergy ensues. With these are joined bishop Caiphas, bishop Annas, the traitor Judas, Ma-

---

[1] [Edit. 1806, i. 191-2.]   [2] disguised in a [sad] garment.
[3] violent.   [4] formerly.   [5] low.
[6] It was a part of the old mundane system, that hell was placed in the centre of the earth. So a fragment, cited by Hearne, *Glossary* [to Peter Langtoft,] ii, 583:

> "Ryght so is hell-pitt, as clerkes telles,
> Amyde the erthe and no where elles."

So also an old French tract, *L'Imaige du Monde, or Image of the world:*—" Saches que en la terre est enfer, car enfer ne pourrait estre en si noble lieu comme est l'air," &c. ch. viii.

homet, Chorah, Dathan, and Abiram. Among the tyrants, or unjust kings, are Nero, Pharaoh, and Herod. Pontius Pilate is hung up by the heels. He sees also many duchesses and countesses, who suffer for pride and adultery. She then gives the poet a view of purgatory :[1]

> A lytill above that dolorous dungeoun,
> We enterit in ane cuntre full of cair;
> Quhare that we saw mony ane legioun
> Greitand and gowland with mony ruthfull rair.[2]
> Quhat place is this, quod I, of blis sa bair?
> Scho answerit and said, Purgatorie,
> Quhilk purgis saulis, or thay cum to glorie.[3]

After some theological reasonings on the absurdity of this intermediate state, and having viewed the dungeon of unbaptized babes, and the limbus of the souls of men who died before Christ, which is placed in a vault above the region of torment, they reascend through the bowels of the earth. In passing, they survey the secret riches of the earth, mines of gold, silver, and precious stones. They mount through the ocean, which is supposed to environ the earth: then travel through the air, and next through the fire. Having passed the three elements, they bend towards heaven, but first visit the seven planets.[4] They enter the sphere of the moon, which is elegantly styled

---

[1] I have [already] mentioned a Vision of Hell under the title of *Owayne Miles*. One Gilbertus Ludensis, a monk sent by King Stephen into Ireland, where he founded a monastery, with an Irish knight called Oen, wrote *De Oeni Visione in Purgatorio*. See Wendover, *apud* Mat. Paris, *sub ann.* 1153. Reg. Stephan. According to Ware, Gilbertus flourished in the year 1152. *Scriptor. Hibern.* p. 111. [There is a printed tract called *Le Voiage du Chevalier Owen au purgatoire de S. Patrix;* it is in double columns, in a rude Gothic type, and consists of very few leaves. "Sir Owain" is one of the *fabliaux*. See a Note, *supr.* p. 157.] Among the MSS. of Magdalene College, Oxford, are the *Visiones of Tundal*, a knight of Ireland. "Cum anima mea corpus exueret." MSS. Coll. Magd. 53. It is printed in Tinmouth's *Sanctilogium*, and in the *Speculum Historiale* of Vincent of Beauvais, lib. xxvii. cap. 88, [and there are several other editions printed separately. See Mr. Turnbull's *Visions of Tundale*, &c. 1843, 8vo. Introd.] He is called Fundalus in a MS. of this piece, Bibl. Bodl. NE. B. 3. 16. He lived in the year 1149. Ware, *ut supra*, p. 55. I believe this piece is in the Cotton Library under the name of *Tundale*, MS. Calig. A. 12. f. 17.

There is a MS. of a knight, called Sir Oweyn, visiting St. Patrick's Purgatory, Bibl. Bodl. MSS. Bodl. 550; MSS. Cott. Nero. A. vii. 4. This piece was written by Henry, a Cistercian monk of Saltry, in Huntingdonshire. See T. Messingham, *Florileg.* p. 86, *seq.* In the catalogue of the Library of Sion Monastery which contained fourteen hundred volumes, in Bennet Library, it is falsely attributed to Hugo de Saltereia. MSS. C.C.C.C. xli. The French have an ancient spiritual romance on this favourite expedition, so fertile of wonders, entitled: *Le Voyage du Puys sainct patrix auquel lieu on voit les peines du Purgatoire et aussi les joyes de paradis.* Lyon, 1506. 4to. [See Brunet, last edit. v. 1377.]

[2] roar.   [3] Signat. D iii.

[4] The planetary system was thus divided. i. The Primum Mobile, or first motion. ii. The crystalline heaven, in which were placed the fixed stars. iii. The twelve signs of the zodiac. iv. The spheres or circles of the planets in this order: viz. Saturn, Jupiter, Mars, Sol, Venus, Mercury, and lastly the moon, which they placed in the centre of universal nature. Again, they supposed the earth to be surrounded by three elementary spheres, fire, air, and water. Milton, in his *Elegy*

Quene of the fey, and bewtie of the nicht.

The fun is then defcribed with great force:

> Than paft we to the fpheir of Phebus bricht,
> That luftye lamp and lanterne of the hevin;
> And glaider of the fterris with his licht;
> And principal of all the planetis fevin:
> And fet in middis of thame all full evin:
> As roy¹ royall rolling in his fpheir
> Full plefandlye into his goldin chair.
> For to difcryve his diademe royall,
> Bordourit with precious ftanis fchyning bricht,
> His goldin cart, or throne imperiall,
> The foure fteidis that drawith it full richt, &c.²

They now arrive at that part of heaven which is called the *Chryftalline*,³ and are admitted to the *Empyreal*, or heaven of heavens. Here they view the throne of God, furrounded by the nine orders of angels, finging with ineffable harmony.⁴ Next the throne is the Virgin

---

on the Death of a fair Infant, makes a very poetical ufe of the notion of a *primum mobile*, where he fuppofes that the foul of the child hovers

> " — Above that high firft moving fphere,
> Or in th' Elyfian fields," &c.

St. vi. v. 39. See *Parad. L.* iii. 483
¹ to be pronounced diffyllabically.
² [Edit. 1806, i. 210.]
³ Moft of this philofophy is immediately borrowed from the firft chapters of the Nuremburg Chronicle, a celebrated book when Lyndfay wrote, printed in the year 149[3]. It is there faid, that of the waters above the firmament which were frozen like cryftal, God made the cryftalline heaven, &c. fol. iv. This idea is taken from Genefis, i. 4. See alfo St. Paul, ii. Epift. Cor. xii. 2. The fame fyftem is in Taffo, where the archangel Michael defcends from heaven, *Gier. Lib.* C. ix. ft. 60, *feq*. And in Milton, *Parad. L.* iii. 481:

> "They pafs the planets feven, and pafs the fixed,
> And that cryftalline fphere," &c.

⁴ Becaufe the fcriptures have mentioned feveral degrees of angels, Dionyfius the Areopagite and others have divided them into nine orders, and thofe they have reduced into three hierarchies. This was a tempting fubject for the refining genius of the fchool-divines: and accordingly we find in Thomas Aquinas a difquifition, *De ordinatione Angelorum fecundum Hierarchias et Ordines*. Quæft. cviii. The fyftem, which perhaps makes a better figure in poetry than in philofophy, has been adopted by many poets who did not outlive the influence of the old fcholaftic fophiftry. See Dante, *Parad.* C. xxviii. Taffo mentions, among *Lq grande ofte dol ciel*,

> "Tre folte fquadre, et ogni fquadra inftrutta
> In tre ordini gira," &c.

Gier. Lib. xviii. 96. And Spenfer fpeaks of the angels finging in their " trinall triplicities." *Fair. Qu.* i. xii. 39. And again, in his *Hymn of Heavenly Love*. See alfo Sannazarius, *De Part. Virgin.* iii. 241. Milton perhaps is the laft poet who has ufed this popular theory. *Parad. L.* v. 748.

> " Regions they pafs'd, and mighty regencies
> Of Seraphim, and Potentates, and Thrones,
> In their triple degrees."

And it gives great dignity to his arrangement of the celeftial army. See *ibid. fupr.* 583.

> " — Th' empyreal hoft
> Of angels, by imperial fummons call'd,

Mary, the queen of queens, "well cumpanyit with ladyis of delyte." An exterior circle is formed by patriarchs, prophets, evangelifts, apoftles, conquerors in the three battles of the world, of the flefh, and of the devil, martyrs, confeffors, and "doctours in divinitie," under the command of St. Peter, who is reprefented as their lieutenant-general.

Milton, who feigns the fame vifionary route with very different ideas, has thefe admirable verfes, written in his nineteenth year, yet marked with that characteriftical great manner which diftinguifhes the poetry of his maturer age. He is addreffing his native language:

> Yet I had rather, if I were to chufe,
> Thy fervice in fome graver fubject ufe;
> Such as may make thee fearch thy coffers round,
> Before thou clothe my fancy in fit found:
> Such, where the deep-tranfported mind may foar
> Above the wheeling poles; and at Heaven's door
> Look in, and fee each blifsfull deitie
> How he before the thunderous throne doth lie,
> Liftening to what unfhorn Apollo fings
> To th' touch of golden wires, while Hebe brings
> Immortal nectar to her kingly fire.
> Then paffing through the fphears of watchfull fire,
> And miftie regions of wide air next under,
> And hills of fnow, and lofts of piled thunder,
> May tell at length how green-eyed Neptune raves,
> In heaven's defiance muttering all his waves.[1]

Remembrance and the poet, leaving heaven, now contemplate the earth, which is divided into three parts. To have mentioned America, recently difcovered, would have been herefy in the fcience of cofmography; as that quarter of the globe did not occur in Pliny and Ptolemy.[2] The moft famous cities are here enumerated. The

---

> Innumerable before th' Almighty's throne,
> Forthwith from all the ends of heaven appear'd,
> Under their Hierarchies in Orders bright.
> Ten thoufand thoufand enfigns high advanc'd,
> Standards and gonfalons, twixt van and rear
> Stream in the air, and for diftinction ferve
> Of Hierarchies, of Orders, and Degrees."

Such fplendid and fublime imagery has Milton's genius raifed on the problems of Thomas Aquinas. See alfo *ibid.* 600. Hence a paffage in his *Hymn on the Morning of Chrift's Nativity* is to be illuftrated. St. xiii. vi. 131:

> " And with your ninefold harmony
> Make up full concert to the angelike fymphony."

That is, the fymphony of the nine orders of angels was to be anfwered by the nine-fold mufic of the fpheres. Thomas Heywood, a moft voluminous dramatic poet in the reign of James I., wrote a long poem with large notes on this fubject, called *The Hierarchie of the Bleffed Angels*, 1635. See alfo Jonfon's *Elegie on my Mufe*, in the Underwoods.

[1] *At a Vacation Exercife*, &c. Newton's *Milt.* ii. p. 11.
[2] For the benefit of thofe who are making refearches in ancient cofmography, I obferve that the map of England, mentioned by Harrifon and Hearne, and belonging to Merton college library, appears to have exifted at leaft fo early as the year 1512. For in that year it was lent to the dean of Wells, William Cofyn, with a caution of forty fhillings. *Regiftr. Vet. Coll. Mert.* fol. 218, b. See its reftitution, *ibid.* fol. 219, b.

poet next desires a view of Paradise; that glorious "garth," or garden, of every flower. It is represented as elevated in the middle region of the air, in a climate of perpetual serenity.[1] From a fair fountain, springing in the midst of this ambrosial garden, descend four rivers, which water all the east. It is inclosed with walls of fire, and guarded by an angel:

> The cuntrie closit is about full richt
> With wallis hie of hote and birnyng fyre,
> And straitly keipit be ane angell bricht.[2]

From Paradise a very rapid transition is made to Scotland. Here the poet takes occasion to lament, that in a country so fertile, and filled with inhabitants so ingenious and active, universal poverty and every national disorder should abound. It is very probable, that the poem was written solely with a view of introducing this complaint. After an enquiry into the causes of these infelicities, which are referred to political mismanagement, and the defective administration of justice, the *Commonwealth of Scotland* appears, whose figure is thus delineated:

> We saw a bousteous berne[3] cum ovir the bent,[4]
> But[5] hors on fute, als fast as he micht go;
> Quhose rayment wes all raggit, revin,[6] and rent,
> With visage lene, as he had fastit Lent:
> And fordwart fast his wayis he did advance,
> With ane malicious countenance:
> With scrip on hip and pykstaff in his hand,
> As he had purposit to pas fra hame.
> Quod I, Gude man, I wald fane understand,
> Gif ye pleisit,[7] to wit quhat is your name?[8]
> Quod he, My sone, of that I think greit schame.
> Bot sen thow wald of my name have ane feill,
> Forsuthe thay call me Jhone[9] the Common-weill.[10]

The reply of *Sir Commonwealth* to our poet's question is a long and general satire on the corrupt state of Scotland. The spiritual prelates, he says, have sent away Devotion to the mendicant friars: and are more fond of describing the dishes at a feast than of explaining the nature of their own establishment:

> Sensual Plesour hes baneist Chaistitie.

Liberality, Loyalty, and Knightly Valour, are fled:

> And Cowardice, with lordis is laureate.

From this sketch of Scotland (here given by Lyndsay), under the reign of James V., who acted as a viceroy to France, a Scotish historian might collect many striking features of the state of his country, during that interesting period, drawn from the life.

---

[1] "Paradisus tantæ est altitudinis, quo est inaccessibilis secundum Bedam; et tam altus, quod etheream regionem pertingat," &c. *Chron. Nur.* ut supr. f. viii. b.
[2] [Edit. 1806, i. 229.]   [3] [strong, powerful.]
[4] coarse grass, [also, an open field, or plain.]
[5] without.   [6] riven.   [7] if you please.   [8] know.
[9] John, for what reason I know not, is a name of ridicule and contempt in most modern languages.
[10] [Edit. 1806, i, 237-8.]

The poet then supposes, that *Remembrance* conducts him back to the cave on the sea-shore, in which he falls asleep. He is awakened by a ship firing a broadside.¹ He returns home and, entering his oratory, commits his vision to verse. To this is added an exhortation of ten stanzas to James V. in which he gives his majesty advice, and censures his numerous instances of misconduct with incredible boldness and asperity. Most of the addresses to James V. by the Scotish poets are satires instead of panegyrics.

I have not at present either leisure or inclination to enter into a minute enquiry how far our author is indebted in his *Dream* to Tully's *Dream of Scipio*, and the *Hell*, *Purgatory* and *Heaven* of Dante.²

Lyndsay's poem, called *The Monarch*, is an account of the most famous monarchies that have flourished in the world: but, like all the Gothic prose-histories or chronicles on the same favourite subject, it begins with the creation of the world, and ends with the day of judgment.³ There is much learning in this poem. It is a Dialogue between Experience and a Courtier. This mode of conducting a narrative, by means of an imaginary mystagogue, is adopted from Boethius. A descriptive prologue which consists of octave stanzas, and in which the poet enters a delightful park, opens the poem.⁴ The sun clad in his embroidered mantle, brighter than gold or

---

¹ "Thay sparit nocht the poulder nor the *stanis*."
A proof that stones were now used instead of leaden bullets. At first they shot darts, or carrieaux, *i. e.* quarrels, from great guns. Afterwards stones, which they called gun-stones. In the *Brut d'Angleterre*, it is said, that when Henry V., before Harflete, received a taunting message from the Dauphin of France and a ton of tennis-balls by way of contempt, "he anoone lette make tenes balles for the *Dolfin* [Henry's ship] in all the haste that they myght, and they were great gonnestones for the *Dolfin* to playe with alle." But this game at tennis was too rough for the besieged, when Henry " playede at the tenes with his harde gonnestones," &c. See Strutt's *Customs and Manners of the English*, 1775, vol. ii. p. 32.

² In the Medicean library at Florence and the Ambrosian at Milan, there is a long manuscript Italian poem, in three books, divided into one hundred chapters, written by Matteo Palmeri, a learned Florentine, about the year 1450. It is in imitation of Dante, in the "terza rima," and entitled [*Citta di Vita.*] The subject is, the peregrination of the soul, freed from the shackles of the body, through various ideal places and situations, till at length it arrives in the city of heaven. This poem was publicly burnt at Cortona, because the author adopted Origen's heresy concerning a third class of angels who for their sins were destined to animate human bodies. See Trithem. c. 797, Julius Niger, *Scriptor. Florent.* p. 404, [and Muratori (*Rer. Ital. Script.* xiii. xix. and *Suppl.* i. This Palmeri (1405-75) must not be confounded with his namesake of Pisa, who continued his chronicle *De Temporibus.* See Brunet, last edit. in v. for a notice of a work by Palmeri the Florentine, distinct from his *Citta di Vita*, and entitled *Libro della Vita Civile.*]

³ It was printed Hafn. 1552. 4to.

⁴ A park is a favourite scene of action in our old poets. See Chaucer's *Compl. Bl. Kn.* v. 39, [edit. Morris:]

"Toward a park enclosid with a wall," &c.

And in other places. Parks were anciently the constant appendage of almost every considerable manorial house. The old patent-rolls are full of licences for imparcations which do not now exist.

precious ſtones, extinguiſhes the horned queen of night, who hides her viſage in a miſty veil. Immediately Flora began to expand :[1]

> hir tapiſtrie
> Wrocht de dame Nature quent and curiouſlie,
> Depaynt with mony hundreth heuinlie hewis.

Meanwhile, Eolus and Neptune reſtrain their fury, that no rude ſounds might mar the melody of the birds which echoed among the rocks.[2]

In the park our poet, under the character of a Courtier, meets Experience, repoſing under the ſhade of a holly. This portrait is touched with uncommon elegance and expreſſion :

> Into that Park I ſawe appeir
> Ane ageit man, quhilk drew me neir,
> Quhoſe beird was weil thre quarter lang ;
> His hair doun ouer his ſchulders hang,
> The quhilk as ony ſnaw was quhyte ;
> Quhome to behald I thocht delyte ;
> His habitt Angellyke of hew,
> Of culloure lyke the Sapheir blew.
> Onder ane Hollyng he repoſit.
> To ſitt down he requeiſtit me
> Onder the ſchaddow of that tre,
> To ſaif me frome the Sonnis heit,
> Amangis the flowris ſoft and ſweit ;—[3]

In the midſt of an edifying converſation concerning the fall of man and the origin of human miſery, our author, before he proceeds to his main ſubject, thinks it neceſſary to deliver a formal apology for writing in the vulgar tongue. He declares that his intention is to inſtruct and to be underſtood, and that he writes to the people.[4] Moſes, he ſays, did not give the Judaic law on mount Sinai in Greek or Latin. Ariſtotle and Plato did not communicate their philoſophy

---

[1] [The enſuing extracts have been collated with the Early Engliſh Text Society's edit. of the *Monarke* (from the 2nd edit. printed by John Scot, *circâ* 1560).]

[2] Inſtead of Parnaſſus he chooſes Mount Calvary, and his Helicon is the ſtream which flowed from our Saviour's ſide on the croſs, when he was wounded by Longinus, that is Longias. This is a fictitious perſonage in the Goſpel of Nicodemus. I have mentioned him before. Being blind, he was reſtored to ſight by wiping his eyes with his hands which were bloody. See more of him in Chaucer's *Lamentat. Mary Magd.* v. 176. In the Gothic pictures of the Crucifixion, he is repreſented on horſeback, piercing our Saviour's ſide : and in Xavier's Perſic Hiſtory of Chriſt, he is called a horſeman. This notion aroſe from his uſing a ſpear, or lance : and that weapon, λογχη, undoubtedly gave riſe to his ideal name of Longias, or Longinus. He is afterwards ſuppoſed to have been a biſhop of Ceſarea, and to have ſuffered martyrdom. See Tillemont, *Memor. Hiſt. Eccleſiaſt.* tom. i. pp. 81, 251, and Fabric. *Apoc. Nov. Teſtam.* tom. i. p. 261. In the old Greek tragedy of *Chriſt ſuffering*, the converted Centurion is expreſsly mentioned, but not by this name. Almoſt all that relates to this perſon, who could not eſcape the fictions of the monks, has been collected by Wolfius, *Cur. Philol. et Crit. in S. Evangel.* tom. i. p. 414, ii. 984, edit. Baſil. 1741. See alſo Hoffman, *Lexic. Univerſal. Continuat.* in v. tom. i. p. 1036, col. 2, Baſil. 1683.

[3] Signat. B i.

[4] " Quharefore to Colyearis, Cairtaris, and to Cukis,
To Iok and Thome, my Ryme ſal be diractit."

in Dutch or Italian. Virgil and Cicero did not write in Chaldee or Hebrew. Saint Jerom, it is true, tranſlated the Bible into Latin, his own natural language; but had Saint Jerom been born in Argyleſhire, he would have tranſlated it into Erſe. King David wrote the pſalter in Hebrew, becauſe he was a Jew. Hence he very ſenſibly takes occaſion to recommend the propriety and neceſſity of publiſhing the Scriptures and the miſſal, and of compoſing all books intended for common uſe, in the reſpective vernacular language of every country. This objection being anſwered, which ſhows the ideas of the times, our author thus deſcribes the creation of the world and of Adam:

> Qvhen God had maid yᵉ heuinis brycht,
> The Sone, & Mone, for to geue lycht,
> The ſterry heuin & Chriſtellyne,
> And, be his Sapience diuyne,
> The planetis, in yair circlis round
> Quhirling about w[ith] merie ſound,
> He cled the erth with herbis and treis;
> All kynd of fyſches in the ſeis,
> All kynd of beſt he did prepair,
> With fowlis fleying in the air.
> Quhen heuin and erth, and thare contentis,
> Wer endit, with thare Ornamentis,
> Than, laſt of all, the Lord began
> Off moſt vyle erth to mak the man:
> Nocht of the Lille nor the Roſe,
> Nor Syper tre, as I ſuppoſe,
> Nother of gold, nor precious ſtonis,
> Off erth he mad fleſche, blude, and bonis.
> To that intent God maid hym thus,
> That man ſulde nocht be glorious,
> Nor in hym ſelf no thyng ſuld ſe
> Bot matere of humylite.[1]

Some of theſe nervous, terſe, and poliſhed lines need only to be reduced to modern and Engliſh orthography, to pleaſe a reader accuſtomed ſolely to reliſh the tone of our preſent verſification.

To theſe may be added the deſtruction of Jeruſalem and Solomon's temple:

> Prince Tytus with his Chewalrye
> With ſound of trompe Tryumphandlye
> He enterrit in that gret citie, &c.
> Thare wes nocht ellis bot tak and ſlay;
> For thare mycht na man wyn away.[2]
> The ſtrandis of blude ran throuch the ſtretis,
> Off deid folk trampit vnder ſetis;
> Auld Wedowis in the preis wer ſmorit,[3]
> Joung Virginis ſchamefully deflorit;
> The gret Tempyll of Salamone,
> With mony A curyous caruit ſtone,
> With perfyte pinnakles on hycht,
> Quhilkis wer rycht bewtyfull and wycht,[4]
> Quhare in ryche Iowelli[s] did abound,
> Thay ruſcheit[5] rudlie to the ground,

---

[1] Signat. C iii. [2] eſcape. [3] ſmothered. [4] [fair or comely.]
[5] ſ. raſed [or daſhed].

And sett in tyll thare furious yre,¹
Sancta Sanctorum in to fyre.²

The appearance of Christ coming to judgment is poetically painted, and in a style of correctness and harmony, of which few specimens were now seen:

> As fyreflaucht haistely glansing,³
> Discend sall the maist heuinly kyng;
> As Phebus in the Orient
> Lychtnis⁴ in haist, the Occident,
> Sa plesandlye he sall appeir
> Amang the heuinlye cluddis cleir.
> The Angelli[s] of the Ordoris Nyne
> Inueron sall that throne Diuyne.
> In his presen[s] thare salbe borne
> The signis⁵ of Cros, and Croun of thorne,
> Pillar, Nalis, Scurgis, and Speir,
> With euerilk thyng that did hym deir,⁶
> The tyme of his grym Passioun:
> And for our consolatioun
> Appeir sall, in his handis and feit,
> And in his syde, the prent compleit
> Off his fyue Woundis Precious,
> Schynand lyke Rubeis Radious.

When Christ is seated at the tribunal, judging the world, he adds,

> There sall ane Angell blawe a blast
> Quhilk sall mak all the warld agast.⁷

Among the monarchies, our author describes the papal see: whose innovations, impostures and errors he attacks with much good sense, solid argument, and satirical humour; and whose imperceptible increase, from simple and humble beginnings to an enormity of spiritual tyranny, he traces through a gradation of various corruptions and abuses with great penetration and knowledge of history.⁸

Among ancient peculiar customs now lost, he mentions a superstitious idol annually carried about the streets of Edinburgh:

> Of Edinburgh the gret Idolatrye
> And manifest abominatioun
> On thare feist day all creature may se:
> Thay beir ane auld stock Image throuch yᵉ toun
> With taibrone,⁹ troumpet, schalme and Clarioun,
> Quhilk hes bene vsit mony one ȝeir bigone,
> With priestis and freris in to processioun,
> Siclyke¹⁰ as Bell wes borne throuch Babilone.¹¹

He also speaks of the people flocking to be cured of various infirmities to the "auld rude" (or cross) of Kerrail.¹²

---

¹ in their rage. ² Signat. L iii. ³ [lightning.]
⁴ lightens. ⁵ representations. ⁶ [hurt].
⁷ Signat. P iii. ⁸ Signat. M iii. ⁹ tabor. ¹⁰ so as.
¹¹ [The "auld stock-image" which is here reprobated by Lyndsay was the image of St. Giles, the patron saint of Edinburgh, and which was yearly, on the 1st of September, carried through the town in grand procession.—*Chalmers*.]
¹² For allusions of this kind the following stanza may be cited, [satirizing the licentiousness which had crept into an old religious usage:]

Our poet's principal vouchers and authorities in the *Monarch* are Livy, Valerius Maximus, Josephus, Diodorus Siculus, Avicen (the Arabic physician), Orosius, Saint Jerom, Polydore Vergil, Cario the chronicler, the *Fasciculus temporum*, and the *Chronica Chronicarum*. The *Fasciculus temporum* is a Latin chronicle, written at the close of the fifteenth century by Wernerus Rolewinck, a Westphalian and a Carthusian monk of Cologne, and is a most venerable volume.[1] The [*Chronicorum Liber*, usually known as the *Nuremberg Chronicle*,] written by Hartmannus Schedelius, a physician at Nuremberg, and from which our author evidently took his philosophy in his *Dream*, was printed at Nuremberg in 1493.[2] This was a most popular compilation, and is at present a great curiosity to those who are fond of history in the Gothic style, consisting of wonders conveyed in the black letter and wooden cuts. Cario's chronicle is a much more rational and elegant work: it was originally composed about the beginning of the sixteenth century by [Johannes] Cario, an eminent mathematician, and [revised, at the author's request,] by Melancthon. [It was first published in German at Wittenberg in 1532, and its popularity was so great that it saw eight-and-twenty editions. It possesses, however, little merit, and is now completely forgotten. There is an early English translation.] Of Orosius, a wretched but admired Christian historian, who compiled in Latin a series of universal annals from the creation to the fifth century, he cites a translation:

> The translatour of Orosius
> Intill his cronicle wryttis thus.[3]

I know of no English translation of Orosius, unless the Anglo-Saxon version by King Alfred, which would perhaps have been much more difficult to Lyndsay than the Latin original, may be called such: yet Orosius was early translated into French[4] and Italian.[5] For the

---

> "This wes the practick of sum pilgramage,
> Quhen fillokis into Fyfe began to fon
> With Joke and Thom than tuke thai thair vayage
> In Angus till the feild chapell of Dron :
> Than kittock thare als caidgie as ane con,
> Without regarde outher to sin or schame,
> Gave Lawrie leif at laiser to loup on,
> Far better had bene till have biddin at hame."

[A *fillok* is a wanton girl; literally *a mare*.] I will here take occasion to explain two lines, Signat I iii :

> "Nor yit the fair maydin of France
> Danter of Inglis ordinance."

That is, Joan of Arc, who so often daunted or defeated the English army. To this heroine, and to Penthesilea, he compares Semiramis.

[1] [First printed in 1474. See Brunet in v.] See it also among *Scriptor. German.* per J. Pistorium, tom. i. p. 580.
[2] Again 1497, fol.
[3] Signat. F ii.
[4] By [Antoine Verard, 1491, fol. See Brunet, last edit. in v. for a notice of this and later editions. Brunet omits to mention the Italian version indicated by Warton below.]
[5] By Benaccivoli, Ven. 1528, 4to.

story of Alexander the Great, our author seems to refer to [the] poem on that subject written in the reign of Edward II.:[1] a work which I never remember to have seen cited before, and of which, although deserving to be printed, only two manuscripts now remain, the one in the library of Lincoln's Inn and the other in the Bodleian Library at Oxford.

> Alexander the conquerour,
> Gif thow at lenth wald reid his ring,[2]
> And of his crewell conquessing
> In Inglis toung in his greit buke,
> At lenth his lyfe thare thow may luke.[3]

He acquaints us, yet not from his own knowledge, but on the testimony of other writers, that Homer and Hesiod were the inventors in Greece of poetry, medicine, music, and astronomy.[4]

Experience departs from the poet, and the dialogue is ended, at the approach of the evening, which is described with these circumstances:

> Behald, quhow Phebus dounwart dois discend,
> Towart his palyce in the Occident.
> The dew now dounkis[5] the rossis redolent:
> The Mareguldis, that all day wer reiosit
> Of Phebus heit, now craftelly ar closit.[6]
> The Cornecraik in the croft, I heir hir cry;
> The bak, the Howlat,[7] sebyll of thare eis,
> For thare pastyme now in the ewinnyng fleis.
> The Nychtyngaill with myrthfull melody
> Hir naturall notis persith throw the sky.[8]

Many other passages in Lyndsay's poems deserve attention. Magdalene of France, married to James V. of Scotland,[9] did not live to see the magnificent preparations made for her public entry into Edinburgh. In a poem, called the *Deith of quene Magdalene*, our author, by a most striking and lively prosopopeia, an expostulation with Death, describes the whole order of the procession. I will give a few of the stanzas:

> Theif, saw thow nocht the greit preparatyvis
> Of Edinburgh, the nobill famous toun?
> Thow saw the pepill lauboring for thair lyvis,
> To mak tryumphe with trump and clarioun!

* * * * *

---

[1] See *supr.* vol. ii. p. [205, *et seq.*] [2] If thou at length would read his reign.
[3] Signat. K iii. He also cites Lucan for Alexander, Signat. L i. For an account of the riches of Pope John, he quotes Palmerius, Signat N i. This must have been [Matteo Palmeri of Florence, or rather his namesake and continuator. See above. The former] wrote a general chronicle from the fifth century to his own times, entitled *De Temporibus*, and, I believe, first printed at Milan, 1475, fol.; afterwards reprinted with improvements and continuations; particularly at Venice, 1483, by Grynæas at the end of Eusebius, 1570, [and by Muratori, *ut supr.*]
[4] Signat. K iii. [5] moistens. [6] are closed.
[7] owlet, owl. [8] Signat. R.
[9] Not inelegantly, he compares James making frequent and dangerous voyages into France to address the princess, to Leander swimming through the Hellespont to Hero.

> Thow saw makand[1] richt costlie scaffalding,
> Depaintit weill with gold and asure fyne,
> Reddye prepairit for the upsetting,
> With fontanis flowing water cleir and wyne:
> Disgysit[2] folkis, lyke creaturis divyne,
> On ilk scaffold to play ane sundrie storie:[3]
> Bot all in greiting[4] turnit thow that glorie.
>
> Thow saw mony ane lustie fresche galland
> Weill ordourit for resaiving of thair quene,
> Ilk craftisman with bent bow in his hand,
> Ful galȝeartlie in schort clething of grene, &c.
>
> * * *
>
> Syne nyxt in ordour passing throw the toun,
> Thow suld haif hard the din of instrumentis,
> Of tabrone, trumpet, schalme, and clarioun,
> With reird[5] redoundand throw the elementis;
> The herauldis with thair awful vestimentis,
> With maseris[6] upon ather of thair handis,
> To rewle the preis, with burneist silver wandis, &c.
>
> Thow sulde haif hard[7] the ornate oratouris,
> Makand hir hynes salutatioun,
> Baith of the clergy town and counsalouris,
> With mony notabill narratioun.
> Thow suld haif sene hir coronatioun
> In the fair abbay of the haly rude,
> In presence of ane myrthfull multitude.
>
> Sic banketting, sic awfull tornamentis
> On hors and fute, that tyme quhilk suld haif bene,
> Sic chapell royall with sic instrumentis,
> And craftie musick, &c.[8]

Exclusively of this artificial and very poetical mode of introducing a description of these splendid spectacles, instead of saying plainly that the queen's death prevented the superb ceremonies which would have attended her coronation, these stanzas have another merit, that of transmitting the ideas of the times in the exhibition of a royal entertainment.[9]

Our author's *Complaint* contains a curious picture, like that in his *Dream*, of the miserable policy by which Scotland was governed under James V. But he diversifies and enlivens the subject, by supposing the public felicity which would take place, if all corrupt ministers and evil counsellors were removed from the throne. This is described by striking and picturesque personifications:

> For Iustice haldis hir sweird on hie
> With hir ballance of Equitie.
> Dame Prudence hes the be the heid,
> And temperance dois thy brydill leid.

---

[1] making. [2] men, actors disguised.
[3] plays and pageants acted on moveable scaffolds.
[4] to grief. [5] found. [6] maces. [7] heard.
[8] [Edit. 1806, ii. 183-4.]
[9] The curious reader may compare "The ordynaunce of the entre of Quene Isabell into the towne of Paris," in Froissart. Berners's *Transl.* tom. ii. c. clvii. f. 172, b.

> I se dame Force mak affiftance,
> Berand thy Targe of affurance:
> And lufty lady Chaftitie
> Hes baneift Senfualitie.
> Dame Ryches takis on the fic cure,
> I pray God that fcho lang indure,
> That Pouertie dar nocht be fene
> In to thy hous, for baith hir Ene,
> Bot fra thy grace fled mony mylis
> Amangis the Hountaris in the Ylis.[1]

I know not whether it be worth obferving, that playing at cards is mentioned in this poem among the diverfions or games of the court:

> Thare was na play, bot cartis and dyce.[2]

And it is mentioned as an accomplifhment in the character of a bifhop:

> Bot gif thay can play at the cartis.[3]

Thus, in 1503, James IV. of Scotland, at an interview with the Princefs Margaret in the Caftle of Newbattle, finds her playing at cards:—"The kynge came prively to the faid caftell, and entred within the chammer [chamber] with a fmall cumpany, whar he founde the quene *playing at the Cardes.*"[4]

---

[1] Signat. G i. I here take occafion to explain the two following lines:
> "Als Jhone Makrery, the kingis fule,
> Gat dowbill garmentis agane the yule."

That is, "The king's fool got two fuits of apparel, or garments doubly thick, to wear at Chriftmas." Signat. G i. So James I. in his declaration at an affembly of the Scotifh Kirk at Edinburgh, in 1590, "The church of Geneva keép Pafche and Yule," that is, Eafter and Chriftmas. Calderwood's *Hift. Ch. Scot.* p. 256. Our author, in the *Complaynt of the Papyngo*, fays that his bird fang well enough to be a minftrel at Chriftmas. Signat. A iii.

> "Scho micht have bene ane menftrall at the *gule*."

Thus Robert of Brunne, in his chronicle, fpeaking of King Arthur keeping Chriftmas at York:

> "On ʒole day mad he feft
> With many barons of his gefte."

See Hearne's *Rob. Glouc.* vol. ii. p. 678. And Leland's *Itin.* vol. ii. p. 116. In the north of England, Chriftmas to this day is called *ule, yule,* or *youle*. Blount fays, "in the northern parts they have an old cuftom, after fermon or fervice on Chriftmas-day; the people will, even in the churches, cry ule, ule, as a token of rejoycing, and the common fort run about the ftreets finging:

> "Ule, Ule, Ule,
> Three puddings in a pule,
> Crack nuts, and cry Ule."

Diction. voc. *Ule.* In Saxon the word is ʒehul, ʒehol, or ʒeol. In the Welch rubric every faint's day is the *Wyl* or *Gwl* of that faint: either from a Britifh word fignifying *watching*, or from the Latin *Vigilia*, Vigil, taken in a more extended fenfe. In Wales *wyliau* or *gwyliau* hadolig fignifies the *Chriftmas* holidays, where *wyla* or *gwyliau* is the plural of *wyl* or *gywl*.

I alfo take this opportunity of obferving, that the court of the Roman pontiff was exhilarated by a fool. The pope's fool was in England in 1230, and received forty fhillings of Henry III. *de dono regis.* MSS. James, xxviii. p. 190.

[2] Signat. F. iii. [3] Signat. G i.

[4] Leland. *Coll. Append.* iii. p. 284, *ut fupr.*

In our author's *Tragedie of Cardinal Betoun*, a foliloquy fpoken by the cardinal, he is made to declare, that he played with the king for three thoufand crowns of gold in one night, at *cartis* and dice.[1]

> Halking, hunting, and fwift horfe rynning,
> Are changit all in wrangus wynning;
> Thar is no play bot *cartis* and dyce.

Where, by the way, horfe-racing is confidered among the liberal fports, fuch as hawking and hunting, and not as a fpecies of gaming.[2]

Cards are mentioned in a ftatute of Henry VII.[3] Du Cange cites two Greek writers, who mention card-playing as one of the games of modern Greece, at leaft before the year 1498.[4] It feems highly probable, that the Arabians, fo famous for their ingenuity, more efpecially in whatever related to numbers and calculation, were the inventors of cards, which they communicated to the Conftantinopolitan Greeks. Carpentier fays that cards, or *folia luforia*, are prohibited.[5] But the age of thefe ftatutes has not occurred to me.[6]

Benedictus Abbas has preferved a very curious edict, which fhews the ftate of gaming in the Chriftian army, commanded by Richard I. king of England and Philip of France, during the crufade in the year 1190. No perfon in the army is permitted to play at any fort of game for money, except knights and clergymen; who in one whole day and night fhall not each lofe more than twenty fhillings: on pain of forfeiting one hundred fhillings to the archbifhops of the army. The two kings may play for what they pleafe: but their attendants, not for more than twenty fhillings. Otherwife, they are to be whipped naked through the army for three days,[7] &c.

Prophecies of apparent impoffibilities were common in Scotland: fuch as the removal of one place to another. Under this popular prophetic formulary may be ranked the prediction in Shakefpeare's *Macbeth*, where the *Apparition* fays, that Birnam-wood fhall go to Dunfinane. In the fame ftrain, peculiar to his country, fays our author:

> Quhen the Bas and the ifle of May
> Beis fet upon the mont Sinay,
> Quhen the Lowmound befyde Falkland
> Beis liftit to Northumberland.

But he happily avails himfelf of the form, to introduce a ftroke of fatire:

> Quhen Kirkman yairnis[8] na dignite,
> Nor wyffis na foveranite.[9]

---

[1] Signat. I ii. They are alfo mentioned in an old anonymous Scotifh poem *Of Covetice*. Anc. Sc. P. ut fupr. p. 168, ft. iii.
[2] See alfo *ibid*. p. 146, ft. v.
[3] xi. Hen. VII. cap. ii. That is, in 1496.
[4] *Glofs. Gr.* tom. i. v. Xaptia. p. 1734.
[5] *Statuta Crimin. Saonæ*. cap. xxx. p. 61.
[6] *Supplem. Lat. Glofs*. Du Cange, v. *Cartæ*, tom. i. p. 342.
[7] *Vit. Ric.* I. p. 610, edit. Hearn, tom. ii. King Richard is defcribed playing at chefs in this expedition. MSS. Harl. 4690:
> "And kyng Rychard ftode and playe
> Att the cheffe in his galleye."

[8] earn, gain. [9] *Ibid*. Signat. H i.

The minority of James V. was diffipated in pleafures, and his education moft induftrioufly neglected. He was flattered, not inftructed by his preceptors. His unguarded youth was artfully expofed to the moft alluring temptations. Even his governors and preceptors threw thefe temptations in his way; a circumftance touched with fome humour by our author:

> Thare was few of that garnifoun
> That lernit hym ane gude leffoun.
> Quod ane, The devill ftik me with ane knife,
> Bot, Schir, I knaw ane maide in Fyfe,
> Ane of the luftieft wantoun laffis!
> Hald thy toung brother, quod ane uther,
> I knaw ane fairer be fyftene futher.
> Schir, when ye pleis to Linlithquow pas,
> Thare fall ye fe ane luftie las.
> Now *tritill tratill trow low*,
> Quod the third man, thow dois bot mow;
> Quhen his grace cummis to fair Stirling
> Thare fal he fe ane dayis darling.
> Schir quod the fourt, tak my counfell,
> And go all to the hie bordell,
> Thare may we loup at liberte
> Withoutin any gravite,[1] &c.

It was in this reign that the nobility of Scotland began to frequent the court, which foon became the theatre of all thofe idle amufements which were calculated to folicit the attention of a young king. All thefe abufes are painted in this poem with an honeft unreferved indignation. It muft not in the mean time be forgotten, that James poffeffed eminent abilities, and a love of literature; nor is it befide our prefent purpofe to obferve, that he was [probably] the author of the celebrated ballad called *Chrift's Kirk on the Green*.[2]

The *Complaint of the Papingo* is a piece of the like tendency. In the Prologue, there is a curious and critical catalogue of the Scotifh poets who flourifhed about the fourteenth, fifteenth, and fixteenth centuries. As the names and works of many of them feem to be totally forgotten, and as it may contribute to throw fome new lights on the neglected hiftory of the Scotifh poetry, I fhall not fcruple to give the paffage at large, with a few illuftrations. Our author declares, that the poets of his own age dare not afpire to the praife of the three Englifh poets, Chaucer, Gower, and Lydgate. He then, under the fame idea, makes a tranfition to the moft diftinguifhed poets, who formerly flourifhed in Scotland:

> Or quho can now the workis cuntrafait[3]
> Off Kennedie,[4] with termes aureait?

---

[1] *Ibid.* Signat. G. Compare Buchanan, *Hift.* lib. xiv. *ad fin.*

[2] Printed at Oxford, by Edm. Gibfon, 1691, 4to. with Notes. [But there is an edition printed as a broadfide in 1663, in the Chetham Library.] He died in 1452.

[3] imitate.

[4] [Walter Kennedy. All his known poems are inferted in Mr. Laing's edition of Dunbar. Mr. Laing fays, that he was born in Ayrfhire before the year 1460, and that he was the third fon of Gilbert, firft Lord Kennedy.] Kennedy wrote a

Or of Dunbar, quhilk language had at large,
As maye be fene in tyll his Goldin Targe?
Quintyng,[1] Merfar,[2] Rowle,[3] Henderfon,[4] Hay[5] & Holland.[6]
Thocht thay be ded, yar libells bene leua[n]d,[7]
Quhilkis to reheirs makeith redaris to reiofe.
Allace for one quhilk lampe was of this land,
Of Eloquence the flowand balmy ftrand,[8]
And in our Inglis rethorick the rofe,
As of Rubeis the Charbunckle bene chofe !
And as Phebus dois Synthia prefell;
So Gawane Dowglas, Byfchope of Dunkell,
Had, quhen he wes in to this lande on lyue,
Abufe vulgare Poetis prerogatyue,
Boith in pratick and fpeculatioun.
I faye no mare; gude redaris may difcryue
His worthy workis, in nowiner mo than fyue.
And fpeciallye the trew Tranflatioun

---

poem in Scotifh metre on the *Paffion of Chrift*. MSS. Coll. Grefham. 286. Some of Kennedy's poems are in MSS. Hyndford. The *Flyting* between Dunbar and Kennedy is in the *Evergreen*. He exceeds his contemporary Dunbar in fmoothnefs of verfification.

[1] He flourifhed about the year 1320. He was driven from Scotland under the devaftations of Edward I., and took refuge at Paris. He wrote a poem, called the *Complaint of the Miferies of his Country*, printed at Paris, 1511. [Quintyne Schaw is the author of a poem called *Advyce to a Courtier*, printed in Sibbald's *Chronicle of Scottifh Poetry*, vol. i. p. 348. He is mentioned by Dunbar in his *Lament for the Makaris* by the name of Quintyne, (as in the text) without any addition.—*Price*.]

[2] [So little is known regarding his perfonal hiftory, that we cannot afcertain the Chriftian name of a poet, who was thought worthy of commemoration by Lyndfay, as well as by Dunbar. In the treafurer's accounts, we find a Peter Merfar, who received articles of drefs, "quhen he paffit in Denmark," in November, 1494; a James Merfar, whofe name occurs as receiving fometimes the fum of £10 from the king, between 1494 and 1497; and a Wille or William Merfar, who was one of the royal houfehold, and apparently a favourite attendant upon the king from 1500 to 1503. Which (if any) of thefe perfons was the poet muft be left to conjecture. There was alfo an Andro Merfar, from 1503 to 1508, who was one of the grooms of the prince's chamber.—*Laing*.]

[3] Dunbar mentions Rowll of Aberdeen and Rowll of Coftorphine, " twa bettir fallowis did no man fie." *Ibid.* p. 77. [It is very uncertain which is here meant, or who was the real author of *Rowlls Curfing*, printed by Mr. Laing (from the Hyndford MS.) in *Rem. of the Early Popular Poetry of Scotland*, 1822. Mr. L. mentions that there is another copy, fupplying fome deficiencies in this text, in Maitland's MS.] There is an allufion in the piece to Pope Alexander VI., who prefided from 1492 to 1503.

[4] [Robert Henryfon, fchoolmafter at Dumfermling. As full an account of him and his writings as we can perhaps ever expect, is given in Mr. Laing's edition of his *Poems and Fables*, Edin. 1865, 8vo.]

[5] Sir Gilbert Hay was chamberlain to Charles VII. of France, and, in 1456, tranflated from French into Scotifh the book of Bonet, prior of Salon, upon battles. From the teftimony of Dunbar, it appears that Sir Gilbert alfo wrote poems, but his fubfcription does not occur in any of the ancient collections.—*Sibbald*. [Hay's *Buke of the Order of Knighthood* has been printed by the Abbotsford Club, 1847.]

[6] [" This poet flourifhed about the middle of the fifteenth century. His poem of the *Howlatt* is preferved in Lord Hyndford's MS. and in the Auchinleck MS."—*Laing*. The *Howlat* has been printed two or three times. It is in Sibbald's collection. The beft edition is that printed for the Bannatyne Club, 1823, 4to., from a collation of the Afloane and Bannatyne MSS.

[7] living. [8] ftream.

Off Virgill, quhilk bene confolatioun
To cunnyng men, to knaw his gret Ingyne,
Als weill in Naturall Science as Deuyne.

And in the courte bene prefent in thir dayis,
That ballatis breuis luftelie and layis,
Quhilk tyll our Prince daylie thay do prefent.
Quho can fay more than fchir Iames Inglis fayis
In ballatis, farfes, and in plefand playis?[1]
Bot Culrofe hes his pen maid Impotent,
Kyde in cunnyng[2] and pratick rycht prudent.
And Stewarte, quhilk difyrith one ftaitly ftyle,
Full Ornate werkis daylie dois compyle.

Stewart of Lorne wyll carpe rycht curiouflie,[3]
Galbreith, Kynlouch,[4] quhe[n] thay lyft tham applie
In to that art, ar craftie of Ingyne.
Bot now of lait is ftarte vpe haiftelie
One cunnyng Clerk, quhilk wrytith craftelie,
One plant of Poetis callit Ballentyne;[5]
Quhofe ornat workis my wytt can nocht defyne:

Gett he in to the courte auctoritie,
He wyll prefell Quintyng and Kennetie.

---

[1] [Mr. Laing in his Notes to Dunbar, fpeaking of *A General Satire*, fays: "This poem is preferved in the manufcripts of Bannatyne and Maitland. In the firft of thefe it is attributed to Dunbar; in the other, and probably more correctly, to Sir James Inglis." An account of Inglis follows, and it appears that there were two perfons of this name about the fame time. To the fecond, who was living in 1550, fhould perhaps be afcribed *The Complaynt of Scotland*, printed at St. Andrew's about 1548. See Mr. L.'s remarks (Dunbar, ii. 396).]

[2] [Proved or practifed in knowledge.—*Price*.]

[3] See fome of his fatirical poetry, *Anc. Sc. P.* p. 151.

[4] Thefe two poets are converted into one, under the name of *Gabriell Kinlyck*, in an edition of fome of Lyndfay's works "firft turned and made perfect Englifhe," printed [in 1566.] This edition often omits whole ftanzas; and has the moft arbitrary and licentious mifreprefentations of the text, always for the worfe. The editor (or tranflator) did not underftand the Scotifh languuge, and is, befides, a wretched writer of Englifh. But the attempt fufficiently expofes itfelf. [It may be fufpected that the Anglicizer of Lyndfay was the fame perfon who performed a fimilar operation on Henryfon's *Moral Fables* in 1577. See *Handb. of E. E. Lit.*, art. *Æfop*.]

[5] I prefume this is John Balantyn or Ballenden, archdeacon of Murray, canon of Roffe, and clerk of the regifter in the minority of James V. and his fucceffor. He was a doctor of the Sorbonne at Paris. (Conœus *de duplici ftatu religionis apud Scotos*, [1628,] lib. ii. p. 167.) At the command of James V. he tranflated the feventeen books of Hector Boece's *Hiftory of Scotland*. Edinb. by T. Davidfon [(1536), repr. 1821.] The preface is in verfe, "Thow marcyal buke pas to the nobyll prince." Prefixed is the *Cofmography* of Boece's Hiftory, which Mackenzie calls *A Defcription of Albany*, ii. 596. Before it is a Prologue, a vifion in verfe, in which Virtue and Pleafure addrefs the king, after the manner of a dialogue. He wrote an addition of one hundred years to Boece, but this does not appear in the Edinburgh edition; alfo *Epiftles to James the Fifth*, and *On the Life of Pythagoras*. Many of his poems are extant. The author of the article *Ballenden* in the *Biographia Britannica*, written [about 1747,] fays that, "in the large collection of Scotifh poems, made by Mr. Carmichael, there were fome of our author's on various fubjects; and Mr. Laurence Dundafs had feveral, whether in manufcript or printed, I cannot fay," vol. i. p. 461, [edit. 1747-66.] His ftyle has many gallicifms. He feems to have been a young man when this compliment was paid him by Lyndfay. He died at Rome, 1550. Dempft. ii. 197. Bale, xiv. 65. Mackenz. ii. 595, *feq*.

The Scots, from that philosophical and speculative cast which characterizes their national genius, were more zealous and early friends to a reformation of religion than their neighbours in England. The pomp and elegance of the Catholic worship made no impression on a people whose devotion sought only for solid edification, and who had no notion that the interposition of the senses could with any propriety be admitted to co-operate in an exercise of such a nature as appealed to reason alone, and seemed to exclude all aids of the imagination. It was natural that such a people, in their system of spiritual refinement, should warmly prefer the severe and rigid plan of Calvin; and it is from this principle that we find most of their writers, at the restoration of learning, taking all occasions of censuring the absurdities of popery with an unusual degree of abhorrence and asperity.

In the course of the poem before us, an allegory on the corruptions of the church is introduced, not destitute of invention, humour and elegance; but founded on one of the weak theories of Wickliffe who, not considering religion as reduced to a civil establishment, and because Christ and his Apostles were poor, imagined that secular possessions were inconsistent with the simplicity of the Gospel.

In the primitive and pure ages of Christianity, the poet supposes that the Church married Poverty, whose children were Chastity and Devotion. The Emperor Constantine soon afterwards divorced this sober and decent couple; and, without obtaining or asking a dispensation, married the Church with great solemnity to Property. Pope Silvester ratified the marriage: and Devotion retired to a hermitage. They had two daughters, Riches and Sensuality, who were very beautiful, and soon attracted such great and universal regard that they acquired the chief ascendancy in all spiritual affairs. Such was the influence of Sensuality in particular, that Chastity, the daughter of the Church by Poverty, was exiled; she tried, but in vain, to gain protection in Italy and France. Her success was equally bad in England. She strove to take refuge in the court of Scotland, but they drove her from the court to the clergy. The bishops were alarmed at her appearance, and protested they would harbour no rebel to the See of Rome. They sent her to the nuns, who received her in form with processions and other honours. But news being immediately dispatched to Sensuality and Riches of her friendly reception among the nuns, she was again compelled to turn fugitive. She next fled to the mendicant friars, who declared they could not take charge of ladies. At last she was found secreted in the nunnery of the Burrowmoor, near Edinburgh, where she had met her mother Poverty and her sister Devotion. Sensuality attempts to besiege this religious house, but without effect. The pious sisters were armed at all points, and kept an irresistible piece of artillery, called *Domine custodi nos*:

> Within quhose schote thare dar no Enemeis
> Approche thare place for dreid of dyntis doure;[1]

---

[1] hard dints.

> Boith nycht and daye thay wyrk lyke befye beis,[1]
> For thare defence reddye to ftand in ftoure;
> And hes fic watcheis on thare vtter toure,
> That dame Senfual with feage dar not affailye,
> Nor cum within the fchote of thare artailye.[2]

I know not whether this chafte fifterhood had the delicacy to obferve ftrictly the injunctions prefcribed to a fociety of nuns in England who, to preferve a cool habit, were ordered to be regularly blooded three times every year, but not by a fecular perfon; and the priefts who performed the operation were never fuffered to be ftrangers.[3]

I muft not difmifs this poem without pointing out a beautiful valediction to the royal palace of Snowdon; which is not only highly fentimental and expreffive of poetical feelings, but ftrongly impreffes on the mind an image of the romantic magnificence of ancient times, fo remote from the ftate of modern manners:

> Adew, fair Snawdoun, with thy touris hie,
> Thy Chapell royall, Park, and tabyll rounde![4]
> May, Iune, and Iuly, walde I dwell in the,
> War I one man to heir the birdis found,
> Quhilk doth agane thy royall roche redounde![5]

Our author's poem, *To the Kingis grace in contemptioun of fyde taillis*, that is, a cenfure on the affectation of long trains worn by the ladies, has more humour than decency.[6] He allows a tail to the queen, but thinks it an affront to the royal dignity and prerogative that

> Every lady of the land
> Suld have hir taill fo fyde trailland.[7]
> Quhare ever thay go, it may be fene
> How kirk and calfay[8] thay foup clene.
> Kittok that clekkit was yeftrene,[9]
> The morne wyll counterfute the quene.
> Ane mureland[10] Mag that milkid the yowis
> Claggit[11] with clay above the howis,
> In barn nor byir fcho will nocht byde
> Without hir kirtill taill befyde.
> Thay waift mair claith [cloth] within few yeiris
> Nor wald cleith fyftie fcore of freiris.[12]

In a ftatute of James II. of Scotland[13] about the year 1460, it was ordered that no woman fhould come to church or to market with her face "muffaled," that is muzzled[14] or covered. Notwithftanding

---

[1] bufy bees.   [2] artillery. Signat. C ii.
[3] MSS. James, xxvi. p. 32. Bibl. Bodl. Oxon.
[4] round table, tournaments.   [5] Signat. B iii.
[6] Compare a MS. poem of Occleve, *Of Pride and waft clothing of Lordis men which is ayens her aftate*. MSS. Laud, K. 78, f. 67, b. Bibl. Bodl. His chief complaint is againft pendent fleeves fweeping the ground, which with their fur amount to more than twenty pounds.
[7] Signat. L ii.   [8] caufey, ftreet, path.   [9] Kitty that was born yefterday.
[10] moor-land.   [11] clogged.
[12] [Edit. 1806, ii. 201-3.] He commends the ladies of Italy for their decency in this article.   [13] ch. 70.
[14] [*Muffler* appears to have been the term ufed in England for the fame half-

this seasonable interposition of the legislature, the ladies of Scotland continued "muzzled" during three reigns.[1] The enormous excrescence of female tails was prohibited in the same statute, "That na woman wear tails unfit in length." The legitimate length of these tails is not, however, determined in this statute; a circumstance which we may collect from a mandate issued by a papal legate in Germany, in the fourteenth century. "It is decreed, that the apparel of women, which ought to be consistent with modesty, but now, through their foolishness, is degenerated into wantonness and extravagance, more particularly the immoderate length of their petticoats, with which they sweep the ground, be restrayned to a moderate fashion, agreeably to the decency of the sex, under pain of the sentence of excommunication."[2] The orthodoxy of petticoats is not precisely ascertained in this salutary edict: but as it excommunicates those female tails which, in our author's phrase, "keep the kirk and causey clean," and allows such a moderate standard to the petticoat as is compatible with female delicacy, it may be concluded, that the ladies who covered their feet were looked upon as very laudable conformists; an inch or two less would have been avowed immodesty; an inch or two more an affectation bordering upon heresy.[3] What good effects followed from this ecclesiastical censure, I do not find: it is, however, evident that the Scotish act of parliament against "long tails" was as little observed as that against "muzzling." Probably the force of the poet's satire effected a more speedy reformation of such abuses than the menaces of the church or the laws of the land. But these capricious vanities were not confined to Scotland alone. In England, as we are informed by several antiquaries, the women of quality first wore trains in the reign of Richard II.: a novelty which induced a well-meaning divine of those times to write a tract *Contra caudas dominarum*, against the tails of the ladies.[4] Whether or no this remonstrance operated so

---

masked article of dress, which was a thin piece of linen that covered the lips and chin.—*Park*.]

[1] As appears from a passage in the poem before us:

"Bot in the kirk and market placis
I think thay suld nocht hide thair facis."

He therefore advises the king to issue a proclamation:

"Baith throw the land and borrowstounis,
To schaw thair face, and cut thair gounis."

He adds that this is quite contrary to the mode of the French ladies

"Hail ane France lady quhen ye pleis,
Scho wil discover mouth and neis."

[2] "Velamina etiam mulierum, quæ ad verecundiam designandam eis sunt concessa, sed nunc, per insipientiam earum, in lasciviam et luxuriam excreverunt, et immoderata longitudo superpelliceorum quibus pulverem trahunt, ad moderatum usum, sicut decet verecundiam sexus, per excommunicationis sententiam cohibeantur." Ludewig, *Reliq. Diplom.* tom. ii. p. 441.

[3] See Notes to *Anc. Sc. Poems*, ut supr. p. 256.

[4] See *Collectanea Historica*, ex *Diction. MS.* Thomæ Gascoign. *apud* Hearne's *W. Hemingford*, p. 512.

far as to occasion the contrary extreme, and even to have been the distant cause of producing the short petticoats of the present age, I cannot say. As an apology, however, for the English ladies in adopting this fashion, we should in justice remember, as was the case of the Scots, that it was countenanced by Anne, Richard's queen: a lady not less enterprising than successful in her attacks on established forms; and whose authority and example were so powerful, as to abolish, even in defiance of France, the safe, commodious, and natural mode of riding on horseback hitherto practised by the women of England, and to introduce side-saddles.[1]

An anonymous Scotish poem has been communicated to me, belonging to this period: of which, as it was never printed, and as it contains capital touches of satirical humour, not inferior to those of Dunbar and Lyndsay, I am tempted to transcribe a few stanzas.[2] It appears to have been written soon after the death of James V.[3] The poet mentions the death of James IV., who was killed in the battle of Flodden-field, fought in the year 1513.[4] It is entitled *Duncane Laider, or Macgregor's Testament*.[5] The Scotish poets were fond of conveying invective, under the form of an assumed character writing a will.[6] In the poem before us, the writer exposes the ruinous policy and the general corruption of public manners prevailing in Scotland, under the personage of the *Strong Man*,[7] that is, tyranny or oppression. Yet there are some circumstances which seem to point out a particular feudal lord, famous for his exactions and insolence, and who at length was outlawed. Our testator introduces himself to the reader's acquaintance, by describing his own character and way of life, in the following expressive allegories:

> My maister houshold was heich[8] Oppressioun,
> Reif[9] my stewart, that cairit of na wrang;[10]
> Murthure, Slauchtir,[11] aye of ane professioun,
> My cubicularis[12] has bene thir yearis lang:
> Recept, that oft tuik in mony ane fang,[13]
> Was porter to the yettis,[14] to oppin wyde;
> And Covatice was chamberlane at all tyde.[15]
>
> Conspiracie, Invy, and False Report,
> Were my prime counsalouris, leve[16] and deare;

---

[1] Chaucer represents his *Wife of Bath* as riding with a pair of spurs. *Prol.* v. 475:
"And on her feete a paire of spurris sharpe."

[2] For the use of this MS. I am obliged to the ingenious Mr. Pennant, whose valuable publications are familiar to every reader of taste and science.

[3] v. 162.   [4] v. 78.

[5] "Copied," says my MS. "at Taymouth, in September, 1769, from a MS. in the library there, ending August 20th, 1490." The latter date certainly cannot refer to the time when this poem was written.

[6] See *The Testament of Mr. Andro Kennedy* [Laing's *Dunbar*, i. 137.]

[7] viz. Laider.   [8] named, *hight*.   [9] robbery.

[10] that scrupled to do no wrong.   [11] murder, slaughter.

[12] The pages of my bed-chamber; called, in Scotland, *chamber-lads*.

[13] took many a booty.   [14] gates; *yates, yattis*.   [15] all times.   [16] beloved.

Then Robberie, the peepill to extort,
And common Thift¹ tuke on them fa the fteir,²
That Treuth in my prefince durft not appeir,
For Falfheid had him ay at mortal feid,³
And Thift brocht Lautie finallie to deid.⁴

Oppreffioun clikit Gude Reule⁵ be the hair,
And fuddainlie in ain preefoun him flang;⁶
And Crueltie caft Pitie our the ftair,⁷
Qhuill Innocence was murthurit in the thrang.⁸
Then Falfheid faid, he maid my houfe richt ftrang,
And furnift weill with meikill wrangus geir,⁹
And bad me neither god nor man to feir.¹⁰

At length, in confequence of repeated enormities and violations of juftice, Duncane fuppofes himfelf to be imprifoned, and about to fuffer the extreme fentence of the law. He therefore very providently makes his laft will, which contains the following witty bequefts:

To my Curat Negligence I refigne,
Thairwith his parochinaris¹¹ to teche;
Ane ather gift I leif him als condigne,¹²
Slouth and Ignorance fendill¹³ for to preche:
The faullis he committis for to bleiche¹⁴
In purgatorie, quhill thaie be wafchin clene,¹⁵
Pure religion thairbie to fuftene.

To the Vicar I leif Diligence and Care
To tak the upmoft claith and the kirk kow,¹⁶
Mair nor¹⁷ to put the corps in fepulture;
Have pouir wad fix gryis and ane fow,¹⁸
He will have ane to fill his bellie fowe:¹⁹
His thocht is mair upon the pafche fynit,
Nor the faullis in purgatorie that pynis.²⁰

Oppreffioun the Perfone I leif untill,²¹
Pouir mens corne to hald upon the rig,²²

---

¹ theft.   ³ fteer, fteerage; the management.
² enmity, hatred.   ⁴ brought loyalty to death.
⁵ caught Good Rule. Read *clekit*, clecked. Cleik is crooked iron, *Uncus*.
⁶ threw him into prifon.   ⁷ over the ftairs.   ⁸ murthered in the croud.
⁹ furnifhed it well with much ill-gotten wealth.   ¹⁰ v. 15, *feq*.
¹¹ parifhioners.   ¹² as good.   ¹³ feldom.
¹⁴ to be bleached; whitened, or purified.   ¹⁵ till they be wafhed clean.
¹⁶ Part of the pall, taken as a fee at funerals. [The *kirk-kow* is the Mortuary.—Ritfon.]
¹⁷ more than.   ¹⁸ If the poor have fix pigs and one fow.
¹⁹ His belly full. Belly was not yet profcribed as a coarfe indelicate word. It often occurs in our tranflation of the Bible: and is ufed, fomewhat fingularly, in a chapter-act of Weftminfter-abbey fo late as the year 1628. The prebendaries vindicate themfelves from the imputation of having reported that their dean, bifhop Williams, repaired the abbey, "out of the diet and Bellies of the prebendaries, and revenues of our faid church, and not out of his own revenues," &c. Widmore's *Weftminft. Abbey*, p. 213. Append. Num. xii. Lond. 1751. Here, as we now think, a periphrafis, at leaft another term, was obvious. How fhocking, or rather ridiculous, would this expreffion appear in a modern inftrument, figned by a body of clergy!
²⁰ He thinks more of his Eafter-offerings, than of the fouls in purgatory. Pafche is *pafchal*. Pais, Eafter.
²¹ I leave Oppreffion to the Parfon, the proprietor of the great, or rectorial tythes.
²² [The *rig* is the *ridge* of the open field, where the Parfon is fo oppreffive as to

Quhill he get the teynd alhail at his will :[1]
Suppois the barins thair bread fuld go thig,[2]
His purpois is na kirkis for to big ;[3]
Sa fair an barne-tyme[4] god has him fend'n,
This seven years the queir will ly unmendin.[5]

I leif unto the Dean Dignite, bot faill,[6]
With Greit Attendence quilk he sall not miss,
Fra adulteraris [to] tack the buttock-maill ;[7]
Gif ane man to ane madin gif ane kiss,[8]
Get he not geir, thai sall not come to bliss :[9]
His winnyng[10] is maist throw fornicatioun,
Spending it shur with siclike[11] occupatioun.

I leif unto the Prioure, for his part,
Gluttony, him and his monkis to feid,
With far better will to drink ane quart,[12]
Nor an the bible ane chaptoure[13] to reid ;
Yit ar thai wyis and subtile into deid,[14]
Fenzeis thame pouir,[15] and has gret sufficence,
And takith wolth away with gret patience.

I lief the Abbot Pride and Arrogance,
With trappit mules in the court to ryde,[16]

---

detain the whole of the poor people's corn, till he thinks fit to draw his *tithe*.—*Ritson*.]

[1] Until he get the tythe all at his will.
[2] Suppose the children should beg their bread. *Barins*, or Bearns.
[3] To build no churches. [4] So fair a harvest.
[5] The choir or chancel which, as the rector, he is obliged to keep in repair. The more tythe he receives, the less willing he is to return a due proportion of it to the church.
[6] without doubt.
[7] A fine for adultery. Mailis is duties, rents. Maile-men, Mailleris, persons who pay rent. Male is Saxon for tribute or tax. Whence Maalman, Saxon for one paying tribute. See Spelman and Ducange, *in vocibus*.
[8] If a man give a maid one kiss. Chaucer says of his *Sompnour* or Apparitor, *Prol.* v. 651.

" He would suffer for a quart of wine
A good fellow to have his concubine."

See the *Freeres Tale*, where these abuses are exposed with much humour.
[9] If he does not get his fine, they will not be saved. Geir is properly goods, chattels.
[10] his profits, in the spiritual court. [11] surely in the same manner.
[12] an English gallon. [13] to read one chapter.
[14] unto death. [15] feign themselves poor.
[16] to ride on a mule with rich trappings. Cavendish says, that when Cardinal Wolsey went ambassador to France, he rode through London with more than twenty sumpter-mules. He adds, that Wolsey " rode very sumptuouslie like a cardinal, on a mule ; with his spare-mule, and his spare-horse, covered with crimson velvett, and gilt stirrops," &c. *Mem. of Card. Wolsey*, edit. 1708, p. 57. When he meets the king of France near Amiens, he mounts another mule, more superbly caparisoned. *Ibid.* p. 69. See also p. 192. [See a MS. of this Life, MSS. *Laud*. i. 66. MSS. *Arch.* B. 44, Bibl. Bodl.] The same writer, one of the cardinal's domesties, says, that he constantly rode to Westminster-hall, "on a mule trapped in crimson velvett with a saddle of the same." *Ibid.* pp. 29, 30. In the Computus of Maxtoke Priory, in Warwickshire, for the year 1446, this article of expenditure occurs, " Pro pabulo duarum mularum cum harnesiis domini Prioris hoc anno." Again, in the same year, " Pro freno deaurato, cum sella et panno blodii coloris, mulæ Prioris." *MS. penes me supr. citat.* Wickliffe describes a Worldly

Not in the clofter to make refidence;
It is na honoure thair for him to byde,[1]
But ever for ane bifchoprik provyde:[2]
For weill ye wat ane pouir benefice
Of ten thoufand markis[3] may not him fuffice.

To the Bifchop his Free will I allege,[4]
Becaus thair [is] na man him [dares] to blame;
Fra fecular men he will him replege,[5]
And weill ye wat the pape is fur fra hame :[6]
To preich the gofpell he thinkis fchame,
(Suppofis fum tym it was his profeffioun,)
Rather nor for to fit upon the feffioun.[7]

I leif my Flatterie, and Fals Diffembling,
Unto the Freris, thai fa weill can fleitche,[8]
With mair profit throwe ane marriage-making
Nor all the lentrane[9] in the kirk to preiche.[10]
Thai gloifs[11] the fcripture, ever quhen thai teache,
Moer in intent the auditouris to pleifs,
Nor the trew worde of god for to appeifs.[12]

Thir[13] gifts that dame Nature has me lent
I have difponit[14] heir, as ye may fee:
It nevir was, nor yit is, my intent,
That trew kirkmen get acht belongis to me :[15]
But that haulis[16] Huredome and Harlottrie,
Gluttony, Invy, Covatice, and Pryde,
My executouris I mak tham at this tyde.

Adew all friends, quhill[17] after that we meit,
I cannot tell yow quhair, nor in quhat place;
But as the lord difpoufis for my fpreit,
Quher is the well of mercie and of grace,
That I may [ftand] befoirr his godlie face :

Prieft, "with fair hors and jolly, and gay faddles and bridles ringing by the way, and himfelf in coftly clothes and pelure." Lewis's *Wiccl.* p. 121.
  [1] continue.   [2] look out for a bifhoprick.
  [3] mares.   [4] give, affign.
  [5] He will order trial in his own court. It is therefore unfafe to attack him.
  [6] You well know the pope is at a great diftance.
  [7] He had rather fit in parliament.
  [8] fawn.   [9] Or, Lentron, Lent.
  [10] Who get more by making one match than by preaching a whole Lent. The mendicants gained an eftablifhment in families, and were confulted and gave their advice in all cafes. Chaucer's *Friar*

      "Hadde i-made many a fair mariage
       Of yonge wymmen, &c.—*Prol. C. T.* v. 212.

  [11] expound.
  [12] explain. The mendicants not only perverted the plaineft texts of fcripture to cover their own fraudulent purpofes, but often amufed their hearers with legends and religious romances. Wickliffe, the grand antagonift of thefe orders, fays that "Capped [graduated] friers that been eleped [called] mafters of divinitie, have their chamber and fervice as lords and kings, and fenden out idiots full of covetife to preche, not the gofpel, but chronicles, fables, and lefinges, to plefe the peple, and to robbe them." Lewis's *Life of Wiccl.* p. 21, xiii.
  [13] thefe.   [14] difpofed, bequeathed.
  [15] A true churchman, a **chriftian** on the reformed plan, fhall never get anything belonging to me.
  [16] whole.   [17] till.

> Unto the devill I leif my synnis¹ all,
> Fra him thai came, to him agane thei fall.²

Some readers may perhaps be of opinion, that Macgregor was one of those Scotish lairds, who lived professedly by rapine and pillage: a practice greatly facilitated, and even supported, by the feudal system. Of this sort was Edom o'Gordon, whose attack on the castle of Dunse is recorded by the Scot[is]h minstrels in a pathetic ballad [of questionable antiquity] which begins thus:

> It fell about the Martinmas,
>   Quhen the wild blew schril and cauld,
> Said Edom o'Gordon to his men,
>   We maun draw till a hauld:
>
> And quhat a hauld sall we draw till,
>   My mirry men and me?
> We wil gae to the house o' the Rodes,
>   To see that fair ladie.³

Other parts of Europe, from the same situations in life, afford instances of the same practice. Froissart has left a long narrative of an eminent robber, one Amergot Marcel, who became at length so formidable and powerful, as to claim a place in the history of France. About the year 1380, he had occupied a strong castle for the space of ten years in the province of Auvergne, in which he lived with the splendour and dominion of a petty sovereign: having amassed, by pillaging the neighbouring country, one hundred thousand francs. His depredations brought in an annual revenue of twenty thousand florins. Afterwards he is tempted imprudently to sell his castle to one of the generals of the king for a considerable sum. Froissart introduces Marcel, after having sold his fortress, uttering the following lamentation, which strongly paints his system of depredation, the feudal anarchy, and the trade and travelling of those days: " What a joy was it when we rode forthe at adventure, and somtyme found by the way a ryche priour, or marchaunt, or a route of mulettes, of Montpellyer, of Narbone, of Lymons, of Fongans, of Tholous, or of Carcassone, laden with clothe of Brusselles, or peltre ware comynge from the fayres, or laden with spycery from Bruges, from Damas, or from Alysaunder! Whatsoever we met, all was ours, or els raunsomed at our pleasures. Dayly we gate newe money; and the vyllaynes of Auvergne and of Lymosyn dayly provyded, and brought to our castell, whete mele, breed [bread] ready baken, otes for our horses and lytter, good wynes, beffes, and fatte mottons, pullayne, and wylde fowle. We were ever furnyshed, as though we had been kings. Whan we rode forthe, all the country trembled for feare. All was oures, goynge or comynge. Howe toke we Carlaste, I and the Bourge of Compayne! and I and Perot of Bernoys toke Calusset. How dyd we scale with lytell ayde the strong castell of Marquell pertayninge to the erle

---

¹ sins. ² v. 309, seq.
³ [Percy's Rel. ed. 1812, i. 123, compared with Maidment's Scotish Ballads and Songs, 1868, i. 227.]

Dolphyn! I kept it not paſt fyve dayes, but I receyved for it, on a fayre table, fyve thouſand frankes; and forgave one thouſand, for the love of the erle Dolphyn's chyldren. By my faithe, this was a fayrie and goodlie life!" &c.¹

But on the whole I am inclined to think, that our teſtator Macgregor, although a robber, was a perſonage of high rank, whoſe power and authority were ſuch, as to require this indirect and artificial mode of abuſe. For the ſame reaſon, I believe the name to be fictitious.

[To this period belongs the writer, who is only known to us as Blind Harry. No particulars of his life are known, except that, as Mr. Laing² has pointed out, "in the treaſurer's accounts we find that ſmall gratuities were occaſionally given to 'Blind Harye' by James IV. between April, 1489, and January, 1492[-3]." Blind Harry's performance is a narrative in verſe of the *Acts and Deeds of Sir William Wallace*, firſt printed, ſo far as can be now aſcertained, by Walter Chepman and Andro Myllar at Edinburgh, about 1520, folio.]³ This poem,⁴ which conſiſts of twelve books, is tranſlated from the Latin of Robert Blare, or Blair, chaplain to Sir William Wallace. The [poem may be regarded as a valuable relic in its vernacular dreſs, inaſmuch as it ſtands in the ſame relation to the Scotiſh poetical literature of the fifteenth century that the *Brus*, noticed in an earlier ſection, does to that of the fourteenth. There ſeems to be good ground to aſſume that the date ſupplied by Dempſter, in which he has been hitherto too implicitly followed, is only wrong by a figure, and that his 1361 ſhould be 1461.⁵ We ſhall annex Blind Harry's verſion of his author's] deſcription of the morning, and of Wallace arming himſelf in his tent:⁶

---

¹ See tom. ii. cap. 170, fol. 115, a. And tom. i. cap. 149, fol. 73. See alſo *ibid.* cap. 440, fol. 313, b. Berners's Tranſlation.

² [Dunbar's Poems, ii. 358.]

³ [The only known fragment of this edition is printed with Chepman and Myllar's peculiar types.]

⁴ Tit. *Geſta Willelmi Wallas*. See Dempſt. ii. 148. [Blair] flouriſhed in 1800. He has left another Latin poem, *De liberata tyrannide Scotia*. Arnold Blair, mentioned in the title page in the text, probably Robert's brother, if not the ſame, was alſo chaplain to Wallace, and monk of Dumferling about the year 1327. *Relat.* ut ſupr. p. 1. But ſee pp. 9, 10. In the fifth book of the Scot[iſ]h poem we have this paſſage, p. 94, v. 533:

"Maiſter Jhone Blayr was offt in that meſſage,
A worthy clerk, bath wyſs and rycht ſawage,
Lewyt he was befor in Paryſs town, &c.
He was the man that pryncipall wndirtuk,
That fyrſt compiled in dyt the Latyne huk,
Off Wallace lyff, rycht famouſs of renowne,
And Thomas Gray perſone of Libertoune,
With him thai war and put in ſtory all
Oftt ane or bath mekill of his travaill," &c.

⁵ [Mr. Skeat's inform. Mr. Skeat ſuggeſts that the error is a mere ſlip of the preſs in Dempſter.]

⁶ B. viii. v. 65. Dr. Jamieſon's text [1822, 4to.] has been adopted for this

> In till a waill be a fmall rywer fayr,
> On athir fid quhar wyld der maid repayr,
> Set wachis owt that wyfly couth thaim kepe,
> To fouppar went, and tymyfly thai flepe,
> Off meit and fleip thai cefs with fuffifiance,
> The nycht was myrk, ourdrayff the dyrkfull chance,
> The mery day fprang fra the oryent,
> With bemys brycht enlumynyt the occident,
> Efter Titan, Phebus wp ryfyt fayr,
> Heich in the fper, the fignes maid declayr.
> Zepherus began his morow courfs,
> The fwete wapour thus fra the ground refourfs;
> The humyll breyth doun fra the hewyn awaill
> In every meide, bathe fyrth, forreft and daail.
> The cler rede amang the rochis rang
> Throuch greyn branchis quhar byrdis blythly fang,
> With joyus woice in hewynly armony.
> Than Wallace thocht it was no tyme to ly:
> He croyffit him, fyne fodeynli upraifs,
> To tak the ayr out off his palyon gais
> Maifter Jhon Blar was redy to rawefs,
> In gud entent fyne bownyt to the mefs.
> Quhen it was done, Wallace can him aray,
> In his armour, quhilk gudly was and gay;
> His fchenand fchoyis that burnyft was full beyn,
> His leg-harnes he clappyt on fo clene,
> Pullane greis he braiffit on full faft,
> A clofs byrny with mony fekyr cla'p,
> Breyft-plait, brafaris, that worthy was in wer:
> Befid him furth Jop couth his bafnet ber;
> His glytterand glowis grawin on aither fid,
> He femyt weill in battaill till abid.
> His gud gyrdyll, and fyne his burly brand,
> A ftaff off fteyll he gryppyt in his hand.
> The oft him blyft, &c.
> Adam Wallaice and Boid furth with him yeid
> By a revir, throu out a floryft meid.
> And as thai walk atour the feyldys greyn,
> Out off the fouth thai faw quhar at the queyn
> Towart the oft come ridand fobyrly,
> And fyfty ladyes was in hyr cumpany, &c.

The four following lines on the fpring are uncommonly terfe and elegant:

> Gentill Jupiter, with his myld ordinance,
> Bath erb and tre revertis in plefance;
> And frefch Flora hir floury mantill fpreid,
> In euery waill bath hop, hycht, hill, and meide.[1]

A different feafon of the year is here ftrongly painted:

> The dyrk regioun apperand wondyr faft,
> In November quhen October was paft,
> The day faillit throu rycht courfs worthit fchort,
> Till banyft men that is no gret comfort:

---

edition (1822, 4to).—*Price.* The edit. of 1570, printed by R. Lekprevik at Edinburgh, is the earlieft impreffion at prefent known in an at all complete ftate, and the only copy of this difcoverable appears to want fomething.]

[1] Lib. ix. v. 22, ch. i. p. 250.

With thair power in pethis worthis gang,
Hewy thai think quhen at the nycht is lang.
Thus Wallace faw the nychtis meffynger;
Phebus had loft his fyry bemys cler:
Out of the wood thai durft nocht turn that tyd
For adverfouris that in thair way wald byde.[1]

The battle of Black Ernfide fhows our author a mafter in another ftyle of painting :

Kerlé beheld on to the bauld Heroun,
Upon Fawdoun as he was lukand doune,
A futtell ftraik wpwart him tuk that tide
Wndir the chokkeis the grounden fuerd gart glid,
By the gude mayle, bathe halfs and his crag-bayne
In fondyr ftraik ; thus endyt that cheftayne,
To grounde he fell, feile folk about him thrang,
Trefoune, thai criyt, traytouris was thaim amang.
Kerlye, with that, fled out fone at a fide,
His falow Stewyn than thocht no tyme to bide.
The fray was gret, and faft away thai yeid,
Sawch towart Ern ; thus chapyt thai of dreid.
Butler for woo off wepyng mycht nocht ftynt.
Thus raklefly this gud knycht haiff thai tynt.
They demyt all that it was Wallace men,
Or ellis himfelf, thocht thai couth nocht him ken;
He is richt ner, we fall him haiff bot faill,
This febill woode may him littill awaill.
Fourtie thar paft agayne to Sanct Jhonftoun,
With this dede corfs, to beryfing maid it boune.
Partyt thar men, fyne diverfs wayis raid,
A gret power at Dipplyn ftill thar baid.
To Dalwryoch the Butler paft bot let,
At fyndry furdis the gait thai umbefet,
To kepe the wode quhill it was, day thai thocht.
As Wallace thus in the thik forreft focht,
For his twa men in mynd he had gret payne,
He wift nocht weill, gif thai war tayne or flayne,
Or chapyt haile be ony jeperte.
Threttene war left with him, no ma had he ;
In the Gafk-hall thair lugyng haif thai tayne.
Fyr gat thai fone, bot meyt than had thai nane ;
Twa fcheipe thai tuk befid thaim of a fauld,
Ordanyt to foupe in to that feemly hauld :
Graithit in haift fume fude for thaim to dycht :
So hard thai blaw rude hornys wpon hycght.
Twa fende he furth to luk quhat it mycht be ;
Thai baid rycht lang, and no tithingis herd he,
Bot houftoufs noyis fo brymly blewand faft ;
So othir twa in to the woode furth paft.
Nane come agayne, bot bouftoufly can blaw,
In to gret ire he fend thaim furth on raw.
Quhen he allayne Wallace was lewyt thar,
The awfull blaft aboundyt mekill mayr;
Then trowit he weill thai had his ludgyng feyne ;
His fuerd he drew of nobill mettall keyne,
Syn furth he went quhar at he hard the horne.
With out the dur Fawdoun was him beforn,

---

[1] Lib. v. ch. i. p. 78, v. 1.

As till his fycht, his awne hed in his hand;
A croyss he maid quhen he faw him fo ftand.
At Wallace in the hed he fwaket thar,
And he in haift fone hynt it by the hair,
Syne out agayn at him he couth it caft,
In till his hart he was gretlye agaft.
Rycht weill he trowit that was no fpreit of man,
It was fum dewill, at fic malice began.
He wyft no waill thar langar for to bide.
Up throuch the hall thus wicht Wallace can glid,
Till a closs ftair, the burdis raiff in twyne,
Fyftene fute large he lap out of that in.
Wp the wattir he fodeynelye couth fair,
Agayne he blent quhat perance he fawe thair,
Him thocht he faw Fawdoun, that hugly fyr,
That haill hall he had fet in a fyr;
A gret raftre he had intill his hand.
Wallace as than no langar walde he ftand.
Off his gud men full gret mervaill had he,
How thai war tynt throuch his feyle fantasé.
Traiftis rycht weill all this was futh in deide,
Suppofs that it no poynt be of the creide.
Power thai had with Lucifer that fell,
The tyme quhen he partyt fra hewyn to hell.
Be fic myfcheiff giff his men mycht be loft,
Drownyt or flayne amang the Inglis oft;
Or quhat it was in liknefs of Faudoun.
Quhilk brocht his men to fuddand confufioun;
Or gif the man endyt in ewill entent,
Sum wikkit fpreit agayne for him prefent.
I can nocht fpek of fic divinité,
To clerkis I will lat all fic matteris be:
Bot of Wallace, furth I will yow tell.
Quhen he was went of that perell fell,
Yeit glad wes he that he had chapyt fwa,
Bot for his men gret murnyng can he ma.
Flayt by him felf to the Maker off buffe
Quhy he fufferyt he fuld fic paynys pruff.
He wyft nocht weill giff it wes Goddis will;
Rycht or wrang his fortoun to fullfill,
Hade he plefd God, he trowit it mycht nocht be
He fuld him thoill in fic perplexité.
Bot gret curage in his mynd evir draiff,
Off Inglifmen thinkand amendis to haiff.
As he was thus walkand be him allayne
Apon Ern fide, makand a pytuouss mayne,
Schyr Jhone Butler, to wache the furdis rycht,
Out fra his men of Wallace had a fycht;
The myft wes went to the montanys agayne,
Till him he raid, quhar at he maid his mayne.
On loude he fperde, quhat art thow walkis that gait?
A trew man, Schyr, thocht my wiagis be layt;
Erandis I pafs fra Doun to my lord,
Schir Jhon Sewart, the rycht for till record,
In Doune is now, new cummyn fra the king.
Than Butler faid; this is a felcouth thing,
Thou leid all out, thow has beyne with Wallace,
I fall the knaw, or thow cum of this place,
Till him he ftert the courfer wondyr wicht,
Drew out a fuerd, fo maid him for to lycht.

Abown the kne gud Wallace has him tayne,
Throw the and brawn in fondyr ftraik the bayne.
Derfly to dede the knycht fell on the land.
Wallace the horfs fone fefyt in his hand,
Ane awkwart ftraik fyne tuk him in the ftede.
His crag in twa ; thus was the Butler dede.
Ane Ingliffman faw thair chiftayne wes flayn,
A fper in reyft he keft with all his mayne,
On Wallace draiff, fra the horfs him to ber ;
Warly he wrocht, as worthi man in wer.
The fper he wan with outyn mor abaid,
On horfs he lap, and throw a gret rout raid ;
To Dawryoch he knew the forfs full weill :
Befor him come feyll ftuffyt in fyne fteill.
He ftraik the fyrft, but baid, in the blafoune,
Quhill horfs and man bathe flet the wattir doune.
Ane othir fone doune fra his horfs he bar,
Stampyt to grounde, and drownyt with outyn mar.
The thrid he hyt in his harnefs of fteyll
Throw-out the coft, the fper to brak fum deyll.
The gret power than efftir him can ryd.
He faw na waill no langar thar to byd.
His burnift brand braithly in hand he bar,
Quham he hytt rycht thai folowit him no mar.
To ftuff the chafs feyll frekis folowit faft,
Bot Wallace maid the gayaft ay agaft.
The mur he tuk, and throw thair power yeid,
The horfs was gud, bot yeit he had gret dreid
For failyeing or he wan to a ftrenth,
The chafs was gret, fcalyt our breid and lenth,
Throw ftrang danger thai had him ay in fycht.
At the Blakfurd thar Wallace doun can lycht,
His horfs ftuffyt, for the way was depe and lang,
A large gret myile wichtly on fute couth gang.
Or he was horft rydaris about him keft,
He faw full weyll lang fwa he mycht nocht left.
Sad men in deid wpon him can renew,
With retornyng that nycht twenty he flew,
The forfeaft ay rudly rabutyt he,
Kepyt hys horfs, and rycht wyfly can fle,
Quhill that he cum the myrckeft mur amang.
His horfs gaiff our, and wald no forthyr gang.[1]

I will clofe thefe fpecimens with an inftance of our author's allegorical invention :

In that flummir cummand him thocht he faw,
Ane agit man faft towart him couth draw,
Sone be the hand he hynt him haiftele,
I am, he faid, in wiage chargit with the.
A fuerd him gaiff oft burly burnift fteill,
Gud fone, he faid, this brand thou fall bruk weill.
Off topas ftone him thocht the plumat was,
Baith hilt and hand all glitterand lik the glas.
Der fone, he faid, we tary her to lang,
Thow fall go fe quhar wrocht is mekill wrang ;
Than he him lad till a montane on hycht,
The warld him thocht he mycht fe with a ficht.

---

[1] p. 82.

He left him thar, syne sone fra him he went,
Tharof Wallace studiit in his entent,
Till se him mar he had still gret desyr,
Tharwith he saw begyne a felloune fyr,
Quhilk braithly brynt on breid throu all the land,
Scotland atour, fra Ross to Sulway-sand.
Than sone till him thar descendyt a qweyne,
Inlumyt, lycht, schynand full brycht and scheyne;
In hyr presens apperyt so mekill lycht,
At all the fyr scho put out off his sycht,
Gaiff him a wand off colour reid and greyne,
With a saffyr sanyt his face and eyne,
Welcum, scho said, I cheiss the as my luff;
Thow art grantyt be the gret God abuff,
Till help pepill that sufferis mekill wrang,
With the as now I may nocht tary lang,
Thou sall return to thi awne oyss agayne,
Thi derrast kyne ar her in mekill payne;
This rycht regioun thow mon redeme it all,
Thi last reward in erd sall be bot small;
Let nocht tharefor, tak redress off this myss,
To thi reward thou sall haiff lestand blyss.
Off hir rycht hand scho betaucht him a bok,
Humylly thus hyr leyff full sone scho tuk,
On to the cloud ascendyt off his sycht.
Wallace brak up the buk in all his myght.
In thre partis the buk weill wrytyn was,
The fyrst wrytyng was gross letteris off bras,
The secound gold, the thrid was silver scheyne.
Wallace merveld quhat this wrytyng suld meyne;
To rede the buk he besyet him so fast,
His spreit agayne to walkand mynd is past,
And wp he raiss, syne sodandly furth went.
This clerk he fand, and tald him his entent
Off this wissoun, as I haiff said befor,
Completly throuch; Quhat nedis wordis mor.
Der sone, he said, my witt unabill is
To runsik sic, for dreid I say off myss;
Yit I sall deyme, thocht my cunnyng be small,
God grant na chargis efftir my wordis fall.
Saynct Androw was gaiff the that suerd in hand,
Off sanctis he is the wowar off Scotland;
That montayne is quhar he the had on hycht,
Knawlage to haiff off wrang that thow mon rycht;
The fyr sall be fell tithingis, or ye part,
Quhilk will be tald in mony syndry art.
I can nocht witt quhat qweyn at it suld be,
Quhethir Fortoun, or our Lady so fre,
Lykly it is, be the brychtnes scho brocht,
Modyr off him that all this warld has wrocht.
The prety wand, I trow, be myn entent,
Assignes rewlle and cruell jugement;
The red colour, quha graithly wndrestud,
Betaknes all to gret battaill and blud;
The greyn, curage, that thow art now amang,
In strowble wer thou sall conteyne full lang;
The saphyr stayne scho blissit the with all,
Is lestand grace, will God, sall to the fall;
The thrynfald buk is bot this brokyn land,
Thou mon rademe be worthines off hand;

The bras lettris betakynnys bot to this,
The gret oppress off wer and mekill myss,
The quhilk thow sall bryng to the rycht agayne,
Bot thou tharfore mon suffer mekil payne ;
The gold takynnis honour and worthinas,
Wictour in armys, that thou sall haiff be grace ;
The silver shawis cleyne lyff and hewynys blyss,
To thi reward that myrth thou sall nocht myss,
Dreid nocht tharfor, be out off all despayr.
Forthir as now heroff I can na mair.

[From Chepman and Myllar's (reputed) edition of 1520 or thereabouts, the episode of John of Lynn, the English reaver, and his discomfiture off the mouth of the Humber, is now taken as a specimen of the oldest printed text of the poem :[1]

With egir will he wald haue bene away
Bad wynd ye saill in all ye haist yai may
Bot fra ye scottis yan micht yai nocht eskey
The schippis sa fair on athir side yai wey
Thai saw na thing yat micht be to yame eis
Craufurd on loft yair saill brynt in ane bleis
Or Johne of lyn schupe for to leif yat stede
Of his best men sexty war brocht to dede
Thair schip by ouris ane burde was mare of hicht
Wallace lap in amang yai revaris wicht
Ane man he straik our schip burd in ye see
On the our loft he slew sone vthir thre
Longaveill enterit and als ye maister blair
Thai gaif na grace to freik yat yai fand yair
Wallace him self with Johne of lyn was met
At his collair ane felloun straik he set
Baith helm and hede fra ye schulderis he draif
Blaiz our ye burd in ye sey kest ye laif
Of his body yan all ye remanand
Enterit and slew ye brigantis yat yai fand
The schip yai tuke grete gold and vthir gere
That yai revaris had gaderit lang in were
Bot maister blair spak na thing of him sell
In deid of armys quhat eventure yat befell
Schir thomas gray was yan preist to wallace
Put in ye buke how yame hapnit yis cace
That blair was in and mony wourthy deid
Of quhilk him self had na plesance to reid
Wallace gart reull ye schip with his avne men
And saillit furth ye richt cours for to ken
In ye sluce havyne quhill yai enterit be
The marchaindis weill he helpit in saufte
Of gold and gere he tuke part yat yai fand
Gaif yame ye schip syne passit to the land
Throw flandris raid vpone ane gudly wise
Enterit in france and socht to parise
The glad tithingis yat to ye king was brocht
Of wallace come it comfortit al yair thocht
Thai trowit be him to get reddres of wrang
The suthroun had in gyane wrocht sa lang
The peris of france war stil at yair parliament
The king command with trew and haill entent

[[1] *Golagrus and Gawane*, &c. 1827. Introd. 25-8.]

> Thai fuld forfe a lordfchip to wallace
> The lordis all yan demyt off yis eace."
> Wallace and his yan fone to harneis ʒeid
> Quhen yai war graithit into yare wourthy weid
> Him felf and blare and ye knycht longaveill.
> Thir thre has tane to keip ye mydfchip weill
> Before was aucht and fex be eft he kend.
> Syne twa he chefit ye top for to defend.
> [And gray he maid] yare fteir man for to be
> [The merchandis yan faw thaim fa manfulle]
> Defend yame felf becaus yai had no weid
> Out of ye how yai tuke fkynnis gude fpeid
> Ay betuix twa ftuffit woll as yai micht beft
> Agane ye ftraik yat yai micht fum part left
> Than Wallace leuch and commendit yame aw
> Of fic harnes before he neuer faw
> Be yat ye barge come on yame woundir faft
> Sevin fcore hir in yat was na thing agaft
> Quhen Johne of lyn faw yame in armour bricht
> He lewch and faid yir haftane wourdis on hicht.
> ʒone glaikit fcottis can ws nocht undirftand
> Fulis yai ar is new cūmyn of ye land.
> He cryit ftrike bot nane anfuer yai maid
> Blair with ane bow fchot faft withoutin baid
> Or yai clippit he fchot bot arowis thre.
> And at ilk fchot he gart ane revar dee
> The brigantis yan yai bikkerit woundir faft
> Amang ye fcottis with fchot and gūmys caft
> And yai agane with fperis hedit weill
> Fele woundis maid throw platis of fyne fteill
> Athir vthir feftnit with clippis kene
> Ane cruell countir yair was at fchipburd fene
> The derfschot draif als thik as haill fchour
> Contenit yair with neir ye fpace of ane hour
> Quhen fchot was gane ye Scottis grete comfort had
> At hand ftrakis yai war ficker and fad
> The marchaindis als with fir thing as yai mycht
> Previt full weill in defence of yair richt
> Wallace and his at neir ftrakis quhen yai fe
> With fcharp fwerdis yai gart fele brigantes dee
> Thai in ye top fa wychtly wrocht with hand
> In the fouth top yair micht na revar ftand
> All ye mydfchip of revaris was maid waift
> That to gif our in poynt yai war almaift
> Than Johne of lyn was richt gretly agaft
> He faw his folk about him failʒe faft.

John Major, the Scotifh hiftorian, who was born about the year 1470, remembered Blind Harry to have been living, and to have publifhed a poem on the achievements of Sir William Wallace, when he was a boy. He adds that he cannot vouch for the credibility of thofe tales which the bards were accuftomed to fing for hire in the caftles of the nobility. I will give his own words.[1] That,

---

[1] "Integrum librum Gulielmi Wallacei Henricus, a nativitate luminibus captus, meæ infantiæ tempore cudit : et quæ vulgo dicebantur carmine vulgari, in quo peritus erat, confcripfit. Ego autem talibus fcriptis folum in parte fidem impertior ; quippe qui hiftoriarum recitatione coram principibus victum et veftitum, quo dignus erat, nactus eft."—*Hift. Magn. Britan.* L. iv. c. xv. f. 74, a, edit. 1521. Compare Holinfh. *Scot.* ii. p. 414 ; Mack. tom. i. 423 ; Dempft. lib. viii. p. 349.

in this poem, Blind Harry has intermixed much fable with true history, will appear from some proofs collected by Sir David Dalrymple in his judicious and accurate annals of Scotland.[1]]

Robert Henryson, the contemporary of Dunbar, was, according to the received account, a member of the family of Henderson or Henryson of Fordell, Co. Fife. Mr. Laing supposes that he may have been born about 1425; at any rate, he received a liberal education; and there seems to be little reason to doubt that he is the same person who is described as being admitted a member of the University of Glasgow on the 10th September, 1462. He was at that time by no means a young man, if the identification should be correct, for he is mentioned as the "Venerable Master Robert Henrysone, Licenciate in Arts, and Bachelor in Decrees." The reader who desires to be possessed of such few particulars of the poet's history as it has been possible with the utmost diligence to collect together, must be referred to Mr. Laing's Introduction. Henryson is generally known to have been a schoolmaster at Dunfermling, and this was his occupation, probably, during all the latter part of his life. Mr. Laing observes: "the fact seems to be, that the Grammar School of Dunfermline was within the precincts of the Abbey, and under the jurisdiction of the Abbots." Henryson is said to have lived to be very old, and to have died of a diarrhœa or flux. His editor places the time of his decease towards the close of the fifteenth century.

Several excellent judges have spoken highly of Henryson's powers of description. He was the earliest of our pastoral writers, and also the first who put into a British dress the series of Fables, which pass under the name of Æsop. At what period of his career this writer produced his *Morall Fabillis of Esope the Phrygian* is as uncertain as the date of the composition of his *Robene and Makyne* and *Testament of Cresseid*. The Fables have come down to us only in a comparatively modern impression, made at Edinburgh in 1569. That nothing from his pen was committed to the press in his lifetime, almost amounts to a certainty; but an edition of his *Orpheus and Euridice* is still extant, printed at Edinburgh in 1508, 4to, when the poet had perhaps not been dead many years. With the exception of one or two of his minor pieces, which were also included by Walter Chepman and Andrew Myllar in their popular series of publications during the reign of James IV., this is the only tribute which his countrymen paid to his memory till very long afterwards. Like Dunbar, he seems to have fallen into utter neglect. But we may be prejudging here, for editions upon editions of old Scotish authors have doubtless completely disappeared, and Henryson's poems may have been republished more frequently and continually than in our present state of information we can positively affirm to have been the case. There is unfortunately scarcely

---

[1] See p. 245, edit. 1776. [For an account of all the known early printed editions of the *Wallace*, see *Handb. of E. E. Lit.* art. *Wallace*.]

space for an extended series of extracts from Henryson's Poems and Fables, highly deserving as they are of wider notice and appreciation. The Editor must content himself with giving the two opening stanzas of *Robene and Makyne*:

> Robene sat on gud grene hill,
>   Kepand a flok of fe:
> Mirry Makyne said him till,
>   " Robene, thow rew on me;
> I haif thee luvit lowd and still,
>   Thir yeiris two or thre;
> My dule in dern bot gif thow dill,
>   Doutless but dreid I de."
>
> Robene answerit, " Be the Rude,
>   Na thing of lufe I knaw,
> Bot keipis my scheip undir yone wude,
>   Lo! quhair thay raik on raw:
> Quhat hes marrit thee in thy mude,
>   Makyne, to me thow schaw?
> Or quhat is lufe, or to be lude,
>   Fane wald I leir that law."

This admirable production is probably not less than two hundred and fifty years older than Allan Ramsay's *Gentle Shepherd*. It appears to be considered, and the Editor is inclined to concur in the opinion, that the author's *Orpheus and Euridice* was a youthful production; it wants the grace and polish which are found in those pieces which may be presumed to have come from his pen in his maturer years. But for the time when it was (conjecturally) composed, it is a work remarkable for the richness and beauty of its descriptions.

His best known work, however, is his sequel to Chaucer's *Troylus and Cresseide*, under the title of *The Testament of Cresseide*. All the early MSS. (if there were any except Asloane's) and printed copies have perished; and the 4to of 1593 in the British Museum is the most ancient and authentic text which remains. *The Testament of Cresseid* is correctly (the Editor thinks) regarded as one of Henryson's latest performances, and, on the whole, it is certainly the most finished and masterly of his poems. Henryson's ballads have also considerable merit. His genius was both versatile and opulent.

A few words must be said here of ALEXANDER SCOT, whom Pinkerton termed " the Anacreon of old Scotish poetry." Scot follows Dunbar at an interval of about a quarter of a century in the strict order of time; but the distance between them is really greater, when it is considered that Dunbar had attained some celebrity in 1490, while Scot does not appear to have written any of those poems which are extant from his pen much before the middle of the sixteenth century. Mr. Laing, who collected these productions in 1821, says: " Alexander Scot has uniformly been reckoned the most eminent of the early minor Scotish poets, and we cannot assume for him a higher character. His poems, with the few exceptions at the beginning [versions of the Psalms,] are all of the amatory kind, and are chiefly to be viewed as the light and sportive effusions of an elegant and ingenious mind." Scot flourished at a middle period in the hiftory of Scotish poetry, when the old allegorical and picturefque fchool of writers had died out, and before Scotish verfification arrived at a higher perfection and refinement in the works of the later Makars.

A verfion of Hector Boece was executed about 1530 by William Stewart, of whofe identity there feems to be fome doubt, fince at the time when he flourifhed (early part of the fifteenth century) there were two perfons of the fame name, both of whom were attached to the court of James V. of Scotland. The late Mr. Turnbull, who edited this Scotifh tranflation of Boece for the firft time in 1858, fuppofed that the author was the fame Stewart of whom Lyndfay, in his *Complaynt of the Papingo* [*circâ* 1530], fays that he

Full ornate warkis daylie dois compyle.

But the affignation is, after all, a little uncertain.

But although Stewart merely purported to render Boece out of Latin into the vernacular Scotifh, he in fact did more, for in fome cafes he introduces notices of curious incidents, overlooked by his original, from fources with which Boece does not appear to have been converfant. As a fpecimen of Stewart's ftyle and language, I fhall avail myfelf of one of Mr. Turnbull's extracts, as it is an account of a matter which is defcribed imperfectly by Boece, and for which Stewart is fuppofed to have been indebted to Fordun:

> The Inglifmen, as my author did tell,
> Had Coupar caftell in keiping that da,
> In falt of victuall on the nycht awa,
> Richt quyetlie out of the houfs tha ftall,
> That famen nycht on to one ferry all,
> Quhilk Donybriffis callit than that wes,
> In that purpois attonir Forth than to pas.
> To that fame ferry fyne quhen tha come till,
> The ferriar, in magir of his will,
> Out of his bed at midnycht gart him ryis.
> The ferrear that fubtill wes and wyifs,
> Quhen that he faw that na better micht be,
> With thame richt fone he paffit to the fe.
> In mid water as thame he afkit fraucht,
> Said ane, "Ʒow fall haif all that euir we aucht;"
> And with his fift vpoun the face him fmet.
> And he agane, "Gramercy, gentill met!
> Haif it be fo, the laif fall all be fre."
> Ʒit nevirtheles he thocht rycht fone to haif
> Ane trew mendis for him and all the laif.

It would be improper to overlook in this place Alexander Montgomery, whom Dr. Irving characterizes, juftly enough, as "one of the moft popular of the early Scotifh poets." The fame writer obferves: "Some of thofe poets undoubtedly poffeffed higher powers of invention; and the rank of Sir David Lyndfay, together with the acknowledged efficacy of his fatires on the tottering church, rendered him more confpicuous among his contemporaries; but few Scotifh poems of equal antiquity feem to have obtained fo permanent a hold of public attention as the *Cherrie and the Slae*."

As several of Montgomery's pieces occur in the Bannatyne MS., written in 1568, he was probably not born later than 1540, and it is supposed by Mr. Laing that he was still living in 1605. He appears to have been at one time of his life in the service of the regent Morton, and there is also little doubt that he held some military preferment, although he is not described as Captain Montgomery in any but the posthumous impressions of his poems. Dr. Irving and Mr. Laing have collected his remains and all the notices of his life which were discoverable; but the latter partake of the scantiness and obscurity incidental to poetical biography. As a writer midway between Lyndsay and Drummond, exhibiting the Scotish language in its state of slow transition, Montgomery clearly merits some degree of attention, and his works unquestionably possess unusual merit. Some of his sonnets are as smooth and polished as the poet of Hawthornden's, and his pastoral is a production which, in the editor's opinion, places him at least on a level with Drummond as a man of genius. *The Flyting betwixt Montgomery and [Sir Patrick Hume of] Polwart* is a strange, grotesque performance, reminding us of Dunbar's similar contest with Walter Kennedy, and Skelton's poems against Garnesche. If Montgomery had produced nothing but this *Flyting* and his select version of the Psalms, entitled, *The Mindes Melodie*, he would have only been remembered as a person whose versatility of talent enabled him to leave to posterity specimens of the broadest satire and of the devoutest common-place. But, as it is, his *Cherrie and the Slae* and his *Sonnets* justly claim for him a high rank among the Scotish writers of the latter half of the sixteenth century and of the beginning of the seventeenth. His poems have not enjoyed quite so extensive a popularity as those of Lyndsay which, it ought to be recollected, have a strong *religious* interest, apart from any other fascination; but the *Cherry and the Slae* has never lost its hold on the public memory and affection, while nothing but modern zeal has restored to notice Henryson's *Robene and Makyne* and the sublime creations of Dunbar.]

I cannot return to the English poets without a hint, that a well-executed history of the Scotish poetry from the thirteenth century would be a valuable accession to the general literary history of Britain.[1] The subject is pregnant with much curious and instructive information, is highly deserving of a minute and regular research, has never yet been uniformly examined in its full extent, and the materials are both accessible and ample. Even the bare lives of the vernacular poets of Scotland have never yet been written with tolerable care, and at present are only known from the meagre outlines of Dempster and Mackenzie. The Scots appear to have had an early propensity to theatrical representations; and it is probable that, in the prosecution of such a design, among several other interesting and unexpected discoveries, many anecdotes, conducing to illustrate the rise and progress of our ancient drama, might be drawn from obscurity.

---

[1] [This has now, to a certain extent, been accomplished by the publication of the *History of Scotish Poetry*, by the late Dr. Irving, edited by Dr. Carlyle, 1861, 8vo.]

SECTION XXXII.

MOST of the poems of John Skelton were written in the reign of Henry VIII. But as he was laureated at Oxford [before] the year [1490],[1] I consider him as belonging to the fifteenth century.

Skelton, having studied in both our universities,[2] [and at Louvaine,[3] took holy orders in 1498,[4] and] was promoted to the rectory of Diss in Norfolk.[5] But for his buffooneries in the pulpit, and his satirical ballads against the Mendicants, he was

---

[1] [" For a notice of Skelton's laureation at Oxford, the Rev. Dr. Bliss obligingly searched the archives of that University, but without success. 'No records,' he informs me, 'remain between 1463 and 1498, that will give a correct list of degrees.'"—*Dyce.* But the question is, whether, being a mere honorary academical distinction, Skelton's inauguration would have been registered in the *Books of Degrees* at all.]

[2] [He was admitted *ad eundem* at Cambridge in 1493.—*Dyce.*]

[3] [Dyce's *Skelton*, i. xv.]

[4] [*Ibid.* xx.]

[5] [Probably as early as 1504. See Dyce's *Skelton*, i. xxvi.] At the end of his *Trentale for old John Clarke*, there is this colophon. " Auctore Skelton rectore de Dis, Finis, &c. Apud Trumpinton, script. per Curatum ejusdem quinto die Jan. A.D. 1507." He was ordained both deacon and priest in the year 1498. On the title of the monastery de Graciis near the tower of London. Registr. Savage. Episc. Lond. There is a poem by Skelton on the death of King Edward IV., who died A.D. 1483. This is taken into the *Mirrour for Magistrates*. [But perhaps Skelton's earliest production was his lost poem on the *Creation of Prince Arthur* in 1489. See Dyce's *Skelton*, i. xxi. There is an imperfect copy of the *Garlande of Lawrell* in Cotton. MS. Vit. E x. 200. A second, supplying some matter wanting in the printed copies, was in a MS. volume formerly in the library at Eshton Hall.] Caxton, in his [prologue] to Virgil's *Eneidos*, says, [" For he hath late translated the epystlys of Tulle and the boke of dyodorus syculus, and dyuerse other werkes owte of latyn in to englyshe." The former is not known, but of the latter there is an unique but imperfect MS. in the library of C.C.C. Cambridge. (See a description of it communicated by Mr. Thomas Wright to Dyce's *Skelton*, i. cii.) In the Preface to the prose *Eneid*, Caxton also remarks, "But I pray mayster John Skelton, late created poete laureate in the vnyuersite of oxenforde, to ouersee and correcte this sayd booke:—for hym I knowe for suffycyent to expowne and englyshe euery dyffyculte that is therin." This, however, does not seem to have flattered him into the service of becoming Caxton's critical overseer, as the book had no re-impression.—*Park.* But Caxton does not seem to indicate an intention of reprinting the work, merely a wish that, if Skelton discovered any errors, he should correct them.] Bale mentions his *Invectiva* on William Lily the grammarian. I know nothing more of this, than that it was answered by Lily in *Apologia ad Joh. Scheltonum* [at present unknown. See Dyce's *Skelton*, i. xxxvii.; but Wood has preserved the beginning :] " Siccine vipereo pergis me," &c. Skelton's *Elinour Rummyng* or *Rumpkin* [occurs in all the editions of the little volume called *Certaine Bokes*, &c.] The last of the old editions is in 1624, 4to. In the title page is the picture of our genial hostess, an old woman, holding a pot of ale [in each hand] with this inscription:

" When Skelton wore the laurell Crowne
My Ale put all the Ale wiues downe."

severely censured, and perhaps suspended by Nykke his diocesan, a rigid bishop of Norwich, from exercising the duties of the sacerdotal function. Wood says, he was also punished by the bishop for "having been guilty *of certain crimes*, as most poets are."[1] But these persecutions only served to quicken his ludicrous disposition, and to exasperate the acrimony of his satire. As his sermons could be no longer a vehicle for his abuse, he vented his ridicule in rhyming libels. At length, daring to attack the dignity of Cardinal Wolsey, he was closely pursued by the officers of that powerful minister; and, taking shelter in the sanctuary of Westminster Abbey, was kindly entertained and protected by Abbot Islip,[2] to the day of his death. He died, and was buried in the neighbouring church of Saint Margaret, in 1529.

Skelton was patronised by Henry Algernon Percy, the fifth earl of Northumberland, who deserves particular notice here; as he loved literature at a time when many of the nobility of England could hardly read or write their names, and was the general patron of such genius as his age produced. He encouraged Skelton, almost the only professed poet of the reign of Henry VII., to write an elegy on the death of his father, which is yet extant. But still stronger proofs of his literary turn, especially of his singular passion for poetry, may be collected from a very splendid MS., which formerly belonged to this very distinguished peer, and is at present preserved in the British Museum.[3] It contains a large collection of English poems, elegantly engrossed on vellum, and superbly illuminated, which had been thus sumptuously transcribed for his use. The pieces are chiefly those of Lydgate, after which follow the aforesaid Elegy of Skelton and some smaller compositions. Among the latter are a metrical history of the family of Percy, presented to him by one of his own chaplains, and a prolix series of poetical inscriptions, which he caused to be written on the walls and ceilings of the principal apartments of his castles of Lekinfield and Wressil.[4] Three of the apartments in the latter, now destroyed, were adorned with poetical inscriptions. These are called, in the MS. above mentioned, *Proverbes in the Lodgings in Wressill.*[5]

1. *The proverbes in the sydis of the innere chaumbre . . . . at Wressill.* This is a poem of twenty-four stanzas, each containing seven lines: beginning thus,

> When it is tyme of coste and greate expens,
> Beware of waste and spende be measure:

---

[1] [See Dyce's *Skelton*, i. xxviii. "The following entry occurs among the Acts and Orders of the Court of Requests: 'An. xvii. Hen. VII. (1501) 10 Julij, apud Westminster *Jo. Skelton* commissus carceribus janitoris domini regis.'"—*Park*.]

[2] His Latin epitaph or elegy on the death of Henry VII. is addressed to Islip, A.D. 1512.

[3] MSS. Reg. 18 D. [ii.]

[4] See [Dyce's *Skelton*, i. 178.] MSS. C.C.C. Cant. 168.

[5] [They are partly printed in the second edition of the *Antiquarian Repertory*, 1807, iv. 411-21.]

> Who that outrageyusly makithe his dispens,
> Causythe his goodis not longe to endure, &c.

2. *The counsell of Aristotill, which he gayse to Alexander, kinge of Massydony; which are writyn in the Syde of the Utter Chamber above of the house in the Gardynge at Wresylls.* This is in thirty-eight lines; beginning thus,

> Punyshe moderatly and discretly correcte,
> As well to mercye as to justice havynge a respecte, &c.

3. *The proverbis in the syde of the Utter Chamber above of the hous in the gardying at Wresyll.* A poem of thirty stanzas, chiefly of four lines, viz.

> Remorde thyne ey inwardly,
> Fyx not thy mynde on Fortune, that delythe dyversly, &c.

The following apartments in Lekinfield had poetical inscriptions: as mentioned in the said MS. *Proverbis in the Lodgings at Lekingfield.*

1. " The proverbis of the garett over the Bayne at Lekyngfelde." This is a dialogue in 32 stanzas, of four lines, between *the Parte Sensatyve* and *the Part Intellectyve*; containing a poetical comparison between sensual and intellectual pleasures.

2. "The proverbis in the garet at the new lodge in the parke of Lekingfelde." This is a poem of 32 stanzas, of four lines, being "a discant on Harmony, as also on the manner of Singing, and playing on most of the instruments then used: *i. e.* the Harps, Claricordes, Lute, Virgynall, Clarisymballis, Clarion, Shawme, Orgayne, Recorder." The following stanza relates to the Shawme, and shews it to have been used for the Bass, as the Recorder was for the Meane or Tenor:

> A Shawme makithe a sweete sounde for he tunithe Basse,
> It mountithe not to hy, but kepithe rule and space.
> Yet yf it be blowne with a too vehement wynde,
> It makithe it to misgoverne out of his kynde.

3. "The proverbis in the rooffe of the hyest chawmbre in the gardinge at Lekingfelde." If we suppose this to be the room mentioned by Leland, where the Genealogy was kept, the following jingling reflections on the family motto (in thirty distichs) will not appear quite so misplaced :

> *Esperaunce en Dyeu*,
> Trust in hym he is most trewe.
> *En Dieu esperance*,
> In hym put thyne affiance.
> *Esperaunce* in the worlde ? nay ;
> The worlde varieth every day.
> *Esperaunce* in riches ? nay, not so,
> Riches slidithe and sone will go.
> *Esperaunce* in exaltacion of honoure ?
> Nay, it widderithe . . . lyke a floure.
> *Esperaunce* in bloode and highe lynage ?
> At moste nede, bot esy avauntage.

The concluding diſtich is:

> *Eſperaunce en Dieu*, in hym is all;
> Be thou contente and thou art above Fortunes fall.

4. "The proverbis in the rouſe of my Lorde Percy cloſett at Lekyngfelde." A poetical dialogue, containing inſtructions for youth, in 142 lines.

5. "The proverbis in the rouſe of my Lordis library at Lekyngefelde." Twenty-three ſtanzas of four lines, from which I take the following ſpecimen:

> To every tale geve thou no credens.
> Prove the cauſe, or thou give ſentens.
> Agayn the right make no dyffens,
> So haſt thou a clene conſciens.

6. "The counſell of Ariſtotell, whiche he gave to Alexander kinge of Macedony; in the ſyde of the garet of the gardynge in Lekynfelde." This, [which was alſo at Wreſyll,] conſiſts of nine ſtanzas, of eight lines: Take the laſt [four lines from the laſt] ſtanza but one [as a further ſpecimen]:

> If ye be moved with anger or haſtynes,
> Pauſe in youre mynde and your yre repreſs:
> Defer vengeance unto your anger aſſwagede be;
> So ſhall ye mynyſter juſtice, and do dewe equyte.

This caſtle is alſo demoliſhed. One of the ornaments of the apartments of the old caſtles in France, was to write the walls all over with amorous Sonnets.

The Earl's cultivation of the arts of external elegance appears, from the ſtately ſepulchral monuments which he erected in the minſter or collegiate church of Beverley in Yorkſhire, to the memory of his father and mother; which are executed in the richeſt ſtyle of the florid Gothic architecture, and remain to this day the conſpicuous and ſtriking evidences of his taſte and magnificence. In the year 1520, he founded an annual ſtipend of ten marcs for three years for a preceptor or profeſſor, to teach grammar and philoſophy in the monaſtery of Alnwick, contiguous to another of his magnificent caſtles.[1] A further inſtance of his attention to letters and ſtudious employments occurs in his *Houſehold-book*, dated 1512, yet remaining; in which the Libraries of this earl and of his lady are ſpecified:[2] and

---

[1] From the Receiver's accompts of the Earl's Eſtates in Com. Northumb. A. xv. Henr. VIII. A.D. 1527. "Soluciones denariorum per Warrantum Domini. Et in denariis per dominum receptorem doctori Makerell Abbati monaſterii de Alnewyk ſolutis, de exitibus hujus anni, pro ſolucione vadii unius pedagogi, ſive Magiſtri, exiſtentis infra Abbathiam predictam, et docentis ac legentis Grammaticam et Philoſophiam canonicis et fratribus monaſterii predicti, ad x marcas per annum pro termino iij annorum, virtute unius warranti, cujus data eſt apud Wreſſill xx^{mo} die Septembris anno xij Regis predicti, ſigno manuali ipſius Comitis ſignati, et penes ipſum Abbatem remanentis, ultra vj lib. xiij s. iv d. ſibi allocatas anno xiij Henr. viij^{vi}, et vj lib. xiij s. iiij d. ſimiliter ſibi allocatas in anno xiiij ejuſdem Regis ut per ii acquietancias inde confectas, et penes Auditorem remanentes." From *Evidences of the Percy family*, at Sion-houſe. C. iii. Num. 5, 6. Communicated by Dr. Percy.

[2] Pag. 44 [edit. 1770. The work was reprinted in 1827.]

in the same curious monument of ancient manners it is ordered, that one of his chaplains should be a Maker of Interludes.[1] With so much boldness did this liberal nobleman abandon the example of his brother peers, whose principal occupations were hawking and tilting, and who despised learning as an ignoble and petty accomplishment, fit only for the purposes of laborious and indigent ecclesiastics. Nor was he totally given up to the pursuits of leisure and peace: he was, in the year 1497, one of the leaders who commanded at the battle of Blackheath against Lord Audley and his partisans; and he was often engaged, from his early years, in other public services of trust and honour. But Skelton hardly deserved such a patronage.

It is in vain to apologise for the coarseness, obscenity, and scurrility of Skelton, by saying that his poetry is tinctured with the manners of his age.[2] Skelton would have been a writer without decorum at any period. The manners of Chaucer's age were undoubtedly more rough and unpolished than those of the reign of Henry VII. Yet Chaucer, a poet abounding in humour, and often employed in describing the vices and follies of the world, writes with a degree of delicacy, when compared with Skelton. That Skelton's manner is gross and illiberal, was the opinion of his cotemporaries; at least of those critics who lived but a few years afterwards, and while his poems yet continued in vogue. Puttenham, the author of the *Arte of English Poesie*, published in 1589, [but written long before,] speaking of the species of short metre used in the minstrel-romances, for the convenience of being sung to the harp at feasts, and in Carols and Rounds, "and such light or lascivious Poemes, which are commonly more commodiously vttered by these buffons or vices in playes then by any other person," and in which the sudden return of the rhyme fatigues the ear, immediately subjoins: "Such were the rimes of Skelton . . . . being in deede but a rude rayling rimer,

---

[1] Pag. 378. I am indebted to the usual kindness of Dr. Percy for all the notices relating to this earl. See his Preface to the *Household Book*, pag. xxi. *seq.* [edit. 1770.]

[2] ["Warton has undervalued him (Skelton); which is the more remarkable, because Warton was a generous as well as a competent critic. He seems to have been disgusted with buffooneries which, like those of Rabelais, were thrown out as a tub for the whale; for unless Skelton had written thus for the coarsest palates, he could not have poured forth his bitter and undaunted satire in such perilous times." *Southey*, 1831 (quoted by Dyce). "That Warton undervalued Skelton is very apparent; but Southey's *for* is not equally so. But our historian was tainted by Pope's antipathy to him. A reprint of Marshe's edition of Skelton's *Workes* having appeared in 1736, Pope took occasion, during the next year, to mention them in the following terms, casting a blight on our poet's reputation, from which it has hardly yet recovered:

'Chaucer's worst ribaldry is learn'd by rote,
And *beastly* Skelton Heads of Houses quote.'"
—*Dyce*, 1843.

Warton enumerated among Skelton's lost works, a better account of which is to be found in Dyce's edition, the *Peregrination of Mannes Lyfe*, which he thought it possible Skelton might have taken from a Latin metrical tract printed by Pynson in 1508. But Skelton's original was in *prose*.]

& all his doings ridiculous, he vſed both ſhort diſtaunces and ſhort meaſures, pleaſing onely the popular eare."[1] Meres, in his *Palladis Tamia*, or *Wit's Treaſury*, 1598, alſo obſerves: " as *Sotades Maronites* yᵉ Iambicke Poet gaue himſelfe wholy to write impure and laſciuious things: ſo *Skeltō* (I know not for what great worthines ſurnamed the Poet Laureat) applied his wit to ſcurrilities and ridiculous matters, ſuch amōg the Greeks were called *Pantomimi*, with vs Buffons."[2]

Skelton's characteriſtic vein of humour is capricious and groteſque. If his whimſical extravagances ever move our laughter, at the ſame time they ſhock our ſenſibility. His feſtive levities are not only vulgar and indelicate, but frequently want truth and propriety. His ſubjects are often as ridiculous as his metre: but he ſometimes debaſes his matter by his verſification. On the whole, his genius ſeems better ſuited to low burleſque, than to liberal and manly ſatire. It is ſuppoſed by Caxton, that he improved our language;[3] but he ſometimes affects obſcurity, and ſometimes adopts the moſt familiar phraſeology of the common people.

---

[1] Lib. ii. ch. ix. p. 69, [edit. 1811.]

[2] [This quotation is not accurately given in the former editions of Warton. *Palladis Tamia* purports to be a ſequel to Ling's *Politeuphuia*, 1597, 8vo. Biſhop Hall characterized both the temper and metre of this lampooner with forcible brevity, when he ſpoke of "*angry* Skelton's breathleſſe rhymes." *Virgidemiarum*, lib. iv.— Park. I reckon the interval of time when Skelton began to write, and when Puttenham publiſhed, to be infinite as to the refinement of manners. Yet even in this laſt period, and later, the commentators of Shakſpeare are glad to ſhelter his ribaldry and puns under the manners of his age.—*Aſhby*.]

[3] [Caxton ſpeaks of Skelton's tranſlations from the Greek and Latin, as not rendered in rude and old language, but in poliſhed and ornate terms craftily. He adds, "And alſo he hath redde the ix. muſes, and underſtande theyr muſicalle ſcyences, and to whom of theym eche ſcyence is appropred. I ſuppoſe he hath dronken of Elycons well." *Prologue to Æneid*. Vide *ſupr.—Park*. That Churchyard indulged the ſame ſtrange notion appears from the following curious encomium, [prefixed to Skelton's *Poems* in 1568,] in which he tells us that the converſation of Skelton reſembled the taunting perſonality of his writings:

" diuers men of late
Hath helpt our Engliſhe toung,
That firſt was baes and brute:
Ohe! ſhall I leaue out Skeltons name
The bloſſome of my frute,
The tree wheron indeed
My branchis all might groe:
Nay, Skelton wore the lawrel wreath,
And paſt in ſchoels, ye knoe;
A poet for his arte,
Whoes iudgment ſuer was hie,
And had great practies of the pen,
His works they will not lie;
His termes to taunts did lean,
His talke was as he wraet,
Full quick of witte, right ſharp of words,
And ſkillful of the ſtaet.
Of reaſon riep and good,
And to the haetfull mynd,
That did diſdain his doings ſtill,
A ſkornar of his kynd.

He thus describes (in the *Boke of Colin Cloute*[1]) the pompous houses of the clergy:

> Buyldyng royally
> Their mancyons curyously
> With turrettes and with toures,
> With halles and with boures,
> Stretchynge to the starres;
> With glasse wyndowes and barres:
> Hangynge aboute the walles
> Clothes of golde and palles;
> Arras of ryche arraye,
> Freshe as flours in May:
> Wyth dame Dyana naked;
> Howe lusty Venus quaked,
> And howe Cupyde shaked
> His darte, and bent his bowe,
> For to shote a crowe
> At her tyrly tyrlowe:
> And howe Parys of Troye
> Daunced a *lege de moy*,
> Made lusty sporte and ioy
> With dame Helyn the quene:
> With suche storyes bydene,[2]
> Their chambres well besene;
> With triumphes of Cesar,
> And of Pompeyus war,
> Of renowne and of fame
> By them to get a name:
> Nowe[3] all the worlde stares
> How they ryde in goodly chares,
> Conueyed by olyphantes
> With lauryat garlantes;
> And by vnycornes
> With their femely hornes;
> Vpon these beestes rydynge
> Naked boyes strydynge,
> With wanton wenches winkynge
> Nowe truly, to my thynkynge,
> That is a speculacyon
> And a mete meditacyon
> For prelates of estate
> Their courage to abate;
> From worldly wantonnesse,
> Their chambres thus to dresse
> With suche parfyetnesse
> And all suche holynesse,
> How be it they let downe fall
> Their churches cathedrall.[4]

These lines are in the best manner of his petty measure, which is

> Most pleasant euery way,
> As poets ought to be,
> And seldom out of princis grace,
> And great with eche degre."]

[1] [This, and all the other, extracts from Skelton have now been collated with ed. Dyce, 1843.]
[2] [*By dene*, seems to signify, besides, moreover.—*Jamieson*.]
[3] This is still a description of tapestry.
[4] [Skelton's Works, 1843, i. 347-9.]

made still more disgusting by the repetition of the rhymes. We should observe, that the satire is here pointed at the subject of these tapestries. The graver ecclesiastics, who did not follow the levities of the world, were contented with religious subjects, or such as were merely historical. Rous of Warwick, who wrote about 1460, relates that he saw in the Abbot's hall, at St. Alban's Abbey, a suite of arras, containing a long train of incidents belonging to a most romantic and pathetic story in the life of the Saxon king Offa, which that historian recites at large.[1]

Hugh de Foliot, a canon regular of Picardy, so early as the year 1140, censures the magnificent houses of the bishops, with the sumptuous paintings or tapestry of their chambers, chiefly on the Trojan story.[2] Among the MSS. *Epistles* of Gilbert de Stone, a canon of Wells, who flourished about 1360, there is a curious passage concerning the spirit for fox-hunting which anciently prevailed among our bishops. Reginald Bryan, bishop of Worcester, in 1352, thus writes to the Bishop of St. David's: "Reverende in Christo pater et domine, premissa recommendatione debita tanto patri. Illos optimos canes venaticos, duodecim ad minus, quibus non vidimus meliores, quos nuper, scitis, vestra reverenda Paternitas repromisit, quotidie expectamus. Languet namque cor nostrum, donec realiter ad manus nostras venerit repromissum." He then owns his eagerness of expectation on this occasion to be sinful; but observes, that it is the fatal consequence of that deplorable frailty which we all inherit from our mother Eve. He adds that the foxes in his manor of Alnechurch and elsewhere had killed most of his rabbits, many of his capons, and had destroyed six of his swans in one night.[3] He then describes the very exquisite pleasure he shall receive, in hearing his woods echo with the cry of the hounds and the music of the horns; and in seeing the trophies of the chace affixed to the walls of his palace.[4]

From a want of the notions of common propriety and decorum, it is amazing to see the strange absurdities committed by the clergy of the middle ages, in adopting the laical character. Du Cange says, that the deans of many cathedrals in France entered on the dignities habited in a surplice, girt with a sword, in boots and gilt spurs, and a hawk on the fist.[5] Carpentier adds, that the treasurers

---

[1] J. Ross. Warwic. *Hist. Reg. Angl.* edit. Hearne, p. 64.

[2] "Episcopi domos non impares ecclesiis magnitudine construunt. Pictos delectantur habere thalamos: vestiuntur ibi imagines pretiosis colorum indumentis.—Trojanorum gestis paries, purpura atque auro vestitur.—Græcorum exercitui dantur arma. Hectori clypeus datur auro splendens," &c. Bibl. Bodl. MSS. James, ii. p. 203. But I believe the tract is published in the works of a cotemporary writer, Hugo de Sancto-Victore.

[3] "Veniant ergo, Pater Reverende, illæ sex Caniculorum copulæ, et non tardent," &c.

[4] MSS. Bibl. Bodl. Super. D. 1. art. 123; MSS. Cotton. Vitell. E. x. 17. [See MSS. James, xix. p. 139.]

[5] *Latin. Gloss.* v. Decanus, tom. i. p. 1326. See also *ibid.* p. 79, and tom. ii. p. 179, *seq.*

of some churches, particularly that of Nivernois, claimed the privilege of assisting at mass, on whatever festival they pleased, without the canonical vestments, and carrying a hawk; and the Lord of Sassay held some of his lands, by placing a hawk on the high altar of the church of Evreux, while his parish priest celebrated the service, booted and spurred, to the beat of drum, instead of the organ.[1] Although their ideas of the dignity of the church were so high, yet we find them sometimes conferring the rank and title of secular nobility even on the Saints. St. James was actually created a baron at Paris.[2] Thus Froissart, "Or eurent ils affection et devotion d'aller en pelerinage au Baron Saint Jaques." And in a fabliau:[3]

> Dame, dist il, et je me veu,
> A dieu, et au Baron Saint Leu,
> Et s'irai au Baron Saint Jaques.

Among the many contradictions of this kind, which entered into the system of these ages, the institution of the Knights Templars is not the least extraordinary. It was an establishment of armed monks, who made a vow of living at the same time both as anchorets and soldiers.

In the poem, *Why come ye not to Court*, Skelton thus satirises Cardinal Wolsey, not without some tincture of humour:

> He is set so hye
> In his ierarchy[4]
> Of frantyck frenesy,
> And folysshe fantasy,
> That in the Chambre of Starres[5]
> Al maters ther be he marres,
> Clappyng his rod on the borde,
> No man dare speke a worde;
> For he hathe al the sayenge
> Without any renayenge.
> He rolleth in his recordes:
> He sayth, "How saye ye, my lordes?
> Is nat my reason good?
> Good euyn, good Robyn Hood!
> Some say yes, and some
> Syt styll as they were dom,
> Thus thwartyng ouer thom,
> He ruleth all the roste
> With braggynge and with bost;
> Borne vp on euery syde
> With pompe and with pryde,
> With, trompe up, alleluya,[6]
> For dame Philargerya,[7]
> Hath so his hart in hold, &c.—
> Adew, Philosophia!
> Adew, Theologia!
> Welcome dame Simonia;[8]

---

[1] *Suppl.* tom. i. p. 32.   [2] Tom. iii. c. 30.
[3] Tom. ii. p. 182, cited by Carpentier, *ubi supr.* p. 469.
[4] hierarchy.   [5] the star-chamber.
[6] The pomp in which he celebrates divine service.
[7] love of money.   [8] simony.

> With dame Caftrimergia ;[1]
> To drynke and for to eate
> Swete ypocras[2] and fwete meate.
> To kepe his flefshe chaft,
> In Lent, for repaft
> He eateth capons ftewed,
> Fefaunt and partriche mewed,—
> Hennes, checkynges, and pygges
> He foynes, and he prygges,
> Spareth neyther mayde ne wyfe,
> This is a poftels lyfe!²

The poem called the *Bouge of Court* [*Bouche de la Cour*], or the *Rewards of a Court*, is in the manner of a pageant, confifting of feven perfonifications. Here our author, in adopting the more grave and ftately movement of the feven-lined ftanza,[4] has fhown himfelf

---

[1] Or gulæ concupifcentia, gluttony. From the Greek, Γαςριμαργια, Ingluvies, helluatio. Not an uncommon word in the monkifh latinity. Du Cange cites an old Litany of the tenth century, "A Spiritu Caftrimargiæ .... Libera nos, domine!" *Lat. Glofs.* [edit. Henfchel, in v.] Carpentier adds, among other examples, from the ftatutes of the Ciftercian order, 1375, "Item, cum propter deteftabile Caftrimargiæ vitium in labyrinthum vitiorum defcendatur," &c. *Suppl.* tom. i. p. 862, [or edit. *ut fupr. ibid.*]

[2] I have before fpoken of Hypocras, or fpiced wine. I add here that the fpice, for this mixture, was ferved, often feparately, in what they called a fpice-plate. So Froiffart, defcribing a dinner in the caftle of Toulouse, at which the King of France was prefent. "After dyner, they toke other paftymes in a great chambre, and hereyng of inftruments, wherein the erle of Foiz greatly delyted. Than wine and fpyces was brought. The erle of Harcourt ferved the kyng of his fpyceplate. And fir Gerard de la Pyen ferved the duke of Burbone. And fir Monaunt of Noailles ferved the erle of Foiz," &c. This was about the year 1360. *Chron.* tom. ii. cap. 164, f. 184, a. Again, *ibid.* cap. 100, f. 114, a. "The kynge alyghted at his palis [of Weftminfter] whiche was redie apparelled for him. There the kynge dranke and toke fpyces and his uncles alfo: and other prelates, lordes, and knyghtes." Lord Berners's Tranfl. In the Computus of Maxtoke priory [MS. *fupr. citat.*] an. 1447, we have this entry, "Item pro vino cretico cum fpeciebus et confectis datis diverfis generofis in die fancti Dionyfii quando Le fole domini Monfordes erat hic, et faceret jocofitates fuas in camera orioli." Here, I believe, vinum creticum is raifin-wine, or wine made of dry grapes; and the meaning of the whole feems to be this. "Paid for raifin wine with comfits and fpices, when [the Lord] Montford's fool was here, and exhibited his merriments in the oriel-chamber." With regard to one part of the entry, we have again, "Item, extra cameram vocatam le geftis chamber, erat una lintheamina furata in die fancti Georgii Martiris quando le fole de Monfordes erat hic."

[3] He afterwards infinuates, that the cardinal had loft an eye by the French difeafe: and that Balthafar, who had cured the fame diforder Domingo Lomelyn, one who had won much money of the king at cards and hazarding, was employed to recover the cardinal's eye, p. 175. In the *Boke of Colin Clout*, he mentions the cardinal's mule, "wyth golde all betrapped." [Dr. Lort fuggefted to Mr. Afhby, that the above lofs was the reafon why the cardinal is always reprefented in profile, to hide his blemifh. But how comes it, fays Mr. Afhby, that we have no pictures of him prior to the accident, *i.e.* before he was a cardinal, for as fuch he is always dreffed; yet he was as great a man before?—*Park.*]

[4] But in this ftanza he fometimes relapfes into the abfurdities of his favourite ftyle of compofition; for inftance, in *Speke Parrot*, p. 97:

> "*Albertus de modo fignificandi*
> And *Donatus* be dryuen out of fchole;

not always incapable of exhibiting allegorical imagery with spirit and dignity. But his comic vein predominates.

Riot is thus forcibly and humorously pictured:

> Wyth that came Ryotte rufshynge al at ones,
> A rufty galland,[1] to-ragged and to-rente;[2]
> And on the borde he whyrled a payre of bones;[3]
> *Quater treye dews* he clatered as he wente:
> Now baue at all by faynte Thomas of Kente,[4]
> And euer he threwe, and kyft[5] I wote nere what:
> His here was growen thorowe oute his hat.
>
> Thenne I behelde how he dyfgyfed was;
> His hede was heuy for watchynge ouer nyghte,
> His eyen blereed, his face fhone lyke a glas;
> His gowne fo fhorte, that it ne couer myghte
> His rumpe, he wente fo all for fomer lyghte;
> His hofe was garded wyth a lyfte of grene,
> Yet at the knee they were broken I wene.
>
> His cote was checked with patches rede and blewe,
> Of Kyrkeby Kendall was his fhorte demye;[6]
> And ay he fange *in fayth decon thou crewe:*
> His elbowe bare, he ware his gere fo nye:
> His nofe a droppynge, his lyppes were full drye:
> And by his fyde his whynarde and his pouche:
> The deuyll myghte daunce therin for ony crowche.[7]

> Prifians hed broken now handy dandy,
> And *Inter didafcolos* is returned for a fole:
> Alexander a gander of Menanders pole,
> With *Da Caufales* is caft out of the gate,
> And *da Racionales* dare not fhew his pate."

Here by *da Caufales* he perhaps means *Concilia*, or the canon law. By *da Racionales* he feems to intend *Logic*. Albertus is [Sigandus Albertus, author of the treatife *Liber Modorum Significandi*, printed at St. Albans, 1480, 4to.] To which add that Ingulphus fays, in Croyland Abbey library there were many Catones and Donati in the year 1091. *Hift. Croyl.* Ingulph. *Script. Vet.* i. p. 104. And that no perfon was admitted into the college of Boiffy at Paris, founded in 1358, "nifi Donatum aut Catonem didicerit." Bul. *Hift. Univ Paris.* tom. iv. p. 355. *Interdidafcalos* is the name of an old grammar. Alexander [Gallus, or *De Villa Dei,*] was a fchoolmafter at Paris about the year 1290, author, [among other works,] of the *Doctrinale*, which for fome centuries continued to be the moft favourite manual of grammar ufed in fchools, and was firft printed at [Parma in 1478.] It is compiled from Prifcian and in Leonine verfe. See Henr. Gandav. *Scriptor. Eccles.* cap. lix. This admired fyftem has been loaded with gloffes and lucubrations; but, on the authority of an ecclefiaftical fynod, it was fuperfeded by the [*Syntaxis* and *Grammatica* of Defpauterius about 1515.] It was printed in England as early as 1503. Barclay, in the *Ship of Fooles*, mentions Alexander's book, which he calls "The olde Doctrinall, with his diffufe and unperfite brevitie." Fol. 53, b, [edit. 1570.]

[1] galant. [2] all over tatters and rags. [3] dice.
[4] Saint Thomas Becket. [5] caft; he threw I know not what.
[6] doublet, jacket.
[7] The devil might dance in his purfe without meeting with a fingle fixpence. *Crouche* is *Crofs*, a piece of money fo called from being marked with the crofs. Hence the old phrafe, "to crofs the hand," for, to give money. In Chaucer's *Marchaunt's Tale*, when January and May are married, it is faid the prieft "*Crouchid* them, and bad god fhould them blefs," ver. 1223, Morris. That is, "He *croffed* the new-married couple," &c. In the poem before us, *Ryotte* fays,

There is also merit in the delineation of Dissimulation, in the same poem; and it is not unlike Ariosto's manner in imagining these allegorical personages:

> Than in his hode I sawe there faces tweyne;
> That one was lene and lyke a pyned goost,
> That other loked as he wolde me haue slayne:
> And to me warde as he gan for to coost,
> Whan that he was euen at me almoost,
> I sawe a knyfe hyd in his one sleue,
> Wheron was wryten this worde Myscheue.
> And in his other sleue, me thought, I sawe
> A spone of golde, full of hony swete,
> To fede a fole, and for to preue a dawe,[1] &c.

The same may be observed of the figure of Disdain:

> He looked hawte, he sette eche man at noughte;
> His gawdy garment with scornys was all wrought,
> With indygnacyon lyned was his hode;
> He frowned, as he wolde swere by Cockes blode,[2]
>
> He bote[3] the lyppe, he loked passynge coye;
> His face was belymmed, as byes had hym stounge:
> It was no tyme with hym to jape nor toye,
> Enuye hathe wasted his lyuer and his lounge;
> Hatred by the herte so had hym wrounge,
> That he loked pale as ashes to my syghte:
> Disdayne, I wene, this comerous crabes[4] hyghte.
>
> Forthwith he made on me a prowde assawte,
> With scornfull loke meuyd all in mode;[5]
> He wente aboute to take me in a fawte,
> He frounde, he stared, he stampped where he stoode:
> I lokyd on hym, I wende[6] he had be woode:[7]
> He set the arme proudly vnder the syde,
> And in this wyse he gan with me chyde.

In the *Garland of Laurel* our author attempts the higher poetry; but he cannot long support the tone of solemn description. These are some of the most ornamented and poetical stanzas. He is describing a garden belonging to the superb palace of Fame:[8]

"I have no coyne nor *crosse*," p. 72. Carpentier mentions a coin called in Latin Crosatus, and in old French Crosat, from being marked with the cross. Hence Croisage, Fr. for tribute; v. *Crosatus*, Suppl. Du Cange, *Lat. Gloss.* tom. i. p. 1208. In Shakespeare's *Timon of Athens*, Flavius says:—

> "—— (*Aside*.) More jewels yet?
> There is no crossing him in 's humour;
> Else I should tell him—well, ifaith, I should,
> When all's spent he'd be *cross'd* then, an he could."

Act i. sc. [ii. edit. Dyce, 1868, vi. 520.] That is, not thwarting him in his humour, but giving him money. Yet a jingle is intended. So in *As You Like It*, ii. iv. [edit. *ut supr.* iii. 25.] "Yet I should bear no cross if I did bear you; for I think you have no *money* in your purse." A Cruzado, a Portuguese coin, occurs in Shakespeare.

[1] [Dyce's *Skelton*, i. 46.] To catch a silly bird.
[2] The Host's oath in Lydgate. See *supr.*   [3] bit.
[4] [So old editions and ed. Dyce, i. 41; but (?) *crab is*, as Warton read.]
[5] in anger.   [6] weened, thought.   [7] mad.
[8] [Dyce's *Skelton*, i. 387.]

In an herber[1] I saw brought where I was;
There birdis on the brere sange on euery syde,
With alys ensandid about in compas,[2]
The bankis enturfid with singular solas,
Enrailid with rosers[3] and vinis engrapid;
It was a new comfort of sorowis escapid.

In the middis a coundight, that coriyusly was cast
With pypes of golde engusshing out stremes
Of cristall, the clerenes theis waters far past,
Enswymmyng with rochis, barbellis, and bremis,
Whose skales ensilured again the son beames
Englisterd that ioyous it was to beholde,
Then furthermore aboute me my syght reuolde.

Where I sawe growyng a goodly laurell tre,
Enuerdurid with leuis continually grene;
Aboue in the top a byrde of Araby,
Men call a phenix: her wynges bytwene
She bet up a fyre with the sparkis full kene,
With braunches and bowghis of the swete olyue,
Whos fragraunt flower was chefe preseruatyue

Ageynst all infeccyons with cancour enflamyd:
Ageynst all baratows broisiours of olde,
It passed all bawmis that euer were namyd,
Or gummis of Saby so derely that be solde:
There blewe in that gardynge a soft piplyng colde,
Enbrethyng of Zepherus, with his pleasant wynde;
All frutis and flowres grew there in there kynde.

Dryades there daunsid vpon that goodly soile,
With the nyne Muses, Pierides by name;
Phillis and Testalis ther tresses with oyle
Were newly enbybid: and rownd about the same
Grene tre of laurell moche solacyous game
They made, with chapelettes and garlandes grene;
And formest of all dame Flora the quene:

Of somer so formally she fotid the daunce:
There Cintheus sat, twynklyng vyon his harpe stringis:
And Iopas his instrument did aduaunce,
The poemis and storis auncient inbryngis
Of Athlas astrology, &c.

Our author supposes, that in the wall surrounding the palace of Fame were a thousand gates, new and old, for the entrance and egress of all nations. One of the gates is called *Anglia*, on which stood a leopard. There is some boldness and animation in the figure and attitude of this ferocious animal:

The beldynge thereof was passynge commendable;
Wheron stode a lybbard crownyd with golde and stones,
Terrible of countenaunce and passynge formydable,
As quikly towchd as it were fleshe and bones,
As gastly that glaris, as grimly that gronis,
As fersly frownynge as he had ben fyghtyng,
And with forme fote he shoke forthe this writynge.

---

[1] See *supr.* p. 65.   [2] It was surrounded with sand-walks.
[3] rose-trees. See Chaucer's *Rom. R.* ver. 1651, *seq.* And our author, *infr.*:
   "The ruddy *rosary*,
      The pretty rosemary," &c.

Skelton, in the course of his allegory, supposes that the *poets laureate* (or learned men) of all nations were assembled before Pallas. This group shews the authors, both ancient and modern, then in vogue. Some of them are quaintly characterised. They are, first, *Olde* Quintilian, not with his *Institutes* of eloquence, but with his *Declamacyons:* Theocritus, with his *bucolycall relacyons:* Hesiod, the [*Iconomicar*][1] Homer, *the fresshe historiar : The prynce of eloquence,* Cicero: Sallust, who wrote both the *history* of Catiline and Jugurth: Ovid, *enshryned with the Musis nyne:* Lucan[2] Statius, writer of *Achilliedos:* Persius, with *problemes diffuse:* Virgil, Juvenal, Livy: Ennius, *that wrate of mercyall war:* Aulus Gellius, that *noble historiar:* Horace, with his *New Poetry:*[3] *Maister* Terence, *the famous comicar,* with Plautus: Seneca the tragedian: Boethius: Maximian, *with his madde ditiis how dotynge age wolde iape with yonge foly:*[4] Boccaccio, *with his volumys grete:* Quintus Curtius : Macrobius, who treated of *Scipions dreme:* Poggius Florentinus, with many a mad tale:[5] a friar of France *syr* Gaguyne, who frownyd on me *full angerly:*[6] Plutarch and Petrarch, two *famous clarkis:* Lucilius,

---

[1] ["*i.e.* Hesiod the writer on husbandry."—*Dyce.*]
[2] Of the popularity of Lucan in the dark ages, I have given proofs in the *Third Dissertation,* vol. i. To which I will here add others. The following passage occurs in Lydgate's *Prologue to the Lyff and Passioun of the blessid Martyr seynt Alboon* [Alban] *and seynt Amphiballus* [printed at St. Albans, 1534, 4to.]

"I not acqueyntyd with Muses of Mars,
Nor with metris of Lucan nor Virgile;
Nor with sugred diteys of Cichero,
Nor of Omere to folowe the fressh style."

And again, speaking of Julius Cæsar, Lydgate refers to Lucan's *Pharsalia,* which he calls the *Records of Lucan.* Ibid. fol. 2, b. Peter de Blois, in writing to a professor at Paris about the year 1170, says, "Priscianus et Tullius, *Lucanus* et Persius, isti sunt dii vestri." *Epistol.* iv. fol. 3, edit. 1517. Eberhardus Bethuniensis, called *Græcista,* a philologist who wrote about the year 1130, in a poem on *Versification,* says of Philip Gualtier, author of the *Alexandreis,* that he shines with the light of Lucan. "Lucet Alexander Lucani luce." Of Lucan he observes, "Metro *lucidiore* canit." It is easy to conceive why Lucan should have been a favourite in the dark ages.

[3] That is, Horace's *Art of Poetry.* Vinesauf wrote *De Nova Poetria.* Horace's *Art* is frequently mentioned under this title.

[4] His six Elegies *De incommodis senectutis.* Reinesius thinks that Maximinian was the bishop of Syracuse in the seventh century: a most intimate friend, and the secretary, of Pope Gregory the Great. (*Epist. ad Daum.* p. 207.) These Elegies contain many things superior to the taste of that period.

[5] Poggius flourished about the year 1450. By his *mad tales,* Skelton means his *Facetiæ,* a set of comic stories, very licentious and very popular. See the *Works of Poggius* by Thomas Aucuparius, Argentorat. 1513, f. 157, 184. The obscenity contained in these compositions gave great offence, and fell under the particular censure of the learned Laurentius Valla. The objections of Valla Poggius attempts to obviate by saying, that Valla was a clown, a cynic, and a pedant, without any ideas of wit or elegance: and that the *Facetiæ* were universally esteemed in Italy, France, Spain, Germany, England, and all countries that cultivated pure Latinity. *Invect. in Laurent. Vallam.* f. 82, b. edit. *ut supr.*

[6] Robert, or Rupert, Gaguin, a German, minister-general of the Maturines, who died at Paris in 1502. His most famous work is *Compendium super Francorum Gestis,* from Pharamond to the author's age. He has written among many other

Valerius Maximus, Propertius, Pifander,[1] and Vincentius Bellovacenfis [Vincent of Beauvais], who wrote the *Speculum Hiftoriale*. The catalogue is clofed by Gower, Chaucer and Lydgate, who firft adorned the Englifh language:[2] in allufion to which part of their characters their apparel is faid to fhine beyond the power of defcription, and their tabards to be ftudded with diamonds and rubies. That only thefe three Englifh poets are here mentioned, may be confidered as a proof, that only thefe three were yet thought to deferve the name.

No writer is more unequal than Skelton. In the midft of a page of the moft wretched ribaldry, we fometimes are furprifed with three or four nervous and manly lines, like thefe :

> Ryot and Revell be in your court roules,
> Mayntenaunce and Mifchefe thefe be men of myght,
> Extorcyon is counted with you for a knyght.

Skelton's modulation in the octave ftanza is rough and inharmonious. The following are the fmootheft lines in the poem before us: which yet do not equal the liquid melody of Lydgate, whom he here manifeftly attempts to imitate :

> Lyke as the larke vpon the fomers daye,
> Whan Titan radiant burnifhith his bemis bryght,
> Mountith on hy with her melodious lay,
> Of the foes hyne engladid with the lyght.

The following little ode deferves notice; at leaft as a fpecimen of the ftructure and phrafeology of a love-fonnet about the clofe of the fifteenth century :

> *To maiftrefs Margary Wentworth.*
> With margerain[3] ientyll
> The flowre of goodlyhede,[4]
> Embrowdered the mantill
> Is of your maydenhede.[5]
> Plainly I can not glofe;[6]
> Ye be, as I deuyne,[7]

---

pieces, Latin orations and poems, printed in 1495. The hiftory of Skelton's quarrel with him is not known. But he was in England as ambaffador from [Charles VIII] of France, in 1490. He was a particular friend of Dean Colet.

[1] Our author got the name of Pifander, a Greek poet, from Macrobius.

[2] In the *boke of Philip Sparow*, he fays, *Gower's Englyfhe is old*, but that Chaucer's *Englyfhe is wel allowed:* he adds that Lydgate writes *after an hyer rate*, and that he has been cenfured for his elevation of phrafe; but acknowledges, "No man can amend thofe matters that he hath pend." [Dyce's *Skelton*, i. 75.] In [*Terens in englyfh*, printed perhaps by J. Raftell, but *fine ullâ nota*, about 1510], thefe three are mentioned in the Prologue, which is in ftanzas, as the only Englifh poets.

[3] *Margelain*, the herb Marjoram. *Afs. Lad.* 56 :
"And upon that a potte of Margelain."

[4] goodlihed, goodnefs. [5] virginity.

[6] In truth I cannot flatter or deceive. Or *glofe* may be, fimply to *write.*

[7] As I imagine. So Morris's *Chaucer*, *Non. Pr. T.* vol. iii. p. 242, v. 446.
"I can noon harme of *no* woman *divine.*"

> The praty primrose,
>   The goodly columbyne,
> With margerain iantill, &c.
>
> Benynge, corteife, and meke,
>   With wordes well deuyfid;
> In you, who lift to feke,
>   Be vertus well compryfid.
> With margerain iantill,
>   The flowre of goodlyhede,
> Embrawderid the mantill
>   Is of yowre maydenhede.

For the fame reafon this ftanza in a fonnet to *Maiftrefs Margaret Huffey* deferves notice.

> Mirry Margaret
>   As mydfomer flowre,
> Ientyll as faweoun,
>   Or hawke of the towre.[1]

As do the following flowery lyrics, in a fonnet addreffed to *Maiftrefs Ifabell Pennel*:

> Your colowre
> Is lyke the dafy flowre,
> After the Aprill fhowre:
>   Sterre of the morow gray,
> The bloffom on the fpray,
> The frefsheft flowre of May:
>   Maydenly demure,
> Of womanhode the lure, &c.

But Skelton moft commonly appears to have miftaken his genius, and to write in a forced character, except when he is indulging his native vein of fatire and jocularity in the fhort minftrel metre above mentioned: which he mars by a multiplied repetition of rhymes, arbitrary abbreviations of the verfe, cant expreffions, hard and founding words newly-coined, and patches of Latin and French. This anomalous and motley mode of verfification is, I believe, fuppofed to be peculiar to our author.[2] I am not, however, quite certain that it originated with Skelton.[3]

---

[1] f. 41. In the king's mews in the tower.

[2] ["Skelton has been frequently termed a Macaronic poet, but it may be doubted, if with ftrict propriety; for the paffages, in which he introduces fnatches of Latin and French, are thinly fcattered through his works."—*Dyce*.]

I have given fpecimens. But the following paffage in the *Boke of Colin Clout* affords an appofite example at one view:

> "Of fuche vagabundus
> Speketh *totus mundus*.
> Howe fome fynge lætabundus, &c.
> *Cum ipfis vel illis
> Qui manent in villis,
> Eft uxor vel ancilla*,
> Welcome Jacke and Gilla,
> My prety Petronilla,
> And you wyll be ftylla,
> You fhall haue your wylla:
> Of fuche paternofter pekes
> All the worlde fpekes."

[3] ["He (Warton) ought to have been 'quite certain' that it did not."—*Dyce*.]

About the year 1512, [Merlinus Cocaus or Cocaius, of Mantua,] whose true name was Theophilo Folengo, a Benedictine monk of Casino in Italy, wrote a poem entitled [*Macaronices Libri* xvii.] This is a burlesque Latin poem, in heroic metre, checkered with [Mantuan] words, and those of the plebeian character, yet not destitute of prosodical harmony. It is totally satirical, and has some degree of drollery; but the ridicule is too frequently founded on obscene or vulgar ideas. [One of the divisions of the work (in the edition of 1521) is entitled] *Zanitonella, or the Amours of Tonellus and Zanina*;[1] [another, *Phantasiæ Macaronicæ*, in twenty-five macaronics, "de gestis magnanimi et prudentissimi Baldi;" a third, *Moschææ facetus liber*.] The author[2] died in 1544.[3] Cocaus is often cited by Rabelais, a writer of a congenial cast.[4] The three last books, containing a description of hell, are a parody on part of Dante's *Inferno*. In the preface or *Apologetica*, our author gives an account of this new species of poetry, since called the *Macaronic*, which I must give in his own words.[5] Vavassor observes that Coccaus [or Folengo] in Italy, and Antonius de Arena in France, were the two first, at least the chief authors of the semi-latin burlesque poetry.[6] As to Antonius de Arena, he was a civilian of Avignon, and wrote in 1519 a Latin poem in elegiac verses, ridiculously interlarded with French words and phrases. It is addressed to his fellow-students, or in his own words, " Ad suos compagnones studiantes, qui sunt de persona friantes, bassas dansas, in galanti stilo bisognatas, cum guerra Romana, totum ad longum sine require, et cum guerra Neapolitana, et cum revoluta Genuensi, et guerra Avenionensi, et epistola ad falotissimam garsam pro passando lo tempos."[7] I have gone out of my way to mention these two obscure writers with

---

[1] Perhaps formed from Zanni or Giovanni, a foolish character on the Italian stage. See Riccoboni, *Theatr. Ital.* ch. ii. p. 14, *seq.*
[2] See his Life, Jac. Phil. Thomasin's *Elog.* Patav. 1644, p. 71.
[3] [See Brunet, last edit. in v. Folengo. The first known edition appears to be that of 1517.] See De Bure's curious catalogue of *Poetes Latins modernes facetieux, vulgairement appelles Macaroniques*, Bib. *Instruct. Bel. Lett.* tom. i. § 6, p. 445, *seq.*
[4] See Liv. iv. c. 13, ii. 1, xi. 3.
[5] " Ars ista poetica nuncupatur Ars Macaronica, a *Macaronibus* derivata: qui *Macarones* sunt quoddam pulmentum, farina, caseo, butyro compaginatum, grossum, rude, et rusticanum. Ideo Macaronica nil nisi grossedinem, ruditatem, et Vocabulazzos, debet in se continere." See Menag. *Diction. Etymol. Orig. Lang. Franc.* edit. 1694, p. 462, v. *Macarons;* and Oct. Ferrarius, *Orig. Italic.*
[6] *Dict. Ludr.* p. 453.
[7] I believe one of the most popular of Arena's Macaronic poems is his *Meygra entreprisa Catoloqui Imperatoris*, printed at Avignon in 1537. It is an ingenious pasquinade on Charles V.'s expedition into France. The date of the Macaronic Miscellany in various languages entitled, *Macharonea varia*, and printed in the Gothic character, without place, is not known. The authors are anonymous; and some of the pieces are little comedies intended for representation. There is a Macaronic poem in hexameters, called *Polemo-Middinia*, by Drummond of Hawthornden, printed with notes and a preface on this species of poetry by Bishop Gibson, 1691.

so much particularity,[1] in order to observe that Skelton (their cotemporary) probably copied their manner: at least to show, that this singular mode of versification [which, however, is not strictly macaronic] was at this time fashionable, not only in England, but also in France and Italy. Nor did it cease to be remembered in England, and as a species of poetry thought to be founded by Skelton, till even so late as the close of Queen Elizabeth's reign, as appears from the following poem on the Spanish Armada, which is filled with Latin words:

> A Skeltonicall Salvtation,
> Or condigne gratvlation,
> And iust vexation,
> Of the Spanish nation;
> That in a bravado
> Spent many a crusado
> In setting forth an armado
> England to invado.[2]

But I must not here forget, that Dunbar, a Scotish poet of Skelton's own age, already mentioned, wrote [somewhat] in this way. His *Testament of Master Andro Kennedy*, which represents [says Lord Hailes,] the character of an idle dissolute scholar, and ridicules the funeral ceremonies of the Romish communion, has almost every alternate line composed of the formularies of a Latin will and shreds of the breviary, mixed with what the French call

---

[1] Erythræus mentions Bernardinus Stephonius as writing in this way. *Pinacoth.* i. p. 160. See also some poems in Baudius, which have a mixture of the Greek and Latin languages, and which others have imitated, in German and Latin.

[2] Printed at Oxford, 1589. See also a doggrel piece of this kind, in imitation of Skelton, introduced into Browne's *Shepherd's Pipe*, 1614. [I have searched in vain for the doggrel mentioned by Warton, unless it be the lines at p. 196 of vol. ii. of Browne's Works, by Hazlitt. More probably it is in the portion of the volume not written by Browne.] Perhaps this way of writing is ridiculed by Shakespeare, *Merry Wives of Winds.* a. ii. sc. i. Where Falstaffe says, " I will not say, pity me, 'tis not a soldier-like phrase, but I say, love me: by me

> ' Thine own true knight,
> By day or night,
> Or any kind of light,
> With all his might,
> With thee to fight.' "

[Dyce's edit. 1868, i. 360.] See also the Interlude of *Pyramus and Thisbe*, in the *Midsummer Night's Dream*, [which was printed by Kirkman in his *Sport upon Sport*, a collection of drolls performed at Bartholomew Fair. Here it was called the *Merry Conceited Humours of Bottom the Weaver*.] Skelton, however, seems to have retained his popularity till late. For [he is the chorus in Munday and Chettle's *Downfall of Robert Earle of Huntington*, 1601.] The second part [*The Death of Robert Earle of Huntington*, 1601,] is introduced by Friar Tuck. Friar Tuck is mentioned in Skelton's *Magnificence*, f. 5, b.

> " Another bade shave halfe my berde,
> And boyes to the pylery gan me plucke,
> And wolde have made me Freer Tucke
> To preche oute of the pylery hole."

Latin de cuisine. There is some humour, arising from these burlesque applications, in the following stanzas:[1]

> *In die meæ sepulturæ,*
> I will nane haif bot our awen gyng,
> *Et duos rusticos de rure,*
> Berand a barrell on a styng;
> Drynkand and playand cop out, evin
> *Sicut egomet solebam;*
> Singand and gretand with hie stevin,[2]
> *Potum meum cum fletu miscebam.*
>
> I will na priestis for me sing,
> *Dies illæ, dies iræ;*[3]
> Na yit na bellis for me ring
> *Sicut semper solet fieri;*
> But a bag pipe to play a spryng,
> *Et unum ail wosp ante me,*
> In stayd of baneris for to bring,
> *Quatuor lagenas cervisiæ,*
> Within the graif to set sic thing,
> *In modum crucis juxta me,*
> To fle the feyndis[4] than hardely sing
> *De terra plasmasti me.*[5]

We must, however, acknowledge that Skelton, notwithstanding his scurrility, was a classical scholar; and in that capacity he was tutor to Prince Henry,[6] afterwards Henry VIII., at whose accession to the throne he was appointed the royal orator. He is styled by

---

[1] [Dunbar's Works, ed. Laing, i. 140-1. But Warton was mistaken in supposing that either Skelton or Dunbar ought to have a place among Macaronic writers. The intermixture of Latin with English words does not constitute Macaronic poetry. It is the use of burlesque Latinity, or vernacular words (in whatever language), with Latin terminations.

[2] With that verse or stanza in the Psalms, "I have mingled my drink with weeping."

[3] A hymn on the resurrection in the missal, sung at funerals.

[4] Instead of a cross on my grave to keep off the devil.

[5] A verse in the Psalms. In [the Bannatyne MS.] are many examples of this mixture: the impropriety of which was not perhaps perceived by our ancestors. See a very ludicrous specimen in Harsnet's [*Declaration,* 1603,] p. 156. Where he mentions a witch who has learned "of an old wife in a chimnies end *Pax, max, fax,* for a spell; or can say Sir John of Grantam's curse for the miller's eels that were stolen.

> "All you that have stolen the millers eeles,
> *Laudate dominum de cœlis,*
> And all they that have consented thereto,
> *Benedicamus domino.*"

[But this is one of the stories in *A C. Mery Talys,* 1526, and was copied by Scot into his *Discovery of Witchcraft,* 1584, whence perhaps Harsnet got it.]

See a poem on Becket's martyrdom, in Wasse's *Bibl. Liter.* Num. i. p. 39. Lond. 1722. Hither we must refer the old Carol on the *Boar's Head,* Hearne's *Spicileg. ad Gul. Neubrig. Hist.* vol. iii. p. 740. Some of the metrical hymns in the French *Fete de l'Ane* are in Latin and French. See *Mercure de France,* Avril, 1725, p. 724 *suiv.*

[6] [Mr. Ashby expresses his surprise that such a man should be chosen; and he adds with appearance of probability, that Skelton's having conceived his disappointment of preferment to be owing to Wolsey may have been the cause of his extreme irritation against that prelate.—*Park.*]

Erasmus "Britannicarum literarum decus et lumen."[1] His Latin elegiacs are pure, are often unmixed with the monastic phraseology; and they prove that, if his natural propensity to the ridiculous had not more frequently seduced him to follow the [whimsical school of poetry, which passes under the name of Walter Mapes, and which has derived its name of *Goliard* from Golias, an appellation bestowed on an imaginary person, who was supposed to represent the ecclesiastics][2] than to copy the elegances of Ovid, he would have appeared among the first writers of Latin poetry in England at the general restoration of literature. Skelton could not avoid acting as a buffoon in any language or any character.

I cannot quit Skelton, of whom I yet fear too much has been already said, without restoring to the public notice a play or Morality, written by him, not recited in any [early] catalogue of his works or annals of English typography; and (I believe) totally unknown to the antiquarians in this sort of literature. It is, The *Nigramansir*, a morall *Enterlude* and a pithie written by Maister Skelton laureate, and plaid before the king and other estatys at Woodstoke on Palme Sunday. It was printed by Wynkyn de Worde in a thin quarto, in the year 1504.[3] It must have been presented before Henry VII. at the royal manor or palace at Woodstock in Oxfordshire, now destroyed. The characters are a Necromancer or conjuror, the devil, a notary public, Simony,[5] and Philargyria[4] or Avarice. It is partly a satire

---

[1] See *Op.* pp. 1019, 1021.
[2] [Poems attributed to Walter Mapes, ed. Wright, Introd. ix.-x.]
[3] My lamented friend Mr. William Collins, whose *Odes* will be remembered while any taste for true poetry remains, shewed me this piece at Chichester, not many months before his death: and he pointed it out as a very rare and valuable curiosity. He intended to write the *History of the Restoration of Learning under Leo the Tenth*, and with a view to that design had collected many scarce books. Some few of these fell into my hands at his death. The rest, among which, I suppose, was this *Interlude*, were dispersed.

In the *Mystery of Marie Magdalene*, written in 1512, a Heathen is introduced celebrating the service of Mahound, who is called *Saracenorum fortissimus ;* in the midst of which he reads a Lesson from the Alcoran, consisting of gibberish, much in the metre and manner of Skelton. MSS. Digb. 133. [These *Mysteries* have since been published entire, and Mr. Park's description of their contents in the *Additional Notes* to Warton did not therefore appear worth retaining.]

[4] Crowley [printed and perhaps] wrote "The Fable of *Philargyrie*, the great gigant of Great Britain, what houses were builded, and lands appointed, for his provision," &c. 1551, [8vo.]

[5] Simony is introduced as a person in *Sir Penny*, an old Scotish poem, written in 1527 by Stewart of Lorne. See *Antient Scottish Poems*, 1770, p. 154:

"So wily can syr Peter wink,
And als sir Symony his servand,
That now is *gydar of the kyrk.*"

And again, in an ancient anonymous Scotish poem, *ibid.* p. 253. At a feast, to which many disorderly persons are invited, among the rest are:

"And twa lerit men thairby,
Schir Ochir and schir Simony."

That is, Sir Usury and Sir Simony. Simony is also a character in Langland's *Vision.* Pass. sec. fol. viii. b, edit. 1550. Wickliffe, who flourished about the year 1350,

on some abuses in the church; yet not without a due regard to decency and an apparent respect for the dignity of the audience. The story, or plot, is the trial of Simony and Avarice: the devil is the judge, and the notary public acts as an assessor or scribe. The prisoners, as we may suppose, are found guilty, and ordered into hell immediately. There is no sort of propriety in calling this play the *Necromancer*: for the only business and use of this character is to open the subject in a long prologue, to evoke the devil, and summon the court. The devil kicks the necromancer for waking him so soon in the morning: a proof, that this drama was performed in the morning, perhaps in the chapel of the palace. A variety of measures, with shreds of Latin and French, is used: but the devil speaks in the octave stanza. One of the stage-directions is, " Enter Balsebub with a Berde." To make him both frightful and ridiculous, the devil was most commonly introduced on the stage, wearing a visard with an immense beard.[1] Philargyria quotes Seneca and St. Austin: and

---

thus describes the state of simony in his time. "Some lords, to colouren their Symony, wole not take for themselves but keverchiefs for the lady, or a palfry, or a tun of wine. And when some lords wolden present a good man and able, for love of god and cristen souls, then some ladies bene means to have a dancer, a tripper on tapits, or hunter or hawker, or a wild player of summers gamenes," &c. MSS. C.C.C. Cant. O. 161, 148. There is an old poem on this subject, MSS. Bodl. 48.

[1] Thus in Turpin's *History of Charlemagne*, the Saracens appear, "Habentes larvas barbatas, cornutas, Dæmonibus consimiles." c. xviii. And in *Lewis the Eighth*, an old French romance of Philip Mouskes:

"J ot apries lui une barboire,
Com diable cornu et noire."

There was a species of masquerade celebrated by the ecclesiastics in France, called the *Shew of Beards*, entirely consisting of an exhibition of the most formidable beards. Gregory of Tours says, that the abbess of Poictou was accused for suffering one of these shews, called a *Barbatoria*, to be performed in her monastery. *Hist.* lib. x. c. vi. In the *Epistles* of Peter de Blois we have the following passage: "Regis curiam sequuntur assidue histriones, candidatrices, aleatores, dulcorarii, caupones, nebulatores, mimi, *Barbatores*, balatrones, et hoc genus omne." Epist. xiv. Where by Barbatores we are not to understand Barbers, but mimics or buffoons, disguised in huge bearded masks. In Don Quixote, the barber who personates the squire of the Princess Micomicona, wears one of these masks, "una gran barba," &c. Part. prim. c. xxvi. l. 3. And the countess of Trifaldi's squire has "la mas larga, la mas horrida," &c. Part. sec. c. xxxvi. l. 8. See *Observat. on Spenser*, vol. i. Section ii.

About the eleventh century, and long before, beards were looked upon by the clergy as a secular vanity, and accordingly were worn by the laity only. Yet in England this distinction seems to have been more rigidly observed than in France. Malmesbury says that King Harold, at the Norman invasion, sent spies into Duke William's camp; who reported that most of the French army were priests, because their faces were shaven. *Hist.* lib. iii. p. 56, b, edit. Savil. 1596. The regulation remained among the English clergy at least till the reign of Henry VIII.: for Longland bishop of Lincoln, at a Visitation of Oriel College, Oxford, in 1531, orders one of the fellows, a priest, to abstain under pain of expulsion from wearing a beard and pinked shoes like a laic; and not to take the liberty, for the future, of insulting and ridiculing the governor and fellows of the society. *Ordinat.* Coll. Oriel. Oxon. *Append. ad Joh. Trokelowe*, p. 339. See Edicts of King John, in Prynne, *Libertat. Eccles. Angl.* tom. iii. p. 23. But among the religious, the Tem-

Simony offers the devil a bribe. The devil rejects her offer with much indignation: and swears by the "foule Eumenides," and the hoary beard of Charon, that she shall be well fried and roasted in the unfathomable sulphur of Cocytus, together with Mahomet, Pontius Pilate, the traitor Judas, and King Herod. The last scene is closed with a view of hell and a dance between the devil and the necromancer. The dance ended, the devil trips up the necromancer's heels, and disappears in fire and smoke.[1] Great must have been the edification and entertainment which Henry VII. and his court derived from the exhibition of so elegant and rational a drama! The royal taste for dramatic representation seems to have suffered a very rapid transition: for in [1528] a goodly comedy of Plautus [probably in Latin,] was played before Henry VIII. at Greenwich.[2] I have before mentioned Skelton's [interlude] of *Magnificence*. It contains sixty folio pages in the black letter, and must have taken up a very considerable time in the representation. The substance of the allegory is briefly this. Magnificence becomes a dupe to his servants and favourites, "Fansy, Counterfet Countenance, Crafty Conveyance, Clokyd Colusion, Courtly Abusion, and Foly." At length he is seized and robbed by "Adversyte," by whom he is given up as a prisoner to "Poverte." He is next delivered to Despare and Mischefe, who offer him a knife and a halter. He snatches the knife to end his miseries by stabbing himself; when "Good Hope" and "Redresse" appear, and persuade him to take the "rubarbe of repentance" with some "gostly gummes" and a few "drammes of devocyon." He becomes acquainted with "Circumspeccyon" and Perseverance, follows their directions, and seeks for happiness in a state of penitence and contrition. There is some humour here and there in the dialogue, but the allusions are commonly low. The poet hardly ever aims at allegorical painting, but the figure of Poverty is thus drawn:

---

plars were permitted to wear long beards. In the year 1311, King Edward II. granted letters of safe conduct to his valet Peter Auger, who had made a vow not to shave his beard, and who, having resolved to visit some of the holy places abroad as a pilgrim, feared, on account of the length of his beard, that he might be mistaken for a knight-templar and insulted. Pat. iv. Edw. II. in Dugdale's *Warwickshire*, p. 704. Many orders about beards occur in the registers of Lincoln's-inn, cited by Dugdale. In the year 1542, it was ordered that no member, wearing a beard, should presume to dine in the hall. In 1553, says Dugdale, "such as had beards should pay twelve-pence for every meal they continued them; and every man to be shaven, upon pain of being put out of commons." *Orig. Jurid.* c. 64, p. 244. In 1559, no member is permitted to wear any beard above a fortnight's growth, under pain of expulsion for the third transgression. But the fashion of wearing beards beginning to spread, in 1560 it was agreed at a council, that "all orders before that time made, touching beards, should be void and repealed." Dugd. ibid. p. 245.

[1] In the *Myftery of Mary Magdalene*, just mentioned, one of the stage directions is, "Here enters the prynfe of the devylls in a stage, with hell onderneth the stage." MSS. Digb. 133. [Another direction is, "With this word vii. dyvyls fall de woyde from the woman, and the bad angyll enter into hell with thondyr."—*Park.*]

[2] Holinsh. iii. 850, [and Stow's *Annales*, edit. 1615, p. 539.]

>   A, my bonys ake, my lymmys be fore,
>   Alaffe, I haue the cyatyca full euyll in my hyppe,
>   Alaffe, where is youth that was wont for to fkyppe!
>   I am lowfy, and vnlykynge, and full of fcurffe,
>   My colour is tawny-colouryd as a turffe:
>   I am Pouerte, that all men doth hate,
>   I am baytyd with doggys at euery mannys gate:
>   I am raggyd and rent, as ye may fe,
>   Full few but they haue envy at me.
>   Nowe muft I this carcaffe lyft up,
>   He dynyd with Delyte, with Pouerte he muft fup.[1]

The ftage-direction then is, "Hic accedat ad levandum Magnyfycence." It is not impoffible that "Defpare," offering the knife and the halter, might give a diftant hint to Spenfer. The whole piece is ftrongly marked with Skelton's manner, and contains every fpecies of his capricious verfification.[2] I have been prolix in defcribing thefe two dramas, becaufe they place Skelton in a clafs in which he never has yet been viewed, that of a dramatic poet. And although many Moralities were now written, yet thefe are the firft that bear the name of their author. There is often much real comedy in thefe ethic interludes, and their exemplifications of Virtue and Vice in the abftract convey ftrokes of character and pictures of life and manners. I take this opportunity of remarking that a Morality-maker was a profeffed occupation at Paris. Pierre Gringoire is called, according to the ftyle of his age, "Compofiteur, Hiftorien et Facteur de Myfteres ou Comedies," in which he was alfo a performer. [One of his numerous pieces,] written at the command of Louis XII., in confequence of a quarrel with the pope and the ftates of Venice, is entitled [*Le jeu du prince des fotz*, to which (in a later edition) is added, *ioue aux halles de pis le mardy gras* (1511). This latter impreffion purports to have been printed for the author.][3]

Moralities feem to have arrived at their height about the clofe of the feventh Henry's reign. This fort of fpectacle was now fo fafhionable, that John Raftell, a learned typographer and brother-in-law to Sir Thomas More, extended its province, which had hitherto been confined either to moral allegory or to religion blended with buffoonery, and conceived a defign of making it the vehicle of fcience and philofophy. With this view he publifhed *A new interlude and a mery, of the nature of the iiii Elements, declarynge many proper poynts of phylofophy naturall and of dyuers ftrange landys, &c.* [*circa* 1520, 8vo.][4] In the cofmographical part of the play, in

---

[1] [Skelton's Works, 1843, i. 290-1.]
[2] [*Counterfet Countenance* fays:
>   "But nowe wyll I [that they be gone,]
>   In *baftarde* ryme after the *dogrell* gyfe
>   Tell you where of my name doth ryfe."]
[3] See Goujet, *Bibl. Franc.* tom. xi. p. 212.
[4] ["Dr. Dibdin and others have fuppofed hence [the allufion to the New World] that this interlude was written about 1510, as Columbus difcovered the Weft Indies in 1492, but the author fays nothing of Columbus, and does not feem to

which the poet professes to treat of " dyvers straunge regyons, and of the new founde landys," the tracts of America recently discovered, and the manners of the natives, are described. The characters are, a Messenger who speaks the prologue, Nature, Humanity, Studious Desire, Sensual Appetite, a Taverner, Experience, and Ignorance. Rastell appears to have been a scholar. He was educated at Oxford, and took up the employment of printing as a profession, at that time esteemed liberal and not unsuitable to the character of a learned and ingenious man. He wrote and printed many other pieces which I do not mention, as unconnected with the history of our poetry. I shall only observe further, in general that he was eminently skilled in mathematics, cosmography, history, our municipal law, and theology. He died in 1536.

I have before observed that the frequent and public exhibition of personifications in the pageants, which anciently accompanied every high festivity, greatly contributed to cherish the spirit of allegorical poetry, and even to enrich the imagination of Spenser and of Shakespeare. There is a passage in *Antony and Cleopatra* where the metaphor is exceedingly beautiful, but where the beauty both of the expression and the allusion is lost, unless we recollect the frequency and the nature of these shows in Shakespeare's age.[1] I must cite the whole of the context, for the sake of the last hemistich :

> Sometime we see a cloud that's dragonish,
> A vapour sometime like a bear or lion;
> A tower'd citadel, a pendent rock,
> A forked mountain, or blue promontory
> With trees upon't, that nod unto the world
> And mock our eyes with air: thou hast seen these signs;
> They are black vesper's pageants.

The Moralities, which now began to acquire new celebrity, and in which the same groups of the impersonated vices and virtues appeared, must have concurred in producing this effect; and hence, at the same time, we are led to account for the national relish for allegorical poetry, which so long prevailed among our ancestors. By means of these spectacles, ideal beings became common and popular objects; and emblematic imagery, which at present is only contemplated by a few retired readers in the obsolete pages of our elder poets, grew familiar to the general eye.

[Hawkins, in the *History of Music*, has printed a song written by Skelton, alluded to in the *Garlande of Lawrell*, and set to music by William Cornish, a musician of the chapel-royal under Henry VII. It begins :

> Ah, beshrew you, by my fay,
> These wanton clarkes are nice alway.

Cornish seems to have been master of the children of the chapel in 1514-15, in the Christmas of which year the interlude of the

---

have known of his existence, attributing the finding of America to Americus Vespucius, who did not sail from Cadiz till 1497."—*Collier*.]

[1] Act iv. sc. [xiv. edit. Dyce, 1868, vii. 576.]

Triumph of Love and Beauty was performed by the children before Henry VIII., at Richmond, on a very fumptuous fcale, at the fame time that Medwall's interlude of *Nature* was played by the king's players.[1]

A dull poem by this perfon is introduced improperly into the edition of Skelton's Works in 1568. He received 13s. 4d. from Elizabeth of York for a Chriftmas carol compofed by him for Chriftmas, 1502. This appears to have been the ufual payment for fuch a performance.

Cornifh has alfo two fongs in the Fairfax MS. (Add. MSS. B. M. 5465) for three voices; there he is defcribed as "William Cornyfsh *junior.*" In Harl. MS. 1709 there is a *Salve Regina* by the fame hand.[2]]

SECTION XXXIII.

N a work of this general and comprehenfive nature, in which the fluctuations of genius are furveyed, and the dawnings or declenfions of tafte muft alike be noticed, it is impoffible that every part of the fubject can prove equally fplendid and interefting. We have, I fear, been toiling for fome time through materials not perhaps of the moft agreeable and edifying nature. But as the mention of that very rude fpecies of our drama, called the *Morality*, has incidentally diverted our attention to the early ftate of the Englifh ftage, I cannot omit fo fortunate and feafonable an opportunity of endeavouring to relieve the wearinefs of my reader, by [reverting to the drama, and] introducing an obvious digreffion on the probable caufes of the rife of the *Myfteries* which, as I have before remarked, preceded, and at length produced, thefe allegorical fables. In this refpect I fhall imitate thofe map-makers mentioned by Swift, who

> O'er inhofpitable downs,
> Place elephants for want of towns.

Nor fhall I perhaps fail of being pardoned by my reader if, on the fame principle, I fhould attempt to throw new light on the hiftory of our theatre, by purfuing this enquiry through thofe deductions which it will naturally and more immediately fuggeft.

About the eighth century, trade was principally carried on by means of fairs, which lafted feveral days. Charlemagne eftablifhed many great marts of this fort in France: as did William the Conqueror and his Norman fucceffors in England. The merchants, who frequented thefe fairs in numerous caravans or companies,

---

[1] [Collier, *H. E. D. P.* i. 63-5.]
[2] [Ellis's *Orig. Letters*, 3rd Ser. ii. 50.]   [3] [See fect. vi.]

employed every art to draw the people together. They were therefore accompanied by jugglers, minstrels, and buffoons, who were no less interested in giving their attendance, and exerting all their skill, on these occasions. As now but few large towns existed, no public spectacles or popular amusements were established; and as the sedentary pleasures of domestic life and private society were yet unknown, the fair-time was the season for diversion. In proportion as these shews were attended and encouraged, they began to be set off with new decorations and improvements: and the arts of buffoonery, being rendered still more attractive by extending their circle of exhibition, acquired an importance in the eyes of the people. By degrees the clergy, observing that the entertainments of dancing, music, and mimicry, exhibited at these protracted annual celebrations, made the people less religious by promoting idleness and a love of festivity, proscribed these sports, and excommunicated the performers. But finding that no regard was paid to their censures, they changed their plan, and determined to take these recreations into their own hands. They turned actors, and (instead of profane mummeries) presented stories taken from Legends or the Bible. This was the origin of sacred comedy. The death of Saint Catharine, acted by the Monks of Saint Denis, rivalled the popularity of the professed players. Music was admitted into the churches, which served as theatres for the representation of holy farces. The festivals among the French, called *La fete de Foux, de l' Ane*,[1] and *des Innocens*, at length became greater favourites, as they certainly were more capricious and absurd, than the interludes of the buffoons at the fairs. These are the ideas of a judicious French writer, who has investigated the history of human manners with great comprehension and sagacity.

Voltaire's theory on this subject is also very ingenious, and quite new.[2] Religious plays, he supposes, came originally from Constan-

---

[1] For a most full and comprehensive account of these feasts, see *Memoires pour servir a l'histoire de la Fete de Foux*. Par M. du Tilliot, 1741. Grosseteste, bishop of Lincoln in the eleventh century, orders his dean and chapter to abolish the *Festum Asinorum, cum sit vanitate plenum, et voluptatibus spurcum*, which used to be annually celebrated in Lincoln Cathedral on the feast of the Circumcision (Grossetesti *Epistol.* xxxii. *apud* Browne's *Fascicul.* p. 331, edit. 1690, tom. ii. Append.) and p. 412. Also he forbids the archdeacons of his diocese to permit Scot-ales in their chapters and synods, (Spelm. *Gl.* p. 506) and other ludi on holidays. Ibid. *Epistol.* xxii. p. 314. See in the *Mercure Francois* for September, 1742, an account of a mummery celebrated in the city of Besançon in France by the canons of the cathedral, consisting of dancing, singing, eating and drinking, in the cloisters and church, on Easter-day, called *Bergeretta*, or the *Song of the Shepherds*; which remained unabolished till the year 1738. [*Bergerette* was the title also of a species of pastoral poetry.—*Park*.] From the *Ritual* of the church, p. 1930, *ad ann.* 1582. See Carpentier, *Suppl.* Du Cang. *Lat. Gloss.* tom. i. p. 523, in v. And *ibid.* v. *Boclare*, p. 570.

[2] ["Warton, referring to both these conjectures, inclines to Voltaire without perceiving that they might be reconciled."—*Collier*. Mr. Collier imagines that Warton's "judicious French writer" may be Du Tilliot, author of *La Fete de Foux*, Lausanne, 1741. "The reign of Charles V. (says Anderson, from Pasquier

tinople, where the old Grecian stage continued to flourish in some degree, and the tragedies of Sophocles and Euripides were [still] represented. [It may be worth while to offer a few illustrations of this position.¹ The Imperial edict of 399, which abolished the feast of Majuma, gave free permission for the continuance of all other public entertainments; and among these the theatre was of course included. The petition of the African bishops, drawn up in the same year according to Godefroy, or in 401 according to Baronius, merely solicits the suppression of plays upon Sundays, and other days observed as festivals in the Christian church, and begs an exemption for all Christians from being *compelled* to attend them. Nor was it till the year 425, that the prayer of this petition was confirmed by Theodosius the Younger, and then restricted to the most important feasts in the calendar. Four years after, the same emperor found it necessary to rescind the law, which prohibited female Christian proselytes from appearing upon the stage; who were thus allowed to resume their profession without the fear of spiritual censure.² The capture of Carthage (439) was effected by Genseric, whilst the inhabitants were at the theatre; and the language of Theodoret upon this occasion, unless we are to accept it as a mere rhetorical flourish, might be strained to imply, that the dramas of Æschylus and Sophocles were still exhibited in the Empire, or at least that they were generally known. An edict of Justinian only forbids deacons, priests, and bishops, from attending any species of scenic representation; and under the same emperor (588) Gregory Bishop of Antioch was publicly defamed by the spectators at the theatre, and ridiculed by the actors on the stage. In the year 692 the council of Trullo prohibited all christians, both clergy and laity, under pain of suspension or excommunication, from following the occupation of a player, and from frequenting the games of the circus and the theatre (Can. 51). Lastly, the canons of Nicephorus and of Photius, both framed in the ninth century, only re-echo the edict of Theodosius, that the theatre ought to be closed upon Sundays and days of solemn festival. The history of the West will afford us nearly similar notices. The theatres of France and Italy,

---

and Brantome) gave rise to the French drama and theatre. The actors, being erected into a company by letters patent, represented the *Mysteries of Christ's Passion* which, with some additional pieces called *Moralities*, continued to be the theatrical entertainment for more than 130 years. Though in the time of Louis XII. some farces or comedies were written, the French drama received no sort of improvement, but continued in the reign of Francis I. under the direction of the Fraternity of the Passion, who only added some burlesque pieces to their Moralities. Under Henry II., Francis II., and Charles IX., Jodella was the dramatic poet, and produced two tragedies and two comedies. His *Cleopatra* together with a comedy, being acted at Paris, he is said to have been rewarded for this new entertainment by his monarch with 500 crowns. But the genius and the relish for such compositions remained suspended for a considerable time after this exhibition of them." *Hist. of France, temp. Francis I. and Charles IX.* vol. ii. p. 427.—*Park.*]

¹ [Mr. Price's addition.]
² Mimas diversis adnotationibus liberatas ad proprium officium summa instantiâ revocari decernimus. L. xv. Cod. Th. Tit. 7, L. 13.

especially those of Rome and Marseilles, continued in high celebrity long after the first incursions of the barbarians; and the policy of Theodoric found it expedient to tolerate a pastime which he secretly condemned, and to encourage an abuse he could neither chasten nor correct.[1] For a period indeed these amusements appear to have been suspended by the ravages of Attila in Italy and of the Franks in France. But, in the time of Charlemagne, the *Mimi* and *Histriones* are spoken of in much the same terms of invective, cast upon their profession by the early Christian teachers; nor does the language of Agobard warrant a belief, that he was characterizing a different order of men from those who fell under the denunciations of his predecessors.[2]]

About the fourth century, Gregory Nazianzen, an archbishop, a poet, and one of the fathers of the church, banished pagan plays from the stage at Constantinople, and introduced select stories from the Old and New Testament. As the ancient Greek tragedy was a religious spectacle, a transition was made on the same plan; and the choruses were turned into Christian hymns. Gregory wrote many sacred dramas for this purpose, which have not survived those inimitable compositions over which they triumphed for a time: one, however, his tragedy called Χριστος πασχων, or *Christ's Passion*, is still extant.[3] In the prologue it is said to be in imitation of Euripides,[4] and that this is the first time the Virgin Mary has been produced on the stage. The fashion of acting spiritual dramas, in which at first a due degree of method and decorum was preserved, was at length adopted from Constantinople by the Italians, who framed in the depth of the dark ages, on this foundation, that barbarous species of theatrical representation called *Mysteries* or sacred comedies, which were soon afterwards received in France.[5] This opinion will acquire probability, if we consider the early commercial intercourse between Italy and Constantinople: and although the Italians, at the time when they may be supposed to have imported plays of this nature, did not understand the Greek language, yet they could understand, and consequently could imitate, what they saw.

In defence of Voltaire's hypothesis it may be further observed, that the *Feast of Fools* and of the *Ass*, with other religious farces of that sort so common in Europe, originated at Constantinople. They

---

[1] Hæc nos fovemus necessitate populorum. Expedit interdum desipere, ut possumus populi desiderata gaudia continere.

[2] [Satiat præterea et inebriat Histriones, Mimos, turpissimosque et vanissimos Joculares, cum pauperes Ecclesiæ fame discruciati intereant. Agobard, (*de Dispens.* p. 299). See *Discours sur la Comedie par Pierre Le Brun*. Paris, 1731.—*Price*.]

[3] *Greg. Nazianz.* tom. ii. p. 253. In a MS. cited by Lambeccius, it is called Δραμα κατ' Ευριπιδην. iv. 22. It seems to have been falsely attributed to Apollinaris, an Alexandrian, bishop of Laodicea. It is, however, written with less elegance and judgment than most of Gregory's poetical pieces. Apollinaris lived about the year 370.

[4] [Such an imitation Mr. Ashby thinks as probable as Otway and Dryden's imitations of Shakspeare.—*Park*.]

[5] *Hist. Gen. Addit.* p. 138.

were inftituted, although perhaps under other names, in the Greek church about the year 990 by Theophylact, patriarch of Conftantinople, probably with a better defign than is imagined by the ecclefiaftical annalifts: that of weaning the minds of the people from the pagan ceremonies, particularly the Bacchanalian and calendary folemnities, by the fubftitution of Chriftian fpectacles, partaking of the fame fpirit of licentioufnefs. The fact is, however, recorded by Cedrenus, one of the Byzantine hiftorians, who flourifhed about the year 1050, in the words below.[1] "Theophylact introduced the practice, which prevails even to this day, of fcandalifing God and the memory of his faints, on the moft fplendid and popular feftivals, by indecent and ridiculous fongs, and enormous fhoutings, even in the midft of thofe facred hymns, which we ought to offer to the divine grace with compunction of heart, for the falvation of our fouls. But he, having collected a company of bafe fellows, and placing over them one Euthymius, furnamed Cafnes, whom he alfo appointed the fuperintendent of his church, admitted into the facred fervice diabolical dances, exclamations of ribaldry, and ballads borrowed from the ftreets and brothels. [Perhaps Theophylact was only the firft who admitted thefe buffooneries within the walls of a church, and thus prepared the way for their reception among the Chriftians of the Weft. Their origin may with more probability be referred to an earlier period, when the Iconoclaft Emperors fought to degrade the Roman Pontiffs by an abfurd mockery of the papal election, the ceremonies of the Weftern Church, and all its obfervances both civil and fpiritual. Gibbon has detailed in part the conduct taken by the Emperor Michael III. in fuch a fcene, and has noticed the fources whence the curious reader may derive a confirmation, or rather a ftrong corroboration, of this opinion.[2]] This practice was fubfifting in the Greek church two hundred years afterwards; for Balfamon, patriarch of Antioch, complains of the grofs abominations committed by the priefts at Chriftmas and other feftivals, even in the great church at Conftantinople; and that the clergy, on certain holidays, perfonated a variety of feigned characters, and even entered the choir in a military habit and other enormous difguifes.[3]

In return, he forbids the profeffed players to appear on the ftage in the habit of monks. Saint Auftin, who lived in the fixth century, reproves the paganifing Chriftians of his age for their indecent fports

---

[1] "Εργον εκεινου, και το νυν κρατουν εθις, εν ταις λαμπραις και δημοτελεσιν εορταις ὑβριζεσθαι τον θεον, και τας των ἁγιων μνημας, δια λογισματων ατρεπων και γελωτων, και παραφορων κραυγων, τελουμενων των θειων ὑμνων· οὑς εδει, μετα καταλυξεως και συντριμμων καρδιας, ὑπερ της ἑμων σωτηριας, προσφερειν τω θεω. Πληθος γαρ συστησαμενος ετιρρητων ανδρων, και εξαρχον αυτοις επιστησας Ευθυμιον τινα Κασνην λεγομενον, ὁν αυτος Δομεστικον της εκκλησιας προυβαλλετο· και τας σατανικας ορχησεις, και τας ασημους κραυγας, και τα εκ τριοδων και χαμαιτυπειων πραισμενα ασματα τελεισθαι εδιδαξεν."
Cedren. Compend. Hift. p. 639, B. edit. 1647. Compare Baron. Annal. fub ann. 956, tom. x. p. 752, C. edit. Antw. 1603.

[2] [Mr. Price's addition. Decl. and Fall of the Rom. Emp. cap. 49, n. 18.—Price.]

[3] Comment. ad Canon. lxii. Synod. vi. in Trullo. Beverigii Synodic. tom. i. 1672, pp. 230, 231.

on holidays; but it does not appear that thefe fports were celebrated within the churches.¹

I muſt however obſerve here, what perhaps did not immediately occur to our lively philoſopher on this occaſion, that in the fourth century it was cuſtomary to make Chriſtian parodies and imitations in Greek of the beſt Greek claſſics for the uſe of the Chriſtian ſchools. This practice prevailed much under the Emperor Julian, who forbade the pagan poets, orators, and philoſophers to be taught in the Chriſtian ſeminaries. Apollinaris, biſhop of Laodicea, above mentioned, wrote Greek tragedies adapted to the ſtage on moſt of the grand events recorded in the Old Teſtament, after the manner of Euripides. On ſome of the familiar and domeſtic ſtories of ſcripture he compoſed comedies in imitation of Menander. He wrote Chriſtian odes on the plan of Pindar. In imitation of Homer, he wrote an heroic poem on the Hiſtory of the Bible, as far as the reign of Saul, in twenty-four books. Sozomen ſays that he compiled a ſyſtem of grammar, (Χριστιανικῳ τυπῳ,) on the Chriſtian model, and that his imitative compoſitions (now loſt) rivalled their great originals in genius, expreſſion, and conduct. His ſon, a biſhop alſo of Laodicea, reduced the four goſpels and all the apoſtolical books into Greek dialogues, reſembling thoſe of Plato.²

But I muſt not omit a much earlier and more ſingular ſpecimen of a theatrical repreſentation of ſacred hiſtory than this mentioned by Voltaire. Some fragments of an ancient Jewiſh play on the Exodus or Departure of the Iſraelites from Egypt under their leader and prophet Moſes are yet preſerved in Greek iambics.³ The principal characters of this drama are Moſes, Sapphora, and God from the Buſh, or God ſpeaking from the burning buſh. Moſes delivers the prologue or introduction in a ſpeech of ſixty lines, and his rod is turned into a ſerpent on the ſtage. The author of this piece is Ezekiel, a Jew, who is called 'Ο των Ιουδαικων τραγῳδιων ποιητης, or the tragic poet of the Jews.⁴ The learned Huet endeavours to prove that Ezekiel wrote at leaſt before the Chriſtian Era.⁵ Some ſuppoſe that he was one of the ſeventy or Septuagint interpreters of the Bible under the reign of Ptolemy Philadelphus. I am of opinion that Ezekiel compoſed this play after the deſtruction of Jeruſalem, and even in the time of Barocbas, as a political ſpectacle, with a view to animate his dejected countrymen with the hopes of a future deliverance from their captivity under the conduct of a new Moſes,

---

¹ "In ſanctis feſtivitatibus choros ducendo, cantica luxurioſa et turpia, &c. Iſti enim infelices ac miſeri homines, qui balationes ac ſaltationes ante ipſas baſilicas ſanctorum exercere nec metuunt nec erubeſcunt." S. Auguſt. *Opera*, edit. 1529, x. fol. 763, b (*Serm.* ccxv.) See alſo *Serm.* cxcvii. cxcviii. *opp.* edit. Benedictin. v. p. 904, *et ſeq.*

² Socrates, iii. 16, ii. 46. Sozomen, v. 18, vi. 26. Niceph. x. 25.

³ Clemens Alexandrin. lib. i. *Strom.* p. 344, *ſeq.* Euſebius, *Præparat. Evang.* c. xxviii. xxix. Euſtathius *ad Hex.* p. 25. They are collected, and tranſlated into Latin, with emendations, by Fr. Morellus (Paris, 1580). See alſo *Corpus Poetar. Gr. Tragicor. et Comicor.* Genev. 1614. And *Poetæ Chriſtian. Græci,* 1609.

⁴ See Scaliger, *ad Euſeb.* p. 401. *Demonſtrat. Evangelic.* p. 99.

like that from the Egyptian servitude.¹ The author of this Jewish tragedy seems to have belonged to that class of Hellenistico-Judaic writers of Alexandria, of which was the author of the apocryphal *Book of Wisdom*, a work originally written in Greek, perhaps in metre, full of allusions to the Greek poets and customs, and containing many lessons of instruction and consolation peculiarly applicable to the distresses and situation of the Jews after their dispersion.

Whether a theatre subsisted among the Jews, who by their peculiar situation and circumstances were prevented from keeping pace with their neighbours in the culture of the social and elegant arts, is a curious speculation. It seems most probable, on the whole, that this drama was composed in imitation of the Grecian stage, at the close of the second century, after the Jews had been dispersed, and intermixed with other nations.

Boileau seems to think, that the ancient Pilgrimages introduced these sacred exhibitions into France:

>   Chez nos devots ayeux le théatre abhorré
>   Fut long-tems dans la France une plaisir ignore.
>   De Pelerins, dit on, une troupe grossiere
>   En public à Paris y monta la prémiere ;
>   Et sotement zélee en sa simplicité,
>   Iöua les Saints, la Vierge et Dieu par piété.
>   Le Savoir, a la fin dissipant l'Ignorance,
>   Fit voir de ce projet la devote imprudence :
>   On chassa ces docteurs prêchant sans million ;
>   On vit renaitre Hector, Andromaque, Ilion.²

The authority to which Boileau alludes in these nervous and elegant verses is Menestrier, an intelligent French antiquary.³ The pilgrims who returned from Jerusalem, Saint James of Compostella, Saint Baume of Provence, Saint Reine, Mount Saint Michael, Notre Dame du Puy, and other places esteemed holy, composed songs on their adventures: intermixing recitals of passages in the life of Christ, descriptions of his crucifixion, of the day of judgment, of miracles, and martyrdoms. To these tales, which were recommended by a pathetic chant and a variety of gesticulations, the credulity of the multitude gave the name of *Visions*. These pious itinerants travelled in companies; and taking their stations in the most public streets, and singing with their staves in their hands, and their hats and mantles fantastically adorned with shells and emblems painted in various colours, formed a sort of theatrical spectacle. At length their performances excited the charity and compassion of some citizens of Paris, who erected a theatre in which they might exhibit their religious stories in a more commodious and advantageous manner, with the addition of scenery and other decorations. At length professed practitioners in the histrionic art were hired to perform these solemn mockeries of religion, which soon became the principal public amusement of a devout but undiscerning people.

To those who are accustomed to contemplate the great picture of human follies which the unpolished ages of Europe hold up to our

---
¹ See Le Moyne, *Obs. ad Var. Sacr.* tom. i. p. 336.
² *Art. Poet.* cant. iii. 81.   ³ *Des Represent. en Musique*, p. 153, seq.

view, it will not appear surprising that the people, who were forbidden to read the events of the Sacred History in the Bible, in which they were faithfully and beautifully related, should at the same time be permitted to see them represented on the stage, disgraced with the grossest improprieties, corrupted with inventions and additions of the most ridiculous kind, sullied with impurities, and expressed in the language and gesticulations of the lowest farce.

On the whole, the *Mysteries* appear to have originated among the ecclesiastics, and were most probably first acted, at least with any degree of form, by the monks. This was certainly the case in the English monasteries. I have already mentioned the play of Saint Catharine, performed at Dunstable Abbey by the novices in the eleventh century under the superintendence of Geoffry, a Parisian ecclesiastic: and the exhibition of the *Passion* by the mendicant friars of Coventry and other places. Instances have been given of the like practice among the French. The only persons who could read were in the religious societies: and various other circumstances, peculiarly arising from their situation, profession, and institution, enabled the monks to be the sole performers of these representations.[1]

As learning increased and was more widely disseminated from the monasteries, by a natural and easy transition the practice migrated to

---

[1] We are sure that religious plays were presented in our churches long after the reformation. Not to repeat or multiply instances, see *Second and Third Blast of Retrait from Plaies*, 1580, p. 77, and Gosson's *Schoole of Abuse*, p. 24, b. As to the exhibition of plays on Sundays after the reformation, we are told by John Field, in his *Declaration of Gods Judgement at Paris Garden*, that in the year 1580, "The Magistrates of the citty of London obteined from queene Elizabeth, that all heathenish playes and enterludes should be banished upon sabbath dayes." fol. ix. It appears from this pamphlet, that a prodigious concourse of people were assembled at Paris Garden, to see plays and a bear-baiting, on Sunday Jan. 13, 1583, when the whole theatre fell to the ground, by which accident many of the spectators were killed. [As this accident happened three years after the above order was issued, Dr. Ashby supposes that the order extended only to the city, and that Paris Garden was out of that jurisdiction.—*Park*.] (See also Henry [Carre's] *Narration of the Fall of Paris Garden*, 1588, and Beard's *Theater of Gods Judgements*, 1631, lib. i. c. 35, p. 212. Also *Refutation of* [Heywood's] *Apologie for Actors*, p. 43, by J[ohn] G[reen], 1615. And Stubbes's *Anatomie of Abuses*, pp. 134, 135, edit. 1595.) We learn from Richard R[aw]lidges's *Monster lately found out and discovered, or the Scourging of Tiplers*, a circumstance not generally known in our dramatic history, and perhaps occasioned by these profanations of the sabbath, that "Many godly citizens and wel-disposed gentlemen of London, considering that play-houses and dicing-houses were traps for yong gentlemen and others,—made humble suite to queene Elizabeth and her Privy-councell, and obtained leave from her Majesty, to thrust the Players out of the city; and to pull downe all Play-houses and Dicing-houses within their liberties: which accordingly was effected, and the Play-houses, in Gracious [Grace-church] street, Bishops gate street, that nigh Paules, that on Ludgate-hill, and the White-friers, were quite put downe and suppressed, by the care of these religious senators." 1628, pp. 2, 3, 4. Compare Whetstone's *Mirrour for Magistrates of Citties*, 1586, fol. 24. But notwithstanding these precise measures of the city magistrates and the privy-council, the queen appears to have been a constant attendant at plays, especially those presented by the children of her chapel. [So, also, she retained some relics of popery, as tapers on the altar, &c. which greatly offended the puritans.—*Ashby*.]

schools and univerſities, which were formed on the monaſtic plan, and in many reſpects reſembled the eccleſiaſtical bodies. Hence a paſſage in Shakeſpeare's *Hamlet* is to be explained: where Hamlet ſays to Polonius, "My lord, you played once i' the Univerſity, you ſay." Polonius anſwers, "That did I, my Lord, and was accounted a good *actor*.—I did *enact* Julius Ceſar, I was killed i' the capitol."[1] Boulay obſerves that it was a cuſtom, not only ſtill ſubſiſting, but of very high antiquity (*vetuſtiſſima conſuetudo*) to act tragedies and comedies in the univerſity of Paris.[2] He cites a ſtatute of the College of Navarre at Paris, dated 1315, prohibiting the ſcholars from performing any immodeſt play on the feſtivals of Saint Nicholas and Saint Catharine.[3] Saint Nicholas was the patron of ſcholars. Hence at Eton college Saint Nicholas has a double feaſt. The celebration of the Boy-biſhop began on St. Nicholas's day.[4] Carpentier mentions an indecent ſport, called *Le Vireli*, celebrated in the ſtreets on the feaſt of St. Nicholas, by the vicar and other choral officers of a collegiate church.[5] The tragedy called *Julius Ceſar*, and two comedies, of Jaques Grevin, a learned phyſician and an elegant poet of France, were firſt acted in the college of Beauvais at Paris in 1558 and 1560.[6] Reuchlin, one of the German claſſics at the reſtoration of ancient literature, was the firſt writer and actor of Latin plays in the academies of Germany. He is ſaid to have opened a theatre at Heidelberg, in which he brought ingenuous youths or boys on the ſtage, in the year 1498.[7] In the prologue to one of his comedies, written in trimeter iambics, and printed in 1516, are the following lines:

> Optans poeta placere paucis verſibus,
> Sat eſſe adeptum gloriæ arbitratus eſt,
> Si autore ſe Germaniæ Schola luſerit
> Græcanicis et Romuleis luſibus.

The firſt of Reuchlin's Latin plays ſeems to be one entitled *Sergius, capitis caput, Comoedia*, a ſatire on bad kings or bad miniſters, and printed in 1507;[8] [but this had been preceded by the ſame writer's *Scenica Progymnaſtica*, publiſhed nine years earlier]. He calls the *Sergius*, however, his *primiciæ*. It conſiſts of three acts, and is profeſſedly written in imitation of Terence. But the author promiſes,

---

[1] Act iii. ſc. [2, edit. *ut ſupr.* vii. 155.]
[2] *Hiſt. Univ. Paris*, tom. ii. 226. See alſo his Hiſtory *De Patronis quatuor Nationum*, edit. 1662.
[3] "In feſtis ſancti Nicolai et beatæ Catharinæ nullum ludum inhoneſtum faciant." *Hiſt. Univ. Paris*, tom. iv. 93.
[4] In a fragment of the Cellarer's *Computus*, of Hyde Abbey, near Wincheſter, A.D. 1397: "Pro epulis Pueri celebrantis in feſto S. Nicholai." That is the Choriſter celebrating maſs. MSS. Wulves. Winton.
[5] *Suppl.* Du Cang. *Lat. Gloſſ.* in v. tom. iii. p. 1178.
[6] Verdier, ut ſupra, ii. 284. La Croix du Maine, i. p. 415, *ſeq.*
[7] "Nunquam ante ipſius ætatem Comoedia in Germanorum ſcholis acta fuit," &c. Lizelius, *Hiſtor. Poetar. German.* 1730, p. 11.
[8] It is publiſhed with a gloſs by Simlerus his ſcholar. [See Brunet, laſt edit. art. *Reuchlin*.]

if this attempt should please, that he will write *integras Comedias*, that is, comedies of five acts.[1]

An old biographer affirms, that Conradus Celtes [or Celtis] was the first who introduced into Germany the fashion of acting tragedies and comedies in public halls, after the manner of the ancients.[2] Not to enter into a controversy concerning the priority of these two obscure theatrical authors, which may be sufficiently decided for our present satisfaction by observing, that they were certainly contemporaries: about the year 1500, Celtes wrote a play or masque, called the *Play of Diana*, presented by a literary society or seminary of scholars before the Emperor Maximilian and his court.[3] It consists of the iambic, hexameter and elegiac measures, and has five acts, but is contained in eight quarto pages. The plot, if any, is entirely a compliment to the emperor; and the personages, twenty-four in number (among which was the poet), are Mercury, Diana, Bacchus, Silenus drunk on his ass, Satyrs, Nymphs, and Bacchanalians. Mercury, sent by Diana, speaks the Prologue. In the middle of the third act, the emperor places a crown of laurel on the poet's head: at the conclusion of which ceremony the chorus sings a panegyric in verse to the emperor. At the close of the fourth act, in the true spirit of a German shew, the imperial butlers refresh the performers with wine out of golden goblets, with a symphony of horns and drums: and at the end of the play they are invited by his majesty to a sumptuous banquet.[4]

---

[1] I give a few lines from the Prologue:

"Si unquam tulistis ad jocum vestros pedes,
Aut si rei aures præbuistis ludicræ,
In hac nova, obsecro, poetæ fabula,
Dignemini attentiores esse quam antea;
Non hic erit lasciviæ aut libidini
Meretriciæ, aut tristi senum curæ locus,
Sed histrionum exercitus et scommata."

[2] "Primus comœdias et tragœdias in publicis aulis veterum more egit."— *Viror. Illustr. Vitæ*, &c. published by Fischardus, Francof. 1536, 4to. p. 8, b. Celtes himself says, in his *Descriptio Urbis Norinbergæ*, written about 1500, that in the city there was an "Aula prætoria, ubi publica nuptiarum et chorearum spectacula celebrantur, hystoriis et ymaginibus imperatorum et regum nostrorum depicta." Cap. x.

[3] It was printed in 1502, at Nuremberg, with this title, *Incipit Ludus Dyanæ, coram Maximiliano rege, per Sodalitatem Litterariam Damulianam in Linzio*. See Conradi Celtis *Amores*, Noringb. 1502, ad calc. sign. q. There is also a work [edited by] Conradus Celtes, containing six Latin plays in imitation of Terence, under this title, *Hrosvite, illustris virginis et Monialis Germanæ, Opera: nempe, Comoediæ sex in æmulationem Terentii, Octo Sacræ Historiæ versibus compositæ, necnon Panegyricus*, &c. 1501.

[4] In the Colleges of the Jesuits in Italy this was a constant practice in modern times. Denina says, that father Granelli's three best tragedies were written, for this purpose, between 1729 and 1731, (ch. v. § 9). The tragedies of Petavius, Bernardinus and Stephonius, all Jesuits, seem intended for this use. See Morhoff, *Polyhist. Literar*. lib. vii. cap. iii. tom. i. 15, pag. 1069, edit. Fabric. Riccoboni relates that he saw in the Jesuits' college at Prague a Latin play acted by the students on the subject of Luther's heresy; and the ridicule consisted in bringing Luther on

It is more generally known that the practice of acting Latin plays in the Colleges of Oxford and Cambridge continued to Cromwell's usurpation. The oldest notice I can recover of this sort of spectacle in an English university is in the fragment of an ancient accompt-roll of the dissolved college of Michael House in Cambridge: in which, under 1386, the following expense is entered: "Pro ly pallio brusdato et pro sex larvis et barbis in comedia," that is, for an embroidered pall or cloak, and six visors and six beards, for the comedy.[1] In 1544 a Latin comedy, called *Pammachius*, was acted at Christ's college in Cambridge, which was laid before the privy council by Bishop Gardiner, chancellor of the university, as a dangerous libel, containing many offensive reflections on the papistic ceremonies yet unabolished.[2] This mode of attack was seldom returned by the opposite party; the catholic worship, founded on sensible representations, afforded a much better hold for ridicule than the religion of some of the sects of the reformers, which was of a more simple and spiritual nature. But I say this of the infancy of our stage. In the next century, fanaticism was brought upon the English stage with great success, when polished manners had introduced humour into comedy, and character had taken place of spectacle. There are, however, two English interludes, one of the reign of Henry VIII. called *Every Man*, the other of that of Edward VI. called *Lusty Juventus*, and written by R. Weever: the former defends, and the latter attacks, the church of Rome.[3]

The comedy of *Gammer Gurton's Needle* was acted in the same society [according to Malone, in 1566; but Udall's *Ralph Roister Doister*, as appears from a passage in Wilson's *Rule of Reason*, printed in 1551, had been performed before the latter date, and was probably printed about 1566.][4] In an original draught of the statutes of Trinity College, at Cambridge, founded in 1546, one of the chapters is entitled, *De Præfecto Ludorum qui Imperator dicitur*, under whose direction and authority Latin comedies and tragedies are to be exhibited in the hall at Christmas, as also *Sex spectacula* or as many dialogues. Another title to this statute, which seems to be substituted by another and a more modern hand, is, *De Comediis ludisque in natali Christi exhibendis*. With regard to the peculiar business and office of Imperator, it is ordered that one of the Masters of Arts shall be placed over the juniors every Christmas for the regulation of their games and diversions at that season of festivity. At the same time he is to govern the whole society in the hall and chapel, as a republic committed to his special charge, by a set of laws which he is to frame in Latin or Greek verse. His sovereignty is to last during the twelve days of Christmas, and he is to exercise the same power on Candle-

---

the stage, with a Bible in his hand, quoting chapter and verse in defence of the Reformation.
[1] MSS. Rawlins. Bibl. Bodl. Oxon.
[2] MSS. Coll. C. C. Cant. (*Catal. Nasmith.* p. 92.)
[3] [Both these pieces will be found in Mr. Hawkins's *Origin of the English Drama*, vol. i.—*Price*.]
[4] [*Ralph Roister Doister* was reprinted in 1818 and 1847.]

mas-day. During this period, he is to see that six spectacles or
dialogues be presented. His fee is forty shillings.¹ Probably the
constitution of this officer (in other words, a Master of the Revels)
gave a latitude to some licentious enormities, incompatible with the
decorum of a house of learning and religion; and it was found
necessary to restrain these Christmas celebrations to a more rational
and sober plan. The spectacula also and dialogues (originally appointed) were growing obsolete, when the substitution was made, and
were giving way to more regular representations. I believe these
statutes were reformed by Queen Elizabeth's visitors of the University of Cambridge under the conduct of Archbishop Parker in
1573. John Dee, the famous occult philosopher, one of the first
fellows of this noble society, acquaints us that by his advice and
endeavours, both here and in other colleges at Cambridge, this
master of the Christmas plays was first named and confirmed emperor.
"The first was Mr. John Dun, a very goodly man of person, habit,
and complexion, and well learned also."² He also further informs
us, little thinking how important his boyish attempts and exploits
scholastical would appear to future ages, that in the refectory of the
college, in the character of Greek lecturer, he exhibited before the
whole university the Εἰρήνη or Pax of Aristophanes, accompanied by
a piece of machinery, for which he was taken for a conjuror: "with
the performance of the scarabeus his flying up to Jupiter's palace,
with a man and his basket of victuals on her back: whereat was
great wondering, and many vain reports spread abroad, of the means
how that was effected."³ The tragedy of *Jephtha*, dedicated to Henry
VIII. by a very grave and learned divine, John Christopherson,
another of the first Fellows (and afterwards Master) of Trinity
College, Cambridge, subsequently Dean of Norwich and Bishop of
Chichester, was written about 1546, in Latin and Greek, being taken
from the eleventh chapter of the Book of Judges; it was most
probably composed as a Christmas-play for the same society. It is
to be noted, that this play is on a religious subject.⁴ Roger Ascham,
while on his travels in Flanders, says in one of his *Epistles*, written
about 1550, that the city of Antwerp as much exceeds all other

---

¹ This article is struck out from cap. xxiv. p. 85. MSS. Rawlins. Num. 233.
Only that part of the statute is retained in which comedies and tragedies are ordered
to be acted. These are to be written, or rather exhibited, by the nine lecturers.
The senior lecturer is to produce one: the eight others are charged with four
more. A fine of ten shillings is imposed for the omission of each interlude.
Another clause is then struck out, which limits the number of the plays to three,
if five " commode exponi non queant."
² *Compendious Rehearsall of John Dee*, &c. written by himself, A.D. 1592, ch. i.
pp. 501, 502. Append. *J. Glastoniensis Chron.* edit. Hearne.
³ *Ibid.* p. 502.
⁴ Buchanan has a tragedy on this subject, written in 1554. [In *Hamlet*, 1603,
is quoted a ballad of *Jephthah Judge of Israel*. See *Handb. of E. E. Lit.* art.
Jephthah.] There is an Italian tragedy on this subject by Benedict Capuano, a
monk of Casino. Florent. 1587, 4to. [Respecting Buchanan, see Ellis, *Or. Let.*
3rd S. iii. 373, and Harvey's *Foure Letters*, &c. 1592, repr. Collier, 52.]

cities, as the refectory of St. John's College in Cambridge, exceeds itself, when furnished at Christmas with its theatrical apparatus for acting plays.¹ [Grimoald's *Archi-Propheta*, 1548, has been noticed elsewhere.²] This play coincided with the author's plan of a rhetoric lecture which he had set up in the college. In an auditbook of Trinity College, Oxford, I think for the year 1559, I find the following disbursements relating to this subject. " Pro apparatu in comoedia Andriæ, vii*l*. ix*s*. iv*d*. Pro prandio Principis Natalicii eodem tempore, xiii*s*. ix*d*. Pro refectione præfectorum et doctorum magis illustrium cum Bursariis prandentium tempore comoediæ, iv*l*. vii*d*." That is, for dresses and scenes in acting Terence's *Andria*, for the dinner of the Christmas Prince, and for the entertainment of the Heads of the Colleges and the most eminent doctors dining with the bursars or treasurers, at the time of acting the comedy, 12*l*. 3*s*. 8*d*. A Christmas Prince, or Lord of Misrule, corresponding to the Imperator at Cambridge just mentioned, was a common temporary magistrate in the colleges at Oxford, [and in the Inns of Court;] but at Cambridge they were censured in the sermons of the Puritans in the reign of James I. as a relic of the pagan ritual.³ The last article of this disbursement shows, that the most respectable company in the university were invited on these occasions. In some great families, this officer was called the " Abbot of Misrule." In Scotland, where the Reformation took a more severe and gloomy turn, these and other festive characters were thought worthy to be suppressed by the legislature;⁴ and this under very severe penalties, viz. : In burghs, to the choosers of such characters, loss of freedom, with other punishments at the queen's grace's will, and those who accepted such offices, to be banished the realm. In the country, the choosers forfeited ten pounds, with an arbitrary imprisonment. " And gif onie women or uther about summer hees [hies, goes,] singand [singing] . . . thorow Burrowes and uthers Landward tounes, the women . . . sall be taken, handled, and put upon the cuck-stules," &c.⁵ Voltaire says that, since the Reformation, for two hundred years there had not been a fiddle heard in some of the cantons of Switzerland.

In the French towns there was *L'Abbe de Liesse*, who in many towns was elected from the burgesses by the magistrates, and was the director of all their public shews. Among his numerous mockofficers were a herald and a *Maitre d'Hotel*. In the city of Auxerre

---

¹ Or, in his own words, " Quemadmodum aula Johannis, theatrali more ornata, seipsam post Natalem superat."—*Epistol.* 1581, p. 126, b.
² [*Infra*, sect. 39 (vol. iv. p. 49.)]
³ Fuller, *Ch. Hist.* (Hist. of Cambridge, p. 159, edit. 1655.) See *Observat. on Spenser*, ii. 211, [and present work, sect. 48.]
⁴ See *Parl.* vi. of Queen Mary of Scotland, 1555. " It is statute and ordained, that in all times cumming, na maner of person be chosen Robert Hude nor Little John, Abbot of Un-reason, Queenis of May, nor utherwise, nother in burgh, nor to landwart, [in the country,] in onie time to cum." [See Dr. Jamieson's *Dictionary*, in voc. Abbot of Un-ressoun.]
⁵ See Notes to the *Northumberland Houshold Book*, 1827, p. 441.

he was especially concerned to superintend the play which was acted on Quinquagesima Sunday.¹

At length our universities adopted the representation of plays, in which the scholars by frequent exercise had undoubtedly attained a considerable degree of skill and address, as a part of the entertainment at the reception of princes and other eminent personages. In the year 1566, Queen Elizabeth visited the University of Oxford. In the magnificent hall of the College of Christ Church, she was entertained with a Latin comedy called *Marcus Geminus*, the Latin tragedy of *Progne*, and an English comedy [by Richard Edwards] on the story of Chaucer's *Palamon and Arcite*, all acted by the students of the University. The Queen's observations on the persons of the last-mentioned piece deserve notice, as they are at once a curious picture of the romantic pedantry of the times, and of the characteristical turn and predominant propensities of the Queen's mind. When the play was over she summoned into her presence the poet, whom she loaded with thanks and compliments; and at the same time (turning to her levee) remarked that Palamon was so justly drawn as a lover, that he certainly must have been in love indeed: that Arcite was a right martial knight, having a swart and manly countenance, yet with the aspect of a Venus clad in armour: that the lovely Emilia was a virgin of uncorrupted purity and unblemished simplicity, and that although she sang so sweetly, and gathered flowers alone in the garden, she preserved her chastity undeflowered. The part of Emilia, the only female part in the play, was acted by a boy of fourteen years of age, a son of the Dean of Christ Church, habited like a young princess, whose performance so captivated her majesty, that she gave him a present of eight guineas. This youth had before been introduced to the Queen's notice, in her privy chamber at her lodgings at Christ Church, where he saluted her in a short Latin oration with some Greek verses, with which she was so pleased that she called in Secretary Cecil, and (encouraging the boy's modesty with many compliments and kind speeches) begged him to repeat his elegant performance. By Wood he is called *summæ spei puer*.² During the exhibition a cry of hounds, belonging to Theseus, was counterfeited without, in the great square of the college: the young students thought it a real chase, and were seized with a sudden transport to join the hunters: at which the Queen cried out from her box, "O excellent! These boys, in very troth, are ready to leap out of the windows to follow the hounds!"³ In the year 1564, Queen Eliz-

---

¹ Carpentier, *Suppl. Gloss. Lat. Du Cange*, tom. i. p. 7, v. *Abbas Lætitiæ*. See also, *ibid.* v. *Charavaritum*, p. 923.
² *Hist. Antiq. Univ. Oxon.* lib. i. p. 287, col. 2. See also *Athen. Oxon.* i. 152, and Peck's *Desid. Curios.* vol. ii. lib. vii. Num. xviii. p. 46, *seq.* [For a detailed account of this and subsequent exhibitions of the same kind see Nichols's *Progresses of Queen Elizabeth.*—Price.]
³ Wood, *Athen. Oxon.* ubi supr.

abeth had honoured the University of Cambridge with a royal visit.[1] Here she was present at the exhibition of the *Aulularia* of Plautus and the tragedies of *Dido* [by John Rightwise,] and *Hezekiah* [all in Latin,] which were played in the body or nave of the chapel[2] of King's College, on a stage extended from side to side, by a select company of scholars, chosen from different colleges at the discretion of five doctors, "especially appointed to set forth such plays as should be exhibited before her grace."[3] The chapel on this occasion was lighted by the royal guards, each of whom bore a staff-torch in his hand.[4] Her majesty's patience was so fatigued by the sumptuous parade of shows and speeches, with which every moment was occupied, that she could not stay to see the *Ajax* of Sophocles, [also] in Latin, which was prepared. Having been praised both in Latin and Greek, and in prose and verse, for her learning and her chastity, and having received more compliments than are paid to any of the pastoral princesses in Sydney's *Arcadia*, she was happy to return to the houses of some of her nobility in the neighbourhood. In the year 1583, Albertus de Alasco, a Polish prince Palatine, arrived at Oxford.[5] In the midst of a medley of pithy orations, tedious sermons, degrees, dinners, disputations, philosophy, and fire-works, he was invited to the comedy of the *Rivales* and the tragedy of *Dido*, which were presented in Christ Church Hall by some of the scholars of that society and of St. John's College. [Both were in Latin. The first was] written by William Gager, admitted a student of Christ Church in 1572. By the way, he is styled by Wood the best comedian of his time, that is dramatic poet. But he wrote only Latin plays. His Latin *Meleager* was acted at Christ Church before Lord Leicester, Sir Philip Sydney, and other distinguished persons, in 1581.[6] Gager had a controversy with Dr. Rainolds, president of Corpus at Oxford, concerning the lawfulness of plays, which produced from the latter a book, called *The Overthrow of Stage-plays*, &c., printed in 1599. Gager's letter, in defence of his plays and of the students who acted in them, is extant.[7] It appears by a pamphlet written by one W. Heale, and printed at Oxford in 1609, that Gager held it lawful, in a public Act of the University, for husbands to beat their wives. In the latter play, Dido's supper and the destruction of Troy were represented in a marchpane or rich cake; and the tempest which drove Dido and Eneas to the same cave was counterfeited by a snow of sugar, a hailstorm of comfits, and a shower of rose-water.[8] In the

---

[1] For a minute account of which see Peck's *Desid. Curios.* Num. xv, and [MSS. Baker, vol. x. 7037, p. 109, Brit. Mus.]

[2] [Mr. Ashby conceived that the anti-chapel must be here meant; though the whole, he adds, is one plain room of uniform dimensions, and no separation of any kind except the organ; but the anti-chapel is more superbly fitted up than the chapel, *i. e.* with roses and shields of arms in alto-relievo.—*Park.*]

[3] Peck, *ut supr.* pp. 36, 39.   [4] *Ibid.* p. 36.

[5] Supposed to be the person whom Shakespeare, in the *Merchant of Venice*, called the Count Palatine, act i. sc. i.

[6] *Ath. Oxon.* i. p. 366.   [7] Bibl. Coll. Univ. MSS. J. 18.

[8] Holinsh. *Chron.* iii. 1355.

year 1605, James I. gratified his pedantry by a visit to the same university.[1] He was present in Christ Church hall at three plays, which he seems to have regarded as childish amusements in comparison with the more solid delights of scholastic argumentation. Indeed, if we consider this monarch's insatiable thirst for profound erudition, we shall not be surprised to find that he slept at these theatrical performances, and that he sat four hours every morning and afternoon with infinite satisfaction to hear syllogisms in jurisprudence and theology. The first play during this solemnity was a pastoral comedy called *Alba*, in which five men almost naked, appearing on the stage as part of the representation, gave great offence to the queen and the maids of honour; while the king, whose delicacy was not easily shocked at other times, concurred with the ladies, and availing himself of this lucky circumstance, peevishly expressed his wish to depart, before the piece was half finished.[2] The second play was *Vertumnus* which, although learnedly penned in Latin and by a doctor in divinity, [Matthew Gwinne,] could not keep the king awake; he was wearied in consequence of having executed the office of moderator all that day at the disputations in St. Mary's church. The queen was not present; but next morning, with her ladies, the young prince, and gallants attending the court, she saw an English pastoral by Daniel, called *Arcadia Reformed*.[3] Although the anecdote is foreign to our purpose, I cannot help mentioning the reason why the queen, during this visit to Oxford, was more pleased to hear the oration of the professor of Greek than the king. "The king heard him willingly, and the queen much more, because, she sayd, she 'never had heard Greek.'"[4] The third drama was the *Ajax* of Sophocles in Latin, at which the stage was varied three times. "The king was very wearie before he came thither, but much more wearied by it, and spoke many words of dislike."[5] But I must not omit that, as the king entered the city from Woodstock, he was saluted at the gate of St. John's College with a short interlude, which probably suggested a hint to Shakespeare to write a tragedy on the subject of Macbeth. Three youths of the college, habited like witches, advancing towards the king, declared they were the same who once met the two chiefs of Scotland, Macbeth and Banquo, prophesying a kingdom to the one, and to the other a generation of monarchs: that they now appeared a second time to his majesty, who was descended from the stock of Banquo, to show the confirmation of that prediction.[6] Immediately afterwards, "Three young youths, in habit and attire like Nymphs, confronted him, representing England, Scotland, and Ireland; and talking dialogue-wise (each to the other) of their state,

---

[1] See *Preparations at Oxford*, &c., *Append. Lelandi Coll.* vol. ii. p. 626, *seq.* edit. 1774. [MSS. Baker, *ut supr.* Brit. Mus.] They were written by one present.
[2] *Ibid.* p. 637.
[3] *Ibid.* p. 642. [This was the piece printed in 1606 under the title of *The Queenes Arcadia*.]
[4] *Ibid.* p. 636.
[5] *Ibid.* p. 639.
[6] *Rex Platonicus, sive Musæ Regnantes*, 1607, p. 18.

at laſt concluded, yielding themſelves up to his gracious government."[1] Towards the end of the hall was a ſcene like a wall, "painted and adorned with ſtately pillars, which pillars would turn about, by reaſon whereof, with the help of other painted clothes, their ſtage did vary three times in the acting of one tragedy."[2] "The machinery of theſe plays, and the temporary ſtages in St. Mary's church, were chiefly conducted by one Mr. Jones, a great traveller, who undertook to further them much, and furniſh them with rare devices, but performed little to what was expected."[3] Notwithſtanding theſe ſlighting expreſſions, [there is no doubt whatever] that this was Inigo Jones, afterwards the famous architect. He was now but thirty-three years of age, and had recently returned into England. He was the principal contriver for the maſques at Whitehall.[4] Gerard, deſcribing Queen Henrietta's popiſh chapel, ſays [under 1635]: "Such a glorious ſcene built over the altar! Inigo Jones never preſented a more curious piece in any of the maſks at Whitehall."[5]

It would be unneceſſary to trace this practice in our univerſities to later periods. The poſition advanced is beſt illuſtrated by proofs moſt remote in point of time which, on that account, are alſo leſs obvious and more curious. I could have added other ancient proofs; but I choſe to ſelect thoſe which ſeemed, from concomitant circumſtances, moſt likely to amuſe.

Many inſtances of this practice in ſchools, or in ſeminaries of an inferior nature, may be enumerated. I have before mentioned the play of *Robin and Marian* performed, according to an annual cuſtom, by the ſchool-boys of Angiers in France in the year 1392. But I do not mean to go abroad for illuſtrations of this part of our preſent inquiry. Among the writings of Udall, a celebrated maſter of Eton about the year 1540, are recited *Plures Comediæ*[6] and a tragedy *de Papatu*, on the papacy: written probably to be acted by his ſcholars. [His *Ralph Roiſter Doiſter* has already been mentioned.] In the ancient *Conſuetudinary*, as it is called, of Eton School,[7] it is ſaid that about the Feaſt of Saint Andrew, November 30, the maſter is accuſtomed to chooſe, according to his own diſcretion, ſuch Latin ſtage-plays as are moſt excellent and convenient; which the boys are to act in the following Chriſtmas holidays before a public audience, and with all the elegance of ſcenery and ornaments uſual at the performance of a play. Yet he may ſometimes order Engliſh plays; ſuch, at leaſt, as are ſmart and witty. In the year 1538,

---

[1] Lel. *Append.* ut ſupr. p. 636. [2] *Ibid.* p. 631.
[3] *Ibid.* p. 646.
[4] [See Peter Cunningham's *Life of Inigo Jones*, 1848, p. 5, *et ſeq.*]
[5] Strafford's *Letters*, i. 505. [6] [See Royal MS. 18. A. lxiv.]
[7] [Theſe rules are] ſuppoſed to have been drawn up about the year 1560. But containing all the ancient and original cuſtoms of the ſchool. MSS. Rawlins, Bibl. Bodl. The following is the original paſſage: "Circa feſtum divi Andreæ, ludimagiſter eligere ſolet, pro ſuo arbitrio, ſcenicas fabulas optimas et accommodatiſſimas, quas Pueri feriis Natalitiis ſubſequentibus, non ſine ludorum Elegantia, populo ſpectante, publice aliquando peragant. Interdum etiam exhibet Anglico ſermone contextas fabulas, ſiquæ habeant acumen et leporem."

Ralph Radcliffe's Plays.

Ralph Radcliffe, a polite scholar and a lover of graceful elocution, opening a school at Hitchin in Hertfordshire, obtained a grant of the dissolved Friary of the Carmelites in that town: and converting the refectory into a theatre, wrote several plays, both in Latin and English, which were exhibited by his pupils. Among his comedies were *Dives and Lazarus*, Boccaccio's *Patient Grisilde*, *Titus and Gesippus*, and Chaucer's *Melibeus*: his tragedies were, the *Delivery of Susannah*, the *Burning of John Huss*, *Job's Sufferings*, the *Burning of Sodom*, *Jonas*, and *The Fortitude of Judith*. These pieces were seen by the biographer Bale in the author's library, but are now lost.[1] It is scarcely necessary to remind the reader, that this very liberal exercise is yet preserved, and in the spirit of true classical purity, at Westminster School.[2] I believe, the frequency of these school-plays suggested to Shakespeare the names of Seneca and Plautus as dramatic authors, where Hamlet, speaking of a variety of theatrical performances, says, "Seneca cannot be too heavy, nor Plautus too light."[3] Jonson, in *The Staple of Newes*, has a satirical allusion to this practice (yet ironically applied), where Censure says: "For my part, I beleeve it, and there were no wiser than I, I would have neer a cunning schoole-master in England: I mean a Cunning-man a schoole-master; that is, a conjuror, or a poet, or that had any acquaintance with a poet. They make all their schollers Play-boyes! Is't not a fine sight to see all our children made Enterluders? Doe we pay our money for this? Wee send them to learne their grammar and their Terence, and they learne their play-bookes. Well, they talk we shall have no more parliaments, god blesse us! But an wee have, I hope *Zeale of the Land Buzzy*, and my gossip *Rabby Trouble-*

---

[1] Bale, viii. 98. *Ath. Oxon.* i. 73. I have seen an anonymous comedy, [by William Hawkins,] *Apollo Shroving*, composed by the Master of Hadleigh School, in Suffolk, and acted by his scholars, on Shrove Tuesday, Feb. 7, 1626, printed 1627, 8vo. Published, as it seems, by E. W. Shrove Tuesday, as the day immediately preceding Lent, was always a day of extraordinary sport and feasting. So in the song of [Master] Silence in [the second part of *Henry IV.* act v. sc. 3:]

"Tis merry in hall when beards wag all,
And welcome merry Shrovetide."

[The first line is in the metrical *Life of Alexander*, attributed to Adam Davie, circa 1312.] In the Romish church there was anciently a feast immediately preceding Lent, which lasted many days, called Carniscapium. See Carpentier, in v. *Suppl. Lat. Gl.* Du Cang. tom. i. p. 831. In the *Northumberland Houshold-book*, 1512, it appears that the clergy and officers of Lord [Northumberland's] chapel performed a play "before his lordship upon Shrowtewesday at night," p. 345, [edit. 1770 or 1827].

[2] It appears anciently to have been an exercise for youth, not only to act but to write interludes. Erasmus says that Sir Thomas More, "adolescens Comoediolas et scripsit et egit." *Epistol.* 447. But see what I have said of More's *Pageants*, *Observat. on Spens.* ii. 47, [and *infra*, section xliii.] We are told that More, while he lived a page with Archbishop Morton, as the plays were going on in the palace during the Christmas holidays, would often step upon the stage without previous notice, and exhibit a part of his own, which gave much more satisfaction than the whole performance besides. Roper's *Life and Death of More*, p. 27, edit. 1731.

[3] Act ii. sc. 7.

truth, will ftart up, and fee we have painfull good minifters to keepe fchoole, and catechife our youth; and not teach em to fpeake Playes, and act fables of falfe newes," &c.¹

In tracing the hiftory of our ftage, this early practice of performing plays in fchools and univerfities has never been confidered as a circumftance inftrumental to the growth and improvement of the drama. While the people were amufed with Skelton's [*Nigramanfir*],² Bale's *God's Promifes*, and *Chrift's Defcent into Hell*, [the laft-named, an anonymous miracle-play prefented before Henry VII. in 1487 by the choir-boys of Hyde Abbey and St. Swithin's Priory at Winchefter Caftle on a Sunday], the fcholars of the times were compofing and acting plays on hiftorical fubjects, and in imitation of Plautus and Terence. Hence ideas of a legitimate fable muft have been imperceptibly derived to the popular and vernacular drama; and we may add, while no fettled or public theatres were known, and plays were chiefly acted by itinerant minftrels in the halls of the nobility at Chriftmas, thefe literary focieties fupported fome idea of a ftage: they afforded the beft accommodations for theatrical exhibition, and were almoft the only, certainly the moft rational, companies of players that exifted. But I mean yet to trefpafs on my reader's patience by purfuing ftill further this inquiry which, for the fake of comprehenfion and connection, has already exceeded the limits of a digreffion.

It is perhaps on this principle, that we are to account for plays being acted by finging-boys: although they perhaps acquired a turn for theatrical reprefentation and the fpectacular arts from their annual exhibition of the ceremonies of the boy-bifhop; which feem to have been common in almoft every religious community that was capable of fupporting a choir. In a fmall college, for only one provoft, five fellows, and fix chorifters, founded by Archbifhop Rotherham in 1481, in the obfcure village of Rotherham in Yorkfhire, this piece of mummery was not omitted. The founder leaves by will, among other bequefts to the college, "A Myter for the 'barne-bifhop' of cloth of gold, with two knoppes of filver, gilt and enamelled."³ This eftablifhment, but with a far greater degree of buffoonery, was common in the collegiate churches of France.⁴ A part of the ceremony in the church of Noyon was, that the children of the choir fhould celebrate the whole fervice on Innocents' Day.⁵ This privilege, as I have before obferved, is permitted to the children of the choir of Winchefter College, on that feftival, by the founder's

---

¹ Act iii. p. 50, edit. fol. 1631, [or edit. 1816, v. 262]. This play was firft acted in the year 1625.
² [Warton, in his original text, fpeaks of this as *The Trial of Simonie*, which according to him (and there is no doubt he faw a copy of this now loft drama,) formed part of the groundwork of Skelton's production.]
³ Hearne's *Lib. Nig. Scacc. Append.* pp. 674, 686.
⁴ See Dom. Marlot, *Hiftoire de la Metropole de Rheims*, tom. ii. p. 769.
⁵ Brillon, *Dictionnaire des Arrets*, Artic. *Noyon* edit. 1727.

S. 33.   *Performance of Plays by Choristers.*   311

statutes given in 1380.¹ Yet in the statutes of Eton College, given in 1441, and altogether transcribed from those of Winchester, the chorister-bishop of the chapel is permitted to celebrate the holy offices on the feast of St. Nicholas, but by no means on that of the Innocents.² The same clause is in the statutes of King's College at Cambridge.³ The parade of the mock-bishop is evidently akin to the "Fete des Foux," in which they had a bishop, an abbot, and a precentor, of the fools. One of the pieces of humour in this last-mentioned show, was to shave the precentor in public on a stage erected at the west door of the church.⁴ It is surprising that Colet, Dean of Saint Paul's, a friend to the purity of religion, and who had the good sense and resolution to censure the superstitions and fopperies of popery in his public sermons, should countenance this idle farce of the boy-bishop in the statutes of his school at St. Paul's; which he founded with a view of establishing the education of youth on a more rational and liberal plan than had yet been known, in 1512. He expressly orders that his scholars " shall every Childermas [Innocents'] daye come to Paulis churche, and hear the childe-byshops [of S. Paul's cathedral] sermon. And after be at the hygh masse; and each of them offer a penny to the childe-byshop, and with them the maisters and surveyors of the scole." ⁵ I take this opportunity of observing, that the anniversary custom at Eton of going " ad Montem," originated from the ancient and popular practice of these theatrical processions in collegiate bodies.

In the statutes of New College in Oxford, founded about 1380, there is the subjoined remarkable passage.⁶ Hearne endeavours to explain this injunction, by supposing that it was made in opposition to the Wickliffites, who disregarded the laws of Scripture, and (in this particular instance) violated the text in *Leviticus*, where this custom is expressly forbidden:⁷ " Neither shalt thou mar the corners of thy beard."⁸ Nothing can be more unfortunate than this elucida-

---

¹ [See *supr.* vol. ii.]
² " In festo sancti Nicolai, in quo et nullatenus in festo sanctorum Innocentium, divina officia (præter Missæ Secreta) exequi et dici permittimus per Episcopum Puerorum, ad hoc de eisdem [pueris choristis] annis singulis eligendum." *Statut. Coll. Etonens.* cap. xxxi.
³ Cap. xlii.
⁴ Tilliot, *Mem. de la Fete des Foux, ut supr.* p. 13. In the Council of Sens, A.D. 1485, we have this prohibition : " Turpem etiam illum abusum in quibusdam frequentatum ecclesiis quo, certis annis, nonnulli cum mitra, baculo, ac vestibus pontificalibus, more episcoporum benedicunt, alii ut reges et duces induti, quod Festum Fatuorum, vel Innocentium, seu Puerorum, in quibusdam regionibus nuncupatur," &c. *Concil. Senon.* cap. iii. Harduin. *Act. Concil.* 1714, tom. ix. p. 1525, E. See also *ibid. Concil. Basil.* Sess. xxi. p. 1122, E; and 1296, D. p. 1344, A.
⁵ Knight's *Life of Colet* (*Miscell.* Num. v. *Append.*), p. 362. [See also Mr. Strutt's *Sports and Pastimes of the People of England.—Price.*]
⁶ " Ac etiam illum ludum vilissimum et horribilem radendi barbas, qui fieri solet in nocte præcedente Inceptionis Magistradorum in Artibus, infra collegium nostrum prædictum, vel alibi in Universitate prædicta, ubicunque, ipsis [sociis et scolaribus] penitus interdicimus, ac etiam prohibemus expresse." *Rubr.* xxv.
⁷ xix. 27.   ⁸ *Not. ad. Joh. Trokelowe*, p. 393.

tion of our antiquary. The direct contrary was the case: for the Wickliffites entirely grounded their ideas of reformation both in morals and doctrine on Scriptural proofs, and often committed absurdities in too precise and literal an acceptation of texts; and (to say no more) the custom, from the words of the statute, seems to have been long preserved in the university, as a mock ceremony on the night preceding the solemn Act of Magistration. It is styled *Ludus*, a play: and I am of opinion that it is to be ranked among the other ecclesiastic mummeries of that age; and that it has some connection with the exhibition mentioned above of shaving the precentor in public.

I have just given an instance of singing-boys performing a Morality on a Sunday in 1487. In the accompts of Maxtoke Priory near Coventry in 1430, it appears that the eleemosynary boys or choristers of that monastery acted a play (perhaps every year) on the Feast of the Purification in the hall of the neighbouring castle belonging to Lord Clinton: and it is specified that the cellarer should take no money for their attendance, because his lordship's minstrels had often assisted this year at several festivals in the refectory of the convent, and in the hall of the prior, without fee or gratuity.[1] The charge for the extraordinary breakfast of the children of the almonry, or singing-boys of the convent, when they went to the hall in the castle to perform the Play on the Feast-day, was fourteen-pence.

So early as 1378, the scholars or choristers of St. Paul's cathedral in London presented a petition to Richard II. that his majesty would prohibit some ignorant and inexperienced persons from acting the *History of the Old Testament* to the great prejudice of the clergy of the church, who had expended considerable sums for preparing a public presentation of that play at the ensuing Christmas.[2] From Mysteries this young fraternity proceeded to more regular dramas; and at the commencement of a Theatre, they were the best and almost only comedians. They became at length so favourite a set of players, as often to act at Court, and on particular occasions of festivity were frequently removed from London, for this purpose only, to the royal houses at some distance from town. In 1554, while the Princess Elizabeth resided at Hatfield House, in Hertfordshire, under the custody of Sir Thomas Pope, she was visited by Queen Mary. The next morning, after mass, they were entertained with a grand exhibition of bear-baiting, with which their highnesses were right well content. In the evening the great chamber was adorned with a sumptuous suit of tapestry, called *The Hanging of*

---

[1] [This is the original Latin:] "Pro jentaculis puerorum eleemosynæ exeuntium ad aulam in castro ut ibi ludum peragerent in die Purificationis, xiv*d*. Unde nihil a domini [Clinton] thesaurario, quia sæpius hoc anno ministralli castri fecerunt ministralsiam in aula conventus et Prioris ad festa plurima sine ullo regardo."

[2] See *Rise and Progress*, &c. *Life of Colley Cibber*, vol. ii. p. 118.

Antioch: and after supper, a play was presented by the children of Paul's.[1] After the play, and the next morning, one of the children, named Maximilian Poines, sang to the princess, while she "plaid at the virginalls."[2] Strype, perhaps from the same manuscript chronicle, thus describes a magnificent entertainment given to Queen Elizabeth in the year 1559 at Nonsuch in Surrey by [Henry, Earl of Arundel, who had acquired it from the crown by exchange[3] in Queen Mary's reign]. I choose to give the description in the words of this simple but picturesque compiler. "There the queen had great entertainment, with banquets, especially on Sunday night, made by the said earl; together with a Mask, and the warlike sounds of drums and flutes, and all kinds of musick, till midnight. On Monday was a great supper made for her: but before night, she stood at her standing in the further park, and there she saw a course. At night was a Play by the *Children of Paul's*, and their [music] master Sebastian. After that, a costly banquet, accompanied with drums and flutes. This entertainment lasted till three in the morning. And the earl presented her majesty a cupboard of plate."[4] In the year 1562, when the Society of Parish-Clerks in London celebrated one of their annual feasts, after morning service in Guildhall chapel, they retired to their hall where, after dinner, a goodly play was performed by the choristers of Westminster Abbey with waits and regals and singing.[5] The children of the chapel-royal were also famous actors, and were formed into a company of players by Queen Elizabeth under the conduct of Richard Edwards, a musician and a writer of Interludes already mentioned, and of whom more will be said hereafter. All Lyly's plays and [some] of Jonson's were originally performed by these boys:[6] and it seems probable that the title given by Jonson to one of his comedies, called [*The Fountaine of Self-Love, or Cynthia's revels*, privately acted at the Blackfriars theatre by the Children of the Chapel, and first printed in 1601,] was an allusion to

---

[1] Who perhaps performed the play of *Holophernes* the same year, after "a greate and rich maskinge and banquett" given by Sir Thomas Pope to the princess, in the "grete hall at Hatfelde." *Life of Sir Tho. Pope*, sect. iii. p. 85.

[2] *Annales of Q. Maries Reigne* (MSS. Cotton. Vitell. F. 5). There is a curious anecdote in Melville's *Memoirs*, 1752, concerning Elizabeth, when Queen, being surprised from behind the tapestry by Lord Hunsdon, while she was playing on her virginals. Her majesty, I know not whether in a fit of royal prudery or of royal coquetry, suddenly rose from the instrument and offered to strike his lordship: declaring, "that she was not used to play before men, but when she was solitary to shun melancholy." *Mem.* pag. 99. Leland applauds the skill of Elizabeth both in playing and singing. *Encom.* fol. 59, p. 125, edit. Hearn:

"Aut quid commemorem, quos tu, testudine sumpta,
Concentus referas mellifluosque modos?"

[3] [Lysons' *Environs of London*, first edit. i. 155-6. The palace is long since destroyed.]

[4] *Ann. Ref.* vol. i. ch. xv. p. 194, edit. 1725.

[5] Stow's *Surv.* edit. 1720, B. v. p. 231.

[6] Six of Lyly's nine comedies were reprinted together in 1632, 12mo. [under the title of *Court Comedies*]. His last play is dated [1601].

this establishment of Queen Elizabeth, one of whose romantic names was Cynthia.[1] The general reputation which they gained, and the particular encouragement and countenance which they received from the queen, excited the jealousy of the grown actors at the theatres: and Shakespeare, in *Hamlet*, endeavours to extenuate the applause which was idly indulged of their performance, perhaps not always very just, in the following speeches of Rosencrantz and Hamlet:— " There is, sir, an aery of children, little eyases,[2] that cry out on the top of question, and are most tyrannically clapped for't: these are now the fashion, and so berattle the common stages, so they call them, that many wearing rapiers are afraid of goose quills, and dare scarce come thither.—*Ham.* What, are they children? Who maintains 'em? How are they escoted?[3] Will they pursue the quality no longer than they can sing,"[4] &c. This was about the year 1599. The latter clause means, " Will they follow the profession of players, no longer than they keep the voices of boys, and sing in the choir?" So Hamlet afterwards says to the player, " Come, give us a taste of your quality: come, a passionate speech."[5] And perhaps he glances at the same set of actors in *Romeo and Juliet*, when a play or masque is proposed:

> We'll have no Cupid, hood-wink'd with a scarf,
> Bearing a Tartar's painted bow of lath.—
> Nor a without-book prologue faintly spoke
> After the prompter.[6]

Some of these, however, were distinguished for their propriety of action, and became admirable comedians at the theatre of Blackfriars. There is a passage in Strafford's *Letters*, which seems to show, that the dispositions and accommodations at the theatre of Blackfriars were much better than we now suppose. " A little pique happened betwixt the duke of Lenox and the lord chamberlain, about a box at a new play in the Black-friers, of which the duke had got the key." The dispute was settled by the king.[7]

[There is, by the way, a] curious account of an order of the Privy

---

[1] They very frequently were joined by the choristers of Saint Paul's. It is a mistake that these were rival companies; and that because Jonson's *Poetaster* was acted in 1601 by the boys of the chapel, his antagonist Decker got his *Satiromastix*, an answer to Jonson's play, to be performed (out of opposition) by those of St. Paul's. Lyly's comedies, and many others, were acted by the children of both choirs in conjunction. It is certain that Decker sneers at Jonson's interest with the Master of the Revels, in procuring his plays to be acted so often at court. " *Sir Vaughan.* I have some coffen-germans at court shall beget you the reversion of the master of the king's revels, or else to be his lord of misrule nowe at Christmas." Sign. G 3, Decker's *Satiromastix*, 1602. Again, sign. M. " When your playes are misselikt at court, you shall not crie mew like a puffe-cat, and say you are glad you write out of the courtier's element." On the same idea the satire is founded of sending Horace (or Jonson) to court, to be dubbed a poet, and of bringing " the quivering bride to court in a maske," &c. *Ibid.* signat. I 3.
[2] nest of young hawks.   [3] paid.
[4] Act ii. sc. [2, edit. *ut supr.* vii. 140.]   [5] Ibid. [p. 143.]
[6] Act i. sc. [4, edit. *ut supr.* vi. 401.]
[7] G. Garrard to the Lord Deputy, Jan. 25, 1635, vol. i. p. 511, edit. 1739.

Council, in 1633, " hung up in a table near Paules and Black-fryars, to command all that refort to the play-houfe there, to fend away their coaches, and to difperfe abroad in Paules Church-yard, carter-lane, the conduit in fleet-ftreet."[1] Another of Garrard's letters, dated 1637, mentions a play at this theatre, which "coft three or four hundred pounds fetting out; eight or ten fuits of new cloaths he [the author] gave the players, an unheard of prodigality!"[2]

It appears by the Prologue of Chapman's *All Fools*, a comedy prefented at Blackfriars, and printed in 1605, that only the fpectators of rank and quality fat on the ftage:

> To fair attire the ftage
> Helps much; for if our other audience fee
> You on the ftage depart before we end,
> Our wits go with you all, &c.

Among the children of Queen Elizabeth's chapel, was one Salvadore Pavy, who acted in Jonfon's two dramas *Poetafter* and *Cynthia's Revels*, and was inimitable in his reprefentation of the character of an old man. He died about thirteen years of age, and is thus elegantly celebrated in one of Jonfon's epigrams:

> *An Epitaph on S. P. a child of queene Elizabeth's chapell.*
>
> Weep with me, all you that read
>   This little ftory:
> And know, for whom a teare you fhed
>   Deaths felfe is forry.
> Twas a child, that fo did thrive
>   In grace and feature,
> As Heaven and Nature feem'd to ftrive
>   Which own'd the creature.
> Yeares he numbred fcarce thirteene,
>   When Fates turn'd cruell;
> Yet three fill'd zodiackes had he beene
>   The Stages Jewell:
> And did acte, what now we moane,
>   Old men fo duely;
> As, footh, the Parcæ thought him one,
>   He plaid fo truely.
> So, by errour, to his fate
>   They all confented;
> But viewing him fince, alas, too late,
>   They have repented:
> And have fought, to give new birthe,
>   In bathes to fteep him:
> But, being fo much too good for earthe,
>   Heaven vowes to keep him.[3]

To this ecclefiaftical origin of the drama we muft refer the plays acted by the Society of the Parifh Clerks of London for eight days fucceffively at Clerkenwell (which thence took its name) in the prefence of moft of the nobility and gentry of the kingdom, in the years 1390 and 1409. In the ignorant ages, the Parifh Clerks of London might juftly be confidered as a literary fociety. It was an effential

---

[1] *Ibid.* p. 175.   [2] *Ibid.* vol. ii. 150.
[3] *Epigrammes*, Epig. cxx. [edit. 1816 of Works, viii. 229-30.]

part of their profession not only to sing but to read: [the latter] an accomplishment almost solely confined to the clergy: and on the whole they seem to come under the character of a religious fraternity. They were incorporated into a guild or fellowship by Henry III. about 1240 under the patronage of St. Nicholas. It was anciently customary for men and women of the first quality, ecclesiastics and others, who were lovers of church-music, to be admitted into this corporation: and they gave large gratuities for the support or education of many persons in the practice of that science. Their public feasts, which I have already mentioned, were frequent, and celebrated with singing and music; most commonly at Guildhall Chapel or College.[1] Before the Reformation, this society was constantly hired to assist as a choir, at the magnificent funerals of the nobility or other distinguished personages, celebrated within the city of London or in its neighbourhood. The splendid ceremonies of their anniversary procession and mass in 1554 are thus related by Strype, from an old chronicle. "May the sixth, was a goodly evensong at Guildhall college by the Masters of the Clarks and their Fellowship, with singing and playing; and the morrow after was a great mass at the same place, and by the same fraternity: when every clark offered an halfpenny. The mass was sung by diverse of the queen's [Mary's] chapel and children. And after mass done every clark went their procession, two and two together; each having on a surplice and a rich cope, and a garland. And then, fourscore standards, streamers, and banners; and each one that bare them had an albe or a surplice. Then came in order the waits playing: and then thirty clarkes, singing *Festa dies*. There were four of these choirs. Then came a canopy, borne over the Sacrament by four of the masters of the clarkes, with staffe torches burning,"[2] &c. Their profession, employment and character naturally dictated to this spiritual brotherhood the representation of plays, especially those of the scriptural kind: and their constant practice in shews, processions and vocal music easily accounts for their address in detaining the best company which England afforded in the fourteenth century, at a religious farce for more than a week.

Before I conclude this inquiry, a great part of which has been taken up in endeavouring to shew the connection between places of education and the stage, it ought to be remarked that the ancient fashion of acting plays in the Inns of Court, which may be ranked among seminaries of instruction, although for a separate profession, is deducible from this source. The first representation of this sort which occurs on record, and is mentioned with any particular circumstances, was at Gray's-inn. John Roos or Roo, student at Gray's-Inn, and created a serjeant at law in the year 1511, wrote a comedy which was acted at Christmas in the hall of that society in the year 1527. This piece, [although written many years before, when the cardinal was unknown, was construed personally by] Wolsey, and the

---

[1] Stow's *Surv. Lond.* [edit. 1720,] lib. v. p. 231.
[2] *Eccles. Mem.* vol. iii. ch. xiii. p. 121.

author was degraded and imprifoned.¹ In 1550, under the reign of Edward VI., an order was made in the fame fociety that no comedies, commonly called Interludes, fhould be acted in the refectory in the intervals of vacation, except at the celebration of Chriftmas: and that then the whole body of ftudents fhould jointly contribute towards the dreffes, fcenes, and decorations.² In 1561, Sackville's tragedy of *Ferrex and Porrex* was prefented before Queen Elizabeth at Whitehall by the gentlemen of the Inner Temple.³ In 1566, the *Suppofes*, a comedy, [a profe paraphrafe of the *Suppofiti* of Arioſto by George Gafcoigne, and *Jocafta*,⁴ a dramatic adaptation of the *Phœniſſæ* of Euripides, the joint work of Gafcoigne, Francis Kinwelmerſh, and Chriſtopher Yelverton, were produced at Gray's-Inn.] Decker, in his *Satiromaſtix*, 1602, accufes Jonfon of having ſtolen fome jokes from the Chriſtmas plays of the lawyers. "You fhall fweare not to bumbaſt out a new play with the old lyning of jeſtes ſtolne from the Temple-revells."⁵ In the year 1632 it was ordered in the Inner Temple, that no play fhould be continued after twelve at night, not even on Chriſtmas-Eve.⁶

But thefe focieties feem to have fhone moſt in the reprefentation of Mafques, a branch of the old drama. So early as the year 1431, it was ordered that the fociety of Lincoln's-Inn fhould celebrate four revels on four grand feſtivals every year, which I conceive to have confifted in great meafure of this fpecies of imperfonation. It is not, however, exactly known whether thefe revels were not fimply Dances: for Dugdale fays that the ftudents of this inn "anciently had dancings for their recreation and delight;⁷ and he adds that in 1610 the under barriſters, for example's fake, were put out of commons by decimation, becaufe they offended in not dancing on Candlemas-day, when the Judges were prefent, according to an antient order of the fociety. In an old comedy, called *Cupid's Whirligig*, acted in 1616 by the children of his majeſty's revels, a law ftudent, one of the perfons of the drama, fays to a lady, "Faith, lady, I remember the firſt time I faw you was in quadrageſſimo-fexto of the queene, in a michaelmas tearme, and I think it was the morrow upon *menfe Michaelis* or *craſtino Animarum*, I cannot tell which. And the next time I faw you was at our Revells, where it pleafed your ladyſhip to grace me with a galliard; and I ſhall never forget it, for my velvet pantables [pantofles]

---

¹ [Collier's *Hiſt. of Dram. Poetry*, 1831, i. 104.]
² Dugdale, *Orig. Jurid.* cap. 67, p. 285.
³ [Printed in 1565, 8vo., and 1590, 4to.; but both thefe impreſſions are fpurious. The genuine edition, printed by John Day (*circa* 1570, 8vo.), purports to be "fet forth, without addition or alteration, but altogether as the fame was ſhewed on ſtage before the queenes maieſtie."]
⁴ [A copy of this drama, apparently the MS. prefented in 1568 by Gafcoigne, to Roger, Lord North, was fold among the Guilford MSS. It is a folio of 38 leaves, beautifully written, and contains the autograph fignature of Gafcoigne to thofe portions which he contributed.]
⁵ *Satiromaſtix*, edit. 1602, *ut fupr.* fignat. M.
⁶ Dugd. *ut fupr.* cap. 57, p. 140, *feq.* alfo c. 61, 205.
⁷ *Ibid.* ⁸ *Ibid.* col. 2.

were ſtolne away the whilſt." But this may alſo allude to their maſques and plays.[1]

[On the 15th February, 1612-13,] the Inns preſented at Whitehall a maſque before James I. in honour of the marriage of his daughter the Princeſs Elizabeth with the Prince Elector Palatine of the Rhine, at the coſt of more than 1,080*l*.[2] The poetry was by Chapman and the machinery by [Inigo] Jones.[3] But the moſt ſplendid and ſumptuous performance of this kind, played by theſe ſocieties, was the maſque which they exhibited at Candlemas-day, in the year 1633, at the expenſe of [upwards of 21,000*l*.] before Charles I., which ſo pleaſed the king and probably the queen, that he invited one hundred and twenty gentlemen of the law to a ſimilar entertainment at Whitehall on Shrove Tueſday following.[4] It was called the *Triumph of Peace*, and written by Shirley [a member] of Gray's-Inn. The ſcenery was the invention of Jones, and the muſic was compoſed by William Lawes and Simon Ives.[5]

---

[1] Sign. H 2, edit. 1616.

[2] Dugdale, *ibid.* p. 246. The other ſocieties ſeem to have joined. *Ibid.* cap. 67, p. 286. See alſo Finett's *Philoxenis*, pp. 8, 11, edit. 1656, and *ibid.* p. 73.

[3] "With a deſcription of the whole ſhew, in the manner of their march on horſeback to the court from the Maſter of the Rolls his houſe," &c. It is dedicated to Sir E. Philipps, Maſter of the Rolls. But we find a maſque on the very ſame occaſion [exhibited on the 20th February, 1612-13] at Whitehall before the king and queen, called *The Maſque of* [*the Inner Temple and Grayes-Inne*] by Beaumont in the works of Beaumont and Fletcher, [edit. Dyce, ii.]

[4] Dugd. *ibid.* p. 346.

[5] It was printed [three times in 1633. "The third impreſſion has conſiderable variations from the others both in the deſcription and in the performances of the anti-maſks."—*Collier.* Mr. Dyce ſeems unable to decide which appeared firſt. As to the coſt of the maſque, compare Shirley's works, edit. 1833, i. xxvii.-viii.] The author ſays, that it exceeded in variety and richneſs of decoration, anything ever exhibited at Whitehall. There is a little piece called *The Inns of Court Anagrammatiſt*, or *The Maſquers Maſqued in Anagrams*, written by Francis Lenton, [who calls himſelf] the queen's poet, 1634. In this piece, the names and reſpective houſes of each maſquer are ſpecified; and in commendation of each there is an epigram. The maſque with which his majeſty returned this compliment on the Shrove-Tueſday following [Feb. 18, 1633-4], at Whitehall was Carew's *Cœlum Britannicum*, written by the king's command, and played by his majeſty, with many of the nobility and their ſons who were boys. The machinery by Jones, and the muſic by H. Lawes. [It is alluded to in Strafford's Letters, 360. The liſt of the maſquers is on the laſt page of the 4to edit. of 1634. See Carew's Works, by Hazlitt, 1870, p. 235.] Middleton [wrote the] *Inner Temple Maſque, or the Maſque of Heroes*, preſented as an entertainment for many worthy ladies, by the members of that ſociety, [and printed in 1619]. I have alſo ſeen the *Maſque of Flowers*, acted by the ſtudents of Gray's-inn, in the Banquetting-houſe at Whitehall, on Twelfth Night in 1613. It is dedicated to Sir F. Bacon, and was printed in 1614. It was the laſt of the court-ſolemnities exhibited in honour of Carr, Earl of Somerſet. [In the library of the Muſic School at Oxford, are two large volumes in the hand-writing of W. Lawes, one of which contains ſome fragments of the muſic which he wrote for the celebrated maſque, *The Triumph of Peace*. W. Lawes, as well as his brother Henry, whoſe character and attainments procured him the proud diſtinction of Milton's friendſhip, was rather diſtinguiſhed as a compoſer by the ſimplicity and eaſy flow of his melodies, than by any diſplay of thoſe maſterly combinations of harmony which adorn the church and chamber muſic of the preceding age.—*Edgar Taylor*]

Masques at Court.

Some curious anecdotes of this exhibition are preserved by a contemporary, a diligent and critical observer of those seemingly insignificant occurrences, which acquire importance in the eyes of posterity, and are often of more value than events of greater dignity. "On Monday after Candlemas-day, the gentlemen of the inns of court performed their *Masque* at Court. They were sixteen in number, who rode through the streets,[1] in four chariots, and two others to carry their pages and musicians; attended by an hundred gentlemen on great horses, as well clad as ever I saw any. They far exceeded in bravery [splendour] any Masque that had formerly been presented by those societies, and performed the dancing part with much applause. In their company was one Mr. Read of Gray's-inn, whom all the women and some men cried up for as handsome a man as the duke of Buckingham. They were well used at court by the king and queen. No disgust given them, only this one accident fell: Mr. May, of Gray's-inn, a fine poet, he who translated Lucan, came athwart my lord chamberlain in the banquetting-house,[2] and he broke his staff over his shoulders, not knowing who he was; the king was present, who knew him, for he calls him his poet, and told the chamberlain of it, who sent for him the next morning, and fairly excused himself to him, and gave him fifty pounds in pieces. This riding-shew took so well, that both king and queen desired to see it again, so that they invited themselves to supper to my lord mayor's within a week after; and the Masquers came in a more glorious show with all the riders, which were increased twenty, to Merchant-taylor's hall, and there performed again."[3] It is added, "On Shrove-Tuesday at night, the king and the lords performed their Masque. The templars were all invited, and well pleased," &c.[4] It seems the queen and her ladies were experienced actresses: for the same writer says (Jan. 9, 1633-4): "I never knew a duller Christmas than we had at Court this year; but one play all the time at Whitehall! .... The queen had some little infirmity, which made her keep in: only on Twelfth-night, she feasted the king at Somerset-house, and presented him with a play, newly studied, long since printed, the *Faithful Sheperdefs* [of Fletcher] which the king's players acted in the robes she and her ladies acted their *Pastoral* in the last year."[5] Again, Nov. 9, 1637, "Here are to be two maskes this winter; one at Christmass, which the king and the young noblesse do make; the other at Shrovetide, which the queen and her ladies do present to the king. A great room is now building only for this use betwixt the guard chamber and the banquetting-house, and of fir"[6] .... Finett observes:

---

[1] They went from Ely house. [2] at Whitehall.
[3] *Strafford's Letters*, Garrard to the Lord Deputy, dat. Feb. 27, 1633, vol. i. p. 207.
[4] See also p. 177, and Fr. Osborn's *Tradit. Mem.* vol. ii. p. 134 (Works, edit. 1722).
[5] *Ibid.* p. 177.
[6] *Ibid.* vol. ii. p. 130. See also p. 140, *Philoxenis*, p. 198.

"There being a maſke in practice of the queen in perſon, with other great ladies."[1] .... She was [alſo] an actreſs in Davenant's maſque of the *Temple of Love*, with many of the nobility of both ſexes. We have Jonſon's *Chloridia* at Shrovetide, 1630: his Maſque called *Love freed from Ignorance and Folly*, printed [1616: the Honourable Walter] Montagu's *Shepheard's [Paradiſe]*, a Paſtoral, printed in [1659]: *Albion's Triumph*, the Sunday after Twelfth-night, 1631 [by Aurelian Townſhend]: *Luminalia, or The Feſtival of Light*, a maſque on Shrove-Tueſday in 1637: *Salmacida Spolia*, at Whitehall in 1639, the words by Davenant, and the muſic by Lewis Richard, maſter of her majeſty's muſic. *Tempe reſtored* was performed by fourteen ladies on Shrove-Tueſday at Whitehall, 1631. The words were by Aurelian Townſend. The king acted in ſome of theſe pieces. In the preceding reign, Queen Anne had given countenance to this practice; and (I believe) ſhe was the firſt of our queens that appeared perſonally in this moſt elegant and rational amuſement of a court. She acted in Daniel's maſque of *The Viſion of the twelve Goddeſſes*, with eleven other ladies, at Hampton-court, in 1604; in Jonſon's *Maſque of Queens*, at Whitehall, in 1609; in Daniel's *Tethys Feſtival* [or the *Queens Wake*],[2] a maſque at the creation of Prince Henry, Jun. 5, 1610. Daniel dedicates to this queen a paſtoral tragi-comedy, in which ſhe perhaps performed, called *Hymen's Triumph*. It was preſented at Somerſet-houſe, where ſhe magnificently entertained the king on occaſion of the marriage of Lord Roxburgh. Many others, I preſume, might be added. Among the entertainments at Rutland-houſe, compoſed in the reign of Charles I. there [are two pieces by Davenant, deſcribed elſewhere, and ſaid to have been performed by declamation and muſic.

After the Reſtoration, when the dignity of the old monarchical manners had ſuffered a long eclipſe from a Calviniſtic uſurpation, a feeble effort was made to revive theſe liberal and elegant amuſements at Whitehall. For, about the year 1675, Queen Catherine ordered Crowne to write a Paſtoral called *Califto*, which was acted at court by the ladies Mary and Anne daughters of the duke of York, and the young nobility. About the ſame time Lady Anne, afterwards queen, played the part of Semandra in Lee's *Mithridates*. The young noblemen were inſtructed by Betterton, and the princeſſes by his wife; who perhaps conceived Shakeſpeare more fully than any female that ever appeared on the ſtage. In remembrance of her theatrical inſtructions, Anne, when queen, aſſigned Mrs. Betterton an annual penſion of one hundred pounds.[3]

This was an early practice in France. In 1540, Margaret de Valois, Queen of Navarre, wrote Moralities which ſhe called *Paſtorals*, to be acted by the ladies of her court.

---

[1] Whitelock, *ſub an.* 1632.
[2] Winwood, iii. 180. [*Handb. of E. E. Lit.* art. *Davenant.*]
[3] Langb. *Dram. P.* p. 92, edit. 1691. Cibber's *Apol.* p. 134.

But it was not only by the parade of processions and the decorations of scenery, that these spectacles were recommended. Some of them, in point of poetical composition, were eminently beautiful and elegant. Among these may be mentioned a masque on the story of Circe and Ulysses, called the *Inner Temple Masque*, written by William Browne, a student of that society, [and presented by the members on the 13th January, 1614-15.][1] From this piece, as a specimen of the temple-masques in this view, I make no apology for my anticipation in transcribing the following ode, which Circe sings as a charm to drive away sleep from Ulysses, who is discovered reposing under a large tree. It is addressed to Sleep:

> THE CHARME.
> Sonne of Erebus & Nighte,
> Hye away, and aime thy flighte,
> Where consorte none other fowle
> Than the batte & sullen owle:
> Where, upon the lymber grasse,
> Poppy & Mandragoras,
> Wth like simples not a few,
> Hange for euer droppes of dew:
> Where flowes Lethe, wthout coyle
> Softly like a streame of oyle.
> Hye thee hither, gentle Sleepe,
> Wth this Greeke no longer keepe.
> Thrice I charge thee by my wand,
> Thrice wth moly from my hand
> Doe I touch Vlysses eyes,
> And wth the Jaspis. Then arise,
> Sagest Greeke.[2]

In praise of this song it will be sufficient to say, that it reminds us of some favourite touches in Milton's *Comus*, to which it perhaps gave birth. Indeed one cannot help observing here in general, although the observation more properly belongs to another place, that a masque thus recently exhibited on the story of Circe, which there is reason to think had acquired some popularity, suggested to Milton the hint of a masque on the story of Comus. It would be superfluous to point out minutely the absolute similarity of the two characters: they both deal in incantations conducted by the same mode of operation, and producing effects exactly parallel.

When the societies of the law performed these shows within their own respective refectories at Christmas or any other festival, a Christmas-prince or revel-master was constantly appointed. At a Christmas celebrated in the hall of the Middle-temple in the year 1635, the jurisdiction, privileges, and parade, of this mock-monarch

---

[1] [The original MS. is still in the library of Emmanuel College, Cambridge. It was printed, not very correctly, by Davies in his edition of Browne, 1772. A complete edition of Browne's works has been included by the present writer in the *Roxburghe Library* Series, 1869-70, 2 vols. 4to. where it is thought that the reader will find all that we can ever hope to learn of Browne's life or to recover of his poetry.]

[2] [Collated with the orig. MS.]

are thus circumstantially described.¹ He was attended by his lord keeper, lord treasurer, by eight white staves, a captain of his band of pensioners and of his guard; and by two chaplains, who were so seriously impressed with an idea of his regal dignity, that when they preached before him on the preceding Sunday in the Temple church, on ascending the pulpit, they saluted him with three low bows.² He dined, both in the hall and in his privy-chamber, under a cloth of estate. The pole-axes for his gentlemen pensioners were borrowed of Lord Salisbury. Lord Holland, his temporary justice in Eyre, supplied him with venison on demand, and the lord mayor and sheriffs of London with wine. On Twelfth-day, at going to church, he received many petitions, which he gave to his master of requests; and, like other kings, he had a favourite whom with others, gentlemen of high quality, he knighted at returning from church. His expenses, all from his own purse, amounted to 2000*l*.³ We are also told that in the year 1635, " On Shrovetide at night, the Lady Hatton feasted the king, queen, and princes, at her house in Holborn. The Wednesday before the *Prince of the Temple* invited the Prince Elector and his brother to a masque at the Temple,⁴ which was very completely fitted for the variety of the scenes, and excellently well performed. Thither came the queen with three of her ladies disguised, all clad in the attire of citizens. This done, the prince was deposed, but since the king knighted him at Whitehall."⁵

But these spectacles and entertainments in our law societies, not so much because they were romantic and ridiculous in their mode of exhibition as that they were institutions celebrated for the purposes of merriment and festivity, were suppressed or suspended under the false and illiberal ideas of reformation and religion which prevailed in the fanatical court of Cromwell. The countenance afforded by a polite court to such entertainments became the leading topic of animadversion and abuse in the miserable declamations of the Puritan theologists, who attempted the business of national reformation without any knowledge of the nature of society, and whose censures

---

¹ See also Dugd. *Orig. Jurid.* p. 151, where many of the circumstances of this officer are described at large; he also mentions, at Lincoln's-inn, a *King of the Cockneys* on Childermas-day, cap. 64, p. 247. [This has been preceded in the former edits. of Warton by a long argument respecting a passage in Hen. IV., part 2, iii. 3, where there is a conversation touching on Shallow and Falstaff's old recollections of the archery meetings on Mile-End Green, mistaken by Warton for dramatic entertainments.]

² This ceremonial, to the honour and pious memory of George III. was laid aside in his reign.

³ Strafford's *Letters*, ut supra, vol. i. p. 507. The writer adds, "All this is done to make them fit to give the prince elector a royal entertainment, with masks, dancings, and some other exercises of wit in orations or arraignments, that day they invite him."

⁴ This was Davenant's *Triumphs of the Prince d'Amour*, written at their request, for the purpose, in three days. The music by H. and W. Lawes. The names of the performers are at the end. [Compare Hazlitt's *Popular Antiquities of Gr. Britain*, i. 275-6.]

⁵ *Ibid.* p. 525.] The writer adds, "Mrs. Basset, the great lace-woman of Cheapside, went foremost, and led the queen by the hand," &c. See *ibid.* p. 506.

proceeded not so much from principles of a purer morality as from a narrowness of mind, and from that ignorance of human affairs which necessarily accompanies the operations of enthusiasm.

SECTION XXXIV.

E have now arrived at the commencement of the sixteenth century. But before I proceed to a formal and particular examination of the poetry of that century, some preliminary considerations of a more general nature which will have a reference to all the remaining part of our history, for the purpose of preparing the reader and facilitating our future inquiries, appear to be necessary.

On a retrospect of the fifteenth century, we find much poetry written during the latter part of that period. It is certain that the recent introduction into England of the art of typography, to which our countrymen afforded the most liberal encouragement, and which for many years was almost solely confined to the impression of English books, the fashion of translating the classics from French versions, the growing improvements of the English language, and the diffusion of learning among the laity, greatly contributed to multiply English composition, both in prose and verse. These causes, however, were yet immature, nor had they gathered a sufficient degree of power and stability to operate on our literature with any vigorous effects.

But there is a circumstance which, among some others already suggested, impeded that progression in our poetry which might yet have been expected under all these advantages. A revolution, the most fortunate and important in most other respects, and the most interesting that occurs in the history of the migration of letters, now began to take place; this, by diverting the attention of ingenious men to new modes of thinking and the culture of new languages, introduced a new course of study, and gave a temporary check to vernacular composition. I mean the revival of classical learning.

In the course of these Annals we must have frequently remarked, from time to time, striking symptoms of a restless disposition in the human mind to rouse itself from its lethargic state, and to break the bonds of barbarism. After many imperfect and interrupted efforts this mighty deliverance, in which the mouldering Gothic fabrics of false religion and false philosophy fell together, was not effectually completed till the close of the fifteenth century. An event, almost fortuitous and unexpected, gave a direction to that spirit of curiosity and discovery, which had not yet appeared in its full force and extent for want of an object. About the year 1453 the dispersion of the Greeks, after Constantinople had been occupied by the Turks, became the means of gratifying that natural love of novelty which has so frequently led the way to the noblest improvements, by the introduction of a new language and new books, and totally changed the state of letters in Europe. But it should be remembered that some learned Grecians, foreseeing the persecutions impending over their country, frequented Italy, and taught their language there before the taking of Constantinople. Some Greeks who attended the Florentine council, and never returned for fear of the Turks, founded the present royal library in the city of Turin. In 1401 the Greek emperor, unable to resist the frequent insults of these barbarians, came into England to seek redress or protection from Henry IV. He landed at Dover attended by many learned Greeks, and the next day was honourably received at Christ Church priory at Canterbury by the Prior, Thomas Chyllenden.[1]

This great change commenced in Italy, a country (from many circumstances) above all others peculiarly qualified and prepared to adopt such a deviation. Italy, during the darkest periods of monastic ignorance, had always maintained a greater degree of refinement and knowledge than any other European country. In the thirteenth century, when the manners of Europe appear to have been overwhelmed with every species of absurdity, its luxuries were less savage and its public spectacles more rational than those of France, England and Germany. Its inhabitants were not only enriched but enlightened by that flourishing state of commerce which its commodious situation, aided by the combination of other concomitant advantages, contributed to support. Even from the time of the irruptions of the northern barbarians, some glimmerings of the ancient erudition still remained in this country; and in the midst of superstition and false philosophy, repeated efforts were made in Italy to restore the Roman classics. To mention no other instances, Alberto [or Albertino] Mussato[2] of Padua, a commander in the Paduan army against the Veronese, wrote two Latin tragedies: *Ecerrinis*[3] (or the fate of the tyrant Ecerinus of Verona) and *Achilleis*, on the plan of the Greek drama and in imitation of Seneca, before the year 1320. The many monuments of legitimate sculpture and architecture, preserved in Italy, had there kept alive ideas of elegance and grace; and the Italians, from their familiarity with those precious remains of antiquity so early as the close of the fourteenth century, had laid the rudiments of their perfection in the

---

[1] In a manuscript called *Speculum Parvulorum*, lib. 5, c. 30. MSS. Bibl. Lambeth.

[2] He was honoured with the laurel, and died 1329.

[3] Printed at Venice, 1636, fol. with his *Epistolæ, Elegi, Soliloquia, Eclogæ, Cento Ovidianus, Latin History of Italy*, and *Bavarus ad Filium*. And in Muratori's *Rer. Ital. Scriptor.* tom. x. Mediolan. 1727, pp. 1, 123, 569, 769, 785. See also in *Thesaur. Ital.* tom. vi. part ii. Lugd. Bat. 1722. Among his inedited works are mentioned, *Liber de Lite Naturæ et Fortunæ*, on natural causes and fate, and three books in heroic verse, on the war against the Veronese above mentioned. The name and writings of Mussato were hardly known, till they were brought forward to the public notice in the *Essay on Pope* [by Dr. Joseph Warton], which I shall not be accused of partiality (as I only join the voice of the world) in calling the most agreeable and judicious piece of criticism produced by the age.

ancient arts. Another circumstance which had a considerable share in clearing the way for this change, and which deserves particular attention, was the innovation introduced into the Italian poetry by Petrarch who, inspired with the most elegant of passions, and clothing his exalted feelings on that delicate subject in the most melodious and brilliant Italian versification, had totally eclipsed the barbarous beauties of the Provençal troubadours; and by this new and powerful magic had in an eminent degree contributed to reclaim, at least for a time, the public taste from a love of Gothic manners and romantic imagery.

In this country, so happily calculated for their favourable reception, the learned fugitives of Greece, when their empire was destroyed, found shelter and protection. Hither they imported, and here they interpreted, their ancient writers whose works had been preserved entire at Constantinople. These, being eagerly studied by the best Italian scholars, communicated a taste for the graces of genuine poetry and eloquence, and at the same time were instrumental in propagating a more just and general relish for the Roman poets, orators, and historians. In the meantime a more elegant and sublime philosophy was adopted: a philosophy more friendly to works of taste and imagination, and more agreeable to the sort of reading which was now gaining ground. For the scholastic subtleties and the captious logic of Aristotle were substituted the mild and divine wisdom of Plato.

It was a circumstance, which gave the greatest splendour and importance to this new mode of erudition, that it was encouraged by the popes, who, considering the encouragement of literature as a new expedient to establish their authority over the minds of men, and enjoying an opulent and peaceable dominion in the voluptuous region of Italy, extended their patronage on this occasion with a liberality so generous and unreserved, that the court of Rome on a sudden lost its austere character, and became the seat of elegance and urbanity. Nicholas V., about 1440, established public rewards at Rome for composition in the learned languages, appointed professors in humanity, and employed intelligent persons to traverse all parts of Europe in search of classic manuscripts buried in the monasteries.[1] It was by means of the munificent support of Pope Nicholas, that Cyriac of Ancona, who may be considered as the first antiquary in Europe, was enabled to introduce a taste for gems, medals, inscriptions, and other curious remains of classical antiquity, which he collected with indefatigable labour in various parts of Italy and Greece.[2]

---

[1] See Dominici Georgii *Dissertatio de Nich. quinti erga Lit. et Literat. Viros Patrocinio*, Rom. 1742. Added to his *Life*.

[2] See Fr. Burmanni *Præfat. ad Inscription. Gruterian.* Amstel. 1707, Baluz. *Miscell.* tom. vi. p. 539. Ant. Augustini *Dialog. de Numismat.* ix. xi. Voss. *De Histor. Lat.* p. 809. His *Itinerarium* was printed at Florence, 1742. See Leon. Aretini *Epistol.* tom. ii. lib. ix. p. 149. And *Giornal. de' Letterati d' Italia*, tom. xxi. p. 428. See the *Inscriptiones*, [many of which, however, are fabrications,] by P. Apianus and B. Amantius, Ingoldstat. 1634, at the *Monum. Gaditan.*

He allowed Francis Philelphus, an elegant Latin poet of Italy about 1450, a stipend for translating Homer into Latin.[1] Leo X., not less conspicuous for his munificence in restoring letters, descended so far from his apostolical dignity as to be a spectator of the *Poenulus* of Plautus, which was performed in a temporary theatre in the court of the Capitol by the flower of the Roman youth, with the addition of the most costly decorations:[2] and Leo, while he was pouring the thunder of his anathemas against the heretical doctrines of Martin Luther, [issued a licence for the publication of the poems of Ariosto, couched in the usual denunciatory terms against piracy].[3] It was under the pontificate of Leo, that a perpetual indulgence was granted for rebuilding the church of a monastery, which possessed a manuscript of Tacitus.[4] It is obvious to observe how little conformable this just taste, these elegant arts, and these new amusements proved in their consequences to the spirit of the papal system: and it is remarkable that the court of Rome, whose sole design and interest it had been for so many centuries to enslave the minds of men, should be the first to restore the religious and intellectual liberties of Europe. The apostolical fathers, aiming at a fatal and ill-timed popularity, did not reflect that they were shaking the throne, which they thus adorned.

Among those who distinguished themselves in the exercise of these studies, the first and most numerous were the Italian ecclesiastics. If not from principles of inclination and a natural impulse to follow the passion of the times, it was at least their interest to concur in forwarding those improvements, which were commended, countenanced and authorised by their spiritual sovereign: they abandoned the pedantries of a barbarous theology, and cultivated the purest models of antiquity. The cardinals and bishops of Italy composed Latin verses (and with a success attained by few in more recent times) in imitation of Lucretius, Catullus and Virgil. Nor would the encouragement of any other European potentate have availed so much in this great work of restoring literature: as no other patronage could have operated with so powerful and immediate an influence

---

[1] Philelph. *Epist.* xxiv. 1, xxxvi. 1. In the *Epistles* of Philelphus and in his ten books of *Satires* in Latin verse, are many curious particulars relating to the literary history of those times. Venet. fol. 1502. His *Nicolaus*, or two books of Lyrics, is a panegyric on the life and acts of Nicholas V.

[2] It was in 1513, on occasion of Juliano de Medicis, Leo's brother, being made free of Rome. P. Jovius, *Hist.* lib. xi. *ad calc.* and *Vit. Leon.* lib. iii. p. 145. Jovius says, that the actors were *Romanæ juventutis lepidissimi*, and that several pieces of poetry were recited at the same time. Leo was also present at an Italian comedy, written by Cardinal Bibiena, called *Calander*, in honour of the Duchess of Mantua. It was acted by noble youths in the spacious apartments of the Vatican, and Leo was placed in a sort of throne. Jov. in *Vit.* p. 189.

[3] [See Roscoe's *Life of Leo X*. vol. iv.—*Price*.]

[4] Paulus Jovius relates an anecdote of Leo X. which shows that some passages in the classics were studied at the court of Rome to very bad purposes. I must give it in his own words: "Non caruit etiam infamia, quod parum honeste nonnullos e cubiculariis suis (erant enim e tota Italia nobilissimi) adamare, et cum his tenerius atque libere jocari videretur." *Vita Leonis X*. p. 192.

on that order of men who, from the nature of their education and profession, must always be the principal instruments in supporting every species of liberal erudition.

[Not only on the *terra-ferma*, but at Venice, about this time in the zenith of her power and prosperity, rapid progress had been made in the cultivation of all liberal arts. The Venetians, not content with reading contemporary history, with mastering the intricacies of diplomacy, or with attaining the highest honours in the military profession, studied the language which Cicero spoke, the language of the *Anabasis*, and the language of Holy Writ. They applied themselves to the liberal, mechanical and occult sciences, and to the fine arts. They became diligent scholiasts. They searched for MSS. with an avidity eclipsing that of De Bure. They formed libraries, some of which were far larger than the public collections at Oxford or Paris. Some gave gratuitous instruction in the *Elements of Euclid*; others lectured on *Ethics* or *Metaphysics*. A Trevisano devoted ten years to the composition of a single treatise, which he never lived to finish. A Giorgio naturalized among his countrymen the literature of the troubadours and the songs of Provence. To a Polo scientific men were indebted for the first book of travels in China, Kamtschatka, and Japan.][1]

Here we cannot but observe the necessary connection between literary composition and the arts of design. No sooner had Italy banished the Gothic style in eloquence and poetry, than painting, sculpture and architecture, at the same time and in the same country, arrived at maturity, and appeared in all their original splendour. The beautiful or sublime ideas, which the Italian artists had conceived from the contemplation of ancient statues and ancient temples, were invigorated by the descriptions of Homer and Sophocles. Petrarch was crowned in the Capitol, and Raphael was promoted to the dignity of a Cardinal.

These improvements were soon received in other countries. Lascaris, one of the most learned of the Constantinopolitan exiles, was invited into France by Louis XII. and Francis I.: and it was under the latter of these monarchs that he was employed to form a library at Fontainebleau, and to introduce Greek professors into the University of Paris.[2] Yet we find Gregory Typhernas teaching Greek at Paris so early as 1472.[3] About the same time, Antonius Eparchus of Corsica sold one hundred Greek books to the Emperor Charles V. and to Francis I.,[4] those great rivals who agreed in nothing but in promoting the cause of literature. Francis I. maintained even a Greek secretary, the learned Angelus Vergerius, to whom he assigned in 1541 a pension of four hundred livres from his exche-

---

[1] [*History of the Venetian Republic*, 1860, iv. 198.]
[2] Du Breul, *Antiquitez de Paris*, 1639, liv. ii. p. 563. Bembi *Hist. Venet.* part ii. p. 76; and R. Simon, *Critique de la Bibl. Eccles.* par du Pin, tom. i. pp. 502, 512.
[3] Hody, p. 233.   [4] Morhoff, *Polyhist.* iv. 6.

quer.¹ He employed Julius Camillus to teach him to speak fluently the language of Cicero and Demosthenes in the space of a month; but so chimerical an attempt necessarily proved abortive: yet it shewed his passion for letters.² In 1474 the parliament of Paris which, like other public bodies eminent for their wisdom, could proceed on no other foundation than that of ancient forms and customs, and was alarmed at the appearance of an innovation, commanded a cargo of books (some of the earliest specimens of typography) which were imported into Paris by a factor of the city of Mentz, to be seized and destroyed. Francis I. would not suffer so great a dishonour to remain on the French nation; and although he interposed his authority too late for a revocation of the decree, he ordered the full price to be paid for the books. This was the same parliament that opposed the reformation of the calendar and the admission of any other philosophy than that of Aristotle. Such was Francis's solicitude to encourage the graces of a classical style, that he abolished the Latin tongue from all public acts of justice, because the first president of the parliament of Paris had used a barbarous term in pronouncing sentence;³ and because the Latin code and judicial processes, hitherto adopted in France, familiarised the people with a base Latinity. At the same time, he ordered these formularies to be turned, not into good Latin which would have been absurd or impossible, but into pure French:⁴ a reformation which promoted the culture of the vernacular tongue. He was the first of the kings of France, who encouraged brilliant assemblies of ladies to frequent the French court: a circumstance, which not only introduced new splendour and refinement into the parties and carousals of the court of that monarchy, but gave a new turn to the manners of the French ecclesiastics (who of course attended the king), and destroyed much of their monkish pedantry.⁵

When we mention the share which Germany took in the restitution of letters, she needs no greater panegyric than that her mechanical genius added, at a lucky moment, to all these fortunate contingencies in favour of science an admirable invention, which was of the most singular utility in facilitating the diffusion of the ancient writers over every part of Europe: I mean the art of printing. By this observation, I do not mean to insinuate that Germany kept no pace with her neighbours in the production of philological scholars. Rodolphus Langius, a canon of Munster and a tolerable Latin poet, after many struggles with the inveterate prejudices and authoritative threats of German bishops and German universities, opened a school

---

¹ Du Breul, *ibid.* p. 568. It is a just remark of P. Victorius, that Francis I., by founding beautiful Greek and Roman types at his own cost, invited many students, who were caught by the elegance of the impression, to read the ancient books. *Præfat. ad Comment. in octo libr. Aristotelis de Opt. Statu Civitat.*

² Alciati *Epistol.* xxiii. inter *Gudianas*, p. 109.

³ Matagonis de Matagonibus *adversus Italogalliam Antonii Matharelli*, p. 226.

⁴ Varillas, *Hist. de François I.* livr. ix. p. 381.

⁵ Brantome, *Mem.* tom. i. p. 227. Mezerai, *Hist. France, sous Hen. III.* tom. iii. pp. 446, 447.

of humanity at Munster which supplied his countrymen with every species of elegant learning, till it was overthrown by the fury of fanaticism and the revolutions introduced by the barbarous reformations of the anabaptistic zealots in 1534.[1] Reuchlin, [dictus] Capnio, co-operated with the laudable endeavours of Langius by professing Greek before 1490 at Basle.[2] Soon afterwards he translated Homer, Aristophanes, Plato, Xenophon, Æschines and Lucian, into Latin, and Demosthenes into German. At Heidelberg he founded a library, which he stored with the choicest Greek MSS. It is worthy of remark, that the first public institution in any European university for promoting polite literature, by which I understand these improvements in erudition, appears to have been established at Vienna. In 1501, Maximilian I. who, like Julius Cæsar, had composed a commentary on his own illustrious military achievements, founded in the University of Vienna a College of Poetry. This society consisted of four professors: one for poetry, a second for oratory, and two others for mathematics. The professor of poetry was so styled, because he presided over all the rest: and the first person appointed to this office was Conradus Celtes [already mentioned,] one of the restorers of the Greek language in Germany, an elegant Latin poet, a critic on the art of Latin versification, the first poet-laureat of his country, and the first who introduced the practice of acting Latin tragedies and comedies in public after the manner of Terence.[3] It was the business of this professor to examine candidates in philology, and to reward those who appeared to have made a distinguished proficiency in classical studies with a crown of laurel. Maximilian's chief and general design in this institution was to restore the languages and the eloquence of Greece and Rome.[4]

Among the chief restorers of literature in Spain (about 1490), was Antonio de Lebrixa, one of the professors in the University of Alcala, founded by the magnificent Cardinal Ximenes, archbishop of

---

[1] D. Chytræus, *Saxonia*, l. iii. p. 80. Trithem. p. 993, *De S. E. Et de Luminarib. German.* p. 239.

[2] See *Epistol. Claror. Viror. ad Reuchlin.* p. m. 4. 17. Maius, *Vita Reuchlini*, &c.

[3] Celtes dedicates his *Amores* or Latin Elegies to Maximilian in a Latin panegyric prefixed; in which he compliments the emperor thus: "You who have this year endowed most liberally the muses long wandering, and banished from Germany by the calumnies of certain unskilful men, with a college and a perpetual stipend: having, moreover, according to a custom practised in my time at Rome, delegated to me and my successors, in your stead, the authority of creating and laureating poets in the said college," &c. *Paneg. Prim. ad Maximilian. Imp.* signat. a ii. *Amores*, &c. Noringb. 1502, 4to. The same author, in his *Description of the City of Nuremburgh*, written in 1501, mentions it as a circumstance of importance and a singularity, that a person skilled in the Roman literature had just begun to give lectures in a public building to the ingenuous youth of that city in poetry and oratory, with a salary of one hundred aurei, as was the practice in the cities of Italy. *Descript. Urb. Noringb.* cap. xii.

[4] See the imperial patent for erecting this college, in Freherus *German. Rerum Scriptor. Var*, &c. tom. ii. fol. Francof. 1602, p. 237, and by Van Seelen, Lubec, 1723; and in his *Select. Literar.* p. 488. In this patent, the purpose of the foundation is declared to be, "restituere abolitam prisci sæculi eloquentiam."

Toledo. It was to the patronage of Ximenes that Lebrixa owed his celebrity.[1] Profoundly versed in every species of sacred and profane learning, and appointed to the respectable office of royal historian, he chose to be distinguished only by the name of the grammarian,[2] that is, a teacher of polite letters. In this department he enriched the seminaries of Spain with new systems of grammar in Latin, Greek, and Hebrew; and with a view to reduce his native tongue to some critical laws he wrote comparative lexicons in the Latin, Castilian, and Spanish languages. These, at this time, were plans of a most extraordinary nature in Spain, and placed the literature of his country which, from the phlegmatic temper of the inhabitants was tenacious of ancient forms, on a much wider basis than before. To these he added a manual of rhetoric, compiled from Aristotle, Tully and Quintilian: together with commentaries on Terence, Virgil, Juvenal, Persius, and other classics. He was deputed by Ximenes, with other learned linguists, to superintend the grand complutensian edition of the Bible: and in the conduct of that laborious work, he did not escape the censure of heretical impiety for exercising his critical skill on the sacred text (according to the ideas of the Holy Inquisition) with too great a degree of precision and accuracy.[3]

Even Hungary, a country by no means advanced uniformly with other parts of Europe in the common arts of civilization, was illuminated with the distant dawning of science. Mattheus Corvinus, king of Hungary and Bohemia in the fifteenth century, and who died in 1490, was a lover and a guardian of literature.[4] He purchased innumerable volumes of Greek and Hebrew writers at Constantinople and other Grecian cities, when they were sacked by the Turks: and (as the operations of typography were now but imperfect) he employed at Florence many learned librarians to multiply copies of classics, both Greek and Latin, which he could not procure in Greece.[5] These, to the number of 50,000, he placed in a tower which he had erected in the metropolis of Buda;[6] and in this library he established thirty amanuenses, skilled in painting, illuminating and writing: who, under the conduct of Felix Ragusinus, a Dalmatian, consummately learned in the Greek, Chaldaic, and Arabic languages, and an elegant designer and painter of ornaments on vellum, attended incessantly to the business of transcription and decoration.[7] The librarian was Bartholomew Fontius, a learned Floren-

---

[1] See Nic. Anton. *Bibl. Nov. Hispan.* tom. i. pp. 104-9.
[2] L. Vives, *De Causis Corruptarum Art.* ii. p. 72.
[3] See Alvarus Gomesius *De Vita Ximenis*, lib. ii. p. 43. Nic. Anton. *ut supr.* p. 109. Imbonatus, *Bibl. Latino-Hebr.* p. 315.
[4] See *Notit. Biblioth. Thoruniensis*, p. 32, by Petrus Jaenichiis, who has written a Dissertation *De meritis Matthiæ Corvini in rem literariam.*
[5] See Joh. Alex. Brassicani *Præfat. ad Salvianum*, Basil. 1530; and *Maderus de Bibliothecis*, pp. 145, 149.
[6] Anton. Bonfinii *Rer. Hungar.* Decad. iv. lib. 7, p. 460, edit. 1690.
[7] Belius, *Apparat. ad Histor. Hungar.* Dec. i. cap. 5.

tine, the writer of many philological works,[1] and a professor of Greek and oratory at Florence. When Buda was taken by the Turks in 1526, Cardinal Bozmanni offered for the redemption of this inestimable collection 200,000 pieces of the imperial money, yet without effect; for the barbarous besiegers defaced or destroyed most of the books, in the violence of seizing the splendid covers and the silver bosses and clasps with which they were enriched.[2] The learned Obsopaeus relates, that a book was brought him by an Hungarian soldier, which he had picked up (with many others) in the pillage of the library of Corvinus, and had preserved as a prize, merely because the covering retained some marks of gold and rich workmanship. This proved to be a MS. of the *Ethiopics* of Heliodorus; and from it, in 1534, Obsopaeus printed at Basle the first edition of that elegant Greek romance.[3]

But as this incidental sketch of the history of the revival of modern learning is intended to be applicable to the general subject of my work, I hasten to give a detail of the rise and progress of these improvements in England: nor shall I scruple, for the sake of producing a full and uniform view, to extend the enquiry to a distant period.

Efforts were made in our English universities for the revival of critical studies much sooner than is commonly imagined. So early as the year 1439, William Byngham, rector of St. John Zachary in London, petitioned Henry VI. in favour of his grammar scholars, for whom he had erected a commodious mansion at Cambridge, called God's House, which he had given to the College of Clarehall: to the end that twenty-four youths, under the direction and government of a learned priest, might be there perpetually educated, and be thence transmitted (in a constant succession) to different parts of England, to those places where grammar schools had fallen into a state of desolation.[4] In the year 1498, Alcock, Bishop of Ely, founded Jesus College in Cambridge, partly for a certain number of scholars to be educated in grammar.[5] Yet there is

---

[1] Among other things, he wrote Commentaries on Persius, Juvenal, Livy, and Aristotle's Poetics. He translated the *Epistles of Phalaris* into the Tuscan language; and this version was published in [1471]. Crescimbeni has placed him among the Italian poets. Lambeccius says, that in the year 1665, he was sent to Buda by the Emperor Leopold, to examine what remained in this library. After repeated delays and difficulties, he was at length permitted by the Turks to enter the room: where he saw about four hundred books, printed and of no value, dispersed on the floor, and covered with dust and filth. Lambeccius supposes, that the Turks, knowing the condition of the books, were ashamed to give him admittance. *Comment. de Bibl. Vindobon.* lib. ii. c. ix. p. 993.

[2] *Collectio Madero-Schmidiana, Access.* 1, p. 310, *seq.* Belius, *ut supr.* tom. iii. p. 225.

[3] In the Preface. See Neandri *Præfat. ad Gnomolog. Stobæi,* p. 27.

[4] "Ubi scholæ grammaticales existunt desolatæ." Pat. Hen. VI. ann. reg. xvii. p. 2, memb. 16.

[5] Rymer, *Fœder.* xii. 653. We find early establishments of this sort in the Colleges of Paris. In the year 1304, Queen Jeanne founded the college of Navarre at Paris for thirty theologists, thirty artists, and twenty grammarians, who are also

reafon to apprehend, that thefe academical pupils in grammar (with which the art of rhetoric was commonly joined), inftead of ftudying the real models of ftyle, were chiefly trained in fyftematic manuals of thefe fciences, filled with unprofitable definitions and unneceffary diftinctions: and that, in learning the arts of elegance, they acquired the barbarous improprieties of diction which thofe arts were intended to remove and reform. That the foundations I have mentioned did not produce any lafting beneficial effects, and that the technical phrafeology of metaphyfics and cafuiftry ftill continued to prevail at Cambridge, appears from the following anecdote. In the reign of Henry VII. that univerfity was fo deftitute of fkill in latinity, that it was obliged to hire an Italian, one Caius Auberinus, for compofing the public orations and epiftles, whofe fee was at the rate of twenty-pence for an epiftle.[1] The fame perfon was employed to explain Terence in the public fchools.[2] Undoubtedly the fame attention to a futile philofophy, to unintelligible elucidations of Scotus and Aquinas, notwithftanding the acceffions accruing to fcience from the eftablifhment of the Humfredian library, had given the fame tincture to the ordinary courfe of ftudies at Oxford. For, about the year 1468, the univerfity of Oxford complimented Chadworth, bifhop of Lincoln, for his care and endeavours in reftoring grammatical literature which, as they reprefent, had long decayed and been forgotten in that feminary.[3]

---

called "Enfans efcholiers en grammaire." They are ordered to hear "lectiones, [readings], materias, et verfus, prout in fcholis grammaticalibus confuevit." Boul. *Hift. Acad. Paris.* vol. iv. p. 74. But the college of Ave Maria at Paris, founded in 1339, is for a Mafter and fix boys only, from nine to fixteen years. Boul. *ibid.* p. 161. The fociety of Merton college in Oxford, founded in 1272, originally maintained in the univerfity fuch boys as claimed kindred to the founder, Bifhop Walter de Merton, in grammar learning and all neceffaries, fometimes till they were capable of taking a degree. They were placed in Nunhall, adjoining to the college on the eaft. " Expens. factae per Thomam de Herlyngton, pro pueris de genere fundatoris a feft. Epiph. ufque ad feft. S. Petri ad vincula, 21 Edw. III, A.D. 1347."—*Item*, in filo albo et viridi, et ceteris pertinenciis, ad reparationem veftium tam artiftarum quam grammaticarum, vi d. *Item*, Mag. Joh. Cornubienfi pro falario fcholae, in tertio quadragefimali. x d. Et hoftiario [ufher] fuo, ii d. ob. *Item*, Mag. Joh. Cornubienfi pro tertio eftivali. x d. Et hoftiario fuo, ii d. ob." A. Wood, *MS. Coll. Merton Collectan.* [Cod. MSS. Ballard. Bibl. Bodl. 46.]

[1] MSS. Bibl. C.C.C. Camb. *Mifcell.* P. p. 194. *Officium magiftri Glomeriae.* I obferve here, that Giles du Vadis, or Ægidius Dewes [or Du Wes,] fucceffively royal librarian at Weftminfter to Henry VII. and VIII. was a Frenchman [?]. The laft king granted him a falary for that office, of ten pounds, in the year 1522. *Priv. Sig.* 13 *Henr. VIII. Offic. Pell.* He was preceptor in French to Henry VIII. Prince Arthur, Princefs Mary, the kings of France and Scotland, and the Marquis of Exeter. Stow's *Survey of London,* p. 230. He wrote at the command of Henry, *An Introductorie for to lerne to rede, to pronounce, and to fpeak French trewly compyled for the* [&c.] *princefs Mary* [firft printed about 1525.] See Pref. Palfgrave's *Lefclairciffement.*] He died in 1535 [and was buried at St. Olaves, Southwark. His *Introductory* is reprinted in the Paris edition of the *Eclairciffement,* 1852.]

[2] " Quod fecit admodum frigide, ut ea erant tempora." *Lib. Matt. Archiep. Parker.* (MSS. Baker), MSS. Harl. 7046, f. 125, 6.

[3] *Regiftr. Univ. Oxon.* FF. [*Epiftol. Acad.*] fol. 254. The Epiftles in this Regifter contain many local anecdotes of the reftoration of learning at Oxford.

But although these gleams of science long struggled with the scholastic cloud which enveloped our universities, we find the culture of the classics embraced in England much sooner than is supposed. Before the year 1490, many of our countrymen appear to have turned their thoughts to the revival of the study of classics: yet, chiefly in consequence of their communications with Italy, and (as most of them were clergymen) of the encouragements they received from the liberality of the Roman pontiffs. Such of our countrymen as wrote in Latin at this period, and were entirely educated at home without any connection with Italy, wrote a style not more classical than that of the monkish Latin annalists who flourished two or three centuries before. I will instance only Rofs of Warwick, author of the *Historia Regum Angliæ*, educated at Oxford, an ecclesiastic, and esteemed an eminent scholar. Nor is the plan of Rofs's *History*, which was finished so late as the year 1483, lefs barbarous than his latinity; for in writing a chronicle of the kings of England he begins, according to the constant practice of the monks, with the creation and the first ages of the world, and adopts all their legends and fables. His motives for undertaking this work are exceedingly curious. He is speaking of the method of perpetuating the memories of famous men by statues: "Alfo in our churches, tabernacles in stone-work, or niches, are wrought for containing images of this kind. For instance, in the new work of the College of Windsor [i.e. St. George's Chapel,] such tabernacles abound, both within and without the building. Wherefore, being requested, about the latter end of the reign of King Edward IV. by the venerable master Edward Seymor, Master of the Works there, and at the desire of the said king, to compile a history of those kings and princes who have founded churches and cities, that the images placed in those niches might appear to greater advantage, and more effectually preserve the names of the persons represented; at the instance of this my brother-student at Oxford, and especially at the desire of the said most noble monarch, as also to exhilarate the minds of his royal fuccessours, I have undertaken this work," &c.[1]

Millyng, Abbot of Westminster about 1480, understood the Greek language, which yet is mentioned as a singular accomplishment in one, although a prelate, of the monastic profession.[2] Adam Efton, educated at Oxford, a Benedictine monk of Norwich, and who lived at Rome the greatest part of his life, is said to have written many pieces in Hebrew, Greek, and Latin. He died at Rome in 1397.[3] Leland mentions John Bate, a Carmelite of York about 1429, as a Greek scholar.[4] Robert Flemmyng studied the Greek and Latin languages under Battista Guarini at Ferrara,[5] and, at his return into England, was preferred to the deanery of Lincoln [on the

---

[1] Edit. Hearne, p. 120.
[2] Leland, *Scriptores*, in v.
[3] *Ibid.*
[4] *Ibid.* v. *Batus*.
[5] Tanner's *Bibl. Brit.* p. 266.

21ft January, 1451-2.]¹ During the reign of Edward IV. he was at Rome, where he wrote an elegant Latin poem in heroic verse, entitled *Lucubrationes Tiburtinæ*, which he inscribed to Pope Sixtus, his singular patron.² It has these three chaste and strong hexameters, in which he describes the person of that illustrious pontiff:

> Sane, quisquis in hunc oculos converterit acreis,
> In facie vultuque viri sublime videbit
> Elucere aliquid, majestatemque verendam.

He was prothonotary to Pope Sixtus. In this poem he mentions Baptista Platina, the librarian at Rome who, together with most of the Italian scholars, was his familiar friend.³ I know not whether one John Opicius, our countryman as it seems, and a Latin poet, improved his taste in Italy about this time: but he has left some copies of elegant Latin verses.⁴

Leland assures us, that he saw in the libraries of Oxford a Greco-Latin lexicon, compiled by Flemmyng, which has escaped my searches. He left many volumes beautifully written and richly illuminated to Lincoln College in Oxford, where he had received his academical education.⁵ [Not long after] the same period, John Gunthorpe, [elected in 1472] Dean of Wells, keeper of the privy seal, and Master of King's Hall in Cambridge, also attended the philological lectures of Guarini: and for the polished latinity with which he wrote *Epistles* and *Orations*, compositions at that time much in use and request, was appointed by Edward IV. Latin Secretary to [his consort Anne] in the year 1487.⁶ The MSS. collected in Italy, which he gave to both the universities of England, were of much more real value than the sumptuous silver image of the Virgin Mary, weighing 143 ounces, which he presented to his Cathedral of Wells.⁷ William Grey imbibed under the same preceptors a knowledge of the best Greek and Roman writers: and in 1454 was advanced by Nicholas V. equally a judge and a protector of scholars, to the bishopric of Ely.⁸ This prelate employed at Venice and Florence many scribes and illuminators⁹ in preparing

---

¹ Wood, *Hist. Univ. Oxon.* ii. 62. Wharton, *Append.* p. 155. Bale, viii. 21. [Le Neve, *Fasti*, edit. Hardy, ii. 33.]

² Printed at Ferrara, 1477, in two books.

³ See Carbo's Funeral Oration on Guarini.

⁴ MSS. Cotton. Vespas. B. iv. One is, *De regis Henrici Septimi in Galliam progressu.* It begins: "Bella canant alii Trojæ, prostrataque dicant." Another is, *De ejusdem laudibus sub prætextu rosæ purpureæ*, a dialogue between Mopsus and Melibeus. One of the poems, *On Christmas*, has the date 1497.

⁵ Lel. *ibid.*

⁶ Pat. 7. Edw. IV. m. 2. Five of his *Orations* before illustrious personages are extant, MSS. Bodl. NE. F. ii. 20. In the same MSS. are his *Annotationes quædam Criticæ in verba quædam apud poetas citata.* He gave many books (collected in Italy) to Jesus College at Cambridge. Lel. *Coll.* iii. 13. He was ambassador to the king of Castile, in 1466 and 1470. Rymer, *Fœd.* xi. 572, 653. Bale mentions his *Diversi generis Carmina* (viii. 42) and a book on rhetoric.

⁷ *Regijtr. Eccles. Wellens.*

⁸ Wharton, *Angl. Sacr.* i 672. [Le Neve, edit. 1854, i. 339.]

⁹ One of those was Antonius Marius. In Baliol College library, one of Bishop

copies of the classics and other useful books, which he gave to the library of Baliol College in Oxford,[1] at that time esteemed the best in the university. John Phreas, or Free, an ecclesiastic of Bristol, [and provost of Baliol College, Oxford,] receiving information from the Italian merchants who trafficked at Bristol, that multitudes of strangers were constantly crowding to the capitals of Italy for instruction in the learned languages, passed over to Ferrara, where he became a fellow-student with the prelate last mentioned, by whose patronage and assistance his studies were supported.[2] He translated Diodorus Siculus and many pieces of Xenophon into Latin.[3] On account of the former work, he was nominated Bishop of Bath and Wells by Paul II., but died before consecration in the year 1464,[4] ["non sine veneni suspicione."] His Latin Epistles, five of which are addressed to his patron the Bishop of Ely, discover an uncommon terseness and facility of expression. It was no inconsiderable testimony of the taste of Phreas, that he was requested by some of his elegant Italian friends to compose a new epitaph in Latin elegiacs for Petrarch's tomb: the original inscription in monkish rhymes not agreeing with the new and improved ideas of Latin versification.[5] William Sellynge, a fellow of All Souls College in Oxford, disgusted with the barren and contracted circle of philosophy taught by the irrefragable professors of that ample seminary, acquired a familiarity with the most excellent ancient authors, and cultivated the conversation of Politian at Bologna,[6] to whom he introduced the learned Linacer.[7] About 1460, he returned into England; and being elected prior of Christ Church at Canterbury, enriched the library of that fraternity with an inestimable collection of Greek and Roman MSS. which he had amassed in Italy.[8] It has been already stated

---

Gray's MSS. has this entry: "Antonius Marii filius Florentinus civis transcripsi ab originalibus exemplaribus, 2 Jul. 1448," &c. MSS. lxviii. [*Apud* MSS. Langb. Bal. p. 81.] See Leland. *Coll.* iii. p. 21.
[1] Leland. *Coll.* ut supr. p. 61.
[2] Among Phreas's *Epistles* in Baliol library, one is *Preceptori suo Guarino*, whose epistles are full of encomiums on Phreas, MSS. Bal. Coll. Oxon. G. 9. See ten of his epistles, five of which are written from Italy to Bishop Grey, MSS. Bibl. Bodl. NE. F. ii. 20. In one of these he complains, that the bishop's remittances of money had failed, and that he was obliged to pawn his books and clothes to Jews at Ferrara.
[3] He also translated into Latin the *Panegyric on Baldness* of Synesius. Printed, Basil. 1521, 8vo. [Whence Abraham Fleming made his English translation, 1579. See *Handb. of E. E. Lit.* art. *Fleming.*] Leland mentions some flowing Latin heroics, which he addressed to his patron Tiptoft, Earl of Worcester, in which Bacchus expostulates with a goat gnawing a vine. *Coll.* iii. 13; and *Scriptor. v. Phreas.* His *Cosmographia Mundi* is a collection from Pliny. Leland, *Coll.* iii. p. 58. See MSS. Br. Twyne, 8, p. 285.
[4] See Leland, *Coll.* iii. 58. Wood, *Hist. Univ. Oxon.* ii. 76. [Le Neve, edit. 1854, i. 141.]
[5] See Leland, *Coll.* iii. 13, 63. Leland says that he had the new epitaph, "Novum ac elegans." *Scriptor. v.* Phreas. "Tuscia me genuit," &c.
[6] Leland, v. *Cellingus.* [7] Id. *Itin.* vi. f. 5.
[8] Wood, *Hist. Univ. Oxon.* ii. 177. In a monastic *Obituary*, cited by Wharton, he is said to be "Latina quoque et Græca lingua apprime institutus." It is added,

that among these books, which were all soon afterwards accidentally consumed by fire, there is said to have been a complete copy of Cicero's Platonic system of politics *De Republica*.[1] Cardinal Pole expended two thousand crowns in searching for Tully's Six Books *de Republica* in Poland, but without success.[2] Sturmius, in a letter to Ascham [dat. 30 Jan. 1552] says that a person in his neighbourhood had flattered him with a promise of this ineftimable treasure. Barthius reports, that they were in the monastery of Fulda on vellum, but deftroyed by the soldiers in a pillage of that convent.[3] Isaac Bullart relates that in 1576, during the siege of Moscow, some noble Polish officers, accompanied by one Voinufkius, a man profoundly skilled in the learned languages, made an excursion into the interior parts of Muscovy, where they found, among other valuable monuments of ancient literature, Tully's *Republic*, written in golden letters.[4] It is to be wished, that the same good fortune which may discover this work of Cicero, will also restore the remainder of Ovid's *Fasti*, the lost *Decads* of Livy, the *Anticatones* of Cæsar, and an entire copy of Petronius. Henry VII. sent Sellynge in the quality of an envoy to the king of France, before whom he spoke a most elegant Latin oration.[5] It is mentioned on his monument, now remaining in Canterbury Cathedral, that he understood Greek.[6]

> Doctor theologus Selling, Græca atque Latina
> Lingua perdoctus.

This is an uncommon topic of praise in an abbot's epitaph. William Grocyn, a fellow at New College at Oxford, pursued the same path about the year 1488: and having perfected his knowledge of the Greek tongue, with which he had been before tinctured, at Florence under Demetrius Chalcondylas and Politian, and at Rome under Hermolaus Barbarus, became the first voluntary lecturer of that language at Oxford, before the year 1490.[7] Yet Polydore Vergil, perhaps only from a natural partiality to his country, affirms that Cornelius Vitellus, an Italian of noble birth and of the most accomplished learning, was the first who taught the Greek and Roman classics at Oxford.[8] Nor must I forget John Tiptoft, the

---

that he adorned the library over the prior's chapel with exquisite sculptures, and furnished it with books, and that he glazed the south side of the cloisters of his monastery for the use of his studious brethren, placing on the walls new texts or inscriptions, called *Caroli* or carols. *Angl. Sacr.* i. p. 145, seq.

[1] This is afferted on the authority of Leland. *Scriptor.* ut supr. [See *supr.* i. 214, note ⁴.]

[2] *Epistol. Afchami ad Sturm.* dat. 14 Sept. 1555, lib. i. p. 99.

[3] Christiani Fueftell. *Miscellan.* p. 47. Compare Mabillon. *Mus. Italic.* tom. i. p. 79.

[4] *Acad. Art. Scient.* tom. p. 87.

[5] From his *Epitaph*.

[6] [In the library of the Earl of Leicefter at Holkham is a MS. copy of a Homily of St. Chryfoftom tranflated in 1488 from the Greek into Latin by Sellyng. A second copy is in the British Museum among the Additional MSS.—Madden.]

[7] Wood, *Hist. Univ. Oxon.* i. 246. See Fiddes's *Wolfey*, p. 201.

[8] *Angl. Hiftor.* lib. xxvi. p. 610. 30, edit. Basil, 1534. But he seems to have

unfortunate Earl of Worcester who, in the reign of Henry VI. rivalled the most learned ecclesiastics of his age in the diligence and felicity with which he prosecuted the politer studies. At Padua, his singular skill in refined Latinity endeared him to Pius II. and to the most capital ornaments of the Italian school.¹ His Latin Letters still remain, and abundantly prove his abilities and connections. In this correspondence, four letters are written by the earl, viz. To Laurence More, John Fre or Phreas, William Atteclyff, and Magister Vincent. To the earl are letters of Galeotus Martius, Baptista Guarini, and other anonymous friends.² He translated Cicero's dialogue on *Friendship* into English,³ [and also the Commentaries of Cæsar *De Bello Gallico*, which were published about 1530. There is, moreover, from his pen *Ordinances for Justes of Peace Royal*, prepared in 1466 in the Earl's official capacity as Lord High Constable of England. These are printed in the *Antiquarian Repertory*]. He was the common patron of all his ingenious countrymen, who about this period were making rapid advances in a more rational and ample plan of study; and, among other instances of his unwearied liberality to true literature, he prepared a present of chosen MSS. books, valued at 500 marks, for the increase of the Humphredian library at Oxford, then recently instituted.⁴ These books appear to have been purchased in Italy, at that time the grand and general mart of ancient authors, especially the Greek classics; for the Turkish emperors now seated at Constantinople, particularly Bajazet II., freely imparted these treasures to the Italian emissaries who, availing themselves of the fashionable enthusiasm, traded in the cities of Greece for the purpose of purchasing books, which they sold in Italy: and it was chiefly by means of this literary traffic, that Cosmo and Lorenzo de Medici, and their munificent successors the dukes of Florence, composed the famous Florentine library.⁵

---

only been a schoolmaster of Magdalen or New College. See Nic. Harpsfield, *Hist. Eccles.* p. 651, who says that this Vitellius spoke his first oration at New College. "Qui primam suam orationem in collegio Wiccamensi habuit."

¹ See Ware, *Script. Hibern.* ii. 133; Camd. *Brit.* p. 436; and the Funeral Oration of Ludovico Carbo on Guarini. [Tiptoft, Earl of Worcester, occupied one of the professorships at Padua for some time. See *Hist. of the Venet. Rep.* iii. 426.]

² MSS. Eccles. Cathedr. Lincoln.

³ See *supra*, iii. 110-11, note. See MSS. Harl. 4329. 2. 3. [It may be added here that Tiptoft is said by Caxton to be also the translator of the Declamation (attached) of Bonacursus de Montemagno (the younger). See Blades, ii. 92.] He has left other pieces.

⁴ Epist. Acad. Oxon. 259. Regist. F. F. f. 121. I suspect that, on the Earl's execution in 1470, they were never received by the university. Wood, *Antiq. Un. Oxon.* ii. 50. Wood adds, that the Earl meditated a benefaction of the same kind to Cambridge.

⁵ Many of them were sent into Italy by Lorenzo de Medicis, particularly John Lascaris. Varillas says, that Bajazet II. understood Averroes' commentaries on Aristotle. *Anecdot. de Florence*, p. 183. P. Jovii *Elog*. c. xxxi. p. 74. Lascaris also made a voyage into Greece by command of Leo X. and brought with him some Greek boys, who were to be educated in the college which that pope had founded on

As the Greek language became fashionable in the course of erudition, we find the petty scholars affecting to understand Greek. This appears from the following passage in Barclay's *Ship of Fools* written, as we have seen, about the [beginning of the sixteenth century]:

> Another boasteth himself that hath bene
> In Greece at scholes, and many other lande;
> But if that he were apposed[1] well, I wene
> The Greekes letters he scant doth understand.[2]

With regard to what is here suggested, of our countrymen resorting to Greece for instruction, Rhenanus acquaints us that Lilly (the famous grammarian) was not only intimately acquainted with the whole circle of Greek authors, but with the domestic life and familiar conversation of the Greeks, he having lived some time in the island of Rhodes.[3] He stayed at Rhodes five years. This was about the year 1500. I have before mentioned a translation of the *Tactics* of Vegetius, written at Rhodes in 1459 by John Newton, evidently one of our countrymen, who perhaps studied Greek there.[4] It must, however, be remembered, that the passion for visiting the holy places at Jerusalem did not cease among us till the reign of Henry VIII.[5] William Wey, fellow of Eton College, celebrated mass *cum cantu organico* at Jerusalem in 1472.[6]

Barclay, in the same stanza, like a plain ecclesiastic, censures the prevailing practice of going abroad for instruction which, for a time at least, certainly proved of no small detriment to our English schools and universities:

> But thou, vayne boaster, if thou wilt take in hand
> To study cunning,[7] and ydelnes despise,
> Th'royalme of England might for thee suffice:—
> In England is sufficient discipline,
> And noble men endowed with science, &c.

And in another place:[8]

Mount Quirinal, and who were intended to propagate the genuine and native pronunciation of the Greek tongue. Jov. *ut supr* c. xxxi. [But the *original* Medicean library, or a portion of it, formed the basis of St. Mark's Library at Venice, having been given to the republic under the reign of Francesco Foscari, while Cosimo de Medici was an exile on her territory. It was presented by the Duke Cosimo to San Giorgio Maggiore, but was afterwards amalgamated with the national collection. *Hist. of Venet. Rep.* iv. 370.]

[1] examined. [2] Edit. 1570, *ut supr.* fol. 185, a.
[3] *Præfat. ad T. Mori Epigram.* edit Basil. 1520.
[4] MSS. Laud. Bibl. Bodl. Oxon. K. 53.
[5] See 1. *The Way to the Holy Land*, printed in 1515, and twice afterwards, by Wynkyn de Worde, and republished for the Roxburghe Club, 1824; 2. [*the pylgrymage of Sir Richarde Guylforde*, (*Controller to Henry VII.*) *to the Holy Land*, printed in 1511, and reprinted for the Camden Society, 1851; and] 3. *The pylgrymage of Syr Richard Torkyngton, parson of Mulberton in Norfolk, to Jerusalem*, An. 1517 [now lately added to the Additional MSS. British Museum].
[6] MSS. James, Bibl. Bodl. vi. 153. See his *Itineraries*, MSS. Bibl. Bodl. NE. F. 2. 12. [Printed for the Roxburghe Club, 1857.] In which are also some of his English rhymes on *The Way to Hierusalem*, [of which there are other copies.] He went twice thither.
[7] knowledge.   [8] *Ibid.* fol. 54, a.

> One runneth to Almayne, another into Fraunce,
> To Paris, Padway,[1] Lombardy, or Spayne;
> Another to Bonony,[2] Rome, or Orleaunce,
> To Cayns, to Thoulous,[3] Athens, or Colayne:[4]
> And at the laſt returneth home agayne,
> More ignoraunt.

Yet this practice was encouraged by ſome of our biſhops, who had received their education in Engliſh univerſities. Richard Pace, one of our learned countrymen and a friend of Eraſmus, was placed for education in grammar and muſic in the family of Thomas Langton, Biſhop of Wincheſter, who kept a domeſtic ſchool within the precincts of his palace for training boys in theſe ſciences. "Humaniores literas" (ſays my author) "tanti eſtimabat, ut domeſtica ſchola pueros ac juvenes ibi erudiendos curavit," &c. The biſhop, who took the greateſt pleaſure in examining his ſcholars every evening, obſerving that young Pace was an extraordinary proficient in muſic, thought him capable of better things, and ſent him, while yet a boy, to the univerſity of Padua. He afterwards ſtudied at Bologna: for the ſame biſhop by will bequeaths to his ſcholar, Richard Pace, ſtudying at Bononia, an exhibition of ten pounds annually for ſeven years.[5] At Padua, Pace was inſtructed by Cuthbert Tunſtall, afterwards Biſhop of Durham, and the giver of many valuable Greek books to the Univerſity of Cambridge; and by Hugh Latimer.[6]

We find alſo Archbiſhop Wareham, before 1520, educating at his own expenſe for the ſpace of twelve years Richard Croke, one of the firſt reſtorers of the Greek language in England, at the univerſities of Paris, Louvain, and Leipſic: from which returning a moſt accompliſhed ſcholar, he ſucceeded Eraſmus in the Greek profeſſorſhip at Cambridge. Croke dedicated to Archbiſhop Wareham his *Introductiones in Rudimenta Græca*, printed in the ſhop of Eucharius Cervicornius at Cologne in 1520.

With regard to what has been here ſaid concerning the practice of educating boys in the families of our biſhops, it appears that Robert Groſſeteſte, Biſhop of Lincoln in the thirteenth century, educated in this manner moſt of the nobility in the kingdom, who were placed there in the character of pages.[7] Cardinal Wolſey, Archbiſhop of York, educated in his houſe many of the young nobility.[8] Fiddes cites a record remaining in the family of the Earl of Arundel, written in 1620, which contains inſtructions how the

---

[1] Padua.
[2] Bologna.
[3] Caen and Touloufe.
[4] Cologne in Germany.
[5] See Pace's *Tractatus de fructu qui ex doctrina percipitur*, edit. Baſil. 1517, pp. 27, 28, in which the author calls himſelf Biſhop Langton's *a manu miniſter*. See alſo Langton's Will. (*Cur. Prærog. Cant. Regiſtr. Moone*, qu. 10). Biſhop Langton had been provoſt of Queen's College at Oxford, [and Biſhop of Saliſbury,] and died in 1501.
[6] *Tractat.* ut ſupr. pp. 6. 99. 103. Leland, *Coll.* iii. 14.
[7] "Filios Nobilium procerum regni, quos ſecum habuit domicellos." Joh. de Athona. in *Conſtit. Ottobon.* Tit. 23, in voc. *Barones*.
[8] Fiddes's *Wolſey*, p. 100. See what is ſaid above of the quality of Pope Leo's *Cubicularii*, p. 411.

younger son of the writer, the Earl of Arundel, should behave himself in the family of the Bishop of Norwich, whither he is sent for education as page: and in which his lordship observes, that his grandfather the Duke of Norfolk, and his uncle the earl of Northampton, were both bred as "pages with bishopps."[1] Sir Thomas More was educated as a page with Cardinal Morton, Archbishop of Canterbury, about 1490.[2]

It is obvious to remark the popularity which must have accrued to these politer studies, while they thus paved the way to the most opulent and honourable promotions in the church: and the authority and estimation with which they must have been surrounded, in being thus cultivated by the most venerable ecclesiastics. It is indeed true that the dignified clergy of the early and darker ages were learned beyond the level of the people. Peter de Blois, successively Archdeacon of Bath and London, about the year 1160, acquaints us that the palace of Becket, Archbishop of Canterbury, was perpetually filled with bishops highly accomplished in literature; who passed their time there in reading, disputing, and deciding important questions of the state. He adds that these prelates, although men of the world, were a society of scholars: yet very different from those who frequented the universities, in which nothing was taught but words and syllables, unprofitable subtleties, elementary speculations, and trifling distinctions.[3] De Blois was himself eminently learned, and one of the most distinguished ornaments of Becket's attendants. He tells us that in his youth, when he learned the *Ars Versificatoria*, that is, philological literature, he was habituated to an urbanity of style and expression: and that he was instituted, not in idle fables and legendary tales, but in Livy, Quintus Curtius, Suetonius, Josephus, Trogus Pompeius, Tacitus, and other classical historians.[4] At the same time he censures with a just indignation the absurdity of training boys in the frivolous intricacies of logic and geometry, and other parts of the scholastic philosophy which, to use his own emphatic words, " Nec domi, nec militiæ, nec in foro, nec in claustro, nec in ecclesia, nec in curia, nec alicubi profunt alicui."[5] The Latin Epistles of De Blois, from which these anecdotes are taken, are full of good sense, observations on life, elegant turns, and ingenious allusions to the classics. He tells Jocelyne, Bishop of Salisbury, that he had long wished to see the Bishop's two nephews, according to promise: but that he feared he expected them as the Britons expected King Arthur or the Jews the Messiah.[6] He describes, with a liveliness by no means belonging to the archdeacons of the twelfth century, the difficulties,

---

[1] Fiddes, ibid. *Records*, No. 6, c. 4, p. 19.
[2] Mori *Utop.* cited by Stapleton, pp. 157, 138. And Roper's *More*, p. 27, edit. *ut supr.*
[3] *Epist.* vi. fol. 3, a. *Opera.* edit. Paris, 1519.   [4] *Epist.* cii. fol. 49, b.
[5] Ibid. That is, "Which are of no real use or service, at home, in the camp, at the bar, in the cloyster, in the court, in the church, or indeed in any place or situation whatsoever."
[6] *Epist.* li. fol. 24, a.

disappointments and inconveniences of paying attendance at court.[1] In the course of his correspondence, he quotes Quintilian, Cicero, Livy, Sallust, Seneca, Virgil, Quintus Curtius, Ovid, Statius, Suetonius, Juvenal, and Horace, more frequently and familiarly than the fathers.[2] Horace seems his favourite. In one of the letters, he quotes a passage concerning Pompey the Great from the *Roman History* of Sallust in six books (now lost) which appears at present only in part among the fragments of that valuable historian.[3] In the *Nugæ Curialium* of Mapes, or some other Latin tract written by one of the scholars of the twelfth century, I remember to have seen a curious and striking anecdote, which in a short compass shews Becket's private ideas concerning the bigotries and superstitious absurdities of his religion. The writer gives an account of a dinner in Becket's palace, at which was present (among many other prelates) a Cistercian abbot. This abbot engrossed almost the whole conversation, in relating the miracles performed by Robert, the founder of his order. Becket heard him for some time with patient contempt: and at length could not help breaking out with no small degree of indignation: And these are your miracles![4]

The inferior clergy were in the mean time extremely ignorant. About 1300, Boniface VIII. published an edict, ordering the incumbents of ecclesiastic benefices to quit their cures for a certain time, and to study at the universities.[5] Accordingly our episcopal registers are full of licences granted for this purpose. The rector of Bedhampton, Hants, being an acolyte, is permitted to study for seven years from the time of his institution *in literarum scientia*, on condition that within one year he is made a sub-deacon, and after seven years a deacon and priest.[6] Another rector is allowed to study for

---

[1] "Ut ad ministeriales curiæ redeam, apud forinsecos janitores biduanam forte gratiam aliquis multiplici obsequio merebitur. Regem dormire, aut ægrotare, aut esse in consiliis, mentientur. Ostiarios cameræ confundat altissimus! Si nihil dederis ostiario actum est. Si nihil attuleris ibis, Homere, foras. Post primum Cerberum, tibi superest alius horribilior Cerbero, Briareo terribilior, nequior Pygmalione, crudelior Minotauro. Quantacunque tibi mortis necessitas, aut discrimen exhæredationis incubat, non intrabis ad regem." *Epist.* xiv. fol. 8, b.

[2] Latin and French, the vernacular excepted, were the only languages now known. [Gilbert] Foliot, Bishop of London, cotemporary with De Blois and Becket, was esteemed, both in secular and sacred literature, the most consummate prelate of his time. Becket, *Epistol.* lib. iii. 5. Walter Mapes, their contemporary, giving Foliot the same character, says he was "vir trium peritissimus linguarum, Latinæ, Gallicæ, Anglicæ, et lucidissime disertus in singulis. [Walter Mapes *De Nugis Curialium*, edit. 1850, pp. 19, 20.]

[3] "De magno Pompeio refert Sallustius, quod cum alacribus saltu, cum velocibus cursu, cum validis vecte certabat," &c. *Epist.* xciv. fol. 45, a. Part of this passage is cited by Vegetius, a favourite author of the age of Peter de Blois. *De Re Milit.* lib. i. c. ix. It is exhibited by the modern editors of Sallust, as it stands in Vegetius.

[4] [The anecdote is in Mapes, *ubi supr.* pp. 41-2.]

[5] See his ten *Constitutiones*, in the *Bullarium magnum* of Laertius Cherubinus, tom. i. p. 198, *seq.* Where are his *Erectiones studiorum generalium in civitate Firmana, Romæ, et Avenione*, A.D. 1303.

[6] Mar. 5, 1302. *Regist. Pontissar. Winton.* fol. 38.

seven years, *in loco quem eligit et ubi viget studium generale.*[1] Another receives the same privilege, to study at Oxford, Orleans, or Paris.[2] Another being desirous of study, and able to make a proficiency, is licensed to study in *aliquo studio transmarino.*[3] This, however, was three years before Boniface became pope. Another is to study *per terminum constitutionis novellæ.*[4] But these dispensations, the necessity of which proves the illiteracy of the priests, were most commonly procured for pretences of absence or neglect. Or, if in consequence of such dispensations, they went to any university, they seem to have misspent their time there in riot and idleness, and to have returned more ignorant than before. A grievance to which Gower alludes in the *Vox Clamantis*, a poem which presents some curious pictures of the manners of the clergy, both secular and monastic.[5]

> Et sic Ars nostrum Curatum reddit inertem,
> De longo studio fert nihil inde domum:
> Stultus ibi venit, sed stultior inde redibit, &c.

By Ars we are here to understand the scholastic sciences, and by Curatus the beneficed priest. But the most extraordinary anecdote of incompetency, which I have seen, occurs so late as the year 1448. A rector is instituted by Waynflete, bishop of Winchester, on the presentation of Merton Priory in Surrey, to the parish of Sherfield in Hampshire. But previously he takes an oath before the bishop, that on account of his insufficiency in letters, and default of knowledge in the superintendence of souls, he will learn Latin for the two following years; and at the end of the first year he will submit himself to be examined by the bishop, concerning his progress in grammar; and that, if on a second examination he should be found deficient, he will resign the benefice.[6] [This state of ignorance probably led to the circulation of some of the ludicrous stories of the illiterate condition of the early English minor clergy, which are to be found in *A C. Mery Talys*, 1526, and other books of the same class.] In the Statutes of New College at Oxford, given in 1386, one of the ten chaplains is ordered to learn grammar, and to be able to write; in order that he may be qualified for the arduous task of assisting the treasurers of the society in transcribing their Latin evidences.[7] In the statutes of Bradgare college in Kent, given in 1398, it is required that the governor of the house, who is to be a priest, should read well, construe Latin well, and sing well.[8] At an episcopal visitation of St. Swithin's priory at Winchester, an ample society of Benedictines,

---

[1] 16 kal. Octobr. 1303, *ibid.* fol. 40.
[2] A.D. 1304, *ibid.* fol. 42.   [3] A.D. 1291, *ibid.* fol. 84.
[4] A.D. 1302, *ibid.* fol. 37, b.
[5] Cap. xvii. lib. 3. *MSS. Coll. Omn. Anim. Oxon.* xxix. [Printed for the Roxburghe Club, 1850.] " Hic loquitur de Rectoribus illis, qui sub episcopo licentiati fingunt se ire scolas, ut sub nomine virtutis vitia corporalia frequentent."
[6] Registr. Waynflete, Winton. fol. 7.
[7] Statut. Coll. Nov. Rubric. 58.
[8] " Sciat bene legere, bene construere, et bene cantare." Dugd. *Monast.* tom. iii. Eccles. Collegiat. p. 118, col. 2.

William of Wykeham orders the monastery to provide an Informator or Latin preceptor, to teach the priests who performed the service in the church without knowing what they were uttering, and could not attend to the common stops, to read grammatically.[1] These, indeed, were not secular priests: the instance, however, illustrates what is here thrown together.

Wickliffe says, that the beneficed priests of his age "kunnen [know] not the ten commandments, ne read their sauter, ne understand a verse of it."[2] Nor were even the bishops of the fourteenth century always very eminently qualified in literature of either sort. In 1387, the Bishop of Worcester informed his clergy that the Lollards, a set of reformers whose doctrines, a few fanatical extravagances excepted, coincided in many respects with the present rational principles of protestantism, were followers of Mahomet.[3]

But at this time the most shameful grossness of manners, partly owing to their celibacy, prevailed among the clergy. In the statutes of the college of Saint Mary Ottery in Devonshire, dated 1337, and given by the founder Bishop Grandison, the following injunction occurs. "Item statuimus, quod nullus Canonicus, Vicarius, vel Secundarius, pueros choristas [collegii] secum pernoctare, aut in lectulo cum ipsis dormire, faciat seu permittat."[4] What shall we think of the religious manners and practices of an age, when the subjoined precautions were thought necessary in a respectable collegiate church, consisting of a dean and six secular canons, amply endowed?[5]

From these horrid pictures let us turn our eyes, and learn to set a just value on that pure religion, and those improved habits of life and manners, which we at present enjoy.

We must view the liberal ideas of the more enlightened dignitaries of the twelfth century under some restrictions. It must be acknowledged, that their literature was clogged with pedantry, and depressed by the narrow notions of the times. Their writings show that they knew not how to imitate the beauties of the ancient classics. Exulting in an exclusive privilege, they certainly did not see the solid and popular use of these studies: at least they did not choose, or would not venture, to communicate them to the people, who on the other hand were not prepared to receive them. Any attempts of that kind, for want of assistances which did not then exist, must have been premature; and these lights were too feeble to dissipate the universal darkness. The writers who first appeared after Rome was ravaged by the Goths, such as Boethius, Prudentius, Orosius, Fortunatus, and Sedulius, and who naturally (from that circumstance, and because they were Christians) came into vogue at that period, still continued

---

[1] Feb. 8, 1386, MSS. Harl. 328.   [2] *Life of Wicliffe*, p. 38.
[3] Wilkins, *Concil.* tom. iii. 202.
[4] Cap. 50. MS. apud Archiv. Wulves. Winton.
[5] "Statutum est, quod siquis convictus fuerit de peccato Sodomitico, vel arte magica," &c. From the statutes of Stoke-Clare College in Suffolk, given by the dean Thomas Barnesley, in 1422, Dugd. *Monast.* ut supr p. 169, col. 1.

in the hands of common readers, and superseded the great originals. In the early ages of Christianity a strange opinion prevailed, in conformity to which Arnobius composed his celebrated book against the gentile superstitions, that pagan authors were calculated to corrupt the pure theology of the gospel. The prejudice, however, remained, when even the suspicions of the danger were removed. But I return to the progress of modern letters in the fifteenth century.[1]

---

[1] [It is necessary to point out that a gap in the numbering of the Sections has been occasioned here by the re-arrangement of a portion of the work, and by the circumstance of the last volume having been printed *first*; but the text is complete.]

END OF VOLUME III.

www.ingramcontent.com/pod-product-compliance
Lightning Source LLC
Chambersburg PA
CBHW031848220426
43663CB00006B/534